The Kenneth Anderson Omnibus

Dear Ishan,
Happy Diwali 'and
Best wishes for the
whole year.
Love
Aji.

Nov. 2000.
Nagpur.

The Kenneth Anderson Omnibus

KENNETH ANDERSON

Volume -II

Rupa & Co

First Published by
Rupa & Co.
7/16, Ansari Road, Daryaganj, New Delhi 110 002
15 Bankim Chatterjee Street, Calcutta 700 073
135 South Malaka, Allahabad 211 001
P. G. Solanki Path, Lamington Road, Mumbai 400 007

ISBN 81-7167-456-9

Typeset in ClassGarmond by
Nikita Overseas Pvt Ltd
19-A, Ansari Road,
New Delhi 110 002

Printed in India by
Gopsons Paper Ltd
A-14 Sector 60
Noida 201 301

Rs. 195

Contents

CONTENTS

The Black Panther of Sivanipalli

Introduction

THE FIRST FIVE CHAPTERS OF THIS BOOK ARE DEVOTED TO PANTHERS. Perhaps you may wonder why I have concentrated on panthers and not written of the other animals of the jungle too. Well, for one reason, panthers are still very common in India. Secondly, they are comparatively easy to find, inasmuch as to this day they are met within a few miles of some of the big towns. For a third reason, hunting panthers is fairly inexpensive and well within the reach of the average person's pocket. A panther will come for such bait as a dog, a goat or a donkey; whereas a tiger must be attracted by a buffalo or a bull, which costs much more.

In return, shooting panthers by the sporting method of sitting on the ground instead of in the safety of a treemachan offers quite as great a thrill as tiger hunting.

I have also written a chapter about tigers and other animals, and something more about snakes. Why I have included snakes in because, although a great deal has been written and is known about tigers, elephants, lions and big animals in various parts of the world, not much has been written about

3

snakes, and most people know very little regarding them, except that in general they should be avoided. I hope I am able to throw some light upon these equally interesting creatures. Nor must the reader think for a moment that tigers, panthers, bears and elephants are the most dangerous creatures to be encountered in an Indian jungle. Far quicker, far less visible, and far more potent is the poisonous snake that lurks in a bush or in the grass.

I have also told the story of a very gallant bison and two adventures with tigers. These last two will give you an idea of the many difficulties, hardships and disappointments involved in trying to shoot a man-eating tiger. In one case I failed completely; in the other I succeeded, but only by pure chance. I have closed with a brief account of a tiger that behaved very strangely. He is alive as I write this — and he is still an engima.

As I record these adventures' the sights and sounds of the present fade way and memories come rushing in. The blackness of the forest night with the star-filled sky above and the twinkling gems of the jungle carpet below, the myriads of fire-flies that glitter together like elfin lamps amidst the dark foliage; and those other, brighter, living lights, the glowing eyes of a tiger, panther or bison, and the green eyes of graceful deer tripping daintily through the undergrowth, reflecting the beams of my torch as I walk beneath the whispering trees.

Come with me for the few hours it may take you to read this book into the domain of the tiger, the panther and the elephant, amidst the stupendous swaying heights and deep shade of the giant trees whose boles form the structure of this marvellous edifice. Forget the false values and ideas of what is called civilization, those imposed rules on the free and simple truths of life. Here in the jungle you will find truth, you will find peace, bliss and happiness; you will find life itself. There is no room, no time at all, for hypocrisy, for make-believe, for that which is artificial and false. You are face to face with the primitive, with that which is real, with that which is most wonderful — which is God.

If I can succeed in spiriting you away for a few moments from all that is mundane in your life, into the marvels of a tropical jungle and its excitements, where your life depends on your senses, your wits, your skill, and in the end on Providence, as you creep on the blood-trail of a wounded man-eater through dense verdure or among piled boulders, then I shall feel myself amply rewarded.

One

A Panther's Way

EVERY PANTHER DIFFERS FROM ANY OTHER PANTHER. SOME PANTHERS are very bold; others are very timid. Some are cunning to the degree of being uncanny; others appear quite foolish. I have met panthers that seemed almost to possess a sixth sense, and acted and behaved as if they could read and anticipate one's very thought. Lastly, but quite rarely, comes the panther that attacks people, and more rarely still, the one that eats them.

A man-eating beast is generally the outcome of some extra-ordinary circumstance. Maybe someone has wounded it, and it is unable henceforth to hunt its natural prey — other animals — easily. Therefore, through necessity it begins to eat humans, because they offer an easy prey. Or perhaps a panther has eaten a dead human body which was originally buried in a too-shallow grave and later dug up by jackals or a bear. Once having tasted human flesh, the panther often takes a liking to it. Lastly, but very rarely indeed, it may have been the cub of a man-eating mother, who taught it the habit.

Generally a panther is an inoffensive and quite harmless animal that is fearful of human beings and vanishes silently into the undergrowth at the sight or sound of them. When wounded, some show an extraordinary degree of ferocity and bravery. Others again are most cowardly and allow themselves to be followed up, or even chased like curs.

If from a hill-top you could watch a panther stalking his prey, he would offer a most entertaining spectacle. You would see him taking advantage of every bush, of every tree-trunk, and of every stone behind which to take cover. He can flatten himself to the ground in an amazing fashion. His colouration renders him invisible, unless you have the keenest eyesight. I once watched one through a pair of binoculars and was amazed at the really wonderful sense of woodcraft the panther had. Then comes the final rush. In a couple of bounds, and with lightning speed, he reaches his prey.

With unerring aim, he seizes the throat with his powerful fangs from above and behind, so that when the animal falls to earth the panther may be on the side opposite and away from its threshing hooves, which might otherwise cause serious injury. The prey is forced to the ground and that vice-like grip never relaxes till the animal is dead. Even then, the panther retains his vicious hold while sucking the life-blood of his victim through the deep punctures he has made in its throat.

Imagine, then, the stillness of the jungle and the stealthy coming of the panther as he approaches his kill or stalks the live bait that has been tied out for him. If you want to hunt the panther, watch very carefully: try to penetrate every bush, look into every clump of grass, be careful when you pass a rock or a boulder, gaze into hollows and ravines. For the panther may be behind any of these, or be lying in some

7

hole in the ground. Not only your success, but even your life will depend upon your care, for you have pitted your wits against perhaps the most adept of jungle dwellers and a very dangerous killer.

One of the most difficult and exciting pastimes is to try to hunt the panther on his own terms. This is known as 'still-hunting'.

To still-hunt successfully, you must have a keen sense of the jungle, a soft tread, and an almost panther-like mind; for you are going to try to circumvent this very cunning animal at his own game. You are about to hunt him on your own feet — and remember, he is the most skilful of hunters himself.

The first thing to know is the time of the day he comes out to search for his prey. He is generally a nocturnal animal, and stalks the forest at night. You, being human, cannot see in the dark unless you are aided by a torch-light. But that would not be still-hunting. The next best time would be the late evening just before it grows dark. Then there is a chance of meeting an early panther. It is useless to go out during the day, for at that time he is resting. Besides, he does not like the hot sun.

Secondly, where are, generally speaking, the best places in which to look for him? To answer this, you should know the answer to the next question — on what does a panther normally prey in the jungle? The reply to that question is not going to be very helpful, for a panther will eat anything that is alive, provided it is not too large to be tackled. Jungle-fowl, pea-fowl, rabbits, monkeys, wild pigs, and any of the deer family, excepting the very large stags. Near villages, domestic pigs, dogs, goats, sheep, donkeys and average-sized cattle are his staple diet. Even a stray village cat will fill the bill, provided it is foolish enough to stray too far from the huts.

Let us suppose for the moment that we are in a jungle where the panther hunts his natural food. How does the panther go about his hunting? Remember, he has marvellous sight and acute hearing, but hardly any sense of smell. What would you do, if you were in the panther's place?

Obviously, one of two things. You would either move around silently in localities where the food is to be found, or you would hide yourself near some spot where your food is likely to come. The panther does just that.

He moves about stealthily, on padded feet, in places where he thinks the birds and animals he is seeking are likely to be, or he lies in wait for them near some waterhole or salt-lick that they generally visit.

If he is stalking and wants to be silent, he cannot always move in the undergrowth, or among dead leaves, for they will crackle or rustle. So he walks stealthily along footpaths, game-trails, a forest fire-line, or in the shelter of the banks of a nullah or a stream. Alternatively, he hides at the approaches to water, or a salt-lick, where he can pounce upon his quarry as it passes by. It is in such places that you must look for him.

Further, movement on your part will attract his attention. Therefore, take a walk around the jungle in the daytime and see if you can discover pug-marks — not just a stray set of pugs, but a series of marks, old and new. When you have found them, you will know you have hit upon a well-used panther trail. Try to select a point where two or more such trails meet or cross, or a spot where such a trail or a fire-line crosses a stream.

When you have found it, return the same evening and hide yourself behind a convenient tree-trunk or bush; and then, whatever you do, sit perfectly still while keeping a sharp lookout along the paths or sections of fire-line or stream-bed that are in view. If you are lucky, you may see a hunting panther walking along one of these, perhaps looking up now and again into the trees in search of a monkey or one of the larger jungle birds. It goes without saying, of course, that in such vigils you might also spot a tiger, an elephant, or one of the several deer species.

But let us continue to suppose for the moment that you are only after a panther. If you can locate a jungle pool or a salt-lick, it would be convenient to lie down under some cover beside it, or behind an ant-hill, if available. You will derive much entertainment in observing the various denizens of the forest as they visit such a rendezvous. Don't be too surprised if, after a time, you notice a panther or tiger taking up a somewhat similar position to your own, although I may warn you that it will be very hard for you to become aware of them, so silently do they move. As I have already said, such places are favoured by carnivora when lying in wait for their natural food.

I remember that I was once lying in the grass behind the trunk of a tree overlooking a salt-lick formed in a corner of a shallow ravine. Earlier examination had shown that spotted-deer and sambar visited this salt-lick in large numbers. It was growing dusk when the faintest of rustles a little behind me caused me to turn my head slowly and glance back. There I saw a panther regarding me with very evident surprise. Seeing he was discovered, he stood up and half-turned around with the intention of getting away. Then he looked back at me once again, as much as to say, 'Can't you get to hell out of here?' Finally he moved off.

It is fascinating to watch one of these animals with her cubs, or a tigress with hers. The solicitude of the mother is very noticeable. Carnivora do not bring their cubs out of the cave where they are born until old enough to walk stably and understand the rudiments of hunting. Till such time, they are sheltered carefully in the cave. When very young, they are fed entirely on milk. When they grow a little older, the mother begins to feed them on raw meat which first she herself eats and partially digests, and then vomits out for the cubs to feed on. As the cubs themselves become able to digest stronger meat, the mother brings her kills to the cave — perhaps a jungle-fowl or pea-fowl, and as time passes, small animals, increasing to the leg of deer, or perhaps a deer itself.

Cubs are very greedy and if left to themselves will overeat and make themselves ill. I have kept a number of panther and tiger cubs, and have found the former particularly prone to gastritis. They will stuff themselves by gobbling chunks of raw meat, and will drink bowls of blood, till almost unable to move. Once they are attacked by gastritis, the malady proves practically incurable, and they die in three or four days in great agony. This complaint seems to affect them until they are about eight months old, and I have lost quite a few by it.

In the wild state, a mother appears to know this instinctively and gives her young just enough to eat, supplementing raw meat with natural milk till the cubs are quite big and start to bite and scratch her while she is suckling them.

If danger threatens the cave, in the form of intruding human beings or the male of the species, which is rather fond of eating his young, she will move them to a safer abode. This she does by carrying them in her mouth by the scruff of the neck, one at a time.

When the cubs are old enough to walk, the mother takes them out for education in the art of stalking and killing for themselves. This is quite a lengthy process. She begins by killing the prey herself, while the cubs hide in the undergrowth. Then she calls them with a series of guttural mewing-like sounds, allowing them to romp over the dead animal, bite it and get the taste of a fresh kill and warm blood. The ferocious sounds emitted by the cubs when doing this are quite amusing to hear. They bolster up their courage and lash themselves into a fury, growling and snapping at each other and even at their mother.

The next lesson starts when she only half-kills the prey, or hamstrings it, allowing the youngsters to finish the task as best they can. This they begin doing by attacking the throat and biting the animal to death — a very cruel process.

Education in the art of killing goes much farther in the case of tiger cubs than in that of panthers. Panthers choke their victims to death by gripping the throat and hanging on, whereas the tiger very scientifically breaks the neck. Hence tiger cubs take much longer to teach, and it is a common occurrence for a tigress to kill four or five cattle in a herd while teaching her young which, equally often if left to themselves, make a mess of the job by merely biting or mauling an animal, which eventually escapes.

I have mentioned that a tiger is a very scientific and neat killer. He generally leaps half across the back of his quarry, bending over and seizing the throat on its other side, while hanging on with his fore-paws in a powerful shoulder-grip. Then he wrenches upwards and backwards in a swift, violent jerk which topples the animal over. It is the combined weights of the quarry and the tiger, coupled with the sudden mighty twist of the neck, that breaks the victim's neck.

When a mother tiger or panther comes out on the hunting trail with her young, they follow behind, copying every action of the parent and sinking to the ground or behind the cover exactly as she does. At such times it is dangerous to be too near a tigress. She is liable to attack you in defence of her young. A pantheress is less likely to attack, although she will demonstrate by growling ferociously. Even so, one never can tell, and it is wise to have your rifle ready when a family procession comes into view.

But whatever you do, and unless utterly unavoidable and in self-defence, please do not shoot the mother, be it panther or tiger, for if you do the cubs will invariably escape into the jungle where they may starve to death, or if they are big enough they may develop into man-eaters. You should remember they have not yet learned properly the art of killing their natural food, other animals. If you interrupt their education at this stage they may, by force of circumstances which you have created, turn to killing human beings to appease their hunger. Bear in mind always that a human being is much easier to stalk, attack and kill than any of the larger animals.

An interesting period to indulge in this pastime of stalking is during the Indian winter — that is, the months of November, December and January — for then is the mating season of both these species of carnivora.

Of course, you should remember that these animals are mostly active during the night, and that there is only an off-chance of hearing or seeing them towards dusk. It is thrilling to listen to the sound of a tigress calling her mate, and one can almost detect the note of impatience in her summons. I should warn you, however, that tigers are definitely dangerous during this season, particularly when courting the female, or in the act of mating. Their method is exceedingly rough, both the tiger and tigress often biting and scratching each other freely.

You may have observed the strange behaviour of domestic cats during mating. Multiply this many, many times, and you will have some idea of the savagery of tigers when making love. They lash themselves into a frenzy and a fury, and woe betide a human who intrudes upon their privacy at this time of sexual excitement. The tigress has the reputation of being even more excitable and consequently more dangerous than the tiger at this period. A tigress on heat, calling lustily, has often stopped forest operations and bullock-cart traffic through the jungle over large areas.

Panthers are much the same in this respect, but generally lack the courage to attack a human intruder, although they will demonstrate in no uncertain manner.

A panther resembles a cat more closely than does a tiger. The scratching up of sand or dead leaves by the side of a game-track reveals where a panther has answered the call of nature and then covered up the excreta, exactly in the same way as a domestic cat. A tiger, however, will not bother to do this, but leaves it exposed in the manner of a dog. The excreta, in both cases, consists mostly of the undigested hair of the last kill.

The hyaena, which is a carrion eater, swallows bones and all complete. So the droppings of this animal are easily recognisable as hard, white lumps of semi-digested bones. The track of a hyaena is identifiable in the great difference between the size of the fore and hind-paws; the fore-paws are much larger.

Panthers, like tigers, retract their claws when walking, so that the difference between a panther's pug-marks and those of a hyaena, which are about the same in size, is that the 'ball' of the panther's pug is much larger than the hyaena's, while the points of the claws do not show at all. The hyaena, being unable to retract its claws, leaves their imprint clearly on the ground.

In the past there has been much controversy between those sportsmen who have claimed that the panther and the leopard are two entirely different species of animal and those who have said that they are one and the same. This argument has died out with modern times, when it has been recognized that they are indeed one and the same. Difference in environment and diet has caused some animals to grow to a much larger size than others. The forest-dwelling panther, with his richer diet of game-animals, generally grow, much bigger and has a darker and thicker coat than the panther that lives near villages, where his food is restricted to dogs and goats. Also, living among rocks and boulders as the latter generally does, his coat is paler, and the hair short and coarse. Incidentally, the darker coat of the forest-dwelling panther helps to camoulflage him very effectively against the dense vegetation of the jungle, while the paler coat of the 'village panther', as he is sometimes called, makes it very difficult to detect him among the rocks where he lives.

Very occasionally, however, there are exceptions in both cases, and Nature appears unaccountably to break her own rule. I have shot some very large panthers living near villages and far from the regular jungle, possessing dark rich coats of hair, and some quite small ones within the forest with pale coats.

Much the same applies to tigers. Those that have accustomed themselves to eating cattle become heavy and fat, while the true game-killers are sleek and muscular, carrying no fat at all, for they have a far more strenuous time hunting wild game than does the cattle-lifter, which procures its prey with little or no effort. Strenuous exercise reduces fat, not only in human beings, but in tigers also.

Man-eaters of both species are distinct anomalies and the products of unnatural circumstances, some of which have been mentioned already.

Panthers can climb quite well and they sometimes ascend trees after monkeys, or to escape when pursued by wild dogs. Tigers do not, although I have known one in the Mysore Zoological Gardens that has accustomed itself to climbing quite high and lying on a platform that had been specially built for it on a tree within its enclosure. This is an instance of the fact that tigers, like human beings, as individuals differ from the another.

Both panthers and tigers hunt monkeys by a quite unique method. Jungle monkeys are very vigilant and keep a sharp look-out for carnivora, which are their natural enemies. At the sound or sight of any of these animals they climb to the topmost branches, where they are safe. Knowing this, panthers and tigers charge at the foot of the tree up which the monkeys have climbed, uttering a series of terrific growls and roars. These fearsome sounds quite unnerve the poor monkeys, which, instead of remaining on their perches where they are safe, attempt to leap to the next tree; or, if that is too far away, jump to the ground from enormous heights with the intention of making a run to climb another tree. In this process some of them injure themselves or are stunned, and fall easy victims to the clever hunter.

One of the most intelligent animals, if not the most intelligent, in the Indian jungle is the wild dog. Shikaris of earlier days have variously given this place to the wild elephant, tiger and panther, but if you have studied the habits of the wild dog you may be inclined to disagree with them. When hunting deer they send out 'flankers', which run ahead of the quarry and ambush it later. In large packs of thirty or more, these animals are fearless hunters, and will ring, attack and kill any tiger or panther by literally tearing it to bits, despite the number of casualties they may suffer in the process.

Particularly in the forests of Chittoor District, in the former Presidency of Madras, they have earned quite a reputation for this, and I know of at least three instances where a very gory battle had been waged, resulting eventually in the tiger being torn to shreds, but not before he had killed a half-dozen of the dogs and maimed many others. I have never come across a panther destroyed in this fashion because, as I have said before, of their ability to escape by climbing trees.

The tiger takes to water and will swim across large rivers freely. Especially in hot weather, he is very fond, during the mid-day hours, of taking his siesta by the banks of a shady stream or pool, sometimes lying in the water itself. He hunts freely on rainy days, and his pug-marks are often seen in the morning after a night of pouring rain. This is not so with the panther. A true cat in every respect, he detests water, abhors rain, and is not given to swimming, although he can do so in emergencies, such as to escape from a pack of wild dogs.

The tiger was originally an immigrant into India from the colder regions of Mongolia. Hence his liking for cool spots in which to shelter from the heat. The panther is a true native of India and of the tropics.

Tigers very occasionally mimic the calls of sambar, obviously to attract and ambush them. Such mimicry is heard very rarely and only in forests where deer are plentiful. Panthers, however, do not follow this practice but rely entirely on their silent stalking, their ability to flatten themselves to the ground and hide in incredibly small places, and their final quick rush upon their quarry.

It was often said by the sportsmen of the past that the tiger is a 'gentleman' while the panther is a 'bounder'. I think these sayings have gained popularity from the experiences some of those hardy, old stalwarts have gained while following wounded animals of both species with their old-fashioned guns, frequently muzzle-loaders. Hats off to them, indeed. Ill-armed and awkwardly clad in the fashions of those days, wearing heavy boots and cumbersomely thick solar to pees, they followed a wounded animal fearlessly on foot. How different from the modern 'hunter' who shoots at night from

17

the safety of a motorcar, the lights of which dazzle the poor animal and give it not the ghost of a chance!

A wounded tiger generally betrays his whereabouts by growling as his pursuer approaches, but a wounded panther often lies silent and concealed, and attacks the hunter from behind, when he has passed. Hence their seems to be some justification for those who labelled the panther a 'bounder'. Actually, a tiger is generally far braver and certainly much more formidable, and when he attacks to kill he finishes that job very thoroughly. A panther, however — unless he is a man-eater — will maul his pursuer and then escape rather than kill him outright.

Panthers gnaw at the bones of their kills, even when they are in a very far advanced state of decomposition. As a rule, tigers do not visit their kills after the second day. For one thing, they eat much more and so have finished all there is to eat, after two or three meals. Also, on the whole, they are cleaner feeders. Decomposed flesh becomes embedded beneath the claws of both species. This breeds dangerous germs, and it is the scratches inflicted by these animals, more than their bites, that lead to blood-poisoning. Tigers are very conscious of this foreign matter under their claws, and clean them, in addition to sharpening them, by scratching upon the soft bark of certain trees. Panthers do this very rarely, so that their claws are generally more infected. Trees bearing such claw-marks at the height of six or seven feet, where a tiger has reared up on his hind legs and cleaned the claws of his fore-paws, are a happy sign to the hunter of the presence of his quarry.

In other ways also, the tiger is a much cleaner feeder. Whereas a panther starts his meal by burrowing into his kill from the stomach end, and soon has the stomach, entrails, offal and so on, all mixed up with the meat of his kill, the tiger makes a vent near the anus into which he inserts his paw and removes the intestines and stomach, dragging them about ten feet away before he begins to eat a clean meal. To facilitate this procedure, he often removes the tail of the animal by biting it off near the root. The larger type of panthers found in forests occasionally do the same thing, but never the normal and smaller beasts, which soon get themselves mixed up in a repast in which the guts and excreta are all included.

The cave or den of a tigress and her cubs is very cleanly kept compared with that occupied by a family of panthers, and seems conspicuously free of bones and other waste matter which is almost always present where panthers live.

Apart from the mating season, tigers advertise their presence in a jungle much more than panthers do. The tribes of aborigines living in the forests of India will confirm this and will tell you the rough direction of the trails generally followed by tigers while out hunting. Their melodious, deep-throated and long-drawn moaning call, terminating in that never-to-be-forgotten 'oo-oo-ongh' that reverberates down the aisles of the valleys and across the wooded glens of the jungle in the stygian darkness beneath the giant forest trees, or in the phosphorescent moonlight, is music to the jungle-lover's ears. The harsher but less distance-carrying call of the panther, very closely resembling a man sawing wood, that occasionally penetrates the still darkness of the jungle night, is much less frequently heard.

Another habit peculiar to the tiger is his way of following a particular beat on his hunting expeditions. This may extend for miles and miles, maybe a hundred miles; but it invariably follows the same course; perhaps the bed of a certain dry nullah, along the banks of a river or stream, through some wooded valley or the shoulder of a hill. On a favourite trail you may find the pug-marks of the hunting tiger, imprinted in the powdery dust; and, once having found them, be sure you will find them again. Some days may pass, extending into weeks, a month, or perhaps longer, depending on the distance covered by his beat; but you may be almost certain that the tiger will pass that way again. He rarely returns by the route he has gone, but works around in an enormous circle, coming back to the place where you found his pug-marks and going on in the same direction once more.

While on his beat, if he is successful in killing an animal, the tiger will remain in the vicinity for a couple of days till he demolishes it, when he will resume his itinerary.

It is important to bear this peculiar habit in mind when trying to anticipate the movements of a man-eater, for he will always return to the same locality within a roughly calculable number of days, depending upon the stretch of territory covered by his beat. You may come to know the number of days and the line of his beat approximately by plotting on a map the human kills he has made, and the dates on which he has made them, followed by some very elementary mental arithmetic.

A panther never seems to follow any such pattern, but is here, there and everywhere. Like looking for the 'elusive Pimpernel'; this habit of appearing anywhere and disappearing just as abruptly, makes the movements of a man-eating panther almost impossible to anticipate or forecast. He will turn up quite unexpectedly to claim his human victim, at a time and place very far from that predicted by the most experienced and astute of shikaris.

In this chapter I have tried to give you some hints on 'still-hunting', as well as telling you about some of the habits and peculiarities of the larger carnivora. I have deliberately abstained from recounting instances of animals shot by me on such occasions, as I feel they may not interest you much.

After all, the fun of the game lies in pitting your skill, woodcraft, endurance and cunning against that of these animals and in beating them at their own game, rather than in merely killing them. In fact, I would very strongly advocate that you carry a camera along with you, and I would ask you to confine yourself to taking photographs of these very beautiful creatures in preference to shooting them. Take your rifle with you by all means, as a protection in emergencies; but try to abstain from needless killing if you can resist the temptation.

Remember always that a good, cleverly-taken photograph is a far more meritorious and commendable achievement than any stuffed trophy hanging on the wall or decorating the floor of your drawing-room. With the first you can view the animal as often as you wish in all the beauty of its living grace and strength; whereas a stuffed trophy, like a cast cocoon or broken egg-shell, is just the husk of a once-beautiful animal which sooner or later will deteriorate and be destroyed by time and insects.

Two

The Man-eating Panther of the Yellagiri Hills

IT WAS MID-AFTERNOON. THE TROPICAL SUN BLAZED OVERHEAD, A veritable ball of fire. The jungle lay still and silent under its scorching spell. Even the birds and monkeys that had chattered all morning were now quiet, lulled to sleep in the torpid air.

Beneath the dark shadows of the forest trees some relief was to be found from the golden glare, even though the shadows themselves throbbed and pulsated in that temperature. Not the least movement of the air stirred the fallen leaves that thickly carpeted the jungle floor, forming Nature's own luscious blanket of crisp yellow-brown tints. When the monsoons set in, these same crisp leaves would be converted into mouldering manure, which in course of time would serve to feed other forest trees, long after the jungle giants from which they have fallen had themselves crashed to earth.

The heavy stillness was occasionally broken by a hollow sound from the wooden bells hanging from the necks of a herd of cattle that had been driven into the jungle for grazing. These wooden bells serve two purposes. The first and main object is to enable the herdsmen to locate in the thick under-brush the whereabouts of the animals that wear them. The second object is to frighten off any carnivora that becomes disposed to attack the wearers. Quite often the second purpose is successfully achieved, as tigers and panthers are suspicious animals and hesitate to attack a prey from whose neck is suspended a strange wooden object emitting queer sounds. But sometimes, again the ruse does not succeed, depending upon the nature of the particular tiger or panther concerned, and even more on its hunger at the given moment.

This particular afternoon was to witness one such exception. A fat and brown young bull was browsing on the outskirts of the herd, munching mouthfuls of grass beneath the shade of a clump of ficus trees. With each mouthful that it tore from the ground it would raise its head a little to gaze in idle speculation at the surrounding jungle, while its jaws worked steadily, munching the grass. Nothing seemed to stir and the brown bull was at peace with itself and the world.

It would not have felt so complacent, however, if it had gazed behind. Not a rustle rose as a tuft of grass parted to show two malevolent green eyes that stared with concentrated longing at the fat brown bull. The eyes were those of a large male panther of the big forest variety, and his heavy body, nearly equalling that of a tigress in dimensions, was pressed low to the ground, the colouring of his rosettes merging naturally with the various tints of the grasses.

Slowly and noiselessly the panther drew his hind legs to a crouching position. His muscles quivered and vibrated with tenseness. His whole form swayed gently, to gain balance for the death-charge that was to follow.

Then, as a bolt from the blue, that charge took place. As a streak of yellow and black spots, the heavy body of the panther hurtled through the air and, before the brown bull was aware that anything was happening, the cruel yellow fangs buried themselves in its jugular. For a moment the bull struggled to maintain his equilibrium with its forefeet apart, hoping to gallop into the midst of the grazing herd. But with his air supply cut off, and his life-blood jetting from the torn throat, his resistance was but momentary. He crashed to earth with a thud all four feet lashing out desperately in an attempt to kick off the attacker. The panther adroitly squirmed his body out of reach of the lashing hooves, but never released his merciless grip on the bull's throat. A snorting gurgle burst from the gaping mouth of the stricken animal, the feet kicked less vigorously, and then his terror-stricken eyes slowly took on a glazed and lifeless expression as death came within a few minutes of the attack.

Thus did Nathan, the herdsman, lose one of his best beasts, as the rest of the herd, alarmed by the noise made by the dying bull, galloped through the jungle for safety to the forest-line that eventually led to the village, a couple of miles away.

But this was not to be Nathan's only loss. In the next three months he lost four more of his cattle, while the other two herdsmen who lived in the same village each lost a couple. On the other hand, the panther responsible for these attacks concluded, and no doubt quite justifiably, that he had found a locality where food was plentiful and easy to get. He decided to live nearby in preference to moving through the forest in his normal hunt for game, which was far more arduous anyhow.

The monsoons then came and with the heavy rains pasture grew up everywhere and it became unnecessary to drive the herds of cattle into the jungle for grazing. Grass sprang up near the village itself, and in the few adjacent fields, and the herds were kept close to the village where they could be more carefully watched.

This change, of course, was not relished by the panther, and he became bolder, as he was forced by circumstances to stalk the herds in the new pastures.

The forest thinned out in the vicinity of village, while the fields themselves were completely tree-less. This made the panther's approach more and more difficult, and often enough the herdsmen saw him as he tried to creep towards their charges. On such occasions they would shout, throw stones at him and brandish the staves they carried. These demonstrations would frighten him away.

Then his hunger increased, he found that he must choose between abandoning the village herds altogether as prey and go back to stalking the wild animals of the forests, or adopting a more belligerent policy towards the herdsmen.

The panther decided to adopt the latter policy.

One evening he crept as far as possible under cover and then dashed openly towards the nearest cow. Two herdsmen, standing quite near, saw him coming. They shouted and waved their sticks, but his charge never faltered till he had buried his fangs in the cow's throat. The herdsmen stood transfixed for the few minutes it took for the cow to die. Then they began to hurl stones and invectives at the spotted aggressor while he lay with heaving flanks across the still-quivering carcass of his prey.

When the stones thudded around, the panther let go his grip on the cow and with blood-smeared snout growled hideously at the men, his evil countenance contorted and his eyes blazing with hatred. Faced with that hideous visage and those blood-curdling growls the herdsmen ran away.

At this stage of affairs the villagers requested the local forester to do something to help them; otherwise to enlist help from some other quarter. The forester, whose name was Ramu, had done a bit of shooting himself and owned a single-barrelled twelve-bore breech-loading gun. Although it was part of his duties as the representative of the government to check poachers, he himself was accustomed to indulge in a little poaching over water-holes and salt-licks, his quarry being the various kinds of deer that visited such spots, or an occasional jungle pig. As often as was possible he avoided letting his subordinates, the forest guards, know of these surreptitious activities, but when that was not possible he made sure of the guards' silence by giving them a succulent leg from the animal he had shot, together with a string of dire threats of what he would do to them if a word about it was breathed to the range officer. Despite all these precautions, however, the range officer had come to know of Ramu's favourite pastime. He was a conscientious young officer, keen to uphold the government's policy of game preservation, and tried to catch his subordinate in the act. But that worthy had so far succeeded in keeping a clean official slate. Perhaps he was too wily, or his threats to the guards so fearsome that the R.O. had not yet succeeded.

So far Ramu had not tried his weapon against any of the larger carnivora, and when the villagers approached him for help to shoot the panther he was not over-keen to tackle the proposition. But the villagers persisted in their requests, and soon it was made very evident to Ramu that his honour was at stake, for he could not delay indefinitely with vague excuses of being too busy to come to the village, or of having run out of stock of ammunition, and so forth.

Therefore Ramu arrived at the village one morning carrying his weapon. He was hailed as the would-be saviour of the situation and immediately took full advantage of the fact by settling down to a very hearty meal provided by the villagers. After washing this down with a loath of coffee, he belched contentedly and announced his intention of indulging in a nap for an hour before tackling the business for which he had come.

Ramu awoke a couple of hours later, by which time it was past mid-day. He then demanded of the headman that a got should be provided as bait. This was done and Ramu set out for the jungle, accompanied by five or six villagers.

Being the forester in charge of the section he was well-acquainted with the locality and had already selected, in his mind, the tree on which to build his machan. This was a large banyan, growing conveniently at the point where the track from the village and the forest fire-line met. It also happened that a nullah intersected the fire-line near the same spot. The panther was known to traverse all three of these approaches as had been evidenced by his frequent pug-marks, so that Ramu's choice was indeed a wise one; for if the panther walked along the fire-line or came up the nullah he could not help spotting his goat, while he himself, in the machan, could see up and down both these approaches as well as part of the track leading to the village.

On this tree, then, Ramu instructed the villagers who had accompanied him to build a machan twenty feet or so off the ground, and being well-skilled in the art of making hide-outs himself, contrived to conceal it cleverly with leaves, so that it would be quite unnoticeable to the panther.

It was past four o'clock that evening before the work was completed. Ramu climbed into the machan and the goat was then tethered by a rope round its neck to a stake that had been driven into the ground.

When the villagers left, the goat, finding itself alone, gazed in the direction of the village path and bleated lustily. Conditions were as perfect as could be, and the panther heard the goat and pounced upon it at about six, while the light was still good. Ramu had loaded his gun with an L.G. cartridge which he fired at the panther while the latter was holding the goat to the ground by its throat. There was a loud cough; and the panther somersaulted before dashing off into the undergrowth. The goat, which was already dying from suffocation and the wound inflicted in its throat, was killed outright by a pellet that passed through its ear into the brain.

Ramu waited awhile, then descended the banyan tree and hastily retreated to the village, where he told the people that he was sure he had hit the panther and had no doubt that they would find him dead the next morning.

With daylight a large party of men assembled and, headed by Ramu, went down to the banyan tree. There they found that the goat had been completely eaten during the night by a hyaena. Ramu pointed out the direction in which the panther had leaped and the whole party of men searched in close formation. It was not long before they came upon a blood-trail on the leaves of the bushes and lantana, indicating that in truth he had scored a hit. But of the panther there was no sign, although the party followed the trail for over a mile before it eventually petered out.

For two months after this no fresh attacks on cattle or goats were recorded, and everyone, including Ramu, was sure that the panther had gone away into some thicket and died.

Then one evening a lad of about 16 years was returning to the village along the same forest line. He was alone. Coming around a bend he saw a panther squatting on his haunches about twenty yards away, looking directly at him. He halted in his tracks, expecting the panther to make off as an ordinary panther would do. But this panther did nothing of the kind. Instead, he changed his position to a crouch and began to snarl viciously.

The boy turned around and ran the way he had come, and the panther pursued him. Luckily, at the place he overtook the boy, a piece of rotting wood happened to be lying across the forest line. As the panther jumped on his back and bit through his shoulder near the neck, the boy was borne to earth by the weight, and in falling saw the piece of rotting wood. Terror and desperation lent strength to his hands and an unusual quickness to his mind. Grasping the wood, he rolled sideways and jammed the end into the panther's mouth. This caused the panther to release his hold, but not before he had severely scratched the boy's arm and thighs with his claws. Springing to his feet, the boy lashed out at him again; this unexpected retaliation by his victim caused the panther to lose courage and he leaped into the bushes. Still grasping the wood that had saved his life, and with blood streaming down his chest, back, arms and legs, the boy made a staggering run for the village.

That was the first attack made upon a human being. The next followed some three weeks later, and this time the panther did not run away. It happened that a goat-herd was returning with his animals when a panther attacked them and seized upon one. The herdsman was poor and the herd represented all his worldly wealth. So he tried to save his goat by screaming at the panther as he ran towards him, whirling his staff. It was a brave but silly thing to have done, knowing that a panther was in the vicinity that had recently attacked a human being without provocation. He paid for his foolish bravery with his life, for the panther left the goat and leapt upon him to clamp his jaws firmly in his throat.

The goats ran back to the village. Seeing no herdsman

returning with them, some of the villagers wondered what had occurred, but for the moment did not attach any significance to what they had noticed. It transpired that this herdsman was alone and had no relatives, so that it was nearly an hour later and growing dusk before his absence was really accepted as a fact, and it became evident that something had happened to him. It was too late by then to do anything.

Next morning the villagers gathered in a party of about thirty persons, armed with clubs and staves, and left the village to try to find the goat-herd. They went down the track leading from the village to the jungle. The hoof-marks of the herd of goats as they had run back to the village the previous evening were clearly visible along the trail. They proceeded a little further and there they came upon the spot where the panther had made the attack. Clearly impressed in the dusty earth were the·pug-marks of the large spotted cat. There was also a distinct drag-mark where the panther had hauled his victim away. Scattered at intervals were a few drops of blood from the throat of the man that had trickled to the ground. But the earth away from the track was sun-baked and hard and had absorbed the blood, and it was difficult to locate, though the drag-mark was quite clear.

The panther had taken his victim off the track along which the man had been driving his goats, and had hauled the body into the jungle. But he had not gone very far from where he had originally made his kill, and within about a hundred yards the group of villagers discovered the body of the victim. The chest and a small portion of one thigh had been eaten. Thus the maneater of the Yellagiris came into existence.

The Yellagiris are a crescent-shaped formation of hills lying immediately to the east of Jalarpet Junction railway station on the Southern Railway. The opening of the crescent faces away from the Junction, while its apex, so to speak, rises abruptly some three thousand feet above sea level about two miles from the station. A very rough zigzag path winds up the steep incline, and in places one has to clamber from boulder to boulder.

Many years ago — in 1941 in fact — I had purchased a farm of small acreage at the top of this ridge. I had intended keeping this farm, which is about ninety-five miles from Bangalore, as a week-end resort, but had not found the time to visit it regularly. As a result, the open land was quickly being encroached upon by the ever-prolific lantana shrub.

I had decided to visit this place for about three days to supervise the removal of the lantana, and when I made this visit I happened to arrive a few days after the death of the goat-herd. The coolies I had engaged for the work told me about the panther, of which no news had been published in any of the newspapers. They assured me that it continued to haunt the precincts of the village, for they had again seen its pug-marks only the previous day.

The news interested me and I thought I might as well make an attempt to bag the animal. I had brought neither of my rifles with me, but only my twelve-bore shot gun, as the Yellagiris abound in jungle-fowl and during the few visits I had made there I had always shot a couple each time for the pot. Further, with this object in view, I had brought along with me only two L.G. cartridges for emergencies, the rest being number six shot for the jungle-fowl. Therefore I would have to make sure of the panther with the only two L.G. shells available.

I stopped work on the lantana about mid-day and went back with the labourers to reconnoitre the ground. It was much as I had expected. The jungle fell away into a narrow belt of lantana which ceased only at the few fields that bordered the village. Clearly visible on a footpath at the end of one of these fields was the trail of a panther — a fairly large adult male, judging from his pugs. He had passed that way only the night before.

I went to the village and introduced myself to the Patel, or headman, whom I had never met before, and told him how I came to be there. He expressed great pleasure at my presence and was most enthusiastic in his promises of every co-operation. We held a discussion and I told the Patel that I would like to buy a goat to tie up as a bait in the initial stage of my operations against the panther.

And here was where the Patel's co-operation was needed, as no goats were available in his village. It was only with much difficulty and considerable delay that he was able to procure one for me from a neighbouring hamlet, a kid that was small enough in size to ensure that it would bleat when tied up. The Patel himself accompanied me, and four other men, one of them leading the goat, the rest carrying hatchets with which to construct a machan.

They led me back along the track to the place where the herdsman had been attacked, and finally to the spot at which they had found his remains. It was densely overgrown with small bushes of the Inga dulcis plant, known as the 'Madras thorn' or 'Korkapulli' tree. It was out of the question to sit on the ground there, as the thorns grew so close together as to prevent one from seeing any animal beyond the distance of a couple of yards. So we were compelled to retrace our steps along the track for about a quarter of a mile.

There we came upon quite a large and leafy jak-fruit tree which, with its thick leaves growing in profusion, seemed to provide the ideal setting for the construction of a machan. At about the height of eight feet the first branch led off the main stem of the tree. The third branch after that extended over the track itself and bifurcated conveniently at about fifteen feet from the ground.

Across this bifurcation I instructed my followers to build the machan. This they set about doing by first lopping small branches off the neighbouring tree and removing the leaves. They then laid the lopped sticks across the bifurcation, tying them to the two arms with vines cut from the jungle. By this means they had soon made a platform about four feet long by three feet wide. This would be sufficient for me to sit on. Finally, the four sides of the machan were well camouflaged with the leaves they had just removed from the small branches they had cut down to build the base of the machan. We also took great care to conceal the base of the platform itself with leaves, so that to a panther standing anywhere around at any angle, or even directly below, nothing would be visible of the occupant sitting in the machan, nor would anything seem to be out of place to arouse his suspicions unduly.

I got one of the men to make a stake out of a piece of wood, sharpened it a little at one end and then hammered it into the hard ground with a boulder at a distance of just over twenty feet from the machan, keeping in mind the fact that I was using a shot-gun.

When all this was ready I climbed into the machan myself and made an opening in the leaves to face the stake and in such a position that I would have a clear view of the goat and a small portion of the ground around it. By the time we were ready it was nearly five in the evening.

As I have already stated, I had not come to the Yellagiris to shoot big game, so I had not brought my night equipment, the torch that I used to clamp to the barrel of my rifle. Instead, I had brought a small two-cell affair which I only used in camp. It threw only a diffused beam and was quite inadequate for the work which I now had in hand. Further, having no clamp, I would have to hold the torch itself in my left hand and close to the barrel of the gun. The outlook was not so good, since I had come during the moonless period of the month and would have to rely on sounds and my own senses to judge the presence and exact whereabouts of the panther in the darkness, would he turn up.

Bearing all these facts in mind, I settled down in the machan and made myself as comfortable as possible. Then I instructed the men to tether the goat to the stake and walk back to the village, talking loudly to each other. Not only would their withdrawal in this fashion cause the goat to begin bleating as it saw them going away, but should the panther be watching anywhere in the vicinity, their noisy departure, coupled with the bleating of the goat, would induce him to come out early to dinner.

According to instructions, the men tied the goat to the stake and began to walk back in the direction of the village, talking loudly. The goat immediately strained at the rope that held it to the stake and started to bleat so loudly and persistently that I mentally congratulated the Patel on the choice of the bait he had selected. I became certain that if the panther was anywhere around within a mile of this goat he would surely hear its cries and hasten to his intended victim.

But nothing that I expected came to pass. The goat called persistently and loudly, so much so that by the time the sun had set it had become quite hoarse and its cries dwindled to husky squeaks. Twilight found the goat so hoarse that it appeared to resign itself to the inevitable and a night in the open. Folding its forelegs first, it settled down on the ground and fell asleep. I now knew there was but little chance of the panther locating the goat unless it actually happened to pass by and practically stumble upon it. Still, I decided to wait till about nine o'clock and chance my luck.

The next two and a half hours were like many others that I had spent in the jungle under similar circumstances. The calls of the feathered denizens of the forest had long since died away at least those that belonged to the day. The only sound that could be heard occasionally was the peculiar low whistle of the 'herdboy' bird. This is a grey night-bird, some eight inches in length which emits a low but very penetrating cry exactly resembling the sounds invariably made by herdsmen as they tend their cattle while grazing in the forest, to keep them together. Hence its name, or to give it its Tamil original, 'mat-paya kurvi', by which it is known throughout Southern India. Incidentally, it is a bird that appears to live only in jungly regions, or their immediate vicinity, as I have never come across it in the cultivated areas.

There is nothing more that I can tell you, beyond the fact that at 9.15 p.m. I decided to abandon the vigil. I shone the torch in the direction of the goat, but the spreading beam hardly reached the sleeping animal, which I could just detect as a faint blur as I heard it scramble to its feet. Had the panther attacked that goat I would not have been able to see it properly, so I consoled myself with the thought that perhaps it was just as well the panther had not turned up.

Climbing down from the tree I untied the goat and, taking it is tow, went back to the village, where I left it with one of the men who had helped to put up the machan, instructing him to look after it until the next day.

Early the following morning I returned to the village to glean as much additional information about the panther as I could. But there was nothing more that anybody could tell me, beyond the facts already related at the beginning of this story, which I slowly pieced together. Nobody knew exactly from where the panther had come and nobody could suggest any particular locality in which he might be living.

The work on my land occupied the next three days, and each evening of those three days I spent in the same machan, sitting up with different goats as baits till a few hours before midnight. But all those three evenings drew a blank, in that I heard no sound of the panther. Each morning I would scour the vicinity of the machan, the forest-lines, and various stream-beds, but there were no fresh pug-marks of the animal for which I was looking, showing that he had not passed anywhere nearby during those nights. Very probably he had moved off to some distant part of the Yellagiri Hills.

On the fourth morning I left for Bangalore, after handing the village Patel my name and address and money for a telegram which he was to send by a runner to Jalarpet railway station.

Over a month passed. No telegram came and I decided that the panther was not a regular man-eater or had perhaps left the Yellagiri Hills to cross the intervening belt of cultivated plain to reach the much more extensive range of forest that clothed to reach the Javadi Hills. This latter range is a wide one and leads far beyond the Yellagiris in a south-easterly direction towards Tiruvannamalai, which is a sacred hill inhabited by a sage said to be possessed of many gifts.

I was quite wrong, as events were to prove.

Seven weeks passed before the telegram, which I had almost forgotten, arrived. It told me that the 'mail-carrier', who brought the 'tappal', or post, from Jalarpet up the hill to the various villages and settlers at the top, had been killed by the panther.

The telegram did not reach me till after three in the afternoon. Nevertheless, by hurrying I was able to catch the Trichinopoly Express which left Bangalore at seven o'clock and reached Jalarpet at 10.30 p.m. I had brought my petromax lantern with me, and by its bright light walked from the station up the hill to reach the village, eight miles away, just before 2 a.m. Normally I would not have dared to risk that rough and steep boulder-covered track by night with a man-eating panther in the vicinity, but I knew that it would be quite safe as long as I had the petromax burning. My 405-rifle and haversack of equipment strapped to my back, plus the light hanging from my left hand, made quite a sizeable and uncomfortable load up that steep track, and I was drenched in perspiration by the time I reached the top of the hill. The village was still a mile away, and a cold breeze chilled my damp clothes as they dried on my back while I walked along.

I awoke the Patel, who in turn awoke most of village, so that a concourse of a hundred dusky faces and gleaming white teeth surrounded me in the light of the petromax.

The Patel offered me food, which I politely declined, but I told him I would be grateful for some hot tea. This was soon prepared, and while sipping it from a large brass utensil belonging to the Patel, I heard the story he had to tell me.

Actually there was nothing much to tell. After my last visit everybody had been very careful when moving about in the day, particularly in the vicinity of the forest. At night they had remained indoors. Then as the weeks had passed without any further signs of the panther, as always happened vigilance was correspondingly relaxed.

The mail-carrier used to ascend the hill early in the morning, leaving Jalarpet at about 6 a.m. from the small post office situated adjacent to the railway station. All the mail trains passed during the night, from Bangalore as well as from Madras on the east coast and Calicut on the west coast. Postal traffic to the Yellagiris was comparatively small, and the few letters or articles that were destined for the hill-top were placed in individual bags by the sorters on the various mail trains and unloaded at Jalarpet Station. The mail-carrier, who was to ascend the hill, would open these bags in order to place all their contents into the one bag he carried up, slung across his shoulders or sometimes balanced on his head.

His one protection — which was intended not as much as a weapon of protection but as an emblem and badge of office, as well as a sound-device to frighten away snakes — was a short spear, on the shaft of which were fitted a number of iron rings. This spear he would carry in his hand, striking the base of it against the ground at every few paces. The rings would jangle against the iron shaft and against each other, making the loud jingling-jangling noise that has been known to the mail carriers for almost a hundred years throughout the length and breadth of India.

On that fateful day the mail-carrier had as usual set out from the small post office at Jalarpet at about six o'clock in the morning. But he never reached the top of the hill. The villagers had become accustomed to hearing him and seeing him as he jingled and jangled his daily route through the main street of the village. But that morning they had not heard the familiar sound. With the indifference and apathy peculiar to the East, nobody worried or thought anything about it.

After the mid-day meal, a party of men had started to descend the hill, bound for Jalarpet. About a quarter of the way down, they noticed the rusty colour of dried blood splashed on the rocks that formed a trail. They had stopped to wonder about it, when the sharp eyes of one individual had noticed the mail-carrier's spear lying away from the track and near a bush. Guessing what had happened, the whole party turned tail and hurried back to the village. There they had gathered reinforcements, including the Patel, and returned eventually to find the partly eaten corpse of the unfortunate mail-carrier.

The Patel had written out the telegram and sent it by the same party of men to be despatched to me from Jalarpet

Station. With all the confusion it had not reached me till after three the following evening, a delay of some twenty-four hours, although Jalarpet is just eighty-nine miles from Bangalore,. I was also informed that the police authorities at Jalarpet had removed the body for inquest and cremation.

By the time all this conversation was over and I had elicited all the information I required, or perhaps it would be more correct to say all the information that the Patel and the villagers knew about the panther, it was past four in the morning. The Patel lent me a rope cot which I carried to the outskirts of the village, where I lay down upon it for a brief sleep of two hours till dawn, when I awoke, not to the familiar calls of the forest, but to the loud yapping of a couple of curs who were regarding me on the rope cot with very evident suspicion and distaste.

As I have said, the Yellagiri Hills do not hold a great deal of regular forest, and there is therefore a complete absence of aboriginal jungle-folk of any kind. I realised that I would have to rely upon the villagers and myself to try to discover ways and means of locating the panther.

One of the questions I had asked earlier that morning concerned the panther's possible hide-out. No definite reply had been given to this, but a couple of cattle-grazers had stated that they had on three or four occasions during the past few weeks observed a panther sunning himself in the afternoon on a rocky ledge of a hill named 'Periamalai' or 'Big Hill', to give it its English translation. The Yellagiris themselves form a plateau at the top, and this Periamalai is the one and only hill rising above the level of the plateau and forms the highest peak of the crescent-shaped Yellagiri range. It is nearly 4,500 feet above mean sea level.

I went to the Patel's house and found him still asleep, but he soon woke up and offered me a large 'chumbo', which is a round brass vessel like a miniature water-pot, of hot milk to drink. I then asked him to call the cattle-tenders who had seen the panther on Periamalai and to ask them to accompany me to the hill and point out the particular ledge which the panther was said to frequent.

It took some time before these two individuals could be persuaded to go with me. They were most unwilling and I could see that they were definitely scared. However, the Patel used his own methods of persuasion, which included threats of retribution if they refused, so eventually I was able to set out accompanied by them.

Periamalai is situated about three miles to the east of the village and in the opposite direction to the path from Jalarpet, which ascends to the west. In all, about five miles lay between this hill and the spot where the unfortunate mail-man had been killed. In addition, practically all the land between was cultivated. The jungle covering Periamalai itself receded down the slopes of the Yellagiri range in the direction of that portion of the crescent that faces north. I was not happy about this as I felt that the cattle-grazers might have seen another panther entirely, and not the one that had killed the postman.

Arriving at the base of Periamalai, my two companions pointed to a ledge of rock that jutted out some 300 feet above, and stated that that was the spot where they had seen the panther sunning himself on several afternoons. Thick lantana scrub grew from the foot of the hill right up to the base of the ledge and to about half-way up Periamalai, where the regular forest began. I could see that, as was happening with so many of the smaller forest tracks in southern India, the lantana pest was slowly but surely encroaching on the jungle proper and smothering the original trees. Like the Yellagiri range itself, Periamalai is a rocky hill consisting of piles of boulders and to look for a panther in that sea of lantana and among those rocks would be a hopeless task, as the former was impenetrable.

So I marked out a place under a tree growing at the foot of the hill and told the men that we would return to the village and procure a bait, and that they should come back with it and tie it at the spot I had selected.

Accordingly we went back and the Patel procured for me a donkey. A goat would have been of no use in this case as I did not intend to sit up with it. Should it be killed, the panther would devour it at one meal and there would be nothing left to justify his return the following night, whereas the donkey was big enough to warrant the panther coming back for what remained after the first meal. Against this was the disadvantage that a goat would more readily and quickly attract the panther by its bleating, whereas a donkey would be silent.

But I relied on the fact that if the panther lived anywhere on the hill, from his elevated position he would be able to see the donkey tied on the lower ground. So I borrowed some stout rope and instructed the cattlemen to take the donkey up and tether it at the spot I had already pointed out to them.

This done, the Patel himself and three or four villagers came along with me to point out the place where the mail-carrier had been done to death. It turned out to be at a spot about a mile and a half from the village, just where the track from Jalarpet passed through a belt of lantana and rocky boulders. I had, of course, passed the place myself the previous night when ascending the hill with the lantern, but had not noticed the blood in the lantern-light. No doubt this had been just as well or my tranquility would have been greatly perturbed.

We came upon a few dried splashes of blood on the trail, and my companions pointed out me a spot nearby to where the unfortunate man had been dragged and partly eaten. As

I have already said, his remains had been removed to Jalarpet for cremation, so that there was nothing to be gained by remaining there any longer.

A cashew-nut tree stood beside the trail about three hundred yards higher up, and beneath this tree I asked the Patel to tie another donkey.

Then we walked back to the village, and I suggested that a third donkey be tied at some place where the scrub jungle came closest to the village. The Patel once more used his influence to procure two more donkeys and sent them out by different parties of men to be tied as I had instructed.

It was past one in the afternoon by the time all this had been done, and I realized that there was nothing more for me to do but await events. I could only hope the panther would kill one of three donkeys that night, provided of course he chanced to come upon it. Since the panther had made but only a few human kills thus far, it was clear that he was mainly existing upon other meat.

The Patel set a hot meal before me, consisting of rice and dhal curry, mixed with brinjals and onions grown on his land and made tremendously hot with red chillies which had been liberally added. I must say I enjoyed that meal, though the sweat poured down my face in rivulets as a result of the chillies. My host was highly amused at this sight and began to apologise, but I stopped him with the assurance that I did enjoy such a meal. Copious draughts of coffee followed, and when I finally arose I was a very contented person.

To pass the time I went down to my small farm and; pottered about for the rest of that evening. You may be interested to know that this farm of mine consists of only one and a half acres of land, but it is a very compact farm at that. There is a 'marking-nut' tree, from the of nut which a black fluid is extracted for making a marking-ink generally used by

launderers and dhobis for writing the initials of the owners
on the corner of each article they send to the wash. Once
marked, this 'ink' cannot be washed out. Three 'jak' trees,
which are of a grafted variety, produce fruit weighing from
two to twelve pounds each or even more. There are a few
guava trees, some peaches and a vegetable garden. The two
existing buildings, or 'kottais' as they are called are mud-
walled affairs with thick thatched roofs made from a mixture
of jungle grass and the stalks of 'cholam' grain. A small rose
and croton garden fronts them. At that time I had about three
dozen fowls, including leghorns, rhodes and black minorcas,
and a few ducks. My drinking-water comes from a small well
into which I introduced some fish, which I had originally
brought from Bangalore to keep the water clean. A small
stream in front forms one of my boundaries, and bamboo
trees line the other three sides. Although such a small place,
it is extremely 'cosy', and an ideal retreat for a quiet Sunday
visit from Bangalore.

About half the land is low-lying and borders the stream
I have just mentioned. I have tapped some water from this
rivulet and grown a variety of black rice, known as "Pegu rice'
and originally imported from Burma. To my knowledge, my
farm was one of the very few spots in Southern India where
this black Burma-rice then grew. I knew it had been sown in
many places, but its cultivation had proved a failure for one
reason or another.

An interesting feature about this farm was a story that one
of the two kottais was haunted by the ghost of the brother
of the Anglo-Indian lady from whom I had purchased it in
1941, lock, stock and barrel, poultry included, for the sum
of Rs. 500/-; about £35 in English money. This man had died
of a reputedly mysterious disease which I was told occurred
in sudden attacks of excruciating pain in his left arm and chest

— probably angina pectoris. He had been very much attached to the small farm and was said to have spent over twenty-five years there after purchasing it as waste land. Then he gave it to his sister, as he had no family of his own. However, as the story went, after his death, passing villagers had frequently seen him standing before his kottai in the evenings just as dusk was falling. Thereafter, needless to say, the villagers avoided the place.

His sister told me nothing about the alleged haunting till the day after I had purchased the farm and paid the cash before the sub-registrar when I had registered the sale deed, probably thinking the 'ghost' would put me off the transaction. Then she told me that her dead brother would sometimes roam about the two kottais at night, and also that she had clearly seen him many times in the moonlight attending the rose trees which had been his special hobby. She hastened to add that the 'spirit' was quite harmless, made no sound or troublesome manifestation, and just faded away if approached.

I have failed to mention that some very ancient furniture came to me with the kottais: a bed in each building, a broken-down dressing table, two almirahs and some three or four rather rickety chairs. The beds were of the old-fashioned sort, having battens.

I well remember the first night I slept in one of the kottais (incidentally the one in which the brother had died), for it was a rainy night and the roof of the other kottai was leaking. I had spread my bed-roll, without mattress, on the battened cot and had lain down to sleep. The hard battens, however, were irksome and pressed against my shoulder blades and back. After failing to woo slumber for some time, I had decided that the floor would be far more comfortable. Of course, there were no electric lights, so I had lighted a candle to enable me to remove the bed-roll and place it on the floor, when I had extinguished the candle and lain down to sleep. This time I was successful and had fallen asleep immediately.

I do not know when I awoke. It was pitch dark. Something heavy and cold and clammy moved and rested against my throat, and what seemed like two icy wet fingers extended across either side of my neck.

Now I am not an imaginative person. I am not afraid of the dark. Nor am I superstitious. But in a rush of memory I recollected the dead brother and his ghost, the fact that I had left my torch on the window-sill some feet away, and also that I did not know where I had left the matchbox. These thoughts came simultaneously, while the cold clammy wet thing distinctly moved and seemed to press its two extended fingers even more tightly on either side of my throat. I could feel my hair rising. To lie there any longer was impossible. With what seemed superhuman energy I scrambled to my feet and dashed towards the unfamiliar window-sill where I had left my torch. Probing wildly in the dark, I at last found that elusive torch. I pressed the button, expecting to see the ghost and its clammy hands, cold from the grave, before me! Instead, there on the floor was quite the largest toad I had ever seen in my life. A huge, black, slimy fellow, almost a foot long. He had come into the kottai because of the rain.

This just goes to show what human nerves can do. Hardly a few seconds earlier I had been scared stiffy by the thought of the supernatural and the unknown. Now I laughed to myself as I guided the toad with the toe of my slippered foot to the door of the kottai, and then out into the rain.

Next morning all three donkey baits were alive, and so I spent the day on my land. No one had any news to give about the panther. Another night passed and the following morning found all three of the donkeys still in the land of the living. This time there was a little news. After the death of the mail — carrier the post was conveyed up the hill by three men instead of one, the party consisting of the relief mail-carrier who had replaced the poor fellow that had been killed, together with two 'chowkidars' — literally, 'watchmen' — who had been pressed into service to accompany him as bodyguards. They were armed with crude spears in addition to the 'emblem of office' spear which had once been the equipment of the deceased mail-carrier and now automatically fell to his successor.

These three men excitedly reported at the village that they had seen a panther sunning himself on a ledge of a rock about a quarter of a mile downhill from the place where the previous mail-carrier had been done to death.

Upon hearing this news the Patel had despatched a villager to run and tell me. Taking my rifle, I accompanied him back to the village, where both the chowkidars offered to come along with me to point out the rock. We covered the distance of little over two miles in good time. But only the bare rock-ledge stared us in the face. The panther that had been lying there, man-eater or otherwise, had gone, and it was too hot, too rocky and too hopeless to search for him among the piles of boulders. However, the news was encouraging, as it indicated the panther was still in the vicinity. Before returning to the village and my small farm, I once again examined the bait under the cashew-tree and mentally selected the branch on which I would fix my machan if occasion arose.

That night brought good luck, though bad for the donkey beneath the cashew-nut tree, for the panther killed and ate about half of him during the hours of darkness.

Early next morning this fact was discovered by the party of men whom I had delegated to inspect, feed and water each one of the three baits in turn. They came back and told me, after having taken the precaution to cover the remains of the donkey with branches to protect it from being devoured to the bones by vultures.

I finished an early lunch and with my great-coat, torch and flask of tea and some biscuit, proceeded to the village, where I readily obtained the loan of a charpoy from the Patel. Four willing helpers carried this to the cashew-nut tree, where it was slung up and secured with the ropes we had brought along with us. I personally supervised the camouflaging of the charpoy with small branches and leaves, till it was invisible from every direction, as well as from below. That this job should be done very thoroughly was, I knew, most essential when dealing with man-eating carnivora. The slightest carelessness might make all the difference between success and failure. A leaf turned the other way, with its under-surface showing uppermost, or any portion of the charpoy being visible from any angle, a remnant of twigs or fallen leaves at the base of the tree, any of these would be sufficient to arouse the suspicion of a man-eater, which is always extremely cautious in returning to its kill.

All arrangements were eventually completed to my satisfaction, and the only fault that I could find was that the machan was rather low, not more than ten feet from the ground. Also that the cashew-nut tree was easy to climb. It was about two-thirty in the afternoon when the party of men who had accompanied me left, after I had instructed them to return at dawn in case I did not go back to the village myself during the night.

I sat back on the machan and made myself as comfortable as possible.

It was a sweltering afternoon, the heat being reflected by the boulders that were piled around in all directions. The tree itself afforded little protection from the afternoon sun that beat down upon me. Indeed, I was glad when evening approached and the sun began sinking towards the Mysore plateau to the west. Far below me I could see Jalarpet railway station on the plains, and the puffs of cream-coloured smoke from the shunting-engines in the yard. At intervals a train would arrive or leave, and the whistles of the locomotives could be clearly heard. All else was silent.

Towards dusk a single peacock wailed in the distance and a couple of night-jars flitted around the tree. Except for them there were no signs of any other animals or birds.

Then the shadows of night descended. Sitting on the slope of the hill facing the west, I could see the plains grow dark as if covered by a black mantle, while yet the last vestiges of day-light lingered on the hill-top above me. The lights of Jalarpet began to twinkle one by one, prominent among them being the blue-tinted neon lamps of the station platforms and shunting yards. Here and there I could make out the red and green lights of the railway signals. From the north a train rolled towards Jalarpet, the bright head-lamp of the engine cutting a swath of light before it. Then the train encountered an incline and the engine began to labour under its load. 'If she can do it ... I can do it ... if she can do it ... I can do it.' Her puffs as she struggled to top the rise formed the words in my imagination, and I listened to the clanking of her worn big-end bearings. All these sounds seemed so close to me — and yet they were so far; they were over five miles away at least, as the crow flies.

Darkness fell around me. It was a moonless night. The heavy clouds scuttled across the sky, some of them merging with the tops of the Yellagiri range. No friendly stars shone down, and the darkness became intense. I would have to rely on my sense of hearing.

Insects were conspicuous by their absence, and even the friendly chirp of the wood-cricket was not to be heard. I sat still on the cot. Now and then a passing mosquito buzzed around my head, to settle on some part of my face or hands. Then came the faint sharp sting of pain as it imbedded its needle-pointed proboscis into my skin. I would move my fingers or hand a little, or noiselessly blow against my own face by slightly protruding my lower lip. This would disturb the mosquito, which would either go on its way or fly around in a further effort to take another bite at me.

I am accustomed to sitting up in the jungle on machans or in hideouts and so lost count of the time, for in any case it served no purpose to keep looking at my wrist watch unnecessarily. I could not anyway make time pass quicker.

Thoughts of all kinds screep into a man's mind on such occasions, some pleasant, some otherwise, and some reminiscent. I remember that, that evening, for some unaccountable reason, I began thinking of some way of inventing a new sort of bicycle something that one could propel fast and for long distances with the minimum of effort. Is it not strange what the human mind may think of when it is forced to be idle?

My reveries concerning this bicycle were disturbed by what seemed like a faint sigh. I knew the panther had arrived and was standing over the dead donkey. The muffled sound I had heard had been made by his expelled breath as he slightly opened his mouth.

I reasoned that to switch on my torch and fire at this juncture might be premature. Better to let him settle down to his meal. I wish I hadn't, for in doing so I lost what might have been a successful shot and caused the death of another human being.

I waited expectantly for the sound of the meat being torn, and bones being crunched, which would have assured me that the panther was tucking in at the donkey, but instead I heard nothing. The moments slipped by and then I became uncomfortably suspicious that something had gone wrong.

I know from experience how noiseless any of the carnivora can be when they want to; particularly a panther which can come and go not only soundlessly, but also without being seen, and that too in broad daylight. Under the present conditions of intense darkness this animal might have been a yard away, or a mile away, for all the difference it made in that gloom.

I glanced down at the luminous dial of my watch, which showed that it was twenty minutes to nine. I waited without moving. Nine o'clock came and passed, and then, from a section of boulders to my right, I heard a deep growl, followed in a few seconds by another.

Somehow the panther had become aware of my presence. He could not have smelt me, as panthers have little or no sense of smell. He could not have heard me, for I had made no sound. Therefore, he had either looked up inadvertently and become aware of the machan, or some intuition had warned him. In either case, he now knew a human being was there. He might then have tried climbing up into the tree to pull me down, but as likely as not his sense of self-preservation had warned him that this particular human being was dangerous to him and not of the same sort as the men he had killed.

Of course, this panther might not be a man-eater, although in the light of his present conduct this seemed the less reasonable explanation.

The growls were initially intended as a warning. As they increased they were also clearly meant to bolster up the animal's own courage. Perhaps he would lash himself into a fury after a sufficient number of growls to attack the tree on which I was sitting and try to climb up. As I have had occasion to remark before, panthers frequently do this with monkeys, whom they terrify with a series of loud growls before rushing at the trunk of the tree. Then the monkeys generally fall of or jump down in sheer terror. As likely as not he expected the noise he was making to have the same demoralising effect on me.

Very soon the growls increased both in volume and tempo. The panther was now making a terrific noise. As I had just thought, he was either trying to frighten me away completely or off my perch; alternatively, he was building up his own courage to rush the tree. I prepared for the latter eventuality.

Some more minutes of this sort of thing went on and then out he came with the peculiar coughing roar made by every charging panther. As he reached the base of the cashew-nut tree I leaned over the edge of the cot, pushing aside the camouflaging twigs to point the rifle downwards while depressing the switch of my torch. I knew I had to be quick because, as I have told you, the machan was only about ten feet off the ground and, the tree being easy to climb, the panther would reach me in no time.

As bad luck would have it, one of the camouflaging branches fell down upon the panther. No doubt this served to delay, if not actually to deter, his progress up the tree. But it also served to screen him completely from the light of the torch. As I looked downwards I just saw the branch shaking violently and guessed that it covered the panther.

At that moment I did a foolish thing. Instead of waiting till the animal could break clear of the offending branch, I quickly aimed at the spot where. I felt his body would be and pressed the trigger. The report of the shot was followed by the sound of a falling body as the panther went hurtling backwards to the ground. For a second I thought I had succeeded in killing him, but that thought lasted only for a second, for no sooner did he touch the ground than he jumped clear of the branch in which he had become entangled, and I caught a momentary glimpse of his yellow form leaping into the undergrowth before I had a chance to work the underlever that would reload my rifle.

I shone the torch at the spot where he had disappeared, but neither sight nor sound of him or his further progress came to me. Silence reigned supreme. He might be lying dead in the bushes, or he might be wounded there, or he might have disappeared and be a long way off. There was no way of knowing.

I continued to shine the torch around for some time and then decided to sit in darkness in the hope of hearing some sound of movement. But there was absolutely nothing. I waited for another hour and then made up my mind to fire a shot into the bushes in the direction in which he had gone, hoping it would elicit some reaction if he were lying there wounded. So, switching on the torch, I fired the rifle at the approximate spot where he had vanished. The crash of the report reverberated and echoed against the hill-side, but there was no sound or response from the panther.

A goods train started from Jalarpet and began to climb the gradient to Mulanur on the ghat section that led to Bangalore. The banking engine at the rear, whose duty it was to help by pushing till the top of the gradient was reached, began to push vigorously and its puffing and clanking eclipsed the sounds made by the engine at the front, whose driver was perhaps taking it easy because of the ready help behind him.

I waited until 11.30 p.m. The loud whistling from the engine of the incoming Madras-Cochin Express decided me to come down from the tree and go back to my kottai for a comfortable night's sleep. I felt quite safe in doing this as, had the panther been wounded and in the vicinity, he would have responded to the noise of my last shot. Either he was dead or far away. Even if he had been lying in wait, that last shot would have frightened him off.

I came down from the cashew-nut tree and by the light of my torch made my way back to the village, where, before going on to my kottai, I related all that had happened to the Patel and the excited villagers.

Early next morning I came back to the village, where at least twenty willing men assembled and offered to help me. They in turn, under my advice and directions, gathered half-a-dozen village curs. Thus, safe and strong in numbers, we proceeded to the cashew-nut tree and the site of the previous night's occurrences.

The remains of the donkey had been untouched. A hole in the ground, directly below the tree, showed where my bullet had buried itself in the earth, nor was a speck of blood to be seen anywhere. We thoroughly searched among the bushes into which the panther had disappeared and into which I had fired my second shot, as well as the surrounding boulders and bushes for quite a wide area, but it was clear that I had missed entirely and that my bullet of the night before had failed to score the lucky hit I had hoped for. The panther had got completely away.

Ill-tempered and disgusted with myself, I returned with the men to the village, where I told the Patel that my time was up and that I would have to return to Bangalore. However, I asked him to send me another telegram should there be further developments. Then I went to the kottai, gathered my belongings and packed them in my haversack, and soon was repassing the cashew-nut tree on my descent to Jalarpet, where I caught the evening express from Madras that got me home by eight-fifteen the same night.

That was the end of the first round of my encounter with the Yellagiri man-eating panther.

Contrary to expectations, I heard nothing more from the Patel. When two months had elapsed I wrote him a letter and received a reply within a few days stating that there had been no further news of the animal. This made me think that it may have relinquished its man-eating habits or have crossed over to the Javadi range of hills which lay scarcely fifteen miles south of the Yellagiris. On the other hand, had the latter been the case I would still have heard through the Press or by Government notification if any people had been killed on the Javadi Hills. I was therefore inclined to the former theory and felt that the panther had given up his tendency to attack human beings. Of course, my chance shot might have found its mark, and the animal may have crept away to die in some secluded place. But this last theory was hardly tenable.

Nine more weeks passed before the next news arrived in the form of a telegram from the Patel, despatched from Jalarpet railway station, stating that the panther had reappeared and once again killed a human being. The telegram asked me to come at once, and with two hours to spare I caught the next train.

This happened to be a slow train which brought me in to Jalarpet station at about half-past eight that night. There was no purpose in my climbing the hill immediately, for there was nothing I could do just then; so I decided to take a few hours' sleep in the waiting-room and make the ascent at dawn. This plan did not prove very successful, however. To begin with, the noise of the passing trains disturbed me each time I fell asleep, being a light sleeper. Secondly, the attacks of mosquitoes and bed-bugs, with which the chair seemed to abound, impelled me to walk about the platform, which I did till five in the morning, when I set off for the foot of the Yellagiris about two miles away. It was dawn as I began the climb and I reached the Patel's village by 7-15.

My friend the Patel greeted me with his usual hospitality and brass 'chumbo' of heavily-milked hot coffee. Then he told me that the panther had attacked and killed a young woman three mornings previously, when she had gone to draw water from a stream running past the base of Periyamalai hill. He also informed me that the people of the village to which the girl had belonged had arrived shortly afterwards and recovered the remains of the victim for cremation. Apparently the panther had eaten but little of the unfortunate woman, perhaps because it had been disturbed by the party of men searching for her and had not had time to settle down to his meal.

This time I decided to tie a live bait in the form of a goat and sit up over it, as my stay on the Yellagiris could not exceed four days, as I had only that much leave. So the Patel offered to procure one for me from the same neighbouring village where he had got them the last time, but said that it would cost a tidy sum of money — about twenty rupees — as not only were goats scarce on the Yellagiris but their owners in that village, which was about three miles away, had become aware of the demand and had raised their prices accordingly. I agreed and handed over the money, and in the time that it would take for the goat to be brought, went down to my farm to see how things were getting along.

At noon, after consuming the cold lunch I had brought with me from Bangalore, I returned to the Patel's village only to find that the goat had not yet arrived.

It was two in the afternoon before the man who had been sent to fetch the animal returned with a black goat that was rather old, in the sense that it was past the stage where it would bleat for a long time when left alone, and so help to attract the panther. Secondly, as I have said, it was a black goat. Black or white goats occasionally cause suspicion among certain panthers. A brown bait, whether goat, dog or bull, is generally the best to use, in that they resemble in colour the wild animals that form the panther's natural food. However, there was no time now to change the goat and I would have to make the best of circumstances.

The Patel and four or five men accompanied me, the latter carrying axes, ropes and the same charpoy I had used on the last occasion. We reached the village to which the girl had belonged in a little under an hour. There another couple of men joined my party, who offered to point out the exact spot at which the young woman had been killed.

It was perhaps three-quarters of a mile from the village. A stream, bearing a trickle of water, ran from west to east and skirted the base of Periamalai Hill perhaps a half-mile away. This stream was sandy and bordered by a thick outcrop of mixed lantana and wait-a-bit thorns. At the spot where the girl had been attacked a shallow hole had been dug by the villagers to form a pool for watering their cattle when the weather became dry and the rest of the stream ceased to flow. It was to this place that the girl had come for water when she had been killed the previous day. The lantana grew quite close to the pool, and it was evident that the man-eater had stalked her under cover of this thicket, and from there had made his final pounce.

As matters stood, this panther had again confirmed that he was most unusual in his habits, even for man-eater. He had repeatedly attacked his human victim in broad day-light. Only tigers do this, as man-eating panthers, being inherent cowards at heart, usually confine their activities to the hours of darkness. I was inclined to think that this animal was perhaps already lying up in the thicket before the girl arrived and could not resist the temptation of a meal so readily offered.

With this idea in mind, I went down on hands and knees and began a close examination of the lantana bushes and the ground in the vicinity, where I shortly found confirmation of my theory, for one of the bushes provided ample shelter for a regular lie-up. Beneath it the carpet of dried lantana leaves rendered impossible the chance of finding any visible track, but a faintly prevailing odour of wild animal inclined me to confirm my guess as correct, and that the panther used this place now and then to lie up, as it offered ideal proximity for attack on any prey that might approach the pool to drink.

This was encouraging for, if the panther had used it before, there was every likelihood that he would use it again. Further, as I have already told you, Periamalai Hill lay about half a mile away. The panther might have his regular den among the rocks and caves higher up the hill and would find this lantana lair a most convenient place in which to await the coming of an unsuspecting victim.

As I studied these conditions an idea suddenly came to me. I would create a scene as close as possible to what the panther might expect it to be. I would tether the goat to a stake beside the pool to make it appear like an animal that had come there to drink. And I would forestall the panther's arrival by hiding myself beneath that very same lantana bush. Should he hear the goat, or catch a glimpse of it from higher up the hill, from where it would be clearly visible, he would make straight for this point of attack and would find me waiting for him.

I explained my idea to the Patel and the men who had acompanied me. They thought it clever, but the Patel decided it was foolish, in that it entailed too great a risk. I convinced him that there was really little danger as, due to the denseness of the surrounding lantana and the thickness of the bush itself, the panther would have difficulty in getting at me from any of the sides or rear, and could only reach me through the entrance to this under-cover shelter, while I would be expecting him to arrive from that direction and would be ready. Further, his attention would be concentrated on the goat and he would scarcely suspect an enemy would await him in his own lair.

The stake which we had brought along was accordingly hammered deep into the sand with the aid of a stone from the stream-bed. I crept under the bush and took my time in making myself quite comfortable for the night. I also clamped the torch to the barrel of my rifle, and tested it to see that it was in good order. This torch I had lately purchased. It was a three-cell arrangement of the fixed-focus type. Finally, I took a long drink of tea from my water-bottle before ordering the men to tether the goat to the stake by its hind legs.

While all these preliminaries were going on the goat had been kept some distance away, so that it should not come to know that a human being was sheltering in the bushes so close by; for once it knew that, there was very little chance of it bleating from a sense of loneliness. On the other hand, if the goat really felt it had been left alone, there was much more reason why it should cry out.

While the goat was being tied I remained perfectly silent. After finishing their job, the Patel and his men went away and I was left by myself to await what might happen.

It was hot and still beneath the lantana, and long before sunset it was quite dark where I was sitting. The goat had bleated a few times at the beginning and then had stopped. I could only hope that it would begin calling again when darkness fell. But I was sorely disappointed. Occasionally I had heard the sounds made by the goat as it kicked and struggled against the tethering rope, but these had now lapsed into silence and I came to the inevitable conclusion that the damned animal had gone to sleep.

Of necessity, in my position I had to keep wide awake and

alert the whole night and could not share the goat's slumbers. I envied that blasted goat.

Mosquitoes worried me, and insects of all kinds ran over my body. Bush mice, which are even smaller than the domestic variety, rustled the leaves and crept along the stems of the lantana. Once something long and soft slithered through the dry leaves and along the sides of the bush. It was a snake. Whether harmless or poisonous I could not know. I sat absolutely motionless in spite of the mosquitoes and insects, and the slithering died away.

The panther did not come. No sounds penetrated the silence under the bush, not even the calls of a night-bird. Time moved on its long and tedious course. The luminous hands of my wrist-watch very slowly clocked the passing hours. I felt drowsy but dared not give in to my inclination to close my eyes even for a few fitful seconds. I tried to think of other things and other events to get my mind off the panther. The only thing I could think of was to damn the goat.

The greying light of a new day gradually filtered in, not even heralded by the call of a jungle-fowl, pea-fowl, or any other bird. I came out of that bush the most disgusted man in the whole of India. The goat, which had been lying curled up and fast asleep by the stake, lazily got to its feet, stretched leisurely, wagged its stumpy tail and regarded me in a quizzical fashion as much as to say, 'Come now, who is the real goat, you or me?' Knowing the answer, I refrained from a spoken confession.

Instead, I untethered that wretched animal, which followed me back to the village where the Patel lived. That worthy, with the same party of men who had accompanied us the day before, was just about to set forth to see how I had fared. Telling him to return the black goat, I said that I would snatch a few hours' sleep and then go myself to find a more satisfactory bait. I went to my kottai and slept till noon.

I was feeling hungry when I awoke, so I opened a tin of salmon, which I ate with some bread I had brought with me from Bangalore. The bread had become rather dry, but was improved by the tinned butter I spread thickly upon it. This served to fill me for lunch. I had already set my portable Primus stove to boil water for tea and the beverage was indeed refreshing. While eating my lunch I brewed a second kettle of tea to put into my water-bottle. Gathering the necessary equipment for another night's vigil, I returned to the Patel's village. Fortunately the weather was warm as the previous night, so that an overcoat was unnecessary.

I took the Patel along with me to add force to my argument, and walked to the village where the goats were available. There, after some picking and choosing, followed by some red-hot bargaining, I was able to select a half-grown animal that was more likely to bleat. It was past 3.30 p.m. when we set out for the place where I had sat up the night before, but really there was no hurry, as the spot had already been selected and there was no machan to fix.

Before five o'clock I had crept into the bush, the new goat was tethered and the men were on their way back.

Hardly were they out of sight and ear-shot than the goat began to bleat, and he kept this up incessantly. I silently congratulated myself on my selection.

With evening it again became quite dark beneath the lantana, the goat called loudly and I waited expectantly for the panther. An hour passed. Then I heard an almost imperceptible rustle, the faintest sound of a dry twig being trodden upon, and I sensed the panther was coming. The crucial moment had almost arrived. Now I had to be careful not to shine the torch before the panther was fully in view.

If I did so, I knew he would disappear. On the other hand, if I delayed too long, he might see me first and perhaps make a charge, or even vanish.

With all my senses at full stretch, I waited. There were no fresh rustlings or other sounds. Then I heard a faint hiss. Instinctively I knew the panther had seen or sensed me. He had curled back his lips in a snarl, preparatory to the growl that would most likely follow. That curling of his lips had occasioned the slight hissing sound I had heard. It was now or never. My thumbn went down on the switch-button of the torch. Its beam sprang right into the twin reddish-white eyes of the panther. I could clearly see his face and chest perhaps ten feet away. Aiming quickly at the throat I pressed the trigger of the Winchester. The panther appeared to come forward a pace. Then he reared up on his hind legs, but not before my second bullet took him full in the chest. He fell over backwards out of sight and threshed the bushes for a few seconds. Next came the unmistakable gurgling sounds of a dying animal; then silence.

I waited another half-hour before deciding to take the risk of leaving the bush. I thought it reasonably safe to do so, as I was almost sure the panther was dead. Holding the cocked rifle before me, I crawled out of cover and stood beside the goat. My first impulse was to cut it loose and take it in tow along with me. Then the thought came to my mind that the panther I had fired at might not have been the man-eater after all, but just an ordinary animal. If that were so, I would need to exercise every precaution in returning to the Patel's village in the darkness and could not afford to hamper myself by leading a goat that would necessarily distract my attention. So I left it where it was and set out for the Patel's abode, where I arrived after slow and cautious walking. The people were still awake and I told them what had happened. Then I went to my kottai for a sound night's sleep.

Next morning we found the panther where he had fallen. An old male, with a somewhat craggy and pale coat, he showed every sign of being the man-eater, for his canine teeth were worn down with old age and his claws were blunt and frayed.

But only time would tell whether I had bagged the real culprit.

By noon I was on my way down the hill with his pelt.

Many years have elapsed since that incident took place, but no more people have been killed on either the Yellagiri or Javadi ranges, and so I am reasonably sure I succeeded that night in bringing the man-eater to bag.

Three

Old Munuswamy and the Panther of Magadi

THE TOWN OF BANGALORE, WHERE I LIVE, LIES PRACTICALLY IN THE centre of a straight line drawn from the city of Madras, on the east coast of India bordering the Bay of Bengal, to the town of Mangalore, on the west coast bordering the Arabian Sea. Bangalore is on a plateau just over three thousand feet above mean sea level. Nobody who has lived there can ever forget its; unique climate — neither too hot nor too cold, and neither too rainy nor too dry — with lovely misty mornings in the cold weather, from November to the middle of February, and with bracing cool mornings even in summer. The name, Bangalore, is an Anglicised version of the Kanarese words 'bengal uru' meaning 'bean town' as translated literally, whence it has become known as the 'city of beans'; and nobody who has eaten them can ever forget Bangalore's

63

luscious fruits and vegetables of both tropical and European varieties.

Bangalore was far from being a city until the end of the Second World War, when its strategic military position, its great potential to grow into a large industrial city, and all its othr assets have joined together to make it the most popular place in India. Following a wide influx of refugees both during and after the war, it has trebled its population, has become highly industrialised and is now a fast-growing city.

But this is not going to be a description of the merits of Bangalore; it was merely to say that I live in a very beautiful city. Bangalore is built on a number of hills, and if you stand on any one of them and look around, you will see thre very high hills on the horizon, respectively to the north, the north-west and the west. They are all within a radius of thirty-five miles and each is above four thousand feet in height. The hill to the north is the highest. It is really not one but three hills, consisting of three peaks together which make up the Nundydroog group. 'Droog' means 'hill fortress', and the eastern-most of these three peaks is crowned by the remains of an old fort, still in a good state of repair, built by that redoubtable Mahommedan warrior Tippoo Sultan, the 'Tiger of Mysore'. It embraces a point overlooking a sheer drop of some 600 feet. This is known as 'Tipoo's Drop', because it was here that this hoary soldier dispensed with those who annoyed him by making them walk, blind-folded, on a narrow swaying plank out over the abyss. If they could walk to the end of the plank and return, they were spared. There seems to be no record of anyone accomplishing this feat. Perhaps the plank swayed too much — or maybe it was made to sway too much. Who knows? Historians are not very clear on this point.

To the north-west of Bangalore is the hill called Sivanaganga. It has a temple at the summit and is a place of pilgrimage for Hindus. It also has a well at the top that is said to be so deep that it is bottomless. Another version is that this well is the beginning of a secret underground passage running all the thirty-five miles to Bangalore.

The third hill to the west is known as Magadi Hill. Viewed from rising ground in Bangalore it appears to be sugar-loaded in shape; but when you get there you find it has two humps like a dromedary. Between them is a heavily-wooded valley difficult to enter, for the approaches are slippery; if you should slip, you will not end much better off than did those blindfolded prisoners with whom Tippoo amused himself on Nundydroog.

This is the valley that brings me to the beginning of the story, for it was here that the panther that terrorized Magadi was said to have his cave.

Magadi Hill is surrounded by gorgeously wooded and hilly country. To the south lies a stretch of reserved forest, covering a series of hills, extending southwards for over seventy miles to the Cauvery River, near a place called Sangam. Not all of this area is reserved forest, but a large part is, while the rest is thickly covered with scrub-jungle. About midway down this line of hills, and between the towns of Closepet and Kankanhalli, the peaks cluster particularly high and closely, and the area swarms with panthers. This hunting-ground is my son, Donald's, particular paradise. He has shot forty panthers there and over a dozen bear, I think, and he is little more than twenty-three years old.

To the west of Magadi Hill are plains of low scrub. Black-buck, hare, pea-fowl, partridge and quail abound. The hills continue to the north, but there they are much lower. To the east lies more hilly country, and Bangalore, about thirty-five miles away. The Arkravarthy River, a comparatively small stream, crosses the road to Bangalore near the twenty-three milestone, and it has been dammed just there. The catchment area is big enough to ensure an ample supply of water to Bangalore throughout the driest year. This dam is known as Tippagondahalli, and huge pumps send the water the remaining twenty-three miles to Bangalore.

There you have the full setting of the country where this leopard first appeared. It must not be thought that there is anything special about this animal because I have used the name 'leopard'. A leopard and a panther are one and the same creature. For no good reason that I know of, in India we more often call them panthers.

The events that I am going to relate took place before the last war.

This panther killed some goats and a village cur or two at some of the few scattered hamlets and lie at the foot of Magadi Hill. Nobody took much notice of him, for panthers had been doing that sort of thing in that part of the country for generations and generations of panthers and the people have grown up with them.

Time passed and he grew more confident of himself. He killed some young bulls — and some cows too.

Now the bull is a sacred animal in India and no Hindu will touch his flesh. Nevertheless, the bull does all the hard work. He ploughs the fields and he draws the bullock-carts. He even turns the huge stone wheels that grind 'chunam' or limestone. But with all his many uses and considerable value, people do not begrudge a panther eating one of their bulls now and again — provided he does not become too greedy. But when he goes in for killing cows — which supply milk and butter, from whence comes 'ghee', which is melted-butter and a cooking medium used throughout the length and breadth of the country and of much value — he commits an unpardonable offence and it is high time something is done.

In Bangalore there lives — and I use the present tense because he is still there — an individual named 'Munuswamy', who claims to be a professional 'gentleman's shikari' guide. He is also a rogue. He brings in items of shikar news to town and passes them on to novices and greenhorns in the game. "Master, there is herd of forty wild pigs can shoot near Whitefield, only twelve miles away." Or, "Master, on tenth mile on Magadi Road and eighteenth mile on road to Mysore City there plenty herds of black bucks got, fifty animals in each, which master very easily can shoot." He demands a reasonable advance of money for the information, and should he turn up on the day appointed to accompany the novice to the place, the latter generally wonders what has become of those many wild-pigs and black-buck that were said to abound. But do not underestimate Munuswamy for a moment. He is quick-witted and a ready liar. "See, master," he will say, "I told you come soon long time back. You no come. Only yesterday big crowd military officer sahibs come in car. Them shoot two pigs. All run away now. Master come again another day, eh?"

Wild pigs and blackbuck are only 'chicken feed' to Munuswamy. To see him at his best is to watch him bringing news of a panther to some unfortunate greenhorn who is about to learn the lesson of his life. He will present himself at the gate of the bungalow, or accost the sahib on the road, with somethihg like this: "Sar, me big gentleman-shikari-guide. Me show master blackbucks, wild pigs, peacocks, hares, partridge and green-pigeons. Or master like snipes and wild ducks? Them come plenty, plenty in December month — Kistmiss time got. Master like shoot very very big panther? Him large one got. Only fifteen miles from here, Kankanhalli road. Master give fifteen chips advance, me tie live donkey. Panther kill donkey, me come tell Master. Me also build machan very fine. Master shoot panther very easy."

The novice is astounded. Only fifteen rupees for a live-bait? A panther only fifteen miles away? Who said hunting was an expensive or difficult hobby?

So the fifteen rupees are handed over to Munuswamy, who then remembers that master must give him another two rupees towards his food and three rupees for bus charge, when he brings master news of the kill. The greenhorn thinks this is very reasonable and forks out another five rupees. Munuswamy goes away most contented.

His first call is at one of the many local toddy-shops. He drinks only 'toddy' and eschews spirits in the form of 'arrack', which he says is too strong for him anyhow. But he drinks three bottles of toddy. This is the fermented juice of the coconut palm. Then old Munuswamy goes into a deep sleep.

The next day he wakes up and sets about the business of baiting the 'panther' in right earnest.

In Bangalore there are two animal 'pounds' for stray cattle, dogs and donkeys. The official charge for reclaiming your donkey, if it has been so impounded, is one rupee. After an interval of about ten days, unclaimed animals are sold by public auction to repay part of the expenses incurred in feeding them during those ten days. These auctions take place about twice a week, and it is a very simple matter for Munuswamy to attend one of them and purchase a donkey for about two rupees. Or he may even wrongfully pose as the owner of one of the impounded animals and claim possession of it. After all, one donkey looks much alike another, and there is no means by which the official in charge can test the truth of Munuswamy's claim, particularly if he sends a friend or agent to make it.

So Munuswamy gets the donkey, for which the sahib paid him fifteen rupees, for only two rupees, thereby making a profit of thirteen rupees, representing a potential 650 per cent on his initial outlay. A good beginning indeed.

Then he sets out on a long walk of some miles to wherever he has told the sahib the panther is to be found and ties the donkey there for a couple of days. Early in the morning of the third day or so he kills the donkey himself. This is how he does it. He has one of those huge penknives that incorporate about a dozen appurtenances, among them a round sharp-pointed instrument originally intended to be used, I believe, for removing stones from horses' hooves. At least this is what I am told, but I am not quite sure myself. With this crude instrument, he stabs the unfortunate animal in its jugular vein, and when it falls down, he stabs it again, making four wounds in all, two on each side of the throat. With the blade end of the same pen-knife he cuts open the belly, scatters the entrails about and tears off some chunks of flesh from outer skin. Then he covers the carcass with branches. Lastly, he removes from a dirty bag he has brought with him a mysterious object. Can you guess what it is? This is Munuswamy's ace trick. It is a panther's paw, crudely stuffed with straw. With this he makes a series of 'pugmarks' here and there.

With the scene set to his expert satisfaction, for a few annas Munuswamy thumbs a lift to town in a lorry, and in great excitement summons the sahib. The greenhorn becomes excited too. In frantic haste he makes the 'missus' prepare sandwiches for him and tea for his thermos flask, while he himself cleans his rifle, assembles rounds, torchlight, batteries and a number of other odds and ends — most of which he never uses and are quite useless anyhow. Then away he drives with Munuswamy at high speed to the place where, the 'panther' has 'killed'.

Munuswamy points out the 'pug-marks' on the ground and the panther's 'teeth-marks' on the donkey's throat, and the sahib is convinced. He also arranges a machan to be tied, using two coolies to do so, for whose services he charges two rupees each, though he pays them only twelve annas. Finally, before sahib ascends, he strikes a bargain. If master shoots the panther, he must give Munuswamy twenty rupees baksheesh. If master misses — that is master's own fault — he must give his faithful retainer ten rupes. If the panther does not turn up — master should not forget that panthers are very, very cunning animals and sometimes don't return to a kill — well, he, Munuswamy has worked very hard in the hot sun for master's sake and must get five rupees. The bargain is struck.

Strangely enough, Munuswamy trusts master, just as much as he expects master to trust him.

Well, the panther doesn't come — for the best of reasons: there is no panther. Munuswamy takes care to pocket his five rupees first, then consoles master by reminding him that panthers are unpredictable creatures and that this one might come next time. He offers to tie another donkey. And so the story goes on and on, till the greenhorn abandons the idea even of seeing one of these most elusive creatures and decides to confine his attention to wild-duck or partridge. Even here, Munuswamy is still useful.

You may ask me: "How do you know all this about Munuswamy?" I was such a greenhorn once and he 'had' me no less than four times. One day an accident occurred — for Munuswamy. He was pointing out the 'pug-marks' to me. A stray cur had been watching us interestedly and suddenly darted into a bush and came out carrying a cloth bag. Munuswamy, in great consternation, gave chase. The dog ran and something spotted dropped out of the bag. Munuswamy rushed for it and so did I. It was a panther's stuffed foot. Then, at the threat of the most violent death — even more violent than the donkey's — he related his *modus operandi* to me in detail, much as I have told you.

I am a long-suffering individual and believe in the adage to 'live and let live'. If there are greenhorns as foolish as I was, just waiting to be 'plucked' — well, why should Munuswamy not pluck them? So, I have never spoilt his game and Munuswamy rather likes me.

Don't think that, by telling you this, I am spoiling his game now, for Munuswamy assumes a different name each time he presents himself to a new recruit to the band of hunters that abound in Bangalore. He may be Ramiah, Poojah, Pooniah, or have a hundred aliases. But in case you should come to Bangalore at any time and aspire to join our ranks, I will give you one hint about him — a casual description. If an English-speaking 'gentleman's shikari-guide' presents himself to you — a lean, tall, oldish, very black man, with long hair drawn to the back of his head and tied in a knot, and large protruding eyes, whether he is wearing a turban or cap, dhoti, lungothi or baggy trousers or shorts, and even if he says his name is Jack Johnson, keep far from him and lock your purse up safely in a drawer. As likely as not it is my old friend Munuswamy, the happy-go-lucky 'crooked' guide.

In talking about this individual, I am aware that you may think I have strayed very far from my story. But really I have not, because he plays quite a prominent part at the beginning and at the end of it. And I am sure you have enjoyed making the acquaintance of this quite unusual and unique character, anyway.

This Munuswamy had come to bear about the activities of the panther that had begun killing bulls and cows in the Magady Hill area. Do not imagine that, although Munuswamy invariably manufactured his own panthers, he did not know anything about real ones. He did. In years gone by, when he was younger and times were not so hard, he had been a genuine shikari himself and knew a good deal about these animals. So when the information reached him, he went to Magadi by bus and made a first-hand investigation, during which he came to understand the panther had been killing goats and cattle rather frequently.

You will appreciate that, because of his methods and the strange fact that nobody who went out shooting with Munuswamy ever saw a panther, and very rarely saw anything else, his reputation as a guide was getting somewhat tarnished. More than half the homes of gentlemen shikaris, both European and Indian, whether experienced or novices, were fast closed to him. This was a very deplorable state of affairs for Munuswamy and reacted directly on his exchequer and consequently upon his stomach. The time had come to remedy it and vindicate himself.

The fact that the panther was killing boldly and frequently should make him easy to bag, and it awoke Munuswamy's latent hunting instincts. He decided that he would shoot the animal and then advertise the fact in town by a procession, in which the panther would be taken around the streets of Bangalore on a bullock-cart to the tune of tom-toms. Even better than that, Munuswamy would have his photograph taken with the panther and present copies to such of his clients as were still on speaking terms. To those who were not he would post copies. On the back of each he would have a short statement to the effect that shikari Munuswamy had shot this panther on such and such a day, at such and such a place, because the sahibs who had come with him had been unable to do so, in spite of all the help he had given them.

The more he thought of it, the more old Munuswamy thrilled to the idea. That would give them something to think about. And it would give a tremendous fillip to his waning reputation.

Having sold his own gun long ago, he somehow contrived to borrow an old hammer-model .12 bore double-barrelled weapon. Then he revisited the scene and told the villagers that he, Munuswamy the old shikari, who had once served with generals and viceroys, had come to shoot the animal that was causing them such loss. He said he intended to live in the village of Magadi, which is situated about four miles north-west of the hill from which it takes its name, and told them to bring him news immediately if any of their animals were killed.

Two days later the news came that the panther had killed another cow. Taking the solitary ball cartridge, and the three others containing L.G. shot that he had borrowed with the gun, Munuswamy repaired to.the spot, tied his machan and shot the panther high up in the shoulder with the ball cartridge. The L.G. in the other barrel — for he had fired both barrels together to make certain — helped to pepper him too, but the panther got away nevertheless. Reviewing the situation later, Munuswamy decided he was too advanced in years to follow wounded panthers. Moreover, the advantages he might get out of the 'propaganda stunt' that had fired his imagination did not now appear to weigh sufficiently against the dangers of following up the blood trail left by the panther. So he decided to call it a day and returned to Bangalore.

Weeks passed, and then the old story, which invariably begins the same way, took its usual course. A panther began to attack dogs and goats outside some of the villages situated beside the twenty-two miles of roadway that stretches outwards from Magadi to Closepet. In two instances the people in charge of the herds had tried to save their goats and had been attacked. A man and a boy had been mauled in this way.

Then a jutka-man and his pony entered the picture. Three persons had detrained one night at Closepet railway station from the night train from Mysore. As there was no bus service at that hour, these three men had decided to travel to their destination, a village ten miles from Closepet, by jutka. A jutka, for those of you who are unfamiliar with the word, is a two-wheeled vehicle covered by an elliptical roof of matting reinforced with bamboos, and is drawn by a small breed of pony especially reared for the purpose. Jutka ponies resemble the ordinary village 'tat', except that they have shorter manes and shorter tails.

The jutka arrived at its destination and unloaded its passengers. The driver decided to sleep in the village and return to Closepet the next morning. He unharnessed his pony and fed it with some of the dried grass he carried in a gunny-bag, slung just below the floor of the vehicle. Then he went to sleep.

The pony evidently finished the grass and began to stray along the village street, hoping to find some more growing there. In this way it came to the outskirts of the village, which was after all a tiny place.

From the back of the last hut along the street something sprang up suddenly against its side, and began to tear at its throat. Neighing shrilly, the pony galloped back up the street. The something that had attacked it had tried to hold on, but had lost its grip on the pony's throat and fallen off, but not before it had inflicted a nasty wound. That something had been the panther.

The sounds made by the terror-stricken pony and the growls of the panther awoke the jutka-owner, who saw his animal rushing towards him. It halted, quivering with fright, blood pouring from its throat. He raised an immediate alarm.

The pony could not haul the jutka; so next day the owner walked it back to Closepet, where he reported the matter to the police. News spread and it became known that the area was threatened by a panther that might any day become a man-eater.

Shortly afterwards a man was pounced upon within two miles of Magadi village itself and badly mauled. Villagers, tending their fields some distance away, rushed to the rescue and found him on the ground, severely bitten and raked by the animal's sharp claws. They carried him into Magadi, and to the Local Fund Hospital there, for attention. A police report was made, and the local police daffedar, whose rank is about equivalent to that of a sergeant, being the most senior officer in the village and in charge of the police chowki or station, set out to make an on-the-spot examination of the evidence given, accompanied by a constable with a bicycle.

He was taken to the place at which the ryots had picked up the injured man. While he was looking at the blood-marks and pug-tracks, and perhaps making copious notes in the way that policemen do, somebody looked up and said they could see the panther lying on a rocky out-crop at the top of a small hillock, hardly two furlongs away. The daffedar saw him, borrowed his constable's bicycle, and pedalled furiously back to the village for one of the three service-rifles that formed the entire police armoury there.

Though he pedalled furiously back, by the time he reached the place, his constable and one or two villagers who had remained, said the panther had disappeared over the top of the hill. The villagers told the daffedar that if he cared to make a detour around the hillock — the distance wasn't very great — he might yet be able to cut the panther off on the other side.

The daffedar was nothing if not keen and brave, and, taking one of the villagers along to indicate the short-cut, hastened around the hill, loading a single 303 round into the weapon he carried. The constabulary in India are armed with rifles of the same type as the military, with the only difference that the magazines are generally removed, so that only one shell at a time can be fired, thus preventing a trigger, happy copper from using his weapon over-enthusiastically at a time of riot of local disturbance. For this reason, the daffedar had only one round to fire with, and two or three others in his pocket.

They came to the other side of the hill, but they found no signs off the panther. Many boulders were scattered about, and the villager suggested they ascend the hill a little, as the panther was probably around somewhere. This they did, and from between or from behind some rocks the panther emerged. The daffedar was taken by surprise and fired from his hip, missing completely. The next second saw him on the ground with the panther on top, biting and clawing at his chest and arms. His companion was in full flight down the hill.

After the few seconds during which it had vented its rage, the panther, which had not yet become a man-eater, left the wounded policeman and sprang back to the shelter of the rocks whence he had come. The badly hurt daffedar lay where the beast had left him.

Meanwhile the fleeing villager ran back to the constable and the other villager and told them what had happened. The constable leaped upon his bicycle and made for the police station in the village, where he summoned the other three members of the local force and told them their daffedar had probably been killed.

Taking the remaining two rifles from their racks, and two 'lathis' in addition, the four representatives of the law hastened back to the hill, being reinforced as they went along with more and more villagers. A party of over ten people finally picked up the daffedar, who was in a bad way, and carried him back to the Local Fund Hospital. The next day an ambulkance was sent for from Bangalore, which conveyed him to the Victoria Hospital in the city.

The reports of the panther's various attacks had all been registered, but when he attacked one of their own force — and a daffedar at that — the police really got busy. It did not take them very long to find out who had been the root of all this trouble, and at this stage, old Munuswamy, the rascally shikari guide, re-entered the scene.

The police caught him. Witnesses had testified that he had built a machan and sat up for the panther. They also said he had wounded it. To have done that he must have used a firearm. Did he have one? Did he possess an Arms Licence? Was he hiding an unlicensed weapon? Did he borrow it? Who from? Why? When? Where? Did the owner have a licence? How many cartridges did he take?

There were a hundred-and-one questions to answer. Altogether, poor Munuswamy could see he was in for a bad time. The number of charges against him, culminating with the statement that if the daffedar died from his wounds he might be charged with 'potential manslaughter', — filled a page and would undoubtedly send him to jail for a long, long time.

Then Munuswamy's inborn initiative came to his rescue and he made his greatest bargain. He undertook to shoot the panther within four days and lay the body at the feet of the District Superintendent of Police. If he failed, the police could do as they liked with him. If he succeeded, the charges should be forgotten.

The D.S.P., being a practical officer, was more interested in having the panther shot than in prosecuting Munuswamy. For it was obvious that this animal was well on the way to becoming a man-eater; whereas Munuswamy, with all his rascally ways, was unlikely to rise to such heights of evil fame. So the D.S.P. gave him just four days and let him out of the lock-up.

The same afternoon I heard a voice persistently calling, 'sar, sar', at my front door. It was Munuswamy. With tears rolling down his cheeks — how he got them to flow so instantaneously is a secret which he has not yet confided to me — he related his whole tale of woe from beginning to end, and all the information that he knew or had been able to gather about this panther, much as I have told the story here.

He had just four days in which to shoot the panther, he insisted, failing which he would go to 'big, big jail' as he termed it. Laughingly I asked him why he did not run away. The idea had occurred to him, he admitted, but where else throughout the length and breadth of India would he be able to find such sporting sahibs who gave him money so freely; such obliging auctions where he could pick up live donkeys for as little as two rupees; and, oh! the many other advantages which come with living in Bangalore. The old man broke down at these thoughts and his tears flowed faster than ever. I would not have been surprised to learn that a few of them were genuine.

Would I please help him by shooting this panther? I would be saving him, and oh! so many other people that it might yet kill.

I conceded the latter point, but I told Munuswamy frankly that I wasn't too interested in the former. He was not offended. I said I would help him on one condition: that, as he had undoubtedly been the root of all the trouble, he would have to be beside me and not run away when the panther was shot.

The old boy actually smiled as he agreed. Strangely, his tears had vanished entirely.

That very evening I took him down to the house of the D.S.P., to whom I laughingly recounted the circumstances under which Munuswamy had presented himself. I told the police officer that I did not know if he had really been serious in allowing Munuswamy a reprieve of four days in which to kill the panther, but I pointed out that if this was so, such a time-limit was an encumbrance, as I wanted the old rogue with me to assist, and it would be a nuisance if the police butted in on the fifth day and took him away.

The D.S.P. replied that he had really meant to give him only four days in which to fulfil his undertaking, but in view of what I said he would not interfere so long as I went ahead and tried to bag this animal. He also helped by handing me a letter, calling upon all police officials to whom I might show it to render me every assistance.

Of course I did not tell this to Munuswamy. That would have made him relax his efforts. Instead, I mentioned that the D.S.P. sahib was beginning to regret having allowed him as long as four days and wanted to cut them down to three, but that I had interceded on his behalf and saved the situation in the nick of time.

This made Munuswamy more grateful to me than ever, and as impatient to be off on our trip. In the Studebaker we reached Magadi Hill early the next morning and started making inquiries at the various hamlets at its foot, including the place at which Munuswamy had wounded the panther. Asking questions as we went along, we worked our way right up to Magadi village itself, wher I spoke to the police constables who had rescued their daffedar. Thence we set off in the car along the road to Closepet, stopping at each wayside village to ask questions. In this way we came to the village where the panther had attacked the pony, and eventually to Closepet town itself, where the Sub-Inspector of Police, to whom I showed the note given me by the D.S.P., immediately sent for jutka-man. I interrogated him and he told me what had happened to his pony.

It took until late that evening to ask all these questions, but in spite of them I had found nobody who appeared to know where the panther was likely to be living, or his particular habits. Of course, I knew there was no hurry, but Munuswamy's dark countenance was even more haggard when he realised that one out of his four days of grace had passed already with no substantial results.

We came back to Magadi village that night and slept in the travellers' bungalow.

Early next morning a skinny-looking individual presented himself and stated that he earned a living gathering honey from the hives on the surrounding hills, by collecting herbs and other medicinal roots, and by snaring hare, partridge and quail when he got the opportunity. He said he had been told the night before that I had been around with Munuswamy, seeking information about the panther, and he had come to report that he was almost certain the animal lived in a cave in the recesses of the cleft between the two hummocks of Magadi Hill.

I asked him what made him so certain of his. He replied that some weeks earlier he had been there to collect herbs and had observed that an animal, dripping blood, had crossed some rocks, leaving a distinct trail. Following cautiously, he had found panther pug-marks where the animal had left the rocks. He had then stopped following. Later, he came to know that on the previous day someone had wounded a panther not far away. That somebody had been Munuswamy.

He knew of the cave, having taken honey from bee-hive in its vicinity many times in the past. A couple of days previously, just after the daffedar had been atacked but before my informant had come to hear of it himself, through having been away for a week at Closepet, he had approached the cave to see if the bees had begun to build again. He was some distance away from it when an animal had growled at him. Remembering at once the blood-trail he had found weeks earlier, he had left the valley as fast as he could.

This was news indeed.

I started asking questions, and he undertook to lead me to the cave, provided that I was prepared to creep on hands and knees for a furlong or so through the dense lantana that led to the valley and the cave.

I agreed and told Munuswamy that the time had come for him to fulfil his part of the bargain, which was to accompany me and be in at the killing of the panther, to atone for his sin in having wounded it in the first place.

If I had expected him to show fear, I was mistaken. The police had so terrified him that he was more afraid of the remaining three days running out without bagging our quarry than of facing any panther.

I waited for the sun to become hot, while I ate a leisurely 'chota hazri'. This was in order to allow the panther time to fall asleep for the day within his cave. If I arrived there too early, he might hear me coming and beat a retreat.

We left the bungalow by car at exactly ten o'clock and in less than fifteen minutes reached a point on the road almost opposite the valley between the two hummocks of the hill. The lean man, who had given his name as Allimuthu, indicated that we should have to get out. I parked the car in the shade of a tree just off the road and the three of us got down. I worked the under-lever of my rifle, just to check that it was moving freely. Then Allimuthu, Munuswamy and I set off for the cave.

The hill is about two miles from the road. We reached the base and started climbing towards the valley, which was no longer visible, because of the trees around us. Over their tops I could just see the summits of the two hillocks above, and to the right and left of us .

We climbed for a hour and it was a stiff ascent. Then we came to a veritable sea of lantana bushes which had entirely enveloped the trees and the lesser jungle. This was the place. Alimuthu indicated, where we would have to crawl through and under the lantana for some distance.

I can assure you that covering the next furlong or so of ground was a strenuous effort. We were perspiring and scratched by thorns already as it was. Allimuthu crawled ahead; I followed closely, and Munuswamy was even closer behind. By the time we negotiated that lantana-belt we were dripping with sweat and my khaki shirt and pants were torn in many places. I am sure I left small portions of my face, neck and hands hanging from many of the barbed hooks that serrate each branch of lantana shrub.

We eventually broke free of the belt and entered the valley between the hummocks. It was strewn with boulders everywhere, covered to half their height by spear-grass. Allimuthu whispered that the cave was to the left and about three-fourths of the distance along the valley. It was an impossible place in which to spot a panther, even at a short distance. A dozen tigers would have been equally invisible there.

I took the lead now, with Allimuthu behind and Munuswamy immediately behind him. I kept to the right and skirted the foot of the right-hand hummock, so that if the panther charged from the cave, or any cover to our left, I should have a chance to see it coming. We drew opposite the cave. There was an overhanging cleft in the rock above it. I noticed that this rock was pitted with barnacles of wax that had been the sites of old honeycombs, although there appeared to be no fresh ones. The inside of the cavern was hidden by the long grass and piles of rocks that lay scattered outside it, many of which had apparently rolled down the hill-side from above.

Then we heard it. An unmistakable growl. Allimuthu

reached out to touch my shoulder to stop me, but I had already caught the sound.

It might have been made by a panther — or it might have been made by a bear.

I stopped to think. There were two courses open to me. There was no doubt that the sound had come from in front: from the cave or some place very close to it. I could throw stones or advance a little closer. I felt afraid to follow the latter course. The creature, whatever it was, could rush down upon me from the higher level of the cavern. If I failed to see it coming between the grass and rocks, or missed it with my first short, I could expect real trouble.

Discretion got the better of valour and I whispered to Allimuthu and Munuswamy to hurl stones in that direction. They did so.

Nothing happened.

With my rifle cocked and ready, I watched for the slightest movement in the scene before me.

They hurled more stones, but still nothing happened.

Then I noticed a slight movement of the long grass away to the right, leading up the hill, beyond the side of the cavern where it adjoined the sloping ground behind.

That movement might have been caused by the breeze or by some animal slinking through the grass. Of one thing I was certain, it was definitely not a bear. Bruin is black in Southern India, and I would easily have picked out such a black object against the brown grass. Nor, for that matter could Bruin sneak about in such fashion — not even if he tried. He is a blundering type, who either bursts upon a scene or bursts away from it.

I strained my eyes and then saw part of the spotted shape as it drew level with the height of the rock that overhung the cavern.

The animal had stopped moving now and was undoubtedly looking back at us, although I could not make out its head or face in the grass. A couple of seconds more and it might be gone.

I covered that spotted patch in my sights and gently pressed the trigger.

The panther shot up and out of the grass, bent up double like a prawn, and then rolled backwards down the slope and was hidden from view in the grass. Scrambling upon a boulder, I tried to look down and see him. There was nothing to be seen.

I waited for ten minutes; then I crept forward, after motioning to Allimuthu and Munuswamy to take cover. Every now and then I leaped on to a boulder to see if I could catch a glimpse of the animal.

Eventually I did, and all my caution was unnecessary, for the panther was quite dead. That snap shot of mine had been a lucky one. The .405 bullet had passed through the back of his neck and into his skull.

Examination showed where the ball from Munuswamy's gun had travelled clean through the animal's back, high up and behind the shoulder-blades. It had made a big hole in leaving and had caused a nasty open wound in which maggots were crawling. Two L.G. pellets were embedded in the skin, but the wounds caused by them appeared to be healing. The main wound, however, would eventually have caused the animal's death, if it had not made him a man-eater before then. This was a middle-aged male, just under seven feet in length.

We had a lot of trouble lugging his body through that infernal lantana thicket, but we made it after more toil and sweat.

That evening we laid the body before the D.S.P's feet. Exactly forty-eight hours had passed since I had asked him to extend the time limit of four days. But Munuswamy and I had accomplished the task in half that time. The D.S.P. was all smiles.

Four

The Black Panther of Sivanipalli

SIVANIPALLI HAS ALWAYS BEEN A FAVOURITE HAUNT OF MINE BECAUSE of its proximity to Bangalore and the fact that it lends itself so conveniently to a week-end excursion or even a visit of a few hours on a moonlit night. All you have to do is to motor from Bangalore to Denkanikotta, a distance of forty-one miles, proceed another four miles by car, and then leave the car and walk along a foot-path for five miles, which brings you to Sivanipalli. The hamlet itself stands at the edge of the Reserved Forest.

Nearly three miles to the west of this small hamlet the land drops for about three hundred feet, down to a stream-running along the decline. To the south of the hamlet another stream flows from the east to west, descending rapidly in a number of cascades to converge with the first stream that runs along the foot of the western valley. To the east of Sivanipalli itself the jungle stretches to a forest lodge, Gulhatti Bungalow, situated nearly five hundred feet up on a hillside. East of Gulhatti itself, and about four and a half miles away as the crow flies, is another forest bungalow at a place called Aiyur. Four miles north-east — again is a Forestry Department shed located near a rocky hill named Kuchuvadi. This is a sandalwood area, and the shed houses an ancient huge pair of scales which are used for weighing the cut pieces of sandalwood as they are brought in from the jungle, before being despatched to the Forestry Department's godowns at the block headquarters at Denkanikotta.

Northwards of Sivanipalli, thick scrub jungle extends right up to and beyond the road, five miles away, where you have to leave the car, before setting out for the hamlet on foot.

Sivanipalli itself consists of barely half-a-dozen thatched huts and is hardly big enough to be called even a hamlet. A considerably larger village named Salivaram is found three miles to the north, just a little more than half-way along the foot-path leading to the main road.

Fire-lines of the Forestry Department surround Sivanipalli on all four sides, demarcating the commencement of the surrounding reserved forest at distances varying from half a mile to a mile from the hamlet. There is a water-hole almost at the point where two of these fire-lines converge at the south-eastern corner. The two streams that meet the west of the village at the foot of the three hundred-foot drop wind on through jungle in the direction of another larger village named Anchetty, about eight miles south-westward of Sivanipalli itself.

I have given this rather detailed description of the topography of the surrounding region to enable you to have in mind a picture of the area in which occurred the adventure I am about to relate.

It is an ideal locality for a panther's activities, with small rocky hills in all directions, scrub-jungle, heavy forest and two streams — apart from the water-hole — to ensure a steady water supply, not only for the panthers themselves, but for the game on which they prey. Because of this regular supply of water, a fairly large herd of cattle is quartered at Sivanipalli, which is an added attraction, of course, so far as these felines are concerned!

As a result, quite a number of panthers are more or less in permanent residence around the area. That is the main reason why I was attracted to Sivanipalli the first day I visited it in 1929.

The jungle varies in type from the heavy bamboo that grows in the vicinity of the water-hole to the thick forest on the southern and western sides, with much thinner jungle and scrub, interspersed with sandalwood trees, to the east and north.

The countryside itself is extremely beautiful, with a lovely view of hills stretching away to a hazy and serrated blue line on the western horizon. Banks of mist float up from the jungle early in the morning and completely hide the base of these hills, exposing their tops like rugged islands in a sea of fleecy wool. On a cloudy day, the opposite effect is seen, for when storm-clouds settle themselves along the tops of the hills, entirely hiding them from view, only the lower portions of their slopes are visible, giving the impression of almost flat country.

I have spent many a moonlit night 'ghooming' — derived, from the Urdu verb 'ghoom', meaning 'to wander about' — the jungles around little Sivanipalli. They hold game of every description, with the exception of bison, in moderate numbers. There is always the chance of encountering an elephant, hearing the soughing moan of a tiger, the grating sawing of a panther, or the crash of an alarmed sambar as it flees at your approach while you wander about the moonlit forest. You will not be able to see them — except perhaps the elephant, for both species of carnivora, and the sambar as well, are far too cunning and have long ago seen or heard you coming.

You may stumble upon a bear digging vigorously in the ground for white-ants or tuber-roots, or sniffing and snuffling loudly as he ambles along. You will undoubtedly hear him, long before you see him as a black blob in the confused and hazy background of vegetation, looking grey and ghostly in the moonlight.

As far back as 1934 Sivanipalli sprang a surprise. A black panther had been seen drinking at the water-hole by a herdsman returning with his cattle from the forest where he had taken them for the day to graze. It was shortly after five o'clock in the evening, which is the usual time for the cattle to be driven back to the pens in the village to be kraaled for the night. It is the custom to drive them out in the mornings to the jungle for the day's grazing at about nine, or even later, and to bring them back fairly early in the evening, the apparently late exodus and early return being to allow time for the cows to be milked twice a day.

Thus it was only a little after five and still quite light when the herdsman saw this black panther standing beside a bush that grew close to the water's edge, calmly lapping from the pool. He swore that it was jet black and I had no reason to dis believe him, for there seemed no real point in a deliberate lie. When the herd approached, the panther had gazed up at the cattle; but when the herdsman appeared amidst his beasts it just melted away into the undergrowth.

Now the black panther is not a separate or special species. It is simply an instance of melanism. A black cub sometimes, but very rarely, appears in a litter, the other cubs being of normal size and colour. Black panthers are said to occur more in the thick evergreen forests of Malaya, Burma, Assam and similar localities than around this district. They have also been seen and shot very occasionally in the Western Ghats of India. I have every reason to believe the view that they prevail in these heavy evergreen forests, for then their dark colour would afford considerably better concealment. At the same time, as they are simple instances of melanism, they should occur anywhere and everywhere that panthers exist, regardless of the type of the jungle prevailing. I have only seen one other black panther in its wild state, and that was when it leapt across the road on the ghat section between Pennagram and Muttur near the Cauvery River, at about six one evening. They are one of Nature's — or rather the jungle's — mysteries that has never been quite satisfactorily solved.

If you look closely at a black panther in a zoo, you will discover that the rosette markings of the normal panther are still visible through the black hair, although of course they cannot be seen very distinctly.

When the herdsman saw this black panther, he came to the village and told the people all about it. A black panther had never before been seen or heard of in this area and his tale was generally disbelieved. Having seen the animal with his own eyes, of course, he had no doubts, although he sincerely believed that it had not been a normal or living animal he had laid eyes upon but Satan in just one of the numerous forms he often adopts in the jungle to frighten poor villagers like himself.

Some weeks passed and no one saw or heard of the black panther again. The herdsman's story was forgotten.

One day, some months later, in mid-afternoon, with the sun shining brightly overhead, another herd of cattle was taking its siesta, squatting with closed eyes or lazily munching the grass in the shade of neighbouring trees. The beasts lay in little groups of two to half-a-dozen. The two herdsmen had finished their midday meal of ragi balls and curry, which they had brought along with them, tied up in a dirty piece of cloth, and were fast asleep, lying side by side in the shade of another tree.

It was indeed a peaceful scene, as from an azure sky the tropical sun sent down its fiery rays that were reflected from the earth in waves of shimmering heat. The herd of cattle was relaxed, drowsy and unwatchful when the black panther of Sivanipalli took his first toll.

Appearing unexpectedly, the panther fastened his fangs in the throat of a half-grown brown and white cow, but not before she had time to bellow with pain and leap to her feet, lifting her assailant off the ground with his teeth locked in her throat.

The cow's agonized cry awakened one of the sleeping herdsmen, who was astounded by what he saw. He awoke his companion to look upon the Devil himself in an unexpected black form, and they watched as the stricken cow dropped to earth to ebb out her life, kicking wildly. The black panther maintained his grip. Thus she died. The men had leapt to their feet.

Ordinarily, in the event of an attack by a panther on one of their cattle, they would have rushed to its rescue, brandishing their staves and shouting at he tops of their voices, if not actually to save the life of the victim, at least to drive off the attacker before he could drag away the kill.

In this case neither of them found the nerve to do so. They just stood rooted to the spot and gazed in astonishment. As they did so, the panther released his hold on the throat of the dead cow and looked in their direction. Although he was some fifty yards away they could clearly see the crimson blood gushing from the cow's torn throat and dyeing the muzzle of the panther a deep scarlet against the black background of fur.

They turned tail and fled.

When the few villagers of Sivanipalli heard this account, they were very reluctant to go out and bring back the carcase before it was wholly eaten. This they would most certainly have done had the killer been a normal panther, but the presence of this unheard-of black monstrosity completely unnerved them. They had been told of a panther described as being jet black by the herdsman who had first seen him at the water-hole. Being villagers themselves, they had allowed a wide margin for exaggeration in that case, but here were two more herdsmen, both saying the same thing. Could it be really true?

After that day, the black marauder began to exact a regular toll of animals from Sivanipalli. He was seen on several occasions, so that there was no more doubt in the minds of any of the villagers as to his actual existence and colour.

When the people came to know of his presence in the jungle, forcibly brought home to them by these frequent attacks on their animals, even their usual lethargy and apathy was shaken and they became more and more careful. Eventually a stage was reached when the cattle were not driven out to graze beyond a radius of about a quarter of a mile from the village.

Finding that his food supply was being cut off, the black panther started to extend his field of operation. He killed and ate animals that belonged to herds coming from Anchetty to the south-west and from Gulhatti and Aiyur to the east. He even carried off a large donkey from Salivaram which, as I have said, lay to the north of Sivanipalli and well outside of the forest reserve proper.

Just about this time I happened to pay a visit to Sivanipalli accompanied by a friend. We had gone there after lunch on a Sunday, intending to take an evening stroll in the forest and perhaps get a jungle-fowl, or a couple of green pigeon for the pot. The story of the advent and activities of the black panther greatly interested me. Only once beforehad I seen one of its kind outside a zoo, and I was therefore determined to bag this specimen if possible.

I offered to pay the villagers the price of the next animal killed by this panther if they would leave it undisturbed and inform me. They must go by bus to the small town of Hosur Cattle Farm, which was the closest place to a telegraph office, where a message could be sent to me at Bangalore. I also asked them to spread the same information to all persons living at places where the panther had already struck. Finally, as a further incentive and attraction, I said that I would not only pay for the dead animal, but give a cash baksheesh of fifty rupees to him who carried out my instructions carefully.

Anticipating a call within the next few days I kept my portable charpoy-machan and other equipment ready at Bangalore to leave within a few minutes of receiving the telegram. But it was over a fortnight before that call eventually came. Moreover it arrived late! That is to say, it reached me just before four o'clock in the evening. I was on my way by four-fifteen, but it was about seven-fifteen and quite dark by the time I reached Sivanipalli.

I noticed that the telegram had been handed in at Hosur Cattle Farm at about one-thirty that afternoon, which was far too late, apart from the additional delay that had taken place at the Bangalore end because it had been classed as an ordinary message, instead of an express telegram, as I had specified.

There was a man named Rangaswamy living at Sivanipalli, who had assisted me as shikari on two or three previous occasions, and it was this man who had sent the telegram from Hosur Cattle Farm to say that the panther had made a kill at ten that very morning, shortly after the cattle had left the village for grazing. The herdsman in charge, who like the rest had been told of my offer to pay for the animal that had been killed, with a cash bonus as well, had very wisely, not touched the carcase but had run back to Sivanipalli with the news which he had given to Rangaswamy, who in turn had made a great effort to reach Denkanikotta in time to catch the twelve-fifteen bus. This he had just managed to do, reaching the Hosur Cattle Farm telegraph office by one o'clock.

Commending Rangaswamy and the herdsman for their prompt action in sending me the news, I now had to decide between trying to stalk the panther on his kill with the aid of torchlight or waiting at Sivanipalli until the following evening to sit up for him. The former plan was a complete gamble as there was no certainty whatever that the panther would be on the kill, or anywhere near it, when I got there. At the same time I could not find any very convincing excuse to justify spending the next twenty-four hours cooped up in the hamlet doing nothing.

I enquired where the kill had taken place and was informed that it was hardly half a mile to the west of the village, where the land began its steep descent to the bed of the stream about three miles away. It seemed too temptingly close and this decided me to tell Rangaswamy and the herdsman that I would endeavour to bag the panther that very night while he was eating the kill, if they would lead me to a quarter of a mile from the spot and indicate the direction in which the kill lay. I felt I could trust my own sense of hearing and judgement to guide me from there on.

They were both against this plan and very strongly

advocated waiting till the following evening, but I said that I would like to try it anyhow.

By the time all this talk was finished it was ten minutes to eight and there was no time to be lost, as the panther would probably be eating at that very moment. I clamped my three-cell, fixed-focus electric torch, which was painted black to render it inconspicuous, to my rifle and dropped three spare cells into my pocket, together with five spare rounds of ammunition. Four more rounds I loaded into the rifle, keeping three in the magazine and one in the breech. Although the .405 Winchester is designed to carry four rounds in the magazine and one 'up the spout', I always load one less in the magazine to prevent a jam, which may occur should the under-lever be worked very fast in reloading. Lastly, I changed the boots I had been wearing for a pair of light rubber-soled brown 'khed' shoes. These would to a great extent help me to tread lightly and soundlessly. I was wearing khaki pants and shirt at the time, and I changed into the black shirt I generally wear when sitting up in a machan.

Rangaswamy and the herdsman came along with me up to a dry rivulet. Then the latter told me that this rivulet ran almost directly westwards with just two bends in its course to the spot where the panther had killed. He said the dead cow had later been dragged about two hundred yards inside the jungle roughly northwards of the place where the rivulet completed the second bend.

Their instructions were clear enough and I was grateful for the two bends in the stream which enabled them to be so specific. Telling the men to go back, as I would eventually be able to find my own way to Sivanipalli, I started out on my attempt.

I considered the wisest and most silent approach would be along the bed of this dry stream rather than along the top of either of its banks. Any slight sounds I might inadvertently make would then be muffled and less audible to the panther. Secondly, by walking along the bed of the stream I could easily follow its course without having to shine my torch to see where I was going, which I might have to do if I were to walk along the bank where the vegetation would impede me, the more so because it was very dark indeed and the sky very overcast, the clouds completely hiding the stars and whatever pale light they might have cast.

Accordingly I moved forward very carefully and soon felt the stream making its first curve, which was in a south-westerly direction. After a while the stream started to turn northwards again, and then straightened out to resume its westerly course. I had passed the first of the two bends the herdsman had mentioned.

Not long afterwards it curved into its second bend, but this time in a northerly direction. I moved as carefully as possible to avoid tripping upon any loose stone or boulder that might make a noise. Although, from the information I had been given, I knew the kill was still about three hundred yards away, panthers have very acute hearing, and if my quarry were anywhere in the immediate vicinity, if not actually eating on the kill, he would hear me and, as like as not, make off again.

·Fortunately the rivulet was more or less clear of boulders and bushes along this part of its course and this helped me to edge along silently. A little later it had completed its northward turn and it began to curve southwards. After a few yards it straightened out once more and resumed its main westerly direction.

I halted. I had reached the place at which the panther had killed the cow and from where he had dragged the kill into the jungle for about two hundred yards to the north. I knew that I must now leave the rivulet and strike off into the undergrowth to try and locate the carcass and the killer, whom I hoped to surprise in the act of eating. In the deep gloom I had only my sense of hearing to guide me.

I tip-toed towards the northern bank of the stream which was, at that spot, only breast-high. With my feet still on the sandy bed, I gently laid the rifle on the bank and, folding my arms across my chest, leaned against it, listening intently.

Five minutes passed, but there was no sound of any kind to disturb the silence. Perhaps the kill was too far away to allow me to hear the panther eating; that is, if he was on the kill and if he was eating.

Putting my weight on my hands, I gently drew myself up to the top of the bank, making no sound as I did so. I then picked up the rifle and started to move forward very, very slowly. The darkness was intense. At the same time I knew I had really little, if anything, to fear from the panther should he discover me, as he was not a man-eater and had shown no inclination at any time to molest human beings. Nevertheless, this was my first experience with a black panther and I had heard several of the usual stories about them being exceptionally dangerous and aggressive. That made me quite nervous, I can honestly tell you.

Inching forward, I stopped every few yards to listen for sounds that would indicate that the panther was busy eating. Only they could guide me, as it was hopeless to expect to see anything without the aid of my torch, which could only be used when I was close enough to fire. The slightest flicker of the beam now would drive the panther away should he happen to see the light.

I went along in this fashion, taking what seemed an interminable time. Perhaps I had progressed seventy-five yards or more when, during one of the many stops I made to listen,

I thought I heard a faint sound coming from in front and a little to the right. I listened again for some time, but it was not repeated.

Bushes and trees were now growing thickly around me, and my body, in pushing through the undergrowth, was making some noise in spite of the utmost care I was taking to prevent this. So were my feet as I put them down at each tread. I tried pushing them forward by just raising them off the ground and sliding them along, but I was still not altogether silent. I did this not only to try and eliminate noise, but to disguise my human footfalls should the panther hear me. He would certainly not associate any sliding and slithering sounds with a human being, but ascribe them to some small nocturnal creature moving about in the grass and bushes; whereas the sound of an ordinary footfall would immediately convey the fact that there was a man in the vicinity. An uncomfortable thought came into my mind that I might tread on a poisonous snake in the dark, and the rubber shoes I was wearing did not protect my ankles. I dispelled that thought and tried walking around the bushes and shrubs that arose before me. This caused me to deviate to some extent from the northerly course towards the dead cow I had been instructed to follow.

I stopped every now and then to listen, but the sound I had last heard was not repeated. It was some time later that I concluded that I had far exceeded the distance of two hundred yards from the rivulet at which the kill was said to be lying and also that I had hopelessly lost all sense of direction, enveloped as I was amongst the trees and scrub, under an overcast sky.

Then suddenly I heard the sound I had so long been hoping to hear — the unmistakable sound of tearing flesh and crunching bones.

I had been lucky indeed. The panther was on his kill at

that moment and, what was more, was actually engrossed in feeding. Now all I had to do was to try to creep sufficiently close to enable me to switch on my torch and take a shot. But that was all very well in theory. The idea was far easier than its execution.

To begin with, the sounds did not come from the direction in which I was moving, but to my left and some distance behind me, indicating that I had not steered a straight course in the darkness. I had veered to the right, by-passing the kill. Perhaps the reason I had not heard the sound of feeding earlier was because the panther had only just returned. Or — and it was a most discomforting thought that came into my mind — maybe he had heard me in the darkness as I passed and deliberately stayed quiet.

I paused for a few moments and listened so as to make quite sure of the direction from which the sounds were coming. In the darkness I guessed the panther to be anything from fifty to a hundred yards away.

I now started to slide my feet forward very slowly and very cautiously towards the noise.

If the panther had dragged his kill into or behind a bush it would be impossible for me to get the shot I hoped for. On the other hand, all the advantages would be with the panther were I to fire and wound him, and if he attacked — the proposition was altogether a most unpleasant one.

At the same time, I tried to encourage myself by remembering that never before had this panther molested a human being, and that the light from my torch, when eventually I flashed it would fill him with fear and keep him from attacking me, if it did not drive the animal off entirely.

It is difficult to describe truthfully the minutes that ensued, or to recount what I actually did. My mind and senses were so alert and intense, that I negotiated all obstacles in the way of trees and undergrowth automatically. I knew that as long as I could hear the sounds made by the panther as he feasted I could be certain that he was fully engaged on the task at hand and was unaware of my approach. It was only when these sounds ceased that I would have to look out, for then the panther had heard me and had stopped his feeding to listen.

The sounds continued and so did I, creeping forward cautiously, never putting my foot down till I had tested each step with my toe. When I heard or sensed a leaf rustle beneath me, I groped for a place where I could tread more silently. All the while I kept my eyes strained upon the darkness before me and my ears pricked for the sounds of feeding.

Then suddenly those sounds stopped, and an absolute, awful silence engulfed me.

Had the panther stopped eating for a while of his own accord? Had he finished and gone away? Was he just going away? Or had he heard my stealthy approach and was even at that moment preparing to attack? The alternatives raced through my mind and I came to a halt too.

I remained thus, silent and stationary, for some time. Just how long I have no idea, but I remember that I was thinking what I should do next. To move forward, now that he had stopped eating, would certainly betray my approach to the panther — that is, if he was not already ware of my presence. However careful I might be, it would be impossible for a human being to move silently enough in the darkness to be inaudible to the acute hearing of such an animal. On the other hand, if I stayed put and kept quiet, there was a chance that I might hear the panther, should he approach, although panthers are well known to move noiselessly.

Of the two courses of action, I decided on the latter, so just stood still. As events were shortly to prove, it was lucky that I did so.

For a few moments later a very faint rustling came to my straining ears. It stopped and then began again. Something was moving have been anything. It was a continuous sort of noise, such as a snake would make as it slithered through the grass and undergrowth. But a panther could just as easily cause it by creeping towards me on his belly. I can assure you that it was a very frightening thought.

One thing was certain. The sound did not come from a rat or a frog, or some small jungle creature or night-bird. Had such been the case, the faint noise would have been in fits and starts; in jerks, as it were, each time the creature moved. But this was continuous sort of noise, a steady slithering or creeping forward, indicating slow but continuous progress. It was now certain beyond all doubt that the sound was being made by one of the two things: a snake or the panther.

I have taken some time in trying to describe to you my innermost thoughts as they raced through my mind. In fact, they raced through so fast that I had made up my mind within a few seconds of hearing that ominous, stealthy, creeping approach.

Another few seconds longer and I had decided that the panther was certainly creeping towards me, but as long as I could hear him I knew I was safe from any attack. Then abruptly the noise ceased.

Next came the well-known hissing sound comparable to that made by an angry cobra when it exhales the air from its body in a sudden puff. The panther was beginning to snarl. Very shortly he would snarl audibly, probably growl, and then would come the charge. I had heard the same sequence of noises often enough before and knew what to expect. Quickly raising the rifle to my shoulder, I pressed the switch of the torch.

Two baleful reddish-white eyes stared back at me, but I could make out nothing of the animal itself till I remembered

I was dealing with a black panther, which would be practically invisible at night.

Perhaps it had at first no vicious intentions in approaching me, but had just sneaked forward to investigate what it had heard moving about in the vicinity of its kill. But having identified the source as a hated human being, that hissing start to the snarl showed that the black panther had definitely decided to be aggressive. His eyes stared back at the light of my torch without wavering.

I had plenty of time in which to take careful aim. Then I fired.

Instead of collapsing as I hoped and expected, or at least biting and struggling in its death-throes, the panther sprang away with a series of guttural roars. Had I missed entirely, or had I wounded the beast?

I felt certain that I could not have missed, but that was a question that could only be settled by day-light. I turned to retrace my steps.

This time, of course, I was free to use my torch, and with its aid I walked back roughly in the direction I had come.

I had thought wrong, however, and floundered about for half an hour without being able to regain the rivulet up which I had approached.

I looked at the sky. It was still cloudy and I could not pick out a single star that would help set me, even roughly, in the right direction to Sivanipalli village. Then I remembered that the land sloped gently westwards from the hamlet towards the ravine formed by the two rivers to the west. Therefore, if I walked in a direction that led slightly uphill I could not go wrong and would surely come out somewhere near the village.

I started walking uphill.

But I did not reach Sivanipalli or anywhere near it. To

cut a long story short, it was past eleven-thirty that night when I landed, not at Sivanipalli or its precincts as I had expected, but more than half-way up the track leading northwards to Salivaram. After that, of course, I knew where I was and within half-an-hour had reached the village.

There I awoke Rangaswamy and related what had happened. There was nothing more to do then than bed down for the night.

I have told you already that Sivanipalli was a small place boasting scarcely half-a-dozen huts. Rangaswamy himself was a much-married man with a large household of women and children and I could not expect him to invite me into his hut. So I lay down in a hayrick that stood a little off the main path and pulled the straw, already damp with dew, over me to try and keep warm.

If you should ever wish to undergo the lively experience of being half-eaten alive by the tiny grass ticks that abound in and round forest areas in southern India, I would recommend you to spend night in a hayrick at Sivanipalli. You will assuredly not be disappointed. The grass tick is a minute creature which is normally no larger than the head of a pin. After it has gorged itself on your blood it becomes considerably larger. But it is a most ungrateful feeder. Not only does it suck your blood, but it leaves a tiny wound which rapidly develops into a suppurating sore. This increase in size in direct proportion to the amount of scratching you do to appease the intolerable itch and eventually turns into quite a nasty sore with a brown crust-like scab, and a watery interior. Moreover, should many of these creatures favour you with their attention at the same time, you will surely get a fever in addition to the sores.

I hardly slept at all during the rest of that confounded night, but spent the remaining hours of darkness scratching myself all over. Dawn found me a very tired, a very disgruntled and a very sore individual, who had most certainly had the worst of that night's encounter with the enemy — in this case the almost microscopical little grass tick.

The first thing to do, obviously, was to make some hot tea to raise my morale, which was at decidedly low ebb, and with this in view I went to Rangaswamy's hut, only to find the door closed fast. It was evident that the inmates intended making a late morning. This did not fit in with my plans at all, so I pounded on the solid wooden structure and called aloud repeatedly. After quite a time I heard sounds of movement from within. Eventually the wooden bar that fastened the door on the inside was withdrawn, and a very tousled-headed, sleepy Rangaswamy emerged.

I instructed him to light a fire, which he started to do on the opposite side of the village road by placing three stones on the ground at the three points of a triangle, and in the middle making a smoky fire with damp sticks and straw. I had not brought any receptacle with me for boiling water, so I had to borrow one of his household earthenware pots, which he assured me was absolutely clean, a statement which I myself was not quite prepared to believe from its appearance.

However, the water eventually boiled. I had put some tea leaves into my water bottle, after emptying it of its contents, poured in the boiling water, re-corked it and shook it in lieu of stirring. In the meantime the inmates of the other huts had come to life. They watched me interestedly. Some offered little milk, and someone else contributed some jaggery, or brown sugar, for which I was very grateful, having also forgotten to bring sugar. We boiled the milk and put some lumps of jaggery into my mug, adding tea and boiling milk. Believe it or not, it brewed a mixture that did have some resemblance to tea.

Breakfast consisted of some eggs which I purchased and hard-boiled over the same fire. By about seven I had restored enough interest in myself and events, after my dreadful encounter of the previous night with those obnoxious little ticks, to think of doing something about the panther.

I asked Rangaswamy to get the herdsman who had accompanied us the previous night and who had not put it an appearance so far that morning, or one of his companions, to collect a herd of buffaloes if they were obtainable and drive them into the thick undergrowth to dislodge the panther, as I felt confident that I had not missed the brute entirely with my one shot.

All present answered that there were no buffaloes in Sivanipalli; and no one was willing to risk his cattle being injured in a possible encounter with the panther. Just then my missing companion of the night before — the herdsman who had accompanied me — turned up. He said that he had a friend at Salivaram who owned a muzzle-loading gun. He had wanted to borrow the gun so as to come along and assist me, and with that in view he had set out to Salivaram early that morning while it was yet dark. Unfortunately, his friend was away with his gun and so he had been unable to borrow it. He had returned empty-handed.

I thanked him for his thoughtful intention to assist me, but inwardly I am more than thankful that he had been unsuccessful in borrowing the muzzle-loader. With an inexperienced user, a muzzle-loader can become mighty deadly weapon and I confess I would have felt most nervous with him and that gun behind me.

Having failed to obtain the use of buffaloes, I then tried to enlist the cooperation of the owners of such village curs as there were at Sivanipalli. After some humming and hawing, one solitary cur was produced. She was a lanky bitch, with ears cut off at their base, entirely brown in colour, with a tremendously long curved tail. The typical example of village 'pariah dog', as they are called, whose ears had been amputated when a puppy because of the ticks which would in later life have become lodged on and inside them. With villagers, it is a simple process of reasoning to come to the conclusion that it takes less effort, and far less time, to cut off the ears of their dogs when they are puppies than periodically to remove scores of ticks in later life.

By a strange coincidence, this bitch was named 'Kush', which reminded me of the name of the dog 'Kush Kush Kariya' owned by my old friend of jungle days,* Byra the Poojaree. I don't know if this name is a favourite among the dog owners of the forest areas of Salem District, or whether it just lends itself to a natural sound emitted to attract the attention of any dog. Personally I am inclined to the latter idea. Whatever it may be, I did not know then that this bitch Kush would conduct herself every bit as precociously as her namesake, the animal owned by Byra.

Finally, accompanied by Rangaswamy, the herdsman, Kush and her owner, we set off to try and find out what had become of the panther.

We retraced our steps of the night before to the spot where my companions had left me, then followed in my own footsteps along the two bends in the rivulet and finally climbed its northern bank at the place I had chosen the previous night.

Thereafter I led the way with cocked rifle, Kush running between me and her owner, who came last in file. Between us came Rangaswamy, with the herdsman behind him.

As I had already discovered the night before, the

---

* See *Nine Man-eaters and One Rogue* (Allen & Unwin, London).

undergrowth was dense, so that there was no means of tracing the exact course I had followed only twelve hours previously; nor, being daylight, was I able to pick out any of the trees or bushes I had negotiated in the darkness, although I knew roughly the direction in which I had gone.

The herdsman, of course, knew where the kill lay, but I did not want to go directly to it, my idea being to find, if possible, the place where I had fired at the panther. I did not succeed. Those who have been in jungles will understand how very different in size, shape and location just a small bush appears in daylight compared with its appearance at night. Darkness greatly magnifies the size of objects in the forest, distorts their shape and misleads as regards direction.

To help me find what I was looking for, I got the herdsman to lead us to the dead cow, which he found without difficulty. Incidentally, it had been half-eaten, although of course there was no means of knowing just then whether the panther had fed before my encounter with it, or whether I had entirely missed him and he had returned to feed after I had left. Panthers sometimes return to their kill if they are missed, although such behaviour, in my experience at least, is not very common.

Having reached the kill, I now tried to recollect and recast the direction from which I had come, so as to try and follow my own footsteps from there and eventually come to the spot where I had fired. Unfortunately I had no means of knowing exactly how far the panther had crept towards me, but had to rely entirely on my own judgement as to how far away he had been when I first heard him feeding. Sounds in jungle at night, when both the hearer and the origin of the sound are enveloped by the surrounding undergrowth, can be very deceptive, and the distance they may travel is hard to guess for that very reason. I felt that to the best of my knowledge,

I could have been standing anything from fifteen to fifty yards from the dead cow.

Deciding approximately on the distance where I might have been standing, I paced off those fifteen yards and got one of the men to mark the spot by bending down a small branch. Then I paced another thirty-five yards to attain the maximum distance of fifty yards, which I judged would be about the greatest that could have separated me from the feeding panther I had heard the night before. Here we bent another branch.

Somewhere in between these two markers, and very approximately in the same direction as I was walking, I knew I should find some sign of whether my bullet had struck the panther. If I did not find anything then I would have to conclude that I had completely missed him.

By this time I was also sure that the panther, if he had been wounded, was not lurking anywhere in the immediate vicinity, for had that been the case he would undoubtedly have given some sign by now, hearing us walking about and talking. That sign would have been in the form of a growl, or perhaps even a sudden charge. The absence of any such reaction and the complete silence led me to conclude that even if I had hit him, the wound was not severe enough to prevent him from getting way from the spot.

I instructed my three companions to cast round in a circle, and search carefully for a possible blood-trail. I joined them, and it was not very long before Kush, sniffing at something, attracted her owner's attention. He called out that he had found what we were looking for Gathering around him and the bitch we saw an elongated smear of dried blood on a blade of lemon-grass.

My spirits rose considerably. Here was proof that I had not missed. The height of the blood-mark from the ground indicated that I had wounded my quarry somewhere in the upper part of his body, and as I knew I had fired between his eyes as they had reflected my torch-light, my bullet must have grazed his head. Alternatively, if he had happened to be crouching down with raised hindquarters at that time (a rather unlikely position for a panther to adopt when creeping forward), my bullet might be embedded itself somewhere in the rear part of his back.

This was where Kush showed her merit. She was totally untrained cur, but she instinctively appeared to sense what was required of her. For a little while she sniffed around wildly and at random, then started to whine and run ahead of us.

We followed and found more blood-smears on leaves and blades of grass where the panther had passed. Between the bushes and clumps of high grass there were spots of blood on the ground too. This was an encouraging find, as it showed that the animal had been bleeding freely, clear evidence that the wound was not just a superficial graze.

The blood itself had mostly dried, except in some very sheltered places. There it was moist enough to be rubbed off by the fingers. However, it was neither thick nor dark enough to suggest that my bullet had penetrated a vital organ, such as a lung.

Kush set out very rapidly in a westerly direction, and it was quite obvious she was following a trail that would eventually bring us to the sharp decline in the land, down to the bed of the stream flowing from north to south before it joined the other stream lower down and turned westwards. This stream, before its confluence, is known as the Anekal Vanka. The combined streams are called Dodda Halla, which in the Kanarese language literally means the 'Big Gorge'. It has this name because so many sections flow through ravines and gorges as they twist and twine a torturous path past the village of Anchetty. There the river changes its course abruptly and turns southwards, past Gundalam, to its eventual junction with the Cauvery River. It is this same stream, the Dodda Halla, that was once the haunt of the man-eating tiger of Jowlagiri,* but that is another story. I have explored every section of it, right up to the place where it joins the Cauvery, and have nick-named it the 'Secret River', partly because of the fact that, due to the many miles of rough walking entailed in following its course, few people come that way, and it is delightfully lonely and far away from the sight and sound of human beings; also because I have discovered secrets of geological interest along its banks. I hesitate to divulge them, for with their publicity must automatically follow the next necessary evil, the violation of the sanctity of one of the most delightfully isolated jungle localities in Salem District.

Returning to events as they occurred that morning. The undergrowth was very dense, but to the unerring instinct of Kush this appeared to offer no obstacle. In fact, the trouble lay in keeping up with her. Her small and lithe brown body dodged in and out between bushes and outcrops of 'wait-a-bit' thorn. Our legs, hands and arms were severely lacerated by these thorns because we were moving at a foolish speed in order to keep the bitch in sight, taking no precautions whatever against a sudden attack by the wounded panther if he happened to lie immediately ahead of us. At times the brambles and other obstructions slowed us down, and Kush would get far ahead and disappear. It then became necessary to whistle her back, and when she did so, which was only after some minutes, she appeared to experience some difficulty in picking up the trail again.

---

* See *Nine Man-eaters and One Rogue* (Allen & Unwin, London).

We had no rope with us, so I borrowed the herdsman's turban and knotted one end of the cloth around Kush's neck, giving the other end to her owner. But it was a small turban and the cloth too short. The man had to stoop down to retain his hold, while Kush strained, spluttered and coughed in her anxiety to forge ahead.

In this fashion we progressed until we eventually reached the edge of the plateau where the land began to fall away sharply to the bed of the Anekal Vanka stream, which we could see between breaks in the tree-tops below us, the sun glinting on the silvery surface of the water as it meandered from side to side on its sandy bed. The stream itself was three-fourths dry at that time of the year.

A little later we came across the first concrete evidence that the panther had begun to feel the effects of his wounds. He had lain down in the grass at the foot of a babul tree and had even rolled with pain, as blood was to be seen in patches and smears where he had rested and tossed. Kush spent a long time at this spot and evinced another unusual characteristic by licking at the blood. Ordinarily a village cur is terrified of a panther, but Kush, as I have said already, was an unusual animal, and it was indeed very lucky that her owner had been willing to bring her along. Normally, villagers who will not hesitate to lop off the ears of a puppy at their base, will vote that it is a cruel practice to employ a dog for tracking down a wounded panther or tiger and will flatly refuse to be parties to such a deed. As it was, without the invaluable aid rendered by this bitch, we would never have been able to follow the blood-trail as we did that morning. It would not have been visible to normal human eyesight in the heavy underbrush.

As we descended the deep decline vegetation became sparser and the ground became bare and rocky. Boulders were scattered everywhere, interspersed with tufts of the tough long-bladed lemon-grass.

Then we reached a stage where there were only boulders, big and small, and the descent had almost ended. This was the high-level mark reached by the waters of the stream when in spate during the monsoon.

Here, with the end of the vegetation, tracking became easy. Drops of tell-tale rusty brown, where blood had fallen from the wounded animal and splashed on the rocks, revealed its passage. Judging from the distance we had come and the quantity of blood that the panther had lost, it appeared to be more severely hurt than I had at first imagined. The wound must have been a deep one and the bullet had probably struck an artery. Had it been elsewhere, particularly in some fleshy part of the animal, there was a possibility that the bleeding might have lessened, if not ceased entirely, by the natural fat under the skin coming together and closing the hole made by the bullet.

We reached the narrow bed of the stream in which the water was still flowing. Here the panther had crouched down to drink, and there were two sets of blood-marks, one nearer to the water's edge than the other. The marks further away indicated more bleeding than those closer. This was curious and it puzzled me greatly at the time, considering I had fired only one shot the night before. The solution was an even greater surprise.

At one spot the panther had stepped into his own gore and had left a clear pug-mark on a rock just before he had waded across the stream. The mark had been made by the animal's one of the forefeet and its size suggested a panther of only average proportions that was probably male. The blood had been washed off the foot by the time the animal had reached the opposite bank, but the dried drops on the stones and boulders continued.

After crossing the stream the panther had changed his course and had walked parallel with the edge of the water and alongside it for nearly two hundred yards, then he had turned to the left and begun to climb the opposite incline. The stones and rocks once more gave way rapidly to vegetation, and again we negotiated thickets of long grass, thorny clumps, small scattered bamboos and trees.

Up and up the panther had climbed, and so now did Kush on the trail, conducting herself as if she had been specially trained for the job. Eventually we came to the road which leads from Denkanikotta to Anchetty and which intersects the forest on its way downwards to the latter village. We had come out on this road exactly opposite the nineth milestone, which we now saw confronting us at the roadside. Incidentally this was the road on which I had parked my car near the fifth milestone when I had left it the evening before to walk to Sivanipalli.

Many carts had traversed the road during the night and in the earlier hours of that morning, and the scent was completely lost for a moment in the powdery brown dust. But Kush had no difficulty in picking it up on the other side, and we followed behind her.

The grass and bamboos gradually gave way to more thorns and more lantana, which tore at our clothing and every part of our anatomy they touched. In places, where the panther had crept beneath the lantana and thorn-bushes, an almost impenetrable barrier confronted us. There was no way through and there was no way around, leaving no alternative but to follow by creeping on our bellies beneath the bushes.

My rifle was an encumbrance in such places and conditions, and I cursed and swore as the thorns tore at my hair and face and became embedded in my hands, body and legs. The plight of my three companions was infinitely worse, as they wore

113

thinner and less clothing than I did. Perhaps their skins were thicker — I really don't know. But I am sure that the language that floated from all four of us would have won us prizes in any Billingsgate contest. Only Kush was unperturbed, and from her position ahead she kept looking back at us, clearly impatient at the slow, clumsy progress we were making.

But this time it was also evident that the wounded animal was heading for a large hill that lay about half a mile behind a hamlet named Kundukottai. This village was situated between the 7th and 8th milestones on the Denkanikotta-Anchetty road which we had just crossed. The top of the hill was known to hold many caves, both large and small, and what was worse, the arched roofs of some of the larger caves had been chosen by the big jungle rock-bees as safe and ideal places in which to construct their hives. I had often seen these hives as I had motored along the road to Anchetty on previous occasions.

I felt that my chances of bagging the black panther were becoming very dim indeed. Looking for him amongst those caves would be like searching for the proverbial needle in a haystack. In addition, the panther had the bees to guard him if his place of retreat happened to be one of the many caves they had chosen for their hives. I can assure you that these rock bees, when disturbed, can be most formidable opponents.

We plodded along and broke cover below the line of caves where the thorn bushes thinned out and became less numerous owing to shelves of sloping rock, worn glass-smooth by centuries of rain water as it ran down from above.

The scent led up and across the sloping shelf of rock to one of the larger openings that loomed above us. From where we stood we could see the black masses of at least half-a-dozen bee-hives hanging from the roof of the cave, each about a yard long by about two feet wide. The remains of old abandoned hives were scattered here and there amongst them, the wax sticking out from the rock in flatfish triangles of a dirty yellow-white colour, perhaps nine inches long.

My canvas-soled shoes enabled me to climb the slippery shelf without much difficulty, while the bare feet of my companions helped them even more. Kush's claws made a faint clicking sound as she scampered up the rock ahead of us.

We reached the entrance to the cave where a subdued rustling sound was all-pervading. It came from the movements of millions of bees as they crawled in and about the hanging hives above us. There was also a continuous faint droning, that arose from the wings of the busy insects as they flew in from the jungle with honey from the wild flowers, which they would store in the hives, and from those departing on a trip for more.

The little creatures were absorbed in their duties and paid no attention to us, but we realized that if we happened to disturb them, these same little creatures, so unoffending and peaceful now, would pour on to us in a venomous venomous attack like a torrent of black lava and sting us to death in a matter of a few minutes.

We stood before the entrance of the cave, where the blood trail, very slight now, was still visible in the form of two tiny dried droplets. They showed that the wounded beast had gone inside.

Near its mouth the cave was comparatively large, some twenty feet across by about twenty feet high. Daylight filtered into the interior for some yards, beyond which all was darkness. I counted nine separate bee-hives, all of great size, suspended from the roof of the cave close to the entrance. The floor was of rock and appeared to be free of the usual dampness associated with such places. No doubt this accounted for the cave being inhabited by the panther — and the bees, too. For these animals and insects, particularly the former, dislike damp places.

I whispered to my three companions to remain outside and to climb up the sloping rock by the sides of the entrance to a point above the cave, and on no account to go downhill, as that was the direction in which the panther would charge if he passed me. They disappeared, and Kush and I entered the cave.

From that moment Kush seemed to know there was danger ahead. Gone was her erstwhile courage, and she slunk at my heels, gradually falling behind me.

I walked forward as far as I could see in the dim light that filtered in from outside. At most, this might have been for about thirty feet. Then we came to a halt. I could go no further as, not anticipating that my quarry would enter such a cave, I had not brought my torch with me from the village.

There were now two alternatives either to try to arouse the wounded animal, or to return to Sivanipalli for the torch, telling the men to keep watch from their position of comparative safety above to guard against the panther slinking out before I came back. I should, of course, have followed the second course. Not only was it safer, but more sure. I suppose, really, I felt too lazy to go all that way back and return again. So I thought I would give the first plan a trial and if possible save myself the trouble of a long walk.

I whistled and shouted loudly. Nothing happened. I shouted again. Kush, who had been shimpering, then started to back. Still nothing happened.

The cave had narrowed down to about half its dimensions at the entrance. Only silence rewarded our efforts. The deep, dark interior was as silent as a grave.

Had the wounded animal died inside? This seemed unlikely, as there was no evidence that the panther had lain down again after the first rest he had taken before crossing the Anekal Vanka stream. Had he left the cave before our arrival? This might easily have happened; but again there was no evidence to suggest that such was the case.

I looked around for something to throw. Just one large stone lay close to my feet. I picked it up in my left hand and found it heavy.

I am left-handed, for throwing purposes, although I shoot from the right shoulder. I had already cocked my rifle, and, balancing it in the crook of my right arm, threw the stone under-arm with as much force as I could muster. It disappeared into the blackness of the cave. I heard it strike the rock floor with a dull thud and then clatter on in a series of short bounces.

The next instant there came the all-too-familiar series of coughing roars as the panther catapulted itself at me out of the darkness. Being a black panther, I could not see it till it emerged from the gloom, two or three yards in front of my rifle. I fired — but the impetus of its charge made the panther seem to slide forward towards me. I fired again. The confines of the cave echoed and re-echoed with the two reports.

Then all hell was let loose. The sound of the bees, which had been registering all this while almost subconsciously on my hearing as a faint humming drone, rose suddenly to a crescendo. The daylight coming in at the entrance to the cave became spotted with a myriad of black, darting specks, which increased in number as the volume of sound rose in intensity. The black objects hurled themselves at me. The air was alive with them.

I had aroused the wrath of the bees. Gone was all thought of the panther as I whipped off my khaki jacket, threw it around my exposed back and face and doubled for the entrance.

The bees fell upon me as an avalanche. They stung my hands. They got through the folds of the jacket and stung my

117

neck, my head, my face. One even got down under the collar of my shirt and stung my back.

The stings were horribly painful.

I slid down the sloping rock up which we had climbed just a short while before. As from far away, I could hear Kush yelping in anguish. As fast as I moved, my winged tormentors moved faster; the air was thick with them as they dive-bombed me mercilessly, I remembered comparing them to Japan's suicide pilots, who sacrificed their lives and their machines by literally throwing themselves upon the enemy. Similarly, each bee that stung me that day automatically sacrificed its life, for the end of every bee's sting is barbed, and in trying to extricate the point after it has stung an enemy the insect tears out its sting, with the venom-sac attached. These remain embedded in the skin of the victim. Thus, in stinging, the bee does irreparable damage to itself, from the effects of which it dies very soon.

I reached the foot of the sloping shelf with the bees still around me. In desperation I crawled under the thickest lantana bush that was available. Always had I cursed this shrub as a dreadful scourge to forest vegetation and a pest to man, encroaching as it always does on both jungles and fields, in addition to being an impediment to silent and comfortable movement along game trails; but at that moment I withdrew my curses and showered blessings on the lantana instead. It saved my life. For bees must attack and sting during flight, another resemblance they bear to the aforementioned dive-bombers. Clever as they are, they have not the sagacity to settle down and then creep forward on their feet to a further attack. The code with them is to dive, sting and die. The closeness of the network of lantana brambles prevented their direct path of flight on to my anatomy. And so I was delivered from what would have been certain death had the area just there been devoid of the pestiferous lantana I had so often cursed before.

For no matter how fast I had run, the bees would have flown faster and descended in their thousands upon me.

All the nine hives had been thoroughly disturbed by now, and the buzzing of angry bees droned and drummed in the air above me. I lay still and silent under the protecting lantana, smarting from the many stings the creatures had inflicted on me during my flight.

It took over two hours for the droning to subside and for the bees to settle down to work once more. I felt very sleepy and would have dozed were it not that the pain of the stings kept me awake. The hot burning sensation increased as my skin swelled around each wound.

It was three in the afternoon before I could crawl out of the lantana and wend my way downhill to the road; from there I walked to Kundukottai village. There I found my three followers. They had almost completely escaped the attention of the bees at their vantage point above the entrance to the cave. The bees had evidently concentrated their attack on the moving enemies immediately before them — myself and poor Kush, who was also with the three men now. She had been badly stung, and I had no doubt that the panther had also received their close attention.

All of us walked to the car where I had left it the day before. After we had piled in, I set out for Denkanikotta, where there was a Local Fund Hospital and Dispensary. It was quite late in the evening when we roused the doctor. He took us to his surgery in the hospital and with the aid of a pair of tweezers removed the stings embedded in Kush and myself. We had received, respectively, nineteen and forty-one barbs from those little demons in the cave. The doctor applied ammonia to our wounds.

We spent the night in the forest bungalow at Denkanikotta. The beds there are of iron with no mattresses. So I lay in an arm-chair. The three men slept on the verandah with Kush.

The stings brought on an attack of ague and fever. Kush suffered, too, and I could hear her whimpers. My neck, face and hands were still swollen. One bee had succeeded in registering a sting not far from the corner of my left eye, causing it partially to close.

Down made me look a sorry sight with my swollen eye and puffy face as I stood before the one blurred mirror the bungalow boasted.

We waited till past ten and then drove back to the ninth milestone. Retracing our steps — but this time along cattle and game trails where walking was comparatively easy — we came to the place below the rock-shelf where we had stood the day before.

The bees were once again busy at their hives. All was peaceful and serene.

Leaving the three villagers, I climbed the slope with Kush for the second time and cautiously approached the cave. I knew I was safe from the bees unless I disturbed them again. And I was almost sure my two shots the previous day had killed the panther. Even if they had not, the bees would have completed that work.

I was right. Lying a few paces inside, and curled into a ball, was the black panther, dead and quite stiff. Kush stayed a yard away from it, sniffing and growling. I put my hand over her mouth to quieten her for fear of disturbing those dreadful bees and bringing them down upon us once more.

Walking out of the cave, I beckoned to the men to come up to me. Together we hauled the panther down the slope. The herdsman, who carried a knife, then lopped off a branch to which we tied its feet with lengths of creepervine. All four of us then shouldered the load and carried it to the waiting car, where I slung the dead animal between bonnet and mudguard.

At the Denkanikotta forest bungalow I removed the skin. I was a male panther, of normal size, measuring six feet seven inches in length. The rosettes showed up distinctly under the black hairs that covered them. It was the first — and incidentally the only — black panther I have ever shot.

It was difficult to detect the bee-stings, embedded in the black hair, but I told the men to make a careful count of the barbs they extracted, which I personally checked. There were 273 stings in that animal, confirmed by the number of barbs extracted. There must have been many more that escaped our attention.

I rewarded the men for their services and returned to Bangalore well compensated for the punishment I had received from the bees — for I had a black panther skin, which is something very uncommon — and I had a wonderfully sagacious dog, Kush, whom I purchased from her owner for seven rupees.

There is one thing I nearly forgot to mention. You will remember that I had discovered two separate blood-marks at the spot where the panther had stopped to drink in the Anekal Vanka stream. One of them had shown signs of greater bleeding than the other, and because I had fired only one shot I had wondered about it at the time. The reason was now quite clear. My one bullet, aimed between the eyes, had missed its mark, had furrowed past the temple and ear and embedded itself in the animal's groin. The second wound was the one that had bled severely. The first was only superficial. Evidently the body had been slightly twisted and crouched for the spring as I had fired that night, just in time.

Of the two shots fired in the cave, one (the first) had struck the panther in the chest, and the other, as the panther skidded towards me, had entered the open mouth and passed out at the back of the neck.

Five

Snakes and Other Jungle Creatures

MUCH HAS BEEN WRITTEN ABOUT THE ANIMALS OF THE INDIAN JUNGLE that is of great interest to people to whom any sort of animal and any forest form sources of secret attraction. Yeoman authors like Dunbar-Brander, Champion, Glasfurd, Best, Corbett and a host of others have blazed the trail and have recorded the habits of these animals as they personally experienced them. Some of them wrote a half-a-century ago, a time when, it must be remembered, the jungles of the Indian peninsula were literally alive with game, particularly carnivora. There writings were always appreciated, but it is only now that the real intrinsic value of their momentous works comes to the fore, and it will be safe to say that as the years roll by and the wild life of India becomes a thing of the past, the records of these great men will be of ever-increasing value, preserving for posterity knowledge that no riches could ever hope to buy.

It is a significant fact that the shikaris of India and even the great white hunters of Africa, who started their careers as trophy seekers or, in the latter case, as professionals, have during their lives invariably found an increasing love for the animals of the forests which they once hunted and killed. The great majority of them came to eschew the habit of killing in favour of the worthier but more difficult art of wild animal photography and the study of nature.

In the early years it was considered a rather hazardous undertaking to enter the jungle on a shooting trip. Apart from the dangers from the animals themselves, which were deemed very great, there were the risks in the form of various poisonous snakes, scorpions, spiders and other creatures, and the threats to health in the jungle diseases such as malaria, black-water fever and so on.

For instance, in my father's day a journey to the forest at the foothills of the Nilgiri Mountains, or to the jungles that clothed the Districts of Shimoga and Kadur in Mysore State, or to the area around the Western Ghats, was considered a very risky undertaking. The mists that shroud these tracts in the early hours of the morning were regarded as a direct cause of bronchitis, pneumonia and particularly malaria. The jungle beasts were said to be most bold and terrifying.

The old writers have, on the contrary, shown us that the wild creatures were far from aggressive in their habits, and that almost without exception they were afraid of the human race. Science has since taught us that no poisonous spiders, lizards or frogs exist in India and only a few varieties of poisonous snake; also that bronchitis and pneumonia can be contracted anywhere, even in the hottest and driest cities of India. Sir Ronald Ross has shown that a particular species of mosquito carries the malaria parasite and not the damp mists and air of the forests. That parasite is found not only in jungles but throughout the length and breadth of the land. The malarial mosquito breeds in stagnant water and dirty drains, and such places abound even in the largest cities. Campaigns and measures by the authorities have done much to mitigate these evils, and medical science has produced rapid and almost certain cures for the complaints themselves, so that they no longer arouse the dread they once did.

As regards the dangers from wild animals and snakes, one's own experience has been and always will be the best teacher. But with a very few exceptions, and those in only particular places, it is safe and true to state that the dangers of a sojourn in the thickest of forests are far less than those run by a pedestrian when crossing any busy city street. The writers of the past have all shown this.

Of course a greenhorn to the game sometimes does something foolish that may involve him in trouble, but that trouble is entirely the outcome of his own inexperience and ignorance. Experience, particularly for him who is not only willing out anxious to learn, is easily acquired.

The tiger is acclaimed the king of the Indian jungles because the lion is not to be found anywhere except in the Gir Forest in the Gujarat peninsula, where it is very strictly protected. The tiger is a magnificent, beautiful and lordly animal, but it is the elephant who is in actual fact the real lord of the Indian forests by virtue of his great bulk, enormous strength and sometimes unpredictable temperament. As a rule he is certainly a far more dangerous animal than the tiger, and aborigines living in areas where both these animals abound treat the tiger, with the exception of course of a man-eater, with contempt, while they have the greatest respect for the wild elephant. Walk along a jungle trail with any of these aboriginal tribesmen. Even should you be so lucky as to spot a tiger or panther, he will point it out to you with good-natured indifference. But should the sound of the breaking of a branch come to his ears, he will immediately halt in his tracks and say the one word in his vernacular which means 'elephant', judge the direction from which the sound came and endeavour to find a way that avoids passing anywhere near the locality in which the elephant is feeding.

This inherent caution is the outcome of the accumulated jungle experience of his fore bearers and himself. They and he have come to know the uncertain nature of these mighty beasts, and so they avoid taking any unnecessary risk.

As a result of fact the wild elephant is in general a harmless creature, subject to moods and subject to sudden excitement, fright and irritation. To this generalisation there are four exceptions.

By strange contrast, and unlike African elephants, the greater the number in an Indian elephant herd the less the danger from its individual members. The four exceptions are: the accredited 'rogue' elephant that has already killed a human being, a 'musth' elephant in that periodical sexual state peculiar to the male of the species, occasionally a single male feeding apart from the herd, and a female accompanied by a young calf to protect which she will readily give her life. It is to be noticed that in each of these four cases the danger arises from a single animal and not from the herd. African elephants are reported to have the ability, when occasion demands, of acting collectively when they attempt to charge down upon a hunter *en masse*. The Indian elephant does not do this.

But in any of the four instances listed, the individual animal can be very dangerous and a creature of terrible destructiveness. It will pursue a human being inexorably, sometimes for as much as a mile, provided the man can keep going that far, till it can run him down. Then it will tear him literally limb form limb, or squash him to a pulp by stamping upon him and rubbing him into the ground with its feet, or beat him against the trunk of a tree or whatever happens to be handy, or toss him high into the air.

While sitting at a waterhole deep in the forest I often amuse myself at the expense of the wild elephants that come there for their daily drink and wash-up, by calling like a tiger or imitating the sawing sound made by a panther. In the former instance, the elephants, if in a herd, usually trumpet shrilly and dash away to the accompaniment of much crashing of branches and underbrush. It is delightful to watch mothers with young babies practically carry their youngsters before them by supporting them under their bellies with their trunks, as they hurry away from the presence of that supposed tiger lurking somewhere in the bushes beside the water. Should an elephant have come alone, he invariably stands quite still when he hears the call, flaps his ears forwards to catch the sound and endeavours to scent the whereabouts of the enemy by 'feeling' the air with his trunk. Then he will turn around and slip silently into the jungle. An occasional elephant stamps its feet and tosses its head and trunk to and fro in anger, but within a minute, it too will disappear from the scene. I have not encountered a single elephant that stood its ground while I continued making the tiger-call. Obviously, despite their size and strength, they lack the nerve to remain in the presence of that dreaded feline. I have read somewhere that the elephant's eye has the property of magnifying the object it looks upon. Naturally this would make a tiger or a human being appear relatively larger to the elephant than they are in reality. Perhaps this is the real explanation of why elephants are afraid of tigers, panthers and human beings too.

Panther calls produce a somewhat different effect. If in a herd, the male elephants become aggressive and show signs of being prepared to defend the young. But a single elephant invariably makes off, although not nearly in such a hurry as when a 'tiger' calls. One or two have stamped the water or struck it with their trunks and then continued drinking. But it was clear they were decidedly nervous and uncomfortable.

These amusing little experiments of mine clearly indicate that elephants are far from courageous creatures, despite their great bulk and strength. On the contrary, they are decidedly nervous and timid. Perhaps I am safe in saying that, like all 'bullies', they will only take fullest advantage of a situation in which their enemy shows signs of fearing them. But attack, apart from the four exceptions mentioned, particularly against anything that might retaliate, is not on the bill of behaviour of the average elephant.

Elephants appear to have an instinctive dislike for white objects. For this very reason milestones and furlong stones along roads in elephant-infested areas are painted black, for such objects, if white, would be immediately uprooted and flung away as soon as an elephant caught sight of them. For the same reason it would be unsafe to dress in white and roam in an elephant forest, for it would only invite attack. In years gone by white, solar topees were the vogue on the ground that, besides being sunproof, they kept the head of the wearer cool by reflecting the sun's rays. A gentleman of my acquaintance was once wandering in a jungle wearing such a white helmet. Why he wore it in the jungle I do not know, for apart from the aversion of elephants it would be very conspicuous and render hopeless any chance of successfully stalking living creatures. Anyhow, he wore it. He and his tracker, a Sholaga, were going along the ridge of a hill when they noticed an elephant about two hundred yards away, feeding on the other side of a clearing and a little higher up the hill. At the same moment the elephant saw them. Normally it would not have seen them at that distance, for elephants have extremely poor sight, and the breeze was blowing towards them, so that it could not have scented them. But that shining white helmet could not be missed against the green and brown background of the jungle. The elephant trumpeted and gave chase. The hunter and the Sholaga turned tail and fled. Fortunately the Sholaga was an experienced tracker, with years of recorded service and prestige in taking 'sahib log' into the jungle. He did not desert his protégé, but ran along behind him, telling him in which direction to run. The elephant gained on them rapidly. Then the Sholaga overtook the huntsman, snatched off his white hat and threw it to the ground, while urging the sahib to keep on running. The elephant reached the hat and lost interest in chasing them further. Needless to say, that nice piece of headgear also lost all semblance of shape by the time the elephant was through with it. He had not been interested in pursuing or harming them, but it had been too much to ask him to tolerate that dreadful white object. He just had to obliterate it.

Fights among male elephants have been known to go on, with but a few pauses for rest, for as long as three days. A fight may be occasioned by rival tuskers for the favours of a bulky lady, although such examples are few. More often it happens when driving a male elephant in musth out of the herd when his attentions to the ladies of the herd become too troublesome. Mostly it happens when a young bull, attaining the fitness that comes with the prime of his life, challenges the master bull of the herd for its leadership.

During such struggles, the bulls do great injury to each other by gouging with their tusks at any portion of the foe's anatomy that may offer itself. It goes without saying that during and after these fights the contestants are in the vilest of tempers and woe betide any living thing they may see.

There was an instance of a forester belonging to the Salem District Forestry Department who came upon a pair of bulls engaged in such a struggle in the fastnesses of the Dodda Halla valley of the Salem District. In that case a strange thing happened. The erstwhile contestants forgot their enmity and thundered down upon him together. He was a sorry mess when eventually his departmental colleagues came upon his remains some days later.

I have written about 'rogue' elephants in some of my earlier stories, so I won't add much about them here, beyond saying that they are the nastiest customers one could encounter in a jungle. Once having heard their trumpet-like screams of rage and hate, and seen their huge bodies bearing down upon you through bush and undergrowth, with trunk curled inwards, ears extended and short tail erect, you will remember the experience till your dying day. The degree of punishment they will inflict on a human being if they catch him varies. One rogue in the foot-hills of the Nilgiris tossed a forest guard high into the air. In falling, he became impaled on the broken end of a bamboo stem and eventually died. The rogue elephant of Segur, shot by the Reverend Bull, was a comparatively small animal, but was noted nevertheless for his sagacity and ferocity. He would literally stalk a human being or ambush him from behind a rock or clump of bamboos. He caught a coolie woman on the Segur road, stamped her flat, rubbed her remains into the ground with his feet and then playfully tore off the silver anklet she was wearing, as well as the string of wooden beads around her neck, both of which he threw some yards away. There was the case of a convalescent forester in the Coimbatore District who was suffering from guinea-worm. After long periods on sick leave, he eventually became so lazy that he would not — or more probably could not — work. He was transferred to the Billigirirangan Mountain

Range, which is an area infested with elephants. It also harboured a rogue at that time, which had long been proclaimed as such but had never been shot. One day this man had the misfortune to meet the rogue. It chased him. In running he twisted an ankle while crossing a stream. The rogue caught up with him and tore him apart. It rampaged around his scattered remains for three days after that and would not permit any traffic to pass, before it had the grace to leave and allow his relatives to gather for cremation what remained. There was another rogue near Bailur in the same district which threw a bullock cart with its oxen off the road. It was killed by Mr Van Ingen, the famous taxidermist of Mysore.

It must be remembered that the incidents I have mentioned above were committed by rogue elephants and hence are unusual. The normal elephant, as I have tried to show, is a timid, retiring creature without any signs of boldness or bravery in its make-up.

For sheer, unsung grit, a wounded wild boar is the biggest-hearted animal in the Indian jungle. Within his comparatively small bulk, contrasted against the much larger animals, he packs more courage, more ferocity and determination, and above all more individual dash and stamina and thirst to kill than any animal I know. Wounded elephants, bison, and even tigers and panthers will invariably try to escape at first and only retaliate when cornered. But wound the old wild boar and just let him know where you are, and down he comes upon you. No lancer at Balaclava ever charged with more gallantry and determination than will 'porky' if you wound him and then reveal your position.

The tiger very closely follows the elephant as the most interesting animal in the jungles of India. I think he is fascinating. Except for the periodic man-eater which takes to killing and eating human-beings and becomes a terror within an area perhaps of some hundreds of square miles, the tiger otherwise well deserves the label of 'gentleman'.

Hunting him might very truly and justifiably be considered the king of all sports. Following him up when wounded is indeed a hazardous undertaking and calls for the best possible jungle-craft on the part of the hunter. But to leave a wounded tiger in the jungle without attempting to finish him off is not only cruel, in that the wounded beast continues to suffer, but cowardly too, having regard to the poor folk who live in and near that area. For that very wound may be the point in his life that turns him into a man-eater. Moreover, he is a gallant opponent. He tries at first to avoid a conflict, but if followed and pressed too hard invariably turns and fights to the last.

A well-known military person of Bangalore, the Rev. Mr. Jervis, once followed a wounded tiger in Kumsi in the Shimoga District. It attacked him and practically chewed through his arm. His Indian car driver, who was also acting as his gun-bearer, but unfortunately knew nothing about using firearms, most pluckily drove the beast off his master while it was mauling him, by attacking it with the butt-end of the spare shot-gun he was carrying. Very richly did he deserve the reward he was given by the congregation of the church for this heroic act. The unfortunate padre was carried to the Kumsi travellers' bungalow, where the local doctor, with the best means available to him at that time, amputated the minister's arm, which was torn to shreds. The arm was later buried in the compound of the bungalow beneath a tree. A special carriage was attached to the next train running to Bangalore and the Rev. Mr. Jervis was sent back, though he died in the Bowring Hospital in Bangalore the next day and was duly buried with full military honours.

The panther does not approach the tiger in size, strength or grandeur. He can also be a very mean foe. I have said before that even man-eating panthers, despite their proclivity for human flesh, generally share the fear of the human species that is distinctive of the rest of their kind. They will rarely attack from in front, but will almost without exception creep upon their prey unawares from behind, as a rule favouring the hours of darkness for such an attack.

The average panther has a propensity for dog flesh which he appears to regard as a delicacy. There were a couple of panthers living on a small hillock crowned by a temple, hardly a mile out of Kollegal Town in Coimbatore District. They made themselves a perfect nuisance to the American missionaries who lived not far from the foot of that hill, by eating up their dogs just as fast as the worthy missionaries could replace them. Eventually the panthers became so obnoxious that the local Sub-Inspector of Police, accompanied by some youths of the town, volunteered to get rid of them by smoking them out of the cave in which they lived. As a preliminary step, the grass in the area was fired. When that failed to expel the miscreants, lighted torches were thrown into the cave. This had the effect of bringing them out at the double, and in the fracas that ensued one panther was killed and some boys were hurt. The other got away after mauling one of the older members of the party. A missionary by the name of Buchanan went after it but was mauled, while the panther escaped.

'Bruin', the sloth bear of the South Indian jungles, is a short-sighted, bad-tempered animal; not brave by any means, but extremely excitable. He is generally a coward. Very recently a family party of three sloth bears — father, mother and rather a big junior — walked into a cave near Closepet in which a panther had already taken up his abode. The panther attacked the three bears. Junior fled on the spot. The two older bears tried to resist, but their courage turned to water before the razor-sharp claws of the infuriated panther, and they also fled. Not only that, but the he-bear was in such a hurry to get away that he did not look where he was going and rolled down a rock about a hundred feet high and broke both his fore-legs. The villagers speared him to death the next morning.

Should he see or hear you coming the sloth bear will dash off at speed. If you meet him suddenly at a corner, he will attack without provocation — not impelled by bravery but by fright and a desire to get away from your presence. Possibly he thinks you may try to prevent him doing so, and to make sure that you do not he sets about mauling you. And he will do that very thoroughly, his objective being the eyes and face of the offending being, which he will invariably tear with his blunt four-inch talons. And he will make a better job of it by biting, too. I have seen jungle-folk who had been attacked by bears: the wounds inflicted have been really ghastly, leaving the victims with disfigured faces for the rest of their lives.

Bruin often behaves like a clown when digging for roots or burrowing into the nests of white-ants. The sounds he emits can resemble anything from a bag-pipe being inflated to the droning of an aeroplane, from the buzzing of an angry wasp to the huffing of a blacksmith's bellows, the latter being a sort of background accompaniment to the buzzing and humming sounds. He will twist and contort his body into all shapes provided he can get at those tasty roots or at those most delectable and delicious termites. He is a heavy sleeper, often sleeping in the shallow holes he has dug in the ground, or between rocks, or in caves, or under shady trees and in grassy areas. He snores so audibly as to be clearly heard at a distance. When he is not snoring, an unsuspecting man may almost tread upon him before he awakens. That sudden awakening will almost certainly cause the startled bear to attack without a second thought.

The Sholagas of Coimbatore are very plucky in dealing with bears. They have been known to split open the skulls of many of these animals with their short, sharp axes. The bear rises upon its hind legs to reach for the face of its victim, thereby exposing its own head, face, throat and chest, and rendering it vulnerable to the sweeping stroke of an axe wielded by a powerful and determined man. The short, black woollen blanket, which a Sholaga generally carries wrapped around his left arm, serves as the only shield.

Although a vegetarian or insect-eater by nature, 'Bruin' is not averse to carrion. I have caught him several times robbing rotten meat from a tiger's or panther's kill.

One of the potential dangers of any jungle are the many varieties of reputedly poisonous snakes that are said to infest the forests. Actually the great majority of snake-stories told to the visitor are grossly exaggerated. As a rule, snakes of all varieties are comparatively few in jungle districts and are not often encountered. They exist in much larger numbers in fields and near villages, the reason being that in such places grain is grown. Millions of field-rats live in holes in the ground to eat the grain. And the snakes eat the rats.

Furthermore, as far as humans are concerned, in the whole peninsula there are only five varieties of poisonous snakes capable of inflicting a lethal dose of venom. There are other species of poisonous snakes, too, but their bites would only cause a local swelling and some pain. The deadly varieties are the king cobra or hamadryad, the cobra, the Russell's viper, the saw-scaled viper or 'pursa', and the krait. The coral snake has a very poisonous bite, but its mouth is so tiny as to prevent it from getting a grip anywhere on a human-being; apart from which, it has a very docile nature. The pit-vipers are all poisonous, but a bite from them is never fatal except in very rare cases where the person bitten suffers from a weak heart and dies more from shock than the effects of poison. Most of the sea-snakes are extremely deadly, some of them having venom as much as twelve times the strength of the cobra's; but of course they are only to be found in the sea.

Roughly speaking, the strengths of snake venoms and their consequent fatality, is as follows: a Ressell's viper's poison is about twice as lethal as that of the saw-scaled viper; the cobra's poison three times as strong as that of the Russell's viper; and the krait almost twice as poisonous as the cobra. The king cobra's venom is not quite as strong as that of the ordinary cobra, bulk for bulk, but being a big snake, measuring sometimes fifteen feet and more in length, it makes up in quantity for this slight deficiency of strength, injecting about four times as much as is held in the glands of a cobra, so that a bite from this snake, which is incidentally about the largest poisonous snake in the world, causes death about three times as fast as an ordinary cobra's bite would do.

The hamadryad is found only in hilly regions in the midst of the ever-green forests where the rainfall is very heavy. It lives entirely in jungles and avoids human habitation as far as possible. Its food consists of other snakes, which makes it very difficult to keep in captivity. A specimen died in the Mysore Zoo recently after a full year of starvation, during which every effort was made to provide it with food in the form of various snakes of the non-poisonous varieties, all of which it steadfastly refused to eat till eventually it died of starvation. Its death caused quite a controversy in the Press of Mysore, where some of the people of the city, on religious grounds, ventilated their strong disapproval of this cruel act on the part of the authorities at the zoo.

The hamadryad, as I have said, is a huge snake, generally of an olive-green colour, banded with white. In Burma and the Malayan region the male is said to be almost jet black, although the white bands still persist. The hood is not so well developed in proportion to the length of the snake as in the common cobra, and does not bear the well-known 'vee' mark. It is said to be very aggressive, attacking on sight, particularly the female of the species while guarding her eggs, which she lays in a nest prepared from fallen, mouldering leaves. However, this aggressiveness I have not experienced myself, although I twice met a hamadrayad at very close quarters. The first time I was digging out tree-ferns for my garden in Bangalore, while at the same time attempting to catch some rare fish with flaming-red tails that wee swimming in a stream deep down in a valley of the Western Ghats, near a place called Agumbe. The fish, by the way, were for my aquarium at home. I saw what looked like the head of an iguana lizard peering at me from a thicket of ferns. I was wading in the bed of the stream at that moment and approached to have a closer look, when the hamadryad — and not an iguana as I had thought — reared up and towered quite six feet above me from its elevated position on the bank. The reptile was trembling with rage, and its black eyes glittered as it exhaled the air noisily from its body. I was not carrying even a stick, so I stood perfectly motionless. After some moments the trembling subsided, the inflated hood went down, the snake lowered itself and slithered across the stream not five feet away. Half-way across it halted, and regarded me again to see what I was going to do. I did nothing and I still did not move. Then it resumed its course and disappeared amongst the ferns on the other bank.

On the second occasion I was sitting behind a tree on a forest fire-line near Santaveri, on the Baba Budan hills, while a tiger-beat was in progress. Suddenly I heard a peculiar whistling sound from the jungle behind my back. It somewhat resembled the alarm signal made by a bull-bison, and accordingly I expected the bison to show up, when a hamadryad broke cover and crossed the fire-line quite close to me. In that case, however, I doubt if the snake even saw me as I did not move a muscle.

Most people to whom I have related these two incidents say that I saved my own life by not moving, and that had I done so the snakes would have attacked at once. Having never been attacked before by one of these big reptiles I cannot offer any opinion. However, there is no doubt that I was more lucky than the unfortunate German zoologist who came to Agumbe some years ago to catch a pair of hamadryads for a zoo. He caught the male first without trouble. A couple of days later he attempted to catch the female. She bit him. He died there in the jungle itself. In that instance the old proverb that 'the female of the species is more dangerous than the male' proved itself to be literally true. Against this I remember witnessing many years ago at Maymyo, in Burma, the performance put up by a way-side snake-charmer. Incidentally she was a Burmese lady, and a very beautiful one at that, as I can still recollect. She took a hamadryad out of a basket and danced before it till it had extended itself some feet above the ground with hood inflated. Then she deliberately kissed it on the mouth. I examined the snake later. It had its poison glands and its fangs. But the hamadryad was a male I remember, and as I have said, she was a very lovely Burmese lady. Perhaps that was why she met with more chivalrous treatment than that unfortunate German scientist.

The ordinary Indian cobra is too well-known to require much description. Contrary to the stories told, it rarely exceeds six feet in length. There are two varieties in India, the first with the widely-publicised spectacle 'vee' mark, which is called the 'biocellate' variety, and the other with only a single white spot on its hood, ringed with black. This is known as the 'monocellate' variety. Here and there specimens are met with that have no mark at all, although their hoods are just as well developed.

Colouring is a very unreliable means of identifying cobras, as they are to be found in all varieties and shades from jet black to various kinds of brown and even reddish, whitish or greenish hues. Grey and brown are the most common colours. Even young cobras, when they are hatched and are just six inches long, are deadly venomous. They are also far more aggressive during the first two years of their lives. They mellow in temperament as they grow older, and very old specimens are not given to biting without extreme provocation. At this age they can be completely tamed while in full possession of their fangs and poison sacs.

Cobras lay quite soft-shelled eggs, about fifteen in number, each about the size of a pigeon's egg, in a shallow hole or among decaying leaves. To hatch these eggs successfully requires indirect heat from the sun together with considerable humidity. Without humidity they shrivel up.

The krait averages about three feet in length and is a slender black snake with white rings around its body. It is very swift in movement, but at the same time is very shy and nervous and generally dies in captivity within a day or two of being caught, for no apparent reason.

The king cobra, the cobra and the krait are know as 'colubrine' snakes, and their venom causes a collapse of the entire nerous system as a primary symptom. Each has two fixed fangs, the length of the normal cobra's being about a quarter of an inch, the hamadryad's about half an inch, and the krait's about one-eighth of an inch.

The 'viperine' snakes are the Russell's viper and the saw-scaled viper. They also have two fangs, one on each side. These lie flat against the back of the mouth when not in use, but can be erected and rotated about their base as an axis.

The fangs of a big Russell's viper grow to a full inch and can pierce through a soft-leather boot, putties, pants or thick woollen stockings. A cobra's or krait's fangs, being 'fixed' and not rotatable, cannot do this. The Russell's viper itself is a stout snake growing to a little over five feet in length and possessing three rows of diamond-shaped markings running down its back (one to the centre and one on each side), joined together in chain-like fashion and of a rich dark brown. For this reason it is sometimes called the 'chain-viper'.

The saw-scaled viper hardly exceeds two feet in length and is a brown snake with white 'notch' markings across its back. Its distinctive feature is that it possesses rough keeled-back scales. When annoyed, it coils round and round against itself, the scales producing quite a loud rasping sound in the process. This gives it its Indian name of 'pursa', 'poorsa' or 'phoorsa', which is a phonetic rendering of the sound made by the rasping scales.

The 'colubrine' snakes have grooves down the backs of their fangs alongs which the venom trickles when ejected from the poison-sacs. The 'viperine' snakes have channels down the centre of the fang itself, like the needle of a hypodermic syringe, for the passage of the poison. Naturally, because of this, the wearing of thick socks, putties, long trousers and soft boots is practically no obstruction to the bite of a viperine snake, although they may do so to that of a colubrine, for, being exposed, most of the venom will be absorbed by the material itself or dispersed against the leather of a boot. The longer, rotatable, hypodermic-like fangs of the two deadly vipers ensue that the unfortunate victim receives a letha dose more or less intact, just as it is expelled from the venom glands. This is particularly so in the case of a Russell's viper, the tremendously long fangs of which will penetrate any normal material.

The chief effect of viperine venom is to cause haemorrhage, which gives the victim a good deal of pain.

Of course, it is impossible to name more than average periods of time for a bite by any one of these reptiles to prove fatal to a human being. The other factors involved are the age, health, constitution and physique of the victim; the size of the snake itself and whether it has bitten any other creature recently; and the amount of venom that has actually entered into the victim's blood stream. The average time in which death normally occurs might be as follows:

In the case of the hamadryad, about ninety minutes; the krait, two to three hours; the cobra, four to six hours; the Russell's viper, twelve to thirty-six hours; and the saw-scaled viper, anything from three to seven days.

The non-poisonous snakes of India are very many in number. Perhaps the most interesting is the python or rock-snake, which may measure up to eighteen feet in length, while the Malayan variety grows to thirty-five feet. It kills its victim by coiling around it and crushing it to death, after which it swallows the whole animal. The victims, of course, range in size from rats and rabbits to pigs and small deer, according to the size and capacity of the snake itself. During the Burma campaign against the Japanese an account was given of the shooting of a 'reticulated python' — which is the name given to the Malayan species which is also to be found in Burma — over forty feet in length. In its death-throes it vomited the body of a Jap soldier it had swallowed, complete with helmet. I do not vouch for the truth of this story, although it appeared in the Press. The idea that a python covers its victim with slime before swallowing it is quite erroneous. Its jaws, like those of all snakes, are not hinged together, but are quite separate units. The outer skin being very elastic, it is easy to see that a snake can swallow creatures several times the size of its head and girth.

141

Other non-poisonous snakes include many varieties of ground snakes; several species of very slender whip-like and fast-moving tree snakes; stout, lethargic worm-like sand snakes; and a large number of fresh-water snakes. One of the sand snakes possesses a blunt tail which looks like a second head, so much so that it is still widely believed that this reptile has two heads, one at either end.

I have always been fascinated by snakes, and for no other apparent reason I formed the habit of keeping them as pets at the age of eight years. As a result, I was considered quite frightful among the girls and something of a terror at school. I know I got quite a kick out of releasing reptiles in cinemas, in Sunday school and even in Church. The name of 'snake-charmer Anderson' still clings to me to this day, in my forty-eighth year.

Snake venom has many medicinal uses, and I am certain is a still unknown remedy for many ailments and conditions. The fact is that this field has not yet been thoroughly investigated and exploited owing to the danger consequent upon experimenting on a human being with these venoms. Viperine poison in small diluted doses and in accordance with the laws of homoeopathy, where the small dose of a particular poison is known to counteract a large dose of that same poison has been proved of sterling value for the very condition of haemorrhage which it produces when a large or lethal dose is administered. This venom is used by dentists and others to stop excessive bleeding after a tooth extraction or minor operation.

Similarly, colubrine venoms, which in large doses bring about a complete collapse of the nervous system, are efficacious in minute doses in cases of epilepsy and other nervous complaints.

The Haffkine Institute in Bombay prepares a series of anti-venom injections as an antidote for the bites of all five poisonous species, obtainable separately for any of the varieties, provided the offending snake has been identified; or in a combined form for all the species, if there is no certainty as to by which snake a person has been bitten. The serum is prepared by progressively injecting horses with increasing quantities of snake-venom, beginning with a minute dose, till they become immune and are able to tolerate three to four times a lethal dose without ill-effect. Then blood is drawn from a vein in the thigh of the horse so immunised, and from this blood the anti-venom serum is eventually prepared.

When as I had I came to hear how the serum was prepared I was greatly intrigued and determined to prepare my own stock. I procured two old ponies and a donkey from sources I still hesitate to reveal and started to immunise them with initial doses of cobra poison, injected with a small 3 cc hypodermic syringe I had bought for the purpose. Unfortunately my knowledge in those days of the initial dose to be given was rather sketchy, with the result that within a very few hours I had to arrange for the disposal of the corpses of the said two ponies and the donkey. I also recollect that my father was very annoyed.

Just before the last war I was doing quite a good business in exporting snake venom in crystallised form to interested institutions in the USA, particularly cobra venom. The average cobra produces roughly one cubic centimetre of venom every four to five days, which when crystallised weighs about one gramme, for which I was getting approximately one and a half dollars. I had twenty cobras, which therefore earned me thirty dollars worth of poison every five days, or a hundred and eighty dollars a month. Not a bad business considering the snakes cost me nothing whatever to feed beyond a frog or lizard each every ten days. These were caught for me by a fifteen-year-old Indian boy, such a servant being known as a 'chokra'.

His salary for this work was seven rupees a month which, shall we say, is the equivalent of ten shillings in English money.

The venom is collected from a reptile by holding it by the neck with its mouth pressed against a glass cup covered by a thin piece of diaphragm rubber or bladder-skin. The snake bites the rubber, and in doing so ejects the poison from its glands, which trickles into the cup. The idea of the very thin rubber is to avoid loss of venom at the surface. Some care has to be taken not to injure the reptile by allowing it to break its teeth against the glass. Some layers of electrical insulating-tape around the edge of the cup serves this purpose.

Cobras are easily handled, as they expose their heads by raising themselves for about a third of their length off the ground while inflating their hoods. It is then comparatively simple to press a stick down firmly across the back of the hood, pin the snake to the ground and grip it by the back of its neck. Russell's vipers, saw-scaled vipers and kraits are far more dangerous, both because they hide their heads beneath the coiled folds of their own bodies and are, moreover, exceedingly quick in movement, far outclassing the cobra. In addition, the exceedingly long and rotatable fangs of a Russell's viper make him a nasty customer, requiring very careful handling.

Cobras in general are also easily tamed. The specimens in the itinerant 'snake-charmer's' basket have been rendered harmless by removing their fangs and poisonsacs. The fangs grow again, roughly in a month's time, but once the poison-sac is removed the reptile is harmless for life, as the venom cannot be secreted. A Russell's viper's poison-sacs cannot be removed because they are situated very near the brain and close to a big artery in the mouth. An operation to remove the sac causes this snake to die not only of blood, but it injures the brain, to which it succumbs in a short while. The snake-charmers therefore stitch the upper and lower lips together at both corners with needle and thread, and feed the unfortunate reptile once a week through a bone funnel inserted down the throat from the centre of the mouth. An egg-flip is the usual nourishment. The same artificial and forced feeding is practised on cobras that frequently refuse to swallow their natural food when in captivity.

Their habit of infrequent eating is what makes all snakes so easy to keep. Normally a meal of a rat, frog, lizard or small bird will be sufficient for a period of a week or ten days, according to the size of the snake. In this respect, strange to say, the smaller species are more voracious than the larger. Pythons eat less frequently, at intervals of fifteen days to a month, according to the size of the animal that formed the last meal.

In writing this rather long account of snakes my purpose was to depict the interesting features shown by each of them. One feature is common to all snakes, both poisonous and non-poisonous, except, it is said, the hamadryad; that they are all afraid of and avoid man. They will not go out of their way to attack or bite a human, but will do their utmost to slither away out of sight when hearing one approach, and will only bite if actually trodden upon. This they do out of fear and in self-defence. Incidentally it is useful to know that snakes have no sense of hearing through an organ resembling an ear. Their 'hearing' lies in the ability to feel vibrations through their bodies. Thus the stories we hear of a snake-charmer's flute, and other musical instruments and sounds, 'charming' a cobra are a myth. It is not the snake-charmer's music that holds their attention, but the rhythmic swaying of his body, head and hands when playing the instrument the causes the cobra to move itself from side to side in keeping with his motions while watching them. By this token, shouting, singing or whistling when walking along some dark footpath in India will not serve to frighten away a lurking snake, whereas heavy boots or the tapping of a stick against the ground most definitely will.

Every snake casts its outer layer of skin two to three times a year. This comes off 'inside-out' in the manner of a removed sock or glove, and is accomplished by the snake rubbing and coiling itself against some rough surface or obstacle.

Both poisonous and non-poisonous snakes are classified generally under two headings — oviparous or viviparous. The former lay eggs, which hatch out after some days, whereas the latter give birth to living youngsters. The possession or absence of venom has no bearing on this factor, as both poisonous and harmless species are to be found under each heading. For instance, the cobra lays eggs, whereas the Russell's viper and python give birth to their young alive.

Of all the five species of poisonous snakes, the ordinary cobra lives to a great extent close to human beings and will be found inhabiting ant-hills and other holes in every field or near any dwelling-place. Strangely, he is rarely met with in a jungle. The hamadryad is just the opposite, as I have already said, and keeps entirely to the jungle. Russell's viper are found more in forests and grassy places than near human habitations. Kraits are not very common anywhere, and the saw-scaled viper lives mostly in arid, sandy regions.

When in the jungle, short of carrying tubes of anti-venom injections, which in any case require to be kept in a refrigerator because they decompose rapidly, the only reliable remedy for a bite from a poisonous snake is immediate deep cutting into the wound with as sharp knife, followed by sucking out as much of the poisoned blood in the vicinity as possible, in order to minimise the quantity of venom absorbed. Incidentally, none of the venoms are poisonous if swallowed, so that there is no fear of secondary symptoms due to this sucking-out of poisoned blood. In fact, cobra venom is fed to trained cocks and partridges in order to make them more aggressive when participating in the staged fights often conducted by the Moslems in this part of India. High sums of money are placed as bets on the winner, and this is one of the standard methods of winning the jackpot.

The typing of an effective ligature above the bite requires time and some skill. Also the method is impracticable if the person happens to be bitten anywhere on the trunk. In any case, before the ligature can be effectively tightened, the venom has invariably entered into the blood-stream. Pouring crystals of potassium permanganate into the bite helps to neutralize the venom to a slight extent through chemical action, but deep incisions have first to be made before the crystals can effectively penetrate the tissues and play their part. For this reason I always carry a small razor-sharp penknife in my pocket when in the jungle.

I know a man who was bitten in the foot by a cobra. He was a poacher and he had the presence of mind to pour a heap of the loose gunpowder he was carrying in a bag for his muzzle-loader on to and around the bitten part. Then he ignited the powder with a match, with the result that he burned a deep hole in his leg which still causes him to walk with a slight limp. But he lived. I know another man, a snake-charmer, who was bitten through his thumb by a cobra. He placed a knife over the second joint and brought a heavy stone sharply down on the back of the knife with his free hand, requiring more than one blow to complete the amputation. He must have suffered agony and almost bled to death; nevertheless, he pulled through and is alive today. In a third instance I was once camped at Muttur Forest Bungalow when a man awoke me at dawn to say he had been bitten in the foot by a cobra nearly an hour earlier. He said he was a cartman returning to Pennagram with a cart-load of cut bamboos; the evening before he had encountered a herd of wild elephants by the roadside. Being afraid, he had turned his cart about and returned to the fellers' camp. About 4 a.m. that morning he had set forth again, walking behind his cart so as to be able to escape more easily if he ran into the elephants again. Probably the cart-wheel had passed over the snake and injured it. He said he felt a sharp pain and looked down to see a snake fastened on to his foot. He kicked out, and the snake let go and made off, but not before he had had time to see by the inflated hood that it was a cobra. After being bitten he had walked the two miles to the bungalow, hoping someone could help him. I lost no time in lancing the wound deeply, and with the aid of a forest guard walked him up and down the verandah to keep him from falling into a coma. But it was not long before I could see that my efforts would be in vain. The unfortunate cartman began to drool at the mouth, his eyes rolled upwards, he staggered like a drunken man and his speech became inarticulate. I managed to get his name and that of his family, who lived in the village of Erigollanur, a mile beyond Pennagram. Then he suddenly became a dead weight in our arms. He had lost consciousness. By 8.30 a.m. he was dead. I sent the forest guard to inform his relatives and the Pennagram police. The relatives came in a bullock-cart by 2 p.m., and set up a loud wailing. Then came the police. They wanted to know why there were blood-marks all over the floor of the forest bungalow where we had walked the man about; why I had cut him; why he had died. Finally the corpse was put into the bullock-cart and sent to the police station, and I was asked to go too. I refused point blank. The chief constable pondered over my refusal awhile and then compromised with instructions that I should remain in the forest bungalow till the results of the postmortem, which would be held on the dead man, had been reported. I readily agreed to do that. Then the party left for Pennagram, seven miles away, from where the body was sent by bus to the General Hospital at Salem town, forty-two miles distant, for a post-mortem. Back came the answer after three days. The cartman had died of cobra bite. On the fourth day the police informed me that I was no longer under suspicion.

In the whole thirty-nine years during which I have handled snakes, I have been bitten only once, and then by a cobra. It happened in 1939. I had just caught the snake when it slipped from my grasp and bit me on the second finger of my left hand. But I am still alive; nor did I have to blow up or cut off my finger. For fortunately the incident happened on some land I own nine miles out of Bangalore and I was able to drive in my car to hospital and receive anti-venom treatment. As a result, the bite itself produced no unpleasant symptoms; but the injection certainly did, for on the third day I suffered a very severe reaction and temporary partial paralysis of both legs. However, calcium and other injections put that right within a day.

In conclusion, I would like to mention a strange belief that was widely held in Southern India, that a stationmaster named Narasiah, working at Polreddipalyam Station on the Southern Railway and situated not very far from the city of Madras, could cure any person of poisonous snake-bite provided he was informed by telegram. The belief became so widespread that the railway authorities gave preference on its own telegraph system to any such message addressed to this stationmaster. I had heard many accounts of his miraculous cures from authentic sources, and there are hundreds of people alive in Southern India today whose lives were saved by him. The *modus operandi* was that, as soon as Mr Narasiah received a telegram informing him of someone being bitten, he would go to a certain tree growing in the station yard, tear off a shred of his dhoti or loin cloth' tie it to a branch of the tree, say a prayer, and then send a telegram in reply informing the patient that he would live provided he abstained from tobacco, alcohol and coffee. Invariably the victim survived.

Alas! Mr Narasiah had to answer the great call himself and has since passed away. But he will never be forgotten. I do not know if his secret died with him, but I fear so, as no reports of any successor to his healing work in the realm of snake-bite have come to me since then.

Six

The Killer From Hyderabad

NORTH, OF MYSORE STATE, IN THE DAYS OF THE BRITISH RAJ, LAY THE Districts of Bellary, Anantapur, Kurnool and Nandyal, all belonging to the former Madras Presidency. North of these again lay Hyderabad State, which was the dominion of the Nizam of Hyderabad, a staunch ally of the British regime and a descendant of a ruler who was an off-shoot of the once all-powerful Mohammedan Moghul Emperor at Delhi.

Hyderabad State now no longer exists and part of the Nizam's wide dominions have been amalgamated with Anantapur, Kurnool and Nandyal to form a portion of the linguistic Telugu State of Andhra Pradesh, which is about the second largest in the new Union of India, being exceeded in area only by Madhya Pradesh to the north.

However, this story dates from long ago when these areas, although predominantly Telegu-speaking, belonged to Madras.

In those days these districts were largely undeveloped

151

because the rainfall was scarce, the climate viciously hot for ten months of the year (while the remaining two months are simply uncomfortably hot) and the population by no means dense. Except for the towns of Anantapur, Kurnool and Nandyal, which gave their names to the districts of which they formed the capitals, the rest of the land was peopled by small villages scattered widely over the area.

The railway line from Bombay to Madras was the principal arterial link which traversed the districts. It passed through a railway colony known as Guntakal Junction. This main arterial link was a broad-gauge section, with its lines 5 ft. 6 ins. Apart. At Guntakal three separate metre-gauge sections branched off. One led westwards towards Bellary and Hubli; one led southwards towards Bangalore in Mysore State; the third led eastwards, passing through Dronachellam and Nandyal to Bezwada, and thence to the east coast of India. At Bezwada it linked up with another broad-gauge arterial section joining Madras and Calcutta, while at Dronachellam a metre-gauge line branched north-eastwards to Secunderabad and Hyderabad. The metre-gauge engines and rolling stock were naturally smaller and much lighter than those of the broad-gauge lines.

After leaving Guntakal, Dronachellam and Nandyal, the eastern metre-gauge line passes through an area of forest for five stations, named in order Gazulapalli, Basavapuram, Chelama, Bogara and Diguvametta, before going on to Bezwada. This forested portion, which forms the setting of my story, is more or less in the midst of a jungle belt stretching northwards across the Krishna River into the former Hyderabad State, and southwards towards the town of Cuddapah.

The metre-gauge trains are slow, and it is still a common experience for the drivers of the up and down mails that pass in the night to see wild animals running across the lines in the beam of the engine's headlight, or to run down a wild pig or a deer that attempts a last-minute crossing.

From the five stations which I have named only rough and stony cart-tracks and foot-paths wend their way into the surrounding jungle. There were no motorable roads in those days. This was one of the main factors that helped to preserved the fauna of the locality from being badly shot-up, as has happened in jungle areas traversed by good roads. Enthusiastic but misguided and unsporting hunters use these good roads by spending their time from dusk to dawn shining spot-lights from motor-cars into the jungle and shooting at any animal whose eyes reflect the glare. More often than not these hunters are not even aware of the kind or nature of the animal at which they fire. This wanton and wicked practice has done and continues increasingly to do immense damage to wild animals, as the females and young of all species are being indiscriminately slaughtered, while a still larger number crawl away sorely wounded to die lingering and agonizing deaths in the jungle. The British Government in its time tried to stop this poaching, and the Indian Government is still trying. The first was, and the second is, altogether unsuccessful, and the terrible havoc still goes on. What a more, this will always be the case till either the public becomes conscious of the fact that wild life is a national asset and should not be wantonly destroyed; or alternatively, until wild life itself is completely wiped out.

However, as I have said, because of the fortunate absence of motorable roads, the Gazulapalli-Diguvametta area has so far been spared to some extent the curse of the night-prowling motor-car butcher, and there one may camp in the jungle reasonably sure of not hearing the hum of a car, followed by a dazzling beam of light, the sudden cessation of sound as the car is brought to a halt, the report of a gun or rifle and perhaps the agonized shriek of a wounded or dying animal.

The indigenous inhabitants of this area are a Telegu-speaking tribe known as Chenchus. Like all aborigines, they go about scantily clad, the main items of clothing in both men and women being torn and dirty loin cloths. The men carry bows and arrows, and most of them adorn themselves with beads or feathers around their necks. Peacock feathers are a favourite ornament for special occasions when stuck into their matted hair. They are fond of alcoholic liquor, which they make from the juice of the sticky mhowa flower, or from the bark of the babul tree. Indeed, because of the presence and abundance of the mhowa tree, these people were always a great problem to the excise officers in the days of British rule, and they are a still far greater problem to the Andhra Government where the policy of 'Prohibition' prevails in certain parts of the State.

However, this tale did not set out to be a protest against night shooting from cars, nor as a discussion of the policy of 'prohibition'; nor is it even a sketch of life of the Chenchus. It concerns a man-eating tiger that terrorized the area, off and on, for some four years. This animal began his activities in the forests which belonged to Hyderabad State, where he fed on Chenchus and lonely travellers for half a year before he wandered southwards and dramatically announced his arrival at Chelama by carrying off and devouring a ganger who left the station early one morning on a routine patrol of the railway line in the direction of Basavapuram to the west.

In those days, particularly, the area was always well stocked with tigers, but these, due to the plentiful supply of natural game, seldom interfered with the local people except occasionally to carry off cattle. The disappearance of the ganger was therefore not attributed to a man-eating tiger at the time, as his remains were never found, and it was thought he had just decamped from the area for reasons of his own.

154

Only in the months that followed, when Chenchus vanished here and there, were suspicions aroused that something untoward was happening, and people began to think that a tiger might be the cause of these disappearances. Even then there was no definite evidence of the presence of this man-eater, as tiger tracks along the jungle paths were common and there was nothing to connect the missing ganger and other Chenchus with earlier victims in the more distant northern parts of the jungle within Hyderabad State.

It was some three or four moths after the incident of the ganger that this tiger revealed his presence. Two charcoal burners were returning one evening to a tiny hamlet known as Wadapally, near the fringe of the forest. They were walking one behind the other when about half a mile before reaching their destination the leading man noticed the speckled form of a hen-koel fly from a nest rather high in a tree. Now you may wonder why I stress that this bird was a hen-koel of speckled plumage. It is because the male koel is jet black and therefore quite unidentifiable with the female, which is a deep grey speckled with white. The koel is perhaps the largest member of the cuckoo family, the Indian 'brain-fever-bird' being another. Like all cuckoos, the koels do not build their own nests, but lay their eggs in the nests of other birds and leave the hatching to them.

Now the facts that the leading Chenchu had seen the speckled hen fly from a nest was irrefutable evidence that she had just laid an egg there. Chenchus not only find koel's eggs hard to come by, because they might be laid in any bird's nest, but they regard them as a great delicacy. He drew the attention of his companion to the lucky circumstance. The second man, who was younger, began to climb the tree with the intention of plundering the eggs. He had almost reached his objective when he heard a scream below him. Looking down, he was amazed to see a tiger walking away into the jungle with his companion dangling from the beast's mouth and screaming for help.

The man on the tree scrambled to its topmost branches while the tiger faded from sight with his still-wailing victim.

Night fell, but the Chenchu in the tree dared not risk coming down. He spent the next twelve hours there, shivering with fear and cold, and expecting the return of the tiger at any moment. Next morning, when the sun was well up, he started yelling at the top of his voice in the hope that someone on the outskirts of Wadapally might hear him. The wind happened to be blowing in that direction and his cries were eventually heard, when a party of villagers set forth to find out what it was all about.

Thus it was that the man-eater officially announced his presence in the Chelama area.

The Chenchus from Wadapally conveyed the news to the station-master at Chelama, who telegraphed up the line to Nandyal, from where in turn the news was conveyed to the Police, the Forestry Department, the railway authorities, and to the Collector of the District. Tongues began to wag, and the various mysterious disappearances of the other Chenchus and of the ganger, four months previously, were linked together and laid at the door of the man-eater.

Normally, when the presence of a man-eater in any particular area of jungle is confirmed, the Forestry Department throws open the surrounding forests for 'free shooting' without licence, to encourage hunters to eliminate the killer. This step was automatically taken, but the announcement by the Forestry Department met with no appreciable response, because few sportsmen cared to try their hand at bagging a man-eater in a district almost bereft of roads, where they would need to walk every inch of the ground without any transport.

One or two railway officials made half-hearted attempts by 'trolleying' up and down the line between Gazulapalli and Chelama with loaded rifles expecting, or at least hoping, to come across the tiger very obligingly seated beside the track, just waiting to be shot. But their expectations and their hopes did not work out, nor did the man-eater oblige. And not only did they see no tiger, but more Chenchus began to fall victims to the invisible devil week by week, till the death toll, inclusive of the ganger, rose to eleven. Of these only two victims were followed up by bands of villagers armed with staves, hatchets and bows and arrows, and their scattered remains recovered. No trace was found of the others, due both to the difficult terrain and the unwillingness of the people to risk their lives in attempting to save what they well knew to be carcasses already half-eaten.

Such behaviour may be regarded as indifferent and callous. But I would remind the reader that these poor folk were unarmed and not organized to deal with the man-eater. The jungle covered a vast expanse of heavy forest, with but few footpaths winding through the dense undergrowth, piled boulders and wooded ravines which lay in all directions. Everybody knew that should the man-eater be bold enough to charge a group of persons, at least one of them would fall a victim. Nobody wanted to be that victim. So who could reasonably blame them for not venturing out? In true eastern philosophy there seemed to be no sense in sacrificing another life to find the body of one who was already dead.

After these eleven killings, the man-eater appeared to have left the area for some time, as no further incidents were reported there for three or four months, though they began to appear again near the Krishna River. Then, and then only, did it become apparent that the former Hyderabad man-eater and the man-eater of Chelama were one and the same animal.

In Hyderabad State the call for hunters to kill the tiger met with greater response, and one or two of the Mahommedan Nawabs (or landowners) started active operations against the animal. Eventually the tiger overplayed his role by killing a traveller quite close to a hamlet named Madikonda. In this case he was driven off before he had time to eat even a portion of his victim, and news of the incident was carried to the Nawab of the area, who happened to be in camp a few miles away.

The Nawab answered the call and came post-haste to the spot, very fortunately before the body of the victim had been removed for cremation, and he was able to construct a machan on an adjacent tree in which to await the tiger's return to its undevoured prey. Being a nomad, the unfortunate victim had no relatives in the locality to claim his body, and this factor had provided the only chance this tiger had so far afforded of being shot.

But at this stage the Nawab's good luck was impaired by an unexpected thunderstorm which almost synchronized with the return of the tiger. Or that was what the Nawab claimed. Whatever the cause, he unluckily failed to kill it when he fired, and the morning light revealed a few traces of blood which had not been washed away by the rain. At least, he had the satisfaction of knowing that he had hit the tiger, although nobody was able to follow up and locate its carcass the next day. The Nawab hoped that it was dead, and so did everybody else.

Again an interval of some weeks elapsed. Then a Chenchu, who devoted his time to snaring partridges and jungle-fowl near Gazulapalli, failed to return home for his midday meal. He had set out that morning on a visit to the traps that he had placed in various parts of the jungle the day before, saying he would be back by noon, as was his habit. But midday passed and the shades of evening fell and still he did not show up, and his wife and only son, a boy of twenty, grew anxious. Of course they had heard of the killings in the vicinity of Chelama, but those had taken place some months previously and everyone had since forgotten about the incidents. Now, with the absence of the trapper who was the bread-winner of the family, their misgivings and fears returned in full force.

In recording the exploits of man-eaters, it is rather noticeable that they follow a more or less regular pattern of happenings. The 'villain of the piece,' the aforesaid man-eater, makes his appearance suddenly, generally after being incapacitated from pursuing his natural prey through being wounded by some hunter. More rarely he, or quite as frequently she, has learned the habit from a parent who had a weakness for human flesh. The killings of human beings, few and far between at first, increase in number as the animal gains confidence in its own prowess and power over the helplessness of the human race as a whole. A strange feature in all man-eaters, whether tiger or panther, is the fact that, despite their growing contempt for humanity in general, a subtle sixth-sense of caution, which some hunters think is cowardice, pervades their whole nature. They will always attack the victim unawares, generally when he is alone or at least at the end, or at the head of, a moving file of persons. Instances are very very rare, indeed, when such a man-eater has charged a group of people. On the other hand, instances have been many in which the would-be victim has resisted and somehow fought for his life, and the man-eater has abandoned its attack and fled. This is more the case with panthers than with tigers, for the simple reason that the latter are such powerful animals that few live to tell the tale once a charge has been driven home. It is this inherent caution or cowardice, call it what you like, which is the common feature of all man-eaters and makes their early destruction a most difficult problem. As various attempts to circumvent them are made, and fail, the hunted animal naturally becomes more and more cautious and cunning as it appears to realize that a special price has been placed upon its head.

The man-eating tiger has a habit of following a particular 'beat' or route, which may extend over some hundreds of miles, halting in the vicinity of villages or hamlets for a week or two and then moving on again. In this way, not only does he escape when things are becoming too hot for him, but he arrives at fresh pastures and fields of opportunity where the inhabitants are unaware of his coming. By the same token, when he leaves a particular locality and the killings cease, the natural apathy and forgetfulness of the villagers makes them feel that the danger has passed and they become careless in their movements, ensuring another easy victim for the tiger when he eventually comes that way again. For he works around the territory in a huge and rough circle, and according to the extent of his beat will surely pass that way once more — maybe after a month or two, maybe much longer.

As I have mentioned earlier in this book, if one has the patience, and provided sufficient information is available, which is often most difficult to achieve, with the aid of a map of the area and by means of marking with a cross the locality of each human kill with the date on which it occurred, it is possible to assess not only the whole extent and area of the tiger's range of operations, but to anticipate its return to each locality within the margin of a fortnight. This is one of the main factors that helps the hunter who scientifically plans the killing of a man-eating tiger to accomplish his task.

In the case of a panther there is no evidence of a regular beat. He is here, there and everywhere. He kills mainly at night and very rarely during the hours of daylight. Being small, a man-eating panther can hide anywhere. As he grows bolder and bolder he often reaches a stage where he attacks and drags inmates out of their huts. I believe there are few authenticated cases of tigers doing this. On the other hand, a tiger will attack his human prey at any time of the day, lying in ambush beside forest paths or near the outskirts of a village.

I have related the story of the coming of the 'Chelama Man-eater', or, as he came to be better known, the 'Killer from Hyderabad', as I pieced together the facts at a much later date. To follow his exploits in detail after he killed and partially ate the Chenchu bird-trapper who used to live in Gazulapalli, and whose remains incidentally were recovered by his son, might bore you. Each incident was much the same in nature, the tiger repeatedly changing his location between the Gazulapalli-Chelama section in the south and the Krishna River in Hyderabad to the north. This area of operations was immense, as you will understand if you glance at the map. Moreover, after the wound inflicted on him by the Nawab at Madikonda, he doubled and re-doubled his normal man-eater-like caution, till he gained the reputation of being a very devil incarnate — a sort of super-natural fiend. That unfortunate affairs caused him to adopt the practice of eating as much as possible of his human victim immediately after the killing, when he would abandon the body and very rarely return for a second meal. Not only did this habit immeasurably increase the difficulties of the few shikaris who went after him, but the killings themselves soon increased in number as the tiger was forced to prey on a fresh victim more often than would ordinarily be the case in order to appease his hunger, each time abandoning the remains of the last one. The area being large and remote, little publicity was given to the animal's depredations; and when it was given, all that appeared was a brief paragraph in one of the local newspapers, at infrequent and sporadic intervals, informing a disinterested public that the man-eater had claimed yet another victim. In this manner, in some three and a half years of activity, the tiger accounted for about eighty persons before serious notice began to be taken of the very real menace he had become.

The death of eighty persons in the jaws of a single tiger might appear colossal to the man living in a city. It certainly is so by all Western standards. But in a land as vast as India, where the average expectancy of life is at present well below thirty years, and in former days was very much lower — where famine, flood and sickness account yearly for thousands of lives; where snake-bite causes the deaths of many thousands more; and where the birth-rate is advancing to an alarming figure each year in spite of early mortality and all the causes of death — eighty people being eaten by a tiger was but a drop in the ocean, and nothing to worry about unduly. Indeed, relatively speaking, it reflected in the tiger's favour as a connoisseur in human flesh, considering the fact that he had only achieved this total in a period of some 1,300 days. It not only dubbed him as a very modest eater of human-beings, but what was very important to the hunter, indicated that he was obviously varying his human diet by killing animals for food, both domestic and wild. He would therefore not be averse to taking a bait should the hunter afford him the opportunity.

Apart from the man-eater of course, there were many other tigers, and panthers too, operating both in the Hyderabad jungles and to the south, so that the number of cattle and other domestic animals killed each year was always large. It was impossible under the circumstances even to guess how many of these 'natural' kills could be ascribed to the man-eater, and how many had been made by other carnivora; but it was certain that the man-eater had been responsible for a number of them as, has already been indicated, he could not have subsisted on human kills alone for such a length of time. Here was another favourable feature. The man-eater could be baited with tethered cattle provided the hunter was able to estimate his line of 'beat' and could reasonably forecast his visit to a locality by allowing a plus or minus factor of a fortnight each way, before and after his due date of arrival. This plus or minus factor could be worked out on the map from his earlier record of kills.

I had read accounts in the Press from time to time about the depredations of this animal, and had received quite a few letters from officials in the Forestry Department inviting me to try my luck at bagging it. To these I had turned a deaf ear, mainly because I found it difficult to spare the time from my work for a protracted visit, and also because the area in which it was operating was much too far from Bangalore to permit me to get there in time after receiving news of his arrival in any particular locality or of a human kill. At the same time, I have always been interested in news of the presence of man-eater, be it panther or tiger, and the doings of a 'rogue' elephant. In this case I had already written to the Forestry Department and Police authorities of both the Madras presidency and Hyderabad State to obtain all possible information about the animal, together with the most important data: the localities where human kills had occurred and the dates on which they had been perpetrated. This data I had jotted down on a map of the place and date of each incident. Thereafter, a study of the map indicated that this animal appeared to spend from two to three months operating between Gazulapalli and Chelama, before moving northwards into Hyderabad for the next four months or so. Then it returned again. The distance from Gazulapalli to Basavapuram is six miles, and from Basavapuram to Chelama five miles, and allowing for overlapping forest tracts the whole stretch of jungle between these areas covered a distance of about fifteen miles. Not only were these stations much closer to Bangalore than the more distant areas in Hyderabad, but they were much smaller in area, and were linked by part of the metre-gauge system of railway to Bangalore. The Hyderabad sections were not, and no motorable roads connected them. Lastly, the southern area was more populated, and I could therefore expect greater co-operation and earlier news of a 'kill' than would ordinarily be the case were I to start operations in the Hyderabad jungle.

You will see, then, that I had been toying with the idea of making an attempt for some time, when my indecision was brought to an end by the tiger himself. This happened when a permanent-way inspector on the railway was one morning carrying out a routine inspection of the line from Chelama towards Basavapuram by trolley. On the Indian railways these trolleys are simple wooden platforms on two pairs of wheels. The platform itself is scarcely more than six feet long, surmounted by a rough bench on which the railway officer sits. It is pushed by two coolies called 'trolley-men', who run along barefooted on the rails themselves. Practice makes them experts at placing their feet on the rails, necessitated in addition by the fact that were they to miss the rail and tread on the ballast they would find it very painful. They push the trolley up-hill at a walking pace, run along the rails at some eight miles per hour where level ground prevails, and jump on at the back of the trolley when a downhill section is reached. The officer controls the speed of the trolley by a handbrake, and the whole assembly is lifted off the line at stations to make way for passing trains.

That day the trolley was negotiating a cutting through rising ground, when the P.W.I. applied his brakes and stopped it to get down and examine the ditches which draw off rain water on either side of the track. The party had plenty of time at their disposal, as the next train was not due for another two hours. One of the trolley-men remained seated on the trolley, while the P.W.I. walked along the side of the ditch. The other man climbed up the bank of the cutting, which was about seven feet in height, seated himself on the top and took out a 'beedi'. This is the name given to cheap Indian cigarettes made of uncured tobacco wrapped in its own leaf. He contentedly lit it and began to smoke.

The P.W.I. walked further away from the trolley, the man seated on it lay back and began to doze, while the smoker on top of the bank threw away the stump of his first beedi, took another and lit it, drew the smoke deeply into his lungs and regarded his superior officer with disinterested eyes while expelling the smoke from his nostrils.

The ditch had not unduly eroded and, after walking a hundred yards or so, the P.W.I. turned around to cross the line and retrace his steps along the other side and inspect the ditch there. As he did so, he glanced backwards and saw the trolley with the coolie sleeping on it, and then glanced upwards to the other coolie seated on top of the cutting smoking his second beedi. On either side the jungle bordered the line to within fifty yards, but some stray bushes had sprung up and grew much nearer. The P.W.I. noticed one such bush — a rather larger one — growing a little way beyond the smoker and what appeared to be a round 'something' sticking out from one side of it. This 'something' moved. The glare from the sun was reflected by the leaves of the bush in a myriad of scintillating points of light. In contrast the lower portion of the bush and the round 'something' lay in shadow. The mysterious object moved again, and the P.W.I. stared, wondering what it could be.

Then it seemed to flatten itself and merge with the ground, and was completely lost to sight.

He crossed the track and started walking back to the trolley. Now his eyes scanned the opposite ditch. He had dismissed the object from his mind. But that was only for a few seconds. For he heard a piercing shriek. He looked up in time to see the coolie on the embankment being drawn backwards and then vanishing from sight, still screaming. Wondering what could be the matter with the man, the P.W.I. ran up the bank of the cutting to get a better view, when he saw a large tiger walking calmly away into the jungle with the coolie trailing from his mouth, his hands and legs kicking feebly. Then the tiger and the man were seen no more.

The P.W.I. was too shocked to move, but stood transfixed to the spot for a full minute or so. Then he was galvanised into action. He rushed down the bank to the railway track and pounded back along it towards the trolley as fast as he could. Meanwhile the sleeping coolie had been awakened by his companion's screams. In his confused state of mind he was not aware of what noise had actually awakened him, or of what was happening. He looked up to see his officer running towards him.

When the P.W.I. reached the trolley he shouted at the stupefied coolie, 'Bagh Reddi ku laikka gaiya' (a tiger has taken Reddi) followed by the words, *Trolley ku dhakkalao, juldhi'* (push the trolley quickly). The coolie needed no further exhortation after that. Both of them commenced to push the trolley along the lines as hard as they could, till it reached the downward slope and began to roll on its own accord. Then they jumped on and allowed it to career madly downhill away from that dreadful place.

Much publicity was given in the Press to this latest killing, and the P.W.I. came in for severe criticism from all quarters, being dubbed a coward for deserting a fellow human being at a time of need, a moral murderer, and something which should have been born as an insect and not as a man. I wonder how many of his critics would have acted differently had they been in his place. You should remember it had all happened so suddenly. Further, he was completely unarmed.

I felt the time had come for me to try to meet this man-eater. So that night I was seated in the train that steamed out of Bangalore and the afternoon of the next day saw me detraining at Gazulapalli.

It seemed to me wisest to begin operations from one end of the area and work forwards towards Basavapuram and Chelama, rather than the other way round. To start haphazardly somewhere in the middle was unsystematic and depended too much on luck. Further, and most important of all. I needed local help and a guide, as I had little knowledge of the district, having visited it only casually once before. I had brought along with me the map on which I had marked the tiger's beat, and I hoped to be able to locate the son of the bird-trapper who had been one of the man-eater's earlier victims. I felt the youth would be a promising and useful ally.

As soon as the train drew out of the station I made friends with the station-master and the few members of the railway staff attached to the small station. When they became aware of my mission they clustered around and said that they were very glad that I had come, and that they would do everything they could to help me. I was a bit handicapped because the local dialect was Telegu, of which I could speak only a few words. This was partially compensated for by the fact that most people there seemed to understand a little Tamil and Hindustani, both of which languages I speak fairly well. Somehow we got along and could understand each other. The station-master of course knew English, and he became my main interpreter.

To begin with, I explained that it was essential I should know some more about this tiger, especially any peculiarities regarding his appearance or habits, in order that I should distinguish him from any of the other tigers I might encounter. To this the station staff replied that all they knew was that he was a very large tiger. Of course, they had all seen tigers crossing the railway track from time to time, but they knew of no particular characteristic that would identify this tiger from any of the others. But, they suggested, one or other of the two forest guards who lived in the village might know better and be able to help me.

At this stage I asked if they could summon the son of the trapper who had been eaten by the tiger. They replied that they knew him by sight, but did not know exactly where he lived, beyond the fact that he lived somewhere in the jungle. They were sure the forest guards would be able to give me more information in this respect.

At my request a ganger was sent to call the forest guards, and in a matter of twenty minutes or so these individuals turned up. One of them was a Mahommedan named Ali Baig, with whom I could converse in Hindustani. The other was a Chenchu named Krishnappa, who spoke only Telegu. I waved them to the shade of a large mango tree growing behind the station, seated them on the ground, sat down myself and then got down to real business.

Using Ali Baig as an interpreter for the Chenchu forest guard, I played the opening gambit in the game of contacting the man-eater by offering a substantial reward to whoever first gave me the information that would lead me to it. At this both gentlemen pricked up their ears. Ali Baig said he would lead me to it even if it cost him his life. The Chenchu said — through Ali Baig — that he would do the same, except that he would not like to lose his life, and provided he knew exactly where the tiger was to be found, so as to be able to lead me there.

I appreciated that candid reply. Like all aborigines, I felt that the Chenchu was being truthful and practical too.

I began questioning them about the tiger. Both claimed to have seen him. Since the time the killings had begun they had never ventured into the jungle alone, but always together and armed with axes. Nor had they gone very far from the village. About ten days earlier they had seen a tiger crossing a fire-line about a mile away. The tiger had seen them too and had leapt into the jungle immediately. A month earlier they had encountered another, about nine o'clock in the morning, beside a water-hole. That had also bounded away when they came into view. The occasion before that — it must have been about four months earlier — they had come upon a tiger hardly a quarter of a mile from the village; he had given them an anxious few moments, for he had not run away as other tigers had done. Rather, he had swung around, half-crouched, and growled loudly. They had been on the point of turning tail and running for their lives. But Krishnappa, the Chenchu guard, had whispered to Ali Baig that they should both shout in unison. They had done that. The tiger growled in return but did not charge. He had hesitated and then walked away, looking back at them over his shoulder now and again, still growling. When he was out of sight they had hurried back to the village.

Something clicked in my mind: four months! The interval corresponded with my calculations on the map, and the unusual behaviour of the animal confirmed the idea. They had seen the man-eater on his last visit to Gazulapalli, without a doubt.

They both thought so too.

More exciting was the fact that the four-months cycle had again appeared: the tiger had killed the trolley-coolie between

Chelama and Basavapuram, and he had been the last victim. If my calculations were correct and fate was kind, the tiger should now be anywhere between Basavapuram and Gazulapalli at that moment. I became more excited. Luck seemed to be favouring me. But would it hold out?

I questioned them more closely about the tiger that had growled at them. Had they noticed anything peculiar about him? Ali Baig said that he was a huge tiger. Krishnappa was sure that it was a male. He thought that it had a lighter, yellower coat than the average tiger. 'Remember, sahib,' he explained, 'we were very frightened at that time and had expected the tiger to charge us. Who would notice such things?'

I then asked them if they knew the boy I was looking for, the son of the Chenchu trapper I had read about as having been killed by the tiger much earlier. Of course they knew him. He lived in a hut in the jungle with his mother, wife and one child, over two miles away to the north. He was carrying on his father's profession as a bird-trapper, although how he was doing it with this 'shaitan' prowling about they could not imagine. It was against the Forestry Department's laws to trap birds in the Reserved Forest, and on several occasions during his lifetime they had prosecuted the father. But always he had carried on his profession after each. But always he had carried on his profession after each case, and his son was doing the same thing now. Periodically, in the past, they had received a pea-fowl, or a brace of jungle-fowl for their own stomachs, and this had often caused them to wink at the illegal practices of both father and son. Even these offerings had now ceased. But who could blame the poor boy? He must be finding it hard these days to trap birds for his own family, knowing this devil-tiger might be anywhere, behind or inside any bush.

I grew cheerful at the thought that I had found my first need — allies who would help me to locate my quarry. Scrambling to my feet, and slinging my .405 over my shoulder, I asked the two forest guards to lead me to this boy.

We crossed the railway lines and followed a footpath that wound into the forest. Light scrub gave way to heavier jungle, and soon we were walking in single file, Krishnappa leading with Ali Baig on his heels, while I brought up the rear. I had taken the precaution to load my rifle and carried it in the crook of my right arm, prepared for all eventualities. Not that we expected the tiger to attack just then, for we were three men together; but, should he make up his mind to do so, it was either Krishnappa in the lead, or myself at the end of the line, who were in any real danger. Ali Baig was quite safe as the middle man of the party.

After what appeared to me to be distance of more like three miles than two, we crossed a stony channel through which a stream of water trickled, climbed a small hill and came upon the hut which was our objective. A pleasant-faced lad of about twenty years of age was seated at the open doorway, whittling bamboos with a sharp knife. Near at hand lay a half-completed contraption which I recognised as a bird-trap in the making.

At our approach he rose to his feet and salaamed respectfully. Krishnappa introduced me to him in the Telegu dialect, and the boy replied to him in a pleasant voice. Ali Baig then played his part as interpreter and told me that the boy's name was Bala. From the hut two female heads appeared, one of an old hag whom I took to be the boy's mother, and the other of a girl of about sixteen or seventeen. Supported by her arm, and contentedly sucking at her breast, was a naked infant about a year old. Without doubt, these were the lad's wife and son.

We squatted down on the grass a few feet from the hut and I began to ask questions, each of which Ali Baig translated to the boy in Telegu, translating also his reply. Krishnappa broke in frequently, clarifying some point that was vague to one or other. Yes, he was certainly willing to help the white 'dorai' to kill the tiger, for had it not devoured his own father? No, he would not accept money or reward in any form. His father's spirit would be very angry with him if he did so for, as his only son, the spirit expected him to claim vengeance on his slayer by direct means if possible, or at least to bring about the death of the tiger somehow. Oh yes, he had often seen the man-eater with his own eyes. Once he had gone down to the very rivulet we had just crossed to bring a pot of water to the hut. It had been about noon, just before the family had sat down to their midday meal. As he had dipped the pot into the stream, he had happened to look up and saw a tiger slinking down the opposite bank. Fortunately he had seen the beast in time, perhaps a hundred yards away, creeping directly towards him. He had left the pot of water and bolted for the shelter of the hut, where the family had closed and barricaded the door of thorns as best they could, expecting the man-eater to make an onslaught on the flimsy structure at any moment. Nothing had happened. He had very often heard the tiger calling at night, and he frequently came to drink at the rivulet. He was a large male tiger, with a rather pale yellow coat. Did the sahib want to know if he had seen anything peculiar about this tiger? Then Bala closed his eyes in thought; finally he looked up with a hopeful expression. All he could say was that the black stripes across the pale brownish-yellow skin were abnormally narrow. Would that help the dorai? He had seen very many tigers in his short life, but he could not remember ever having seen another with such narrow stripes.

When had he last seen the tiger? Again there was a slight pause for thought, and then Bala replied, 'About four months ago.' Had he seen any tiger after that? Certainly he had; twice. But they were ordinary tigers, not the slayer of his father. How did he know this? Well, for one thing, they were smaller and darker, and they had disappeared as soon as they had seen him.

Then Bala came out with the news I was hoping so much to hear. He thought the tiger was in the vicinity once again, for although he had not seen or heard him, he had discovered large pug-marks a short distance down the banks of the stream. Those large pug-marks had synchronised on previous occasions with the man-eater's visits. They had been present around the half-devoured remains of his father.

I got to my feet as I made known my wish to see these pug-marks for myself. Bala took the precaution of telling the women folk to keep inside the hut and barricade the door during his absence, and then led us back to the stream almost at the same point at which we had crossed it when coming. He turned, and began to lead us downstream. Some three furlongs away the stream broadened, though the water kept to the centre of the channel. Due to its broadening, however, there was a narrow stretch of sand-bank on either side. This had been crossed by a tiger two nights previously, from east to west. The tiger's pug-marks were so large that they were clearly visible to me long before we reached them.

The spoor was that of a very large animal, undoubtedly male. As I stood looking down upon it, I decided that, even allowing for the exaggeration caused by the imprints spreading in the soft sand, the animal that had made them was exceptionally big.

We returned to the hut, where I suggested to Bala that he should take his family away to Gazulapalli village for the duration of my visit at least. This would leave him free to assist me with an easy mind. The thought of that old woman, the girl wife and her infant son, not to mention Bala himself, in that pitiful hut deep in the jungle, just awaiting the day when one of them would be taken by the man-eater, was something dreadful even to think of. In these modern days of strife and warfare, it is commonplace to read accounts of valour on the battlefield for which men have been awarded medals, for which their praises are loudly sung. We have read, too, of the lonely death of spies and agents who have gone voluntarily into the jaws of death and have sacrificed their lives for their country before a firing-squad, to fill an unmarked grave, their praises unsung. Thrilling tales of bravery, no doubt, that liven the blood in our veins. But my blood that day tingled in humble and respectful admiration for this little aboriginal family that had so bravely but simply faced the long months in their lonely home with the killer literally at their very door — the killer that had already taken the life of the bread-winner and head of their home.

The Chenchus hesitated for quite a while, but when I pressed them further, with the strong backing of both Krishnappa and Ali Baig, they eventually consented. The two forest guards and I sat under a nearby tree and waited while they packed up their few miserable goods into three ragged bundles. Then Bala closed the thorn door of the hut behind him, and with each of them carrying a bundle as a head-load, the mother still suckling her child, we set off in single file for the village.

That night the station-master invited me to his quarters for dinner. He was a vegetarian, but his wife had put up a noble effort and prepared one of the most tasty vegetarian curries that has ever been my good fortune to taste. A large bowl of delicious curd was an outstanding item, the whole being followed by big mugs of coffee. We had decided to hole a 'conference' after dinner to determine my next line of action, and Mr Balasubramaniam, the station-master, suggested that we hold it on the station premises, as his presence was required there during the night when the mail train to Guntakal would pass through, and two or three goods trains as well. So we repaired to the station, where we seated ourselves upon a bench on the open platform, with the two forest guards and Bala squatting on the ground before us.

To my way of thinking, the best plan appeared to be to tie out a couple of live baits the next day, one at the spot where the tiger had threatened the guards, and the other beside the stream midway between Bala's hut and the sand-bank where we had seen the pug-marks. Bala and Krishnappa would remain behind to watch them and report if they were killed, while I would take Ali Baig as interpreter and proceed up the line to make further enquiries at Basavapuram and Chelama. If either of the baits was killed. Mr Balasubramaniam was to receive the report and telegraph the news up the line to me at either Basavapuram or Chelama, wherever I might be camped.

Taking me to his office, the station-master called up his colleagues at both those stations and asked for 'khubbar' or information. They reported no fresh news of the man-eater's presence, but added that everybody was on the alert and not a soul would venture out during the night. The station-master at Chelama also added that the trolley had been brought back to his station and was at present lying on the platform there. He suggested that Balasubramaniam should send a telegram down the line to the P.W.I., whose headquarters were at Nandyal, asking that I should be permitted to use the trolley if I should require urgent transport between the stations. No sooner said than done, my friend Balasubramaniam put his suggestion into practice at once, by transmitting a service telegram to the P.W.I. at Nandyal for urgent delivery, asking for the required permission. I was gratified by the enthusiastic co-operation shown by these railway officers. Throughout this adventure they did everything they could. Leaving the station-master to his work for a short time, I took my three henchmen down to the village. Although it was late at night, we did not want any delays the next day, so went to the house of a cattle-owner, awoke him from his sleep, and explained that our mission was to buy two half-grown bulls to use as baits.

The purchase of animals for this purpose in the jungles around Bangalore and particularly in Mysore State is always most difficult and has to be conducted with the utmost tact, as cattle-owners there consider it an evil practice to tie out live baits to be killed by a tiger or a panther, even with the object of eliminating an animal that has taken toll of human life. The people are not interested in selling for this purpose, and to obtain their co-operation sometimes takes hours of persuasion. To approach an owner for such a sale at dead of night would usually have been a hopeless undertaking. But the people in this particular area appeared to take a very realistic view. No sooner did the herdsman know my purpose than he readily acquiesced. He even became enthusiastic and invited me to make my own selection.

The cattle-kraal stood behind his house, and with the aid of my torch I chose two half-grown brown bulls. The owner sold them to me for thirty-five rupees each — less than three pounds in English currency. I paid him the money, thanked him for his assistance and asked him to allow the animals to be kept with his herd till morning, when my followers would call for them. To this he agreed at once.

We returned to the station to find a goods train had since drawn in and stood on the line. The Anglo-Indian driver was chatting to Balasubramaniam in the latter's office, a thermos flask of coffee in one hand, while he sipped from a mug in the other. Evidently the station-master had been talking to him about me, for at my approach he introduced himself as William Rodgers, offered me his mug of coffee and volunteered the information that only four nights ago he had seen a tiger jump across the track about a mile down the line in the direction of Nandyal. I asked him if he had noticed anything remarkable about the tiger or its colouration. He reminded me that the headlight of his engine would not reveal such details at that distance, but that the tiger appeared to have been quite a large animal. He also told me that if I cared to shoot a good chital or sambar stag, or even wild-pig, they were more plentiful in the vicinity of Diguvametta than around this station.

I thanked Mr. Rodgers for his information and told him I would consider shooting deer after disposing of the tiger. He shook hands with me, took the 'line-clear' token from the station-master, waved us goodbye and sauntered back to his engine. A minute later its shrill whistle broke the stillness, and with a loud puffing and clanking the goods train rumbled on, the red light at the rear being lost to sight as it passed around a curve. Once again the station was shrouded in stillness.

Just then the telegraphic reply from Nandyal arrived, conveying the P.W.I.'s agreement to the use of the trolley lying at Chelama station.

The station-master opened the waiting-room. I struck a match and lit the solitary oil-light that hung from the ceiling. Bala brought in my rifle, bedroll, waterbottles and tiffin-basket. There was no water in the bathroom, and it was far too late to ask Balasubramaniam to arrange for any to be brought to me. Nor was there any bed in the room, but only a table, two armless chairs, and an arm-chair with a large hole in its centre. Grateful that at least I had a roof over my head, I blew out the light and found my way to the arm-chair. Half my rear end sank through the hole in the cane bottom, but the other half managed to keep above. I removed my boots, lay back in the chair, cautiously raised my feet to place them upon the extended leg supports, and was asleep before I even knew it.

Another goods train rumbled through about 4.30 a.m. After that I fell asleep again, but it seemed only a few minutes later that Bala came into the room and called to me softly. I awoke to see that it was daylight. I found out that Balasubramaniam had gone to his quarters to snatch a few hours well-earned rest; so, while Bala got busy on my instructions to gather three stones at the end of the platform, find some sticks and light a fire to brew tea in my travelling-kettle, I got out my small folding Primus stove, lit it and fried some bacon. The tea-water had not yet come to the boil when I finished the bacon, so I sauntered down to the 'water-column' at the opposite end of the platform, which supplied water to such thirsty locomotives as required it. I carried my towel, tooth-brush, toothpaste and soap and a change of clothes with me. Stacking these articles some distance from the water-column, I removed all my clothes and knotted the towel around my waist. Then I got beneath the leather hose and with one hand turned the wheel that opened the valve and let the water into the column from the ten thousand gallon storage tank standing high on its four stone pillars nearby. The quantity of water that suddenly descended upon me was tremendous and almost knocked me off my feet. However, I enjoyed my bath, combining it with my morning tooth-brushing routine. Although I generally do not bother to shave in the jungles, to keep clean and feel fresh is very necessary. I had no second towel to dry myself with, as the one around my waist was wet, but it was of no account, for the morning was far from cold. In a few minutes I was able to don dry clothes and go back to Bala, to find the kettle boiling merrily. The tea, bacon and remains of the chappatis I had brought from Bangalore, which had become bone dry by then, served as 'chotahazri', which is the white man's exalted name for breakfast in India. The Hindustani adjective 'chota' signifies 'small', while 'hazri' indicates 'a meal'.

By the time I had finished all this, the two forest guards had come back from the village where they had gone to spend the latter part of the night. The four of us then set out, after collecting the two young bulls I had purchased the night before, to tie them at the places we had already selected. If you remember, the first of these was to be where the two guards had seen the tiger that had adopted such a threatening attitude. This was a spot on a narrow fire-line within a mile of the village. Krishnappa lopped off a branch with his axe, cut off about three feet and sharpened one end of this. We selected a tree on which a machan could be conveniently tied, provided the tiger obliged us by killing this bait, drove the stake that Krishnappa had just made into the ground at a suitable spot some fifteen yards away, and tethered one of the brown bulls to it by its hind-leg, using a coil of the stout cotton rope I had brought with me in my bed-roll. Then we walked back to the station, crossed the lines and traversed the three miles to the stream near Bala's hut. No fresh tracks were evident, so we tied the second calf beneath another tree on the slope of the stream about fifty yards short of the sandbank on which the tiger had left his pug-marks.

We got back to the station shortly before noon, when the station-master started insisting I should have lunch with him again. So as not to wound his feelings I very politely declined, as I knew my presence in his house was irksome to him as a high-caste individual, although he tried very gallantly not to show it. Instead, I went to the village with the guards and managed to obtain a meal of sorts from the village 'hotel' — a one-roomed zincsheet-cum-grass-roofed affair. That done, we all returned to the station, where I gave instructions to the two Chenchus who were to feed and water the baits: they were to tell the station-master if either was killed. Mr Balasubramaniam needed no reminding of the part he was to play in the affair by sending a message to me should such a kill occur.

Let me here record my appreciation of this gentleman's co-operation. I knew it was violently against his religious principles to aid and abet me, or to assist me in any way by bringing about the death of a bull or cow, which to his caste are sacred animals. But in the larger interests that were at stake, he suborned his principles and went all-out in his efforts to help me.

The train that was to carry me to the next station, Basavapuram, six miles away, steamed in at 2.30 p.m. I asked the driver for permission to travel with him on the engine, which he very readily gave. I wanted to do this so as to view the jungle on both sides of the track. Ali Baig got into the first third-class compartment behind, and away we went.

The train took twenty-five minutes to cover those six miles. As I viewed the thick jungle through which we passed, my hopes of success sank very very low indeed. It was an immense area, heavily forested, and the tiger might be anywhere.

The railway station at Basavapuram closely resembled Gazulapalli. As I got off and thanked the driver, I began to think I had indeed been a super-optimist in tying those two baits at Gazulapalli while the tiger might be here at Basavapuram, or even at the next station, Chelama, five miles further on.

The station-master here turned out to be as obliging as had been his counterpart. He was a non-caste Tamil named Masilamony, and after his first words of greeting, in which he made me feel quite at home, he urged me to make my headquarters in his waiting-room, stating that the tiger would surely be found there in Basavapuram, being the centre of the affected district.

Once again I went through my routine of closely questioning the station staff, and the one forest guard who came from the village. He was a Telegu and told me, through Masilamony, that the other forest guard who shared with him the responsibility of looking after the area was suffering severely from malaria and had gone on sick leave to Nandyal. They had all seen tigers at various time, and each claimed that he had seen the man-eater. But nobody appeared to have noticed anything special about it, either in size or markings. This forest guard, whose name was Kittu, told me there was a water-hole north of the railway line and a little over a mile away, where he had often seen tiger pug-marks when these animals came to drink water.

We walked to the water-hole that evening, where I noticed some old pug-marks of tiger, together with a recent spoor made by a large panther. I was annoyed to see the latter, as I was almost certain he would devour any bait I tied there long before the tiger showed up. It is a nuisance to bait for a tiger at a spot frequented by a panther, as one is almost sure to sacrifice the bait to the latter.

I spent the night in the waiting-room and bought a half-grown buffalo calf in the village next morning. This we tied in a clearing in the jungle half a mile short of the water-hole, and I instructed Kittu to visit it each morning in company with his friends, to feed and water it, and to tell the station-master if it was killed. Masilamony readily agreed to follow

Balasubramaniam's example and send me a message as soon as word was brought to him.

Once again I caught the afternoon train, which came a little late at 3.15 p.m., and travelled on the engine up the line for five miles to Chelama. The engine-driver, who was an Indian, as we passed through it, pointed out the cutting where the trolley-man had been taken. He said it was almost midway between the two stations.

We alighted at Chelama to follow much the same procedure. The station-master came up and greeted me, saying he had been told to expect my arrival by his colleagues in the stations I had recently left. He had also arranged with the two local forest guards to await me; they were, in fact, on the platform.

As a result of the conference that followed, I was told that word had been brought by the guard of a goods train which had passed through Basavapuram while I had been sleeping in the waiting-room there that morning, that a woman had been killed at Diguvametta, sixteen miles further up, at the extreme eastern limit of the jungle belt. The guard had been unable to mention the matter to any of us at Basavapuram, as his train passed the station without stopping.

This latest news upset all my calculations, just as it dashed my hopes to zero. Not only did it increase enormously the area of search for the man-eater, but all my carefully cherished tiger-beat time-table was entirely upset. I had been almost sure that the man-eater would be somewhere in the vicinity of Gazulapalli. Instead, he had killed at Diguvametta, which was twenty-seven miles away.

Then I remembered that twenty-seven miles was, after all, no long walk for a tiger.

I asked the station-master to verify the news if possible on the morse-line to Diguvametta. After about fifteen minutes of tapping on the telegraph key, he said that the station master at Diguvametta had confirmed it with the local policeman at his village, to whom a report had been made that a Chenchu woman, gathering mhowa flowers at the edge of the jungle, had disappeared the morning of the day before. People from her village had found her half-filled basket, but no traces of her. The Diguvametta station-master also sent his advice that, as he had heard I was tying up live baits at the different stations, I should on no account fail to do so at Diguvametta, and also at the small station of Bogada which lay between Chelama and Diguvametta.

Here indeed was a pretty kettle of fish. It seemed as if I would have to tie up baits at each station along this whole line to catch up with the elusive tiger.

It would not be very interesting to give you the details of how I tied up a bait at Chelama next morning. Perhaps you may wonder why I did not leave for Diguvametta by the next train, but you must not forget that two days had passed since the woman had been killed, and the tiger would have picked her bones clean by the time I arrived — assuming, of course, that I was able to find them. So I thought it better to finish tying the bait intended for Chelama before moving on.

But that same afternoon I caught the train to Bogada, where I tied another bait in the evening, catching a goods train for Diguvametta in the early hours of the morning. There I tied two animals, one near the place where the woman had been taken, and the other at a point where a forest line, a large stream and a cattle-track leading into the jungle intersected. Diguvametta boasted of a forester, an intelligent and very helpful Indian Christian. This man assured me that many tiger had been shot in years gone by from machans in the branches of the 'hongee' tree which grew at the spot where the latter bait was tied.

I had now spent some five days in this area, had seven baits tied out, had used up far more money than I wanted or expected to use, and was quite tired of only hearing stories about this elusive tiger without even hearing him roar — or any tiger, for that matter. The jungles had been exceptionally silent since my arrival.

During the evening of the day on which I tied the two baits at Diguvametta, I went for an extensive ramble into the forest, accompanied by Joseph, the Indian Christian forester. As he was a non-vegetarian like myself, and a bachelor withal, at his invitation and assurance that my presence would cause him no discomfort or inconvenience, I decided to remain at least a few days at Diguvametta and sleep on the verandah of his quarters. The station-master had previously offered the use of the station waiting-room, but the passing trains at night disturbed me. Joseph's Malayali servant, whom he had brought along with him from Calicut, who cooked his food and attended to his few requirements, would relieve me of the burden and waste of time each day that I had hitherto been compelled to spend in preparing some of my own meals, snatched and scanty as they had had to be.

Another reason for choosing Diguvametta as my camping-place, at least for the present, was of course the fact that it was here that the tiger had last killed, just over three days previously. You may wonder again why we had made no very serious attempt to locate the remains of the poor woman who had been taken. Firstly, it would have served no purpose. As I have already indicated, the tiger had had more than sufficient time to devour her completely, and at most we might have found but a few gnawed bones. Secondly, the jungle was intensely dry, and although I had cast about at the time of tying up my live-bait (a bull-calf), there had been no clue as to the direction in which the tiger had carried her. We had combed the area in a radius of well over two hundred yards and found nothing, not even a remnant of torn cloth from her garment. Lastly, there being no purpose as I have just said in finding her remains at such a late state, I did not want to disturb the area further, for it had already been disturbed by the party of men who had come searching for the girl and found her basket.

The jungle in the locality was beautiful and indeed a sportsman's paradise as regards feathered game and deer. We came upon several herds of graceful cheetal in the forest glades. The long spear-grass was bone-dry, and the ends of the stems bent down to earth with the weight of the barb-like dry seeds with which they were tufted. This factor greatly increased the range of visibility and enabled us to see between the stems of the trees and into the glades. We even came upon a lordly sambar stag with a beautiful pair of antlers, which crashed away at our approach. It had been a bit early in the evening for a sambar to be about. Nevertheless the presence of the stag advertised the fact that the jungle was undisturbed, but that natural game was so abundant suggested little hope or reason for the tiger to take either of my baits. By the very same token, with such abundance of food available just for the taking, there seemed no cause for the tiger ever to have turned man-eater at all.

I purchased Ali Baig's ticket, instructing him to return by the night mail to Gazulapalli, as his presence was no longer necessary, and made an early night of it myself. At least in Joseph's verandah I was not disturbed by the clanking of trains, so that I slept soundly for ten hours and awoke the next morning in a considerably more hopeful frame of mind. The Malayali servant had performed wonders while we had been sleeping. There was a jug of strong tea and plateful of 'hoppers' and 'put too-rice'. The former is made from finely-ground rice-flour, and the latter from the whole grains of a special variety of rice. They are specialities of Madras, and their presence before me that morning indicated that my new-found friend and host Joseph, undoubtedly came from that city. It proved a delicious and most welcome repast.

Then I had a cold bath inside the enclosure constructed for the purpose, built up against the wall of the house, its three sides consisting of bamboo mats, each about five feet wide. There was no roof.

Joseph was ready and waiting while I dressed. We then visited the two baits we had tied out the day before, in company with both the forest guards who worked under Joseph, and to whom he had delegated the responsibility of feeding and watering these animals. Both the baits were alive and untouched.

There was nothing more I could do but await developments. The area was far too extensive to warrant long walks in the jungle in the hope of stumbling upon the tiger by accident. It might be anywhere between Diguvametta and Gazulapalli, twenty-seven miles away, and searching for it would have been a waste of time and energy. Up to this stage, as I have already said I had not contacted any tiger whatever, but I had done some yeoman spadework, and I might expect to reap the rewards in a little while.

And once started, things really did begin to happen. The telegraph wires hummed at about nine the next morning when Masilamony, the station-master at Basavapuram, relayed the news that my bait had been killed the night before. I was not over exuberant at receiving this information, for you may remember that this was the place where I had come across fresh panther-tracks near the water-hole, and had deliberately tied my bait some distance away to keep it from that panther, if possible.

I asked the station-master at Diguvametta to speak to Masilamony and ask him to question the forest guard, Kittu, closely to find out whether it was a tiger that had taken my bait or the panther. There was only a short delay before the reply came back; Masilamony explained that Kittu was beside him at the telegraph instrument while he was signaling. Kittu stated the bait had been killed by a panther and advised that I should come and shoot it, as otherwise any other baits I might tie up would undoubtedly suffer the same fate at the hands of this animal.

This was sound logic. At the same time, I did not possess a regular game licence for the area, but had come on a special request to shoot the man-eater only, and nothing else, made directly by the Chief Conservator of Forests at Madras, who had issued a permit to cover my visit. I decided I would write to the Chief Conservator later and explain the reason why I had to eliminate the panther, while offering to pay the game licence fee should any objection arise. I therefore made up my mind to answer Masilamony's summons.

There was no passenger train in the direction of Basavapuram during the day, but fortunately a goods train was scheduled to pass through at about eleven that very morning. The station-master stopped the train for me, and I travelled in the guard's van to Basavapuram. Joseph insisted on going with me.

Kittu took me to the kill, which bore every trace of a panther's handiwork, from the fang-marks in its throat to the large hole that had been eaten in the animal's stomach, where entrails and flesh had all become mixed up together to form a repast. The panther had eaten heavily the night before, and because of that I feared it might make a late return. Kittu offered me the loan of his own charpoy or rope-cot, so, rather than build a machan, we went back for it. To return and tie it up took scarcely two hours, and everything was set by four o'clock.

It was far too early to sit up, so we returned to the station, hardly more than a mile away, and had a quick meal, consisting of biscuits, chappatties, bananas and several mugs of tea. Joseph expressed a keen desire to sit up with me, so we both returned and were in position in the machan by 5.30 p.m.

I have said that I expected the panther to come late. I was wrong. We had been in the machan for scarcely twenty minutes, and I was leaning back and taking it easy, when I heard a faint sound below me. I looked down. There was the panther sitting on his haunches beside his kill and contemplating it. A truly nice specimen, I was tempted to spare his life. This temptation I overcame only because his presence there would be a constant source of interference with my baits. I shot him behind the left shoulder.

Our early return to the station surprised both Kittu and Masilamony. Hearing the news, the latter asked me to give him the skin if I was not in need of it, to which I agreed, and we went back with a petromax light and four coolies to retrieve the dead panther. I supervised while Masilamony excitedly watched the skinning operation. I showed him how to preserve the pelt temporarily with a solution of copper-sulphate and salt till such time as he could sent it to a taxidermist at Bangalore.

Next morning I bought another bait to replace the one that had been killed. We took this to the water-hole where I had seen the old tiger pug-marks and there we tied it up.

It had been my intention after shooting the panther to return with Joseph to Diguvametta by the afternoon train, but when we got back to Basavapuram station after tying out the new bait, Masilamony informed me that he had just received a morse message from the station-master at Chelama, stating my bait there had been taken the previous night by a tiger.

This information came before ten o'clock. The train to Chelama would not arrive for at least another four hours. So I decided to walk the five miles to Chelama, to which Joseph at once agreed. We were there shortly after 11.30 p.m.

The station-master who had relayed the message, and the two forest guards who had brought it, were awaiting our arrival. They were all in a state of excitement, and the guards reported that when they had gone to inspect and water the bait that morning they had come upon its partially-devoured remains and the pug-marks of a large tiger in the surrounding earth. Delaying only long enough to cut some branches and place them across the carcass of the dead animal to hide it from vultures, they had hurried back to the station to send their message.

Now in all seven cases, when tying up these baits, I had chosen each spot very carefully and had taken care to place each animal close to a tree on which it would be convenient to tie a machan. This precaution had already made my task easy when shooting the panther.

The forest guards volunteered to get a charpoy for me, while Joseph and I, together with the station-master, went down to the only eating-house in the village for our midday meal. During this meal Joseph said he would like to sit up with me again, and it was with the greatest difficulty that I could dissuade him without wounding his feelings. His company was one thing where the panther was concerned, but quite another when it came to a tiger, especially so if the animal happened to be the man-eater for which we were all searching. The slightest sound or incautious movement by a person in a machan would betray our presence and drive the animal away. I had previously had experience of companions who had sat in machans with me and made involuntary sounds which had rendered our vigil abortive. This is especially likely to happen if the sitting-up becomes a night-long affair and the person gets fidgety and restless. I did not want to run this risk after all the trouble I had taken in tying up my baits over such a wide area.

The kill was about an hour's walk from the station and perhaps three miles inside the jungle, and was reached by traversing a tortuous footpath and then making a short cut downhill. I had the charpoy in position long before 3.30 p.m., but as the leaves to screen it had to be brought from some distance away, so as not to disturb the neighbourhood, and moreover had to be of the same species as the tree in which the charpoy had been fixed (in this instance a tamarind), it was nearly an hour more before I was in position.

While the two guards had been busy fixing the machan, assisted by Joseph, who passed the branches up to them from the ground, I studied the kill and the half-dozen or so pugmarks that the tiger had left. The earth was fairly hard, so that the marks were only partially visible, and in every instance the ball of the pad was not clearly outlined. I could see the tiger was a large one and a male, but it was quite impossible to say with any degree of certainty that he was the same animal whose footprints I had seen beside the stream near Bala's hut in Gazulapalli. There the marks had been made in the soft, damp sand which had served to spread and to some extent exaggerate their size. But here the ground was dry and fairly hard.

Just before 4.30 p.m. I was comfortably settled on the charpoy. I spent a few minutes arranging my tea-filled water-bottle beside the smaller one that contained water. The village 'hotel' had supplied three large chappattis, folded inside a portion of banana-leaf, for dinner. These I placed next to the bottles holding the liquid refreshments; then came my spare torch and cartridges. The nights at this time of the year were warm, so I had brought no blanket or overcoat; only my balaclava cap, which I donned. Finally I fixed my torch into its clamps along the rifle, and then all was ready.

I told Joseph and the guards that I could find my way back to the station on my own. They walked away, leaving me to start my vigil.

It was just getting dark when I became aware of a muffled tread on the grass directly beneath me. The leaves of the tamarind tree are tiny and soft, so that when they become dry and fall to earth they form a malleable carpet and emit no sound when trodden upon, beyond the vaguest rustling noises, hard to recognize or define. In this respect the dried leaves of teak trees provide the ideal medium to warn the watcher of the approach of any living thing, even a rat, for they rustle and crackle long before the intruder appears in sight. But I knew that those muffled sounds heralded the coming of the tiger, and so it was that I was not surprised when, leaning forward and looking down, I saw him almost immediately beneath me. The weight of his body on the grass and tiny fallen tamarind leaves had caused the slight sound that had betrayed his approach.

He then passed out of view for a few seconds, but reappeared soon and strode boldly towards the bull he had killed. This was in a direction away from me, so that I could not make out much of his head, but saw his left flank, hindquarters and tail instead. As I have said, it was just about getting dark. In the forests, at such a time, colours tend to lose their clarity and objects look much bigger than they really are. Anyone who has been in a jungle or even in the English woods at dusk, will tell you the same thing. The animal below me appeared abnormally large, but I could not make out whether his colour was pale or otherwise. The stripes were blurred and hardly visible.

It was too dark to take the shot without the aid of the torch, especially as I would not be able to see the foresight of my rifle clearly. So I pressed the switch with my left thumb. The beam shone forth, lighting up the left side of the tiger, and fell ahead of him on to the kill. As I aimed quickly, I remember noticing that the tiger was not aware of the fact that the light was coming from behind him. Rather, he seemed to think it was coming from the kill itself. He just stood still and looked.

I fired behind the left shoulder. He fell forward against the dead bull and then squirmed around on his right side. The white of his belly and chest came into view. I fired again. The tiger died as I continued to shine my torch on him.

I waited for perhaps twenty minutes, during which time I flashed my light now and again to make sure I had indeed killed him. Then I climbed down and made a close examination of my prize.

He was a large male in his prime, but he was certainly not the same animal that Bala had described to me. This one had a rich dark coat, and his stripes were very far from being abnormally narrow. Had I shot the wrong tiger, or was this the real man-eater? Was the animal that. Bala had seen some other ordinary, oldish, tiger? These questions sprang to mind, but I knew that the answer would only be known if another human was killed — or if there were no more human victims.

By the aid of my flashlight I was able to find the winding track that eventually brought me to the railway station a little before 9 p.m. Joseph was asleep in the waiting-room, while the two guards lay on a mat on the platform. I awoke them and announced what had taken place. Their surprise at my early return gave place to great jubilation at news of my success, and Joseph shook hands with me in warm congratulation.

I thanked him, but said I was far from certain that I had killed the man-eater. He asked why, and I told him. But he and the guards were optimistic and said they were sure I had slain the right tiger.

The station-master then arrived to supervise the passing of the night trains, and he too was very pleased to hear the news. The two guards hurried off to summon a carrying party, returning in another hour or so with some ten men, a couple of stout bamboos, ropes and two lanterns.

We returned to the kill and were back with the tiger by 1 a.m. I had the carcass placed at the end of the platform, just outside the iron railings that marked the precincts of the station yard, and started to skin the animal with the aid of the two lanterns and my spare torch, held by Joseph. I did the job myself as the guards appeared not to know much about the art, and I was closely engrossed and half-way through the operation when the night mail train, going down the line to Guntakal, came to a halt at the station.

Everybody in that train got down, from driver to guard and including all the passengers, and stood around me in an enormous circle to get a clear view. I got much publicity that night and the train left more than fifteen minutes behind schedule. The running staff regarded the delay as of little consequence. Besides, the skin being taken off a large tiger at dead of night on a railway station platform is not exactly a common sight, even in India.

The standard application of a solution of copper sulphate and salt would temporarily preserve it for the duration of my trip.

The next day I rested, while the station-master relayed the news to the stations on both sides of Chelama, and everybody was happy. I was not so pleased myself, and decided to remain for a further week if possible. As I had tied out my baits and come prepared to stay up to a month if needed, I felt it would be better to remain where I was rather than return to Bangalore and then have to come out again and tie out my baits once more. For a strange premonition kept insisting to me that the man-eater was not dead and would kill someone very soon.

Four days passed. Then came the news from Gazulapalli that the tiger had killed Bala's young wife. Unknown to me he had taken his family back to his hut in the forest, thinking that the coast was clear.

The man-eater had kept to his expected schedule after all.

Joseph had meanwhile returned to Diguvametta, so I waited only long enough to send a message to Balasubramaniam to keep Bala in attendance and, borrowing the trolley at Chelama, as no goods train was due to pass for the next four hours, set out for Gazulapalli, propelled by two trolleymen.

We took a little over an hour and a half to get there and found Bala awaiting me, seated on the ground at a corner of the platform, weeping. Balasubramaniam was there, too, and the two forest guards, Ali Baig and Krishnappa.

The young Chenchu's tale was as brief as it was tragic. Hearing I had shot the man-eater at Chelama, and as neither of my live baits had been touched all this time, he had decided that the danger to their lives had passed and had taken his family back to their hut only two days earlier. At dawn that very morning his wife had wakened, laid their baby next to him, and had gone outside to relieve herself. A moment later he heard her cry out faintly. Realising that something terrible had happened, he had seized his axe and rushed outside. There was nothing to be seen.

It was not yet daylight, and Bala said that he could find no trace of anything having happened, except that his young wife was not there. He had called to her but received no answer. Frantically searching, he went to the other side of the hut where he knew she would have gone for the purpose she had had in mind. Still he found nothing.

The grass was wet after a heavy night's dew-fall, and as the light grew stronger he was able to pick out the course made by something that had walked away through it into the jungle.

He had found no blood-trail, but he knew he was gazing at the path made in the wet grass as the man-eater had walked through it, carrying his wife. For the trail through the damp grass was clear, where it had been trodden upon or brushed aside by the passage of the two heavy bodies — the tiger and his victim.

Then Bala had done a very brave and a very foolish thing. Alone, and armed only with his puny axe, he had followed the trail.

With more daylight, after a couple of furlongs, he had come upon the first trace of a blood-trail from the point where the tiger had laid his burden down among the dew-dripping bushes in order to change his grip on his victim. Thereafter, following the grim trail had been easy, and he had caught up with the tiger in the act of settling down to its meal at the foot of an old dead tree.

The man-eater had seen him. He laid back his ears and growled. In another second he would have charged. But the sight of his wife being devoured before his very eyes had proved too much for the young Chenchu. Some demon of recklessness and bravery had possessed him, and, burning with hate and screaming, he rushed upon the tiger brandishing his little axe.

I have often told you that all man-eaters appear to be possessed by a strange streak of cowardice. They will attack a victim unawares but will rarely face up to a direct counter-attack. That early morning the man-eater of Chelama proved himself no exception to the rule. He hesitated till the little Chenchu was almost upon him. Then he turned tail and fled.

Fortunately, wisdom at last came to Bala. Had he attempted to follow the tiger, the latter might well have recovered his morale and wiped him out. Instead, he snatched up the corpse of his wife and ran back with it to the hut.

Hearing this simple tale, simply told by the little aborigine, my heart was filled with admiration and pride that India possessed such heroes, even among her most humble out-caste tribes.

At the hut Bala had wasted no time on tears. Leaving the body inside, and bidding his old mother carry the child, he had secured the door as best he could and set off for the railway station to get word to me. It was lucky that he had acted so quickly, for he and his mother were well on their way to the station before the tiger had time to recover from his fright and return to the body or the hut.

The little man was crying silently as he told me this story, and I made no effort to console him. His tears would be good for him. They were Mother Nature's own salve to the great nervous strain he had been through and an outlet for his pent-up emotions after the shock of bereavement. My lip-sympathy, on the other hand, would be quite useless. I could never even hope to look for an excuse to bridge the tragic gap that had been created tin his young life, so early that very morning.

But the tears did not last for long. The aboriginal is inherently a fatalist. I did not want to interrupt or hurry him, but ten minutes later Bala stood up and announced himself ready for action.

I had been thinking quickly and deeply, and a plan was forming in my mind. To put it into effect would require the utmost sacrifice from Bala, and I hesitated to ask him to make it. Perhaps some affinity of thought between us, born of years of life in the jungle, he by birth and me by choice, bound us together. He looked up into my face, and once again tears welled from his eyes as he gently nodded his head. Then Ali Baig interpreted. 'She was my wife and I love her, dorai. But you shall have her dead body to serve as bait to avenge the death of this dear one, and of my father.'

Enough words had been spoken, and enough time wasted. I was determined to play my part in the role with which this humble but great little man had entrusted me. I waited only to eat a hurried meal of vegetable curry and rice which the ever-solicitous Balasubramaniam had got his wife to prepare for me, filled my two water-bottles with tea and water respectively, and set off for the hut with the two forest guards and Bala, carrying a charpoy.

The dead girl was a pitiful sight. The few rags she had been wearing had been torn away by the tiger, but Bala had covered her loins with the one saree she had possessed. The young face wore a strange expression of calm. Blood had steeped into the mud floor of the hut from her lacerated back, and its dark stream had trickled from her torn throat and breasts and dried on her dusky skin. We stood, all four of us, in respectful silence for a minute, regarding those mangled remains on the floor before us that had, only that morning, been a living and happy mother. Then I closed the door of the hut behind us as I motioned Bala to lead us to the spot where he had found the tiger about to begin his meal.

The sun had long since absorbed the dew, and the heads of spear-grass that had bent with the passage of the man-eater and his victim were standing upright again, gently nodding in the light breeze. Bala walked ahead to the spot where the tiger had laid the girl down for the first time and changed his hold. From there the blood-spoor began and it led us in a short time to an old dead tree, at the foot of which the killer had set her down to begin his meal in real earnest, when Bala had driven him off.

We walked silently and did not speak, although all four of us were on the alert. But there was little actual danger, because of our numbers. At the foot of the tree we halted and looked at the ground. It was hard and covered with short dried grass. No pug-marks were visible, nor was there any need to look for them

I remembered that this tiger was accredited with never returning to his meal of a human victim after his earlier experience in Hyderabad when he was wounded by the Nawab. Would he return now? Would there be any use in my sitting up for him? These thoughts passed dismally through my mind. The only ray of hope in this case was the fact that he had not eaten even a mouthful of the girl. But against that was the fact that Bala had frightened him away. All said and done, the proposition appeared to hold out but little chance of success. But I knew I would have to try, for there was no alternative.

I looked around for a tree on which to put the charpoy.

The tiger had selected a densely-wooded spot for his repast, covered with bushes and undergrowth. The nearest tree, other than the bare dead one, was thirty yards away. When I squatted on my haunches at the approximate height of a tiger, I could see I would have to sit right at the top to see over the undergrowth and have a fair chance to shoot. Most probably the tiger would only return after dark, if he returned at all, and a flashlight could not penetrate the brambles should I sit any lower down.

I walked the thirty yards to the tree and looked up. Its higher branches were no thicker than my two fingers and could not possibly support my weight in the charpoy.

The next sizeable tree was some ten yards further away. I got to it and scrambled up. But I could only see the upper portion of the trunk of the dead tree where the tiger had been. The brambles hid its base and everything else below.

Here was a knotty problem. Where could I sit?

I walked back to the three men and sauntered around the dead tree. It had been a big tree in its day and the bole at its base was twelve to fifteen feet in circumference. There was no apparent reason why it had died: perhaps from some disease or an insect pest. Perhaps its roots had been eaten away underground. Whatever the cause, it had perished some years earlier; only the dead branches forked into the cloudless sky above my head.

White ants had already begun their work of demolition from below, and in a short while the weakened base would no longer be able to sustain the weight of the dead superstructure, and the whole would crash to earth and disintegrate as food for the termites and the myriad wood-beetles and insects of all kinds that would then attack it from the ground.

I walked closer to the trunk. At a spot just level with the top of my head three branches had spread out from the main stem. A crust of dried earth covered the busy white ants below. Raising Myself on tiptoe, I peered into the cavity that led down the stem. The inside of the tree was hollow.

This had not been noticeable from outside, particularly from the spot where the victim's body had been laid.

I motioned to the three men and whispered to Ali Baig to ask Bala to get inside the hollow trunk to see whether a place could be made for me there. Before sending him, however, I took the precaution to shine my spare flashlight into the hole, to make sure it did not shelter a snake or scorpion, or even a centipede. Having made certain it was tenantless except for the white ants, Bala nimbly let himself down. Being at least a foot shorter than me, he disappeared from view, but popped out again and stated that it was a close fit for him and could not possibly accommodate my greater bulk. Some extension of the interior was absolutely necessary.

I then noticed that the white ants had eaten much further into the wood on the opposite side.

With Bala pushing from within, and we three pulling from outside with our hands, aided now and again by a couple of gentle blows from Krishnappa's axe, we started tearing away the rotting wood from the hole by which Bala had entered. The termites had already done most of the work for us, and little by little we enlarged the hole, working downwards towards ground level. We increased the size of the entrance not only at the top, but by dint of removing the wood from the other side of the bole we completely exposed that side down to about knee-level. As the wood came away, to lay open the interior, we were able to get our hands inside and use Bala's short-handled axe as well.

It was hard work and took nearly two hours, but at last I was able to step into a hole that was sufficiently big to accommodate my feet up to my knees. Thereafter, I was free enough to move my hands and my rifle through the opening we had made in the off-side of the trunk.

There were several serious snags in my position. The main one was that I had my back to the point where the tiger had set the woman down, and to which he would most probably return — that is, if he did return. I could not turn and look in that direction because the tree trunk was behind me. Further, we had not been able to remove the wood from this part of the trunk, as the white ants had eaten more on the opposite side, as I have said. To do so we would have had to hack through the wood, for which we did not have the time, apart from the noise we would make.

All these drawbacks combined to suggest that, when we finally put the corpse of the girl-wife into place, it could not be at the spot where the tiger had left it. We would be compelled to change its position a little. If I did not do that and the tiger did come, he would either remove the carcass before I became aware of his presence, or he would sit and eat it within a distance of five yards from me without my being able to do anything about it. Of course, I could step out of cover and creep around the bole of the tree. But I was far too afraid to do that. Further, I would probably make some noise in stepping out of the trunk in the dark. The tiger would hear me and perhaps disappear; or, what was more frightening, he might meet me half-way around the trunk. That thought was difficult to relish.

A second major disadvantage lay in the fact that I would have to stand upright throughout the night. I could not even squat, because the hole below knee-level was just large enough for my legs.

Thirdly, if the tiger reconnoitered the place before approaching the body, as every sensible tiger would do, he would look straight at me as soon as he came opposite the gap we had cut. Of course, I would have the men put up some sort of camouflage to hide in, in the way of leaves and trailing creepers, but would I be able to deceive his jungle-bred eyes if he looked straight in my direction? At lest, would he not become suspicious of these leaves and other things, suddenly appearing on the bole of a tree that had been quite bare only that very morning?

Again, if a cobra, scorpion or some other nasty creeping or crawling thing chose to select the hollow in the dead tree to keep itself warm on a chilly night, I would indeed be in a sorry predicament. There were so many possibilities of trouble that I shrugged them away. I would have to take the chance, although the odds seemed to be ten to one against success.

I laid my coat upon the ground, and on it we piled every bit of the dried wood we had removed, even to the last scrap. We then held the coat at the four corners and carried it away to throw the debris at a distance.

Then we returned to the hut, where Bala bravely lifted his wife's body on his shoulder. In single file and silence we walked back to the tree. I asked him to set the body down a little to the left of the opening we had made, so that the tiger in looking at it would not be in a direct line with the opening and myself. There was no room for anything inside the hollow but myself and the rifle with torch attached, so I swallowed a chappatti and some tea from my water-bottle before giving it to Ali Baig to take back.

I stepped into the hollow. Bala and Krishnappa then placed some sticks across the opening, between which they draped leaves and trails of creepers to screen me as much as possible. This job Bala took very seriously, going back some paces to different angles of vision every now and again, to check whether I could still be seen inside. He wedged a larger bit of stick across the two sides of the opening at the level of my chest, so that I might rest my rifle upon it as I fired. I found I could slide my rifle before me, slowly up my body and then over this stick without making any noise. The two Chenchus draped the stick and the trunk on both sides of my face with creepers, hanging them downwards against the wood from the two higher branches of the tree. Finally, they wedged a great mass of leaves and wood down on the base of the three branches that bifurcated above me. I was truly bottled up inside that hollow.

Before leaving, Bala bade farewell to his dead wife. He kissed the cold forehead and he kissed her feet. Then he got down on his knees beside the body and prostrated himself on the ground, with his palms extended to earth, to seek her pardon for the indignities to which he was exposing her poor body.

When he got up again, there were no tears in his eyes. His face was resolute. He looked at me wordlessly. Once more the telepathy of jungle-loving people passed between us. His look said, far more clearly than any spoken word: 'I have done all I could and have even sacrificed the body of my dear one. The rest is up to you.' I resolved I would not fail him.

A moment later my three followers had gone on their way to the hut and I was alone.

I glanced at my wrist-watch. The time was 4.45 p.m. Patches of bright sunlight filtered through the undergrowth and dappled the red and black of the dead woman's saree which Bala had wrapped around her waist. Her hair had fallen loosely and lay outspread on the ground, framing the head and face, now turned towards me, with its peaceful expression. Rigor mortis had set in and one hand lay folded stiffly across her breast, where perhaps her husband had laid it in the morning when he had carried her body back to their hut. The other had set by her side. The gentle evening breeze, swaying the grass, idly flapped a corner of the saree or lifted a wisp of her jet-black hair.

Except for the breeze stirring the leaves and grass, nothing else moved. Except for the faint tick of my wrist-watch, and a dull thudding sound which took me quite some time to identify as the pounding of my own heart, I could hear no other sound.

I spread my feet gently, inch by inch, and eased them as far forward as possible while leaning back. They would have to bear my weight that whole night, and my least duty to them as to try to distribute that load as evenly as possible.

203

The jungle came of life forty-five minutes later, with the usual cries of roosting pea-fowl and jungle-fowl. One grey cock strutted out into the clearing before me, and crowed his challenge to the dying day. '*Kuck ky'a ky'a khuk'm*', he called, and in a few seconds the cry was answered by another jungle-cock in the distance. '*Wheew, kuck khuke'm*', he replied. The first rooster ruffled his feathers and looked in the direction from which the reply had come. Then a gust of wind blew and the corner of the saree stirred. With a heavy flapping of wings, the rooster was gone.

'*Mi-iao mi-iao*' called a peacock, to be answered by similar cries from his own kind, as the heavy birds flapped one by one to rest in groups in some distant tree. Spur-fowl cackled their fighting notes in the undergrowth, while the last of the butter-flies and beetles sailed or buzzed their homeward way to the particular leaf or other shelter they had chosen for that night.

The daylight faded fast in the manner of all tropical countries. My feathered friends of the sunny hours were no doubt tucking their heads beneath their wings, or at least would do so very soon. With the fading light, something soft descended from the skies and came to rest on the ground a yard away. It was a night-jar, the harbinger of the Indian jungle night. '*Chuck-chuck-chuckoooo*', it trilled, it trilled, while its brown outline on the dried grass resembled just a stone. And then, with a graceful outstretching of its wings, it floated away. '*Cheep-cheep-cheep*' came a sound from directly above me. Two bats circled their rapid flight around the tree, to snap up the belated day-insects that were just going to rest, in addition to some early-arrivals from among the insects of the night.

I had seen and heard it all so very many times before; the diminuendo of the creatures of the day giving place to the crescendo of the creatures of the night. But never in quite the same position and circumstances as I was now in, I had to admit.

Then came darkness for a short while — but not for long, as singly and in groups the stars began to twinkle overhead, shedding a very diffused light on the jungle around me. That would be my only illumination till daylight came again, for this had happened during the moonless nights.

The mosquitoes took some time to find me out, but when their scouts finally made the discovery, they lost but few moments in reporting to headquarters. Then whole squadrons of dive-bombers made full capital out of it. With protruding under-lip, I blew them off my face and I stuffed my hands into my trouser pockets to outwit such of the more enterprising individuals as had flown inside my tree-trunk, bent upon sucking my blood.

Eight o'clock came. I lifted one foot after the other and wriggled my toes inside my canvas shoes in order to restore circulation to the soles of my feet. This tiger had the reputation of never returning to a human kill. And I had placed myself in this awkward and uncomfortable position for the night. Then a picture of Bala's tear-stained face and of that dead countenance, now lying out in the darkness so close to me but hidden from sight, appeared before my mind, and my reason assured me that what I was doing at that moment was the only thing possible for me to do.

My thoughts had been wandering when all of a sudden I became fully alert, every nerve at high tension. I had seen nothing; I had heard not a sound. But just as certain as I was of my own name, I knew the man-eater was near. The hair on my neck was on end and a faint nervous quiver ran through my whole being. Some undefined and indefinable sense had screamed the warning to me. Yes, without doubt, the tiger was there.

I strained my ears to the utmost to hear any sound. There was absolute silence. No warning cry from deer or other jungle creatures had betrayed the feline's movements.

Such complete silence and such delay in approaching the dead body meant only one thing. The tiger was suspicious. Was that the aftermath of the fright Bala had given him that morning, or had he seen or sensed something in his surroundings. Above all, had he seen or sensed me?

I would have given a great deal to know the answer to the last question.

After what appeared to be an eternity. I heard a faint snuffling noise; then that of something being dragged.

There was only one explanation. The tiger was dragging the body of the dead woman away. In another moment he would be gone.

I was on the point of casting caution to the winds and revealing my presence by bringing my weapon out of cover and flashing the torch to risk a shot, when the dragging ceased abruptly. Had the tiger disappeared with the body?

And then the sounds of eating began, and the crunch of bones. They came from the other side of the tree and from behind me.

The explanation was easy. For some unaccountable reason the man-eater had dragged the body back to the very position where he had left it early that morning. Instinct perhaps. At least it indicated one thing: the tiger was not suspicious or alarmed, as I had at first thought. If that had been the case, he would either have slunk away or bounded off with the body. Had he become aware of my presence, he might even have made an attack.

The fact that he had done none of these things clearly indicated that he was not alarmed, but only that he wanted to have his meal exactly where he had left it. Perhaps he had reasoned to himself that some earlier visitor, in the form of a jackal or hyaena, had shifted it.

I breathed a sigh of relief — until I recollected that I would now have to step out of my shelter into the open and around the trunk of the tree if I wanted to take a shot. Then all feeling of relief left me.

You will remember that Bala and Krishnappa had more or less 'fenced me in' with the aid of sticks, leaves, creepers and so forth. To step out, I would first have to remove these obstructions. In doing so some slight noise would undoubtedly result. The tiger would hear. He might run away, or, far worse than that, he might come around the tree to investigate the cause and find me before I was ready.

There was just one thing to do, and I did that thing. I let the tiger tuck into his meal right heartily.

Each time to tore the flesh or crunched a bone and chewed noisily, I gently untangled a leaf or piece of creeper or removed one of the sticks and slid it down the inside of the hollow tree towards my feet. Thus I cleared the way to step out while the tiger was eating.

Then I raised my right foot into the air and poised it for a minute to restore circulation, before lifting it ever so carefully outside the tree-trunk. I waited; but the tiger was still crunching bones. I steadied myself with my left hand against the hole and very cautiously brought my left foot beside my right one.

For a few moments I was unbalanced to take a shot, and it would have indeed been very unfortunate for me had the man-eater discovered me then. But mercifully he was far too engrossed in his meal.

An inch at a time, I shuffled myself forward around the bole of that tree. Then came the moment when another inch would reveal me. If the tiger happened to be facing the tree he would surely see me. If not, there was a chance that I would not be detected immediately.

The moment for action had arrived and I had to risk it. I raised the rifle, pointing skyward, and placed the stock to my shoulder. I edged an inch forward with each foot. Then I slightly craned my neck to look around the trunk.

My eyes had become accustomed to the diffused light and I saw the tiger lying full-length on the ground over a dark mass that was all that was left of the woman. He was half-inclined away from me, facing the direction whence we had come that evening. The foresight of the rifle would not be visible in that light, and I would have to use my flashlight for the shot.

I raised my left arm gently to support my rifle as I brought it to firing position at my right shoulder. My left thumb frantically groped for the torch switch. Something warned the tiger that all was not well. He looked back over his shoulder as the beam shone forth to frame his head and glowing eyes, while flesh and blood drooled from his lips.

My first bullet took him in the neck, and as he catapulted head over heels I worked the under-lever of my Winchester as I had never worked it before in my life. He was writhing furiously as I pumped into him a second shot, followed by a third. I really could not tell you what happened then. But he just disappeared.

He had been roaring with pain and rage after my first shot. He had roared during the fusillade. He was still roaring and tearing up the undergrowth in rage and agony, but I could see him no longer. He had leaped into the shelter of the jungle.

I dived back into the hollow of the dead tree as fast as I could scramble and awaited events. I wanted to replace the three rounds I had just fired, so as to have a full magazine ready. But a .405 Winchester does not lend itself to that kind of thing. A 'jam' is likely to occur when putting more rounds into a half-empty magazine. If that should happen, I would be helpless. I decided to leave well alone. There was still one round with which I could hold off the tiger. Although my rifle magazine held five rounds, I usually load only four, keeping one in the breach and three in the magazine when sitting up for carnivora. This is by way of an added precaution against a 'jam'.

I began to wonder if I had acted wisely in getting back inside the tree. Perhaps it would have been better if I had remained outside. I could at least see the tiger if he charged. Now I could not do so till he came out of the bushes and in front of me.

However, it was too late for regrets. I stood still. Perspiration saturated my body and my hands were slippery from holding the rifle. I felt terribly sick and my head ached.

The tiger was still roaring and tearing at the bushes, but in time the sounds subsided and then faded in the distance. The creature was not dead, but at least it had gone away and I was safe. And I was thankful. Then I retched — and felt all the better for it.

Unfortunately, the direction of the tiger's departing roars had not registered on my confused senses and I was uncertain which way he had gone. Under such conditions it would be suicidal to attempt at once to walk to Bala's hut in the darkness. I would have to use my flashlight to find my way there, and that would betray me if the man-eater was lying up in the undergrowth.

So I spent the rest of the night in that damned hollow, drooping on my tired feet. Dawn found me dejected, till I remembered I was lucky to be alive. For that I was glad.

As soon as it was light enough to see, I stepped out of the hollow tree and sat on the ground outside. Have you ever attempted to remain on your feet all night for a stretch of something like thirteen hours? Try it yourself sometime.

For fifteen minutes or so, while the light grew stronger, I rested. Then I got up to see what could be seen. The time I had taken to free myself from the sticks and leaves, and to step out from the tree, while the tiger had been eating, could not have been much more than ten minutes — perhaps fifteen minutes at the most — but the tiger had eaten more than half of the dead woman. Her head and arms had been parted from the body and lay scattered on the grass. One thigh and leg were there too, and part of the other foot. The rest of her was gone, except for the gnawed vertebrae with a few of the rib bones still attached.

The earth was torn up where the man-eater had ravaged the ground in his agony. Then he had made a jump into the undergrowth a couple of yards away. Here the stems of the bushes had been bitten through and the leaves were smeared with his blood. This had been the place from which I had heard him roaring and rampaging while I had been cowering in the hollow tree. From there the blood trail moved away into the jungle. I followed it for a few yards and found it was leading approximately northwards. I could return to the hut in comparative safety.

I did so. Bala and the guards had heard the sound of shooting from the hut, where they had been lying awake. With the coming of daylight they had advanced for about a furlong and were waiting for me. Indeed, the Chenchus would have come all the way to the dead tree, but Ali Baig cautioned them that I might have only wounded the tiger and there was no knowing where it would be hiding.

I told them all that had happened during that terrible night.

My watch showed that time was 6.25 a.m. I must have fired at the tiger about 8.30 the night before — ten hours previously. He must be dead by now, I thought. Or, if not dead, he must have lost so much blood and become so stiff from his wounds that he would be lying up somewhere in a bad plight. I could no longer restrain myself from following the blood-trail.

As Ali Baig was unarmed, I asked him to go back to the hut and await us there. He replied that he was afraid to stay there alone and that he would rather accompany us and take his chance. So we returned to the dead tree.

I had told Bala that, as much as I had not wanted to do so, I had been compelled to let the tiger eat the body of his wife in order to preoccupy and distract his attention while I was freeing myself from the camouflaging sticks and creepers. He had accepted my explanation then. But when we reached the tree and he saw he torn remains of the poor woman, the shock had been too great for him. The little man broke down completely and wept loudly and bitterly.

He said he would not go on till he had cremated the remains. It took all that the two forest guards and I could do to stop him from setting about this business there and then. In fact, it is doubtful if we would have succeeded had not Ali Baig bluntly told him that all of us, and more particularly he, would be in trouble with the local police, who would expect a report about the incident, after which they would conduct some sort of inquiry and hold an inspection of the remains. They would not look kindly upon him if he should cremate the evidence before they had seen it. So we broke branches and covered the scene of carnage to keep off the vultures that would otherwise soon arrive.

We all hoped we would find the tiger, dead or dying, within a very short distance, and that we would be able to return soon to make the necessary report to the police.

That was where we were greatly mistaken.

The blood trail led through the bushes. As far as I could see, the tiger had been wounded in two places, one of them high up — no doubt by my first shot at his neck. The second wound had left a constantly dripping blood trail, and as we followed it we found a tiny piece of membrane mixed with the clotted blood. To me this indicated a stomach wound.

The animal had first rested beneath a tree within two furlongs of the dead tree. Here mounds of regurgitated, blood-soaked flesh — the flesh of that poor woman — showed that the tiger had suffered a severe fit of vomiting and confirmed that one of my bullets had entered his stomach.

He had carried on from there for another half-mile or so, where he had lain down upon the grass. Two small pools of blood established the fact that he had been hit twice. The stomach wound appeared to be the more severe one, as the bleeding there had been much more copious.

Nevertheless, the animal had still kept going. The blood trail, which had been very prolific at the start, was now less. Outer skin, membrane or fat had perhaps covered the exterior hole made by the bullet where it had entered his stomach, and so had stopped the bleeding. Probably it was only the neck wound that had continued to bleed thereafter and that no doubt accounted for the scantier trail.

We came to a stream between two hills where the tiger had lain in the water, which still held a faint pinkish tinge. A little blood streaked the mud on the further bank. Here the pug-marks were clearly visible for the first time along the whole trail. They were the large quarter-plate-sized pugs of a big male.

Still the trail carried on, but the bleeding had become markedly less. Soon there was only a drop to be seen here and there. I was amazed to say the least of it.

My first shot had been at the tiger's neck. I knew I had

not missed, for he had made a complete somersault, which indicated he had been hit. I had fired twice after that and one of those shots had perforated his stomach. The quantities of vomited human flesh had established that also. We had been following a copious blood trail at the start, commencing from the place where the man-eater had torn up the undergrowth in pain and fury. He had rested more than twice after that. All these factors together, and all my experience over the past many years, cried out that by all the rules of the game the tiger should have died, or have almost bled to death, by now. We should have come across him lying up in a very enfeebled condition in some cover. In fact, we had expected the trail to be a short and easy one.

Instead of any of these expected happenings, however, the man-eater was still pressing on, heading ever northwards. Splashes of blood on the earth and leaves, as it dripped from his wounds or was smeared on the bushes as he passed, were few and far between now and the trail was becoming increasingly difficult to follow. We had travelled far from any footpaths and were many miles into the interior of the jungle, with only a game-path here and there. The terrain had become very hilly, criss-crossed by deep boulder-strewn valleys, each of which was the bed of a tiny, trickling stream. Water was far from scarce, and we could see the tiger had stopped to drink from many of these rivulets. The larger trees of the jungle had given way to dense undergrowth, mostly of lantana and other thorny varieties.

At ten minutes to one o'clock we could find no more blood drops, although the four of us fanned out and cast around in a wide circle. We had reached the journey's end and the trail was dead. The sun beat down mercilessly.

We were a silent party as we made our way back to Gazulapalli, and I was dog-tired when I threw myself into the

213

old arm-chair that had almost no bottom in the station waiting-room. Sleep came before I could take off my boots.

Mr Balasubramaniam made a telegraphic report to the police that night, and next day the officials arrived by the afternoon train from Nandyal. We went with them to the old dead tree.

What had been left of the unfortunate woman was stinking by now. We could smell it a furlong away. Hordes of blue bottles nestled in swarms on the leaves we had thrown over the bits and pieces. But at lest they had been protected from the vultures. I showed the Sub-Inspector of Police the hollow in the tree-trunk where I had hidden the night before, while I related my story.

The notes he made covered some thirteen pages of paper. My statement alone took six.

Bala begged for permission to cremate the remains. The police officer was of the opinion that they should be taken to Nandyal for a post-mortem examination. I vouchsafed no advice, because I could see that the sub-inspector did not regard my action in having set the dead woman out for bait as quite the proper thing to have done. I felt that whatever I advised now might cause him to take exactly the opposite course of action. So I minded my own business. The presence and testimony of the two forest guards, however, eventually turned the tables in Bala's favour, and permission was given to him to cremate the remains. We were silent witnesses as he and the two guards gathered a pile of dried wood, set the decomposed remains thereon, topped-up the pile with more wood and then set fire to the lot. It was a simple and sad ceremony, marred only by the awful stench of burning decomposed flesh. Out of respect for Bala's feelings, I remained there. The police officer went some distance away, leaned against a tree and was terribly sick.

I found it difficult to look Bala in the eye next day. I felt I had let him down. But the little man's intuition sensed this. He came with Balasubramaniam to the waiting-room while I sat there and asked the station-master to interpret what he was about to say. It was just this. 'Tell the "dorai" not to feel worried because he failed to shoot the tiger. I know he did his very best. No other man — no, not even I — could have done more.'

And no man could have said more than that to relieve my feelings. I felt better and told Balasubramaniam to thank him for what he had said, and for all the cooperation he had extended to me. His simple tribute was one of the best I have ever received.

I remained in Gazulapalli for another week, but no more news came to me of the man-eater. A panther killed one of my baits at Diguvametta. I went there to verify this and proved it to be a fact. Joseph was not very pleased when I left the remains for the panther to have another feed that night.

At the end of that week I paid farewell to all my newly-found friends who had helped me so unstintingly and made my visit such a pleasure. The baits I gave away to the various forest guards at the different stations, with something more for Bala.

Three months passed after my return to Bangalore. Then a tiger killed a man near the Krishna River in Hyderabad State. Three months later a Chenchu was killed several miles north of Bogara railway station. News of human kills since then have been very few and far between. But they still come in.

Did the man-eater I wounded recover after all? Has he started operations again? Were there two separate man-eaters operating at the time of my visit, the one that had taken the woman gathering mhowa flowers at Diguvametta being quite different from the one that had killed Bala's wife?

Were the latest kills the work of one or other of these two tigers — if indeed there ever had been two? Or had they been made by quite another tiger, one that had newly appeared on the scene?

These questions worry me sometimes, for I cannot find an answer. But I would give a lot to know.

Seven

The Big Bull Bison of Gedesal

THIS IS NOT THE STORY OF A REGULAR HUNT, CONCLUDING WITH THE shooting or wounding of the Big Bull Bison I am going to tell you about. If you think that, you are in for a disappointment, for I never even fired a shot at this animal at any time, nor would I ever have done so. For I admire him too much.

He was a brave old warrior, and if he is still alive today he well deserves his title as lord and leader of the herd he cared for so faithfully. If he could understand me, I would be proud to call him my friend.

Gedesal is the name of a small Sholaga village standing at the head of what I call the 'bison range' in the forests of North Coimbatore District. A forest bungalow called by the same name borders the road as it reaches the top of the ascent on its southward journey from the town of Kollegal to the hamlet of Dimbum. This road runs down the side of a hill for five of the seven miles that separate Gedesal from Dimbum.

217

For those last two miles it rises again. Dimbum is at the edge of an escarpment. The road falls steeply, in a series of sharp hair-pin bends, from Dimbum to the plains below it to the south, whence it pursues an almost level course to the large town of Satyamangalam.

Gedesal itself is flanked on the west by the towering range of the Biligirirangan Mountains, their slopes a scenic combination of frowning crags jutting out of a green background of lawn-like grass. In the folds of the hills, and along the beds of the myriad water-courses that tumble downhill, clumps of trees and matted jungle have sprung up. These are commonly called 'sholas', or isolated islands of forest, surrounded by open, grassy areas or out-crops of forbidding rock.

To the east lies another range of hills, much less in altitude, size and grandeur than the mountain range of the Biligirirangan to the west. These low hills are entirely covered by forest, consisting mainly of tiger-grass that grows to a height of ten feet, interspersed with thousands upon thousands of the stunted wild date palms. Towards the middle of the year these palms bear long clusters of the yellow wild dates at the ends of drooping stems — dry, tasteless fruit, indeed, but much favoured by birds and animals alike.

Thus the topography, the vegetation and the dates combine to make the area a favourite haunt for bison, sambar and bear.

A long valley runs from north to south between the flanking ranges of mountains and hills, and along the side of this valley the road from Kollegal to Dimbum wends its lonely, southward way, passing between Gedesal hamlet itself and the forest bungalow of the same name.

This building is exceptionally large for a forest bungalow, and has a long line of outhouses at its rear for the occupation of the menials working for the Forestry Department. Moreover it has a big compound, where some nice specimens of the wild hill-rose grow, the flowers of which bloom in large clusters, resembling small bouquets.

Just south of the bungalow is a low-lying stretch of land, holding a small pond and some marshy ground. Because of the tender shoots of green grass that grow there — entirely different from the coarse tiger-grass in the surrounding area — a small herd of spotted-deer is almost always in residence. When I saw them last they were sired and led by quite a sizeable stag with a good head of antlers, his dark brown shoulders being almost black, against which the dappled white spots contrasted markedly.

I hope that no hunter, human or animal, has brought him down, and that he still roams at the head of his harem in that deeply green and refreshingly moist, cool glen — lordly and free as the jungle to which he belongs.

The low range of hills to the east of the road and the deep valley running along the base of the mountains to the west offer wide browsing opportunities to the many separate bison herds that inhabit the area. A perennial stream of considerable size flows down the length of this valley, the road being crossed every now and again by the various tributaries that feed it. A never-failing water supply, even during the hottest summer season, is thereby assured, which is the main factor that contributes towards keeping these animals permanently in residence.

These bison herds number from twenty to forty or even more, the majority being cows and calves of different ages, with perhaps about half-a-dozen sizeable bulls to each herd. The oldest and most mature bull automatically gains supremacy over his younger rivals and becomes the lord and master of that herd until such time as he in turn is overthrown by some younger and more vigorous male, or meets his end in some fashion that accords with the laws of the jungle. Occasionally a big bull will break away from the rest of the herd and pursue his own solitary existence.

Bison suffer severely from diseases such as 'rinderpest', which frequently attack the herds of domestic cattle belonging to the Sholagas, living in the forest or adjacent cattle patties. The cattle are let out to graze in the jungle and spread the infection to the bison. It is quite common to come across bison affected by the 'foot-and-mouth' disease which is so fatal to cattle, or to be led by the sight of vultures to the carcass of one that has succumbed to this most deadly of cattle scourges.

The big bull of which my story tells was the leader of a herd of at least thirty animals. Very frequently have I seen him early in the morning when droplets of dew glittered in the rising sun, and sometimes round about 5.30 in the evening, grazing within sight of the road between the 39th and 41st milestones. It was easy to identify him by his crumpled left horn, which was clearly deformed and turned inwards and forwards.

Perhaps the old bull owes his long life to this deformity, as it renders his head worthless as a trophy, though the right horn is beautifully shaped. True it is that some hunter and collector of oddities might value his head as an unusual specimen, but he has been lucky in that such a curiosity-monger does not so far appear to have met up with him. In battle his deformed horn has proved an invaluable weapon, as I am about to relate. He has the natural advantages that would be those of a unicorn, if this legendary animal actually existed, in that he could transfix an opponent in a frontal attack or badly slash him with a toss of his head.

I have often motored along that road on a dark night, shining the sealed-beam spot-light on my car from side to side, to see what I could see and just for the fun of it. Twice or thrice on such occasions the widely-separated blue eyes of a bison have reflected the lamp's rays and upon closer inspection I have found them to be the eyes of the old bull.

My attention was first attracted to this veteran some years ago when I was out for a walk on the lower slopes of the Biligirirangan Range. There is a road running through the forest from the western side of the main road. It skirts Gedesal village, crosses the stream, and then starts to climb over the foothills of the mountain range to disappear eventually over a saddle-back and descend a valley on the other side. Finally it leads to a beautiful forest lodge, the private property of Mr Randolph Morris who is one of Southern India's biggest and most influential coffee planters. He is also an authority on shikar and a hunter of renown, having contributed many valuable articles on the habits of big game and on big game hunting. He was the honorary game warden of the area, well known to the Viceroys and former Governors of British India, and the owner of some of the most beautiful and well-planned coffee estates in the south.

Long before this road makes its way over the saddle-back there is a pre-fabricated shed, the property of the Forestry Department, which has been erected for the convenience of its officers on tour and for the use of licensed sportsmen on shikar. Some thoughtful soul has made, or caused to make, a ladder of stout twisted vines, which is kept in this lodge and comes in very handy for climbing up to and down from machans erected on trees, to those who are not naturally gifted or adapted to this arboreal art.

That morning I had passed this lodge and was walking along a ridge overlooking a bowl-like shallow valley when I heard a clashing and thudding sound, interrupted with snorts of rage. The evidence pointed to a bison fight, and I hurried along, taking what cover was available, in the direction of the sounds. Very soon I saw in the valley below me, but quite three hundred yards away, two large bull bison locked in fierce combat. With horns entangled and foreheads pressed together, they were pushing against each other with might and main, the outstretched taut legs of each animal indicating the tremendous effort he was making to push his opponent back. At intervals one or other would momentarily disengage his horns and head from his rival to deliver a short quick jab before interlocking again, and before the opposing animal could score a similar thrust.

Then I noticed that one of them had a peculiar horn that gave him a distinct advantage over his antagonist which was bleeding profusely from wounds in his neck, shoulders and side.

The fight raged for the next twenty minutes or so with unabated fury, till the gasps that took the place of the sorts of rage that I had first heard, and the glistening sides of the two bulls, soaked in sweat and blood that was clearly visible even at that range, showed that the gruelling pace and strain of the fight was beginning to tell. Froth drooled from the mouths of the bulls and splattered their bodies, falling in splashes to the ground.

I had never witnessed a bison fight before and was very curious to know how it would end. Fortunately I had come alone. Moreover, the breeze blew in my direction. Therefore the combatants were quite unaware of my presence and fought their fight under natural conditions.

The bull with the crumpled horn seemed to be getting the better of things, and his opponent gave ground, becoming reddened by the gore that flowed from the many wounds in his body. Of course, he had also inflicted some telling jabs on his enemy, but the crumpled horn was obviously giving its owner a decided superiority. After another ten minutes the severely injured animal began to falter. He fell to his knees several times, and at each opportunity that unicorn-like horn embedded itself in some part of the unfortunate animal. Eventually he broke, turned and ran at a staggering trot, the victor following up his advantage by pursuing him and butting his hind-quarters. The two animals passed out of sight at a point where the bowl of the valley merged with the surrounding jungle.

Out of curiosity I walked down to the site of the recent combat. The ground had been torn up by the straining hooves of the two contestants and was flecked with blood and foam in a rough circle some twenty yards in diameter.

It was a considerable time after that when I saw my bull again. The second occasion was on another walk one evening on my way to visit a water-hole situated on the eastern side of the road about a quarter of a mile from and almost level with the 41st milestone. A tiger had killed a couple of head of cattle belonging to the Sholagas of Gedesal village. They told me they had seen it on several occasions in the evenings, walking along — or crossing — the fire-line that leads past this pool and thereafter cuts across the road.

I went to the water-hole at about 4.30 p.m. that day, and walked around its edge to discover what animals had been visiting it. There were the usual tracks of elephant, bison, sambar, spotted-deer and of a few wild pigs. The tiger had also drunk there on about three separate occasions so far as I could judge by the age of his pug-marks, although the last time had been at least three days earlier than my visit.

Among the bison tracks were the pointed hoof-marks of what must have been a truly massive bull. The weight of his body had been so great that he sank almost a foot into the mire that bordered the pond. His tracks were also visible in many places in the vicinity, indicating that he was a frequent visitor to this pool. This was rather strange in view of the fact that he had the river, which I have already mentioned, at which to quench his thirst.

I asked the Sholaga who had told me about the tiger, and who had accompanied me, if he knew anything about this bull. He replied in the affirmative and told me that he and all the villagers had seen him many times, and that he had a deformed horn — the left one — which thrust forwards. Immediately my mind flew back to the scene I had witnessed in that memorable fight, in which a bull with a crumpled horn had completely routed his opponent. I wondered if this could be the same animal and thought it must be so, as such a deformity is extremely rare.

The Sholaga told me the bull frequented the pond, as he kept the herd under his care in that locality; probably because of the exceptionally fine grazing to be had on the low land around the water-hole. Then he went on to say that if I cared to take a walk with him, we might be lucky enough to see this animal for ourselves, or even come across the tiger.

At that time the tiger was my immediate quarry and I was not very interested in the bull, so more with that objective in mind I consented. In any case, stalking a bison in broad daylight is a tricky business and depends upon the direction in which the wind is blowing, the cover available, and of course the lie of the land.

We set off on an aimless walk, following cattle trails and game paths and criss-crossing the fire-line several times. I remember we were ambling along a narrow track when quite suddenly the long grass parted before us, hardly thirty yards away, to reveal the head and shoulders of a massive bull bison which regarded us complacently and obviously without much concern. It was my friend, the bison with the crumpled horn.

He showed no signs of fear, but just stood looking at us. We advanced another ten yards then, with a loud swish of the reedy grass, he turned around and disappeared. After that day, as I have said, I saw him on other occasions, and then came the memorable event which drew him to me.

An unidentified hunter, who was also poacher, came along the road one night and shot a cow bison. Before he knew where he was, a bull attacked his jeep and with a toss of his head tumbled the vehicle down a khud that bordered the road into one of the dry tributaries of the river. Fortunately the bison did not follow up its attack, so the poacher suffered only an injured leg and a smashed rifle. The Sholaga who was with him, and was sitting at the side of the jeep on which the assault was launched, had clearly seen the bull and avowed it was the animal with the deformed left horn.

I heard about the incident some months later, on a subsequent visit, and felt pleased that the old bull had acquitted himself so creditably. No doubt the fact that he had tossed the jeep down the khud had caused him to think, in his own bovine mind, that he had disposed of his foe. Had the khud not been there he would probably have followed up his initial attack with another, found the men inside and eliminated them altogether.

It was some time later, in November, 1953, that I was visiting Dimbum. I had not intended to halt at Gedesal and was motoring along the road when I espied a lone figure walking. Drawing level, I recognised the Sholaga, whose name was Rachen, whom I always employ when I camp at that bungalow. Stopping the car and returning his greeting, I asked him in Tamil: *'Yenna Sungadhi'* — which means: 'What news'?

Rachen replied that just two nights ago the villagers had heard the sounds of a terrific fight in the jungle, not very far from the village, between a tiger and some other animal. From the violence and duration of the combat, which appeared to last for hours, they decided that the tiger's opponent could not be a wild boar, which is the only wild creature of medium-size that fights back against a tiger, and thought it might be an elephant. But then again, had it been an elephant they felt sure they would have heard the trumpeting and screaming which an elephant invariably makes when in trouble or when fighting, or when otherwise excited.

Later in the night the sounds had gradually died away, but they had noticed before that time, from the great noise the tiger had been making, that it had been badly hurt.

Early next morning, impelled by curiosity, the Sholagas had gone to see what had happened and had come upon the scene of the marathon struggle they had heard the night before. The undergrowth had been torn up and trodden down by the combatants, and to one side of this arena lay the carcass of a tiger that had been repeatedly gored and trampled by a bison.

The Sholagas had then promptly removed the skin from the tiger and taken it to the village.

It was about noon when I heard this tale and, having time to spare, felt interested in visiting the spot myself. Seating Rachen beside me, I drove down the narrow track leading to Gedesal village and found the tiger's skin already pegged out on the ground to dry. The raw side was uppermost and had been liberally covered with dry ashes, which is the only preservative known to the Sholagas, salt not being available.

The tiger had been quite a large animal but, judging from the underside of the skin, it had been badly mangled and gored by the bison. There were no less than five distinct holes where the powerful horns had penetrated, and one of them, on the left side, showed where a fateful thrust had pierced the tiger's heart.

I was now more interested than ever and expressed a keen desire to visit the spot where the fight had taken place. Leaving my car, and accompanied by a crowd of Sholagas, I set forth. Less than half a mile away we reached the site of the incident.

'Arena' is the best word I can find to describe it, for indeed there had been a titanic struggle. Great gouts of gore were sprayed on the surrounding grass and bushes in all directions, which had been flattened by the weight of the contestants and were red with dried blood. The Sholagas pointed out the spot where the dead tiger had been lying.

It was obvious from the quantity of blood that the bison had also been severely injured. On a whim I decided I would like to follow him up if possible, to see if he was dead or dying somewhere in the jungle. In either case, I guessed he could not have moved very far from the scene of the fight in his present condition.

Even an entire novice would have been able to follow that trail, as the bison had left a wide path of blood through the jungle. He had passed downhill, heading towards the stream, and I felt certain I would find him there, very likely dead, beside the water.

We forged ahead, not troubling to keep silent. An hour and a halfs quick walking along that tremendous blood trail brought us to the stream, and to the bison standing in shallow water and resting himself against the bole of a large tree that was partly submerged. Due to the noise made by the water as it rushed over the rocks, he had not heard us at first, and we were well out of cover before he turned around to face us.

It was the big bull bison of Gedesal, the bull with the crumpled horn.

From where we stood, with the breadth of the stream separating us, we could clearly see the awful wounds that had been inflicted by the teeth and the talons of the tiger on his face, neck, sides and rump. Even his belly was badly lacerated, and something red protruded from it and hung into the water. Perhaps it was a portion of his bowel, perhaps a piece of torn skin; I could not see clearly into the shadows where he stood.

But his eyes were clear and fearless, although pain-wracked, as he stood and faced us. Then he turned and staggered away into the jungle.

I had thought of shooting him to put him out of his agony, but somehow could not find it in my heart to do so after the gallant victory he had won at such frightful cost. In any case, I never expected to see him again.

But very recently I visited Gedesal, and great was my surprise and pleasure when one evening I happened to see him, surrounded by his beloved herd, browsing contentedly on the long grass that borders the water-hole on the eastern side of the road not far from the 41st milestone — his favourite haunt.

Long may he live in the jungle to which he belongs.

Eight

The Maned Tiger of Chordi

THIS IS THE STORY OF A VERY BIG TIGER THAT GAVE GREAT TROUBLE to the area in which he lived — or rather to the human inhabitants of the area — and was very troublesome to pursue and finally bring to bag.

In telling hunting stories, it is the purpose of the teller to keep his hearers interested. To do that he has to relate the efforts that ended successfully in the killing of his quarry. Perforce he has to leave out many of the failures and disappointments he encounters, for if he were to describe them all his listeners would soon be bored. But to mention only the successes is to give the impression that efforts to kill a man-eater, whether tiger or panther, are nearly always crowned with success, nearly always easy, and can nearly always be accomplished within a comparatively short space of time — a few days, at most.

In reality, all three of these impressions are very far indeed from the truth, and actual circumstances are invariably quite the opposite. Failures are very many and conditions — physical, mental and nervous — are most arduous; and frequently the animal takes months and even years to catch up with. Sometimes he is never shot.

So in this story I am going to tell of a pursuit that began in a casual way and took almost five long and tedious years to bring to a conclusion. Of course it was not a continuous hunt, but a series of sporadic attempts. Between my own efforts there were other hunters from Bangalore and Bombay, not to speak of the local nimrods, who all attempted to bring about the downfall of this wily creature. And we all failed — until those five years had passed.

He was known as the 'maned tiger' because he had an outstanding ruff of hair around his neck, behind his ears and covering his throat and chin. Naturally this outcrop of hair greatly increased the apparent size of his head, which was always described as being 'that big', the witness stretching out his hands sideways, with finger-tips inwardly curved, though very few persons had seen him and lived to tell the tale.

His original habitat was known to be around Chordi, because that was the name of the village where he was first seen and near to which he made his first human kill.

Chordi is a small road-side hamlet, surrounded by jungle, about four miles from the little town of Kumsi, which itself is sixteen miles from Shimoga, the capital town of the district bearing the same name, in the State of Mysore. Shimoga is just 172 miles by a good road from Bangalore. Nearly seventy miles of this road, at the Bangalore end, is of concrete and the rest is tarred, so that a motorist can generally and safely — with the exception of a few nasty, unexpected bends — make quite good time to Shimoga.

From there the road goes on to Kumsi and Chordi, then

to the village of Anandapuram about nine miles further on, then eleven miles to the town of Sagar, and thence about sixteen miles, past another village named Talaguppa, to the famous Gersoppa waterfalls, sometimes known as the Jog falls, where the waters of the Shiravati River descend 950 feet in four separate cascades. That is a sight to be remembered and one that has inspired feelings of awe and reverence in the hearts of the most callous and materialistic of men.

There are two Travellers' Bungalows at the head of the falls. The one on the southern bank of the Shiravati River, which is by far the more modern building, falls within the boundary of Mysore State and is appropriately called the 'Mysore Bungalow'. The opposite bungalow, across the river and on its northern bank, comes under the jurisdiction of Bombay State. It is an older building, very isolated and seldom occupied — for which reason I much prefer it. It is known, of course, as the 'Bombay Bungalow'.

It is rather unusual — and amusing — to find the visitors' books in both bungalows crammed with efforts to write poetry by the various people who have stayed in them from time to time. Undoubtedly the grandeur of the falls has been the cause of awakening this latent desire to wax poetical in minds that perhaps have hitherto remained indifferent. Some of their efforts are really laudable and inspiring; but for the rest I feel it would be difficult anywhere else to assemble such a pile of drivel in one place.

The depredations of the tiger accorded very closely with the pattern of events usually associated with the careers of man-eaters. From being a hunter of the natural game-animals that live in the jungle, he gradually became a cattle-lifter, tempted no doubt by the presence of the thousands of fat kine that are grazed in the reserved forests all over the Shimoga District. Their presence, and the ease with which he could stalk and kill them, in contrast with the difficulties of creeping up on the other wild animals, was the first step that changed him from being an inoffensive game-killer into an exceedingly destructive menace to the herdsmen around Chordi.

Attack followed attack as cattle were killed by the maned tiger, till the normal lethargy of the keepers was sufficiently ruffled to decide to do something about it. Matters came to a head when a more enterprising cattle-owner carried his loaded shotgun into the forest with him when he took his animals there for grazing, although it was against the Forestry Department's regulations for him to enter the reserve with a weapon but without a game-shooting licence.

However, he did just that, and as luck would have it, the maned tiger chose that very day to attack and bring down one of his animals. From a position behind the trunk of a tree he let fly with his shotgun, and the L.G. pellets badly injured the tiger along his right flank. He disappeared from the vicinity of Chordi for the time being, and all the cattle-men were grateful to the owner of the shotgun for ridding them of such a menace.

Then the maned one reappeared a few miles away, in the shrub-jungle that borders Anandapuram. But he still clung to his habit of attacking cattle grazing in the reserve. He had not yet been spoiled — had not yet become a man-eater — because the wound in his side had not incapacitated him in any way.

Once again his unwelcome presence forced itself upon the attention of the cattle -grazers, and once more he was wounded. This time in his right foreleg, and from a machan as he was approaching the carcass of a cow he had killed the previous day. He vanished for the second time. Once more false hopes were raised that his departure was permanent, and once again he reappeared.

232

However, there was a difference with his second return. No longer was he the obnoxious but nevertheless inoffensive tiger that had been so destructive to cattle, but harmless to their attendants. This time it was the other way round; the cattle were comparatively safe but the herdsmen were in danger — in very great and real danger — because he had become that greatest scourge and terror that any jungle can produce: a man-eating tiger.

The ball that had entered his right foreleg had smashed a bone. Nature had healed the bone, but the limb had become shortened and twisted. No longer could he stalk his prey silently and effectively, no longer could he leap upon them and bring them crashing to earth with broken necks. His approach was noisy, his attack clumsy. His ability to hold his prey was greatly hampered by his deformed limb, and very often they escaped. Even the dull cattle heard his approach and eluded him, or shook him from their hacks when he attacked.

Because of his disability he became thin and emaciated, and he was faced with starvation. He — the big maned tiger — was forced to try to catch the rats that ran in the bamboo trees, and even they escaped him.

The only living things that were not too fast for him were the slimy frogs in the pools of scum-covered water stagnating here and there in the jungle, and the sharp-shelled crabs by the water's edge — and men. Sheer necessity, and nothing else, drove him to this new diet of human flesh.

These are the facts about this tiger as I gathered them from time to time. The nature of his wound I only discovered for myself when years later I examined him after I had shot him.

Thus one day a man alighted at Anandapuram bus-stand and began a jungle journey to a tiny hamlet three miles away. He had left the previous morning to go to Shimoga town, and had told his wife to keep his midday meal ready for him the next day, as he would be back in time. The meal was prepared accordingly, but he did not appear. This caused no untoward alarm in the little household because the settlement of business affairs in India, particularly in the lesser towns, is often protracted. Time is of little or no consequence in the East.

Even that evening he did not turn up, nor during the whole of the following day. On the third day his eldest son, a grown lad, was sent to Shimoga to find out what had delayed his father. There he was told that the transaction had been completed three days earlier and that his father had left to return to his home.

Still no untoward anxiety was felt, as it was thought he might have gone to Sagar, which is beyond Anandapuram, in connection with the same affair.

Five days thus passed without a sign, when the family became really anxious and alarmed. The consensus of opinion was that he had been set upon and robbed by badmashes or dacoits on his way home through the jungle and probably killed. The police were informed and a search was made, which brought to light a slipper lying among the bushes beside the track to the hamlet where he lived.

The old slipper was identified by the household as belonging to the missing man, and that gave further credence to the dacoit theory. Several K.D.s — known depredators — living in Anandapuram were taken to the police station and questioned. They avowed their innocence.

A closer and wider search was then made. Shreds of clothing and dried blood-marks were discovered on thorns and bushes, and across the dry bed of a nullah the pug-marks of a tiger. Thereafter, no traces were apparent.

Tigers are — or rather were in those years — quite common in those areas, and as there was no direct evidence to connect the pug-marks with the missing man, there was only a very vague suspicion that a tiger might have had anything to do with his disappearance. The presence of the pug-marks might have been purely coincidental.

The mystery was never solved.

A fortnight later a lone cyclist was pedalling the four miles from Kumsi to Chordi. Half a mile from his destination the road crosses the river by a bridge. A parapet of limestone - or chunam as it is called — flanks the road. Looking over as he was riding along, the cyclist saw a tiger drinking almost below him. He was at a safe distance from the animal so, applying his brakes, he sat in his saddle with one foot on the parapet and watched the tiger.

The tiger finished drinking, turned and began to reclimb the bank. In a couple of seconds he would disappear in the undergrowth, so for the fun of it the cyclist shouted 'Shoo-shoo'. The tiger stopped, looked backwards over his shoulder and up at the cyclist, snarled and growled loudly.

Very hastily, the man removed his foot from the parapet, applied it to the pedal, and rode as fast as he could to Chordi, where he told his friends that along the road he had met a very nasty tiger indeed which had tried to attack him. Only by God's grace had he escaped.

There was a lull for the next-month or so, and then occurred the first authenticated human killing. This happened at a place called Tuppur, which is almost midway between Chordi and Anandapuram. It is a little roadside hamlet, and one of the women had taken her buffalo down to the stream behind the village so that it might take its morning bath. It appears that the buffalo was lying in the water with only its head above the surface, as is the usual habit with buffaloes, when a tiger attacked the woman who was sitting on the bank watching her protégé. Another woman from the village had just drawn water from the stream and had spoken a few words to the woman sitting beside her buffalo and was passing on. She had scarcely gone a hundred yards when she heard a piercing shriek and looked back in time to see a tiger walking off with her erstwhile companion in his mouth.

Tiger and victim vanished into the jungle while the other woman threw down her water-pot and raced for the huts.

What happened was usual with most incidents of this kind. Considerable time elapsed in collecting a sufficient number of men brave enough to go out to look for the woman. Eventually this was done and they found her, or rather what was left of her.

That was the beginning, and thereafter followed a sequence of human victims, whose deaths took place as far away as the road leading to the Bombay Bungalow near the Jog Falls on the further side of the Shiravati River.

Officialdom moves slowly, and it was a considerable time before the reserved forests in these regions were thrown open to the public for shooting this beast.

A number of enthusiasts turned up and the Bombay Presidency was well represented amongst them. They tried hard and diligently, but luck did not come their way. This particular tiger did not seem to be tempted by the cattle and buffaloes tied up as live bait. Meanwhile the human killings continued.

A friend of mine named Jack Haughton, who went by the nickname of 'Lofty' for the very reason that he was about six foot four inches tall and proportionately broad made up his mind to have a try at shooting this animal and asked me to accompany him. As far as I can remember, this trip was undertaken about one year after the tiger had turned man-eater.

It so transpired that for some reason or the other — most probably because I had already used the leave due to me —

236

I went with him for only a week, telling him I would have to return after that time. We travelled in his 1931 'A' Model Ford car, and the arrangement was that I should return to Bangalore by train after the week had expired, while he would remain for a full month or so.

We motored from Bangalore to Shimoga and stopped there for half a day in order to visit the District Forest Officer, Sagar Forest Range, where these killings had been taking place, to find out the names of the different places where people had been attacked and the exact dates of those attacks, in order to establish, if possible, by studying the sequence of the attacks, the precise 'beat' being followed by this tiger.

I have already explained that man-eating tigers generally pursue a definite course or itinerary when they become man-eaters. By noting the names of the villages or localities where they kill on a map, with the date of each incident, it is frequently possible to work out the beat for oneself, and forecast roughly in which direction or area the tiger may be at about the time one undertakes to try and bag him.

Our study of events on a map indicated very clearly that this tiger kept within a few miles of the roadside and operated up and down between Kumsi and the further bank of the Shiravati River, as far as the Bombay Bungalow.

This is a very densely forested region with many scattered hamlets, whole occupants are almost entirely devoted to grazing big herds of cattle. A large number of these animals are always killed in these areas each month by both tigers and panthers, so this fact made it difficult to find out whether our man-eater also killed cattle or not. We felt that it was almost certain he did so, as the human kills were too few and far between for him to have subsisted only on a human diet. Our opinion was quite contrary to the local one, which was that he would not touch any domestic animals.

Lofty chose to make his camp at a small forest bungalow situated half a mile from the Tuppur hamlet. It is a picturesque little lodge, standing in the jungle about two hundred yards from the roadside, and the forest in the vicinity is crammed with game, particularly spotted deer. In that year some of the stags carried magnificent heads and we came across quite a few outstanding specimens.

Lofty started operations in the routine fashion by buying three animals for bait. Two of them were young buffaloes, and the other a very old and decrepit bull. One buffalo was tied near the stream where the cyclist had seen the tiger. The aged bull was tied at about the spot where the woman of Tuppur had been carried off. The remaining buffalo we had taken and tied near Anandapuram along the same path that the man who had disappeared had been following on his way home.

Having completed these arrangements, we motored on to Jog and arranged two baits there — both buffaloes — tying one of them half a mile or so from the Bombay Bungalow and the other on the southern bank of the Shiravati, near the spot where the river is crossed by a ferry plying between the bungalow on the Mysore bank and the Bombay bungalow. This ferry crosses the river about a mile above the waterfalls.

Lofty had therefore five baits in all, and I remember they cost him quite a bit of money. The plan was that we should spend alternate nights at the Tuppur forest lodge and the Bombay bungalow, checking the baits closest to the place where we had spent the previous night before setting out by car for the bungalow where we would spend the next night.

My calculations, made by the method of checking the dates of the human kills, which were now nine in number, seemed to indicate that this tiger might be somewhere in the middle of this region between Sagar and Anandapuram.

So on the third day I bought a buffalo myself, which I then tied up about half-way between these two places and within a furlong of the main road. We tied this animal about two in the afternoon on our way from the Tuppur bungalow to Jog.

Very early next morning we looked up the two baits tied in the vicinity of the waterfalls. Both were alive. So we set out for Tuppur, halting en route to visit the buffalo I had tied up the previous afternoon. It had been killed by a tiger.

Lofty, being a good sportsman and considering the fact that I had paid for this buffalo, insisted that I should take the shot. But I knew how keen he was and so quite an argument arose. Finally we tossed for it, and Lofty won.

Leaving him up a tree, sitting uncomfortably perched in a fork, I drove to Tuppur lodge to fetch his machan, which we had both most thoughtlessly forgotten to take with us on that important day. Lofty's contraption was nothing more than a square bamboo frame about four feet each way, interlaced with broad navaree tape. At each of the four corners was loop of stout rope which helped when tying the affair to a tree. I also brought three men from Tuppur hamlet along with me to assist in putting up this machan.

We ate a cold lunch by the roadside while the man made a good job of fixing the machan and camouflaging it with branches. Lofty then had a nap in the back seat of the car till four o'clock, while I chatted with the three men. This was because, being close to the road, we knew the tiger would not put in an appearance before nightfall.

At four I woke him up and he climbed into the machan with all his equipment. His weapon was a 8 mm Mauser rifle — a really neat and well-balanced job — which Lofty affectionately calls 'Shorty Bill'. Wishing him good luck and saying I would be back by dawn, I drove to Tuppur, where

I left the three men and then returned part of the way to spend the night at the small dak bungalow at Anandapuram, which was closer to where I had left Lofty over the dead buffalo.

By break of day next morning I had reached the spot on the road opposite where he was sitting and tooted the horn of the car. He coo-eed back to me, which was the signal we had agreed upon before parting to signify that all was well.

I set out for his tree and met him half-way, walking towards the car. He told me the good news that he had shot the tiger, which had turned up much earlier the previous evening than we had expected, arriving just after dark.

I was very happy at his success, while Lofty himself was in raptures and simply bubbling over with joy and excitement. I went with him to see the tiger, which was a beautiful large male in the prime of life and handsomely marked with bold, dark stripes.

But I noticed that the he was a very normal tiger. He certainly did not possess the distinctive mane which the official Government Notification had said was the outstanding characteristic of the man-eater. I was surprised to find that in his enthusiasm over his own success Lofty had apparently quite overlooked this fact and I just did not have the heart to tell him.

I congratulated him very heartily on his success and tried my best to appear sincere. Then leaving him to guard his precious trophy, I motored back to Tuppur to bring four men and a bamboo pole for lifting the carcass.

Returning with the men, we tied the feet of the tiger to the pole and carried him upside down to the car. As Lofty had no proper carrier at the back that was strong enough to support the weight, we spread-eagled the carcass across the bonnet of the car, not only bending the metal in the process, but making it very difficult to drive as, in spite of his height,

Lofty could not see the road ahead for some yards because of the body on the bonnet.

In driving through Anandapuram, Lofty stopped to exhibit his prize to the townsfolk who crowded around, and it was then that disillusionment very cruelly came to him. For, no sooner did the people look at the tiger than they exclaimed: 'But, Sahib, this is not the man-eater.' 'Of course it is,' replied Lofty indignantly. 'What other tiger can it be? And in any case, how are you so sure it is not the man-eater?' 'Where is the mane?' they asked in justification.

'The mane?' Lofty looked blank at first. Then understanding crept into his eyes. Finally he looked at me accusingly. 'I forgot all about the mane,' he admitted. 'I have shot the wrong tiger. You knew all the time?'

'Yes, Lofty, I knew,' I admitted. 'But you were so happy when I met you this morning and you told me you had bagged the man-eater, that I just did not have the heart to disillusion you. The mane was the first thing I looked for. Of course, there was nothing else you could have done but shoot.' And then, to make it seem more convincing, I hastily added: 'After all, the tiger came when it was dark, and you could not look for a mane even by torch-light. In any case, it is a magnificent specimen and a trophy to be proud of; so cheer up, old chap.'

But Lofty was not so easily consoled. We drove to Tuppur, where I found him so disheartened as not to be in the least interested in supervising the skinning of the tiger, which he left entirely to me. I watched the men at work while Lofty lay moping in an armchair. Several times I tried to buck him up by drawing his attention to the large teeth and claws of the animal, its dark markings and other aspects, but he was not at all interested and refused to be drawn into conversation. He just said: 'Had I known it was not the man-eater I would not have shot the poor brute.'

Instead of throwing off his gloom, Lofty got more gloomy as the day wore on. Then he announced that, if no kills had taken place by next morning, he would like to return to Bangalore.

We were up early next day, but the three baits at our end of the line were all unharmed. Accordingly, we resold them to their previous owners, as already arranged, at about a quarter of the price which Lofty had paid for them. Then we drove to the Jog end of the beat, but both buffaloes were alive there also. We made the same deal with their owners as we had done at Tuppur, and late afternoon saw us in the 'A' Model on our way back to Bangalore.

For some time after this I did not come across any news of this tiger. It was over a year later, I think, that I read in the papers that a charcoal-burner had been killed and wholly eaten by a tiger quite near to Kumsi town and almost by the roadside.

So I wrote to the District Forest Officer at Shimoga, requesting him to keep me informed about future kills by telegram if possible.

The forests of Shimoga District, unlike those to the south-west of Mysore State, and in the Madras and Chittoor Districts, are heavily sprinkled with villages and hamlets, and widely interspersed with cultivation, particularly great stretches of paddy-fields. The roads are also far more used, both by vehicular and pedestrian traffic. Because of all this, not only may a tiger be anywhere at all and difficult to locate, but tracking is left to the individual hunter's own skill. It is a strange fact that no aboriginal forest tribes inhabit this area, unlike the other jungles of India. The only people who go into the forests are coolies, of Malayalee origin, hired in large numbers from the West Coast of India. Next to them in number are the Lambanis. These last are the 'gypsy tribe' of

India, who strangely resemble their Romany cousins in the western world. But only the women are distinctive in appearance. They are lighter in colour than the local people and dress picturesquely, with many ornaments, big, white bone bangles, necklaces of beads of all colours, shapes and sizes, nose-rings, ear-rings and rings on their fingers and rings on their toes. They do not wear the saree in the same fashion as the other women of India, but a distinctive costume, made up of a very widely-skirted sort of petticoat, covered by a very tightly-fitting backless jacket, often displaying an ill-restrained bosom, over which a large shawl-like cloth is draped that covers the head and shoulders. The two halves of their jackets are held together by strings at the back.

The Lambani men, on the other hand, are darker than the women and dress very ordinarily. In fact, almost exactly like the rest of the local villagers, who are Kanarese. They wear rather nondescript loose turbans, and very ordinary or dirty-white cotton shirts, covering short pants or a loin-cloth tied high about their waists. Their knees and calves are generally uncovered, but rough leather sandals protect their feet against thorns.

A curious fact is that the men and women among the gypsies of Southern India do not resemble each other in either facial or other physical appearances. Most of the women are as graceful and handsome in features as the men are ungraceful and plain.

They are an outstanding tribe of people and have preserved their individuality very strongly throughout the centuries. I am myself surprised at this, as the laziness of the men is such that one would have expected their tribal distinctiveness to have died away generations ago. It is entirely to the women that must go the praise for prizing their own traditions, and their picturesque dress and appearance, keeping the tribe and its customs so well-defined throughout the years.

These Lambanis, as a whole, are nomads and do not stay in one place for long. They prefer their own encampments of small grass huts in cleared spaces to life in the regular villages. As a rule they are not of much worth and they certainly do not excel as trackers. At the same time, the credit must be accorded to them of being far more cooperative than the local Kanarese.

Among the Lambanis, both men and women are hard drinkers, distilling their own very potent liquor from the bark of the babul tree; or from rice, bananas and brown sugar combined; or from the jamun fruit after it has been soaked in sugar; or, for that matter, from almost any material they can find — and they are most ingenious at discovering sources.

They will work more willingly in return for wages in kind — mainly food and drink — than for money, which in any case will be mostly spent in purchasing liquor, if they are unable to make it for themselves. However, they are a nice people, and one of India's finest exhibits among the very many interesting races and tribes of curious and distinctive appearance.

The coffee plantations and orange estates in western Mysore owe much to the Lambanis, particularly the women, who form the bulk of the labour employed by them. The remainder of the labour comes from the West Coast - from people of Malayalam and Moplah stock. These west-coast coolies have one trait in common. They are bound by unbreakable bonds to their homes among the coconut-trees, lagoons, rivers and breakers that tumble on the western shores. It is indeed a beautiful country, and I can well understand their fondness for it. Lack of industry and lack of work of any definite sort drives them into the interior in search of employment. But no sooner have they earned and saved some more — for, unlike the Lambanis, they are very thrifty — then back they go to their homeland to enjoy some months of lazy comfort. This universal characteristic makes them rather unreliable as plantation coolies, because one cannot be sure of their regular attendance unless a portion of their pay is held back as a sort of bond. The law forbids this practice to estate-owners, while on the other hand the usual system is to grant advances to the coolies to enable them to buy stocks of gram and other foodstuffs, blankets and odds and ends. As can well be imagined, this is welcomed by the Malayalee coolies, who draw their pay and whatever advances they can collect and then disappear on French leave to their coast-land areas.

And so the planters encourage, and have come to rely upon, the humble and picturesque Lambani gypsy as a mainstay on the estates. For them he has become almost a 'must'.

·My personal interest in this state of affairs lay only in the fact that I would have to rely almost solely on my own initiative if and when I went after this tiger. As good as they are as estate-workers, Lambanis are not on a part with the other aboriginal jungle tribes — like the Poojarees, Sholagas, Karumbas and Chenchus — in tracking and general jungle lore. I only wished this tiger was operating in one of the other forest districts where I had willing and experienced helpers to rely upon.

A month or so after writing to the D.F.O. at Shimoga I received from him a letter of thanks and the news that the tiger had attacked and killed a woman who had been gathering leaves from the teak trees that grew by the road-side about mid-way between Kumsi and Chordi.

For the benefit of those who have not seen the teak tree or its leaves, I should tell you that the latter are large in size and tough in fibre. They do not tear easily. Hence they are much favoured for the manufacture of leaf-plates, on which meals, particularly rice, are served in Indian hotels. Some four or five teak leaves go to make one such plate, which is an enormous affair by all Western standards. They are joined together at the edges, either by being stitched with a needle and thread, or more frequently by being pinned together with two-inch-long bits of 'broom-grass'. These plates are required in hundreds of thousands to supply the demands of the many eating-houses in Mysore State. Hence their manufacture forms quite an industry in some of the localities where teak trees grow in abundance. The Forest Department sells the right of plucking these leaves to contractors, who bid at an auction for that right. The contractors in turn employ female labour and pay the women a certain sum of money per thousand good leaves plucked. Women are hired for this work rather than men as they ask only about half the rate.

The D.F.O. concluded his long missive with a statement expressing his hope that I would come to Kumsi to try and kill the man-eater.

The extent of the area in which the tiger operated, and even more the other conditions I have already explained at some length, made me feel that the quest was pretty hopeless at this stage. Also the question of leave was a great problem. Searching for a tiger under such circumstances might take several weeks, if not some months.

So I set myself the task of writing a very diplomatic reply. While profusely thanking the Forest Officer for his letter, I endeavoured to convince him of the time factor involved in trying to locate or pin down the man-eater in any particular locality. I explained that I did not have the time to spare just then to undertake a prolonged trip. I also suggested that he inform all forest stations and police stations in the area to warn the inhabitants to beware of the man-eater, and to move in day-light only and in groups, keeping to the main roads; also that grazers and contractors' coolies should temporarily cease operation. Should another human kill occur, I suggested he ask the police, as well as his own subordinates, to urge the relatives of the unfortunate victim to leave his or her remains untouched and send me a telegram. I also suggested that the Forestry Department might materially help by sanctioning the purchase of half-a-dozen buffaloes, and to tie them out at intervals along the area where the tiger operated. I promised to come, upon receiving telegraphic news of a fresh victim, be it animal or human, on the condition that the body of the victim had been allowed to remain where the tiger last left it.

Back came the response to this letter on the third day. It deeply regretted that I had been unable to come, and added that it would be impossible to ensure that all the villagers living in such a wide area followed the precautions I had suggested. Further, relatives would not consent to the body of loved one being left out in the jungle as a bait to entice the man-eater to return. They would demand that they should remove and cremate it at once. Lastly, he said that there was no provision under the rules whereby the Forestry Department could undertake the expense of buying six live buffaloes for tiger-bait.

Of course, I had anticipated the replies I would receive to these two suggestions. As a matter of fact, I had merely made them to bring home indirectly the problem I was up against in looking for the tiger, which was like searching for a needle in a haystack. That first letter, asking me to come to Kumsi at once, gave the impression that the writer had perhaps over-looked some of the snags involved, and I wanted him to appreciate my side of the picture.

Nothing more happened for the next few weeks and then

the man-eater struck again, this time making a double-kill between Chordi and Tuppur. News of this tragedy came to me in a telegram from the D.F.O. — quite a long one — which stated that the tiger had attacked a wood-cutter and his son on the high road opposite the Karadibetta Tiger Preserve near Chordi. He had killed the man and carried off the son. Would I please come at once.

The Karadibetta Tiger Preserve borders the northern side of the road here. It is a large block of teak and mixed jungle, set aside by order of His Highness the Maharaj of Mysore and the State Forestry Department to provide a Sanctuary, where shooting is not allowed.

The enlightened ruler of this State, with the advice and cooperation of his far-sighted and equally enlightened chief conservator, has allocated forest blocks in different districts of Mysore State as game sanctuaries for the preservation of wild life. In such places, shooting in strictly forbidden. This advanced policy of Mysore State was a brilliant example to the rest of India of how a far-sighted ruler and his able assistant have pioneered in game-preservation. Such initiative may well be emulated throughout the sub-continent, where wild life of every kind is being rapidly shot out.

In this particular case perhaps, the man-eater had broken the rules of the game by taking refuge in the Sanctuary, intended to be the home of well-behaved normal tigers. I thought I would go and see for myself, as it was significant that the majority of human kills had occurred between Kumsi and Anandapuram. The Karadibetta Sanctuary is almost at the hub of this area.

I left Bangalore very early in the morning next day, after getting together the necessary kit for a ten-day stay in the jungle, which was the longest I could afford to be absent from town. Owing to large sections of the road being under construction for concreting, it was two o'clock in the afternoon before I could reach the D.F.O. at Shimoga, where I halted briefly to thank him for his communications.

He was good enough to afford me still further assistance by handing me two letters, addressed to his subordinates, the Forest Range Officers stationed at Kumsi and at Chordi. One directed them to render me all possible help, particularly in purchasing live baits, which is sometimes a bit difficult in Mysore State, while the other ordered them to permit me to go armed into the game sanctuary at Karadibetta in pursuit of the man-eater.

Once more I thanked him and then hastened on to drive the sixteen miles to Kumsi. The range officer there, after reading his superior's letter, assured me of the utmost cooperation and said he would come along in the car with me to Chordi to meet his brother officer, the ranger stationed at that place.

We covered the next few miles in short time. The range officer at Chordi was a Mangalore Christian; that is to say, he came from the town of Mangalore on the West Coast, one of the earliest seats of Christianity in India. He was most enthusiastic about helping me, and called his subordinates at once and asked them to summon the other wood-cutters who had witnessed the incident in order that I might talk to them.

These men arrived after a few minutes and related the following story.

A contractor at Shimoga had recently purchased the right to fell trees in a certain sector of forest a mile from Tuppur for charcoal-burning. He engaged the services of both of them, as well as of the wood-cutter who had been killed and his seventeen-year-old son. They all had their homes in Shimoga, but had decided to live temporarily at Chordi village while the felling operations in the area lasted.

They had risen early in the morning of the day when the killing had taken place — which was now two days earlier — and had set forth to walk the three miles to where the felling was being done. They were passing by the Karadibetta block, which was on their right-hand side, when the son asked his father for a 'pan' leaf to chew.

I would like to interrupt my story here for a minute or two, for the benefit of those who do not know what the 'pan' leaf is. It is the longish heart-shaped leaf of the betelvine creeper and is a great favourite among all classes of people in Southern India, more particularly among the labourers. It is made into what is known as a 'beeda'. On the outspread leaf some 'chunam' or white lime is placed, together with three to four tiny pieces of the areca-nut, which is called 'supari', perhaps a few shreds of coconut and some sugar. The betel — or 'pan-leaf', as it is called — is then wrapped around the ingredients and well chewed. The white lime and the 'supari' causes saliva to flow copiously and colours it blood red. As they walk along chewing, these peopole expectorate freely, leaving blood red marks from their saliva on walls, pavements, and indeed everywhere. Europeans, who are newcomers to India and see traces of these marks everywhere, are generally thunderstruck at what they sometimes think to be the large number of cases of advanced tuberculosis in the country.

Returning to our story. The father stopped to hand the leaf to his son. To do so, he first had to remove it from the corner of his loincloth where it had been kept tied up in a knot. Meanwhile, the other two men had walked on. They heard a roar and looked back to see the son lying on the road with a tiger on top of him, while the amazed father stood by, his hand still extended in the act of offering the pan to his son.

They then saw the father perform a magnificent art — which was to be the last of his life and the supreme sacrifice. The old man rushed forward, waving his arms about the shouting at the tiger to frighten it off. What happened next was very quick.

The tiger left the boy for a moment and whisked around on the father, leaping upon him and biting fearfully and audibly at the man's throat and chest. Blood gushed like a fountain from the father's gaping wounds. Then leaving him lying on the road, the tiger leaped back upon the son, who was sitting up dazedly watching his father being done to death.

At that juncture the spell was broken and the two men turned tail and ran as fast as they could to Tuppur, nor did they once look back to see what had happened to the boy or his father after the last scene they had witnessed.

Tuppur, as I related, is quite a small hamlet. Besides, nobody there possessed a firearm. So a dozen men set forth to Anandapuram to tell the police and call someone with a gun.

It chanced that on the way they met a lorry going towards Chordi to collect sand from the stream where it passed under the bridge, at the spot where the cyclist had seen a tiger some time previously.

The men stopped the lorry and asked the driver to turn around and take them quickly to Anandapuram so that they could report what had happened. But the driver was an exceptionally bold individual, or at least appeared to be so. If they would all get into his lorry, he would drive down the road to the spot where this 'fairy-tale' — as he openly described it — had taken place. Then they would all see what they would see. 'What about the tiger?' somebody had asked. 'You have an open truck. Supposing it jumps in amongst us and kills some of us?' 'Brother,' the driver had announced, stoutly, 'I am here; so you have nothing and no one to fear. Do you think I shall be idle, waiting for the tiger to jump? I shall run my truck over the brute in a jiffy.'

Thus encouraged by the brave words of the driver, the twelve men had climbed on to the lorry. Very soon they had reached the spot. I was told the driver was really surprised when he saw the father lying on the road in a great pool of his own blood — quite dead by that time. He had thought the whole story had been concocted from beginning to end.

Of the son there was absolutely no trace.

The driver had lost a good deal of his self-confidence by this time. The thirteen men stopped long enough to put the dead body of the elder wood-cutter into the lorry. Then they had driven to Chordi at top speed. There they had picked up the range officer and driven on to Kumsi where, after some slight delay, they were reinforced by the Kumsi range officer and the Sub-Inspector of Police. The whole party had proceeded in the lorry to Shimoga where detailed reports were made to the police and to the Forestry Department. A perfunctory postmortem, for the sake of formalities, was held on the wood-cutter and his body was handed over to his relatives late that night.

Next day a party of armed police returned in the same truck to look for the son. It was said that a blood-trail could be seen, and a drag-mark where the man-eater had carried his victim through the bushes and into the game sanctuary. After that, nobody appeared to be competent enough in woodcraft to follow the trail, so that the police party returned to Shimoga that evening to report that they had failed to recover the body of the son.

And that, as far as I could see, was the complete story of the Tiger's latest exploit, as I was able to gather the details from the two wood-cutters who had been eye-witnesses to the whole episode and the subsequent events.

The Chordi range officer served coffee, after which he and his colleague who had accompanied me from Kumsi, together with the two wood-cutters and myself, set out for the scene of the attack on the roadside opposite the Karadibetta Tiger Preserve.

I had often travelled along this road before, and this was the second occasion on which a tiger I was after had taken refuge within this game sanctuary. The first time had been when a wounded animal from the village of Gowja had made for the sanctuary, and I was able to bag it just before it had entered within the boundary, which story I have related elsewhere.*

The range officers had visited the place already and were able to point to the exact spot where the tiger had made his attack on the father and son. Traffic had been considerable and all traces of blood had been obliterated during the intervening three days under the wheels of the many buses, trucks, private cars and bullock-carts that had traversed the road.

The sanctuary itself starts a few yards from the road in the form of a teak plantation. The trees at that time were of nearly uniform height, about twenty feet tall, having been planted in straight lines by the Mysore Forestry Department some ten to fifteen years previously. The plantation extended thickly into the sanctuary for about two furlongs before it gave way abruptly to the natural jungle.

Tracking beneath teak-trees, except of a wounded animal leaving a distinct blod-trail, is next to impossible. The ground is carpeted with fallen and dried leaves which take or leave no impression. In this case, the boy the man-eater had carried had apparently bled but little. Although the woodcuters pointed

---

* See Nine Man-eaters and One Rogue (Allen & Unwin, London).

out the exact spot where the beast and its victim had disappeared, we were able with diligent searching to find only three places where blood had dripped on to the teak leaves. It was not worth wastig time on a further search.

I knew the sanctuary extended northwards to a stream and cart-track that connected the village of Gowja on the west with another village named Amligola to the east. The cart-track and stream formed the northern boundaries of the sanctuary proper, although the jungle itself extended for many more miles. A wise plan appeared to be to tie four live-baits on the four boundaries of the sanctuary, and another at its centre, as I had obtained special permission to shoot this tiger within this hallowed area if occasion arose.

I told the two range officers that I would need their cooperation in procuring these five baits, as past experience in this area made me rather sceptical of being able to get as many as five animals because the people opposed the sacrifice of cattle as baits and would not cooperate. They told me not to worry and that they would have the baits sent to me by nine o'clock the following morning.

At Kumsi is a Forest Lodge — the one at which the emergency operation had been performed to amputate the arm of the Reverend Jervis after being mauled by a tiger. I decided to camp at this bungalow, and asked the Kumsi R.O. to let me see the baits he could get before having them driven to Chordi to join the others which his counterpart at Chordi had undertaken to procure. I did this because I am quite particular about the live-baits I use. Very sick or aged cattle, already close to death's door, are often palmed off to a sahib as bait. He then wonders why the tiger does not readily kill them. But the tiger is a shikari and a gentleman, like the sahib himself, and not a jackal to be satisfied with a diseased bag of bones.

My companions had been very fidgety while I had been talking about the baits, for it was six o'clock and the shades of night were fast approaching. I had not been unduly nervous, however, as I knew we were safe as long as the five of us kept close together. We threaded our way through that dense teak plantation in a very closely-knit bunch, I can assure you, till we regained the car standing on the road. It did not take long to drop the Chordi officer and the two wood-cutters at the former's residence, and we were back at Kumsi in less than fifteen minutes.

I slept soundly at the forest lodge that night and went across early next morning to the R.O.'s quarters to see how he was getting along with the job of buying the baits. Despite his confidence of the evening before, I felt that with all his influence as a local forest officer, he had underestimated the difficulties he faced. It was as well I went there, for he had not yet started on the job.

To cut a long story story short, it was past 10 a.m. before he had got three animals together. One was a buffalo-calf. The two others were scraggy old bulls. I did not at all approve of the latter, but the R.O. said it was the best he could do. Moreover, they cost me quite a lot of money.

We assigned three men to do the task of driving them along the four-mile stretch of road to Chordi and set off for that place in my car at eleven, reaching our destination just ahead of the three animals.

The Chordi R.O. had procured a half-grown bull — quite a nice animal, brown in colour — and said the second bait in the quota that he was to fill had been sent for that morning and was coming soon. It took an hour to arrive, and it was twelve-thirty before we had all five animals together. Half the day had already been wasted.

As a result, we were able to tie out only three of them

that day. The best, the half-grown brown bull, I tied in approximately the centre of the sanctuary. The buffalo-calf was tied a few yards inside from the road to the south, where the attack had been made. The bait on the eastern flank of the sanctuary, which was incidentally about five miles north of Chordi, was one of the old white bulls.

Again it was sunset by the time we had finished, and I left the remaining two animals at Chordi, saying I would return very early the next morning to select the places to tie them out, which you remember were to be the remaining two sides of the rough rectangle formed by the sanctuary, on its northern and western flanks.

Before dawn next day I was motoring back to Chordi along with my friend the Kumsi R.O., who had been up and ready, waiting for me. A large sambar stag rag across the road about half-way to our destination and he remarked that it was a lucky sign.

At Chordi, the R.O. there said he would accompany me to tie out the remaining two baits, and he instructed his subordinate, a forester, to take two forest guards and one of the men who had been with us the previous day, and so knew where they were located, to see if the baits to the east and the south of the sanctuary were alive. We ourselves would look up the third one, tied out in the centre of the sanctuary, as we would make a short-cut through it before turning off to the western and northern boundaries. We all set out together, and it was over an hour and a half later that we came to the bull-calf I had tied near the middle of the sanctuary. It was alive and well.

You must not overlook the fact that in tying each live-bait, the question of feeding and watering it each day had to be considered also. To feed it is not much trouble as a bundle of hay or grass is sent along for its consumption each twenty-four hours, but watering often provides quite a problem. Of course a pot or a kerosene tin might be provided and refilled with water each day, but this method has its own snags. Invariably the animal knocks over the receptacle, or breaks it if it happens to be a pot, while the proximity of a kerosene tin often makes a tiger too suspicious to attack. So the best method is for the men who visit the bait each day to untie it and lead it to some pool or stream, water it there and then bring it back. Rarely, however, does such a pool or stream happen to be handy for the purpose, and frequently the beast has to be led for a mile or more to a suitable place. Villagers are mostly lazy and apathetic by nature, and they generally feel such a long walk is unnecessary. In their logic, the animal has been tied out to be killed, anyhow. So why worry about watering it? This is a point that all hunters who tie out live-baits in India should bear in mind. If they do not supervise these daily visits, or at least employ reliable men to do the work for them, and should a tiger or panther not make a kill, it is almost a certainty that the poor bait has spent a very parched and thirsty week, unless the place where they have tied him has water close by, or it has been provided in a container.

In the present case there was a stream half-a-mile away. We led the animal there, allowed it to drink its fill and then brought it back.

You may wonder if it is not easier to tie the bait beside a stream or pond to overcome this problem of watering it. Very often this is done, as the tigers themselves visit such spots to drink. But there are other factors, too, to be considered. Nullahs, game-trails, fire-lines and certain footpaths, cart-tracks and even sections of roads, along which tigers are known to walk frequently, are equally good places to tie-up, and may have an added advantage of tiger pug-marks are noticed there regularly. The places at which there tracks intersect are even better. Tigers do not always stroll along the banks of streams, especially where streams are many. We had tied this particular bait on a game trail along which tigers often walk, so the Chordi range officer had assured me the previous evening, when we had been searching for a likely place.

We secured the two animals we brought with us to the feet of convenient trees at suitable places on the western and northern boundaries of the sanctuary. But it was past noon before we had finished.

Of course you should not for a moment imagine that, by doing all this, we had completely ringed the tiger within the sanctuary. For the sanctuary extended for miles and it by no means followed that, wherever he came out, he would be confronted by one of my baits. I had only done what was possible under the prevailing conditions, and the rest was left to fate or luck, whichever name you prefer. And fate played a fickle game that day.

It was close on three p.m. and we were on our way back and close to Chordi, when a group of men tilling their fields on the outskirts of the clearing that lay around that hamlet informed us that the forest guards we had sent out that morning had found that the buffalo-calf, tied near the spot where the man-eater had killed the two men, had been kiled by a tiger the night before. They said the guards had been unable to get word to us as they did not know exactly which way we had gone or how we would return. So they had told all passers-by to inform us if they happened to meet us on the way.

After hearing this news we hurried back to Chordi, where the two range officers roundly abused the guards for not coming to inform us of what had happened. They were hardly to blame, poor fellows, for we ourselves had been on the move the whole afternoon, and had they come to try and catch up with us they were very likely to have failed and caused still greater delay. In the circumstances, I felt they had done the wisest thing by remaining 'put' at Chordi and sending word by all who passed through the village. In any case, it was not too late to put up a machan if we hurried, and the news that they had taken the precaution to cover the kill with branches — against a visit by vultures — caused me to intercede on their behalf.

By 3.30 p.m. my Studebaker was standing on the road to the south, opposite the place at which we were to enter the teak plantation and walk the little distance to where we had tied up the buffalo-calf. In three minutes we had unroped my folding charpoy from the luggage-carrier at the back of the car. I had made this charpoy quite recently and it was an improvement on the old one, in that the frame was only a little more than half the normal length. It was therefore easy to transport on my luggage-carrier without overlapping the width of the car at either end. Wide khaki navarre tape, for comfort and for unobtrusive colouration, was what I sat upon, the bands of tape being interwoven in the manner of a mat. The ends of the tape were permanently looped around the bamboos that formed the rectangular frame. The four legs at the four corners were but a foot long, extending beyond the rectangular frame for about six inches above and below. This was to allow sufficient purchase by which to tie the machan to a tree. The whole structure was simple, light, very portable and most comfortable; above all it did not crak at the slightest movement, as did any normal machan put together with branches lopped from trees.

Although the average height of the teak trees here was about twenty feet, being comparatively young, there were a few of much greater age and therefore taller; I had tied the buffalo at the foot of one of these, in case the occasion should later arise for putting up a machan. There was no other choice in this instance, for there were no other trees than teak growing in that plantation, and as teak trees have their branches fairly high up, it meant that I had to sit at a greater height from the ground than usual.

That confounded tree gave me a devil of a lot of trouble to climb, as there were no branches for the first twelve feet, and I never excelled as a climber of perpendicular poles. However, I stood on the shoulders of one of the forest guards, when all willingly helped to push and shove my legs a little higher till I could get a grip on the first branch and haul myself up. Due to the large size of the teak leaves, it was a simple matter to hide the machan completely from view. Moreover, as they were the only leaves growing there, the camouflage arrangements we made were most efficient, in that the machan became inconspicuous and blended naturally with the surroundings. The fork of the tree where we had placed the charpoy was over twenty feet from the ground.

The calf's neck had been broken and half the beast had been eaten, but there was just about enough left to justify another visit by its killer.

Neither of the range officers could drive a motor-car, nor could the two forest guards, but as the two wood-cutters had also come along with us, I told the six of them to push my car at least half-a-mile or more away in order not to alarm the tiger should he cross the road anywhere nearabouts. Actually I had not thought of this until we were unroping the charpoy from the car. In any case, the road was more or less level, and the six men should not have too much trouble in trundlng my 'Stude' along.

It was just 5 p.m. when they left me on the teak tree, and

I figured that in another twenty minutes or so they would have moved the car and the way would be clear for the tiger to cross the road, provided he came from that direction. Perhaps I was being unduly optimistic, and he would not come at all.

Well, he came all right; but it was only at about a quarter past eight, when it was quite dark He gave me quite a lot of time to know beforehand, or rather the herd of spotted deer with their shrill calls, and a barking deer, with his hoarse, guttural 'Khar-r-r Khar-r-r' bark, did this for him. They had announced his passing to all the denizens of the jungle for the last mile or so of his journey. No wonder tigers are reticent animals. The popularity — or is it unpopularity? — that is often forced upon them by the humbler inhabitants of the forest must indeed be embarrassing. On this occasion, I am sure that tiger had felt more than embarrassed.

Anyway, he came without undue caution, and I could hear his heavy tread crunch the dry fallen teak leaves long before he stood over his kill.

I shone my flashlight and he looked up at me, full in the face. It took about three seconds for me to notice, even in torch-light, that he did not appear to have any distinctive 'mane'. But I could not take the chance and he dropped to a bullet through his heart.

I waited fifteen minutes, just to make sure he was dead. He did not stir and I was sure. So I descended, having to jump the last seven or eight feet down from that infernal tree. I am perhaps heavier than I should be, and the jolt with which I came to earth did not cause me to think kindly of the practice of leaping from trees. I approached the dead tiger and looked carefully. I muttered invectives then. As I had known, even as I fired, this was not the man-eater; for the dead beast had no ruffle of hair at his neck. Once more the culprit had escaped, and once again an inoffensive tiger had

261

paid the penalty. Besides, I would have some explaining to do to the D.F.O. at Shimoga. He had given me special permission to shoot the man-eater in the tiger sanctuary — but definitely not a harmless beast.

Well, it was just too bad.

I regained the road and walked towards Chordi, expecting to come up with my car where the men had pushed and left it. But there was no car on the road.

Poor fellows, I thought. They had misunderstood me and pushed it all the way to Chordi, which was about two miles.

I came to Chordi and to the Ranger's quarters. Both officers were there. I announced that I had shot a tiger, but that I was almost sure it was the wrong tiger, as it had no mane.

It might be the man-eater after all, they argued. Perhaps he had dropped his mane in the last two years. Or perhaps he never had a mane from the very beginning and that the description was only a myth. That was a point, I conceded; but my hopes did not rise.

Then I asked them where they had left my car. Car? Why, sir, they explained, you left it pointing up the road, away from Chordi. We did not know how to turn it towards Chordi, while you had very definitely instructed us to push it away from that spot for at least half-a-mile. We did that, sir, but in the opposite direction.

Well, life is like that, I said under my breath. It has its ups and downs. Tonight was one of those in which the 'ups' predominated — or was it the 'downs'? I could not find the answer.

Some more coffee followed. Then a carrying party assembled with bamboos, lanterns and ropes, and we made our way back. While the men were securing the tiger to fetch it to the road, I walked in the opposite direction and found my car exactly four furlongs away.

We were back at Kumsi in a little over an hour.

Next morning I skinned the tiger, while the two range officers wrote out their official report to the D.F.O. at Shimoga. I had shot a tiger without a ruff, they wrote. It might not be the man-eater. The special permit I had in my possession enjoined that I should shoot the man-eater and nothing else within the boundaries of the Karadibetta Sanctuary. They closed their joint statement by leaving it to their superior officer to 'take such further and necessary actions you best deem fit'.

Then they apologised to me for having had to write such a report.

I waited till my leave was over, but none of the other baits was killed. The D.F.O. at Shimoga wrote to me officially that his rangers had reported I had shot a tiger within the sanctuary which was said not to be the man-eater, whereas the permit handed to me had been for the man-eater and no other animal. Would I please explain?

Now, I have lived all my life in India. As such, the 'redtapism' that goes with all government transactions was well known to me. But I did not get annoyed at receiving the D.F.O.'s comunication. I wrote back an official letter stating that I regretted he had been misinformed that the tiger I had shot was not the man-eater. I affirmed that it was the man-eater itself, and no other tiger, that I had shot within the sanctuary in accordance with the provisions of the special permit that had been so kindly granted to me for that purpose.

So what? Everybody was happy. Official decorum had been amply satisfied on all sides. All concerned had strictly and very properly performed their duties.

The time came for me to return to Bangalore. I thanked the two range officers for their help, sold the remaining four baits back to their owners for less than a quarter of the price

I had paid for them, and set out on the homeward journey. On the way I stopped at Shimoga to pay my respects to the D.F.O. He informed me that I had replied wisely to his letter asking for an explanation and apologised for having written it, saying he had to do so in face of the report that his two range officers had made to him. I told him not to worry and that I was accustomed to such things, adding that it was I who had told the ranger officers that I had shot the wrong tiger when I discovered it had no mane. We parted good friends.

A whole year went by. There had been no more kills since the old man and his son had fallen victims. That had been somewhere about the beginning of the previous year. Or it may have been a few months later — I really forget now. Everyone thought the story of the maned man-eater had been a fable and that I had shot the actual miscreant. I thought so, too, till disillusionment came.

A tiger killed man on the outskirts of the town of Sagar, which, as I have said, was on the road beyond Kumsi and Anandapuram, before it reached the Jog Falls. A fortnight later he killed a second man near Anandapuram, and then within the next month another man and woman at the villages of Tagarthy and Gowja respectively. Both these places are within a ten-mile radius of Anandapuram. Early in August he carried off a Lambani boy in broad daylight. He had been grazing his cattle close to the main road on the outskirts of Kumsi town.

The man-eater had returned from wherever he had gone after killing the old wood-cutter and his son beside the sanctuary, and now was killing in real earnest. Or if it was not him, he had been replaced by another of his kin who was taking human victims at a far faster rate.

I manipulated matters to get a week's leave, which was the most I could manage, and motored to Kumsi. The D.F.O. at

Shimoga had been transferred and another officer, whom I did not know, had taken his place. But he wished me success. I enquired of him as to whether the two range officers at Kumsi and Chordi were the same that I had met there early the previous year, and was glad when he answered in the affirmative.

It was a meeting of old friends, therefore, that took place at Kumsi when I met the ranger again at his quarters, and the same a little later at Chordi, when I met his colleague. Both the officers were of the opinion that the present man-eater was quite a different animal, and that I had indeed killed the right tiger over a year previously within the sanctuary. Their reason for saying so was the fact that no human kills had taken place since that time, till within the last couple of months. If I had not shot the man-eater, then where had he been for all those months? Once a man-eater, always a man-eater. A tiger has never been known to give up the habit altogether. So wherever this tiger had strayed, he must have killed at least some human beings during that period and we would have heard of it.

I must say their argument appeared very sound, and I was convinced in spite of myself.

We held a conference over what to do what to do next. This tiger had killed at Sagar, Anandapuram, Tagarthy, Gowja, and now at Kumsi. It was the same area as that over which the other man-eater — the so-called maned tiger, if there had ever been such an animal — had operated two years earlier and more. Where was I to tie my baits? Where should I begin? We could not quite make up our minds.

The matter was decided for us the next day. As luck would have it, the tiger took a hered-boy in broad daylight at Amligola, which you may remember was the terminal point of the northern boundary of the Karadibetta sanctuary at its eastern end. In other words, Amligola formed the north-eastern end.

In other words, Amligola formed the north-eastern corner of the rough rectangle that was the sanctuary. The forest guards there hastened to report the matter to their R.O., at Chordi headquarters, who came to Kumsi at once to tell me about it. It was 3 p.m. when he arrived.

To reach this place, Amligola, the two range officers and I had to make a detour and follow a very, very rough cart-track beyond Chordi. Amligola boasts a delightful little forest lodge, with the stream that forms the northern boundary of Karadibetta flowing close behind it. This stream empties itself into a large tank about two miles away. The boy had been grazing cattle by the side of that tank. The tiger had walked up the bed of the stream and had attacked the boy at about nine in the morning. He had not touched the cattle, although they were feeding all around the spot where the boy had been standing. After the killing, the tiger had walked back with his victim along this stream and into the jungle.

I was shown the pug-marks of the tiger as it had come towards the boy, and its tracks on the return journey, where a drag-mark, made probably by the boy's feet as they trailed along, could be clearly seen. There was hardly any blood along the trail.

It was late evening by the time we had seen all tis, and it had become too dark to try to find the body of the poor youngster. This was a great pity. I chafed at the unfortunate circumstance that had brought the news to us at Kumsi so late. Although we had made every possible effort to arrive earlier, the bad cart-track leading to Amligola had wasted time, as I had not wanted to break a spring or an axle. Had I been able to find the remains that evening. I would have sat up over them for the tiger to return. I cursed my bad luck.

The range officers slept in one room of the forest lodge. I slept in the other. The two guards had gone to a godown which adjoined the kitchen as separate building to the main bungalow, where they barricaded and bolted the door.

A tiger started calling shortly after midnight. He appeared to be within a mile of us. He called again and the range officers heard it. They tapped on the door that separated our rooms to attract my attention, in case I should be asleep. I opened the door and let them in, telling them that I had been listening to the calls myself.

I then opened the main door leading on to the narrow front verandah of the lodge. Moonlight poured down on the jungle around us, and shone in at one end of the verandah. Only in a tropical land can one ever hope and appreciate to the full the eerie thrill of a moonlit night in a forest. As I gazed outside, drinking in the wonder of it all, the tiger called again, this time much closer. Suddenly I realized that the beast was walking along the bank of the stream that flowed a few yards behind the bungalow and would probably pass within the next ten minutes. Was this the man-eater?

I decided to chance my luck.

It took only a couple of minutes to fix my flashlight on to its two clamps along my rifle barrel. I ran out of the bathroom door at the back of the lodge, brushed through the thin hedge of young casuarina trees that bordered the compound and ran down the slope at the rear that led to the bed of the small stream.

I could see the surface of the water glistening and twinkling in the moonlight, although it was very dark under the trees which grew by the bank on which I stood. I have told you that this stream formed the northern boundary of Karadibetta. The opposite bank was within the sanctuary. The forest lodge and the bank on which I was now standing were just outside its limits.

The tiger called again. It was fast approaching and hardly

a quarter of a mile away. I would have to act quickly if I wanted to ambush him.

The all-important question was this: along which bank was he walking? If he was on the opposite or Kardibetta bank, I would have to get much closer to the water's edge if I wanted to see him in the moonlight and get in shot. On the other hand, if he was coming along the same bank as the one on which I was standing, and if I went down to the edge of the stream, the tiger, when he passed, would have the advantage not only of seeing me silhouetted against the moonlight on the water, but of himself being on more elevated ground. That could be most dangerous and disadvantageous for me if he made a charge.

He called again — about a furlong away. There was no time whatever to lose. I decided to take a chance. Most probably he was on the opposite bank of the stream and within the sanctuary.

Meanwhile my eyes had been searching desperately for a place to hide. A clump of reedgrass grew about two feet from my bank, completely surrounded by water. I knew the stream was shallow, so I ran down to the edge and silently waded the two feet, taking care not to make any splashing noises. Then I squatted low in the grass. Two or three minutes passed in dead silence. I could not see into the deep shadows cast by the trees on either bank.

Then the tiger moaned again directly opposite me — and on the very bank on which I hd just been standing. He was passing at that very instant.

I counted, one-two-three-four-five, so as not to have him completely level and above me. Then I pressed the switch on the flashlight. There, hardly fifteen yards away, was his striped form.

He halted in his tracks and turned around. He was facing

right side on, so that I had to take the shot behind his right shoulder. He sprang into the air and fell backwards. I fired a second and third time.

Then he realized where I was and came for me, sliding and stumbling down the sloping bank. At a distance of barely five yards, my fourth bullet crashed through his skull.

Later, as I examined him, I marvelled at the unusual ruff of hair growing around his neck. It formed a regular mane.

Some jungle mysteries can never be solved, and one of them is why this tiger had a 'mane' at all.

Nine

Man-eater of Pegepalyam

THIS IS NOT A COMPLETE STORY OF THE EXPLOITS AND DOWNFALL OF a man-eating tiger because the tiger of which I write is very much alive at the moment of writing. There is an official record of it having killed and eaten fourteen persons, although unofficially its tally of victims is said to amount to thirty-seven men, women and children. Of this unofficial estimate about half had actually been wholly or partially eaten, the remainder being just mauled by the animal's claws. The official record considers only individuals killed and eaten, and not those mauled. This accounts for the discrepancy between the official and unofficial death-rolls.

The interesting feature of the story I am about to tell is that I believe this tiger to be the same animal of which I wrote in an earlier book in a story entitled the 'Mauler of Rajnagara'.*

---

* *See Man-eaters and Jungle Killers* (Alen & Unwin, London).

When writing that account, a tiger had taken up his abode at the foot of the Dimbum escarpment, in the district of North Coimbatore, in the scrub jungle bordering the foot of the hilly plateau and about midway between Dimbum to the north, at the top of the steep ghat road up the hill, and the town of Satyamangalam on the arid plains at the foot, to the south.

The nearest village to the scrub jungles at the foot of the hills bears the name of Rajnagara, and since the tiger began his exploits against the human race by persecuting the herdsmen from this village who led their cattle to pasture in these scrub jungles, he became well known as the tiger of Rajnagara. Moreover, he earned a particular reputation because of a peculiarity in his mode of attack — or at least it was so at the time I wrote that story. The peculiarity lay in the fact that he would rush out of cover and severely maul a herdsman by scratching him with his claws and then invariably carry off his own selection from the herd of cattle which would be milling around during the attack on the herdsman. At that time there was no authentic case of him having bitten any of the human beings he had attacked. One or two persons were listed as missing and it was presumed the tiger had devoured them, but there had been no definite evidence to corroborate that presumption. All that was known was that this tiger always mauled his victims by clawing them — not by biting.

This peculiar habit gave rise to a universal belief that he was an animal that had been wounded in the face or jaw in such a way as to prevent him from biting. At the same time it was found that he generally made a very hearty meal of the cattle he killed after mauling their herdsman, which proved that he could bite and eat perfectly well when he was so disposed. Altogether, it was a most unusual and peculiar case, which has never been satisfactorily explained or proved,

271

although many were the ingenious explanations put forward to account for this habit.

I have related how I tried to shoot this tiger and how I failed. He was a most elusive animal. Finally I returned to my home in Bangalore, leaving the 'Mauler of Rajnagara' the undisputed winner of the first round of our encounter. I sincerely trusted the time would come when there would be an opportunity for staging a second round, when I hoped for better success.

A few friends and well-wishers have since written to me, inquiring if there is any sequel to that story. An old acquaintance of mine, Joe Kearney, went as far as to send me a cable-gram from Los Angeles, California, stating he was looking forward to further developments regarding this particular tiger.

Alas, I could not satisfy the curiosity of any of them, for the 'Mauler of Rajnagara' stopped his mauling, and simply faded out shortly after my visit. We all hoped that he had become a reformed character and had perhaps turned over a new leaf with the new year. Or maybe he had just gone away to some distant jungle or even died a natural death. Time passed and the herdsmen of Rajnagara resumed their accustomed cattle grazing in the scrub jungle that surrounded their farmsteads and came home in the evenings, tired but unmauled.

And then, one evening about nine months later, the sun began to set behind the Biligirirangan Range of mountains some fifty miles north of Rajnagara, as the crow flies. Its oblique rays cast elongated shadows to the eastern side of the few huts that comprised the little hamlet of Pegepalyam, set in a clearing of the jungle, with the mountain range to its west, and the road from Dimbum to Kollegal flanking it to the east, barely two miles way. It was the time that the cows come home, and within a few furlongs of the village the local herd was wending its way along the forest tracks that led to Pegepalyam; two herdsmen, a man and a boy, were bringing up their rear.

Ravines, densely wooded, intersected the country. In the rainy season they were rushing torrents of water drained away eastwards, after cascading down the mountain range to the west. But on that balmy evening they were bone-dry, and the twitter of bulbuls and the rustle of several groups of 'seven-sister' birds lent an air of peace and tranquility to the scene.

The cattle crossed one of these dips in the terrain, the adult herdsman was half-way across and the boy was on the further bank as it sloped down to the bed of the ravine. A clump of young bamboos surrounded by nodding grass-stems barred his way, and the tracks made by the cattle herd just ahead passed around it, the dust raised by the many hooves as yet unsettled. The boy followed, engrossed in his own thoughts.

The adult herdsman ahead thought he heard a hollow sound, followed by a sort of gasp and turned around to find the cause. There was nothing to be seen. The track behind him led way to the bamboo clump. Nothing and no one was on it. The herdsman resumed his course in the wake of the herd. No doubt, the boy would come along.

Finally they neared Pegepalyam. The herdsman looked back once more. Again there was no sign of the boy. He called him by name: 'Venkat, Venkat,' he called, but there was no answer. The herdsman hesitated a while and called again, but still there was no response. Meanwhile the cattle were forging ahead towards the village, and as he did not want to leave them alone he followed them into the village. Then only did it become evident that the herdsboy had not turned up.

No serious notice was taken, as there might have been a hundred reasons for the boy's delay. But after an hour or so had passed and the boy had not appeared, the herdsman recollected that he had missed him after the track had circumvented the clump of bamboos. He also remembered the hollow gasping sound he had heard and came to the conclusion that something had happened to the boy. Perhaps he had been bitten by a snake. The thought of a man-eating tiger or panther never entered the herdsman's mind, as such a menace had never yet been heard of in the tranquil vicinity of Pegepalyam.

So he turned back and hastened to the bamboo clump. He circumvented the bend in the track, and there, clearly and boldly superimposed over the hoof-marks of the herd of cattle and his own footprints, were the pug-marks of a tiger, the signs of a brief struggle, and a drag-mark where the killer had hauled away his victim.

And thus the man-eater of Pegepalyam came to public knowledge.

Time passed and desultory human kills were reported from scattered places, south-westwards as far as Talvadi and Talaimalai, perhaps thirty miles away; eastwards at the base of Ponnachimalai Hill, and another on the banks of the Cauvery River at Alambadi, over forty miles distant; and one more in a northerly direction, barely six miles from the big town of Kollegal. That one was the latest, being that of a fifteen-year-old boy who was boldly attacked and dragged off the field where he was working at about 10.30 a.m. in blazing sunlight.

A significant fact about this man-eater is the information that was brought in on the occasion of a kill that occurred some three miles from the spot where he had taken his first victim, the herdboy of Pegepalyam. Three men were traversing a cart track that led into the jungle and had formerly been used by carts for extracting felled bamboos from the forest.

Because of the activities of the man-eater, such felling operations had been almost suspended, and when people entered the jungle they only did so if it was imperative; never alone and always in broad daylight. These three men had urgent business, which accounted for their presence, their number, and the time of day which was just before two in the afternoon. They had eaten their midday meal at Pegepalyam and had almost reached their destination. They expected to be back by 3.30 p.m. at the latest.

Suddenly and without warning, a tiger sprang on to the track just ahead of the leading man. The party came to a halt, transfixed with terror. Then the tiger attacked the leading man, standing up on his hind legs and clawing his face. His companions made for the nearest tree, which was fortunately close by, and scrambled up it. Meanwhile, with commendable presence of mind and great courage, the man who had been attacked swung blindly at the tiger's head with the knife that all Sholagas carry for lopping wood or clearing a path through the undergrowth. The blow caught the animal on the side of its head and glanced off. The tiger roared with pain at this unexpected retaliation, and the natural cowardice with which all man-eaters appear to be imbued caused it to leave its victim and spring back into cover.

Meanwhile the other two men had succeeded in scrambling to the top-most branches of the nearby tree, whence they looked down in terror on the scene below them. Blood poured from the face and chest of their companion, welling from the deep wounds that had been inflicted by the tiger's claws. He was sitting dazedly on the ground, numbed with shock. The men in the tree called to him: 'Brother, come and climb this tree quickly. It is unsafe to remain on the ground. The man-eater may return.'

The wounded man heard them, clambered to his feet and

taking the turban from his head, began to mop up the blood tht poured from the many scratches he had received. Again the men on the tree called to him, and he turned to walk towards its base with the intention of climbing. But fate had decreed that his days on this earth had run out. The man-eater's momentary cowardice had been supplanted by rage, probably caused by pain from the wound where the brave man's knife had cut through the skin on the side of his head. With a rush it was upon him, and this time a mighty blow of his foreleg across the back of the man's head broke the neck. Hardely had his body fallen to the ground than the tiger picked him up in his jaws and walked into the jungle in full view of the two men in the tree.

I visited Kollegal and Pegepalyam soon after this incident and spoke to both these men. Their accounts were unusually consistent with each other's and clear in detail. They both agreed that on both occasions when the tiger had attacked, he had done so primarily with his claws and not with his teeth.

Memory rushed back to me. Could this be that elusive tiger, the 'Mauler of Rajnagara', that had beaten me at the first encounter, grown bolder with the passage of time and become a confirmed man-eater, to appear now as the 'Man-Eater of Pegepalyam'? The evidence of the two men appeared to indicate the likelihood that this tiger was the same animal.

I took a lot of trouble in pursuing my inquiries on these lines, not only at Pegepalyam itself but at one or two of the nearer hamlets where this animal had claimed his victims, and also with the Forest Department at Kollegal. A number of the human victims had been recovered before the tiger had completely eaten them. All had been clawed, but they had also been bitten. There was no conclusive evidence that the tiger killed only by clawing, as had been the method of attack by the 'Mauler'; and in any case, the actions of clawing and biting would both take place on any carcass in the normal process of a tiger eating it.

My first visit to Pegepalyam lasted only a week, but the man-eater did not touch any of the three live-baits I offered. Nor was there any news of him whatever during that period. Duty called and there was no excuse for extending my leave. I returned to Bangalore.

Since then, as I have indicated, the man-eater has killed again — a fifteen-year-old boy in broad daylight and in an open field, with the big town of Kollegal only six miles away. This time my son, Donald, is going after thim and hopes to have more luck than I did.

We would both like to know very much if the man-eater is the mauler of which I have told you, although there seems no possible way of proving this point unless Donald succeeds in finding some reason for the quite unusual habit the mauler had of attacking with his claws rather than his teeth. If he succeeds, Donald will have certainly unravelled a most intriguing jungle mystery.

And as I think these thoughts, these pages and this handwriting once again fade from sight. In imagination I see the roaring flames of a camp-fire before me, from which cascades of sparks shower fitfully into the darkness, while a thick spiral of smoke curls upwards to the sky.

It is a clear night, but few of the myriad stars that spangle the sky are visible owing to the glow from the camp-fire.

With all its vigour, the flickering light is only able to dispel the shadows for about fifteen yards around me. Beyond is blackness — intense, silent and all-pervading, like some solid substance, covering and enveloping everything — the blackness of a jungle night, a blanket of velvety gloom.

Yet more smoke curls from the bowl of my pipe as I puff at it contentedly. The smoke rises to merge with the smoke from the flames and finally disappears in the flickering, fitful radiance from the fire, with its comforting though slightly oppressive heat.

Silence broods around me, broken only by the crackle and hiss of the flames.

Then I hear it. Over the hills and far away, but drawing nearer and nearer. 'O-o-o-n-o-o-n! A-oongh! A-oongh!' It is the call of a tiger!

I have heard it so often before, and the more I hear it the more I thrill to that awful yet wonderfull melodious sound.

'Ugha-ugh! Ugh! Aungh-ha! A-oongh! O-o-n-o-o-n!' There it is again! The tiger is drawing nearer, ever nearer.

And in my imagination I like to think this will be the 'Man-eater of Pegepalyam'.

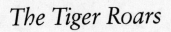

The Tiger Roars

Introduction

PREFACES ARE NOT POPULAR AND ARE SELDOM READ. AFTER ALL, A reader buys a book for what he can get out of it by way of entertainment, excitement or knowledge, as the case may be, and no explanation by the author will increase or diminish these. But before I embark on a few more tales of my adventures in the jungles of Southern India, I merely wish to make a plea for their preservation, that their wild life and their beauty may survive, not only for their own sake, but that future generations may enjoy them as I have done. Time is already short.

It is the duty of the Government of India, of every government in every state of India, of every sportsman who visits her forests – indeed, it is the duty of every Indian – to make a supreme effort to save the country's wild creatures from extinction.

Game and bird sanctuaries have been formed, it is true. But this is not nearly enough. Rules are printed that cannot be enforced. For one thing, the forest guards and watches are not paid enough. For another, corruption is rife.

In the State of Mysore as a whole, and also in the District

of Salem belonging to Madras State, tigers and panthers are now almost extinct, wiped out by the villagers who use a poison supplied to them almost free of charge by the local governments as an insecticide to protect their crops. This poison they smear on the flesh of the kills made by tigers and panthers. These animals invariably return, eat the doctored meat and die within a few yards. So do the jackals, hyaenas, vultures and crows that follow them.

Deer continue to be slaughtered in hundreds every summer by the poachers who wait for them with muskets over the water-holes to which they must come to drink. A few rupees, or a piece of the carcase here and there, silence the officials who are paid by the governments to protect the lives of these animals.

So death stalks the wild creatures of India. Extinction, particularly in South India, will surely and certainly follow unless the governments of the various states and the people themselves wake up to the fact very soon and become realistic. It is almost too late already.

I hope that you will enjoy reading these stories a fraction as much as I have enjoyed writing them, for in doing so I have been carried back to the forest life – not only to memories of bygone days but to its enchanting sights, its myriad exotic smells, its medley of sounds, its joys and its sorrows, the exuberance of life there and its tragedy.

One
The Novice of Manchi

THE NARROW TRAIL WOUND IN AND OUT BETWEEN CLUMPS OF GIANT bamboo that rose on every side, the tall graceful fronds arching like huge bouquets of elegant, feathery blooms. It was the time when the bamboo tree was seeding, when each length of cane was crowded at its tip with tufts consisting of thousands of tiny seeds. These seeds look like ripe grains of wheat but are smaller; yet the weight of thousands of them was enough to bend each frond low to the earth, creaking and groaning under its burden as it moved with the gentle breezes passing along the jungle aisles.

The seeds fell in showers, carpeting the earth and the narrow path with a thick layer that mostly decayed, but here and there showed signs of sprouting into tiny darkgreen seedlings. This carpet felt like sawdust and had a springy consistency: it deadened the sound of anything moving over it, and of the killer that now stalked from bamboo clump to bamboo clump in search of a meal. Overhead, thousands of parakeets screeched as they hung by their feet, head downwards above the twisting trail, pecking the seeds with their razor-sharp curved beaks, deftly severing the husk from the kernel, which they crushed to a fine powder before swallowing. They were small compared with other members of the parrot family, being about twice the size of the domesticated budgerigar, but they were of many hues, ranging from emerald green to peacock blue, some with pale yellow wing-feathers and heads of rose pink or deep purple, and others of a uniform green, ringed around the neck with a narrow collar of red and black.

A lone traveller, walking cautiously along the jungle trail, did not heed the parakeets nor the thousands of other birds, including wild pigeons and doves, that fed on the seeds of the bamboos. He gazed intently ahead and glanced furtively to either side, slowing down and even halting now and then to study a particularly dense clump of bamboo before drawing level with it. His sharp, restless eyes tried to penetrate the thick growth to see if anything was hidden there. His ears, too, were alert for sounds far different from and far more arresting than the raucous, strident screech of the parakeets. The sounds he was listening for, and dreading to hear, were the sharp crack of a bamboo branch being broken, or the deep rumble of contented feeding, or the swishing sweep of ponderous feet brushing through the carpet of seeds and decaying leaves.

The man was afraid of meeting a wild elephant or a herd of them, for there were many in this area, especially at this time of the year. But his hearing was not attuned to the approach of the killer, who first sensed and then saw him. The killer made no sound whatever, unlike the screaming, fluttering birds above or the ponderous elephants beneath, engrossed in their search for vegetable food. This killer was by no means harmless, nor was he a vegetarian. He dealt death swiftly and surely and he was at this moment very hungry indeed.

The man was a Poojaree, a member of an aboriginal jungle tribe that inhabits the forests of the Salem District in southern India, and the trail he was following was the footpath that led through the forest from the hamlet of Aiyur, southwards for about ten miles to the still smaller hamlet of Manchi, nestling on the slopes of a great range of hills. The path ran down a valley, as also did a rocky stream, the two crossing and recrossing frequently, and sometimes running parallel to each other, while the hills towered on both sides, to east and west, in an unbroken chain of jungle. The narrow path was visible now and again, but disappeared as suddenly beneath the tall, bending, swaying bamboos as they moved to the gentle currents of the forest breeze.

Fine webs, almost invisible, frequently caught and tickled the face of the Poojaree whose attention was wholly concentrated on the possible presence of the elephants. He brushed them off angrily with both hands, much to the annoyance of the large, long-legged, yellow-and-black-and-red spiders, six inches and more across, whose webs extended from tree to tree, secured by gossamer-like threads that were unbelievably strong, supporting a central area of a web eight or ten feet in diameter and of an intricate, finely-woven pattern. The dew had condensed on these webs and drops of moisture glistened in the sunlight that filtered through the bamboo fronds. All was still, all was peaceful, except for the din of the feeding birds.

Keera, the Poojaree, passed a dense clump of bamboo after making certain no elephant sheltered behind, but failed to see the killer in its black and rusty coat that crouched low to the earth and stared at him with malevolent, unblinking eyes.

285

The man heard a coughing roar twice: "Aa-arrgh! Aa-arrgh!" Then the tiger charged.

Keera whirled around as a great shape with widely-extended jaws engulfed him. The Poojaree screamed but once: "Aiyooo-oo-oo!" He screamed no more. The birds that had ceased chattering for the moment, when the tragedy was enacted, started to screech again and from the side of the pathway came the crunch and crack of bones as the tiger began his meal.

Away on the hillside a troop of langur-monkeys had been feeding joyously, their cries of "Whoomp! Whoomp, Whoomp!" echoing across the narrow valley. Then the sharp hearing of the langur-watchman caught the distant sound of the tiger's roars and the fainter, futile, agonized human scream. He knew that the tiger had made his kill and the hoarse, guttural, langur alarm-cry issued from his lips as he stood on his hind-legs high up on a branch to discover if possible in which direction the killer was moving.

"Ha-aah! Harr! Harr!" called the watchman, over and over again. The langurs ceased playing and scampered in terror, to huddle in families on the tree-tops; while the deer and other creatures on the floor of the jungle, whose sharp ears had detected the sounds of death and the alarm of the monkeys, raced uphill and away from that valley of doom.

Time passed, and the life of the forest resumed its normal course. The birds forgot the tragedy in a matter of seconds; the monkeys and the other animals took perhaps an hour to calm down; while the Poojarees in the distant hamlet of Manchi would undoubtedly have forgotten the death of their clansman Keera in a month or two had not another of them been killed a fortnight later; and, ten days after that, a third.

These things the Poojarees could not forget. A dreadful

fear overshadowed them. A scourge lay upon their tiny village; a man-eater had come to stay!

These people belong to a tribe that lives on the produce of the forest. They gather wild-honey from giant combs built on high rocks and trees; they catch the iguana-lizard which they eat or sell for the aphrodisiac properties said to exist in its tail; they pick medicinal herbs and roots and berries which are traded as medicine; and they cut and collect bamboos, grass and the pods of the tamarind fruit, according to the season of the year. All for a pittance, less than an ordinary person living in Europe or America would spend on feeding his pet dog. Their work, their very existence depends upon the forest, and into that jungle a fearful menace had now come. No man who left his miserable grass hut in the morning knew whether he would return that night. No woman or child was safe; for the second and third victims had been, respectively, a young girl of nine years and a pregnant bride of fourteen!

None of them did anything about it except one man, and that was my old friend and instructor in jungle-lore, Byra the Poojaree. Once before had he summoned me, in the case of the "Marauder of Kempekarai," about which I have written elsewhere,* and once again he asked me to come to the help of the people of Manchi.

This time Byra arrived in person rather than convey the message through another. He walked ten miles or more from Manchi to Aiyur village, and thence nine miles to Denkanikota town, whence a bus brought him to Bangalore.

From the story he told me it was clear that the three killings had taken place in comparatively quick succession, within a total of twenty-four days and all within a radius of four miles from Manchi, in the vicinity of the track leading

---

* See *Man-eaters and Jungle Killers*, Chapter 1.

from Aiyur to Kempekarai along the deep valley that I have elsewhere referred to as "Spider Valley," because of the large spiders to be found there.

These killings indicated that the perpetrator was a comparative novice so far as man-eaters go. Either he was a young animal that had, for some reason or the other, just launched out on a career of man-eating; or he was a wounded tiger that had been almost incapacitated and was desperately hungry; or perhaps a tigress, killing merely to feed her cubs. This third alternative was extremely unlikely, as there was still a fair amount of game on the surrounding hills, while cattle were plentiful around the villages of Aiyur, Gulhati and Bettamugalam.

The facts pointed more to his being a beginner. No experienced man-eater would have killed in such quick succession or almost in the same place, as had this tiger. Veterans are far too cunning to do that. They follow a circuitous beat of many miles, covering a large tract of land, and slay at sudden and infrequent intervals, all of which habits combine to make them extremely difficult to shoot.

The course for me to follow would be to strike quickly and bag this beast before he began to learn from experience and became more cautious and adept. That caution would come as soon as the villagers tried to retaliate by shooting him or by some other means. He would be frightened then; or perhaps he would be wounded. That would make him a wiser and far more dangerous antagonist.

I knew the terrain well. For many years I had tramped that dense bamboo jungle in the deep, narrow valley flanked by the two parallel ranges of towering hills, running north and south, closely bordering the banks of the narrow stream that also flowed southwards to merge finally into the Chinar River at a place called Sopathy. The eastern range was the loftier of the two, culminating in a high peak named Gutherayan, near which was a picturesque forest bungalow known as the Kodekarai Forest Lodge. Kempekarai hamlet lay on the slopes of the other and western range, a short distance above the little stream. The locale was almost the same as in my earlier adventure, except that the "Marauder of Kempekarai" had been a more experienced man-eater, hunting in an area west and south of the little hamlet of that name. The present animal had so far confined his activities to the north of the settlement of Manchi and near to the Aiyur track, as I have just told you. For this reason he should be a comparatively easy proposition to bag.

Bundling Byra and my camp-kit into the Studebaker, with food to last for about a week in the form of flour for chappattis, bread, butter, vegetables — especially potatoes — and of course tea, coffee and sugar, together with my little tent and bed-roll, we set out for Denkanikota and Aiyur. From the latter place we would have to walk to Manchi and that would mean that Byra and I must carry the load for upwards of ten miles. Fortunately, it would be downhill for most of the way going, but uphill coming back.

As far as possible, I avoid tinned foods on these excursions. I grant that they are convenient to transport. But like the villagers of India I like my food fresh and simple. Thereby I have contrived to avoid much indigestion and the other stomach troubles that appear to afflict half the sophisticated people of the world. Indians and Europeans alike.

I put my tent on Byra's head, slung the bed-roll on to my back, piled the kit-bag with the flour and vegetables on his, and carried the rest of the things, including the rifles, myself. I can assure you we were well weighed down, but Byra seemed to feel no inconvenience as he strode rapidly along in front of me.

The valley was hot and humid and I was bathed in perspiration. While my companion was exposed to greater risk from a wild elephant by walking in front, I was in more danger from the tiger, as man-eaters invariably attack the last person on the trail. In both cases, heavily burdened as we were, neither of us would have been able to do much about it. But I don't think we thought about elephants or tigers, being more bent upon reaching the journey's end as quickly as possible and ridding ourselves of our abominable loads.

We arrived at last, and with a sigh of relief I threw down the things I was carrying (except the rifle) just beyond the little pool of drinking-water that was to figure so prominently in this adventure. The first requirement was tea — gallons of it — and I asked Byra to fill the kettle from the pool and light a fire quickly. Very soon we were pouring scalding tea down our throats and life seemed to be rosy once more.

By this time some of Byra's friends from the hamlet had gathered around us. They were all Poojarees — an underfed, skinny and scantily-clad group — but all as tough as nails. The men wore little moochas and nothing else; the women were bare-breasted, the rest covered by threadbare saris that hung in shreds and hid nothing; the children, both boys and girls, were completely naked.

There were the usual greetings, whereupon Byra launched into a prolonged account of how he had travelled to Bangalore to bring his *dorai*, who had immediately come to their help. There was a murmur of amazement and, being of a practical turn of mind, I took advantage of the situation to despatch some of the elder boys to gather firewood from the brambles growing around the pool, and one of the men to lay in a store of water in the aluminium carrier and the water-bottle I had brought with me. These mundane but essential matters attended to, I set about munching the roasted meat, jam and buttered bread brought from home, while I asked my companions to tell me all they knew about the tiger.

I acquired little information other than the bare facts that Byra had already recounted, but there was one new item. Byra had set forth for Bangalore the previous morning. In the early afternoon of the same day, as nobody would go near the pool later than three o'clock for fear of the man-eater, four of the women had gone for water together. They had kept close to one another, relying on their numbers for safety.

The women had finished the task and were turning away when the eldest noticed a slight movement under one of the bushes bordering the jungle some fifty yards away. She looked closer. Her companions, noticing her staring at something, had all looked the same way. On the ground under that bush was the head of an enormous tiger. It was glaring at them hungrily and snarling! With screams they threw down their water-pots and bolted for the hamlet, less than 200 yards away. This time the tiger did not attack and they all got back in safety.

Two of those four women were among the group around me. One described the tiger's head as "that big," indicating a distance of a yard between outstretched hands. The other, who was a very matter-of-fact and comely young girl, and somewhat of a wit to boot, said it was big enough to eat all four of them and me as well. Her subtle smile after this statement was perhaps a hint that, after it was all over, I would at least be in good company inside the tiger's belly!

The news gladdened me and I noticed the gleam of satisfaction that sprang into Byra's eyes. Old hunter that he was, he knew that things would be easier for us now. If the tiger was there yesterday evening, as likely as not it would come again this evening. For all we knew, it might be watching us at that very moment.

This fresh development made me change my mind about pitching my tent near the pool. It would not fit into the plan that now came to my mind. To make camp within the hamlet itself was a far from attractive proposition, as the Poojarees, who have many good attributes, do not count cleanliness among them. So I got some of the men to carry my things a little beyond the village, to where a wild jack-fruit tree was growing. Beneath its shade I pitched the small tent and put my belongings inside.

The plan that had come to me connected the tiger with the pool. Strange, indeed, that a situation of this nature should be twice destined to arise in waiting for a man-eater. In that earlier adventure at Kempekarai, just a few miles away but many years ago, I had waited all night long at a well for the "marauder" to make an attempt to kill me. But I had waited in vain. Perhaps this tiger, which was certainly not such an experienced animal, would be more obliging and I was glad I had not made the mistake of pitching my tent, that was more or less white in colour, within sight of the pool. Whereas the "marauder" of years ago might have been tempted to attack the occupant, this recruit among man-eaters would surely be frightened away. Or so I reasoned, and Byra agreed with me. Events that night were to prove both of us quite wrong.

At sunset I ate an early supper, finishing the last of the roast I had brought. This time I made no tea and drank hardly any water, for experience had taught me that imbibing liquids does not help when a night-long vigil for a man-eater is contemplated. Nature cannot be diverted from her normal practices, and the slightest fidgeting or movement on the part of the hunter will betray his presence to the tiger when he comes.

The night would be dark, for which reason I did not follow quite the same plan as I had with the "marauder." That had been a moonlit night and I had deliberately advertised my presence at the well by working the squeaking pulley and pretending to draw water in order to attract the tiger. But this night would be totally dark and it would be foolish to show myself openly. He would hear and see me all right; the only trouble being that I certainly would not be able to see him, and might not be able to hear him either till it was too late!

So I decided to modify the scheme a little by sitting with my back against to babul tree some twenty feet from the water and facing the jungle. I would sit quite still and with no movement whatever. The man-eater could hardly attack from the rear. He would have to come from in front or from either side and sitting motionless would not only help me to hear him but it would puzzle him also. He might not notice me at all; or if he did, as a novice he would be perplexed at my immobility and decide to investigate. I hoped he would make some sound in the process.

When Byra heard my plan, he told me that it was a very stupid one. The tiger might attack without making any preliminary sound. He might come from behind. I would hear nothing and see nothing in that darkness; but the man-eater would certainly see me, while he (Byra) would never see me again. For that matter, the tiger might not come this way at all. Why should he be snooping around a pool of water at dead of night? The beast knew very well that people drew water from it — but during the hours of daylight and not at night.

While he was speaking, Byra looked at me significantly, and the meaning of his glance became quite apparent. He was trying to put me off.

"I know all that," I interrupted testily, but it's the only way.

The old fellow was bent upon complicating the situation.

"I never meant that you should not sit for the tiger." he said aggressively. "What I meant was that you should be beside me. We should await his return together."

"Idiot," I interrupted, being as rude as I could, "you have not the brains of a flea! In what way will your presence lessen the darkness? Keep out of this and let me try the plan I have in mind, at least for tonight. Tomorrow you may tell me a better one if you can think of one."

"If you are here to listen," he concluded pointedly.

And so, an hour before sunset, I took up my position near the little pool, my back to the babul tree and facing the jungle, the small stream beyond and the pathway along which we had come that morning. Inwardly, I hoped that the tiger would arrive early and see me and that in turn he would show himself as he had to the four girls, so that the episode might be closed before darkness fell. Unfortunately, the man-eater did not oblige.

The Poojarees in the hamlet drew great clumps of thorns, which they had cut earlier, around the low entrances to their wattle huts, stepped gingerly between them and slipped inside. I could hear the thatched doors of the huts being barricaded from within with large stones, gathered from the stream for the purpose. These people believed in self-help, and it was evident they did not have much confidence in my ability to save them from the killer that now threatened their lives.

The sun had sunk behind the range of hills to the west, outlining their heights against a background of blue, which turned to pink and then to orange. As I was facing north-east, I could just catch brief glimpses of the beauties of this sunset. The orange deepened to blood-red, and then to crimson, green and yellow and violet and purple. An instant later it was quite dark.

While I had been watching the sunset abstractly, I had

been listening to the sounds of the jungle which at all times are pleasant music to my ears, particularly at the close of the day and again at dawn. Two families of langur-monkeys, one on each of the slopes of the opposing ranges of hills, called to each other across the narrow, deep valley. "Whoomp! Whoomp! Whoomp!" cried the males of one batch as they leapt from branch to branch, and back came the joyous notes from the other group on the hill slopes across the stream: "Whoomp! Whoomp! Whoomp!" and "Cheek! Cheek!" from the females and young.

Then the sounds of pleasure suddenly turned to those of fear and danger as the monkey-watchman of the more distant clan issued his staccato barking alarm cry: "Ha-aah! Harr! Harr!" which he continued to repeat at short intervals.

The group nearer to me and on the same side of the valley fell silent, while their watchman in turn took up the note of warning, answering the more distant calls of his colleague: "Haaah! Harr! Harr!" The two monkey sentinels kept answering one another and my nerves tingled pleasantly in expectation.

To one accustomed to such sounds there was a wealth of difference in the timbre of the calls. The voice of the distant watchman was filled with great fear and apprehension, and it was evident that he could see the source of danger. The watchman on this side of the valley, although sounding the alarm also, was merely doing his duty to alert his tribe. His notes were flat and matter of fact. This could be detected by the fact that he called each time immediately after the other watchman, like an echo.

The calls of the two monkeys were becoming less frequent when a jungle cock, somewhere on the stream, screamed suddenly in fright: "Kuck! Kuck! Kuck!" The hen with him, hearing the cries of fright made by her mate, flew quickly away crying: "Krr-r-r-r! Keek! Keek! Keek!" Silence and a great stillness enveloped the jungle. Then a peacock gave sign of nervousness; "Quank! Quank! Quank!" His metallic notes broke the stillness and a moment later I could hear the distant heavy flapping of wings as he launched his weighty body into the air to reach a place of greater safety.

I knew the tiger was afoot! He had descended the opposite range of hills and been discovered by the distant langur-watchman. He had crossed the stream and disturbed the jungle fowls and the peacock. He was now coming straight towards the pool and the spot where I was seated.

It was growing darker with the passing of each minute. Would the keen eyes of the nearer langur-watchman detect him? Although the monkey had the advantage of elevation, he was comparatively far away, and no tiger — not even a beginner among man-eaters — will betray his presence unnecessarily. My doubt was settled the next instant when the watchman on the hillside to my left broke forth hysterically, fearfully: "Ha-aah! Harr! Harr!" His cries were quick now, and independent of his distant colleague, who was still calling, but at long intervals. The note of fear was there this time — of danger and sudden death. He had seen the man-eater. And it was much closer to me than I had thought.

But of the tiger itself I could see or hear nothing. It was growing darker all the time. The bushes at the edge of the jungle before me had lost their individual outlines. They appeared as grey masses against a background of deep chocolate, turning rapidly black. A frightened hush fell over the forest, permeating it, enveloping it. The further langur-watchman had stopped calling altogether, and the nearer one barked only intermittently. He could see the tiger no longer and, having fulfilled his duty by alarming his tribe, was wondering what next to do about it.

The summits of the ranges of hills to my right and left showed themselves as ragged lines of intense blackness against a background of lesser darkness, studded by a myriad of stars, flashing and blazing in a distant glory all their own. I concentrated upon one of them. It seemed to change its colours constantly, like a heavenly gem.

While staring into the blackness before me I glanced alternatively from right to left. I slowed my breathing, even tried to hold my breath altogether, in an effort to hear the very faintest of sounds. But I saw and heard nothing.

Then, with nerve-shattering abruptness, a sambar belled in the thickets just the other side of the pool: "Dhank! Oonk! Oonk!"

The brambles crackled to his departure as he crashed his way through. The sounds of his running were lost in a few seconds, but he continued to call with alarm as he rattled over the pebbles in the stream and scrambled up the slopes of the opposing range of hills, "Oonk! Oonk! Oonk!" came his cries as they grew fainter with the ever-increasing distance.

Grateful, indeed, was I for the warnings of my jungle friends, for they told me as unmistakably as if I had seen him with my own eyes that the tiger was within a few yards of where I was sitting. The questions were: Had he seen me? Would he see me?

I know the value of stillness in the jungle, and so I sat absolutely motionless, hardly daring to breathe. That was my only hope of escaping the tiger's immediate attention.

The seconds ticked interminably by. They appeared to pass into minutes and then into hours, though I knew that they were only seconds. Then I heard a gentle rustle to my right: the faintest of sounds, as of a leaf being turned over, and it came from a direction in line with the pool. Not a breath of air passed which could have caused that dry leaf to be moved and I knew that the author of the sound was moving through the undergrowth, hidden from my sight, and passing the pool at that moment, and that in a few moments more he would have passed behind me.

Holding my breath I listened intently, but I heard no further sound. Every instinct warned me that the tiger had now passed and was somewhere behind the bushes on the other side of the babul tree against which I was leaning. I was filled with an urge to turn around and face the danger, but I knew that if I did so I would certainly make some faint noise. However slight it might be, the tiger would hear it and in all probability would turn to investigate. So I overcame the urge, but turned my head around to see if the beast was creeping upon me from the rear. All I could see was the trunk of the babul tree only a few inches away, and beyond that darkness.

I do not know for how long I endured this suspense, but suddenly the silence was shattered by the high-pitched, fear-laden yelping bark of a village dog in the Poojaree hamlet so close behind me. The tension was relieved for the moment and I breathed more easily. Two things were evident to me now. The tiger had passed the well without detecting my presence, and had gone towards the wattle huts, obviously in search of human prey. Secondly, and beyond any doubt, it was the man-eater, as no ordinary tiger would deliberately wander near human habitation.

At that moment a perfectly silly notion entered my head. I reasoned that I could achieve no useful purpose by remaining where I was. Assuming that the man-eater did not succeed in finding a human victim, there was little chance that he would retrace his steps and pass the pool again. He might wander away in any direction, while if he did return, he would come upon me from the rear and this time he might not fail to detect my presence.

I cannot tell you, however, why I did not think of doing the most obvious thing; just sit where I was, but facing the hamlet. Instead, I made up my mind to go towards the hamlet myself, shine my torch when I came close enough, and pick up the glare of the tiger's eyes in its beam. That should afford me an easy shot.

This was a silly thing to do. Had I remained where I was, the tiger might have returned to drink at the pool, while I would have been in a fair position, behind the stem of the babul tree, for an easy shot. Instead, I got stealthily to my feet, and in a half-crouching position, started advancing towards the hamlet which, as I have already told you, was hardly 200 yards away.

Within a few steps I realized my foolishness, for although there was a well-defined pathway leading from the huts to the pool, in the intense darkness I could not see it and began stumbling among the bushes, making enough noise to scare away the man-eater or urge him to attack. I then thought of going back to the friendly babul, but again decided to advance, this time with the full knowledge that the man-eater might be five yards away, behind any bush, and I would not be able to see it.

The hysterical barking of the cur was taken up by others of its kind, and by now some half-dozen village dogs were yowling their heads off in a perfect frenzy, making enough noise to unnerve the boldest of man-eaters. It was extremely doubtful that the tiger would pursue his original intentions in the face of this din; he would either slink off or turn back. And if he did turn back, he would run into me, face to face, at any moment.

With this thought in mind, I made the second mistake of

the evening. I switched on my torch — far too soon, as it turned out! As the bright beam cut through the darkness the tiger, of which I did not catch a glimpse, true to the cowardly code of most man-eaters, roared shatteringly from somewhere in front, and I could hear him crashing into the dry scrub beyond.

There was no point in further caution. My quarry had fled and I followed the torch-beam dejectedly towards the Poojarees' wattle huts while cursing myself repeatedly for the idiot I had been. Upon reaching the hamlet, I called softly to Byra, who emerged from one of the huts. He had been awake and had listened to the alarm-cries of the langurs at sunset, followed by those other sounds. The barking of the dogs had mystified him till the tiger had roared. Only then had he realized that the man-eater was in the village itself. He was even more surprised at finding me there also.

Quickly I related what had happened and was not comforted with Byra's brief comment, heavy with sarcasm. "Did the *dorai* think he was following a rabbit? Perhaps the years have affected his wisdom!"

It was now just after eight o'clock, and with nothing better to do, I walked to my tent, which you will remember I had pitched under the jack-fruit tree beyond the village, lit the small hurricane lantern hanging from the ventral pole, and made myself a pot of tea. That done, I closed and fastened the flap of the tent, spread my bedding on the ground, not having burdened myself with the weight of a camp-cot, extinguished the lantern because I do not like sleeping with a light burning, and was soon fast asleep.

Something awakened me with a start. In the jungle one does not wake as city folk usually do from the snug warmth of a comfortable bed, to yawn and stretch in luxury and maybe spend another five minutes contemplating with dismay the tasks that have to be performed. The forest teaches its inhabitants to sleep alert. When they awaken, they are keyed to instant action, for a second's delay may be their last.

When I opened my eyes, the vague feeling of danger that filled my mind synchronized with my groping hand and outstretched fingers as they fumbled for the rifle I had placed loaded on the ground beside me. Its comforting hardness brought assurance as I sat up to discover what had awakened me with that urgent, oppressive sense of peril.

For a second I could hear nothing, and then came the faintest of scratching sounds, which stopped and started again after a moment or two — scrape, scrape — stop — scratch, scratch — silence, and then once more. The side of the tent moved slightly and something entered from underneath; something that groped about here and there with a sinister purpose. Was it a snake?

That something encountered the edge of my bedding as it lay on the ground to my left barely a foot away, became entangled with it, and pulled away sharply, wrenching canvas and groundsheet with a sharp, tearing noise. Claws! The man-eater was outside!

He had sensed the presence of a human being within the tent, but fortunately, with no knowledge of its flimsy structure, had tried to feel with his paw under the canvas and along the ground in the hope of reaching his prey, whom he would drag out before the victim was aware of what was happening.

A neat little plan, indeed; the only fault being that the victim was myself! Fortunate, indeed, that a premonition of terrible danger had awakened me in time.

I quickly pulled the rifle across my body as I lay on the ground, pointing the muzzle towards where I knew the tiger must be, and slid my right hand towards the trigger.

Remember, it was pitch dark in the tent when this happened

and I did not know exactly where, and in what position the tiger was standing outside. I waited for the next movement and it came again as the groping paw wrenched once more at the bedroll.

Then I pressed the trigger!

There was a deafening explosion and I scrambled to my feet, working the underlever of the .405 Winchester feverishly to fire two more shots blindly through the canvas side of my tent.

There was no sound from the tiger. Was it dead? Even so, it should have uttered a last gasp or gurgle. Was it wounded? Then surely it would have roared with pain. Had it got away? I must have missed. That could be the only explanation for the unaccountable silence.

Like a fool I had once again made an inexcusable mistake. My torch was clamped to the rifle. Why had I not switched it on for a brief moment before firing? A second or two of torchlight would have sufficed to indicate the direction from which that groping paw was coming and where the tiger was standing outside the tent. Instead I had pressed the trigger blindly in total darkness; three times, moreover, hoping to hit an animal whose whereabouts I did not know.

With torch alight, I hastily opened the tapes closing the entrance to the tent and stepped forth cautiously, to direct the torchbeam in every direction. As I had already guessed, the man-eater had escaped, nor was there the slightest sound to indicate in which direction he had fled.

My three shots had awakened the Poojarees in Manchi hamlet. I could hear the voices of Byra and some others calling anxiously, inquiring if all was well. Knowing that if I did not go to them soon, the poor felows would brave the darkness and come to find out what had happened, I walked the short distance to the huts by torchlight and told a huddled, frightened group of little jungle men just what had taken place.

They insisted in coming back with me right away to see the three bullet holes in the canvas of my tent for themselves, and the ragged edges in my bedding made by the tiger's claws. They called loudly upon God in thanks for protecting me. Then I had to leave them back at the hamlet, where Byra implored me to share the hut in which he slept for the rest of the night and not risk going back to my tent.

But this invitation I declined and marched back once again, and lay down to continue a much disturbed sleep this time with the hurricane lantern brightly burning. Sheer disgust with myself and things in general caused me to awaken long after sunrise. Voices outside greeted me, and opening the tent-flap I found all the Poojarees from the hamlet squatting around in a semi-circle.

The reason for their visit was a simple one. My foolish actions of the previous evening and night, and the misses I had made with the three shots I had fired, was to be explained in just two words, both of them very simple: black magic! Someone had cast a spell upon me and my rifle, so that I and the weapon did not act in coordination. Who had done it? Why? When? How? The spell would have to be removed if I hoped to kill the man-eater.

Superstition of this sort is rife amongst the simple people of the Indian forests, and large numbers of town-folk as well. I knew that no amount of reasoning, persuasion of argument would make the Poojarees thinks otherwise. If I ignored their belief, they would just cease co-operating with me, and then blame my failure on the spell that had been cast on me and my weapon. The shortest and easiest way was to agree.

I said, "Yes; some misbegotten son of a ... has cast a spell without doubt. Will you please remove it, if you can?"

In turn, the eldest among them replied, "Yes, but it will cost five rupees to do this," going on to explain that this sum covered the cost of a fowl that had to be sacrificed, and various other articles, together with the fee for performing the pooja.

I agreed again, paid the five rupees, and went inside the tent to snatch another hour of sleep. But disgust with myself prevented me from sleeping and I fell to thinking about the man-eater. The raucous screeching of an unfortunate chicken having its throat cut, followed by the acrid smell of smoke and incense, announced that pooja was being performed.

In due course Byra's voice called to me from without: "*Dorai! Dorai!* Wake up and come out. The spell is broken. Let us search for the tiger now. We will surely find him, and this time he will fall to your rifle with a single shot, for the weapon will obey your command."

The pooja was not quite complete, however. The grey-beard, who was also the sorcerer of the hamlet, asked for my rifle. Laying it on the ground he made various marks in red and white, using *konkam* powder and lime (*chunam*) respectively, on both sides of the stock. The entrails of the chicken were next looped into a circle and passed up and down the length of the barrel half-a-dozen times to the accompaniment of muttered mantras and some more incense smoke. Finally he scattered the fire in four directions, calling loudly to the tiger to come forth and be shot.

The sun was high in the sky by the time all this was over. Byra and a Poojaree lad of about twenty years of age, who turned out to be the grandson of the old man who had conducted the pooja, then invited me to accompany them into the forest in search of the man-eater. As everybody knows, to look for a tiger in any jungle, especially a man-eater, by walking about in broad daylight is not only hopeless but foolish and a waste of time. My regard for Byra's jungle-craft was boundless, but that a hunter of his experience could lend himself to this sort of foolishness surprised me.

My looks must have shown my disapproval, but Byra and the lad together urged me to waste no further time in idle talk. Evidently they had implicit faith in their sorcerer. We started, Byra leading, then me and next the boy, but as soon as we were out of sight of the hamlet I insisted on altering this marching order and exchanged places with Muthu, for that was the lad's name. If the man-eater did see us, regardless of all the hocuspocus that had just been performed, the chances were that, like all man-eaters, this one would decide to attack the last individual in the line of march, and the unarmed youngster would not have a chance.

We walked downhill to the stream-bed where we cast around in the loose, dry sand for recent tracks. Difficult as it always is in such terrain to differentiate between fresh and old spoors, the two Poojarees were not long in finding the tiger's tracks where he had approached the pool, with me sitting near it, the previous night a little later, and nearly a furlong away, they found his trail again, this time leading away from the village. Whether this was the spoor left by the tiger when my light near the hamlet had alarmed him, or later on after I had fired my three shots through the tent, was settled by the fact that the scooping out of the grains of sand at the toe portions of the tracks, and the marks of all four feet separately on the ground, showed that our quarry was moving very fast when he made them, with no attempt at concealment or caution. Evidently he was hurrying away after being badly frightened and this appeared to indicate we were following the trail left by the man-eater after I had fired those foolish shots. The absence of blood anywhere confirmed that he was uninjured.

We had not gone far when the trail veered abruptly to the right and led straight up the hillside on the eastern bank of the stream. I remembered that this was the direction from which the monkey-watchman of the first batch of langurs had voiced his alarm the evening before, when the tiger was descending the hill. Now the tiger had returned the same way. Very probably his lair was in a cave somewhere higher up that hill, or perhaps some distance further away, on the slopes of the Gutherayan mountain.

With this discovery came difficulties. The ground became hard and stony once we had traversed the low-lying belt of bamboos. Clumps of spear-grass grew in between rocks and small boulders and all signs of pug-marks vanished entirely.

The two Poojarees, experts though they were in woodcraft, were soon at a complete loss. They moved around in small circles, trying to pick up trail. At times Byra, and then his young companion, would come upon a broken stem of grass or an over-turned stone that showed the way the tiger had gone. But this was not for long and very soon they were forced to a halt. Beyond knowing that the tiger had gone up the hill, we had no further indication of his whereabouts.

We discussed the matter in whispers and decided to climb the hill ourselves in the vague hope of coming upon a cave of some sort in which the man-eater might be hiding. To proceed in single file meant covering only a single line of advance, so we decided to fan out slightly in order to search a wider area. Byra went about a hundred yards to my right but remained within sight, while Muthu moved off about the same distance to my left. Then the three of us started to advance cautiously.

The ground became more stony and the boulders increased in size and number, but we came across no signs of a lair. The hillock we were climbing might have been about 500 feet high, but in due course we reached the top and were able to look down the other side. Here the ground dropped sharply to a lush valley, thickly covered with bamboo, before it started to climb the next foothill. Above that hill rose the peak of the Gutherayan mountain.

At a signal from me, and maintaining the same distance apart, the three of us began the steep descent. On this side the hillock was more fertile. There were fewer rocks and boulders, larger and taller clumps of grass, and even bushes and stunted trees that increased in number till we had reached the region of bamboos, where we found ourselves in a green twilit valley beneath the towering fronds. Now we could not longer see each other, and very soon I felt that my companions, unarmed as they were, had exposed themselves to terrible risk, for I could not help them should the tiger decide to attack. The bamboos and heavy jungle afforded ample cover and even the keen eyes of the two aborigines could not possibly penetrate the green wall that enveloped the three of us.

It was as if this thought gave rise to action, for just then I heard a shrill scream of terror from the Poojaree boy, who was about a hundred yards to my left. This was followed by short, sharp "woofs" as the tiger charged him. The roars ended abruptly when Byra, to my right, gave voice to a volley of shouts. Knowing he was doing this in an attempt to frighten off the attacker I added my yells to his as I turned and crashed towards the spot from which the scream and the roars had come.

Short as the distance was, Byra had caught up with me before we found the lad. He was lying on his face just beyond a pile of boulders and long grass, the back of his skull crushed in, while deep fang marks at the base of the neck and over the right shoulder showed where the tiger had first bitten him before smashing his skull with a stroke of the paw. Possibly the man-eater had been seized by a mixture of fear and rage at hearing our shouts, intended, as I have told you, to save the boy's life. But in this instance they had sealed his fate, for the tiger had killed him.

The flattened grass on the opposite side of the pile of boulders showed where the man-eater had been hiding, waiting till the lad had passed before pouncing upon him from behind. We turned the young Poojaree over and were confronted by a ghastly spectacle. The force of the blow upon the back of his head had caused the eyeballs to protrude, while the boy had bitten through his own tongue so that the end hung loosely from his mouth, held by a shred of flesh. Blood seeped into the sand where it was forming a little pool.

Shaken and feeling sick, I turned to my companion. His jet-black face had turned to an ashen hue and his features worked violently with emotion. But not a word did he say. Nor did I. What was there to say? We — and most certainly I — could only blame ourselves for our carelessness and for exposing this unarmed youth to the fiendish cunningness of the tiger.

My watch showed it was just eleven o'clock and the sun beat mercilessly down upon the scene.

It took some minutes to recover from the shock.

Then I said, "You were so sure that we would kill the tiger after that silly pooja. Instead, he has slain one of us!"

Byra did not answer at once. When he spoke there was resentment in his tone. "The sorcerer should have sacrificed a cock. Instead, he slew a hen, for the hen cost him a rupee less. But it has cost his grandson his life!"

I was scarcely listening. An idea had flashed into my mind. I walked through the long grass to the boulders, stepped on one, and looked back at the body. Barely ten yards! The distance was almost too close. There were only four boulders lying haphazardly together, and the largest of them, the one on which I stood, was about three feet high. The others were much smaller.

The idea then became a definite plan. Since there were already some stones on the spot, would the tiger notice if a few more were added? Perhaps not, provided the extra stones were so placed as not to give rise to undue suspicion.

I turned to Byra and said, "The night will be dark and this will tempt the devil we are after to return to his kill early, provided we leave the body where it is. For he is hungry, remember. He was hungry last night. That was why he went so boldly to the huts at Manchi. And he has not eaten since then. Tonight he will be very hungry indeed. So we will bring some more boulders to add to these four and make a hide in which I will sit. At this close range, when my torchlight falls upon him, I cannot miss."

"*Dorai* you're completely mad," commented the old hunter. "As soon as he sees the hide he'll suspect something. Perhaps he may go away. Maybe not! If he should spring over the boulders, he will be on top of you before you know where you are."

"Besides," he continued, "it's our duty to return to Manchi and tell that rascally grandfather what has happened to the poor boy. Then the men from the village will come and bear his body away and burn it tonight. Thus his soul will gain peace. If we leave his remains here to be eaten by the tiger, and not burn them, the soul will wander in these jungles and torment us for failing to do our duty."

"The tiger will not eat them," I cut in sharply, "for I will be among the boulders to prevent him. That I promise you. Is this not a good chance to be avenged upon this devil? If I succeed in slaying him tonight, will I not save many lives, perhaps your own among them? As a hunter yourself, don't you agree it would be foolish for us to lose such a golden opportunity?"

Byra did not reply. I could feel him weakening. Finally he looked at me and there was complete innocence in his expression.

"We've searched everywhere and cannot find the body, *dorai*. Let's go back now and inform the others. Tomorrow morning we will search again. Tonight you will sit at the side of some jungle path to await the tiger, should he pass by, while I will perch like a monkey on a tree, out of sight but not out of hearing, in case you should need my help."

Thus Byra settled the issue with his conscience and we got to work in right earnest.

In order not to arouse the tiger's suspicion, we moved quite 200 yards away to another area strewn with boulders, big and small. Together we carried half a dozen of the larger ones, one at a time, and placed them in a rough circle with the four boulders that were already there. On this foundation we placed smaller stones, so that in time we had built a circular wall maybe three feet high. I realized it would not do to make this wall any higher, for the additional safety thus gained would be of no avail should the tiger become suspicious on seeing a construction before him that had not been there on his last visit.

Next, into crevices between the stones we stuck handfuls of the tough grass which we tore from tufts and clumps growing some distance away. All this took a long time and was strenuous work, for you must realize the sun beat down on us mercilessly, and the stones and the grass had to be brought from a distance to avoid creating suspicion.

When we left Manchi that morning, boosted by the sorcerer's confidence that we would kill the tiger, I had brought only my rifle and no torch or water-bottle. It would be dangerous to send Byra back alone to fetch these things. Either we would both have to go back, or I could go myself and leave the Poojaree up a tree, and if I did that there was always the chance that the tiger might return during my absence and carry away the cadaver of the unfortunate boy to some more remote spot where it would be difficult for us to find it again.

After considering all these factors in whispers, we decided that we had no choice but to take up our positions straight away. I within the small three-foot fort we had constructed and Byra on some tree within hearing distance, and remain in our places till next morning, in the hope that the man-eater would remember his human victim and come back for a meal. We could only hope that the tiger had not been in hiding within hearing distance all this while, for then our movements during the past three hours would undoubtedly have alarmed him and he would have moved off long ago, not to return. Our only chance of success lay in the hope that he might have gone higher up the hill in search of water and had not heard us. It was most unlikely that he had returned to the stream in the valley for, as I have told you, it was quite dry at this time of the year.

We cast around in a wide circle for a suitable tree for Byra, and came upon one about half-a-furlong away, slightly lower down the hill from the spot where the boy had been killed. This was a fairly large tamarind and offered ample scope for the old Poojaree to shelter in comfortably till I called him next morning.

It was two-fifteen in the afternoon, perhaps the hottest time of day, when Byra climbed the tamarind after earnestly advising me to be careful and not fall asleep at any cost. Leaving him there, I returned to my little fort, scrambled over the scorching stones we had placed there to form the wall, and tried to settle down inside. I at once encountered the first difficulty. The ground was so hot that I could not sit on it, but had to remain crouched on my haunches. Apart from being a painful and uncomfortable posture, the wall was not high enough for it. My head showed above the top and would be easily seen from outside, so I had to sit with head bowed to try to conceal myself.

It did not take me long to realize that such a position was absurd and dangerous, for I would not be able to see the tiger should he creep upon me.

I got out of the hide then, walked some distance away, and plucked several handfuls of tough grass stems which I stuck very closely together into the pugaree of my "Gurkha" hat. This took a little time, but I was satisfied with the task eventually. When seen from a distance, there was no hat to be seen, only another clump of grass.

Donning the hat, I returned within my fort of stones, crouched once more on my haunches and attempted to remain motionless. I was just able to look over the rim of the rocks in a half-circle, before and to both sides of me, and by turning my head ever so slowly to right and left, I could even see behind. This movement would not be very noticeable, I felt, as the whole "clump" of grass on my hat would turn with it and might be mistaken by the tiger for the effect of the hot breeze that was blowing from the valley and the stream-bed towards the hill-tops and was rippling the bowed heads of the dried grass in waves from time to time.

I soon found that I could not remain still in that crouching posture for very long. My ankles became painful and the calves of my legs became numb. I had to move this way and that, slowly and a little at a time, till after four o'clock, when the earth cooled sufficiently to allow me to sit down.

Up to this time the surroundings had been abnormally silent. Not an animal or bird had indicated its presence by sight or sound. All creation — and no doubt the tiger, too — was sheltering from the devastating heat. Only twice had I seen movement, firstly when a giant iguana lizard attempted to cross, caught sight of Muthu's body on the ground, turned abruptly and scrambled away, and later, when a small python, hanging unnoticed head downwards from a low tree, had dropped upon a passing ground squirrel to crush it to death. I had seen the squirrel, but had not noticed the snake till I saw the python's coils squirming in the grass and heard the squeaks of the victim being crushed to death.

There was a marked cooling of the air by five o'clock and this reminded me that I had drunk no water since morning. There was not a drop to drink anyhow, and worst of all, I would have to remain thirsty till I returned to Manchi the following morning — a truly formidable thought!

A partridge on the hillside to my left broke the long silence at last "Kee-kok-kik! Kee-kok-kok! Kee-kok-kok!" he called in challenge and within minutes came the acceptance to a fight from another male bird slightly higher up the hill: "Kee-kok-kok! Kee-kok-kok! Kee-kok-kok!"

The two partridges challenged each other frequently as they drew closer together, hastening to the fray, till finally they met. Then with hysterical cries of "Kok! Kok! Kok!", the duel started in earnest. Unfortunately I could not see the birds but could picture the battle in my imagination for the ten minutes or so that it lasted, before one of the contestants gave way to the superior prowess and stamina of his adversary. He flew helter-skelter from the scene of battle. I was just able to glimpse his brown form sailing precipitately downhill to safety, while the other bird remained to voice the victory cry "Kee-kok-kok! Kee-kok-kok! Kee-kok-kik!" once again.

The battle of the partridges had served to while away the time. It was now 5-40 p.m. and the calls of jungle-cocks from the stream-bed in the valley rose to announce the advent of eventide. "Wheew! Kuck-kya-kya-kuckm!" they crowed from down below, to be answered by other cocks on the hillsides in all directions. Occasionally a pea-fowl voiced its meowing cry, while bul-buls in hundreds, on bushes and thickets, joined in the general symphony of calls that remain indelible in the memory of all that have known these beautiful jungles.

But it would not do for me to pay too much heed to these sounds much as I enjoyed hearing them. I would have to remain keenly alert from now onwards, for with nightfall drawing near, the man-eater would remember his victim and might decide to return at any moment. At this time the two tribes of langur monkeys, one of them on the hilltop above me and the other somewhere on the adjacent hill across the stream, started their eventide gambols, frolicking among themselves and calling boldly to each other across the intervening valley. "Whoomp! Whoomp! Whoomp!" they screamed as they leaped from branch to branch. I could not see them from where I was sitting, but could hear the bang and thud of their bodies as they landed heavily among the branches of the trees.

I was grateful for the presence of the langur-monkeys. I knew that each tribe would have its own watchman, sitting alert on a tree-top, serious, silent and intently scanning the ground below for movement and danger.

The sun set behind the range of hills at my back and the shades of evening spread rapidly around me. The grasses and bushes and boulders that had been so clear all this while now became hazy and blurred. Distances lost their perspective. In a few moments there was no background to be seen at all; just the few indistinct bushes that grew in my immediate vicinity. All else was a dark-grey void, rapidly turning to chocolate and then to blackness. Muthu's body, only ten yards away, lost its shape and became merely a darker heap upon the rapidly darkening ground.

There was a whirring flutter of movement behind my head that startled me, accompanied by high-pitched, creaking squeaks. The long-eared bat, intent on its search for insects, had thought there might be a few in the clump of grass adorning my hat and had come to investigate. Softly a nightjar fluttered on to one of the stones forming my rampart. It was so close that by stretching out my hand I could have caught it, and I was pleased with myself at having sat so still, for I had even deceived this bird into not noticing, my presence. The nightjar snuggled low on the hot rock, puffed out its throat with air, and voiced its usual cry:

"Chuck! Chuck! Chuck! Chuck! Chuckoooooo!"

Then it noticed poor Muthu. Suddenly it took fright, fluttered both its wings like a giant moth, and sailed into the heavy air and out of sight. A little later I could hear it again, this time from far away, where the bird thought it was quite safe, voicing its jerky call.

Now I could no longer see the bushes, the grasses, the stones, nor even poor Muthu. A curtain of blackness closed over me with the falling of night. The stars that to a certain extent illumine the darkness in a jungle were few this night as I raised my eyes heavenwards in search of them. The steely blue-black of the usual night sky was covered by a ruffled blanket of small, broken, cirrocumuli clouds, resembling the ringlets of wool on a sheepskin. They stretched between the two ranges of hills and all but hid the stars from sight.

It was a perfect night for the man-eater to discover my presence and add me to his menu without my ever being aware of his nearness. To see him in such darkness was

315

impossible, and I was entirely at his mercy. Suddenly I became very frightened and began to shiver. Why had I been so foolhardy as to place myself in this predicament by not listening to the old Poojaree's experienced advice? I felt like shouting to Byra. I felt like getting up and dashing away from this horrid place to the far-away tamarind tree in which I knew my friend, the jungle man, was sheltering. A feeling of being closed in, of suffocation, of claustrophobia, gripped me. Panic all but overwhelmed me and the sweat of nervous terror streamed down my face. In the distance, a horned-owl hooted dismally: "Whoo! Whoooo! Whoo! Whoooo! Whoo! Whoooo!"

At that moment the calm of the night was shattered by the dying scream of a sambar stag from the stream bed down in the valley.

"Aar-aar-aarrhh-aaarrhh!" it shrieked in its agony, and once again "Aaahhh-gggrrrhhh!" Then there was silence.

I knew the animal that was being done to death at that moment was a stag, for a doe would have uttered a cry of far higher pitch, while the shriek of a spotted deer would have been quite different. Three possible foes could be killing that stag; a pack of wild dogs, a panther or a tiger. I decided against the dogs; a pack would have raised its hunting calls and I would have heard them long ago. Besides, these dogs do not hunt on dark nights. So the slayer was either a large panther of the tendu variety, or a tiger. Nothing else could be killing an animal as big as a sambar stag. Even a tendu would have all its work cut out to bring down a victim of that size.

Very likely the killer was a tiger after all. But was it the man-eater, who was reputed to eat only human flesh? Or was it some ordinary wandering tiger who happened to be in the vicinity too? I knew that the man-eater could not subsist on human flesh alone. His kills were too few and far between. He must be devouring animals as well, and I remembered he was very hungry that night, not having eaten for some time. Very likely it was he who had attacked the stag after all. Perhaps he had been returning for Muthu and had come upon the deer by chance.

The sambar was dead now and all sounds had ceased. The tiger would spend the rest of the night feeding on this new victim and would not come near the body of the Poojaree lad. My vigil would have been in vain. The thought was very mortifying indeed.

Mixed feelings of relief from immediate danger, and sheer disgust with myself at my cowardice, set in when I realized that only a few moments earlier I had been trembling, scared out of my wits at nothing but the darkness and the thought of the man-eater's proximity.

I knew that the old Poojaree, too, must have heard the sambar's death-scream. Like me, he would wonder if the killer was the man-eater or some other animal. I wondered what conclusion he had reached. The slaying of the sambar had brought to an end the nervous tension under which I had been labouring. I was quite calm now as I wondered over and over again whether the man-eater would return or not.

For the next half-hour or so the forest was hushed and strangely silent. It was as if its denizens were aware that danger lurked by the stream-bed, and that sudden and violent death awaited any of them who betrayed his presence. I glanced at my watch. It was not yet ten o'clock. I had many hours of tiring vigil before me.

After that the jungle gradually came to life again. I could hear the stealthy nibbling of grass by a barking-deer a few yards to my right. Down below, on the banks of the stream, an elephant was breaking bamboos.

As the heated air from the valley started to rise, the colder air from the hilltops rushed down to take its place. This caused fitful gusts of breeze to blow and carried to the munching barking-deer the smell of Muthu's body that was now beginning to make itself felt. There was a sudden noise as the little animal dashed away for a few yards. Then it came to a halt to voice its barking alarm-cry: "Kharr! Kharr! Kharr! Kharr!"

The barks came at intervals of a few minutes. It seemed incredible that such a small animal could make such a loud noise. I knew that the call of a barking-deer can be heard for over a mile on a still night.

Shortly afterwards the elephant in the valley, in his hunt for fresh bamboo-shoots, moved upstream. This brought him to the remains of the stag that had been killed a short while earlier. Probably the killer, panther or tiger, was still there, feeding on his prey. Whatever it was, the elephant became excited and began to trumpet repeatedly, the brassy scream of each note disturbing the silence of the forest.

And then I heard it clearly. "Wr-aagh! Wrr-aagh!" — the roars of an angry tiger coming from the same direction. The elephant screamed again and again, and the tiger roared its defiance in between, answer for answer. I could imagine the scene. The tiger had been feeding, or perhaps just sleeping by the sambar's remains, when the elephant had blundered upon him. Would the encounter develop into a fight, or would one or other of the animals lose its nerve and retreat?

The screams of the elephant began to change in timbre. The high-pitched note of fear gave place to the longer, slightly lower note of anger. I could make out that the animal was a bull. He resented the tiger's presence amongst the bamboos, which he no doubt regarded as his own property, and was rapidly losing his temper.

What would the tiger do? The matter was not left in doubt

for long. He suddenly lost his nerve and decided to giver way to the irate elephant, even if it meant abandoning his kill. There was sudden silence when the tiger beat a retreat, while the bull elephant, finding his bluster had succeeded in driving away the foe, slowly regained his composure and ceased to trumpet.

Silence once again descended upon the forest. The fleecy clouds that had been hiding the stars since sunset had disappeared about an hour before, and I could now see the dark form that was Muthu, and the nearer bushes and grasses, reasonably clearly in the light of the stars. Now at least I might be able to see the man-eater should he decide to return to Muthu's body. This caused me to wonder again whether the tiger that had just had that altercation with the elephant was the man-eater or not. His display of cowardice tended to offer an affirmative answer.

My thoughts were disturbed at that instant by a growl! I heard it only once and so I could not quite locate the sound or where it had come from, but it was an unmistakable growl. I fancied it had come from somewhere behind me and lower down the hillside, but I was not quite sure.

As quietly as possible, I turned my body a few inches to the left, so as to be able to observe whether anything was approaching from that direction, but I could still see the smudge that was Muthu, by looking to my right.

And then I heard it again: another growl, louder and closer this time. There was now no doubt whatever: the tiger was coming up the hill, he was coming in my direction.

I could not help smiling to myself as I thought of the great service that the elephant had done me in driving the tiger from his kill. The angry tiger had now been forced to remember that he had made another kill, one of those tasty human beings, earlier that afternoon and higher up the hill. So he was returning to it, voicing his anger all the while against the elephant that had disturbed him.

My luck had been stupendous. Not only was the tiger advertising his presence, which was much in my favour on a dark night, but the bad temper he was displaying, and his smouldering resentment against the elephant, would prevent him from being too cautious when he eventually reached poor Muthu. After all, perhaps he would not discover my presence. I was elated at the thought.

Twice more the tiger growled. Then I dimly saw a long, dark ill-defined shape to my left and a little below me. It seemed to move. It disappeared completely. Then it appeared again, this time much closer. It was certainly moving towards me.

The tiger growled again Apparently he was still thinking of the elephant and could not get him out of mind. The throaty, rasping note came from the long, moving object that was rapidly approaching me.

The dark shadow disappeared behind an intervening bush. A few seconds later the slinking shape moved dimly from left to right, and came to a halt over Muthu, just ten yards away. It had not even glanced at the little stone fort that Byra and I had so painstakingly constructed.

The tiger was in such a vile temper that he voiced a series of loud growls when he bit savagely into the Poojaree lad's dead body and began to worry the carcase. His recent undignified retreat before the bull elephant, and the fact that he had to abandon his sambar kill, was annoying him intensely. He felt he had to vent his spleen on something.

Only now did I realize how difficult was the task that lay before me. I had to kill the tiger with my first shot, or at least cripple it effectively so that it would not turn upon me. My quarry was a mere ten yards away, but I could just see it as a blur. I had no torch, no nightsight, no white card as an index, that we read about so often, to fit to the sights of a rifle to make night shooting easy. My old .405 did not even have a phosphorescent foresight.

I realized I would have to act quickly while the tiger was still venting its wrath upon poor Muthu's remains. Once it became calmer and settled down to feed, it would notice any slight movement of my rifle and attack me. In fact, if it had eaten enough of the sambar it might just pass on, to return later in the night when it became hungry again, or perhaps not return at all.

Very cautiously I raised the stock of the .405 to my shoulder, taking the greatest care not to knock the barrel against any of the stones we had erected. Holding it firmly, I pointed the barrel as best I could at the front portion of the dark shape that was the tiger.

I knew there was no possibility of picking my shot of firing at some vital place. I would have to take a chance. Perhaps I would miss altogether. Very likely I would just wound the tiger superficially and it would then turn and attack me. There was a hundred-to-one-chance that I would kill it with my first shot.

Steadying my hand and holding my breath, I pressed the trigger.

Pandemonium broke loose as the sharp report of the rifle thundered out and echoed against the opposing range of hills. The tiger roared lustily. Fortunately it had been facing away from me when I fired. Not knowing whence the shot had come, it imagined the foe was somewhere in front and sprang upon the nearest bush and began to tear it to shreds. As I feared would happen, I realized I had only wounded the tiger. It had been in a bad temper then. Now it was furious.

And then I made a mistake. Had I done nothing, the tiger

would have reduced the bush to nothing and probably have gone away after that, without discovering my presence. But I fired again at its dark shape.

After that the tiger's behaviour was fearsome. Hit a second time, it catapulted itself into the air, fell to earth with a thud, and then began grubbing around in a circle. Evidently the spine was broken, for the animal appeared to be unable to stand upright. But this time it knew where its attacker was concealed, and the grubbing circle it was taking brought it directly down upon me.

Scrambling to my feet, I fired my third shot into its head at a range of scarcely two yards. Then I vaulted over the stone parapet by using my hands and promptly fell down the other side. My feet pricked as if there were a thousand needles in each, for I had been sitting crosslegged for some eleven hours and they were numbed.

Fortunately the tiger remained on the other side of the stones. A dreadful bubbling, gurgling sound was coming from it, showing that the animal was still alive but grievously hurt and probably dying.

I scrambled to my knees as the blood flowed back to my legs and peeped cautiously over the intervening boulder. The tiger lay on the other side, twitching and gasping and gurgling. My fourth shot ended its suffering.

When the noise died away, I could hear Byra calling to me frantically, asking if all was well. I answered him in the affirmative and told him to come along. A few minutes later my friend appeared out of the darkness and I told him the whole story. On the stream-bed the elephant trumpeted again.

Unerringly Byra led me through the dark jungle back to Manchi hamlet. There, for the second time, I repeated all that had happened. The inhabitants turned out to the last child, brought lights and returned with us to bring in the bodies of Muthu and the tiger.

My first shot had entered the stomach. My second had smashed the spine high up at the shoulder. It was this second shot that had anchored the tiger and prevented it from escaping. As we had anticipated the man-eater turned out to be a young animal, and this accounted for his inexperienced, erratic ways. The Poojarees asked why we had used the body of Muthu as a bait. We asked them why they entertained a sorcerer of such poor calibre in their midst. We also reminded them we had rid them of the man-eater. The end justified the means.

To this they said nothing.

Two

The Lame Horror of Peddacheruvu

IF YOU WERE TO TRAVEL FROM GUNTAKAL BY THE METRE-GAUGE railway eastwards towards the city of Bezwada, now known as Vijayawada, you would traverse some of the best-known and densest forests of the State of Andhra Pradesh soon after leaving Dronachellam Junction, when you pass Nandyal and go through the stations of Basavapuram, Chelima, Bogoda and Diguvametta.

The forests on either side of the track are the only areas in southern India where the once-numerous giant antelope, known as the nilgai or blue-bull, are still to be found. They are especially numerous in the jungles around the Forest Department Rest House at a place named Chinnamantralamanna. These great animals, which once abounded everywhere, are now extinct in all the other forests of the South.

In addition to the blue-bull, the other found in the Indian

subcontinent are numerous here, together with huge sounders of wild pig, and all of these animals in turn attract tigers and panthers who are always to be found where sufficient food is available. But when this natural food becomes scarce for any reason, the carnivora are forced to prey on the herds of cattle, sheep and goats tended by the herdsmen who live on the out-skirts of the villages. Then, and only then, do they fall foul of the men who attend the herds, and who naturally endeavour to drive away the marauders with spears, traps, bullets and other devices. Tigers and panthers are wounded or hurt in other ways too. This incapacitates them for normal hunting, and in time they take to man-eating as the easiest way of appeasing hunger.

In the course of years many man-eaters have appeared in these areas. I have already told of one of them that haunted the railway tracks between some of the stations I have named* and what follows is the story of another that appeared in the same general locality, but some miles to the north.

To reach the spot, you do not alight from the train at Diguvametta, but travel another forty miles to Markapur Road. You detrain there and go by road in a northerly direction for another forty miles. The road winds down a picturesque ghat to an insignificant place known as Srisailam, overlooking the winding course of the Kistna River that formerly separated the Madras Presidency in the south from the dominions of the Nizam of Hyderabad in the north. The British have now gone, and so also have the Nizam's dominions, all these areas having been brought within the extensive State of Andhra Pradesh, the second largest in India, while Srisailam, hitherto merely the site of a large temple and of only religious

_____

* See *The Black Panther of Sivanipalli*, Chapter 4.

significance, is becoming famous as the centre of a great twin project involving an irrigation and electricity scheme.

In former years, when conditions were undisturbed, this road from a point about twenty miles from Markapur Road railway station as far as the Kistna River was covered with the type of forest that tigers delight in — not too dense and not too thorny — with sufficient high grass and low trees to afford cover for themselves and grazing and shelter for the wild deer and pig that form their natural diet. Low, rolling hills with interesting streams provided plenty of water for them in even the hottest weather, while the tiny jungle-ticks that are the scourge of the forests further south, and the voracious leeches of the Western Ghats, both of them hateful to all carnivora, who cannot rid themselves of these pests, seem to be entirely absent. At least the leeches are, while the ticks appear only after the rains and then in insignificant numbers.

So tigers and panthers, particularly the former, were plentiful. They fed on the Nilgai and the deer, and sportsmen did not visit the area very often. Elephants and bison strangely enough, are entirely absent from these jungles. The rare blue bull makes up for them in a way, but as it is protected and there is a total prohibition against shooting them, these areas have never been popular with tourists or sportsmen. The climate, too, is difficult: hot in winter and savagely hot in summer.

Another factor that has saved the carnivora to a large extent is the paucity of motorable tracks into the interior. If you want to travel away from the main road, you either walk or travel by bullock-car. But all this made the jungles of Srisailam very pleasant to me. In their fastnesses I could lose myself, away from the crowd.

There is a village named Peddacheruvu situated to the

west of the road from Markapur to Srisailam. To reach it you go by bullock cart through eighteen miles of forest where you generally do not meet another human being. Peddacheruvu is a small village, and to the south of it lies a pretty lake. The bullock-cart track passes this lake and wends southwards for a few miles more till it reaches a hill. At an impossible gradient the track descends this hill to the hamlet of Rollapenta, where it meets another main road leading from the village of Doranala to the town of Atmakur. Further south yet is the Rest House of Chinnamantralamanna, where the Nilgai abound.

The lake I have just told you about is ringed by the jungle, and in this jungle many tigers are to be found. So many, in fact, that they have killed and eaten all the panthers that at one time lived there too. From November to January each year, during the mating season, after sunset and often during the daylight hours too, you can hear the moaning call of a tigress seeking her mate, and sometimes the awful din of tigers fighting for the female whose roars have summoned them from afar.

. I have told you in earlier stories that the natural food of tigers and panthers is the wild game of the forest, and, when these become scarce, the herds of domestic cattle and goats that are taken out to graze. Man-eating is invariably the result of a tiger or panther becoming unable to hunt its normal food by some injury caused, in every case in my experience, except the one I am going to tell you about, by a wound inflicted by man. Generally it is a gunshot or rifle wound, or injury brought about when escaping from a spring trap, when the animal has had to tear itself free from the teeth of the steel jaws that have fastened on its face or foot.

But in the case of the man-eater of Peddacheruvu it was none of these things. For after I shot him I found that this tiger, well past his prime, had been involved in a fight with

another tiger. He had lost an eye and an ear as the result —
both on the right side, where his adversary had gripped him
— and the tendons of his right foreleg had been chewed
through and through, causing him to drag that limb as he
walked and to leave a distinct trail behind him. These
disabilities, together with his advancing years, had prevented
this animal from being able to kill his normal prey. A tiger's
forepaws, and particularly the right one, are essential to him
in normal attack, for with them he grips his victim while he
bites the neck or throat, causing the animal to topple over
and break its neck by its own weight. With his right foot
maimed, this tiger could not hold any animal larger than a
mouse-deer. So he went through months of starvation while
his wounds healed, and then he took to killing and eating
every human being that came his way, for he found them slow
in movement and quite helpless to resist him, even with his
handicaps.

The people of Peddacheruvu told me later that they had
heard a tigress moaning for some days. That was when this
story really began.

It was just before Christmas and the mating season. Two
tigers had begun to fight for her. The quarrel had started at
sunset and had lasted half the night. Both contestants had
evidently been badly hurt, for one of them had come down
to drink water at the edge of the lake, where he had left a
pool of blood on the muddy edge. The other had crossed the
sandy track leading from Peddacheruvu to Rollapenta, on the
Doronala-Atmakur road. The soft earth showed a distinct
bloodtrail and three sets of pug-marks, while a faint furrow
in the sand showed that the animal had been dragging one
of his limbs and could not put his weight on it.

Time passed, and then a sheep or goat here or a village
dog there disappeared, while as often as not the pug-marks

of the 'limping tiger,' as he came to be known, showed that this contestant at least had survived the epic fight.

The older men in the village shook their heads and conferred in whispers. Some of them had heard of such cases before. A few had actually seen them. But they all knew that the taking of the sheep, the goats and particularly the village curs, meant that a man-eating tiger was in the making. For tigers disdain such food and will only stoop to kill and eat such insignificant prey when they are on the verge of starvation, or when they are unable, for some good reason, to kill anything bigger.

The first human victim was taken very soon after that, and the old men wagged their heads and their tongues yet more. He was a cart-man and had been returning to the village in the evening with his cart laden with bamboos that had been cut in a valley five miles away. The cart track skirted the lake I have told you about, and here the man had stopped to water his bulls without unyoking them, for his cart was too heavily laden and it would have been impossible for him to re-yoke them again single-handed.

Perhaps just before or after watering his animals, the man had got down from his cart to drink himself. That was when the 'limping tiger' took him.

The bulls, terrified at the sight of the tiger, had dashed madly away, dragging the laden cart behind them. They had not kept to the road, as a result of which the cart had fallen down an incline, the weight of the bamboos dragging the two unfortunate bulls with it. One had broken its thigh and the bone, protruding through the outer skin, had stuck into its belly, while the cart lay on top of the animal, effectively anchoring it. The second bull had been more lucky. The yoke had slipped off its neck, leaving the animal free to dash to the village. Its arrival there had caused consternation, but as night had fallen already nobody would listen to the pleadings of the car-man's wife and three children that the men should form a search-party with lanterns to look for the bread-winner.

The sun was already up next day when the able-bodied men of the hamlet, two of them armed with matchlocks and the rest with spears and sticks, eventually left the village. Very soon they came upon the capsized cart, and the unfortunate bull with the broken thigh. Of the owner there was no trace.

They followed the tracks of the cart to the edge of the pool and there they saw in the mud the prints left by the limping tiger. Some of the searchers had wanted to look for the remains of the car-man, but the two individuals armed with matchlocks had become faint-hearted. One said his weapon was useless and would not fire. The other, more truthful, admitted he was too afraid. As a result the whole party returned to the village and the remains of the cart-man were never found.

The second victim was a woman. This incident also took place in the evening, but at a spot within a hundred yards of the village where she had taken her water-pot to the community well. No jungle grew there, but nearby was a grove of peepul trees which, in turn, adjoined a coconut plantation. A thick hedge enclosed this plantation, and on the further side was wasteland, covered with scrub and grass. The jungle proper began more than half a mile away. The well was at a spot where no tiger had ever been known to come within the memory of the oldest inhabitant, and he was well over a hundred years old.

But the limping tiger came that evening. Two other women saw him in the act of carrying away his victim when she screamed. They turned around at the sound and were dumbfounded to see a great tiger, with a distinct limp, dragging the woman by her shoulder and moving at a fast pace towards the peepul trees. They had waited no longer and fled screaming to the village.

Human kills had followed in rapid succession after that, and one day I received a letter from an old friend of mine, a Telegu Indian gentleman named Byanna, who lived near the Markapur Road railway station, telling me of the goings-on at Peddacheruvu village and asking me to come and shoot the tiger. Moreover, Byanna offered to accompany me in order to render what assistance he could, and suggested I should travel by train to Markapur Road, from where he would take me in his Land-Rover to our destination.

Such a summon is impossible to resist, so I sent Byanna a telegram informing him I was leaving by express the following night. The next forenoon found us together on the platform of Markapur Road railway station.

Mr Byanna is meticulous, and looking after a guest is to him a matter of great importance, so important that at times it is all rather embarrassing. I was taken to his house, where a hot bath had been ready for the last two hours. Then a huge dish of chicken pilau was placed before me and I was almost commanded to eat it all. I knew I would have to put up a good show, for Byanna is rather sensitive and would be greatly offended if I did not do justice to the meal.

When this feast was over, I was taken to the garage at the rear of the house. There stood Byanna's Land-Rover, laden to the brim with all manner of unnecessary things intended for my comfort. There was a spring-cot and mattress, camp-chairs, camp-tables, a canvas camp-tub, a comp-basin and stand, a small refrigerator and a fan, both worked by kerosene oil, and heaven knew what else. As for foodstuffs! There were gunny-bags in large numbers crammed with stores; enough, I should think, for a whole month. Four Primus stoves, one of them with a doublerange cooker, had

331

been provided; and pots, pans and storagedrums for water were tied on at inconceivable points and at incredible angles. Where he and I were going to sit seemed an insoluble problem.

Byanna asked me if I would like to sleep the night in his house and start next morning, to which I said I was as fresh as a daisy after that hot bath and marvellous chicken pilau. Could we start right away? Wonderfully obliging, he consented at once, and an hour later the Land-Rover, looking more like one of those covered-wagons from the prairies of America, took the road northwards that led to Srisailam.

We left the main road a little beyond Doranala village and negotiated the rough track of eighteen miles that eventually brought us directly through the jungle to the village of Peddacheruvu, passing another hamlet named Tummalabayalu on the way, the scene of an encounter with a man-eater in my young and inexperienced days. There I tumbled out of the Land-Rover and sat on someone's doorstep, while Byanna rattled away in the Telugu dialect to the throng of villagers that gathered around us.

It transpired he was trying to find a suitable room for us to occupy. This did not take long, for the headmaster of the local school, who had joined the crowd to learn the purpose of our visit, at once volunteered to let us live in the main hall of his little school.

We drove the Land-Rover there and unloaded. By the time we had taken everything out of the vehicle we had crammed that room to capacity, though more than half the objects were quite unnecessary.

Water was fetched for us in pots by several willing villagers. We were conducted to the bathroom, in a separate building, where we bathed; and we were shown the lavatory, in yet another building. It was a long time before we could sit down to our first meal of curry and rice that Byanna had brought from his home at Markapur.

Dusk had fallen by now, but people from the village still kept coming and going, to stare at us and ask innumerable questions which Byanna answered in Telegu at great length. Finally I took matters into my own hands. Selecting three or four of the villagers who seemed to know something about the man-eater, and carrying my rifle, I asked them to follow me outside.

It was moonlight. The main street of the village led directly to the track that skirted the lake on its way to the Doranala-Atmakur road. Half a furlong away the lake began, and I could see the water glinting in the moonlight.

I walked along the street with my companions, who very soon told me that it would be dangerous for us to leave the precincts of the village because of the man-eater, I said I wanted to talk to them where we could have peace and quiet, which was impossible in that infernal schoolroom, and I reassured them about the tiger. Finally we reached the edge of the lake and sat down by the water. It was delightfully cool there and the moonlight was so bright that we could see right across the wide expanse of the lake to the jungle on the other side.

I noticed that my companions kept glancing nervously around, but as we were in the open with no cover for the tiger, there really was no justification for their fear. Little by little I learned of the tiger's doings, as I have already set them out, and my companions ended their narrative with a fervent plea that I should shoot the beast at all costs.

I think Byanna must have wondered at my sudden departure, for he came looking for me with about twenty people and joined us just at the water's edge. We discussed plans as to what to do on the morrow.

And that was when a tiger started to roar. From directly opposite us, on the other side of the lake, where we could see the dark edge of the jungle coming down to the water, he roared at regular intervals. To me that sound was pleasing, exciting, tempting and challenging. I had been told enough to know I would be able to recognize the man-eater at once by his limp, if I could only see him. I had talked enough and eaten enough; and those roars were very, very inviting. And the moonlight was so wonderfully bright.

On an impulse I jumped to my feet and told my companions I was going after the tiger. They were aghast. But before they could remonstrate, I set off almost at a trot along the track that I knew skirted the lake closely for nearly half its circumference till it reached the other side, before breaking away into the jungle. I judged the tiger was roaring at least a mile away, maybe further, and I wanted to reach him before he stopped. Obviously he was coming down to the lake for a drink.

In less than fifteen minutes I was almost there, and the tiger was still calling, although at longer intervals. I knew that very soon he would stop. He was so close now that the earth seemed to tremble with each roar as I left the track I had been following to cut through the jungle towards the sound. That was when my difficulties began.

I knew very well that if I attempted to walk through the undergrowth the tiger would hear me. He would either go away then or, if he was the man-eater, he might creep forward to ambush me by a flank or rear attack. My hope lay in finding a footpath if possible, and in following it in silence so as to try to see him first — an almost impossible thing to do.

Luckily I discovered that footpath. Rather it was a game-trail that went down to the water and not a footpath; but it offered salvation, for it was leading more or less in the general direction from which the tiger's roars were still coming, although at longer and longer intervals.

I started to follow the path, glancing down frequently to make sure I did not stumble or tread upon something that would betray my presence. I judged the tiger was well within 200 yards when he ceased to roar. I stopped advancing as soon as I realized this, for it would be impossible for me to located him. Whereas he would assuredly hear my footsteps in spite of all my precautions in the complete silence that now enveloped us both. I thought quickly and had an idea. An acacia tree grew to the right of the game-trail. Its trunk was hardly thick enough to hide my body when I sheltered behind it, but provided I remained absolutely motionless there was a hope that the tiger would not detect — at least, not too soon.

Quickly I stepped behind the acacia, drew in my breath, and imitated the roar of a tiger with all the force of my lungs. Twice I did this, in rapid succession. Then I remained silent to await events. And happen they did, in real earnest. The tiger in front of me, apparently amazed and greatly annoyed at the impudence of the intruder who dared to come so close to him and roar twice, although those roars must have sounded miserably puny and weak, lost his temper. I could hear him coming, grunting and snarling as he bounded forward. Fortunately, the acacia had been growing at a spot where the pathway followed a straight course for a few yards, rather than at a bend.

Before long, down the pathway came the tiger in short bounds, so intent upon looking for another of his kind that he failed to notice me behind the trunk of that acacia tree. He had passed when I was forced to put him to the test. I coughed almost imperceptibly.

The tiger whisked around in his tracks to face this new

sound. He knew it did not come from another tiger but from a man, and his reaction would show whether he was the man-eater or not.

I did not move a fraction of an inch as the beast started at the acacia. Having no sense of smell, he could not locate me exactly, although he must have seen some part of me and knew that something was sheltering behind that tree. He hesitated, and then stepped three or four paces to his left from where he would be able to get a better view of me.

Recognition came to both of us at once. He found out what I was and where I was standing, while I found out that he was not the man-eater. For there was not the faintest trace of a limp in his walk. We stared at each other.

The next three or four seconds would decide our fate. I certainly had no wish to shoot a harmless tiger provided he left me alone. But would he? I had excited and irritated him by roaring, and had made matters worse by coughing. An angry tiger cannot often control itself.

The tiger sank to his haunches and I knew the charge was coming. I aimed and was about to press the trigger when one of those unaccountable events, that often make a tiger's behaviour unpredictable, occurred. He turned and bounded into the bushes!

Allowing time for him to get away and for my nerves to calm down. I retraced my steps along the game-trail to the roadway and back to the village, where I told Byanna and the others, who admitted they had never expected to see me again, what had happened.

To say I was disappointed would be putting matters lightly, but I was glad I had not made things worse by shooting the wrong tiger.

During the next three days we bought four baits and tied them out at the most likely spots where nallahs and pathways crossed each other, and within a mile or so of the big lake, and above each bait we constructed an almost perfect machan.

That was how I came to meet an individual who, as events were to prove shortly, was as brave a man as any I have met. He was a Chenchu — the name by which the aboriginal jungle men of these areas are known — and he carried a bow and a quiver of arrows like most Chenchus do. These, and a filthy rag as a loin-cloth, were apparently his sole pssessions. One more thing he had, and I think it was his greatest asset. Appu — for that was his name — had a most infectious smile, a marvellous sense of humour. He was as happy as the day was long.

Appu offered his services in selecting suitable place in which to tie my baits and in building the machans, and I was quick to accept, for his smile won me completely. What wonderful machans he built! He concealed them so cleverly that, even when staring at one from the ground and knowing its location, it was difficult for me to realize a machan was there. Indeed, little Appu added greatly to my knowledge of the art of machan-tying, for with him it was an art indeed!

Nothing happened the first night, nor the second. The buffalo heifer that we had tied a quarter of a mile from the spot where I had met the roaring tiger was killed and half-eaten on the third night, so that on the fourth night I sat over his heifer's remains, awaiting the return of the killer.

Would it be the lame tiger — the man-eater — or would it be the 'roaring tiger' — as I had come to call him — that I had encountered a few days earlier? Unfortunately the ground was so hard that no tracks were visible to answer this question in advance. The tiger returned before darkness had set in, which is something rare for a tiger to do, although sunset is the usual time at which panthers come to their kills. He did not even glance upwards at Appu's perfect machan but walked boldly up to the heifer's carcase and gazed down upon it.

There was nothing wrong with his walk. He was not the lame tiger I had been told to look for. He was not the man-eater.

The thought came to me to try a little experiment from that wonderful machan. I made the grating call of a panther. The effect on that tiger was astounding; he was galvanized into fury. He whirled around to locate the puny but audacious panther who had dared to challenge his right to his own kill. Where was this intruder?

'Hah-ah! Hah-ah! I called again. Then stopped.

'Wrauff! Wrauff! Wrauff!' roared the tiger, and charged directly at the tree in which I was hidden. I had carried the joke too far. The tiger was furious and hell-bent upon exterminating what he thought to be his spotted foe, hiding in the tree. Moreover the tree was an easy one to climb and I was only about fifteen feet above the ground.

The tiger disappeared from view as he got below the platform of my machan. The tree shook as he sprang into the first fork and I could hear the scraping of his claws upon the bark as he scrambled upwards, growling furiously. It was not a big tree and his efforts, together with his weight, set up a strange trembling that made my whole machan vibrate.

Matters had gone far enough. In another moment those enormous paws would reach up and tear the platform on which I was seated to shreds. I would be thrown off the tree and the tiger would probably jumps down up me before he could realize I was no panther.

'Shoo! Shoo! Shoo!' I screeched in desperation, leaping to my feet as I pointed the rifle downwards, waiting for his head or paw to show over the edge of the platform. The unfortunate tiger really got the shock of his life. He recognized the human voice and must have wondered what sort of panther could be above him, since it had, all of a sudden, turned itself into a man. And courage was not his strong point, as he had shown a few days earlier when he had met me behind the acacia.

The growling stopped and the tree shook furiously as the tiger hurled his bulk to earth. He did not stop for a moment, but bounded into the undergrowth; then I heard the noise of his precipitate departure through the dry bushes.

When I got back to camp I told Byanna and Appu and my other friends of the joke I had at the tiger's expense. They were all amused, but little Appu was tickled to death. He slapped his thighs with the palms of his hands and laughed and laughed and laughed. Almost gasping for breath, he choked over his words: 'But yesterday, the tiger heard a tiger that turned out to be a man. Today it heard a panther that became a man. It must be thinking it's going mad!'

Next day, I replaced the heifer that had been killed, and that very night this new heifer was killed. We had not changed the spot nor the machan where I had teased the tiger the day before. We were after the lame tiger, the man-eater, so it was an advantage to use the machan from which the other tiger, the stupid 'roaring tiger's as we had named him, had been driven away. By using this machan again, we could at least be sure the 'roaring tiger' would not interfere. So it followed that, when the slaying of the new heifer was reported at about 9 a.m., by Appu and the half-dozen men, armed with axes and staves, who had gone to inspect the various baits, my spirits rose in anticipation. At last I was to come to grips with the man-eater himself, for surely here he was at last!

Filled with this hope, I climbed into the machan early that afternoon and had not been there long when a mongoose appeared. He must have been extremely hungry, for he nibbled at the dead heifer and then started bolting mouthfuls of flesh until he was bloated and could hardly walk, before he toddled away.

As they had been awaiting his departure, a bevy of what are known in this part of India as 'gerjers' — a species of small quail — appeared in the clearing within short time. They did not touch the putrefying flesh but started pecking at the myriads of tiny beetles and other insects attracted by the stench from the carcase that was increasing with the heat of the day. Bluebottle flies settled in hordes upon the expose flesh. There they would lay eggs that in a short while would hatch into myriads of white grubs. These would eat up the flesh and would, in turn be eaten by birds and insects that would come to prey upon them. In less than twenty-four hours that carcase would be reduced to mere bones by the action of maggots alone, apart from the scavengers of the sky — the vultures — that were already gathering for the final feast, and the scavengers of the night — hyaenas and jackals — that would arrive for the scant remains after darkness had fallen.

Then, of course, there was the rightful owner — the lame tiger as I hoped he would be — who should turn up by eight o'clock at the latest.

My reverie was rudely interrupted by the raucous but happy crow of a jungle-cock nearby: 'Wheew! Kuck-kaya-kaya-kuck'm' he called, and I knew without looking at my watch that it was nearing half-past five. Evening had come and I began to hope that the man-eater would be as obliging as his inoffensive cousin, the roaring tiger, by putting in his appearance before nightfall.

Down by the lake which, incidentally, was behind me, two families of peafowl began to call to each other: 'Mi-aow!" while what is known as the 'Golamothy Bird,' from far away, gave her mating call: 'Gol-a-mothy! Gol-a-mo-thy!' Every male within earshot, hearing that irresistible, enticing cry, would fly to her and before sunset she would have a number of suitors from whom to make her choice.

Twilight soon enveloped the jungle, that period of uncertainty between daylight and dark, when the eyesight is most easily deceived and innocent shrubs and bushes assume the menacing appearance of crouching, watching beasts.

Phutt! Phutt! Phutt! A number of birds flapped heavily in headlong flight from a tree somewhere behind me. They give voice to a shrieking alarm 'Kee-ya! Kee-ya! Kee-ya!'

Something has aroused a flock of crimson-headed parrots from their roosting place and they have fled to seek another. Now why did the parrots do that? Maybe they saw a wild cat on the prowl. Or could it be the tiger?

Time slipped by.

'Keech! Keech! Keech! Keech!' A number of miniature bats of the insect-eating variety swooped and dived at their invisible prey, taking them on the wing and screeching in sheer joy in such high notes, I am told, that it is beyond the human ear to register them. And I am right glad of that as the screeching, creaking noises they were making at the moment and that I could hear were loud enough.

A nightjar fluttered overhead and settled somewhere behind me. He started the chorus of calls that would soon be repeated by a number of his fellows: 'Chuck chuck Chuck Chuck Chuckooooo; Chuck Chuck ...'

Then he stopped abruptly and took flight. I could see him sailing over the treetop to my right. And a second later I heard a deep sigh beneath my machan, followed by complete silence. Although I could not see him, I knew the tiger had arrived.

He was standing directly below me, and I sensed that he was inspecting the kill and his surroundings with the utmost care to make quite certain no hidden danger threatened. Would he look up and discover the machan? A nerve-straining period of inactivity followed. Then I heard a continuous small sound which I shall not try to described, although I could easily identify it. The tiger was answering the calls of nature.

I was elated. This was a good sign indeed. It showed he was not at all frightened or suspicious.

The next instant the tiger walked boldly into view from under my tree. In spite of the fact that it had become very dark I could make out those cautious but purposeful strides that took him to the kill. There was not the vestige of a limp in his walk. He was certainly not a lame animal and therefore not the man-eater.

I voiced my disgust beneath my breath. The tiger stopped as if he had heard me. Then he continued till he reached the dead heifer, where he halted to look down upon it.

Without doubt he was my old friend, the roaring tiger. For a moment I was tempted to shoot him, for this animal was becoming a nuisance. He had taken two of my baits and probably would take a lot more. And baits cost money.

Then I stopped to think. Could he be the man-eater, after all? What evidence did I really have that the man-eater was lame, beyond hearsay? Perhaps the story was all wrong. Maybe this was the man-eater, standing there, just waiting to be shot.

But I recalled his behaviour on the two occasions when he had seen me and found I was a man. That was not the conduct of a man-eater: he had acted more like a scared rabbit. Nevertheless, there was no getting away from it. This animal was becoming a nuisance. So I raised my rifle, aimed quickly at the ground under his belly and fired.

The bullet struck the earth between his legs and in spite of the near darkness I could see the puff of dust it raised as it buried itself in the ground. As for the tiger! he arched his back like a frightened cat, then became elongated as he stretched himself for a mighty spring that took him clean out of sight.

I came down from the machan in disgust, shouldered my rifle, and using a pocket torch to light the way in case I trod on a snake, made my way back to the village.

The next day I bough yet another heifer and tied it out at the same spot. Surely the roaring tiger would not take it this time? And I made up my mind that, if he did, I would shoot him without compunction.

This time he did no kill. Oh, he came there all right. The whole village and I heard him. He roared from about ten till near midnight. He had seen the heifer and was very hungry. But, mindful of a tiger that had turned into a man, followed by a panther-man — or shall we say a 'leopard-man' — and then of some strange thing that made an awful bang and hit the ground between his feet with tremendous force, he could not summon enough courage to kill the tempting bait. He roared his frustration and displeasure instead.

Next morning not kills were reported. But little Appu had some news to give. He had found the trail of the lame tiger near one of the further baits. It had passed within a few yards of the heifer, even halting to look at it. Yet it had not killed the buffalo. Appu said he felt that the man-eater was averse to buffalo meat and would therefore not take any of our baits, however long we might try. He suggested I exchange the buffaloes for bulls and try again.

He said he had another plan in mind. I inquired what it was. Appu grinned hugely as he suggested that he and I might go looking for the man-eater every night until we found him.

A good idea, I replied. As good a notion as looking for a needle in a haystack.

It took a little time for Appu to understand me. With haystacks he was familiar. But not with needles. After all, why should he want one? He wore no clothes! I suggested a pin, instead of a needle. That did not register, either. What had Appu to do with pin? Then I had a brainwere. I picked up a dried twig and twisted off the largest thorn growing on it. I went through the motion of hiding the thorn in a haystack and asked Appu how long he might take to find it. He shrugged.

I said that this was like looking for the lame tiger in an area of jungle that extended as he caught my meaning at last. He laughed and he laughed and he laughed.

All this talk had made breakfast late, but we set out as soon as I had finished. Appu led me in a south-westerly direction from the lake, over the brow of a low hill and into a valley on the other side. A dry stream-bed wound along this valley and one of my baits had been tied at a spot where a fire-line crossed this stream.

The path we had just followed from the lake also crossed the stream at its intersection with the fire-break and led onwards to a Chenchu settlement about three or four miles away. Chenchus do not live in villages. One stumbles upon a tiny circular hut of sticks and grass, scarcely noticeable in the surrounding jungle. A whole family of ten persons may live in one such hut. There may possibly be another hut nearby, or you may have to cover many miles before reaching the next.

We had deliberately selected the junction-point as the best spot for tying the bait, for a tiger coming upstream or downstream, or from either side of the fireline or footpath — that is, from any one of six directions — would see it immediately. And now, clearly in the dust of the footpath and coming from the opposite sides, were the footprints of a tiger.

I studied them closely. There were the pug-marks of three feet, instead of the four distinct impressions a tiger makes when he is ambling along, or the two marks he leaves when he is stalking by placing each hind foot upon the place vacated by the corresponding forefoot as it is moved forward to avoid treading upon a dried leaf or a twig. There was no doubt about it: this animal was using only three of his feet, and there was something wrong with the fourth. Hence he was unable to leave the quadruple trail normally made by a roaming tiger.

At last I was looking at the man-eater's pug-marks. The uneven distance between them indicated that he was limping badly, almost hopping along, while an occasional drag-mark in the dust showed where he had tried to put his weight on that right foreleg but could not do so. It was clear that the injury was severe and that the wound had not yet healed. I came to the conclusion that it could not be a very old one.

By tracking backwards for about 200 yards we reached the place where the tiger had come out of the jungle intending to cross or follow the footpath. Here he had spotted our bait and had deliberately walked up to it. We could see where he had halted to inspect the heifer from a distance of ten feet and then continued on his way.

This conduct puzzled me. Judging from the severe handicap from which the beast was suffering, he must be very hungry indeed, if not in a state of starvation most of the time. In that emaciated condition, why had he refused a meal that was his only for the taking? One could only conclude that he was not so very hungry after all, for hunger is an urge that neither a starving human nor a starving tiger can resist.

We followed the tiger's trail after leaving our heifer. He had continued along the pathway for only another five or six yards and had then broken into the jungle where he had turned back to recross the stream-bed and enter the forest on the other side. Here we lost the trail among the dry leaves and hard ground. It appeared as if the tiger had decided to resume his walk to wherever he had been going before he had spotted our buffalo and moved closer to examine it.

Appu and I decided we would ramble in his wake, or rather in the general direction he had been going, for as I have just said, the dry ground afforded no further trail. In a little while we came upon a game-path. The ground was still too hard for us to see any pug-marks, but we could make out the abrasions and scrapes left upon the baked earth by the pointed hooves of sambar and spotted deer, while a little further on a bear had recently been engaged upon heaving over boulders that bordered the path in his search for grubs and roots.

Appu suggested that, after all, the lame tiger might have been making for this game-trail and had probably followed it, although we could see no traces, and I agreed with him. The track seemed to be much used by wild animals, for not long afterwards we found the marks of a sounder of wild pig, coming from the opposite direction. Of the tiger there was still no trace.

But a little further on we found we were right. A nallah cut across the path almost at right angles. The trail we were following led sharpy down an incline into this nallah and up the other side, and clearly imprinted upon the loose earth of this nallah were the tracks of the lame tiger, leading away from us. They had been made the previous night and we had been correct in thinking that the game-trail we were following was the tiger's route. We were interested and decided to find out where the tiger had wanted to go.

We had covered more than a mile along that game-trail when we reached the crest of a small hill and looked down the other side. Below us, leading across a small clearing, we could see a distinct pathway and knew that it was the rough road that led to the Chenchu settlement I have told you about. The game-trail we were following had been but a short cut that had led across the hill instead of going around it, and the lame tiger had been moving towards the settlement.

We continued, and within the next half-mile we discovered that our game-trail led across the Chenchu roadway. Here the tiger had left the game-trail and had walked along the roadway, for his tracks lay clearly in the dust before us. We followed him for nearly another mile, when we heard voices approaching from the opposite direction. Around a bend appeared some ten Chenchus, walking rapidly and talking loudly among themselves. All carried bows and arrows and half of them were armed with crude spears and axes in addition.

They caught sight of us and came forward, talking excitedly, but before they could reach us we had overheard and knew the reason for their agitation. The man-eater had carried off a Chenchu from the hamlet the previous evening.

When they reached us they told us the story. They had all known of the presence of the man-eater for some time and went about, when they had to, in groups armed as they were now. But Kalla, one of the their number, had always been a hunter and held all tigers, including man-eaters, in contempt. He had proclaimed that he was afraid of no tiger, while on the other hand every tiger walked in fear of him. Kalla had taken his axe and his bow and arrows and his long spear that morning and gone out hunting. He had returned for a late lunch and had informed his wife that he had failed to kill anything, but consoled her with the news that he had discovered a beehive in a hole in a tree almost within a stone's throw of the village.

Kalla had left his bow and arrows and spear behind as unnecessary impediments and had taken his axe, a box of matches and some straw with which to hack out the hive and smoke the bees away, and also an empty tin in which to collect the honey. In a short while, some of the Chenchus heard the sound of his axe and had wondered how they had been so foolish as not to detect the presence of the hive before Kalla had done.

At that moment they were startled by a scream: 'Tiger! Tiger!' Kalla had shrieked, and 'Help! Help! Help!' Then there was silence.

Kalla had not been popular and nobody, including his own wife, was in too great a hurry to rush to his rescue. They waited to see when he would return, but Kalla did not show up. In due course the menfolk gathered together, armed themselves as best they could, and went to the hollow tree where Kalla had found the beehive. The tree and the bees were there, and the axe, but no trace of Kalla. Instead they found fresh gum oozing from the deep abrasions that had been made in the trunk of the tree as the tiger had stood on his hind-paw and grabbed at Kalla with the only fore-paw he could use — his left. Necessarily, the operation had been a clumsy one, as the handicapped tiger must have had to support his weight against the tree trunk while reaching for his quarry with one foreleg. This had given Kalla time to scream for help. Had the tiger not been maimed, the Chenchu would not have heard or seen his attacker, while had the tree been a few feet higher, Kalla would have been beyond the reach of the man-eater, which could not have followed him.

The man-eater had dragged Kalla through the bushes into the jungle, where they came across blood and the remnants of his lion-cloth. They had followed for a short distance after that and then stopped, for nobody seemed to have liked Kalla very much. They knew he was dead. What was the use of following? Then they remembered that somebody had told them a couple of *dorais* had come to the village of Peddacheruvu to shoot this man-eater, and they had decided to go there to tell them. But it was too late and darkness had already set in.

So next morning some of the Chenchus had leisurely finished breakfast before setting out to bring Byanna and me the news. That explained how Appu and I came to meet them on the way. My guide and I now knew where the lame tiger had been heading when he had observed our buffalo, and we also knew why he had not killed and eaten the heifer.

Evidently he had made a good meal of the Chenchu the previous night and had then wandered away for water. As likely as not he had visited the lake for a drink. There he had remembered his human kill and had decided to return and finish off what was left. He had been on the way back when he saw our bait but was not hungry enough to kill and eat it, and as likely as not he preferred the taste of the Chenchu's flesh to tough buffalo meat, even though by now there could be little of the Chenchu left.

We told our part in these happenings to the Chenchus, who now became enthusiastic and offered to help in trying to trace where the tiger had gone. We knew that if we succeeded we would find Kalla's remains. But to them this appeared of little importance. Primarily, they wanted me to shoot the tiger, for as long as he remained their lives were in danger. With the eleven Chenchus to follow the trail, we went in the wake of the lame tiger for another few yards before we found he had again turned into the jungle. This time his passage could not escape those eleven pairs of searching eyes and in due course we came to a small, dry nallah, up which our quarry had turned. We could see his footmarks, while one of the Chenchus whispered that their settlement was hardly a quarter of a mile away. Within a short time we got the smell of the cadaver, and a little later we heard the hum of a thousand bluebottle flies. At last we had come to what remained of the unfortunate Kalla, the man who had been a little too cocksure. He had met the fate of many a hunter before him, and the fate that is in store for many more the world over. The fate that comes to those who are over-confident and careless.

There was very little left of the Chenchu. His head had been spared. Also his hands and feet, the usual portions of the human anatomy left by a man-eater. Even his shin-bones had been chewed and splintered, and some of his ribs, while sections of his spinal column lay about with hardly any flesh on them.

The man-eater must have been very hungry. Indeed, he must have been almost starving to have made such a meal. Again I wondered why he had spared my buffalo bait, which would have provided him with a far bigger repast.

A short distance away one of the Chenchus discovered a thigh bone. Of the other there was no trace. A hyaena or jackals had probably carried it way.

We discussed the situation in whispers. My companions were divided in their opinions. About half said that I should sit up for the tiger that night in a machan they offered to construct, while the other half were convinced it was a waste of time, as the man-eater would never return. There was nothing left for him to eat. Yes indeed: a hyaena would come, certainly jackals. A tiger? Never. Tigers were not carrion-eaters!

Then I remembered that the lame tiger appeared to be a very hungry animal, and I had no doubt of the course I should follow. I would sit over the remains of Kalla that night, come what may. There was a chance, albeit a slim one, that the tiger would return. I told my companions this and even the doubtful ones now saw my point. With enthusiasm, one and all set to work, and under the direction of that expert on machans Appu, once again a wonderful structure took shape before my eyes.

Appu had selected a bushy tree that grew some thirty-five yards away, and from the machan the Chenchus built on it, rather higher than usual, being some twenty feet off the ground in order to gain an uninterrupted view of the remains, I would await the doubtful return of the man-eater. We brought the solitary thigh-bone to where the other bones lay, so as to keep them as closely as possible together and offer a more tempting sight that might at least bring the man-eater forward to sniff at them.

Leaving Appu to the task with the other Chenchus, I hurried back to Peddacheruvu for something to eat and also for my night equipment. Byanna was excited when he heard the news and wished me luck.

It was past four o'clock when I returned to find Appu and two others perched on the machan. They had covered the few remains with leafy branches to conceal them from the keen sight of vultures, and these branches they removed when they left for the Chenchu settlement, where Appu had elected to spend the night with the others.

With the departure of my henchman, I began to think about the lame tiger. I wondered if he had really been maimed in a fight with another tiger as reported, or by a gunshot wound fired by some poacher, as frequently is the case. Undoubtedly the animal was very severely handicapped, so much so, in fact, that he must have lacked the confidence to tackle the heifer I had tied out for him. I concluded that this was the real reason why he had left it alone. This tiger would indeed prove to be in a very emaciated condition, necessarily dependent on the few small animals and other creatures that he could stalk and tackle upon his three sound legs till such time as some lucky chance presented itself

351

and he found and killed some unfortunate human being.

With this thought came fresh hope. A tiger as hungry as this would surely be tempted to return to the scraps that were left, even after the full meal he had made the night before.

The evening drew to its close in comparative silence. There were few birds and small animals, such as monkeys, in this part of the jungle, or they were strangely quiet for some unaccountable reason. This was unfortunate, for not only are the sounds of the forest for me endless source of delight, but it is upon the cries of alarm made by these smaller creatures, as well as the members of the deer family, that I largely rely to tell me of a tiger's movements. Once or twice, in the distance, partridge called, but of jungle-fowl and pea-fowl there was no evidence. I wondered about this till the answer came suddenly. The Chenchu settlement! Those little marksmen, with their bows and arrows, had wiped out all the edible birds within a considerable radius.

Darkness began to fall and the birds of the night, being less edible in Chenchu opinion than their unfortunate cousins of the day, and certainly far more difficult to hunt, began their calls. I welcomed the sounds that broke the monotonous silence of the evening I had just passed. A night-heron wailed in despair from the bed of some dry stream, and his cry was answered by a companion further down the valley. Far away, a pair of jackals raised their haunting call.

A squat kind of wood-cricket inhabits the forests of Andhra Pradesh in large numbers, which I have never come across nor heard in the jungles of Madras and Mysore. This little insect chirrups loudly, and when hundreds of them chirrup together the noise is loud enough to drown all other sounds. At times these vibrations synchronize and the resultant throb has the intensity of a tractor working nearby.

I had been listening to this noise that had started soon after sunset. It appeared to be growing steadily in volume and intensity as more and more of the insects joined in the chorus. Nothing else could I hear. Suddenly there was a sharp diminution of the sound. The crickets in the distance appeared to have stopped chirruping, and in a matter of seconds those nearer to me, becoming aware of the silence of their distant companions, stopped chirruping too. It was as if the tractor had come to a sudden halt.

The ensuing hush was relieving to the nerves in one sense but in another way it was strangely foreboding and terrifying. Just what had made the crickets stop their chorus?

The night-herons were still wailing to each other in the distance when I first heard the cause: the call of the man-eater! He roared in the valley. Once, twice and again.

Now I knew why the crickets had ceased their chorus so abruptly. They had heard the first roars of the tiger that had been inaudible to me because of the din they were making. Only after they had stopped was I able to hear him. But what had the man-eater got to do with crickets? Why should they fear him? I fell to wondering at the answer to this question. It intrigued me so much that I decided to put it to a friend of mine in Madras, who is a naturalist. The answer, as I found out later, is a simple one, and I shall tell you about it before I end this story.

The tiger was still roaring. He roared and roared as he came closer and closer. Obviously he intended returning to the remains of Kalla, the Chenchu, but why was he roaring in this fashion? It was as strange as it was unusual. When a tiger returns to his kill he does so in absolute silence, using the utmost caution to conceal his every movement with each step he takes. He certainly does not advertise his presence by roaring.

He was intrigued and awaited the answer in what he would do in the next thirty minutes.

He came as close as about fifty yards from my machan, but there he stayed put, hidden in the undergrowth, while he continued to roar. Never for a moment did he come out or show himself, although after some time he started to move around my machan and Kalla's remains in a wide circle, while his roaring grew louder and more fierce.

It did not take long to realize that the man-eater knew all about my presence in the tree overlooking his kill. But how could he have found out? He certainly could not have discovered my machan, for he had started roaring a long while back and quite a considerable distance away. Thus it was clear that he had known about me and the machan from the very start, and that he was trying to frighten me away.

There was only one way in which he could have found out. The man-eater had been lying in concealment all the time and had watched us build the machan. He knew some hated human enemy was awaiting his return, and that a return spelt great danger to him. Like all man-eaters, this tiger had an inherent fear of the human race, but in this instance the urge to eat again, in spite of his last big feed, was making him bold enough to think he could drive his foe away by roaring loudly and often. He had evidently followed Appu and the other Chenchus as far as their encampment and had now come back in the hope of being able to gnaw a few bones.

The man-eater continued to roar as he circled again and again, and I waited in patience to see what he would do. There could be only one answer to this intriguing situation within the next half-hour or so. Either the man-eater must become impatient and take a chance, or I would become impatient and go down in search of him. The third alternative was that the tiger would go away and I would lose him. At all costs, I must not allow that to happen.

Time passed. Half an hour. Then another ten minutes. But the man-eater did not show himself. Instead of continuing to move around in a wide circle as he had been doing, the tiger was now evidently lying on the ground, or perhaps sitting on his haunches, in a thicket that I could just make out as a big, black void in the darkness that was softened by the stars that shone brilliantly from a clear sky. And from this thicket he was roaring and roaring with unabated vigour and fury to drive away the person or persons he well knew were hidden in the tree where he had noticed such activity in the afternoon.

When there is something to be done, I am not a very patient person, and the urge to act was growing stronger with each moment. So at last I started to descend the tree as silently as possible. As stealthily as I moved, I knew the man-eater would hear me. If only he would give me time to reach the foot of the tree and walk the few steps to where Kalla's bones lay! Danger lay in the risk that he might attack while I was half-way down. Then I would be helpless, as I would not be able to use my rifle. I could feel the sweat of fear pour down my face and my hands were slippery with it. But I controlled my feet to move as silently and surely as possible. To fall now and hurt myself would mean lying on the ground entirely at the man-eater's mercy.

I was about half-way down when the roaring ceased. He had heard me and guessed that his quarry was on the move. Would he come closer to investigate? Naturally, he would. He might even then be only a few feet away.

The thought made me skaky and I quickened my descent, almost slipping once or twice. I had to feel for each foothold, although the stars gave enough light to make the ground visible. A great feeling of relief and thankfulness surged through me as my foot touched the earth at last. Quickly I brought my loaded rifle, which I had to sling over my right shoulder while making the descent, to the ready, while I stood with my back to the tree to meet the charge I expected at any moment.

The quietness was intense. Not a leaf stirred. The crickets were silent. The man-eater must be creeping towards me now. Surely he would make some sound, the faintest of rustles that would tell me where he was and give me a chance. But he made no sound. There was no rustle. Only an unearthly stillness.

Then it happened! The strain on the tiger had been as great as it had been on me, and he could contain himself no longer. With a shattering roar, he charged.

But he came from quite a different direction from what I had expected. He launched his attack from behind and not from the bush in which he had been hiding.

I heard the roar and whirled around. The tree-trunk was in my way and I could not see him coming, although I had switched on the torch. The stream of light was thrown back into my eyes by the trunk before me and a dark void lay beyond.

The tiger could not now check himself despite the bright light that faced him. A mass of snarling fury, he was suddenly before me, appearing out of the darkness from behind the tree-trunk and to my left. I leaped to the right, desperately keeping the tree between us, and fired hastily from the shelter of the trunk at the massive head, not more than two yards away.

The tiger tried to turn while continuing his blind rush forward and had reached the tree before my scattered wits responded to the urge to work the underlever of the .405. The spent cartridge case flew out of the breach and I had time for a hasty second shot at the confused, blurred hindquarters of the tiger.

He disappeared, and silence fell once more. I listened intently for the sounds I hoped to hear: the gurgling death-rattle of a dying animal, or the deep, sad moaning of a badly-wounded beast. At least the angry roar of an infuriated creature that has been hit in some place. I listened for the crackling, crashing noise made by a wounded animal in headlong flight, heedless of where it is going so long as it succeeds in getting away.

But none of these sounds was to be heard: absolutely nothing at all. I waited perhaps for ten minutes — or fifteen — with the beam of my torch still on the spot where the tiger disappeared from view.

Still the silence continued. No distant alarm-cries from sambar or spotted-deer marked the movements of the man-eater. Could my first shot have been fatal? Perhaps the tiger had dropped dead a few yards away.

Then at last I heard a sound. It was the chirruping of a cricket. Others joined in, singly and in twos and threes, till once more the jungle was filled with that vibrating, rasping, uneven sound. It was as if the hidden tractor had been put to work once again.

Of one thing I could then be certain: the man-eater was no longer in the vicinity.

Relieved of the tension, I lowered the beam of the torch on my rifle to examine the ground at the spot where the tiger was when I fired at his head. Then I moved slowly forward, looking closely at the earth in the direction he went. I passed Kalla's bones and reached the place where he disappeared. But nothing was to be seen.

I moved forward till I reached the thick undergrowth and the ground was hidden from view. I examined the leaves, the twigs and the blades of high grass as I moved on in the direction taken by the fleeing man-eater. But there was not a drop of blood to be seen, nor any sign of disturbed, bitten or clawed under-growth, no evidence of any wounded creature having passed that way.

Then I remembered the deep silence that followed my two shots and was convinced at last of the shocking fact that I had missed, not once, but twice, and the first at point-blank range.

Not knowing the way to the Chenchu settlement in the darkness, I climbed back into the machan and spent the rest of the night in bitter self-recrimination. The man-eater would now become more cunning than ever and would never return to a kill again. As a result he would be hungry more often, and this would lead to him killing more frequently. The Chenchus, and other unfortunate people who lived in that area, would have to pay the penalty. The man-eater would not exact an indirect payment for my poor shooting.

It was 4 a.m. before I fell asleep, to be awakened shortly after dawn by Appu and nearly a dozen Chenchus who had accompanied him to ascertain the result of the shots they must have heard the previous night. Shamefacedly, I related what had happened. Appu said nothing. He merely looked at me with one raised eye-brow. There was a wealth of disdain in that look, and he knew I knew it.

There was nothing to do but ask our Chenchu friends to report at once if they heard or saw anything more of the man-eater, and then Appu and I took the weary trail back to Peddacheruvu. Neither of us spoke the whole way. We both felt that, under the circumstances, the less said the better.

Byanna tried to cheer me up when he heard the story by giving a short discourse on the law of averages. In effect he said I had to miss some time if I did not want to miss every time. I was not impressed and went to sleep.

Nothing happened during the next two days and Byanna said that we would have to return to Markapur very shortly for fresh supplies, for, incredible as it might seem, that great stock of foodstuffs we had brought with us was running low. Personally, I think he had given up hope and had come to feel that the man-eater was too cunning for us.

Here was where little Appu showed his mettle. He told Byanna to go to town for the fresh supplies while he and I would scour the jungle from dawn to dusk in an attempt to meet the tiger. My friend agreed, but added that he thought we were wasting our time.

Byanna left for Markapur at six next morning, while Appu and I set off at the same hour to try to meet the lame tiger. This time the Chenchu brought not only his axe but his dog, a lanky, cadaverous cur, whose ears had been cut off as a puppy to avoid attracting the hordes of 'horse-flies,' as they are called in India, that pester horses and dogs in later life by collecting on their ears. I do not know the real name of these pests, but I am told that they belong to the same family as the African tse-tse fly. Their bite, unlike that of their African cousins, is quite harmless, although very sharp and painful.

This apparition of a dog, which Appu addressed as 'Adiappa,' looked as if he had not eaten for at least six months. Now Adiappa is a man's name in the Telegu dialect and definitely not that of a dog. I asked Appu the reason and he replied that Adiappa was this neighbour's name, a person whom Appu disliked intensely. He had, therefore, named the cur after him to insult the neighbour. In this strategy, however, Appu had come off second best, as he went on to add with great resentment that the neighbour, who washed clothes for a living, had retaliated by giving the name Appu to one of his donkeys, which he used for carrying the bundles of dirty linen to the tank for washing.

So Appu and I, with the cur Adiappa dodging between our legs, circled the lake once again, this time along the eastern shore and not by the western approach where the track from Peddacheruvu made its way to the Atmakur-Doranala road. The scrub was thinner at this end of the lake, and as a consequence feathered game like pea-fowl and partridge were quite plentiful. We also put up a small herd of black-buck, an animal normally not found in the vicinity of big jungles and usually confined to wastelands bordering the cultivated areas. One old stag, with a jet-black coat and white underbelly and an enormous pair of corkscrew horns, regarded us with studied indifference till Adiappa took it into his head to give chase with a series of hungry yelps. The stag and his harem disappeared and the cur came back to regard us with mournful, accusing eyes. Very plainly he was upbraiding us in his doggie mind for having missed the chance of giving him something to eat.

The black-buck, which is the most beautiful of the few species of the antelope family in India, was also at one time the most plentiful and roamed the wastelands all over the peninsula in thousands. Since those days they have been relentlessly pursued with bows and arrows, firearms, dogs and all manner of ingenious traps, till today they are but few and far between, scarcely to be seen in their old haunts and in real danger of extermination. Rules for their protection exist on paper, written in Government offices and printed in notifications and gazettes, but nobody pays heed to them, and the eventual disappearance of this beautiful creature from the face of this earth seems a certainty.

To make matters worse, the black-buck belongs to the

order of animals that chew the cud. That is, their food is swallowed after being partly masticated and passes into the stomach where digestion begins. From here it is returned to the mouth again for further mastication before being finally swallowed. During this process the animal is incapable of quick or prolonged movement and tires easily. If chased for a distance, it falls to earth exhausted and helpless. The indigenous hunters and village poachers know this, and they also know exactly how long after grazing the second digestive process begins and for how long it lasts. So when they observe a herd feeding, they watch patiently till the animals squat down to 'chew the cud.' They wait for a few minutes more and then give chase with packs of dogs, guns, bows and arrows and what not. The frightened antelope tries to escape, but the younger members and the females cannot go far. They collapse exhausted and are either torn to bits by the pursuing dogs or killed at close range when the men come up.

To continue with my story! Appu and I had not gone far after seeing the black-buck when we crossed the tracks of a family of four nilgai or blue-bull, as they are better known. As a rule these animals graze alone. This quartet had gone down the previous night to water at lake. These big antelope leave tracks that look very like those of their cousins of the jungles, the giant sambar deer, the difference being that the former are much more pointed and rather more elongated. At this point we halted. For, superimposed over the tracks of the four nilgai were the pug marks of a big male tiger.

Appu and I studied the ground carefully and started to follow the tiger's trail for a short distance. Soon we confirmed that he was not our quarry; the lame man-eater. This animal had all four of his feet intact and was suffering no handicap whatever. Undoubtedly we were looking at the pug-marks of our old friend, the roaring but very timid tiger that seemed to insist on haunting us as well as the precincts of the lake. He was no good to us anyhow, while the lame man-eater, being also a male, was hardly likely to keep him company.

We went on and on, working southwards, till by mid-day we judged we were at least ten miles from the lake which, according to my pocket compass, lay directly north of us. We did not want to go too far as the man-eater had hitherto confined his activities to within about this radius. So after a whispered consultation Appu and I changed direction and set off on a north-westerly course that should, before evening, bring us to a point due west of the lake and within a couple of miles of the little Chenchu settlement where I had met my last adventure.

Here we ran into difficulties. Such game-trails as we did cross ran at right-angles to our course, from south-west to north-east, as the animals that had made them through the years had gone towards the lake for water. So we could not avail ourselves of the natural assistance they afforded by following them, but had to follow a direct course towards our destination by struggling through the jungle. This made for very hard going and slow progress. Every few yards we would come up against thorny bushes or clumps of heavy vegetation. These we had to circumvent. Thus the distance we had to cover was more than doubled and took much more time than planned and required frequent reference to my compass.

The sun was scorchingly hot at 3 p.m., and we were both bathed in perspiration when we reached a small hillock. There was an overhanging rock facing us on one side of this hillock, and from the base oozed a tiny trickle of fresh water, only a few drops at a time, which had formed into a puddle no more than a couple of feet in diameter. The supply of water was so small that a stream could not form and the liquid soaked into the ground at about the same rate as it dripped from the rock. As a result the water was fresh and crystal-clear, and to our overheated and tired bodies as welcome as an oasis in the Sahara.

But there was this difference. Clearly imprinted in the moist earth were the tracks of the tiger we were looking for; in fact there were many pug-marks to be seen, for by accident we had discovered his regular drinking-place. Among the tracks was the blurred drag of his limping foot in places where he had rested it on the ground while he drank.

There was no doubt about it. We were looking at the tracks of the lame man-eater at last! Jubilation filled us, both at discovering the tracks and at finding water to drink. I placed the .405 on the ground and lay on my stomach with just one thought for the moment and that was to drink, and drink and drink. I never bothered to see what Appu was doing or even to think about him. I suppose with the usual sahib's accustomed attitude of taking things for granted, my subconscious mind, if it thought at all, expected Appu to wait till I had finished.

I was good that Appu actually did so, for my subconscious mind was apparently not up to form that day. For, as I was enjoying the ice-cold water, the man-eater decided to charge.

There came a tremendous roar from the right of us; 'Wrr-off!' And again: Wrr-off! Wrr-off!' And then the man-eater was upon us!

Groping for the rifle with my right hand, I crouched on my knees, turning around as best I could to face the rush. A terrifying apparition greeted me. The snarling form of the tiger was racing towards us in lop-sided, bobbing bounds. He

363

was but fifteen feet away! Appu stood his ground, maniacally flourishing his axe in sweeping circles to meet that onslaught. Yelping frenziedly in front of his master, the dog Adiappa, which up to this moment had showed no sign of being any more than a ludicrous, half-starved cur, stood with bared teeth to meet that awful onslaught.

I suppose the tiger, too, thought the sight before him frightening. The people he had so far killed had been taken by surprise. They had screamed but offered no resistance. In this case a man stood before, him, whirling something around and around, while a despicable cur, that he would not have condescended to look at, seemed to want to fight. The only craven thing in the scene and up to the tiger's expectations was the second individual who was rolling on the ground, evidently in abject fear and unable to get up.

The tiger halted for a moment, and in that moment the man-eater had made his greatest and last mistake. The man on the ground — myself — had found his rifle at last and did not get up because he was kneeling to take aim. I fired then, and twice again.

An examination of the dead animal confirmed what I had been told. He had been turned into a man-eater by the severed damage to his right leg suffered during a fight with another tiger. At least, in this case, man was not to blame!

To Appu and his dog, Adiappa, I am grateful that I was able to tell Byanna, when he returned from Markapur very late that evening with a fresh stock of food-stuffs, that his labour had been in vain. Had the stocky little Chenchu and his large-hearted dog not stood their ground but run away, the man-eater would never have paused in his rush and I would not have lived to tell the tale.

To conclude, I will explain why the crickets ceased their chirruping when the man-eater started roaring. My naturalist friend at Madras says it is because the tiger's roars made the ground vibrate. Apparently crickets cannot hear, but they have an acute sense to touch. The vibrations had given them cause for fear — perhaps even an earthquake in the offing? The crickets had stopped shouting at least.

Three

The Queer Side of Things

VISITS TO THE JUNGLE ARE NOT ALWAYS FOR THE PURPOSE OF HUNTING and killing. Far from it. As I grow older, I find that I have no urge to slay, except when occasion calls for it. So for a change I will tell you of few incidents of another kind that I have experienced in my forest wanderings.

Among the foothills to the north of the Nilgiri range of mountains lies undulating country, covered by heavy forest to the west, where the rainfall is plentiful, and slightly lighter jungle to the east, where the monsoon, having expended itself against the lofty Nilgiris, is unable to bring so much rain. Centuries ago, all this land was cultivated and densely populated too, and the remains of quite a number of ruined villages, temples, forts and viaducts are to be found in the forest, covered now by the jungle, where evidently civilization thrived in days gone by.

I have in mind the cattle patty of Chemanath, where half-a-dozen wattle huts now stand, enclosed within a rough circle of perhaps two acres of land. The circumference of the circle is outlined by a low barrier of cut, piled thorns, three feet high. The surface within is inches deep in cow dung, accumulated over decades by the hundreds of cattle that have sheltered in this 'patty.' In summer time, when there is no grazing in the forest and the cattle are taken away, this cow dung dries as hard as cement. Then the rains come, and the cattle return. The rain, and the urine passed by hundreds of animals quartered within the thorn enclosure at night, make a quagmire of the accumulated dung. The herdsmen live in the centre of the enclosure, so if you wish to speak to them you must be prepared to wade through the malodorous morass, which may reach to your ankles or higher.

It is not about this patty itself that I intend to tell you, but about the ruins of a great temple that stand perhaps half-a-mile away. The roots of massive fig trees grow within the temple walls, but the sanctuary, the holy of holies which only the Brahmin priests were allowed to enter, remains fairly well preserved. A courtyard encloses this sanctuary, and you pass great pillars of hewn rock, leaning at a crazy angle, till you reach a massive wooden door at least six inches thick. It is studded with great brass knobs and has a mighty lever for opening the door from the outside. The huge draw-bar that closes it on the inside is still there. The rusty hinges, made of crude wrought-iron, still exist, and the two doors creak eerily when you open them to pass inside. Of their own weight, perhaps, or maybe due to the angle at which they hang, they come together and shut once that you are now immured within the sanctuary and can never escape.

The temple itself is built of solid granite, and a few yards in front are the remains of what must, in its day, have been a magnificent stone well. It is lined with granite and is over

150 feet deep by about the same in diameter. Many of the granite blocks have fallen in now and no sign of water is to be seen at the bottom of the well.

Just over a mile from this temple and well, as the crow flies, stand the remains of a stone fort, surrounded by a moat. The forest now covers everything. Nobody goes there and the Irilas of the jungle give the area a wide berth. For they say the spirits of the thousands who perished there in a matter of a few days still haunt the place. No one knows exactly when the catastrophe happened. The story has been handed down from father to son for many generations and has always been the same. It may have occurred two or three hundred years ago or it may have been much earlier.

The Great Fever came at that time, so they say, and it mowed the people down in thousands. The victims never saw the light of a second day. There were no remedies and no doctors. The people just died where they collapsed and there was nobody to bury them. It is said that the stench of death and decay was so great that people at Kalhatti, seven miles away and half-way up the mountains, could smell it. The few that survived fled from the valley of death, not waiting to take their belongings with them, and civilization came to an end. The jungle took over and blotted out human habitation, while its creatures fed on the rotted flesh and the countless bones of the dead for a whole year.

What this great fever could have been nobody knows, but from the havoc it wrought, its contagious nature and quick end, people say it could only have been that most dreaded of all infectious diseases, the plague, in one of its most virulent forms. Certain it is that human habitation in the area ended completely, and it has never returned.

Into the holies of holes of the temple no outsider was ever allowed in times past, particularly a meat-eater or one of foreign race. The ancient priests, all Brahmins, would attend bare-bodied and with bare feet. This makes you wonder whether you are right when you stand within the sanctuary with your boots on.

There is a raised earthen platform at one end, and resting upon it a number of images, carved in stone, of the sacred animal of the Hindus, the bull. There are about five of them if I remember correctly, varying in size. The bull is always depicted in sitting posture. The largest stands a little over a foot high by about two and a half feet long; the smallest about four inches by ten. To one is an ancient lamp, perhaps six inches high. It is made of brass, completely dulled with age and oxidization, and consists merely of a hollow cavity to hold the oil, and a lip to support the wick that rests in the oil, the whole standing on a pedestal which is a carving of some deity.

And thereby hangs a tale, for some years ago I went to this temple accompanied by some tourists. They were strangers whom I had met casually in the jungle. They had heard of the temple and asked me where it was, and because it was difficult to locate I had brought them there in person. They were four. We stood inside the holy of holies, looking at the stone bulls which, incidentally, are called 'nandies,' when one of the tourists, let us call him Captain Neide, who came from Australia, noticed the brass lamp and took a fancy to it.

'I think I'll keep this as a souvenir,' he remarked, picking it up and thrusting it into his pocket.

'You shouldn't do that.' I remonstrated, and his wife supported me. 'Put it back, John; we don't need it,' was her comment.

'But why not?' argued John. 'I need it.'

The top of the lamp protruded from his pocket as we went away and I could not help thinking to myself that it was a shame that the lamp was leaving its abode after no one knew how many hundreds of years. I returned to my camp, while the party of tourists went up the hill to the town of Ootacamund, seventeen miles away. They had mentioned they were spending four or five day there, before moving on.

Four days later I was walking along the main road when a black and yellow taxi, coming down from Ootacamund, overtook me and then halted. Taxis do not generally come to jungles, so I approached it curiously to see who was inside. To my great surprise I saw Captain Neide at the back, propped up with pillows, covered with a blanket, and looking very sick. Next to him sat Mrs Neide, pale and anxious.

'Thank heaven we met you, Mr Anderson,' she burst out. 'Something terrible has happened to John.'

Then she went on to explain that the very evening her husband and their friends reached Ootacamund, he developed a high temperature and became extremely ill. A doctor was summoned, who diagnosed sunstroke and treated the patient accordingly.

But during the night Neide's temperature rose to 106 degrees. He became delirious. His distraught wife and her friends called the doctor again. Neide was taken to hospital, where it was thought he was developing blackwater fever, or an extremely bad bout of malaria. Quinine was administered, but there was no improvement. On the third day Neide was desperately ill, and the hospital staff confessed they could not discover the cause. Neide himself provided the solution on the morning of the fourth day. Delirious most of the time, due to his high temperature, there were short periods when he regained his senses, and during one of these he gasped to his wife, 'Margaret! That lamp! I must take it back to the temple. Get a car — a taxi — anything. I must take it back to the temple today, or I shall die tomorrow. I must take it myself.'

Halting he explained that he had had a dream in which he had seen the lamp back in its place on the altar of the old temple. His wife told the house doctor, who merely smiled and said briefly, 'Delirium, madam — he imagined it all.'

But Mrs Neide knew this was not so. On the table in their room at the hotel stood that dreadful lamp. It seemed to draw attention to itself and she could not take her eyes from it.

'I thing I shall take him and the lamp by taxi, doctor,' she argued. 'I feel something dreadful is going to happen if we don't return it.'

'Mrs Neide, if you move your husband in his present condition, I'll not be responsible for what happens. He is far too ill and I will not give my permission.'

She went back and told Neide what the doctor had said.

'If you don't help me to return the lamp, I shall be dead by tomorrow. I know it, Margaret,' he gasped.

'I'll take it back in the taxi for you John,' she offered.

'No, no,' he was adamant. 'I brought it away and I must return it,' he insisted. And that was how I came to meet them on the road.

Without comment, I got in beside the driver and directed him to the track that led off the main road to the Chemanath patty. A little beyond was the temple, but the car could go no further. Captain Neide, who was conscious now, wanted to carry the lamp to the temple, but it was obvious he was quit unfit to walk.

So I said to him, 'John, I think you have done enough to show you're sorry for taking the lamp away. You've brought it back as far as you possibly can. The temple deity will understand that. Let Mrs Neide and me take it back for you while you rest here.'

371

He was too exhausted to reply but nodded his consent and, with his wife carrying the lamp and me leading the way, we went back to the temple. The ancient door creaked open and closed of its own volition behind us. We stood at the alter before the five nandies and Mrs Neide reverently replaced the old brass lamp on its pedestal. She was weeping, and I could see she was praying. The we returned in silence to the car.

Neide was sound asleep. Involuntarily, I strected out my hand to touch his forehead. He was perspiring profusely, the sweat running down his forehand and cheeks. The fever had left him, and he was quite cool to my touch. Helped by his wife, I tucked the blanket more closely around him, wound up the glass windows to prevent a draught, and instructed the driver to take him back to the hotel at Ootacamund.

For there was no need to go to the hospital. Neide was cured. There were tears of joy on his wife's face as the taxi drove away.

That, my readers, is exactly what happened. You may offer any explanations you like. Autosuggestion? I will not argue with you. All I know is that it happened!

* * *

Another curious incident that I witnessed recently at a hamlet within half-a-mile of Mavanhalla settlement, which is exactly fifteen miles from Ootacamund, was a case of avowed black magic.

A comely girl living in the hamlet was engaged to be married to man living in the village of Garupalli, twelve miles away. In India couples do not get engaged of their own volition. These things are arranged for them by the parents of both parties, who barter and bargain till they arrive at a settlement. Normally, the principal parties do not even see each other till they are actually married. But in this case there was a difference. The man and his parents visited Mavanhalla. He saw the girl and approved of her, and the date of the wedding was tentatively set.

These people are known as Irilas, and it is their custom for the man's parents to pay the girl's parents a certain sum of money for her hand in marriage. In plain words, they purchase her. This is different from the normal Indian custom of dowry, whereby the girl's parents are required to put down an agreed sum.

In this case, however, the boy's parents at the last moment said they could not, or would not, pay. The girl's parents, in a rage, broke off the engagement and found another candidate willing to pay the price they had fixed for their daughter.

Then things happened. The Garupalli lad, furious at being turned down, and mad with jealousy, walked through the jungle for a distance of over a hundred miles to the town of Kollegal, near the banks of the Cauvery River, where lived a black magician of very great and evil repute. He had to spend money through the nose, for the magician made him buy a whole sheep for sacrifice, its blood being offered to the spirit which was now to take a hand in matters, while its flesh went to the magician. The unholy ceremony was performed at three in the morning of the night of the full moon.

A hundred miles away the girl was sleeping in the hamlet near Mavanhalla when, at precisely three that morning, she awoke with a pain in her stomach and hastened outside the hut to answer the call of nature. A few yards to the rear of each hut is the spot where the inhabitants usually go for this purpose.

She reported that she had finished and was just coming away when two unknown men materialized as if from nowhere, laid hold of her sari, and urged her to come at once with them to Gorupalli. Sensing that this was a ploy by her late betrothed to entice her away, the girl said she would try to come as soon as it was daylight. To this the men replied that she should come immediately, when the girl said that the distance was too great. At this they offered to carry her.

The exchange of words had reached this stage when the girl happened to look down. Horror gripped her when she noticed that neither of the men had feet; at least their feet did not touch the ground, which she could plainly see in the brilliant moonlight. Rather, she could see the ground in the brilliant moonlight, but no feet where there should have been feet!

She screamed after that. The men vanished and people came tumbling out of their huts in response to her yells. She told them what had happened, but the neighbours thought she had had a nightmare, for no men were to be seen.

The girl was upset for the rest of that day and would not eat, but at the usual time of about 7.30 p.m., sat down for her supper, a simple meal of curry and rice. In the usual way she fashioned with her right hand a ball of rice and curry and put it into her mouth. Then her mouth burned as if on fire and the food appeared to become hard. In a panic she spat it out. But what came out of her mouth and into the plate was a stone.

This sort of thing continued for eight days. Then I happened to visit Mavanhalla and was told about it. Apparently the girl could eat her morning meal undisturbed, and also at any other time of the day. The phenomenon occurred only after sundown, when she attempted to eat her supper.

Being always interested in things unusual, I hastened to the hamlet, where I saw the girl and her parents and spoke to them. I spoke also to the neighbours; in fact nearly every adult in that settlement. They had all witnessed the phenomenon and told me the story that I have just related. The father had collected these stones and some other miscellaneous articles that the girl had spat out. I asked him to give them to me, which he did, and they are before me as I write. The items are as follows: stones of various sizes and shapes — six items, the largest weighing three ounces; broken bits of pottery — six items; charcoal — two pieces; lastly, a piece of broken bottle-glass.

As I have said, the time for these phenomena to occur was at the evening meal. So I returned just after seven o'clock that evening to witness things for myself.

The girl was lying on the ground in a sort of daze, with more than a dozen people around her. Her face was damp with sweat, and every little while her mouth would work, twist and pout, as if something was inside.

By nature I am sceptic. The thought came to me that the girl was putting on an act and the reason seemed simple enough. She wanted to marry the man at Garupalli and had invented the whole story. In the course of the day she herself, or perhaps an accomplice acting for her, would procure a stone or a piece of tile in advance and conceal in somewhere on her person. This object the girl would put into her mouth some time before the evening meal and keep it here till the time she spit the object out, together with the food. So I determined that I would expose her trickery before all the people who had gathered around her.

I told her to open her mouth widely. She did so. I had brought my torch with me, as it was dark outside. I shone the torch into her mouth. Nothing appeared to be there. Suddenly, and without asking her permission, and risking a bite from her, I thrust my forefinger beneath her tongue to see if anything was hidden there, then into both the cavities formed between her cheeks and jaws, holding her firmly with my left hand by the back of her neck in order that my probing finger would find the stone I was convinced was hidden in her mouth.

The girl choked, but surprisingly enough did not struggle or protest. Rather, she appeared to be going to sleep. There was nothing in her mouth and finally I released her. The working and pouting and twisting of her mouth stopped after that, and time passed.

In about half-an-hour her evening meal was brought to her. She sat up to eat it, stretching forth her hand to take the first mouthful, but I stopped her. Calling to her mother, I asked the old woman to break up the rice in the girl's hand as the thought came to me that a stone might be concealed in the rice or curry.

The girl stretched out her hand again, took up the grains we had examined between her fingers, mixed them with the curry, made a small ball of them and put it into her mouth. Then she started to chew. Everything was normal. I smiled to myself in satisfaction. The vixen has not been able to dodge me.

The next instant I heard it. A jarring, crunching sound as the girl's moving teeth came down on some hard object in her mouth. The look of abject terror that came into her face was genuine enough. I could see fear in her eyes, genuine fear, not assumed. With a muffled scream she spat the object out. A stone fell with a dull plop into the earthen plate containing the curry and rice.

At that moment I shouted to her to open her mouth, seized the back of her neck again with my left hand, and thrust my right forefinger into her mouth. Believe it or not. There was not a grain of rice or food of any sort in her mouth! The mouthful she had just taken had vanished entirely. The stone had taken its place!

Now the girl had not the time to chew the food, nor could she have swallowed it, for I had been watching intently all the time. To swallow a fistful of rice and curry requires a visible swallowing movement of the muscles of the mouth, throat and gullet. There had been nothing of that sort. The stone she spat out that evening is the one weighing three ounces which is now before me.

But the story does not end there. I witnessed the same thing the next evening. Once more I looked into the girl's mouth and searched carefully for any hidden object as she began to eat her food. As if to reward my diligence, the piece of broken bottle-glass, with jagged edges, emerged this time. It also lies before me as I write. How the broken edges did not cut her tongue and mouth I do not know. And once again there was not a grain of food left in her mouth after the glass had dropped out. This time a larger crowd of people than ever before witnessed the incident.

News of these happenings, as may well be imagined, had spread far and wide, and the next afternoon a healer arrived. He was an Indian of about my own age, a Christian, and an unpretentious individual. I had gone a little early to the girl's hut that evening, for I was still curious and wanted to see this thing once more for my own satisfaction. The strange Indian was squatting at the door when I arrived. He rose and smiled affably. Speaking softly and in faultless English, he introduced himself and said he was on a visit or Ootacamund. He had heard about the girl there and had come down by the evening bus, walking the three miles alone through the jungle from the village of Masinigudi, where the bus had dropped him.

Very modestly, but with strange self-confidence, he claimed that God had given him the power of healing and that he had come to heal the girl. Rather taken aback, I am afraid I spoke somewhat caustically.

'What you mean is, you have come to try to head her!'

'No, sir, I have come to heal her. I was impelled to come from Ootacamund for this purpose. God will not fail, sir. He cannot.'

I felt rather sheepish, faced with such simple confidence, and said nothing. Then this stranger, who had introduced himself by the simple Indian name of Puttaswamy, began to question the girl and her parents. In a short while these, together with several of the bystanders who had witnessed the phenomenon on many occasions, told the whole story. Finally I told him of my own experiences on the two preceding days.

By this time the girl begun to perspire and her mouth had begun to work. The symptoms I had seen twice before were starting. Puttaswamy sat beside her and said nothing. Hie eyes were closed and his lips were moving faintly. He appeared to be muttering to himself — perhaps he was praying.

Once again, regardless of the healer's presence, I made the girl open her mouth and examined it more carefully than ever before, looking down her throat questing with my finger beneath her tongue, between her jaws and cheeks, everywhere I possible could. Very definitely there was nothing concealed in her mouth.

Then came the final act in this strange drama. The evening meal was brought to the girl in the form of the usual rice and curry, for the Irilas knew no other. The girl made and put the ball of food in her mouth and started to chew. Peremptorily the silence was broken by Puttaswamy. In a strangely confident, loud voice, he cried:

'In the name of Jesus Christ of Nazareth, whoever you are, I command you, come out of her!'

There came the unmistakable crack and crunch and crunch of stone in the girl's mouth. She screamed and rolled on the ground in a frenzy as if in an epileptic fit, tearing her hair and grinding her teeth. Puttaswamy knelt beside her. His eyes were like coals and were moist with emotion. Once again he cried:

'In the name of Jesus Christ of Nazareth, leave her this instant!

The girl was violently convulsed, bending backwards as if in the throes of tetanus. She spat out the rice and curry she had taken. A horrid screech came from her throat. She shuddered, then was still. A few minutes later she moved again. Gently Puttaswamy sat her up. There was no stone in her mouth — only a few grains of rice and curry.

Softly, but quivering with deep emotion and joy, Puttaswamy said, 'Thank you, Jesus.'

The girl was cured. Instinctively we all knew it for we could feel the power that radiated from this strange and simple man.

I saw these for myself and know they are true!

* * *

The man I am now going to tell you about was a dacoit — a thief and the murderer of nine people!

The story began many years ago. The man's name was Selvaraj. The police records described him as: 'aged 36 years; height 5 feet 7 inches; of average dark complexion; usually sporting a heavy, twirled moustache reaching almost to his temple; has a distinctly protruding upper lip and a scar reaching from the corner of his right eye to the lobe of his right ear.'

The trouble started with a family feud. Selvaraj's father had quarrelled with a neighbour. The latter assembled a gang of relatives, waylaid the elderly man one night, murdered him and tied the corpse to a tree bordering the highway for everyone to see as an example the following morning.

Selvaraj was a young man then. He knew about the feud, but had contrived to keep himself aloof. But the cruel murder of his father was too much for him. With his brother to assist, and five others, the seven avengers raided the home of the murderers and hacked all nine of them to death with wood-choppers.

There was a hue and cry after that, the cause of mass murders and the identity of the perpetrators being well know. Three of Selvaraj's relatives, who has assisted him, were caught, convicted and hanged. He, his brother and two others went into hiding.

The feud spread and police help was not asked by either side. The relations of the nine men who had been killed came to find out where Selvaraj, his brother and the two others were hiding. As usual, it was because of a woman that the information leaked out. Selvaraj's brother had taken up with another man's wife and was living with her, along with Selvaraj and the other two men. The aggrieved husband gave the information to the relations of the nine men. They came at night with petrol and set fire to the hut in which their enemies were sleeping. The brother and the woman were burned to death, while Selvaraj and his two companions escaped.

The police came again, arrested the avengers, and got two of them convicted and hanged. Both sides had now gone into hiding in the forest, afraid of the police and thirsting for each other's blood.

Bereft of all his possessions, lands and livelihood, Selvaraj had to live somehow. He could not earn an honest living in any town because the police would arrest him on sight, so force of circumstances compelled him to turn to robbery, but even this he tried to do in an honourable way, if one can associate such a term with crime.

Selvaraj became a dacoit, a sort of Robin Hood of South

India. He robbed the rich to feed the poor. Landlords, wealthy business men, shopkeepers and thriving merchants were his prey, but he kept only a portion of his extortions for his own maintenance. The rest he gave away to the maimed, the poor, the sick and the needy. So much so, indeed, that there was a sharp division of feeling about him. The large majority of people, including the farmers and poor ryots, loved and respected him. The small majority of the rich, and of course the police, feared and hated him intensely.

Selvaraj, at about this time, began to acquire a nickname. He had a protruding upper lip and became known as 'Mumptyvayan' meaning 'the man with a mouth like a 'Mumpty.' 'Mumpty' is the local name for a shovel. He lived entirely in the jungle and his domain was here, there and everywhere, over an extent of many miles, ranging from the banks of the Cauvery River into the eastern portion of the District of Kollegal, into Salem District, up Doddahalla or the Secret River and across the mountains to the Chinar River and the outskirts of the town of Pennagram.

He appeared and disappeared like the Scarlet Pimpernel, and the authorities could never catch him. Like Man Singh, the notorious dacoit who ranged the fastnesses of the Chambal valley of Rajasthan in the north of India, Mumptyavayan in the south was equally loved by the poor who inhabited the forest regions and their borders. The authorities could never gain information regarding his whereabouts and could not lay hands on him. On the other hand, people would inform him about the movements of the police when the latter sent armed squads periodically into the jungles to try to catch up with him.

Mumptyavayan's *modus operandi* was simple. From a host of willing informers he would gain information about the sources of income of landlords and merchants. Mysteriously he would then appear at dead of night in the homes of these gentry, threaten them with knife and gun, and make away with the large sums of money they would hurriedly hand over to him in order to save their lives.

Another thing he did was collecting money from timber thieves. At dead of night these poachers would bring lorries and a gang of workers to some quiet corner of the jungle, hack down a tree, cut it up into sections, load the wood on to their vehicles, and disappear before dawn. But just at the crucial moment, as the engine was being started, Mumptyvayan would appear at the driver's cab, his gun pointed at the people inside, and demand fifty rupees as the price of his silence. Invariably the sum was paid.

But on one occasion the enterprising driver engaged his gears and tried to make a run for it. Mumptyvayan did not shoot the man; he shot at both the rear tyres in quick succession. The driver paid up after that. He was put out of business too, for the lorry carried only one spare wheel. Daylight came before the party could go to town and return with a second spare. The poachers tried to off-load the lorry and hide all the timber they had stolen, but they were discovered, arrested and sent to jail, while the lorry was confiscated. In any event, each tyre cost Rs. 600 and the dacoit had only asked for Rs. 50. Mumptyvayan gained much prestige after this incident, while the poacher greatly regretted having refused his reasonable demand.

From reports that were made to the police, it was estimated that Mumptyvayan collected Rs 25,000 a year by robbery, on an average, but the figure could be doubled to include amounts that were taken by him but not reported to the police, as Mumptyvayan was astute enough to rob many whose activities were such as to make it inconvenient, if not impossible, for them to seek police aid.

He invariably worked alone for, very wisely, he distrusted accomplices. His usual costume was a Khaki shirt, rather ragged khaki shorts, a belt around his waist to which a huge knife was strapped on the left side and a dagger on the right, a cartridge-belt across his shoulder, filled with home-loaded 12 bore cartridges, both ball and shot, while he carried an old but well-kept harmless .12 bore Geco gun that he had stolen. Sometimes he wore a green turban to simulate the uniform of a Forest Guard, but generally was bareheaded.

Mumptyvayan was extraordinary courteous to women, of whom he was, unfortunately for himself, rather over-fond. His legal wife lived at the village of Mecheri, ten miles from the Mettur Dam, and he never forgot her in spite of his many concubines who ranged, like his activities, all over the jungle. For six months the police watched the wife's house at Mecheri and still the husband visited her. He came once, disguised as a woman and all covered up, the police only knew about it after he had left.

A month later another muffled figure approached. The police pounced on this one, knocked it down and fastened handcuffs on hands and feet. But to their chagrin, and the open derision of all the villagers who had turned out to enjoy the fun, this figure turned out to be a real woman. She abused the police, but also grinned widely and admitted that Mumptyvayan had sent her to make of them a laughing-stock.

This incident appears to have increased the vagabond's confidence in himself and he regarded the custodians of law and order with contempt, for overnight a notice appeared on the gate of the police station, duly signed by the dacoit, intimating a week in advance that he would visit that very village on a particular day. Two wagons, loaded with constables were rushed to Mecheri and every one of the men was ordered to learn, by heart, a description of the rogue so as to be able to recognize him on sight.

Nobody answering to the description put in an appearance, but at the time of the midday meal a rather troublesome mendicant, without a vestige of hair on head or face and who had met with an accident and lost his right eye, turned up at the police station and begged for food from the constables who were squatting on the verandah and eating their food. One or two of the more kindly-natured gave him a fistful or rice, but the others kicked him out unceremoniously.

Later, they found that a small aluminium tiffin carrier belonging to one of them was missing. The beggar must have taken it — for all beggars are thieves! At dawn, two mornings later, a bleary-eyed policeman found the tiffin-carrier at the gate of the police station. Inside it was a note from Mumptyvayan thanking the owner for the loan of the carrier.

Greatly incensed at his, the authorities are rumoured to have sent about 300 armed policemen, in gangs of fifty, to scour the jungles and bring the dacoit in, dead or alive. They were particularly enjoined to be very alert in dealing with him because, shortly after the tiffin-carrier incident, the rascal had purloined a rifle from a landlord whose house he had raided, although the weapon had had no ammunition with it and it was felt the dacoit would not be in a position to secure any.

While the police were out in the forest searching for him, Mumptyvayan came to town and visited a travelling cinema that had come to the large village of Pennagram. He sat through the show till it was half over, then visited the box-office and relieved the cashier of all the evening's takings. The cashier pleaded that he would be sacked and jailed, as the management would say he had invented the story in order to take the money himself. So the chivalrous dacoit, seeing his point, hastily scribbled a note certifying that it was he,

Mumptyvayan, who had taken the money and not the cashier. He also gave the latter a five rupee note from the takings to buy himself a good meal at the local hotel before news of the robbery was given to the owner and trouble began.

The very next morning he visited the largest shop in the hamlet of Uttaimalai, eleven miles away, and relieved the owner of sixty-three rupees. On that occasion he appears to have been wearing a black muffler, closely wrapped around his neck and up to his ears, and an overcoat, from beneath which he produced two straight double-edged daggers, holding one in each hand to frighten the shopkeeper into silence.

About this time a jail-guard, whose home town was the same village of Pennagram, but who had been working at the prison situated in the city of Salem, was dismissed. He returned to his home at Pennagram very disgruntled and heard there about the recent exploits of Mumptyvayan and how anxious the police were to lay hands on him. The thought came to this ex-guard that, with a little subterfuge, he might be able to find the dacoit and gain his confidence; then he could go to the police and make a bargain in advance. A promise would have to be made to reinstate him in his old job at Salem prison, in return for which he would deliver the dacoit, duly fettered, to the police.

With commendable cunningness the ex-jailer pursued his plan. He gave out that he was an aggrieved man who wanted to work for the dacoit and give him information as to where easy money was to be had from the rich landlords and merchants of Salem City. This news was carried to Mumptyvayan in due course and the dacoit fell for the story. Through an agent he contacted the man and had a preliminary talk with him. It was arranged that they should meet again under a certain tree at a secret place near the cattleshed of Panapatti, about eight miles from Pennagram, at ten the following night and come to an understanding. The man hurriedly informed the police at Pennagram, who planned to swoop on the rendezvous at 10.30 p.m., next day, by which time the dacoit was to have been securely fettered. The police also promised to see that the informer was reinstated as jailer at Salem.

Promptly at 10 p.m. the next night the two men met and sat down to talk. Unfortunately, the ex-jailer was rather careless and allowed the handcuffs, which the police had lent him, to clank against a stone as he sat on the ground. Mumptyvayan's sharp ears caught the sound and he became suspicious.

'What have you got there that sounds like iron brother?' he asked.

'This,' replied the ex-jailer and, realizing that the game was up, leaped upon the dacoit at once. Both men were well-built, powerful individuals and a terrific battle was fought in silence, neither side asking or giving any quarter as they struggled upon the ground like beasts.

Then, for the second time that evening, the stone on the ground aided Mumptyavayan. The ex-jailer was sitting astride him, trying to choke him to death, when the dacoit felt the stone sticking into his side. Gripping it in his right fist, Mumptyvayan smashed it against the side of his antagonist's head. Momentarily stunned, the ex-jailer tumbled off and the dacoit in turn got on top. Once more the struggle began, but Mumptyvayan had his dagger out by now. As his adversary reached up to grapple with him again, a quick slash of the razor-sharp weapon severed three of the man's fingers. He screamed with pain, realizing that the dacoit, in his fury, would kill him for his duplicity. He begged for mercy and said he was sorry for what he had attempted to do.

Just then, Mumptyvayan heard the sound of the approaching police van. He disappeared in the darkness of the forest, leaving the would-be police agent rolling on the ground while trying to staunch the jets of blood that spurted from his injured hand.

The dacoit became a little more cautious after this incident. He disappeared from the jungles for three or four months and was heard of in the towns of Dharmapuri and Krishnagiri, where he robbed shops and people on a petty scale. He also filched a pair of binoculars from the owner of a car three miles out of Dharmapuri. Then Mumptyvayan came back to his old haunts, and the manner of his return was dramatic.

The Superintendent of Police and his family went down to the Hogenaikal Water Falls on the Cauvery River on a Sunday, to enjoy a picnic and a bath beneath the waterfall. They had left their jeep scarcely a hundred yards away. After completing their ablutions, they ate a picnic lunch and returned to the vehicle to find that the camera that had been left there had been stolen. Scribbled upon the grey paint of the jeep, in chalk, and in five separate places, were these words in the Tamil dialect: 'Mymptyvayan, the rajah of dacoits!'

During my visits to these areas from time to time, I had of course heard many tales of Mumptyvayan and his exploits. The early incidents in his history had aroused my sympathy, but this to a large extent disappeared when I learned of his more mundane actions and the thefts he had committed. I then regarded him as a complete rogue. But when I heard from the police of his daring, his sense of humour and his undeniable bravery, I confess I became attracted by this personality and entertained a great desire to meet him.

One day I brought a party of friends on a fishing expedition to Hogenaikal and found much excitement prevailing at that otherwise peaceful and sleepy hamlet. Mumptyvayan had struck again, and dramatically.

For at about this time an engineer from the Government

of Madras State had been commissioned to explore the possibility of constructing a dam across the river above the waterfalls, and survey work of every kind was in progress. Just a mile upstream, at a point where the actual construction was contemplated, a camp site had been made and over a hundred labourers were engaged in building a road, drilling holes and helping generally with the survey work. A shed had been erected for the engineer and his associates. A payroll centre had been established, and a clerk had arrived to pay the labourers at the end of each week.

So had Mumptyvayan — just two days earlier — and he had relieved the pay-clerk of Rs 350 from the pay for the following week without touching an anna of the pay for the week just completed and about to be paid out to the labourers.

Not content with his exploit, he had tapped upon the door of the quarters where the Inspector of Fisheries lived at the neighbouring hamlet of Uttaimalai, a mile away, announcing he was the forest Guard and had urgent news of the presence of fish poachers. The Inspector opened the door to find Mumptyvayan, but no Forest Guard. In a flash the dacoit had stepped within and closed the front door. Then, drawing his usual two double-edged daggers, he had intimidated the official. Luckily there were only Rs. 51 in the house at the time and all of this was handed over to the dacoit.

I met the Fisheries Inspector, and then the engineer, who allowed me to talk to the pay-clerk, and they confirmed the tales I had heard.

But at the moment I was more concerned about the dam than the exploits of the bandit. A dam here would mean the destruction by inundation of thousands of acres of jungle. There would be the erection of quarters for the staff and the township that would follow in the wake of the dam. The whole hamlet of Uttaimalai, including the little hut I had built and owned there for over twenty years, would disappear beneath the water.

I questioned the engineer regarding these things and he very kindly offered to take me around in his jeep and show me exactly where the construction might begin. I accepted his invitation gladly. A third man then joined us, carrying what at first seemed to be a service rifle. He was bareheaded, with a white dhoti around his waist and a khaki shirt hanging over it. Great ammunition boots without socks adorned his feet.

As we drove off, I asked the engineer who the armed man might be. He grinned and replied that the man was a police guard deputed to accompany him whenever he went into the jungle, for fear of what was generally thought that he would certainly be robbed by the dacoit, if not captured and held to ransom. Actually my friend seemed to be enjoying the situation.

Very soon we reached the site of the projected dam, alighted and wandered down the river bank together, followed by the armed policeman, who thumped over the river stones in his great boots or dragged them through the soft river sand. Winking to the engineer, I opened a conversation with the policemen, asking him about the dacoit. The man soon gave voice to his pent-up feeling. He was a government servant, he admitted, but the government consisted of fools. Fancy deputing him, single-handed, with a ridiculous weapon such as he held in his hands, to guard so august a personage as the engineer against such a notorious person as Mumptyvayan!

I asked what was wrong with the rifle. The policeman spat with disdain, unslung the weapon from his shoulder, and handed it to me contemptuously.

'It's not a rifle at all, although made to look like one,' he asserted. 'It's only a gun.'

I took the weapon from him and was surprised to find

it was only a .410 shotgun with a wooden casing to make it look like a .303 service rifle. The policeman then opened the leather punch on his belt and showed me ten rounds of ammunition for the weapon. They were merely .410 cartridges.

'With this pea-shooter,' he continued bitterly, 'the government expects me to guard this great man and outshoot this rascal Mumptyvayan, who is a marksman, as everyone knows.'

'Besides,' he went on, 'these rounds won't carry for more than fifty yards. Mumpty has only to sit on a rock sixty yards away and laugh at me, and I can't do anything about it. From there he can kill me, and the engineer sahib, as full of holes as a sieve. Bah! Thoo!' and the spat again venomously.

Keeping a serious face, I asked, 'What will you do, then, my friend, if Mumpty should suddenly appear from behind yonder rock or tree?'

With a start, the policeman looked up fearfully at the big rock and the phalanx of trees beyond it, some seventy-five yards away. In a burst of confidence, he addressed both of us.

'Sirs, I'm a family man. I have a wife and six children, the youngest yet a baby. Who will feed them if this bastard kills me? Forgive me, sirs; but if he should appear this instant I shall down this toy gun and run away.

We laughed to ease his embarrassment when he realized he had said the wrong thing, and I added, 'Please pass the word to everyone to tell this character Mumptyvayan that Anderson *dorai* is looking forward to meeting him some day.'

Three or four months had passed after this incident when I went to my twelve-acre plot of land on the banks of the Chinar River, a dozen miles upstream from the point where this river joins the Cauvery River at Hogenaikal, to camp for a few days. I had allowed my old friends and shikari, Ranga,

of whom I have spoken in other stories, to live on this land
and cultivate it for himself, and in his usual manner he urged
me to spend the time with him in the hut he had erected at
one corner of the land, rather than pitch the tent I had
brought along with me, and usually occupied, at quite another
spot.

'For there's a bad elephant about, *dorai,* he urged. 'It
sometimes prowls around at night. Seeing your tent, it may
trample upon it you before you can wake.'

'Bad elephant?' I queried. 'How extraordinary! The
Forestry Department has not told me of any such creature.'

It was midsummer. Everything was bone-dry, and the
jungle like timber. There was a not a drop of water in the
Chinar River. This was scarcely the time of year for an
elephant to be around. Elephants would keep strictly to the
banks of the Cauvery River, the only place for many miles
where water was to be found.

'Are you quite certain?' I asked again, and suspicion lurked
in my tone.

Ranga tried to avoid my gaze. The he spoke in a whisper.
'Mumptyvayan is here,' he confided. 'He came to my hut by
moonlight last night and spoke to me. He's known to me,
and will not harm you if you stay with me, *dorai.* But if you
stay alone — who knows? He may rob you! He may kill you!
Who can tell?'

'That's just wonderful.' I exclaimed in ecstasy. 'I have for
long wanted to meet this character. Just you go and tell him
to come along to my tent tonight. I'd like to speak to him.

Ranga feigned surprise and indignation. 'Why should I?'
he asked. 'Am I the friend of a dacoit?'

'You are,' I affirmed 'just that. But have no fear, I won't
tell anyone.'

So we pitched my tent at the corner of the land where

I usually camped. That night, till about 10 p.m., I had a long talk with Ranga beside the camp fire and then retired, while he walked back to his hut at the other end of the plot. I remember that I did not leave the lantern burning, for it usually attracts mosquitoes, which are plentiful in that area. The moonlight made everything almost as bright as day, and I could clearly discern the heavy belt of trees, nearly a quarter of a mile away, that marked the course of the Chinar River. I fell asleep still thinking of the dacoit.

Suddenly I awoke. No sound had disturbed me, but I knew that I was no longer alone. The figure of a man stood at the entrance of my tent, brilliantly lit from head to foot by the moonlight. With both hands the held a shotgun at waist level, the weapon pointed directly at me. A khaki shirt overhung a ragged pair of short, and strapped to the man's belt were two long, wicked-looking daggers, one on either hip. Crosswise from one shoulder was strapped a cartridge-belt, the brass heads of the .12 gauge rounds winking in the moonlight. Across the other shoulder hung a pair of binoculars in leather case! A scarf was wound around his head like a turban, but I could see the enormous black moustache that curled upwards to his temples. Brown, rubber-soled shoes were on his feet.

I blinked and rubbed my eyes, but he was still there. My watch showed that it was exactly 2 a.m.

I sat up and spoke joyously: 'Welcome Mumptyvayan! I've wanted to speak to you for a long time.'

'This is no time to talk, white man. I mean business.' He spoke truculently, in a harsh tone. 'Don't attempt to run, or cry out, or I'll kill you. Just come out of your tent and stand here in the moonlight, where I can keep an eye on you, while I collect your rifle, gun and money. I want all three.'

I was disappointed. I had been looking forward to meeting this fellow, but our meeting was not going to be the pleasant one I had hoped it might be. Well, if he wanted it that way, he could certainly have it.

'Mumptyvayan,' I replied sternly, not attempting to move from where I sat, 'I had been looking forward to meeting you and to talking to you as a friend. I've heard of your exploits and I confess I admired some of them, but not all. At least, I thought you were a brave man. Now I'm disappointed — greatly disappointed. For you're a coward, a braggart, and a bluffer!'

The man choked with rage. 'Do not provoke me too far, white man,' he hissed, 'or —.'

'Look, Mumpty,' I interrupted firmly, but with my heart in my mouth. You can't get away with it. You know that. You know very well you are bluffing. For you dare not shoot me! As it is, the price upon your head is too high. If you murder a white man just to rob him, the government will really come down upon you with a heavy hand. They'll send the *paltanwallahs* (soldiers) here. They will scour every corner of the jungle till they ferret you out like a jackal. Then they'll kill you, like a rat! Besides, I had hoped to be your friend. I had looked forward to meeting you. What a pity things have ended in this way.'

It was a game of bluff. On my part and on his. Nevertheless, fear gripped my heart. This man had murdered many people already. Would he shoot me like a dog? Perhaps kill me with one of his great knives? I could see that he was a man of tremendous physique.

He knew I was bluffing, but I was not quite certain how far he was bluffing. I only wished I knew. He overrated me, for he was certain that I was certain he was bluffing, and the next second his actions confirmed this.

For Mumptyvayan grounded the butt of his gun and leaned upon the weapon. Then he spoke in a changed voice:

393

'*Dorai,* you're a strange man, indeed, and the first one who has not begged for mercy. A man after my own heart. Do you give me your word of honour that you won't try to arrest me or harm me? Will you promise that you'll tell nobody, not even our friend Ranga, that we met tonight?'

'I promise, most willingly, Mumpty,' I said in genuine relief, getting up and walking out into the moonlight. 'Let's shake hands on it.'

The dacoit laid his gun on the ground and very solemnly we shook hands. It would have been a strange sight to a watcher, to see this fierce and ragged multi-murderer vigorously shaking the hand of a white man in blue-and-white pyjamas, whose heart was still beating abnormally fast.

We squatted on the ground there, and we talked and talked. I was clear from the beginning that this poor fellow wanted the company of someone to whom he might talk freely, someone to whom he could pour out his heart. And he did just that. He told me his whole life story, every detail. When he began talking there was pride and boastfulness in his words, but as he proceeded a certain wistfulness crept in. I could see that he was genuinely sorry for all that had happened, that he was genuinely repentant. Mumpytyvayan was earnestly looking for a way out. I was deeply moued by his words and I wanted to help him all I could.

He came to the end of his story at last, and silence fell upon us for quite some time. Looking straight into his face in the moonlight, I began to speak:

'Two wrongs don't make a right, Mumpty,' I said. 'They never have; they never will. Just because those wicked men murdered your father you did not acquire the right to murder them. However, the harm has been done now. I think you can see that for yourself and you'll admit it, eh?'

The dacoit nodded in silence.

So I continued. 'The proper thing for me to do is to advise you to give yourself up, but I am not so sure it would be practical advice so far as your interests are concerned. You would probably be hanged; come to think of it, I'm sure you would be. If I were to advise you continue as your are doing, it would be bad advice, Mumpty. For every man's hand is against you — .'

But here the dacoit interrupted vehemently. 'What about my friends, *dorai?*' he protested impetuously. 'What about my many informers, who tell me so many things, including every movement of the police? They even told me about you!'

The in a burst of confidence he admitted: 'The policeman who escorted the engineer told a constable that you wanted to meet me. That constable passed the message to me, for once I befriended his father, who is very poor. And so he gives information to me about the movements of his brother policemen. Even Ranga is my friend.'

I tried another line of persuasion. 'Don't you feel lonely at times, Mumpty? Don't you long for human companionship? A person to whom you might talk, to whom you may pour out your heart just as you're doing at this moment — to me? How many could you trust to talk to in this way?'

'Indeed I do, *dorai,*' he responded wistfully. 'I realize that inside myself I am most unhappy, most miserable, most lonely. But tell me what I can do!'

I was deeply touched by the man's quite evident sincerity, by the magnitude of the problem confronting him. Silence fell between us as I thought awhile. Then all of a sudden it came to me. I felt I had the solution.

'You can do this, Mumptyvayan. Go to the Cauvery River at night. Throw your rifle, your gun, all the ammunition, your knives, the glasses you stole, everything, into the "Big Bannu," the pool below the Hogenaikal Falls where the water is perhaps 200 feet deep. They will never be seen again. Keep nothing you now have, even your clothes, for they will incriminate you. Throw everything into the "Big Bannu".'

'Remove your moustache and hair. On second thoughts, burn your khakhi clothes and shoes and don't throw them in the river, for they might float. Then walk to Biligundu and onwards to Dodda Halla. Traverse this stream three miles above the place where it reaches the Cauvery and go through the Tagatti forest to the town of Oregaum. Keep straight on, and you will soon cross the Madras State frontier and enter Mysore State. The police there will not know you. You will arrive at a main road eventually. Turn to your right then, and inquire the way to the town of Kankanhalli. Thirty-three miles north of Kankanhalli is the city of Bangalore, where I live. If you reach Bangalore and come to me there, I will help you further.

'It will take you some days to do this journey on foot. Don't ever let your hair or moustache grow again for if you do, you'll certainly be recognized. Try to get work along the way. The money you earn will help you. Don't carry too much money from here or it will make people suspicious. I will give you my address at Bangalore.'

'Money I have enough of, *dorai,* he assured me, 'but write your address on a piece of paper, so that I may find you easily at Bangalore.'

I shook my head sadly. 'That I will not do, Mumpty. For, if you are caught and address found on your person in my handwriting, I shall be in serious trouble. However, I'll give you clear instruction. Memorize them. Okay?'

Mumpty nodded, and I proceeded.

'My name is Anderson. Ask for "Anderson *dorai."* Repeat the name each day to yourself so that you don't forget it.'

He repeated my name several times. Then I proceeded. 'I live next to the 'Tamasha Bangla" (the Museum), close to the statue of the "Great White Queen!" Queen Victoria). Remember that. When you reach Bangalore, ask the way to the statue of the "Great White Queen" and the "Tamasha Bangla" which is close to it. In between is a big red house. That's where I live — Anderson *dorai*. Got it? Now keep repeating these directions to yourself, several times a day, so as to be sure you won't forget.'

We were both sitting on the ground, as I told you, and the dacoit threw himself forward touching my feet. This big man was crying like a child.

'*Dorai*, You are my father and my mother' he cried, 'the only real friend I have in this whole world. And to think that only a little while ago I wanted to kill you. I will do as you say.'

There was strange lump in my throat as I tried to remain calm while patting his matted hair. The muffler he had been wearing as a turban had unwound itself and lay on the ground.

When he began to regain control I raised him to a sitting position, placed a hand on each shoulder and, looking into his eyes, said earnestly:

'You must go now, my friend. You've not realized it, but it's past five o'clock. The jungle-cocks are crowing and the moonlight wanes before the coming sun. Soon dawn will break, and nobody should see you here. Be brave now, my friend; be determined; be true to yourself and to me and do as I have said. And may Krishna be with you till we meet again.'

Impetuously he dropped to his knees, bent to kiss my feet. Then he scrambled to his feet, salaamed, picked up his gun.

The next instant Mumptyvayan the dacoit had vanished into the fading moonlight. I was alone. Or so I thought. For within a couple of minutes my old friend and companion, Ranga, stood before me.

'The *dorai* does not appear to have slept soundly,' he inquired. 'There are dark circles under his eyes. I trust no elephant disturbed him, or was it just the mosquitoes?'

The man could be very annoying at times and I was in no mood for banter.

'I slept soundly enough,' I countered, cutting him short, 'and you know very well that I'm an early riser.'

Ranga coughed, then continued in a casual tone. 'Perhaps I ate too much last night, for I appear to have been dreaming since the early hours of this morning. In my dream I saw two figures sitting in he moonlight, before this very tent. One of them was you, *dorai;* the other was a man in khaki and he carried a gun. You just talked and talked. Wasn't it a strange dream, *dorai?*'

So he had been watching us all the time! Abruptly I swung around and thrust my face forward, almost touching his.

'It was a strange dream, indeed,' I said fiercely. 'But it was only a dream. Only a dream. Remember that always, Ranga. And now, forget about this dream. Don't ever talk about it again. For if you do — to me, or to any other man — our friendship that has lasted for over thirty-five years is over!'

In a changed voice, he spoke cheerfully. 'I slept soundly last night, *dorai*. Nor did I even dream after all that heavy dinner.'

I smiled and laid my hand on his arm, and he smiled in return. Our long friendship was to continue.

Often did I think of Mumptyvayan after that night and nearly three months passed away. Then one day I had finished lunch at home when the dogs barked. My Alsatian, followed by a little woolly nondescript about one-tenth its size, dashed out of the back door. They were barking at a mendicant, one of the many that present themselves almost every day at everybody's house in India.

This beggar was leaning on a staff. He was bald headed and clean-shaven, wore only a dirty loin-cloth and an ancient, broken pair of sandals and large, rounded glasses. Around his neck hung a necklace of wooden beads, each the size of a walnut and covered with grime. Smeared horizontally across his forehead from temple to temple were white and red caste marks alternately.

His coal-black eyes looked at me haughtily, even disdainfully. Almost with contempt he asked, 'Can any charity be expected in the abode of a white man?'

Impertinent blackguard! I felt like throwing him out. I advanced threateningly, my intention to abuse him roundly. The proud black eyes stared back into mine. Then I noticed that, beneath the white and red caste marks, a scar extended from his right eye to his temple, only visible when one came near enough to see it.

Mumptyvayan! By all that was wonderful! He knew then that I had recognized him. His eyes were no longer haughty. They shone and were moist with pleasure.

Donald, my son, had gone to work. My wife was out. Only the *Chokra* (boy-servant) was on the premises.

Motioning with my hand to Mumpty to wait, I shouted to the *Chokra,* and when he came gave him instructions to go the railway station nearly two miles away to inquire the time of the arrival of the mail train from Madras. That should keep him away for the next ninety minutes at least.

When the *Chokra* had gone, I called Mumpty inside, offered him tea and what odds and ends were to be found in the cup-board, and asked him how he fared.

'I did exactly as you instructed me, *dorai*. It broke heart to throw my firearms and cartridges into the "Big Bannu" in the river. But I did so. The rest was comparatively easy. I reached the Mysore State border and the town of Kankanhalli in due course. There I got work as a labourer under a rich landlord. *Dorai*, how that man oppressed his poor workers! How I longed to be Mumptyvayan again, if only for a few minutes, to deal with him suitably! His behaviour made me decide never to work for any other man again.'

'But by this time I had noticed that there were many mendicants on the roads, most of them on some religious guise. None ever appeared to be hungry. Somehow, somebody fed them. So I decided to become a *sadhu*. My name is Omkrishna, and I am making quite a good living out of it. I'm touring the south and hope to make my way to the city of Madras, where I'll settle down eventually.'

'Not Madras, Mumpty — I mean, Omkrishna,' I corrected myself, 'Somebody in uniform might want you there. It's too close and you might be recognized. I suggest you go northwards instead, into Hyderabad State. The further you are from the scene of your operations the better, remember.'

He thought for a moment and then nodded. 'I think you're right, *dorai*.'

Then he rose to go. I offered him money, but the *sadhu* refused it. 'I'm indebted to you, sir,' he said, 'not you to me. Which reminds me, I've brought something for you. It's the only link I have with the old days.'

He rummaged in his loin-cloth and produced a ring — a gold ring!

'Where did you steal it?' I inquired sternly.

'I didn't steal it,' he replied. 'I got it from the engineer who went to Uttaimalai to build a dam.' Mumptyvayan was laughing now, as he thought of the incident. 'He was walking by the riverside with an armed policeman to keep guard over him. The stupid policeman had one of those toy guns disguised as rifles. They didn't know that I knew it.'

Omkrishna grinned more widely at the recollection. The he continued: 'I called to the policeman from the shelter of a rock that I would shoot him dead if he tried to resist.'

'The poor devil was terrified. He threw down his ridiculous gun and bolted. I went to the engineer then, but made sure to throw the policeman's weapon into the river first. Strangely, the engineer sahib was not frightened. He was grinning at the policeman's hasty departure. In my usual rough voice, I demanded money from him. The the engineer spoke strange words to me: 'Don't threaten me, Mumptyvayan. Learn to ask nicely.'

'He gave me ten rupees. He also took this ring off his finger and handed it to me. I tried to return the money and the ring, for the engineer sahib was indeed a good man and a brave one; a gentleman, too. But he refused to take them back. So I wore the ring myself for some time. I knew that if I tried to sell it, I might get caught. However, and this happened before I met you that night, *dorai*,' Omkrishna hastened to add, as if in apology. 'After that meeting I have kept straight and have never robbed again, I can swear to that. And I kept the ring as a gift for you.'

So the unexpected had happened! My friend, the engineer, had longed to meet the dacoit Mumptyvayan. They had met, and as a result I now had his ring!

Omkrishna went away shortly after that and I never saw him again! A whole year passed, during which I often thought of Mumptyvayan but never heard of him. Several times I visited Hogenaikal and other areas that were his old haunts, but nobody spoke of him, nobody had seen him for a long time. Apparently he had disappeared for ever. Two months later the land was agog with the news! Mumptyvayan was dead! He had been shot by a friend who then claimed the reward that the Government of Madras had placed on his head two years earlier. The reward was Rs 500, I think, and five acres of land, dead or alive!

Various stories were abroad about how his death had come about. Some said that Mumptyvayan had gone back to visit his wife, others that he had returned to visit a concubine who had been a great favourite. Wife or concubine — the woman had betrayed him! She had a brother, who was in debt and needed the reward badly. The story went that she had prepared Mumptyvayan's favourite dish for him, but into the food she had put *follidol,* a very powerful chemical supplied to the ryots by the government for killing insect pests that attack their crops. Mumptyvayan ate the food. In a few minutes he was in the throes of death. At that moment the woman's brother, who had been awaiting the propitious moment, came in and shot Mumptyvayan dead! For the reward stipulated that the dacoit should be brought in alive, or shot dead in self-defence, but it did not say anything about poisoning him.

The story has it that the reward was granted. Mumptyvayan's dead body was brought by the police to the town of Dharmapuri, where crowds gathered to witness his hasty burial.

* * *

My next story is about an animal and has nothing to do with magic or evil men. It is the story of a bull elephant, and an unusual one at that.

We met this elephant for the first time at about four-thirty one evening while motoring through the jungle, about two miles short of the Forest Lodge at Anaikutti and about ten miles beyond the old temple I told you about at the beginning of this chapter. He was grazing peacefully in the jungle some fifty yards to our right.

The car was filled with sightseers and amateur photographers, and they took innumerable pictures of the old elephant. He ignored us completely, both cars and people, behaving as if he were all alone, with no other creature within miles of him.

I was seated at the back of the car, on the right side, while a friend was driving. The other members were foreigners who had come to India to see the jungles. One of them, who has seen elephants before but only in zoos and circuses, stepped out from the car and, against our whispered advice, walked around the vehicle and half the distance towards the elephant. This was an extremely dangerous thing to have done and the rest of us called to him to return. So he stopped and took a picture. He took several more and then started asking for trouble by shouting at the elephant, waving his arms about, and finally by hurling stones at the animal. The first missed its mark by a narrow margin. The second struck a branch of the tree under which the bull was standing and bounced off, falling directly on his back. The third stone stuck the elephant in the face at the base of the trunk and rolled down, thudding against the left tusk before falling to the ground.

The bull did not retaliate. He merely turned his back on us, walked behind the tree, faced about and peered at us quietly as if to say, 'Can't you go away and leave me in peace?'

His behaviour was astounding. No other elephant would have acted thus, particularly no bull, after such provocation. The normal reaction would have been to make itself scarce at the first sight, or even the sound of the car. Allowing it had not done this, any wild elephant would certainly have repeatedly, and then hurling stones at him. I confess I made certain it would charge, and the gentleman who had been so brave and foolish would have ceased to exist, together with the car and all of us in it. We could not have done anything to save ourselves, for it is against the rules to annoy wild elephants, to bait them, hurl stones at them, if they show resentment.

With difficulty we got our friend away from the place and continued on our drive in search of other animals to photograph.

It was 6 p.m., when we returned the same way, speculating on whether we would meet the elephant again. We had yet a furlong to go when we saw him once more, this time standing on the opposite side of the road, even closer to the track we were negotiating and facing us. We stopped again to watch, but he went on chewing placidly, every now and then stuffing his mouth with leaves from boughs he had broken down. We noticed that in the process he even ate the wood of the smaller branches on which the leaves were growing.

We studied the animal carefully. He appeared to be in good condition, not emaciated. There were no signs of a wound or of sickness to account for his oddly placid behaviour. The only thing noticeable was that he was an old animal, as could be judged by the fact that the tops of his ears folded over, and by the hollows in his forehead.

Once more my new acquaintance got out of the car and started his stone-throwing. The elephant was closer to us now than at the first encounter, being barely twenty feet away and facing head-on. Something was bound to happen.

But the bull turned his back in obvious disgust and went on feeding. His behaviour was quite unaccountable. Even a domesticated elephant would not have tolerated such treatment from total strangers. To say the least, he would have moved away! Finally our acquaintance — brave, or mad, or both —

called out to us that he was going to walk up to the bull. The rest of us then got out and seized him, practically dragging him back to the vehicle, while the elephant continued to graze placidly.

'Rats to your Indian elephants!' he exclaimed in disdain. 'They're as harmless as rabbits.'

At dinner that night the subject was the same. Questions were fired at me that I could not possibly answer. Was this how fiercely wild elephants actually behaved? I was worried. Why had the bull acted in such a strangely docile manner? I fell asleep determined to solve the puzzle the following day.

After breakfast the next morning, I enlisted the aid of two Karumba trackers and taking my rifle we motored to the place where we had met the elephant the evening before. We left the car there and followed his progress through the jungle. This was an easy task for the Karumbas and we came upon him again, a little over half-a-mile away, headed in the general direction of the Anaikutti River, which was still about a mile and a half distant. He was not grazing now, but standing placidly under a tree.

The Karumbas, of course, acted with great caution; but emboldened by our experience of the evening before, I walked towards the bull, the jungle men following at a considerable distance and ready to take off at the first sign of trouble. Nothing happened, although I came as close to the elephant as had my friend the evening before. The bull took no notice of me whatever.

I walked around him. I was convinced he was sorely injured. Or perhaps he was a very sick animal. Then the idea came to me: maybe he was blind in one or both eyes. Or he was deaf. Or he could not smell. There was something seriously wrong with him; of that I was convinced.

For a second time I circled him. At that moment I noticed

him following my movements with his small eyes. But they were not inflamed, and there was certainly no sign of the discharge that would show on a bull in 'musth.' And the animal was not blind. He then lifted his trunk a little towards me and then I knew he could even smell.

What could be wrong with him? Lazily he lifted his trunk, broke a twig above him and stuffed it into his mouth. He could not be wounded or sick, for then he would not be eating so well. All that I was able to discover was that he was a very old animal indeed. Apart from the hollows in his forehead and temples, and the turned-down skin at the tops of his ears, the ivory of both tusks was blackened at the roots with age.

The two Karumbas had been standing at a safe distance while I had been circling the bull. One of them now called out to me, 'there's no mystery here, *dorai*. The Wise one (the manner in which the Karumbas usually refer to elephants) is very old. His days on earth are over, and he has come to the river to die in it peacefully.'

We left it at that and returned to camp. The following day I had some business at the town of Gudalur, nineteen miles away, which is the headquarters of the district. A string of carts, laden with lengths of sugar-cane, passed me on the main street. I thought of the old elephant then and of an experiment I would like to try with him. So I bought a dozen pieces, each over six feet in length.

Next morning I went to Anaikutti again, this time with three Karumbas. Two of them carrying the sugarcane. We trailed the old tusker from the spot at which we had seen last and found him on the bank of Anaikutti River. He was standing in the shade of a muthee tree.

I approached cautiously with one of the Karumbas who was carrying six of the sugar-can stems. I can assure you he came with the greatest reluctance. The bull saw us and half-turned slowly. Now he was facing us. The Karumba stopped. I took two lengths of the sugar-cane in my left hand, holing my loaded rifle cocked in the crook of my right arm, and advanced slowly and deliberately towards the animal, staring into it eyes but with only conciliatory thoughts in my mind. The next few second would show whether this strange animal's behaviour would culminated in a sort of friendship or in enmity.

When I got to within a few a feet, the bull became very nervous. He blew air through his trunk and began curling it inwards to protect if from possible harm. His ears flapped. They came forwards and then went backwards against the side of his head. Bad signs indeed! He was about to charge!

I halted, extending my arm to hold out the sugarcane towards him. I did not speak, for I know the human voice annoys and frightens animals.

The elephant became less restive and my arms began to ache with the weight of the sugar-cane. After some minutes, I inched forward again, continuing till the broad leaves at the end of the six-foot piece of cane were within reach of his trunk. Then I stopped, holding it out invitingly. With a nervous swish of his trunk the elephant tore the cane from my grasp, pulled it towards himself, and then beat it repeatedly against the ground. He hesitated. I knew he was pondering the question as to what to do next. Put it into his mouth? Stamp upon it and crush it with his weight? Throw it away? Or perhaps attack the puny intruder?

Cautiously, the bull placed the cane sideways in his mouth and bit it. That did it! He tasted the sweet juice, perhaps for the first time in his life, for there were no sugar-cane fields in this area. Or maybe he hailed from far-off parts and had eaten sugar-cane before and remembered the taste. Anyway, he obviously liked it. For he munched at the cane, while his small eyes stared at me unwinkingly. There was no enmity in them, but there was nervousness still.

I handed him the second length of cane after he had finished the first. He took it readily enough and munched it.

The Karumbas, with the rest of the sugar-cane had stopped some distance away and refused to approach any nearer. I knew they regarded my actions as sheer madness. As I was reluctant to dispense with my rifle, I had to make two more trips from the elephant to the Karumbas and back again before I had fed him the remaining ten pieces of cane. But at last they were done and the strangest friendship that ever was heard of had been established between the old wild bull and myself.

The next day I motored to Gunlupet, twenty-one miles away, where sugar-cane could be had, and bought a whole load of the stuff. On the return journey I passed my old friend, Mr Chandran, one of the Forest Range Officers attached to the Mudumalai Game Sanctuary that came very close to the area where the old bull was living out the last days of his existence. I told him the story and he was amazed, adding that he had never heard of anything like it in all his service with the Forest Department. Mr Chandran reminded me of an incident about two years earlier, when he and I had been in a government jeep, conducting a German friend through the sanctuary.

On that occasion, the jeep had been travelling down hill along a narrow track when we had turned a corner and almost ran into a wild tusker feasting on a clump of bamboos he had knocked down, which lay across the road. The tusker saw us and came straight at the jeep. I forgot to tell you that none of us carried firearms, as the area was a game sanctuary and no rifles or guns were allowed. Fortunately the driver kept his head and did not capsize the vehicle by running down the steep slope to our right. The hill banked upwards on the left, so we could not escape that way.

The bull reached the radiator, halted, smacked the bonnet with his trunk and — did nothing more! The driver came to life then and backed the jeep as far as he possibly could. Meanwhile, the tusker had gone. After ten minutes we advanced once more towards the bamboo-clump that lay across the track and got out to cut a clearing for the jeep when back upon us in great rage came the bull!

We scurried into the vehicle while the elephant mounted guard over his precious bamboo. This time we had to reverse the jeep for about a furlong before the track was wide enough to turn it around. Needless to say, we left the tusker with the bamboo as his prize!

Mr Chandran related another incident that had occurred more recently. He was again accompanying a party of tourists in the same jeep and with the same driver. A baby elephant suddenly ran across the track, frightened by the sound of the jeep, and its mother came after it. Fury seized her when she saw this strange thing, which she took to be an enemy, so close to her calf. Without further ado she overturned the jeep and then herded her calf to safety. Fortunately, the presence of the calf and her anxiety to get it out of harm's way had distracted her and prevented her from killing the jeep's occupants. As it was, the vehicle was damaged and several of the inmates injured, although not by the elephant directly.

The docile behaviour of the old bull at Anaikutti was all the more amazing in the light of these occurrences.

I returned the next day to feed him again. He accepted the cane readily enough, but did not seem very hungry, as he took only two pieces. The third and fourth pieces I offered him he refused, merely touching them with the tip of his trunk.

The following day we were back once more, but this time the old bull would accept nothing. He just stood in front of me, acknowledging my offering with the tip of his trunk, but taking nothing. His eyes were watery and seemed to hold a sad expression. When I left him, he even turned his head as if to bid an old friend farewell.

For some reason I could not visit him as usual the next day, but at about nine o'clock on the morning of the fourth day, I went to see him again, along with the Karumbas and the sugar-cane. But he was not there. However, we knew well enough where we would find him. He would be at the 'Big Pool', half a mile upstream, the 'place where the elephants come to die,' as the Karumbas call it in their own language.

And we found him there, right enough. He was dead. The weather had been dry and the pool was only four feet deep. But the tusker had deliberately lain down in it on his side and placed his head and trunk beneath the surface of the water to drown. His flank protruded above and that was how we found him.

There lies the answer to the great secret: where do the elephant go, and how do they die, when they become too old to live? They drown themselves in a river. I had solved the mystery and at the same time had enjoyed a unique friendship with a full grown wild tusker, although it was but a brief one.

Four

The Dumb Man-Eater of Talavadi

I HAVE MET MANY UNFORGETTABLE CHARACTERS IN MY TIME AND most of them have been jungle men; Indian, Anglo-Indian and European. For the forest appears to develop a man's personality. The more time he spends there the clearer his personality becomes. One such character was my friend Hughie Hailstone, who lived in a wonderful home he had built for himself called 'Moyar Valley Ranch,' down at a place named Mudiyanoor, near Talaimalai, in a corner of the North Coimbatore District and not very far away from the Moyar River, which separates North Coimbatore from the Nilgiri Forest Division.

Now Hughie was a character if ever there was one. He attended the same school as I did, but passed out much earlier. From that time he followed a varied career. But the man had brains. Everything he touched turned to gold. With some of this money he bought a large tract of forest land and on it he built his Moyar Valley Ranch.

411

Hughie had a fine collection of firearms, the best that money could buy, but among these he had a great fancy for a .023 Mauser rifle with a hexagonal barrel with which, if I remember rightly, he told me he had shot nine elephants and over twenty tigers. Later, Hughie took a great liking to my son Donald and presented him with this very weapon. Donald was, of course, delighted. But what enhanced the value of the gift was the fact that it was Hughie's favourite weapon. Frankly, I do not believe I could ever part with my ancient, but lovable, old .405. It has been my companion and solace for over forty years.

My story begins at a point where in some part of India Hughie either found or heard of a special kind of grass, the stems of which when dry were stronger than the ordinary match-stick, and not so brittle. They would not break easily, and they burned readily. So Hughie conceived the idea of cultivating this grass on a large scale on the lands of his Moyar Valley Ranch with a view to starting a match factory that would turn out a product to be sold at about half the price of those already on the market, and of much higher quality.

He obtained seeds in quantity, ploughed his lands with the first shower of the monsoon rains, and sowed them. Up came the grass in fine style. Acres of it. The land was virgin and the grass grew to five feet and more. I remember watching it as it bent and rippled to the breeze. But before Hughie's grass could be turned into match-sticks there came herds of deer, particularly chital, and large sounders of wild pigs. The deer, of course, ate the grass, while the wild pigs made it their home and did considerable damage by digging it up at places, though for the most part they burrowed a maze of low tunnels through it, leading here, there and everywhere. In these tunnels they sheltered and multiplied to the extent that Hughie wondered eventually whether he should persevere with the match factory or run a ham and bacon concern!

Best of all, with deer and the pigs came tigers and panthers to eat them. Rather I should say more tigers than panthers, for the former arrived in such numbers as not only to decimate the deer and pig population, but to kill and eat the panthers too, so that in the course of time the smaller cats learned to give the match-grass a very wide berth.

Now Hughie employed an assistant, a man named Sweza (a corruption of D'Souza), who came from Mangalore on the west coast of India. Sweza was a most versatile individual: he did everything for Hughie, whose problems he not only knew but anticipated.

He once said to me with reference to his employer, 'I don't know why master spend much money to make more money. Master got plenty money to enjoy and enjoy. But no; he want to make match-sticks, tooth powder from babul bark, fertilizer from jungle seeds mixed with elephants' dung, invention for finding underground water, digging ground for getting some stones master says got iron, all sort of things. Only spending money. Why for? This very good place. Master should enjoy. Plenty girls got it here. Young girls; not 'nuff husbands here. I tell-it master. He get very angry. He say-it, "Sweza, you bloody rogue you got it one wife and three more women already. I saved you from one more wife. Now you want to put me a in same trouble!"'

But he was a good fellow, this Sweza, game for anything and as keen as mustard. And he ate well! His paunch and his jolly smile showed this.

One Easter, Sweza felt that his master and himself were entitled to roast pork or venison. So he borrowed his master's small-bore rifle after confiding his good intentions to Hughie, and waded into the match-grass, now somewhat withered and

413

thinned down by the summer heat, in search of quarry. Sweza had not gone very far when he saw the snout of a medium-sized wild pig regarding him with grave suspicion from between the stems of the grass. He fired. The pig fell, picked itself up again, and disappeared. Sweza started to follow hard on its trail.

Just then there was a great swishing in the grass where the pig had disappeared, a snarl, and the scream of a dying animal. Sweza beat a hasty retreat and told his master.

Hughie came out with one of his heavy rifles and Sweza led him to the place where he had fired at the pig, pointing out the direction in which it had gone. Hughie went on and Sweza made to follow him from behind, but Hughie very wisely objected to this. He did not want a bullet from Sweza's rifle in his back. So he asked his servant to go back and wait for him in the open.

Hughie came to the spot where the pig had been killed, but there was no trace of its body. The killer had carried it away. Bent and broken stems of dried grass showed the direction he had taken with his burden. Moving cautiously forward, he had gone for quite a hundred yards when suddenly a loud growl from in front told him the killer was feeding somewhere ahead and resented his intrusion. But Hailstone had seen and shot many tigers and was not to be intimidated by a growl. He moved forward stealthily and the tiger growled more loudly. Hughie knew the charge would come at any moment.

A little later the tiger charged. It came in great leaping bounds through the dried match-grass. Hailstone waited till he could see the contorted face clearly, till the final spring would land the beast right on top of him. Then he fired. Thus was born the man-eater of Talavadi! Hughie's bullet struck the tiger full in the face. The impact tended to stop it, but the weight of the body behind still pushed it forward, with the result that the tiger somersaulted just a few yards away. Hughie worked the bolt of his rifle rapidly to get in a second shot. The magazine jammed.

He did the right thing after that. He turned and fled.

Evidently the tiger was temporarily blinded or maybe too hurt to follow. It floundered about in the grass, digging great holes in the earth as, in agony, it bit and tore the ground with its claws and teeth.

Hughie dashed into the bungalow to get another rifle, Sweza running after him and asking what had happened. But by the time Hailstone got to the spot again, advancing one step at a time, the tiger had vanished, while splashes of blood and saliva on the ground made it plain he had received a severe wound in the region of the mouth or throat.

It is a common belief among some hunters that a wounded feline should not be followed up immediately. Sufficient time should be allowed to pass in which the animal might possibly bleed to death. At least, the wounds would stiffen to the extent that the beast would be disinclined to move far, or it might even be incapable of movement. But there is another school of thought which advocates following up at once. The theory in this case is that the wounded animal should not be given time to recover from the shock and pain of its wounds and from its immediate fear. The advocates of this theory feel that, with the passage of time and long hours of pain, the wounded beast becomes vicious and bent upon revenge, whereas immediately after being wounded it seeks only to escape. They also argue that on humanitarian grounds it is very cruel to allow an animal to suffer hours of intense agony with a vital organ shot away.

Now I am not going to give my own judgment on these theories, except to say that both are partly right and partly wrong. Each animal has its individual characteristics and special nature and will react in its own way. Hughie was a firm believer in the second theory and lost no time in following up.

The blood-trail through the long match-grass was clear. It left Hughie's land and entered the forest, where things became a little more difficult. Hughie had to rely on his own abilities as Sweza, still trailing behind with the other rifle, was no tracker. They followed it across a dry ravine, where the tiger had lain down and then continued, and across flat country the other side. The fact that the tiger had lain down indicated that it was badly wounded, and as Hughie had followed up at once, the animal could not be very far away. Probably it had heard him and Sweza and was taking cover in the undergrowth. The third item of information was that this animal appeared to be a coward; it should have taken advantage of the terrain and plenty of cover in the ravine to ambush the two men.

By now the bleeding had lessened and after crossing the flat stretch for another furlong the trail began to lead downhill, where the ground became increasingly stony. Hughie had to slow down and keep looking about for the next drop or two of blood. Soon even this ceased and he could go no further. On that hard ground no pug-marks were visible.

For some unaccountable reason the tracts of forest in the Mudiyanoor area are entirely devoid of jungle tribes or aboriginal population. It is believed this has been so since the days when Tippoo Sultan, the Muslim ruler of Mysore, invaded the surrounding country, sweeping all before him. So Hughie had no opportunity to return later and follow the tiger, as there was nobody in all that area who knew anything about tracking.

The village of Talaimalai is about two miles south of

Mudiyanoor, where Hughie had his farm. It is a small hamlet surrounded by fertile country. Nearly two months later, one of the villagers from this place bought a tract of land from his neighbour, or rather arranged to buy it, for the sale deed pertaining to this transaction had necessarily to be signed and registered in the office of the sub-registrar and the money paid by the purchaser to the seller in the presence of this august individual whose headquarters were at a larger village named Talavadi, situated seven miles north of Mudiyanoor. So the vendor and the prospective purchaser, the latter carrying the money he was going to pay for the land, which came to Rs 400, including the incidental expenses involved in the sale deed, set forth together on foot to cover the nine miles between Talaimalai and Talavadi.

They had covered two-thirds of this distance when they crossed a stream that had a little water in it. Here they stopped under a large tree to eat the curried balls of ragi flour they had brought with them as a midday meal. The purchaser then went down to the stream to drink and wash while his companion watched him with sleepy eyes.

Suddenly something huge leaped down upon the drinking man from the opposite bank of the stream and back again across the stream to disappear as abruptly as it had come, except that there was no longer any sign of the unfortunate purchaser. He had disappeared, along with that horrible apparition!

The vendor, now fully awake, leaped to his feet and ran as fast as he could towards Talavadi, covering the three miles to that place in record time. There he gasped out his story before the sub-registrar and the clerks sitting in the office. All this being something out of the ordinary, the sub-registrar sent the man to the police station, where the whole tale was repeated.

In the opinion of the constable in charge there was nothing strange about the story. As he reasoned it out, here we have A reporting that he is selling some land to B for Rs 400. A and B set out to register the sale, B carrying Rs 400. On the way, A says that some strange creature appeared out of the jungle and disappeared again, taking B with it. A reports he was more than half-asleep and cannot describe what this strange something was. But the facts remain that B has vanished, the Rs 400 have vanished with him, and the land still belongs to A.

Without further ado, the head constable arrested the unfortunate vendor and locked him in the police station's solitary cell. Then he wrote a lengthy report, stating why he suspected he had caught a murderer. He did not forget to add that the sub-inspector at Satyamangalam, which was the headquarters of the Police and Forest Departments and the place to which the prisoner would have to be sent, might please bear in mind when he read the report that it was the humble prayer of the head constable that promotion was long overdue and this brave and dramatic arrest of a dangerous murderer and thief should forthwith clinch matters and lead to the said promotion without delay. He closed the report by saying that he offered daily prayers for the sub-inspector's continued long life and prosperity.

It was not till a week later that the fourth constable attached to the police station at Talavadi returned from leave. The head constable then felt he could manage with two policemen while he sent the other two on escort duty with the prisoner, and his report, to Satyamangalam, where the sub-inspector resided, forty miles away. They should reach there in three days, for they had to walk the whole distance.

Hailstone happened to be standing at the entrance to the grounds of his farm, which abutted on the track leading from

Talavadi to Satyamangalam, when he saw the two policemen coming along with a prisoner handcuffed between them. Conversationally he inquired what wrong the man had done and where he was being taken. The constables, glad of the respite, said they were escorting a murderer, while the poor vendor burst into tears, sobbing out his innocence and his story afresh.

Hughie pricked up his ears.

'Stop weeping, you idiot,' he said kindly but firmly. 'If you want me to help you, just answer a simple question. What was this strange something that you say carried away your companion? At least, what did it look like?'

'Dorai,' the man replied, striving to control himself, 'I saw my friend stoop to drink water. At that instant I must have fallen asleep. I heard nothing, but seemed to see some huge, long body jump down from the jungle across the stream and jump back again. Then only did I notice the man had gone! I woke up and ran all the way to Talavadi. Now these policemen say I have murdered my friend and taken his money.'

Then he started crying once more at the thought of his plight.

Hughie remembered the tiger he had wounded just two months earlier. He had often thought about it and wondered if the animal had died or had recovered from its wound. And if it had recovered, Hughie knew that sooner or later he would hear about the animal again. Could this be it?

'Did it look like a tiger?' he asked abruptly.

The policemen looked at him stupidly, but the man in handcuffs replied quickly, 'Come to think of it, dorai, it might have been a tiger. As I said, I was more than half asleep and the whole thing happened so quickly. But it was nothing in human form that carried away my companion, of that I am certain. It was something long and big.'

'Don't take this poor man to Satyamangalam,' Hughie advised the policemen. 'Save yourself the journey, for he is no murderer. I think I know what really happened.'

But the officers of law and order the world over are dogged in their purposes, especially when they have someone in handcuffs. The policemen continued on their way to Satyamangalam with their captive, while Hughie went in his car to Talavadi. To his mortification, he discovered from the head constable that nobody knew exactly where the incident had taken place except the prisoner himself, as nobody had troubled to investigate the story or make an inspection of the spot.

Hailstone considered telling the head constable about the wounded tiger but decided against it. A man of his temperament, with a one-track mind, might do anything. He might even lock Hailstone up! So he left the police station without further ado and set out for Satyamangalam, overtaking the two policemen and their prisoner some ten miles beyond Mudiyanoor. Glad of the lift, the three men piled into the car and in less than ninety minutes the whole party were with the sub-inspector.

The sub-inspector read the head constable's report and then listened to what Hughie had to say.

'And this man wants a promotion' was his comment after Hughie had told him that the head constable had not even troubled to visit the scene of the tragedy. 'I shall see him reverted! Please take me to Talavadi in your car.'

Back they went, all five of them, to give the head constable at Talavadi the nastiest surprise of his life. Then the vendor took them to the place where the would-be purchaser and his money had vanished. The head constable was made to go too.

Over a week had passed, but when they crawled to the top of the bank they found the pug-marks of a tiger at the spot where it had clambered back with its burden, the unlucky would-be purchaser. Casting around, a little distance away but still to be seen in the sand, were the fainter imprints of the tiger before it had launched its attack.

Hughie had not brought his rifle. The sub-inspector inquired nervously if the tiger might still be there. Hailstone said 'no,' and the six men started searching the immediate surrounding for the remains of the victim. Strangely enough, it was the vendor, now no longer in chains, who stumbled upon the gnawed bones. A few rags and the ten-rupee notes that had been scattered by the breeze in a wide circle in the grass and undergrowth, confirmed that the remains were indeed all that was left of the purchaser. There were only a few, as most of the bones had been removed by the vultures, jackals and hyaenas that had visited the carcase after the tiger had finished.

The man-eater struck a second time scarcely a month later. This was at the village of Nagalur, about half-way between Hughie's place and the Moyar River which bounded the Nilgiri District. The third victim was an old man who was walking behind his two sons on the old Sultan's Battery Road, a couple of miles behind Talaimalai village. This killing took place in broad daylight — at noon, as a matter of fact.

The three men had set out together from Talaimalai to Nagalur, where the second victim had been taken. For some distance their way lay along the old road I have named, a relic of the days of that fierce Muslim conqueror who long ago brought terror to this region. They had not gone far when they came to a mighty wild-mango tree. Monkeys had knocked down some of the ripe fruit and the three men stopped to eat. When they started walking again the father had fallen behind, from where he continued to talk to them about the business that was taking them to Nagalur.

He had reminded them that it was getting late and they had all begun to walk faster, when a sudden choking cry made the two sons turn around to see a huge tiger with its jaws firmly in their father's throat, in the act of springing into the undergrowth that closely bordered the road on both sides.

Where the beast had come from they never knew. It had certainly made no sound whatever, not even a growl or snarl, which was rather unusual, for attacking tigers generally roar or make some sort of noise to inflate their own courage before springing. In this case, all they had heard was their father's last gasp. By this time the attacker had disappeared and the two boys took to their heels, running as fast as they could back to Talaimalai.

Consternation spread among the village folk and the man-eater, as if he knew very well that his name had struck terror in the area, increased the number of his attacks as he began to roam over a wider circle. He killed as far north as the high road connecting Satyamangalam with the large town of Chamrajnagar in Mysore State. He killed to the east as far as Dimbum, a hamlet standing on the escarpment of mountains overlooking the Satyamangalam plain. He crossed the Moyar River and went into the Nilgiri District to the south, and on the west he trespassed into the Bandipur area which lies in Mysore State.

Unfortunately, at just about this time Hughie, who had always been a vigorous man, fell ill. It happened suddenly and unexpectedly. I know he felt deeply about all that had taken place and was happening, for he held himself responsible for starting the tiger on its man-eating career by wounding it, and he chafed at the illness that prevented him from going after it, which he would otherwise have assuredly done. So he wrote to me, and the was what took me in my Studebaker to Moyar Valley Ranch.

Sweza met me at the gate and I found Hughie asleep in a canvas chair on his verandah. He had not heard my car. The change in his appearance since we had last me was almost frightening. A robust man, he had shrunk to half his normal size and looked haggard and very ill. He apologized for dragging me away from home and then, as I sat beside him drinking tea and eating the most delicious mangoes that grew on his land. Hughie told the story as I have told it here, not sparing himself and full of self-recrimination not only for wounding the tiger but for not finishing it off after that.

'These things happen, Hughie,' was all the comfort I could offer. 'You must pull yourself together now and join me in killing it.'

He looked at me wryly and said, 'Kenneth, my hunting days are over. My next shikar will be in the happy hunting grounds — if there's such a place!'

Indeed, he never hunted again. Shortly after the end of this episode he went by air to England. He had already bought a house there, a nice place in the country. But he was not to enjoy it, for he had been there only a few days when he slipped and fell down the staircase, injuring himself severely. Soon afterwards he died of a heart attack.

However, we now discussed what should be done. It was clear that it would not be worth my while to visit Nagalur and Talaimalai and other places where the tiger had killed in order to question the people about the animals habits and peculiarities. Hughie had already done this before falling ill and told me all he had discovered. To begin with, there was scarcely any doubt that it was the animal he had wounded that had now become a man-eater. The few people who had seen it clearly, particularly the two sons of the old man who had been snatched on the Sultan's Battery Road, affirmed that the glimpse they had got of the tiger's face showed there was something seriously the matter with it. The face had been hideously scarred and contorted. Secondly, the animal's uncanny silence on every occasion when there had been a witness to its attack proved that it was either a very strange animal by nature, or that something was wrong with its vocal chords. Moreover, nobody remembered having ever heard this tiger roar.

Of course, tigers had often roared in the area. This was to be expected, because it was full of tigers. But in no locality where any of the human kills had taken place, or at least not for a few days before or after that killing, had any tiger roared in the forest. For this reason the rumour spread that the man-eater was dumb.

The procedure normally followed in trying to shoot a man-eater is as unexciting as it appears to be selfcontradictory. The hunter purchases three or four live baits in the form of buffalo heifers or young bulls and ties them out at pre-selected places where machans have already been put up, in the hope that the tiger may kill one of them. The hunter then sits in the machan the following night to shoot the tiger when it returns for a second meal.

Having heard that man-eaters eat men, you may wonder why an animal bait is tied out. Would a man-eater want to kill it? The answer is that man-eaters do not confine themselves to a diet of human flesh. They merely prefer the flesh of men to other meat. Perhaps a man is easier to find. He is certainly easier to stalk and kill. Maybe there is something appetizing about human flesh. But anyway, one cannot very well tie out a human being as bait.

With Hughie's influence and Sweza's help I purchased four young bulls at Talaimalai village. The two boys whose father had been killed volunteered to help me in tethering the animals and building machans, so I recruited them and two more to assist. With Hughie and Sweza we formed a committee of seven persons when we sat down to deliberate on where to tie our baits. Strangely, it has become customary to tether a bait as near as possible to the spot where a kill has already taken place. I do not really know why this is so. It is certainly wrong reasoning to infer that a man-eater, like a murderer, may have a guilty conscience and come back to the scene of his crime. To a man-eater his action is no crime. It is merely his dinner.

I admit I have fallen into the habit myself, but now I come to think of it, the practice follows faulty reasoning. As a matter of fact, a man-eater is more likely to avoid the scene of one of his former kills rather than go there again, because he knows of the publicity it occasioned and the number of people who have visited the spot since the occurrence.

The real thing to do, as I have related in earlier stories, is to try to work out the line of beat the killer has been following by studying a map of the locality and marking on it the places where each human kill occurred and the date of each event. When the tiger is a man-eater of long standing, with many crimes to his discredit, such a study reveals that he has been following a fixed route over and over again, returning to the same eocalities (but not the exact spot) in which he has killed before, once in so many weeks or months as the case may be. In shikar parlance, this habit or practice is known as the 'man-eater's beat.'

I suppose in a way this answers the question posed earlier as to why it has become more or less an accepted practice to tie a bait near the spot where a human kill has already occurred. One hopes it will be on the tiger's beat and that he will come again. But this may not happen for many weeks or even months, for every man-eater does not follow a beat. Most do, but there are exceptions. And in any case such a

425

beat can only be worked out with a man-eater of long standing. The animal I was after had started recently and his killings so far had been haphazard.

All of which brings me back to the fact that it was difficult for us to decide precisely where to tie out and there was much difference of opinion. The two boys advocated trying the Sultan's Battery Road where their father had been killed. The other two men I had recruited to help me said the track leading from Talaimalai to Talavadi would be best, as tiger pugmarks were seen along it nearly every day. Hughie suggested tying the four baits a mile apart from each other and in a straight line, two to three miles south of Talaimalai, where the ground fell away abruptly to the valley of the Moyar River. Sweza suggested tying up somewhere in Hughie's match-grass, where the tiger was first wounded, because he felt it would return there to eat the spotted deer and wild pig that were still abundant.

Of all these suggestions, I decided the last was the least likely to bring success. The man-eater would never return to a place where it had been so badly hurt. So we ruled it out. All the other suggestions were equally good and it appeared to be a matter of luck where and when the tiger would next show up.

Eventually we decided to lether one of the baits on the Sultan's Battery Road, another one of the baits on the Sultan's Battery Road, another on the Talaimalai-Talavadi track, and the third and fourth baits at two of the most likely spots along the ridge south of Talaimalai that overlooked the Moyar River, as suggested by Hughie. I felt that the kill, if and when it took place, would be one of these two baits, as tigers passed to and from the Nilgiri forests to the Talaimalai Reserve across this ridge. However, as there was more than one tiger in the area, we would not know whether the man-eater or some quite innocent tiger had made the kill, and the only course open would be to shoot it in the hope that it turned out to be the man-eater. The selection of the exact spot for each tie-up was to be left to me.

I told my four helpers to return at dawn the next day with another eight men, so that there would be a dozen of them altogether, allowing sufficient men for the task of erecting each of the four machans that were to be put up before the baits were tied out.

I have found it wise to erect the machan first and only afterwards to tie the bait in a suitable line of fire. Then, when a kill occurs, the hunter is ready to take his place. The other way around much disturbance is caused in tying a machan after the bait has been killed, and should the tiger be lying in concealment within hearing he generally fails to return.

The machan I favoured using at that time, and still think is best, is an ordinary charpoy cot with its four legs cut short. For those of you who don't know what a charpoy cot is, I may explain that it consists of a rectangular wooden or bamboo frame of four pieces, about six feet by three. Rope, or wide cotton tape, is laced across this frame, while four legs at each of the four corners complete the cot. Most villagers sleep on the ground, but in certain places unduly infested with snakes and scorpions, charpoy cots are the only type that are favoured, for they are made in the villages and cost in the region of five rupees each, including the rope used. Where cotton tape or webbing is employed for more comfort — the price, at the most, is doubled.

My machan consisted of a cot of the latter type. Each of the four legs had been shortened to a foot in length, sufficient to provide something by which to tie the cot to the branches of a tree. The cot itself was cut into two and folded on two hinges for convenience of transport. Its advantages are obvious;

it provided maximum comfort with minimum weight and noise should I be forced to move about — which, incidentally, is the one thing you should never do in sitting up!

Hughie favoured another type of machan, which was nothing more than a folding canvas chair with a footrest to keep your legs from dangling downwards. Sitting in one of these always gave me a sense of insecurity — a feeling that I would either fall out of it, or that the whole structure would collapse at any moment. Of course, this was only prejudice, as in reality there was no real risk either way and I was grateful when Hughie offered to lend me his canvas chair-machan to be used in one of the four places we had selected. This meant that the remaining two machans would have to be constructed in the spot with bamboos and wood cut in the jungle.

Work began in earnest next day, when the dozen men arrived carrying their sharp knives. Hughie supplied all the rope we would need, so with four of the men leading, the bulls I had purchased to serve as bait, we were soon on the Talaimalai-Talavadi road, where we were to tie the first machan.

We had gone scarcely a quarter of a mile along this track when we saw, clearly imprinted on the soft earth, the fresh pug-marks of a tiger that had come down the bed of a small nallah that crossed the road. The tiger had passed in the early hours of the morning, which was revealed by the fact that the powdery dust bordering the edges of the track had not yet fallen into the depressions made by the tiger's pads. With the passage of a few hours and the action of the wind, this would certainly have happened were the tracks more than six hours old.

Walking up the nallah, both to the left and right of where it crossed the road, we saw several older tracks, indicating that this dry stream-bed was much used either by the tiger whose tracks we had just seen or by other tigers in the locality. Unfortunately, due to their age, these tracks could not be identified for certain with the fresh ones along the road which undoubtedly had been made by an adult male of rather bigger than average size.

A banyan tree grew on the farther bank of the nallah, just before it crossed the road, and all agreed that this would be the ideal place for the first machan. It was an old tree, and many of the roots that had dropped to the earth from the higher branches had in the course of the years, themselves taken root and grown into the thickness of minor tree-trunks. Within this network of the roots and trunks it would be easy for us to put up an inconspicuous machan, and I decided to save my charpoy and Hughie's chair for one of the other places where natural construction might not be so easy. We completed that machan in ninety minutes, and after tying the first bait in a convenient position, set out for our second selection, which you will remember was the Sultan's Battery Road.

The sons of the old man who had been killed showed me where the tragedy had taken place, and within a couple of furlongs of this spot and once again where a nallah crossed the road, we erected the second machan. This again was constructed on the spot, but took much longer to do, so that it was nearly noon before we set out for the ridge, two miles away, overlooking the Moyar Valley and Niligri jungles whence the tigers generally came.

My guides, who had lived in the area all their lives, pointed out first one then a second game trail that led up from the valley to the south of us, down which in the distance flowed the Moyar River, its course easily recognizable by the thick belt of giant trees on its bank. From the height at which we were standing, the Moyar looked like a great green python, writhing its course through the forest.

On convenient trees we tied our remaining machans, my charpoy first and finally Hughie's canvas chair, while with the tying-up of our fourth unfortunate bull-bait, the work of the day came to an end. The sun was sinking across the jungles of Bandipur to the west when we started on our walk back to Hughie's farm quite five miles away. It had been a long day and we were very tired, but I was very satisfied by the four jobs we had completed. It was very satisfied by the four jobs we had completed. All I had now to do was scour the jungle in other directions by day in the hope of meeting the man-eater accidentally. Meanwhile, I would sleep peacefully at Hughie's place by night till one of my baits was taken.

Little did I know what was going to happen.

The two sons of the old man and the first two men who had volunteered to help me had been instructed to visit the four baits next morning, and every morning thereafter, and to feed and water them, till a kill occurred. They were to begin with the most distant baits, the two animals we had tied on the western ridge, and then work eastwards to the Sultan's Battery Road, and finally to the first bait on the Talaimalai-Talavadi track, which was the closest of the four to Hughie's farm.

It was ten-thirty next morning when I heard them coming up the driveway, talking excitedly, and I knew that a kill had occurred. But the news they brought was surprising — and disconcerting! The last bait we had tied the previous evening — the one under Hughie's canvas-chair machan — had been killed and part eaten, and the first animal at the junction of the nallah with the Talaimalai-Talavadi road had also been killed and about half devoured.

Two kills on the same night, at points at least five miles apart. This clearly pointed to two tigers. Now which of them was the man-eater and in which of the machans should I sit?

Another consultation was held, but his time we were unanimous. The tiger that had killed the first bait — the nearest to the farm — was far more likely to be the man-eater, for its tracks had indicated that it haunted the nallah-bed crossing the Talaimalai-Talavadi road on which a human kill had already taken place and which was frequented by human beings. The other kill on the ridge was at a far less frequented spot, where people hardly ever went, but which was used by tigers coming from the Nilgiri district, or returning to it. As such, the tiger that had killed there was in all likelihood not the man-eater. It was therefore decided that I should sit at the nallah-crossing that night.

With this settled, the next thing to do was to put in a few hours of sleep.

Hughie called me at one o'clock for a hearty lunch and gave me a parcel of sandwiches for the night, a most acceptable gift. By two-thirty I was on the machan, looking down upon the half-eaten young bull as my four assistants removed the branches with which they had covered the carcase that morning to protect it from vultures.

There was silence after their departure and, as was to be expected, no travellers passed along the road, the presence of the man-eater discouraging people, especially towards evening, from using a track on which he had already killed a man. I was surprised, therefore, to hear voices approaching from the Talaimalai village direction some time after five o'clock, and astonished when I recognized the party as my own four attendants, accompanied by Sweza carrying a gun. They came to tell me that the man-eater had killed a woman while she was carrying water from a well near the hamlet of Dimbum, which was seventeen miles away on the Satyamangalam-Chamrajnagar road. Hughie had sent them with the news, as he felt that I might not consider it worthwhile to sit up all night to shoot a tiger which obviously could not be the man-eater. No tiger that had devoured half a bull the previous night would walk a distance of seventeen miles to kill a woman the next morning.

I heartily agreed with the message Hughie had sent and came down from the machan. As far as I was concerned the tiger that haunted the nallah was welcome to the remaining half of his meal. When I got back, Hughie suggested that I go at once to Dimbum and try to find a place to sit up, either near the well or wherever the woman had been killed. No doubt her family would have removed her remains of cremation, but it was just possible that the man-eater might return to the spot during the night in search of the body of his victim. I agreed and started straight away, taking my four helpers along in case of need.

It was almost dark when we left Talaimalai village and I switched on the headlights of the Studebaker. Just a mile farther on, the road descended steeply to cross the first of several intersecting streams, all dry at this time of the year, and strung out across the road on the opposite bank of this stream, reflecting the beams from my lights, were the eyes of a herd of bison! The herd galloped away, disturbed by the noise when I changed gear to cross the stream — that is, all of them except the herd-bull, which stood squarely in the centre of the road, his head partly lowered and pawning the ground in a attitude obviously nasty and threatening.

Bisons are generally quite harmless animals and run away at the slightest sight or sound of human beings. Here was one of them behaving rather differently. Perhaps he felt I constituted a danger to the herd. More likely he was puzzled by the headlights of the car and never realized that human beings were behind them. In any case, I did not wish to risk the consequences of a charge. It meant shooting the bull — which

I had no desire to do — and quickly, for the signs of an impending charge within the next few seconds were unmistakable. If he succeeded, I knew my Studebaker would be a write-off together with some, if not all of us, who were inside. With my own eyes I have seen a loaded trunk overturned by a charging bison on the Tippakadu road in the Nilgiri jungles; the driver had been killed — by the truck itself — while the bison had disposed of his assistant and the cleaner by goring and trampling them to pulp.

These unpleasant thoughts passed quickly through my mind. There was just one chance left before using my rifle, and I would have to take it at once. That chance lay in the old klaxon horn fixed to the right of me on the wind-shield of the Studebaker. Many an elephant had I scared with this same ancient klaxon! Its blatant, brassy blare had made them flee in abject terror. So I tried it again. I pumped the spring lever of that old horn hard and repeatedly. A ghastly sound rent the jungle silence. The bull raised its lowered head, its eyes dilated by fear of what seemed like all hell let loose, and the next moment it plunged into the bamboo undergrowth and vanished from sight.

After that I saw quite a lot of game, which was rather unusual for so early an hour, and incidentally a 'good omen,' so far as hunting superstition goes. Spotted deer and two sambar crossed individually, a sloth bear was digging by the roadside as my lights disturbed him, and a panther leaped from left to right a furlong after I had passed the Honathetti Forest Lodge and was negotiating a valley between two hillocks, just seven miles from Dimbum.

We arrived at our destination shortly before 8 p.m., which, all said and done, was excellent going, for the track was not only steep and winding but had been in places completely obliterated by the long grass. Hidden boulder lay in that grass, enough to tear open the bottom of any crankcase or differential that bumped against it. In such spots I had had to slow down to a snail's pace, slowly following two of the men as they walked side by side a few yards ahead to warn me of hidden rocks before one of the front wheels of the car banged against them. Then we would all help to roll them aside, or if they were too big to move I would circumvent them by going off the track.

Dimbum is a hamlet on the main road from Mysore City, past the town of Chamrajnagar, down to another large town in the plains named Satyamangalam, which was the headquarters of the police and forest departments for the area. Fifty miles on lies the city of Coimbatore.

All that Dimbum could boast were a few huts and a tea shop, owned by a Moplah, a descendant of some Arab trader, who centuries earlier had come to the west coast of India for trade but remained to settle down and marry several Hindu Malayalee women. These men have kept their business acumen through the years and there is hardly any trade in which numbers of them do not excel. The tea shop at Dimbum was kept open by the Moplah and his three wives throughout the twenty-four hours of the day. Tired lorry drivers, ascending the steep ghat-road from Satyamangalam, sixteen miles away, could count on a large mug of steaming tea or coffee at any time of the day or night, together with a hot meal of curry and rice. There was another essential commodity thrown in with the refreshment, and it was free: cool water for their boiling radiators when their trucks arrived in a cloud of steam after that long ascent.

There is a Rest House for travellers, too, and it is beautifully situated upon the edge of the escarpment that overlooks the valley many thousands of feet below. The nearer part of this valley at the base of the escarpment is heavily forested, but the road can be seen winding through the jungle and finally breaking out into the cultivated lands that stretch away to the horizon. In the middle distance is Satyamangalam, while far away on the skyline to the south-west is Coimbatore.

Those jungles at the foot of the hill recall the escapades of the tiger I named 'the mauler of Rajnagara,'* for it was there that I spent some exciting days looking for him without success.

To look upon the plains from this Rest House at nightfall is like looking down into fairyland. The myriad points of electric light, frequently interspersed with coloured lights of every hue, stand out in sharp contrast to the black void. Away to the south-west is an angry glow upon the horizon: the reflection of the lights of Coimbatore, too far away to be seen directly, upon the cloud-layered sky.

I drove to the Moplah's tea shop, for that I knew would be the fountain-head of all the information I wanted. Abdulkunni, the ambitious proprietor, knew me well. In fact, I had dropped in for a cup of tea at his place on my way to Hughie's farm and had told him the reason for my visit. He greeted me loudly now and in his high-pitched, excited voice, began pouring out his news.

'Why do you go to Talaimalai looking for your tiger, sahib, when it's right here? This morning it killed a woman at the well, just behind this tea shop. A damned nuisance, indeed! We need a great deal of water here, for making tea and for the radiators of the hundred or more lorries that need it every day. This requires many visits to the well and many buckets of water. My three wives have all refused to go there since they heard the news. Disobedient, good-for-nothing

_____

* See *Man-eaters and Jungle Killers*, Chapter 8.

bitches, all three of them! I have threatened to kick them out. Even beaten them. But with one accord they told me to go myself. Cannot somebody rid me of these wenches? Now I put it to you, sahib. Can I possibly leave the tea shop? So I have been compelled to engage a servant on daily wages from today. This costs money and in any case she is a lazy slut! Look sahib, as a good Mussulman it is not the custom for me to allow strangers to speak to my womenfolk. But you are a friend, sir. Please talk to my wives and advise them to fetch the water.'

A difficult assignment indeed! Besides, I had better things to do than persuade old Abdulkunni's wives to commit suicide. For that was the fate they would invite by visiting the well with the man-eater about. I could not blame the women for going on strike. Old Abdulkunni thought more of his money than of his wives, but I did not tell him so. It would hurt his feelings.

I said instead, 'I have come to shoot the tiger, Abdulkunni, so if you'll help me, your problem will be solved. Let's not waste time, but tell me exactly how the woman was killed.'

'What is there to say, sahib. She went for water. She was returning with it. Then the *shaitan bagh* leapt from the bushes and carried her off into the jungle. She screamed loudly but the tiger only growled. Another woman was going down for water, too, and was but a few yards away when it happened. She heard and saw everything. She ran back to this very place and told us. I had five or six customers here at the time. We bolted and barred the doors and locked ourselves in for nearly two hours. That was another loss of business. It was only when other drivers arrived and banged on the front door that we opened up. Then a large party of us went down to the well. Of the woman there is no sign. Her broken pot remains where it fell from her hands. There is nothing more to tell you.'

'Have there been earlier reports of a tiger in this locality, Abdulkunni? Has anyone else seen it? Did anybody notice anything distinctive about the animal?' I fired the questions rapidly.

But the old man only laughed. 'What can be distinctive about a tiger?' he inquired. 'They all look alike, with a head, four legs and a tail. Besides, why do you ask such silly questions of me? Have I not told you already that nobody except the other woman who was going herself to the well for water saw the tiger? She said it was a huge beast and looked like *shaitan* (the devil) himself.'

One last question I asked, with visions of possibly being able to sip up over the victim's remains of the next day. 'Has, the woman's body been found?'

Abdulkunni's derisive grin widened. 'Who is there to search for it, sahib? Do you think we are mad? We are alive now. The woman is dead. If we go in search of her body and the tiger finds us, we too will be dead. And that will not help her!'

How often had I not heard those same words before, spoken in so many different languages, when inquiring if a man-eater's victim or the remains, had been found!

It was evident that the Moplah could give me no further help. I would have to do things for myself and think out some plan. So I ordered two mugs of tea for myself, and a mug each for the men I had brought in the car from Talaimalai, and selecting the corner-most table in the grimy tea shop took out my pipe to smoke while considering the best course of action.

The first thing to do was to get rid of Abdulkunni, who had started talking again. Very frankly I asked him to leave me alone as I wanted to think out a plan.

The old man's behaviour was particularly irritating that

day. With a wicked smirk, he remarked, 'If you want the tiger, why not call it?' Then he went to serve the tea.

Four tracks join at Dimbum, almost directly in front of the tea shop. Or rather, two of them are tracks, while the other two consist of the main road that passes through the hamlet, leading northwards towards Mysore and southwards to Satyamangalam. I have intentionally counted this one main road as two because, so far as searching for the tiger went, he might cross it to the north of Dimbum, or go down the ghat road as it fell away to the south towards Satyamangalam,. The third track was the one I had just travelled, leading from Talavadi and Talaimalai, and the fourth track led into the jungle and was hardly noticeable. It began just behind the Rest House and then wound eastwards through the forest for ten miles or more, keeping more or less to the edge of the continuation of the Dimbum escapement that overlooked the plains as far as the watershed of the Cauvery River, fifty miles to the east.

Being the least used of the four, this last track was the one along which most animals were to be seen, especially bison and sambar. Quite a number of bear came up the escarpment and tigers very often crossed it by steep hidden routes on their long trek of more than fifty miles eastwards, through very dense, jungle and mountain terrain, to the Cauvery River. After about ten miles this track dwindled to a mere footpath that threaded through very heavy bamboo jungles, inhabited more by elephants, bison and sambar than by tigers. For the area is infested by tick, and tigers definitely do not like ticks!

It was pitch dark outside — an ideal night for using a spotlight in searching for animals.

I could motor up the road towards Mysore for about five miles and then return, shining my spotlight and hoping the man-eater might cross by sheer chance. I could then repeat the performance along the ghat road in the opposite direction. I could even motor along the road I had come from Talaimalai. But motoring along the fourth track to the east would not be advisable. Here I would have to walk. For this track was not only in a very bad state, littered with big stones and full of potholes, but it twisted and turned, and was full of sharp gradients. It entailed far too much gear work and consequent noise, which would drive away gear work and consequent noise, which would drive away the man-eater and any other animal that happened to be near, before I had a chance of seeing them.

Where to begin was anybody's choice and I decided to walk along the eastern track first, while I was still fresh and because it would take the longest time.

Finishing my tea, I paid Abdulkunni and told my four men to catch up with as much sleep as they could while I took a walk up the eastern trail. Not being old acquaintances of mine, they thought I was mad. Abdulkunni, who had overheard the conversation and who had known me for quite a long time, remarked: 'You think he's mad, eh? That's no discovery! I've known him to be mad for a long time.'

For some reason the old rascal was annoying me more and more that evening. I checked the torch in the .405 and the spare five-cell torch that I intended using for the actual reconnaissance, as it would be far too tiresome to keep pointing the barrel of the rifle about so as to use its torch. Then I walked to the Rest House, stood on the verandah plinth for a few minutes to admire once more the twinkling lights of Satyamangalam, and finally started along the eastern track that began behind the bungalow. With the first turn, that came within a few yards, I was shut off from the friendly light of the petromax lantern hanging in front of the tea shop and from the sounds that came from within.

The man-eater had disappeared with his victim and there was no knowing where he had taken her. Tigers have been known to carry their kills for a distance of half-a-mile and even more, although generally they don't go so far. He had killed the woman that morning and no doubt had eaten part of her. The rest he would have come back for after dark to make a second meal. It was now a little after 9.30 p.m., and as the habits of tigers generally go, the man-eater should have returned by now for his second meal and be enjoying it at this moment, or very likely he would have finished it by now. After all, there is not much meat in an already half-eaten human carcase!

If he had eaten his fill, he would next seek water, and I knew there were three possible places for him to do that. The closest was at a water-hole that was skirted by the very track I was following and lay hardly a furlong ahead. The second was by a regular stream that crossed the road to Mysore about two miles away. The third was another stream that I had already passed in the car that evening and was about three miles from Dimbum on the Talaimalai road. Apart from the waterhole I was approaching, the man-eater could drink at any point throughout the course of the two streams, and the chance of meeting him over water was extremely slim.

I was approaching the water-hole with these thoughts still in my mind, and the first signs of its nearness were a row of blue-green lights in pairs, that kept jerking up and down as they stared into the bright beam of my torch. Spotted deer! Here was a herd, either on its way to the water-hole or returning from it.

I stopped abruptly and put out the light to allow the deer a chance of going away quietly. If any of them caught the human scent behind my light, if would surely voice an alarm cry to warn its companions. That cry would also alert the tiger if it was in the vicinity, and I did not want that to happen.

The night was pitch-dark and not a sound came to me from the spotted deer. The silence was intense. Not even a cricket chirped. I did not like it at all. It was eerie.

I switched on the torch. The bobbing pinpoints of light had gone. The deer had vanished in complete silence. That was good, for they had raised no alarm. I waited a few minutes longer to allow them to get far enough away, so as not to scent me or see my torch-beam. Then I started moving forward silently along the track. The next turn would bring me to the water-hole that lay to the left.

That was when I heard the splashing and gurgling and loud swishing noises. An elephant was at the water-hole and enjoying a bath. I stopped again. His presence was a nuisance, for elephants, like most human beings, like their bath. Once they start, they not only gurgle and drink and bathe and gambol, but they lie in the water and play in it, even if all alone, sometimes for an hour at a stretch. I could not waste so much time waiting for the creature to go away of its own accord. On the other hand, if I advanced and it saw or scented me, the chances were that it might trumpet in alarm and that, again, would warn the man-eater, should he be within earshot, that something strange was moving through the forest, something unusual enough to disturb an elephant. For me to make a noise to frighten away the elephant would be folly for the same reason.

Then I had an idea. I pointed the beam of the torch high up to the treetops in the direction of the water-hole in the hope that it might be seen by the elephant and cause him to move off. Evidently I was too far away at first, because he did not see the light. Then I advanced till I was almost at the bend of the track before trying again. This time I succeeded. All sounds of that most enjoyable bath ceased abruptly.

There came a great squelching as the elephant lifted his big body out of the mud, followed by a rhythmic plop-plop-plop-plop of heavy footsteps as he plodded slowly through the water to the bank. Then followed repeated hissing sounds as of escaping steam. Although disturbed by my light, the elephant did not intend to deny himself the last luxury of a sand-bath, and that was what he was doing at that moment; he was throwing sand over himself.

I allowed him time, while continuing to flash the torch from treetop to treetop to keep him sufficiently disturbed. The hissing stopped eventually. It was followed in a little while by faint crackling sounds as the beast moved its heavy way through the undergrowth bordering the water-hole. Once again came silence. The elephant had moved off and just then the sharp crack of a breaking branch told me that he had stopped for feed, but far enough away not to be alarmed at my passing.

I negotiated the turn in the track and came upon the water-hole lying limpid and dark before me, a few wisps of vapour already rising from its warmer surface into the rapidly-cooling night air. Hundreds of pin-points of brilliant red light, like tiny rubies scattered over the water, shone in my torchlight, and from the nearer bank bordering the pool came the chorus of frogs. Alarmed by my approach, they had leaped off the bank in great numbers. With vigorous thrusts of their hind legs they propelled themselves into the centre of the pool, where they whirled around to face me, their tiny eyes glistening and reflecting like a thousand rubies.

I had been to such pains to avoid the elephant raising an alarm at my approach only to meet with a singular detect at the hands of those most insignificant of creatures — the frogs.

442

The tiger heard them, for he happened to be there, and must have seen me and my light simultaneously.

Fortunately for me, he was on the further bank of the pool, where he must have come to drink, and not on the track, or matters may have turned out differently. Under similar circumstances, any normal tiger would have taken himself off quietly and I would never have known of his presence. But this one growled, and continued to growl, the ominous sound rumbling from the darkness at the other end, across the pool and to me as I came to an abrupt and uncertain halt.

The tiny ruby-red eyes of the frogs floating on the surface disappeared altogether, as if some switch had cut off the power, when they dived beneath the surface to escape that awful sound. On the opposite bank of the pool whence the growling arose there was a great disturbance as the myriad frogs that had been resting on the cool sand by the water's edge threw themselves into the pool for safety and with their tiny legs struck out frantically for the centre.

The growling stopped as abruptly as it had begun. The frogs fell into a hushed silence too. I then directed the beam of my torch around the bushes and undergrowth that grew down to the water's edge at the opposite end. Would I see the tiger's eyes glow in the beam? I saw nothing and heard nothing. My light fell only upon the jungle and a deathly silence covered everything.

The tiger had vanished. Had he made off? A normal tiger would do just that, but no normal tiger would have growled at seeing my torchlight. This beast was far from normal. He was angry, and he was unafraid of the approach of man. Was this the man-eater?

I glanced around nervously. My front was safe. To attack from that direction the tiger would have to charge through water and I knew he was very unlikely to do that. Rather, he would come around the pool and attack me from either flank, or from behind. If he chose a flank attack, he would have to charge along the bank or the track, either from the direction I had just come or from the opposite end where the pathway left the pool. More probably he would attack from the rear, where the jungle bordered the edge of the track and not two yards from where I was standing. Then I would have no chance whatever.

There was but one thing to do and I did it very quickly. I scrambled down the sloping bank into the water and, feeling the way before me with each foot-step, made for the middle of the pool as fast as I could. I knew it was not very deep and there I would be safe from attack from any direction. No tiger — not even a man-eater, at least not in my experience — would attack across water, and even if it did, the tables would be turned entirely in my favour. I would have the tiger in the open and completely at my mercy, long before he could reach me.

The water had reached a little above my knees when the tiger growled again. This time it was a loud growl, almost a roar. And it came from the jungle bordering the track, from the very direction in which I had expected the attack. Had I not sought the safety of the pool just in time, the tiger would have launched itself upon me. He was growling with fury now at finding me beyond reach.

But was I really beyond reach? The next few moments would answer that question. Of one fact I had no doubt whatever: I was dealing with the man-eater and no ordinary tiger. The hate in its behaviour clearly showed that. Hughie's bullet had turned this animal into a fiend.

I waited in vain. The tiger did not emerge. The growling stopped as unexpectedly as it had started, and once again I was plunged into silence with a sea of darkness around me.

I played the beams of my torch in every direction as I turned slowly around, hoping to catch a glimpse of the beast's eyes as they reflected the light, or of the striped body slinking from bush to bush. But I saw and heard nothing.

The myriads of frogs that had experienced such a disturbing night, first with the arrival of the elephant, then myself, and finally the tiger, all went below the surface of the water when I waded into it. But they could not remain submerged for long and had to come up for breath. One by one they came to the surface now, soundlessly, to gulp in air, and soon the nearer edge of the wide circle of light thrown by my torch once more revealed hundreds of pairs of tiny red eyes gazing on me in fear.

A long time seemed to have passed since I left the tea shop, but a quick glance at my watch showed it was only 10.30 p.m. How long would I have to wait for the tiger to move, if he moved at all?

I began to get tired of standing in the water. It grew colder and colder and wreaths of vapour arose from the surface of the pool, obscuring the jungle around its edges and making it difficult for the light of my torch to penetrate. At the same time, I realized that if I got back to the pathway I would be at the mercy of the man-eater should he decide to ambush me at any spot along the track. I felt certain he had not gone away but was biding his time till I came out of the water.

Midnight, and it was biting cold! By now I realized I must not shine my torch continuously, for the five cells would run down and under no circumstances could I risk using up the cells of the other torch, clamped to my rifle, for the accuracy of my shooting depended on them. So I extinguished the light and was plunged abruptly into darkness. That was when I noticed that the night was cloudy, with no stars to be seen.

However, there was no danger so long as I remained in

the water. My hearing would warn me of the approach of any animal.

Very soon, that was what happened. An elephant came, perhaps the same one I had disturbed earlier. Probably another. I was standing still and he did not hear or see me. The wind was blowing from him to me, so he could not scent me. I felt I was safe, for in any case his sight was too poor to penetrate the mist that had settled over the whole pool like a thick bank of fog, and he would not be able to see me.

I heard the loud fooff-foooff-foooff as he exhaled air though his trunk, and then the sucking noises as he drew in water and splashed it into his mouth and over his body. He drank and he drank, a seemingly endless number of gallons of water.

At last he decided to have a regular bath and I heard the tremendous plop-plop-plop of his great feet approaching me as he waded through the water towards the centre of the pool. This would never do, I thought. So I shone the torch straight into his face.

That night was for me one in which I seemed fated to meet animals of strange behaviour. According to all the rules of the game, the elephant should have turned tail and bolted from my bright light, but he did nothing of the kind. He trumpeted shrilly, coiled up his trunk, and charged me.

Taken aback, instead of putting the five-cell quickly into its pouch at the left side of my belt, so as to leave both my hands free to handle my rifle, I missed the pouch and dropped the torch into the water. Out it went.

There was no time to retrieve it. The charging elephant was dangerously close. I brought the .405 to my shoulder while pressing the button of the smaller torch that was clamped to its barrel with my left thumb. The beam cut through the darkness as I aimed a foot above the head of the elephant and fired in an attempt to halt that charge.

No rogue elephant had been proclaimed by the Forestry Department and so, as far as possible, I should try to avoid killing this animal. I had erred by letting him come too close to me and I should not have shone the torch directly in his face.

As these thoughts rushed through my mind, I awaited the result of that deterring shot. If he still came on, I would be forced to stop him with my next bullet or he would kill me. There was no doubt of that.

Luckily it worked. The great beast braked to a halt by planting all four feet firmly in the mud. The impetus of the rush brought him on, skidding ludicrously in the clay till he ended up sitting on his hind-quarters like an elephant at the circus. Encouraged by his failing nerve, I fired a second time, again over his head. The elephant turned and bolted.

When the nose and tumult had died away I felt disgusted, but at the same time relieved. My two shots must have driven away the man-eater. My chance of success were gone. But now I was safe also and could at last get out of the water.

Shivering with the cold, I started my walk back to Dimbum. I knew I had only a short distance to cover, but there was always the danger that the man-eater, driven from the immediate vicinity of the pool by the sound of my shots, might still be lurking somewhere along the pathway and might ambush me.

At last the lights of Satyamangalam, twinkling in the black void of the plains below me, put an end to my tension. I got into the Rest House, took off my wet pants and, as I had brought no change of clothes, went to sleep without them.

A banging on the door awakened me. I had closed all the

windows and it was dark inside, but a glance at my watch surprised me. It was 9.30 a.m.

I put on my pants again. They were still wet. The banging on the door was renewed, this time more urgently, and I could hear the murmur of voices on the verandah.

I opened the front door. Confronting me was Abdulkunni himself, his three wives and four or five other people, all in a great state of excitement. Obviously the tea shop had been closed down. Something very serious must have happened.

'Come quickly, sahib,' called the excited Moplah. 'The tiger has just carried away the girl we employed to fetch the water.'

Grabbing my rifle and some cartridges, I hastened with the group to the tea shop, while he quickly told the story.

Barely thirty minutes earlier the girl had taken a basket of cooking utensils to wash at the well behind the tea shop. She had decided it would be easier that way than carrying a pitcher or more of water to the building for the purpose. One of the wives had been watching her from the back door to ensure she did not linger unduly over the task. The girl, a maiden of about eighteen years, was bending down, absorbed in her work, when a movement behind her had caught the eye of the watching woman. She had glanced in that direction and was horrified to see a tiger, belly to the ground, sneaking stealthily upon the unsuspecting servant girl from behind. The woman had screeched a warning. The girl heard and jumped to her feet. But the tiger drove home his charge. He had leapt upon his victim and, not waiting to kill her, had taken the unfortunate girl in his mouth and leaped back into the cover of the undergrowth. Terrible screams could be heard long after the tiger and victim had disappeared from sight.

Alarmed by his wife's yells and hearing distant wailing, Abdulkunni and the other members of the household had rushed to the rear door to find out the cause of the disturbance. Then they had come in a body to the Rest House. The man-eater had taken another victim at nine in the morning, and exactly where he had killed only a few hours earlier! This was something unheard of in the annals of man-eaters.

Telling everyone to remain indoors, I hastened to the well. The scattered utensils, some washed and the others not, showed that the girl had been taken by surprise while engrossed in her task, and a single sliding pug-mark indicated where the tiger had stopped his rush to seize his victim and had slipped on the wet earth where the girl had been doing her washing. There were no other marks on the surrounding earth, trampled flat as it was by the feet of the many people who came there all day long to draw water, and baked by the sun's rays. The ground was far too hard to carry pug-marks, while the girl had been grabbed so quieckly that there was no blood-trail of any kind.

The woman who had witnessed the killing, Abdulkunni's second wife, called to me from the door-way, pointing out the direction in which the man-eater had gone with his victim, and I followed it. The clearing in which the well stood ended abruptly in a wall of lantana bushes that fringed the jungle. No tiger, carrying his prey, would dream of forcing himself through this tangled obstruction. It would be impossible for any beast. There must be some other way and I started to look for it. I found it eventually, a game-path, close to the ground, tunnelling at a height of not more than four feet through the lower branches of the lantana. It had been made by wild pigs during the rainy season, when they visited the clearing to root and dig in the swamp which would at that season surround the well. In places the tiger had had to crawl along this tunnel, dragging its victim, and I followed suit, crouching low and at times on hands and knees.

Within a few yards I came upon the first evidence of the tragedy. Some torn shreds of a sari and a quantity of blood on the lantana leaves that littered the game-trail. Probably the victim had been struggling to free herself and this was where the tiger had killed her.

After that there was a regular blood-trail, and more shreds of the sari caught on the lantana. There came a bend in the tunnel and here the remains of the girl's clothing had caught on a thorny bush. The man-eater must have become angry and wrenched his victim free, for the scraps of a sari and a skirt had been torn from her body and were hanging on the thorns. With the removal of all her clothing the blood had fallen directly on the ground and leaves, making a ghastly red trail through the tunnel.

I could not know how far the tiger had carried his victim. Probably the screeching and screaming from the tea shop had made him decide to go to a quieter place before commencing his meal. At least, I hoped so. For if he was anywhere near and attacked me from my rear, I was completely at his mercy in this death-trap of a tunnel.

This thought caused me to stop frequently to listen. He might give himself away by growling. Tigers often do that when followed. Partly in anger, partly as a warning, but more often to strengthen their own courage. For all their lives have been spent in pursuing a fleeing prey and it is an unusual and terrifying experience for any tiger to realize he is the object of pursuit himself. Not a sound did I hear. Complete silence filled that twisting tunnel.

At last the lantana began to give way to jungle proper. The tunnel came to an end and I was able to stand upright. There was a grassy glade through which the blood-trail led before it merged into a park-like jungle of babul and box-flower shrubs with grass between. I judged that I had not far to go now before meeting the tiger, who must have started his meal. That is, provided the man-eater had not heard me and realized he was being followed. If that had happened, he might take himself off altogether or lie in wait for me at some spot close to his kill. He might even creep forward to intercept me, or ambush me from either side or from the rear.

Then I heard a crow cawing some distance away. I listened carefully, and there was no mistaking that persistent cawing. The crow was watching the tiger with his victim and was excitedly calling reinforcements to be ready to enjoy the feast that was soon to follow.

Sounds and the distances from which they emanate are difficult to locate and estimate correctly in the forest. Air currents, the density of tree growth and the terrain all make difficulties. In flat country conditions are not quite so bad, but in hilly areas like this, sounds and distances are often unjudgable.

I reckoned the crow was about sixty to seventy yards away, and slowly, very stealthily, studying the ground before me so as not to tread upon a dried twig or stone and so betray myself, I advanced step by step. I do not know how far I had gone when I heard the first sounds of the feast. The sharp crack of a bone being broken, followed by crunching and tearing.

The crow was still cawing excitedly. I reckoned that I was within thirty yards now, possibly a good deal less. I stopped and began to think.

The crow offered a greater risk at that moment than the tiger. For he was sitting on a tree and had the advantage of height. I knew that if he saw me he would cease cawing at once. He might even fly away. The man-eater, engrossed in his meal, knew that the crow was watching him but had ignored the bird and his cawing as a matter of no consequence.

A sudden end to that cawing and the sudden departure of the crow would tell the tiger at once that something had alarmed the bird, that some danger to himself was approaching. For crows fear no other bird and ignore the presence of wild animals. They fear only the human race.

But I had not yet alarmed the crow. At a snail's pace, with infinite caution, I advanced, crouching low, shuffling forward and halting again, watching the ground in front of me before making any movement, glancing to right and left and even looking behind when the tearing and crunching sounds ceased for a moment. For so long as I could hear those sounds I knew the tiger was in front. When they ceased I could no longer know where he was. There lay the greatest danger, for he might creep upon me from behind. Man-eaters generally snatch their victims that way.

Suddenly an uncanny silence fell over everything. At first I could not account for it. Then I knew the cause. The crow had stopped cawing! Undoubtedly something was afoot. Then I saw the crow, but too late. He had seen me first. With what seemed a tremendous fluttering, he flew to another tree.

And I was right: the man-eater had become suspicious. He had started to move. Was he moving away from me or towards me? Was he trying to escape or attack? As these questions raced through my mind, with the corner of my eye I saw the crow rise again. This time he flew out of sight.

I froze in my tracks. But it was too late. The cunning crow flew back to investigate and perched at almost the same spot as the one where I saw him first. He turned his head sideways for a better view of me, cawed and bobbed. Convinced that. I was dangerous, he fluttered his wings and then flew to yet another tree to turn around and watch me.

I stopped watching the crow and stared at the bushes all around. And I turned about to watch the bushes behind me.

There was a pricking sensation at the back of my neck. Every cell of my body warned me that I was in great danger. I knew that the man-eater was about to pounce.

But I simply could not see him, stare as I might at the undergrowth all around. The jungle was ominously silent. Not a twig cracked, not a leaf stirred. The birds and insects were silent, so too were the bushes and the long grass that grew between the trees. I looked in vain for the stirring of a branch or a blade of grass, the bending of a sapling stem that might betray movement below and the passage of a creeping body.

But there was not a movement anywhere, not a sound. I knew that the tiger was employing all his skill to make his last rush a complete surprise.

And then there came to my mind the scene I had witnessed many years before by moonlight, beside a jungle pool in the heart of a deep forest far away. A sambar hind was approaching the water-hole cautiously. All was silent. Suddenly, for no reason whatever, she wheeled noisily and rushed away. The ruse worked then, for the tiger patiently lying in wait to ambush her a few yards further on, now lost his head. He thought his prey was about to escape and he bounded after her. But the hind had too much of a start and got away to safely.

Now I did the same thing. But I did not turn and run back, for something warned me that the man-eater was already there. I stamped noisily and ran forward diagonally, but only for four paces. Then I stopped.

As on that moonlit night so many years before, the simple ruse worked again. The man-eater roared and bounded after me from behind. He took two leaps and then halted in crouching amazement as this strange man before him, instead of continuing to run, turned around and fired rapidly.

The tiger knew no more after that, but I know that if I had not heeded that warning of his very close presence behind me, or if I had run backwards instead of forwards, I would not be here to tell this tale.

Five

The Killer of the Wynaad

TO THE SOUTH-WEST OF THE CITY OF MYSORE LIES THE HEAVILY forested area of the Kakankote jungles, for centuries the home of many herds of wild elephants that are partial to the kind of jungle that grows in this district. The rainfall is heavy and the vegetation is luxurious. Giant bamboos, rank grass and mighty trees grow together in dense profusion, and a passage through the forest, except for the elephants and the large and harmless bison, is almost impossible. Sambar and barking deer are found in the thinner areas, but as one moves farther south-west and the rainfall and the denseness of the jungle increase in direct ratio to each other, the deer become fewer and fewer, leaving the elephants and bison in almost entire possession of what appears from the narrow road to be primeval, virgin jungle.

Still further on is the Kabini River, one of the natural boundaries between Mysore State to the north-east and Kerala

455

State, in the extreme south-west. In my opinion, the state of Kerala, in the extreme south-west of the Indian peninsula, offers a scenery second only in beauty to that of the Himalayas, though very different. It is a land of dense forests, fertile plantations of tea, coffee, cinnamon, rubber and tapioca, and emerald-green fields in the areas bordering the sea; of gently flowing rivers and waterways without number, along which palm-thatched river boats glide among coconut palms laden with huge bunches of green nuts, and a sea coast without parallel, culminating at the southern tip of the peninsula in the famous beach of Cape Comorin.

The town of Manantoddy, on the Kerala side of the border, stands on the Western Ghats, the range of mountains that run down the west coast of India, almost from Bombay to the far south, at an average elevation of about 4,000 feet above sea level. This district is known as the North Wynaad, to differentiate it from the country a few miles further south, which abuts the Nilgiri Mountain and is known as the South, or Nilgiri, Wynaad. Both areas are extremely fertile, enjoy a heavy rainfall, and are the site of many plantations, producing every conceivable crop.

Pleasant as they are in all other respects, these regions abound in leeches throughout the year, and in the rainy season their numbers are enormous. Moreover, that curse of the drier jungles, the tick, thrives in yet greater comfort than it does in the forests of the interior — both the large crab-tick that gives you tick-fever when it bites you in sufficient numbers, and the microscopic jungle, or grass, tick, smaller than a pin's head, that provokes a small sore wherever it has sucked your blood. Since it bites you all over the body, in hundreds of places, you become a very sore creature indeed, covered with sores that last for many months. You scratch and scratch yourself, night and day, into a mental and physical wreck.

Leeches and ticks suck the blood not only of a human being, but of animals as well. Even the bison suffer, while tigers, panthers and deer become covered with them, especially ticks, so that they hang from the softer portions of these animals' bodies, gorged with blood, like bunches of small grapes.

For this reason, the jungles of the Wynaad hold few carnivorous animals or deer. Now and then a stray animal may roam in during the dry summer months to brave the discomforts, but with the advent of the rains they move to the higher ranges of the Western Ghats, or the drier areas of East Kakankote to escape from the leeches and ticks till the monsoon abates with the approach of winter.

Thus it came about that, when a traveller journeying from Kakankote to Manantoddy was taken by a tiger just within a few hundred yards of the outskirts of the latter, it was regarded as a quite unusual event. Tigers had been seen in these parts but were few in number, and no human had been harmed for as long as anybody could remember. The event was soon forgotten and many months passed.

Then, across the border in the State of Mysore, preparations were started for the next kheddah operation, in which many wild elephants were to be caught. Coolies were engaged in hundreds to build the mighty wooden stockade into which they would later drive the elephants before the gate was dropped and the bewildered beasts captured. Much preliminary work was required; timber had to be felled, the forest cleared, bamboos gathered and bound together and then moved to the spot selected for the stockade. This required not only hard work out experienced workers. Men from the jungle tribes, the Karumbas and the Sholagas, provided most of the recruits, for they were experienced not only in tree felling and bamboo binding, but in the ways of the elephants, in driving them into the stockade, and in roping and shackling them and taming them afterwards.

That was when the tiger struck, a second and a third time, before people realized that a man-eater was amongst them.

Two Karumbas vanished within three days of each other and the half-eaten remains of the first showed he had been devoured by a tiger. The body of the second Karumba, like that of the traveller to Manantoddy, was never seen again.

There is another way of getting to Manantoddy from Mysore City, and that is via Coorg, which was for years an independent state but has recently joined Mysore. It is a more circuitous route, but the scenery is even more picturesque. Like the Kakankote road, this route traverses dense jungle inhabited by elephants and bison, where tigers are practically unknown for the reasons already explained.

The Coorgies are a hardly, lively people. In olden days the British conferred a special honour upon them unknown elsewhere in India. Every Coorgie living within the limits of his state was exempted from possessing an arms licence, no matter how many weapons he possessed. This privilege is, I believe, still maintained by the Indian Government. It was a laudable gesture but it had one bad result. The Coorgies never abused their privilege by using their weapons against each other or against other people, but they exercised it against the fauna of their beautiful little state to such an extent that the deer have been practically exterminated.

I know a large number of Coorgie families, most of whom are coffee planters, owning wide estates where the coffee berry flourishes to perfection, with oranges as a profitable secondary crop, and I happened to be a guest of one of these families when news of the man-eater trickled through.

The estate where I was staying was situated about midway between the towns of Sidapur and Virajpet, and at a considerable distance from both Manantoddy and Kakankote, where all three killings had occurred. Further, I had not brought my rifle with me from Bangalore, as I knew there was no shooting, at least of the kind in which I was interested, to be had in Coorg. So, when my friend gave me the news one morning over his breakfast table, I listened to it dispassionately, wondering like him as to how a man-eating tiger had found its way into an area so unpropitious, where ordinary tigers and panthers are almost unknown. But my friend waxed enthusiastic and suggested we go after it.

I told him I did not think much of the idea. In my opinion, the animal was not a confirmed man-eater, but was probably a sick or wounded tiger, or perhaps one that had escaped from one of the many miniature circuses that are always touring the country, and had strayed there because of the heavy jungles. I felt that it would either die of its sickness or wounds, or would soon leave these unfavourable haunts and move into normal tiger country, where it could find an abundance of its natural food, when it would stop man-hunting of its own accord. Besides, as I reminded him, I had not brought my rifle.

Timayya, for that was my host's name, offered to bet that I was wrong. The tiger would remain where he was, he affirmed. As for a rifle! He had five, from which I could make my choice.

I reminded my friend that to do so would be illegal. His weapons were unlicensed. It was a part of the stipulation that he, as a Coorgie, was forbidden to lend his unlicensed weapons to a non-Coorgie. And in any case, it was against the rules for anybody, even a licence-holder like myself, to borrow another man's weapon.

Timayya laughed at me, and said, 'What rot!' Then, banteringly, he bet me ten rupees that the tiger would kill again before the week was out. Rather huffed at his words, I took him on.

Timayya won that bet; for on the third day we heard that the tiger had killed again. This time the victim was a woman. She had been washing clothes on the further bank of the Kabini River, just within the limits of Kerala State. And Timayya's free arms permit was not valid in Kerala State.

My friend had set his heart on going after this tiger. I suppose to him, being something unusual, it became a must, and he stated flatly that I was included in the party.

Frankly, I was not keen; but to continue to refuse would have strained our relations. I had known Timayya for a long time, in fact we had been at school together, and stubbornness had always been his failing and his virtue! The estate, when he had bought it cheaply, was considered by the neighbours to be a complete 'write off.' The soil was said to be no good, the variety of coffee that grew there was no good, the shade trees were no good, and so forth! But Timayya was determined to buy. He bought; he worked hard; and he made good.

So I gave in on one condition. I would go back to Bangalore for my .405 and bring along my .450/400 as a spare rifle. He would accompany me. Then we would return to Mysore City from where we would motor directly to Kakankote and the Kerala border. I stressed that I would much rather incur the expense of the additional 240 miles of motoring than be mixed up in arms licence disputes with the police of two states.

Timayya concurred, left his weapons behind and came with me to Bangalore the same night. We spent the next day in buying provisions for a fifteen-day camp in the jungles of the border where we knew no foodstuff, acceptable to our civilized palates, would be available. Timayya bought a jar of some patent cream and a huge tin of D.D.T. as protection against the leeches and ticks. We carried mosquito nets too, along with my small tent, a portable charpoy machan, batteries and torches, and my two rifles. Timayya said he did not want to shoot but would rather watch the fun. Knowing him as I did, I realized this was not strictly true.

We arrived at Kakankote on the afternoon of the second day and then drove to the kheddah site to try to pick up what information we could about the tiger. As I anticipated, there was little to learn. So many coolies were about, working on the project, that no one appeared to know exactly when and where the tiger had taken his two victims. But rumour and universal fear were rife. The men had just vanished and their absence had not been noticed for two days or so. Even then it was only by mere chance that, being attracted by the stench of putrefying flesh, some travellers had gone to investigate and found some scanty remains.

Many people had theories to account for the presence of a man-eater in that zone, but not one of them had seen the animal. What they had to say boiled down to the belief that an evil spirit was operating in the forest in the guise of a tiger. This instilled an even greater fear into the coolies, so much so that we knew if another of them was killed, the kheddah operation would come to a stop. Such a happening, or even a postponement in the date, would be in the nature of a calamity to the local government, which had invited certain. V.I.P.s from abroad as guests at the trapping.

Next morning, we motored the short distance to the Kerala border and came to the hamlet on the further bank of the Kabini River from which the latest victim — the woman who had been washing clothes — had been taken. Once more, nobody had seen the tiger. Only its pug-marks on the river bank, the trail of something that had been dragged away, and a few drops of blood on the leaves and earth had revealed a man-eater's visit.

We went on to Manantoddy and made inquiries at that small town regarding the first victim, the traveller who had been coming from Kakankote. Here again nobody knew anything. A forest guard, returning to his quarters near the Forest Range Office, had come across an odd sandal by the roadside. As it was good sandal, and people do not usually throw their footwear away, he stopped to look at it. That was when he noticed the other sandal lying on the sloping bank of a stream that ran parallel to the road. He walked down to see that too, and found a turban entangled in the bracken that grew by the waterside. Then he looked at the ground and saw the pug-marks of a tiger in the mud. They were deeply embedded in the ooze, indicating that the animal had been carrying additional weight, while a few carmine splashes on the fern leaves revealed the truth.

Blood! The tiger had been carrying away the wearer of the sandals and the turban.

We interviewed this guard and heard the story from his own lips. And that brought us to the end of the trail. There was nothing more we could learn, and we did not know where to make start. Timayya confessed that he was sorry he had urged me to start upon this wild-goose chase.

Manantoddy is a beautiful place and we spent the night at the inspection bungalow which was fortunately vacant. Unlike most of the bungalows in other states, it is fully furnished with comfortable beds and foam mattresses, has neon lights and electric fans, and stands on a hillside opposite the ruins of an old British dwelling house that had its own private cemetery.

This is the land of fireflies. They come out after dark in their thousands, and the twinkling of their little lights are a fitting background to the chorus of the hundreds of small frogs, known as the 'Wynaad' or 'tok-tok' frog, and the hauntingly-sweet, never-to-forgotten aroma of sprays of the 'Rath-ki-Rani,' the 'Queen of the Night' blooms that open only after dark. We lay in armchairs, smoking tranquilly as we listened to the endless 'tok-tok-tok-tok-tok' of the frogs. Now and again a firefly would find its way into the room through the open window, its little light eclipsed by the brilliance of the neon tube that lit the room.

The next morning we made a leisurely start, our intention being to motor by the direct route to Virajpet in Coorg State, and thence to Timayya's plantation, where I would drop him, stay a day myself, and then go on to Mysore City and back to Bangalore.

We had travelled over ten miles from Manantoddy and were negotiating a stretch of dense forest; mostly of bamboo, on the Kerala bank of the Kabini River, when we saw a party of men approaching us, carrying a litter. And this is where my story really begins, for on the litter was a man, his tattered clothing soaked with his blood.

The bearers told us they were bamboo cutters and had been working on contract by the riverside, just over a mile away, when shortly after dawn that morning and without warning, a tiger had suddenly charged upon two of them, in full view of the others, and struck down one, whom it had grabbed by the shoulder and begun to drag away.

But the two men were brothers, and the one the tiger had ignored was very brave. He had run after the beast with the large curved knife he had been using to cut bamboos.

Seeing he was pursued, the man-eater had started to gallop away, still carrying his victim. The pursuer, realizing he had no hope of catching up with the tiger to save his brother, had then hurled his knife at the departing animal in sheer desperation. Luck favoured him, for the heavy weapon struck the carnivore in its flank. Either in pain, or from fright, the man-eater dropped his victim and bounded into the bamboos.

The hero of this episode, who was one of the men carrying the litter, had then assembled the scattered bamboo cutters and mobilized them into a team to help carry his sorely stricken brother to the nearest hospital, which was at Manantoddy.

There was no time to be lost and we acted quickly. Bundling the mauled man, with two others to help him, into the Studebaker, I told Timayya to turn around and drive them as fast as he could to the hospital, where he could leave the wounded man. He would then drive back to the bamboo cutters' camp, directed by the two men who were with him, while I went ahead on foot with the rest to see if we could find the tiger.

While Timayya was still turning the car I started at a jog-trot for the camp, the brave brother, whose name I learned was Yega, running beside me while the rest of the party followed behind. There was not a minute to be lost. In all probability the man-eater was miles away by this time, but there was just the slimmest of chances that he might still be lingering in the vicinity.

We reached the encampment in good time, but did not stop till we came to the place where the tiger had dropped his victim. There was a rank undergrowth of weeds covering the ground that showed no pug-marks, but on the bright green leaves were splashes of red — fresh blood that had not yet had time to dry. Whether the blood came from Yega's brother, who had been dropped here, or from a wound made by the knife in the man-eater's flank, we could not at that moment tell.

At this spot I halted the men who had followed and whispered to them to return to their camp. Yega and I would see this thing through together. The presence of many people would frighten the man-eater away, if it happened to be still nearby.

The bent heads of the undergrowth showed the direction in which the man-eater had run after dropping his victim, and I followed Yega, alert for a surprise attack at any moment and from any direction, particularly our rear. He tip-toed in front with bent head, examining the foliage and such glimpses of the dark 'black-cotton-soil' type of earth as he could see between the green stems of the crowded plants.

Yega was looking for his knife. We wanted to make sure if his heavy weapon had actually hurt the tiger or not. If it had really done so, we might expect the animal to act quite differently from what he would have done if the blow from the knife had been a glancing one. Most likely, if injured, the tiger would roar and charge us from a fair distance; but if uninjured the man-eater would either attack only when we came fairly close to him, or slink away.

My part of the business now was to watch the jungle more carefully than ever before, ahead on both sides, and also behind, to protect us against a surprise attack. I could not help Yega in his search.

Then we found the knife. Its edge was clean, with no trace of blood. The tiger had not been hurt and the blood we had passed had come from the wounded man.

We crept forward for some distance and stopped. Then Yega shook his head slowly from side to side. The man-eater had stopped running.

We followed for another furlong, when the trail of our quarry petered out. Here the animal had crossed an area of lemon-grass, which is a scented variety with leaves that are largely used for distilling an essential oil. This grass has long, hard tough stems which had bent with the man-eater's passing and then regained their position, so that no trace now remained of the direction in which he had gone. The earth between the large clumps of this lemon-grass was a matted carpet of decaying stems and seedlings, showing not the faintest trace of a pug-mark.

Quickening our pace, we cut directly across the lemon-grass area, which extended for perhaps a quarter of a mile, to where the jungle began again. But the tiger's trail could not be found again and we were forced to conclude that we had lost him.

Apart from his courage, perseverance was another quality in which this little bamboo cutter was strong. He refused to admit defeat and urged in a whisper that we should go on and on till we eventually found the tiger. Stimulated by his keenness, I entered into the spirit of the chase and we pressed forward for many miles and most of the remaining hours of that day. We passed two herds of bison and a family of wild elephants and it was past 3 p.m., before we finally turned back for the bamboo cutters' camp. This we reached after dark, at 7.30 p.m., I was covered with leech bites and with ticks, and I was unutterably tired, although glad that we had at last come to grips with the man-eater and had such a stout henchman as Yega to assist.

Timayya had returned in the car many hours earlier and was eagerly awaiting our news. Unfortunately, I had none to give him.

We decided to return to the inspection bungalow at Manantoddy, which was only eleven miles away, for the night and to the bamboo cutters' camp the next morning. The prospect of spending the night with them, lying on the ground, with the mosquitoes and what not, was too terrible to contemplate.

That was where I made a big mistake. For when we did arrive the next morning we found the little camp in terrible confusion and all the bamboo cutters huddled together in a single hut. They swarmed out, led by Yega, to report that the man-eater had returned in the dead of the night. He had crept up and snatched one of them from beneath the walls of a hut!

Now you may wonder how a tiger could do that, but the explanation is simple. The huts which the bamboo cutters had constructed were but temporary shelters in the jungle which they would leave as soon as their work was done. They were built of split bamboos and leaves, and the sides of the structures were never allowed to touch the ground. For if they did, the termites — or white ants, as they are better known — would creep up into the walls in a matter of hours and the whole hut would be destroyed in no time. So a gap was left right round the hut, the ends of such bamboos as had necessarily to be embedded in the ground being first defended by a coating of tar.

The man-eater must indeed have been starving. Perhaps being deprived of his victim the previous day had whetted his appetite. He had returned in the early hours of the morning and, emboldened by the silence that reigned over the slumbering camp, had wandered up to the four huts. There, through the gap below the wall of one of them, he had seen the form of a sleeping man. The rest was easy to the hungry, daring beast. He had crept up to the hut and stretched his paw under the gap, fastening his claws into the sleeping man. The man had screamed for help, but no one, had had the presence of mind to do anything and the man-eater had dragged his victim out of the hut, tearing down the lower portion of one of the walls in the process.

Unfortunately for the victim, Yega the one person who might have given help, was not in that hut in the one furthest away, enabling the tiger to make a clean getaway. The bamboo cutters related in horror that they had had to listen to the poor man's screams for a very long time after the tiger dragged him out of the hut. Strangely, it had not killed him while he yelled and screamed, as man-eaters generally do when their victims make a noise. This animal had carried him away screaming and his comrades had heard his cries grow fainter and fainter as his captor bore him away.

Yega offered to accompany me at once, but the other coolies were utterly demoralized. They remained huddled in a group, calling to God to help them while they rained invectives upon the tiger. There were nine of them, excluding Yega. So I asked Timayya to squeeze them into the Studebaker, even if it came to letting a couple stand on the footboard, and to take them back to Manantoddy and safety without delay. He was then to return to the camp site and wait for me, but while doing so was not to leave the car on any account. In any case, he had my .405/400 with him, so there was no danger of being unable to protect himself.

Yega and I then took up the trail of the man-eater.

The ground was soft outside the huts and had been cleared of the usual weeds in an effort to keep away the ticks and the leeches. This helped us to find the tiger's footprints, both as he had approached the hut and when he had left, carrying his victim with him. Whatever part of the poor man's anatomy had been grasped by the tiger was clearly not a vital region, for the victim had struggled and kicked the ground, as tell-tale marks revealed. At one place he had grasped the stem of a sapling and must have held on tenaciously. The tiger had literally torn him free, as could be seen by the particles of skin from the palms of the man's hands that still adhered to the stem and the markedly increased quantity of blood on the ground and leaves at that spot. No doubt this had resulted from an enlargement of the wound as the tiger dragged his victim free.

Now we were able to follow the trail with ease. The poor man had bled terribly and splashes of blood on the weeds, grass and leaves marked the way the tiger had passed. A queer sensation of nausea came over me as I pictured that horrible scene at dead of night in the blackness of the jungle, and the victim's realization that he was to be devoured, that nothing and no one could save him, and that he would never see his wife and children again.

At last we reached the spot where the tiger must have felt he had had enough of his victim's cries and struggles. Here he had laid the man on the ground and, releasing his grip, had bitten him again and again till his wails had been stilled for ever.

All this was written in the marks on the ground and the pool of blood that had streamed from those last fierce and fatal bites. After that the man-eater had continued his journey.

We followed for another furlong, and here at last the tiger had decided to begin his meal. He had left the narrow trail and turned into a small hollow in the ground, sheltered by grass, bushes and bracken, where he had set about devouring the unfortunate bamboo cutter. As we had surmised, the beast must have been hungry, for little remained of the man beyond the usual parts: the head, hands and feet, and a small portion of his chest, with rib bones bereft of flesh. The entrails had been torn out and dragged aside. The meat had been removed from the victim's pelvis, exposing the bone, and the thighs had also devoured, here again leaving the bare bones in evidence of the great feast.

Far less than a quarter of the poor man remained, but this was enough to make the tiger return that night for a second meal, provided we played our cards cunningly enough and did not arouse his suspicions.

Yega and I looked around and at this point we encountered our first setback. There was no tree within at least eighty yards, a range far too great, as I well knew from past experience, to risk a shot by torch-light at night.

To the uninitiated this may seem an exaggeration. Eighty yards in daylight might appear a mere stone's throw. But those who have sat on machans in a jungle at night will know what I mean. Bushes, leaves blades of grass and rocks all cause obstructions at this distance, and to attempt to cut them away, to ensure a better view when the tiger returned, might arouse his suspicions and prevent him from returning at all. Remember, I could not risk wounding him. I had to shoot to kill.

Tigers and panthers, and man-eaters especially, are very cautious when they come back to their kills. They reconnoitre the approaches to the spot for a long time before they show themselves, and if they feel or sense anything suspicious, if they find any cut branches scattered about, any removal of bushes or undergrowth or rocks, or any addition of leaves or branches that may conceal a hidden enemy, they will give the spot a wide berth and never return. Although he lacks a sense of smell, the tiger makes up for this handicap with an uncanny caution and an ability almost to read the hunter's mind and anticipate his every action.

As if to compensate for the distance of the nearest tree from the remains of the woodsman, a dense patch of tiger-grass bordered the bank of the small depression into which the tiger had taken him before beginning his meal, and this patch was barely fifteen feet away.

If I could hide in that grass without the man-eater becoming aware of my presence he would offer a point-blank target. The moon would rise early, and conditions would be in my favour, always provided the tiger did not become aware of my presence. Would this be possible? For if he did find out, the situation could turn into a most unpleasant one for me.

As I well knew, all tigers and especially man-eaters, which appear to be endowed with a fiendish cunningness, exceeding even the natural caution of their kind, have a habit of taking advantage of every vestige of natural cover when returning to the remains of their victims for a second meal. The clump of tiger grass in which I contemplated concealing myself lay in the direct path of the man-eater's return and so close to his victim that it was more than likely, if not certain, that he would make use of it to conceal his own approach. And however silent I might be, I knew well enough how silent would be his own coming. Should the man-eater discover me before I discovered him, the bamboo cutter's bones would have those of another to keep them company before many hours had passed. It was a gamble, with a heavy stake, that I would have to take.

In order not to disturb the grass by unnecessary trampling, I walked around it while considering the problem in all its aspects. If I hid in that grass, I would have to keep a careful watch in two opposite directions: over the victim's remains and also in the direction by which the man-eater might be expected to make his approach, which would almost certainly be through this patch of grass. This I could not do; I would have at least to turn my head from side to side, even though I kept my body still. That would mean movement, and movement of any sort would be fatal.

One of two things would happen if the tiger became aware of me: he might take fright and disappear, or he would deliberately stalk and leap upon me before I even suspected his presence. Frankly, I funked that terrible alternative.

At this point, Yega came up with a brilliant idea. He and

I would sit back to back in the grass, one of us watching the bamboo cutter's remains while the other listened for the rustle that would herald the man-eater's entrance into that same clump of grass, by which time he would not be more than five or six feet away.

What transpired next would have a lot to do with whether I happened to be the one who was watching the victim's remains or the tiger's approach through the grass. If I were watching the remains and Yega the grass, he would have to warn me with a nudge, and I would have to turn around in a second to be in time to shoot. And I would have to shoot accurately. But if I chose to watch the approach through the grass and left Yega to watch over the kill, and the man-eater crept up to the latter from some other direction, I would have to react similarly, except that the situation would not be nearly so dangerous. At least, the tiger would be more than a mere five or six feet away and I should have a better chance to shoot.

I hated to risk Yega's life. And I hated to risk my own. But this was our only chance and I nodded assent.

Strangely enough, in the Wynaad Forest area vultures are not nearly so numerous as in drier jungles of south India. Nevertheless, we took no chances of them discovering the remains and finishing what little flesh remained on the bones. So Yega cut a few small branches from the tree that grew eighty yards away, and these we placed over the bones and entrails of the man to hide them from any chance vulture hovering in the sky above. Then we returned to the deserted encampment.

It took another fifteen minutes for Timayya to come back in the car from Manantoddy. I told him of our discovery and our plan of action. Then occurred one of those awkward situations that sometimes appear between friends. Timayya stated bluntly that he would sit with me in Yega's stead, armed with my spare rifle, but I was not happy about his decision. I did not wish to risk my friend's life for one thing.

Secondly, quite frankly and I suppose selfishly, considering my own life was also at stake, I doubted his ability to keep watch for the tiger as efficiently as Yega would, with his lifetime of jungle experience. As tactfully as possible I put these points to my friend. Timmy became angry — and rude, too.

'Damn it, I'm a planter,' he said, 'not a bloody town-dweller like you. What the hell do you think? If you don't feel life sitting with me, at least lend me the .405/400 and . . . off back to Manantoddy yourself. I'll do the rest.'

There was a very nasty look in his eye.

I shrugged. 'Okay Timmy, you win,' I said. 'We'll sit together.'

The nasty look faded and a gleam of pleasure and excitement took its place.

When Yega heard the change of plan he was crestfallen. Now it was his turn to look at me reproachfully. I avoided his glance and studied one of the Studebaker's tyres closely.

We returned to Manantoddy for lunch, bringing Yega with us, after which we put in a couple of hours sleep to fortify us for the long, sleepless night vigil ahead. At three o'clock we were ready. Timmy suggested we take tea and sandwiches along with us, to which I assented after reminding him that these refreshments could only be enjoyed the following morning. No sound or movements of the slightest kind could we risk while we awaited the man-eater's return.

We left Yega at Manantoddy, as it would be dangerous for him to accompany us to the spot where we were going to sit and then return alone. Besides, we did not require his services in any way. By half-past three we had reached the woodcutter's deserted encampment. Here we parked the Studebaker close to the huts and before four we were at the patch of tiger-grass.

I removed the small branches with which Yega and I had earlier covered the scattered remains of the bamboo cutter to protect them from vultures, carrying them to a spot quite a distance away. It was a hot and sunny afternoon and what remained of the woodcutter, little enough though it was, had begun to smell, especially the entrails, which the man-eater had dragged to one side. But we dared not remove them for fear of arousing the tiger's suspicions when he returned.

I had already made it a condition with Timmy that I would face the side from which the tiger might be expected to approach through the grass, while he would face in the opposite direction towards the woodcutter's remains. Fortunately, he had not been difficult about this and had acquiesced readily enough. We had brought two of the foam-rubber cushions from the Rest House to sit upon. They would not only provide comfort, but would deaden any sound we might make in movement. Placing these on the ground, we squatted on them back to back and facing in the directions already described. I crossed my legs and settled down to sit in silence, having trained myself to this position after many years of similar experience in the jungle. Timmy whispered that he could not make himself comfortable that way and stretched both his legs out before him. Straightaway a disquieting thought entered my mind: for how long would Timmy be able to sit thus without moving? To me it appeared physically impossible, and I knew he would become fidgety before sundown.

Jungle life in the forests of the Wynaad and the Western Ghats is rather different from that of the drier areas. Animals and reptiles are fewer in number, but bird and insect life is prolific. We quickly became aware of this, for within a few minutes of our arrival and things quietening down, we heard the twittering calls of birds from all directions, accompanied by the chirping of crickets. The cicada of these regions is different from those of the plains: the latter, to which I was accustomed, emits a shrill and continuous high note, but the hill variety, which abounded here, emits a rasping note of fluctuating volume. It almost dies away and then rises to a cadence that jars the nerves, before fading away, only to rise again.

As evening fell, distant jungle-cocks and spur-fowl began to vie with one another in their usual preroosting chorus, to the accompaniment of an occasional, plaintive, brassy cry from a peacock, feeding amidst the fallen seeds of the giant bamboo that grew so prolifically, or grubbing for caterpillars by scratching up the thick carpet of decaying leaves and mould. Around us, from the grass, itself, came the very faint and indefinable sounds of insects of all kinds on the move : grasshoppers, beetles of countless varieties, and a host of other creatures. A green and slender mantis, that must have been at least eight inches long, appeared just before me, camouflaged so marvellously that I would not have noticed him had he not climbed upon my knee. His body was frail and indefinably delicate, for all the world like a silver of bamboo and not more than a sixteenth of an inch in thickness, while his wings, of a transparent tissue and veined like leaves, folded across his back to resemble a green sepal of no consequence whatever. So wonderful and impartial is nature's camouflage, that both those that prey upon others by habit, and those that seek to escape from being preyed upon, are equally disguised from one another. This inoffensive-looking mantis, that resembled so closely a slender twig with two green leaves attached, was quite as carnivorous and fierce in its own insect world as the man-eating tiger whose return we were awaiting was to the frightened jungle-dwellers.

Darkness came swiftly with the almost instant hushing of the bird-calls. The rustle of activity from the hidden insects in the grass around us increased apace. We felt their movements on all sides, and even upon our bodies. They climbed all over us and got inside our clothing, setting up such an itching that all our self-control was needed to prevent us from moving and scratching ourselves to secure an instant's relief.

I missed my old friends of the jungles of the plains, the night-jars, and thought of them for a few moments. They would be active at this period of twilight, flitting around in their silent, ghost-like fashion, in search of their evening meal, stragglers among the insects of the day that were going to bed late, and early-comers among the insects of the night in search of food.

This diverted my thoughts to the primal instincts of life, the search for food and the urge to procreate that are the two issues that govern all the dwellers of the jungle; to man and his civilization, and the search for wealth, which brings food and power, pleasures and a means of satisfying ourselves in practically any way we desire; and to much similar musing, one idea leading to another. But eventually I pulled myself up with quite a start, discovering that it was now pitch dark and I had forgotten all about the man-eater and how close to me he might be.

The stench that came to us from the human fragments that had been exposed to the hot sun all day was now quite awful. Myriads of bluebottle flies had settle on them for the night.

The humble bluebottle fly is regarded everywhere as an obnoxious insect, associated only with filth and dirt and carrion. Nevertheless, he can be a great and secret friend to the hunter who watches by night; for the flies in their thousands, when they cover a carcase at night, are alert thought resting. Any creature approaching near enough, even if it does not touch the carcase, makes its presence felt to the watchful, restless flies, who rustle in unison. And that rustling can be clearly heard by the watcher in the darkness, provided he is not too far away, is alert enough, has reasonably good hearing, and above all recognizes its significance. The bluebottles were silent now and I was satisfied that neither the tiger, nor anything else for that matter, was anywhere near the carcase.

My friend's back rested against mine tautly, uncomfortably, radiating heat though my sweater. I could sense his nervousness as he strained his eyes into the darkness. This is the most dangerous period for the hunter who risks his life sitting on the ground for a man-eater : the brief fifteen to thirty minutes from twilight till the light of the stars makes itself felt, be it ever so little.

Our greatest danger lay in the direction in which I was facing, the opposite end of the grassy clump in the midst of which we were hiding. If the man-eater approached from there, his keen eyesight, even in that darkness, would enable him to discover our presence while he was yet some distance away. He would not bother to come any closer then. What he would do would depend upon his individual character; he might launch himself from fifteen feet away and be upon us in the fraction of a second, or, if he were a coward, as many man-eaters are, he would just slink noiselessly away.

Then I remembered with considerable trepidation that this tiger could not possibly be called a coward. Barely a few hours ago he had sneaked up to a hut filled with people and dragged a human being away. With tensed nerves and strained ears, I listened for the faintest creak or rustle of grass that might betray the arrival of the man-eater from in front, while hearkening for the buzz of disturbed bluebottles that might herald his advent from behind. There was nothing but complete silence. The immediate danger passed as three things happened almost together. My eyes accustomed themselves to the gloom and I could begin to identify objects around me. The stars came out in their multitude and their gleam seemed to bring back the moments of half-light that had so recently gone. And above all, the fireflies of the Wynaad began their nightly display of living fireworks that would continue till the early hours of the morning, when the mist and the dew would chill the tiny lamp-bearers and force them to seek the shelter of the foliage.

There must have been thousands upon thousands of these little creatures within a few yards of us, wining their way hither and thither in restless flight. The glow of their combined light produced a radiation that dispelled the darkness like a flashlight, then broken again into a myriad of individual lights that sparkled through the darkness.

No sounds broke the stillness. The forest seemed strangely devoid of animal life. No friendly calls of sambar or spotted deer could we hear. No cries of the usual birds of the night. There came to us only the undefinable taint movements of the insects in the grass around us. And to the torment caused by the insect marauders on our bodies, the mosquitoes now began to add their torture. They had not worried us unduly until now, perhaps because they had not discovered our presence; but having done so they apparently decided to make the most of their discovery. I did not dare to betray our presence to the tiger which, at that very instant perhaps, might be approaching us. Faintly I could hear Timmy behind me, trying to blow the mosquitoes away.

It was at this instant that there came clearly to my hearing the faint rustling buzz of angry, disturbed bluebottles flies.

Something was near the remains of the woodsman. Timmy had heard it too, for I felt him tauten against my back, while he ceased blowing at the mosquitoes. His elbows dug into me in the prearranged signal and remained there as he gripped the .450/400 in his lap.

The flies buzzed again as they rose nervously a few inches above the bones and entrails on which they had been resting. They hummed a while, they resettled themselves and the buzzing stopped. The intruder, whatever it was, had not yet reached the kill or the flies would never had resettled. It was approaching.

Something made the faintest sound from beyond the remains and there came the distant thud of a stone being turned over. Undoubtedly the man-eater had arrived. He was reconnoitring and would presently approach the remains of his feast.

Or was he creeping upon us?

Casting caution to the winds I whisked around, bringing the Winchester to my shoulder and pressing the torch-button, fitted to the barrel, with my left thumb, almost in one movement. The bright beam cut a swathe of light through the blackness and was reflected by two baleful eyes. But they were rather more reddish-white in colour than a brilliant whitish-red. And they were set rather too closely together.

Sitting on his haunches like a dog, the torchlight caught the panther in the act of licking his lips. We could see the red of his tongue sweep across the slightly opened mouth.

Could the man-eater be a panther after all? I dismissed the thought as soon as it crossed my mind, for I had seen the man-eater's pug-marks on the trail we had followed. They had certainly been those of a tiger. Besides, he had been seen by Yega and some of the other woodcutters. This panther was merely there by chance. In passing by, he had stumbled on the kill. He was sitting there in doubt, wondering how it had all come about and if he could take a chance.

At that moment the panther became aware of the torch-beam that was shining straight into his eyes.

He stood up, snarled, turned and walked away. Disgust was written in his every movement. Clearly he did not wish to involve himself in such a compromising situation. I extinguished the torch as quickly as possible. Was the man-eater nearby? If so, he would certainly have seen my light. That might cause him to run away. Or, having come to know of our presence and whereabouts, he might at that very moment be creeping upon us. But the attitude of the panther soon dispelled this disquietening thought. He seemed absolutely unconcerned. He would hardly be so indifferent if his hereditary and implacable foe, a tiger, were in the vicinity.

The bluebottles settled down and so did we, to a long and uneventful vigil, while the fireflies kept us company to lend enhantment to an otherwise macabre scene. It became cold, and then colder. The insects in the grass around us stopped their restless movements. Perhaps they were feeling the cold too. The mosquitoes grew less active as well and the fireflies began to disappear.

The tiger should have returned long ago. He should have put in an appearance even before the panther. It seemed as if the man-eater did not intend to come back.

Time dragged on. I began to feel sleepy and perhaps I grew a bit careless too. For, although I heard the sound once or twice, it did not register straight away. Then, all of a sudden, I was wide awake and alert.

Something had approached the grass in which we were hiding. Not directly from in front but a little to my left. There had been a faint rustle and then a definite footfall as something heavy had placed its weight upon the grass. There had followed a faint but distinct creaking and cracking of stems.

And that thing, whatever it was, had now stopped.

Had the man-eater discovered our presence, as he must most surely have done? Was he crouching for a final spring? The answer came the very next second when the tiger snarled. He was not more than ten feet away.

I pressed the button of the torch.

The beam lit up a wild scene of violently swaying grass stems. I had a glimpse of something brown that catapulted itself backwards and was gone. The came a shattering roar from the jungle.

I switched off the torch as the man-eater began to demonstrate by emitting roar after roar. He was very angry; but he was also frightened. I had switched on the torch a fraction too soon. He would otherwise have come on. Perhaps I had done the right thing after all. I might have been too late to stop his charge, once it had been launched.

Timmaya had whisked around and, like me, was facing in the direction from which the tiger was now roaring. The beast began to circle us, snarling and roaring horribly as he did so. It was a war of nerves. Either he was trying to work up enough courage to drive home a charge, or he was trying to scare us away. I felt he was following the second plan.

We waited awhile, hoping he would decide to attack; but this he failed to do. The roars now sank to a series of growls, but they came from different directions as the tiger circled. It seemed he was trying to find out how many human beings were hidden in that grass. Was there only one, whom he could easily overwhelm, or were there many?

This went on for another fifteen minutes. But nothing happened. The tiger would not attack, nor did he go away. It was a game of nerves and I am afraid the tiger won.

I decided to draw him out by precipitating an attack. I whispered to Timmaya to remain where he was, while I got up and started to walk back towards the encampment, which was only a short distance away. The tiger would probably come after me. On the other hand, he might decide that it would be a better proposition to let the hated man-with-the-light depart while he went back for what was left of the kill. This would give Timmy the chance of a shot.

My friend protested vigorously, whispering 'Don't be a fool!'

But, with restraining hand on his shoulder, I got slowly to my feet, stood there a few seconds to restore my circulation, and then started walking deliberately towards the woodcutter's deserted huts, taking care to make the expected amount of sound a man might make in covering such ground.

The effect on the man-eater was instantaneous. He began to roar again; and then he came after me. You must bear in mind that, except for the starlight, it was quite dark. Purposely, I had kept the torch extinguished so as not to frighten the tiger, but the situation had turned into a most unpleasant one.

I had covered about twenty-five yards when the man-eater screwed up enough courage to charge. I remember thinking to myself that it was fortunate he had chosen to be so noisy about it, rather than make a silent and stealthy rush, when I would not have known from which direction he was coming.

There came the all-too-familiar 'Wroof! Wroof! Wroof!' as he launched his attack. I whirled around with the rifle to my shoulder, once again pressing the button of the torch with my left thumb. The bright beam of light cut through the darkness to shine upon the angry eyes of the enraged man-eater, coming towards me in an up-and-down motion as he charged.

It was difficult to hold the eyes in my sights as they

moved, and while this thought flashed through my mind, something quite unexpected happened. I was blinded by another blaze of light that obscured the tiger, and indeed everything else from sight, as it shone fully into my eyes! Timmaya had switched on his torch and was shinning it directly in my face.

Instinctively, I raised my forearm to cover my eyes and jumped backwards to try to get out of the glare.

The next instant everything was plunged into inky darkness. My finger went off the button and my own torch went out while the beam of light from my friend's torch turned away from me.

It cut through the darkness and on to the tiger, which was crouched on the ground hardly four feet away from me in a ludicrous pose. He looked rather foolish with his head bent low, almost to ground level, front paws outstretched, with his rear up in the air behind him, his curving tail upheld and stiff, brought to a halt by Timmy's light.

It was not an instant too soon, for he had been about to spring upon me when Timmy's unexpected light from behind stopped him.

There came an ear-splitting crash and I saw the crouching tiger literally pushed as if by some invisible force. When the bullet from my. 450/400 rifle, fired by Timmy, took him somewhere in the side.

At that instant I stood directly in his path, his nearest enemy, and he came for me with all the hate and speed of which he as capable. My own torch-beam must have completely blinded him when I fired directly into his open mouth, followed by a second shot as he crashed at my feet while I jumped aside.

That was when Timmy fired again. His bullet passed over the tiger and hit the ground almost at my feet, raising a spurt of dust. Everything was over when I found myself running backwards at incredible speed to try to get away from the tiger as he rolled on the ground.

It was Timmy who got the man-eater, for apart from his first shot that had struck the tiger's flank and halted the beast at the instant of springing upon me, he had fired a second which had entered the animal squarely behind the left shoulder. This second shot I had never heard in the confusion. My own bullet had blown out the back of the tiger's head, while my second, also striking his head, had struck the ground near me and had been a complete miss.

Timmy was overwhelmed with delight and executed a war-dance around the fallen enemy. Although the skin, and particularly the head, would not make much of a trophy, ruined as they were by the bullets from my two powerful rifles, he kept chanting and repeating over and over again that he had never heard of a man-eater being killed under such unusual conditions.

Needless to say although I was not nearly so exuberant, I fully concurred with Timmy's sentiments. I might not object to having the same experience all over again providing I could be in Timmy's place. But not where I had been!

Six

The Man-Hater of Talainovu

IN THE KOLLEGAL TALUK OF WHAT WAS FORMERLY COIMBATORE District, part of the Madras Presidency in the days when the British governed India, there is a hamlet called Talainovu. Now the British have gone and with them the Madras Presidency, and Madras State has taken its place; its area is just about half that was covered by the former presidency, for much of the territory has gone to the neighbouring states of Andhra, Mysore and Kerala.

Among these transferred territories is Kollegal Taluk, and with it the hamlet of Talainovu. They have now become a part of Mysore State. Cultivation and buildings have spread, and much of the beautiful forest areas that stretched from Talainovu across rugged hills down to the valley of the Cauvery River have been felled ruthlessly, while what is left has been practically denuded of game.

But it will always be easy for me to remember the little

village of Talainovu, as I knew it long ago, for two reasons. Firstly, in the Tamil language the word 'talainovu' means 'headache' secondly, the wily panther that made its abode by the banks of the Cauvery river, in a steep valley some ten miles from the hamlet, gave me a real headache while trying to deal with it.

Man-eating panthers are rare in southern Indian and have always been so. This panther was never a man-eater in the true sense. Rather, it was a man-hater, filled with deep hostility for the human race, and it treasured this hatred and exacted a toll upon its life-long enemy until its last day.

To begin at the beginning; a pantheress lived on a forest hilltop, ten miles from the village of Talainovu to the south. Six furlongs away and to the north, lay a deep valley where the hill fell away steeply to the bed of the Cauvery River. To the east the forest stretched for miles upon miles, into and across the boundaries of the Salem District and along the twists and turns of the Cauvery River. But to the west it continued only for about six miles, till it gave way to the low scrub that bordered the main road leading from the town of Kollegal, across a bridge, northwards to Maddur and Bangalore.

This pantheress was a young animal, and when she gave birth to her first cubs, three in number, she was a proud and happy mother, devoted to her offspring and prepared to defend them with her life. According to reports and hearsay, picked up by me at a much later date; some circumstances, we do not know what, induced the pantheress to bring her cubs out of the cave in which they were born much earlier than normal, while they were still too young to move about in safety. Perhaps their father had had designs on their young lives and sought to devour them, as male tigers and panthers frequently do. Perhaps a bear trespassed into their cave. Perhaps food was scarce in that locality.

So the pantheress brought her cubs down the hill and hid them in a bamboo thicket on the banks of the Cauvery River. No doubt this was only a temporary measure till the mother could find a better home for them, perhaps some other cave. But fate decided to be unkind to her that early morning. She had left the cubs in the thicket and had probably been out hunting all the night. The sun had topped the parallel range of hills that marked the course of the big river and was glinting on its tumbling, foaming waters when the pantheress was yet a mile away from the bamboos in which she had concealed her cubs.

And then she stopped in her tracks, for far away she heard a noise, a persistent tap-tap-tap! Humans! And in the very area where she had left her three little cubs unprotected.

The pantheress doubtless broke into a bounding gallop to cover the intervening distance as fast as she could, her only thought for the safety of her offspring. But when she was but a short distance away she must have heard their snarls, and she knew what had happened. The hated humans had discovered her cubs.

The pantheress arrived on the scene to find that half-a-dozen or more almost naked black bodies, glistening with sweat, surrounded her cubs. These were on the ground, back to back, and small as they were they snarled defiance at the intruders. The men jabbered to one another, pointing at the cubs with the sharp, curved knives that they used for cutting the bamboos, an expression of gloating excitement on each countenance, but no sign of pleasure at the three pretty balls of for so gamely defied them, nor pity for their helplessness.

Even as she watched, one of the bamboos cutters raised his *koithar* and swiped at the nearest cub. The curved blade bit into the soft body. The cub was flung into the air and fell

487

some feet away, almost cut in two but still living. It groaned faintly as its young blood reddened the grass.

This was the signal for the other bamboo cutters to destroy the remaining two cubs, which they set about doing without further delay. A few slashes of their sharp knives and it was all over. Three mangled scraps of flesh now lay scattered on the ground where previously there had been three living creatures.

Probably an inborn fear of the human to all wild animals, even the worst man-eating tiger and the most ferocious rogue elephant, had held the grief-stricken mother back, but the sight of her dead cubs now drove her crazy. With short, sharp roars, she hurled herself upon the men.

The first man did not know what it was all about for the pantheress tore out his eyes as her raking talons slammed into his face. He fell to the ground, and she leaped over him to bite the second man's chest. He fell, too, his screams joining those of the blinded man who thrashed about on the ground. The remainder, all armed with *koithars,* did not wait. With yells of terror they fled in all directions.

The pantheress made to follow them but then stopped, her attention taken by the two men who writhed upon the ground. With cold fury she set upon the two of them and tore them to shreds.

Then, sniffing at the dead bodies of her three cubs, she picked up the least mangled of them and bore it away in sorrow.

That was how it all began.

When the bamboo cutters returned to their village, they had a harrowing tale to tell of a savage panther of huge dimensions that had attacked them entirely without provocation. They did not mention their part in the incident — at least, not them — and of how they had wantonly destroyed the cubs and infuriated the mother. This admission came later. Naturally, there was a hue and cry. People avoided that part of the jungle where the killings had taken place, or such as had to go there went armed with hatchets and guns, and in groups of as many persons as possible.

The pantheress was not seen or heard of for some weeks after that. People soon forgot the incident, and through apathy or laziness left their weapons behind. The licensed cutters of bamboo and sellers of timber, as well as the poachers, went into the jungle, the former by day to follow their daily routine, and the latter, who lived by stealing and selling the same commodities, renewed their practice of cutting bamboos and wood and floating the stolen material across the river during the bright moonlit nights.

But the vengeful pantheress did not forget. This was her opportunity to strike a second time.

A notorious poacher of sandal-wood, whom the people of the Forest Department and the police knew had been operating for years, but whom they had never succeeded in bringing to book, went into the jungle with his son one moonlit night. They had planned to cut some sandal-wood, float it down the river for a mile or so to a spot where the water became calm and there was no undercurrent, and then tow the cut timber across the river to the northern bank which belonged to Mysore State, using the circular coracle made of bamboo and buffalo hide which they kept permanently hidden on the river for this purpose. Once they were on the Mysore side of the river, they knew they would be safe from pursuit by the authorities on the Madras bank and would be asked no awkward questions.

The two thieves began hacking the sandal-wood saplings they had marked for this purpose on an earlier visit, and the pantheress heard the hated sound of chopping. As likely as not the noise of wood being cut reminded her, by instinctive association rather than thought, of the day when her cubs had been cut to pieces before her eyes. Hatred must have filled her mind as she started stalking towards the noise with but one thought in her brain — to obliterate those who made it.

The father never knew what happened when the pantheress sprang upon him from behind and fastened her fangs in his throat. He could not even scream for help, but toppled to the ground with the sudden weight upon his back. The son, a lad of eighteen years, saw what was happening, but with thoughts only for his own safety and not for his father's life, dropped his axe and fled precipitately.

It took the pantheress a few seconds to kill the man and that saved the boy from sharing the same fate. Running as fast as he could, he reached the coracle, jumped into it and paddled frantically across the river. When he got back to his hut and burst in upon his mother, it was to tell what had just happened to his father.

The villagers had gone to sleep long ago, but the combined wails of mother and son awoke them. They lit their lights and heard the story, but agreed not to do anything till the next day. After all, everybody knew both father and son were thieves.

The sun was high when a large party of villagers, armed with guns, hatchets, knives and spears and led by the poacher's son, returned to the scene. There they found the old thief lying in a pool of his own blood, his gullet torn out and his whole body badly bitten and lacerated. But it was very noticeable that no flesh had been eaten. The killer could certainly not be called a man-eater. To the men who gazed with horror upon the mangled remains, the attack on the poacher had apparently been for no reason and under no provocation whatever, for at that time few people knew the beginning of the story.

Once again there was an uproar and folk went about only in groups and armed to the teeth. The panic lasted for a longer period on this occasion, but once more time and the usual apathy among the people gradually calmed them down. Eventually, the panther was forgotten again and they carried on in their accustomed ways.

Again weeks passed, and again came the moonlit nights, the period when most of the mischief is done in the jungles of India. For it is during this time that the poachers of game sit over water-holes and salt-licks to shoot the sambar, spotted deer and other animals that come there to quench their thirst or eagerly to lick the salty earth, while the timber thieves, who steal the sandal-wood, teak-wood, muthee, giant bambool etc., go into the forest to hack down the trees, cut them to convenient lengths and float the timber down the river or take it stealthily away in bullock carts or, when they are daring enough, by lorry loads.

A third kind of thief also takes advantage of the bright moonlight: the poachers of fish. They do not fish with rods or nets, for the catch would be too small and the work too hard and slow. Instead, in the river pools where they knew the large fish congregate at nights to sleep or to feed, according to species, these men explode their home-made bombs, made in secrecy from crude gunpowder and fuses. Floating gently downstream in one of the circular coracles made of a bamboo frame covered with buffalo hide, in common use on the rivers of India, these prowlers visit every pool for a distance of about five miles down the river. The fuse is lit and the bomb is then floated on the water.

While the explosion does no general damage, the concussion in the water stuns the large fish and slaughters thousands of the smaller ones and all the fry for yards around. These casualties rise to the surface, where the larger fish are quickly scooped into the coracle with the help of nets attached to poles. The thousands of smaller dead fish, including the try, are allowed to go to waste and float downstream to rot and be eaten by other fish and by the crocodiles.

And so the operation is repeated from pool to pool. By this time the poachers have gathered almost more fish into the coracle than it can hold, while the wanton destruction of countless thousands of valuable fry and many species of small fish can be imagined.

Generally a number of men share in the operation, employing two coracles, one from which to launch the bombs, and the other for collecting the catch. The second is often almost at sinking point before the poachers feel they have collected enough. Moreover, there is an unwritten law amongst them that they should not trespass upon the domain of the next batch of poachers, which starts where they leave off, for that would provoke a fight and one or other batch would be bound to sneak to the Forest Department officials or to the police. Everyone is happy, the fish are slaughtered, and the local authorities can do nothing about it. Moreover, to make things absolutely safe, each man receives a basketful after every expedition. Should they prove unlucky and they are discovered by some representative of the law, the poachers have but to present half-a-dozen of the largest fish they have caught to the official and all is well again.

The coracle, loaded with fish, is eventually brought ashore at the end of the five-mile stretch. Here the catch is cleaned and gutted and loaded into gunny sacks that the men have brought with them. Every man shoulders a bag, while two men pick up the coracles and carry them upside down over their shoulders. The light flat paddles taken by one of the others. Now begins the five miles walk back to the point from which they started, for it is not possible to propel the clumsy, circular craft upstream against the strong river currents. This is the hardest part of the whole business.

The same procedure is followed through the ensuing moonlit nights until the dark nights come again, when the poachers rest and laze it out for a fortnight till moonlight returns.

In very lonely regions where there are no Forest Guards or other inconvenient persons to interfere, the bombing of the pools is carried on by daylight, although at the period I am writing about there was some restraint, for the Forest Departments were controlled by British officers. Alas, that restraint has now gone. With Independence, the poachers no longer work by night.

But to return to our story: the moonlit nights came round again and a party of fish poachers systematically bombed pool after pool and netted the stunned fish, filling them into the second coracle, which was propelled by a single man so as to leave more space. They worked steadily until after midnight, when they decided to take time off to go ashore and eat the snacks they had brought with them.

It so happened that the second coracle, the one filled with the catch and paddled by the single boat-man, was nearer the shore when his companions called to him:

'Brother, put ashore. We have worked hard and we've caught much. Let's rest for a while and eat the *shappad* (food) we have brought with us and drink some cold coffee.'

The solitary boatman welcomed the call, for he was lonely. He dug the blade of his paddle into the water, holding the shaft with both hands, first to the right of him and then to the left, with swift, short strokes, to force the clumsy craft across the current which was particularly strong at this place, for not long had passed since the rains had filled the river to overflowing.

Eventually he reached the bank and sprang ashore, carrying in one hand the end of the rope that was attached to the bamboo bottom of the coracle, so as to tie it to the root or trunk of a tree. This he never succeeded in doing. Those of his companions in the other coracle who happened to be watching saw something that looked long and grey spring from behind the *mendhi* (henna) bushes at the water's edge. They heard a rasping roar and saw the black form of their friend go down with a strange grey shape on top of it. They heard his piercing scream and then saw that his coracle, dragging the rope that had fallen from his hands, was rushing downstream on the powerful current.

The boatman who was paddling their craft made a desperate effort to overtake the runway coracle. But he was at a disadvantage with the load of men in his own boat. The runaway coracle gained speed as the current, spinning it around and around, drew it towards midstream where the water bubbled and foamed in the bright moonlight over a low cataract formed by a reef of rocks.

The pursuing boatman was almost rash enough to drive his craft into those dangerous waters when his companions restrained him. They watched in dismay as the unmanned coracle lurched heavily against the rocks, tossed wildly from side to side and then capsized, throwing the whole of their catch into the river. Then it was that they turned towards the shore to abuse and beat their comrade for being so stupid as to let the rope slip from his grasp. Why, a large coracle such as the one they had just lost would cost a hundred rupees to make and much more to buy, not to mention the value of the fish that had been lost in the river. Idiot that he was they would thrash him soundly!

But on the bank no one was to be seen. Then they remembered the grey shape in the moonlight, and the roaring they had heard, and how their friend seemed to stumble and fall. They had been so concerned to intercept the runaway coracle that they had ignored their companion's plight.

Some of the men ordered the boatman, who wanted to go ashore to investigate, not to do so on any account. Perhaps some evil spirit was lurking there. It has got their friend and might get all of them if they ventured too near. For quite a long time nobody thought of the panther. Then somebody remembered, and reminded the rest. They agreed then that the grey form they had seen had been the lurking beast. It had killed their companion and assuredly was devouring him at that moment.

Using the single paddle, the men took turns to propel their weighted craft upstream, as they dared not go ashore. They did this for about half a mile and then found they could go no further. So they made for the river bank, where each man exhorted the other to jump ashore first. Finally they did so in a body, relying on the safety of numbers. So as not to be encumbered by the weighty coracle all the way back to their starting point, they drew it some yards up the bank and made for their village as fast as they could in a group, talking at the top of their voices to keep the panther away.

Next day, when the sun was high, the whole village turned out, the men having armed themselves as best as they could, to discover what had happened to the missing man. They found his remains behind the henna bushes. He had been literally torn to bits, but so far as could be seen, none of his flesh had been eaten.

And so it went on, the pantheress attacking and killing where she could, but never eating her victims. Her handiwork was evident by the manner in which each corpse was bitten and clawed savagely, far beyond what was necessary just to kill the victim. She seemed to be taking savage delight in mangling each body almost beyond recognition.

Now, the stretch of river where these events took place was a favourite spot for catching the great 'mahseer', the king of Indian fishes, in spite of all the poaching. But fishing has never held any attraction for me. I have no patience for it. Yet a great many of my friends are devotees and occasionally I took one or other of them to this river for a couple of days.

These visits had to be few and far between, however, because the rough track from Talainovu, through the jungle to the river, is very steep, with abrupt turns that my Studebaker cannot negotiate. Most of my friends owned English cars, and these were equally unsuitable for the purpose. So our visits were limited to those occasions when we could get someone who owned a jeep to come along with us, or to the lucky occasions when we could borrow or hire such a vehicle.

Well, such an opportunity came our way one day, and this time it seemed to have come to stay. Donald, my son, had bought a jeep! A much-battered vehicle that hailed from Andhra State, painted vivid blue, and with faults in every conceivable part. But Don set to work, and at considerable expense and very great trouble he substituted good parts for bad, so that eventually we possessed a vehicle that would go anywhere.

Then came the day when we set out for the Talainovu fishing grounds, with Donald proudly driving the jeep he had so painstakingly repaired. Next to him sat 'Tiny' Seddon, a great 'mahseer' fisherman, great not only in his fishing potentialities but also in bulk and height. In the back were three of us; an old friend and schoolmate of Donald's, named Merwan Chamar-Baughvala; Thangavelu, who had once been my shikari and had found service in our establishment as table-boy, motor-cleaner, the feeder of our domestic creatures and many wild-animal pets, and general jack-of-all-trades, his particular function on this trip being camp cook. Finally, wedged securely and tightly, at an uncomfortable angle that gave little chance to move, was myself.

It is exactly ninety-nine miles from our house in Bangalore to the camping site on the bank of the Cauvery River, some ten miles beyond the village of Talainovu, where we proposed to do our fishing. We left Bangalore rather late, and when the journey ended the sun was setting in flames of red, with a background of orange, vermilion and indigo. We halted a few yards from the river's edge, under the grove of giant muthee, tamarind and jum-lum trees, beneath which we always made our camp.

There were three things to be done at once, and the trained members of the party — Don, Thangavelu and myself — started on them straight away. Don looked quickly around for fresh elephant tracks, to reassure ourselves that none were in the vicinity to resent our intrusion and come thundering down upon us. Using both feet, I started clearing the ground, in a six or seven yard circle, of all dried leaves, stones and sticks which might shelter scorpions, particularly the small red variety. A sting from such a scorpion is guaranteed to take your mind off all other problems, including the demands of the Income Tax *wallahs*, for the next eight hours or more. Thangavelu hurried to gather dry logs, a task in which Don soon began to help him, for the camp fire that was to be kept blazing all night in case an elephant came our way while we were asleep.

Tiny Seddon jumped on to a rock half-submerged in the water and gazed pensively at the swirling eddies. No doubt he was seeking inspiration as to where to start fishing the next morning. Merwan Chamarbaughvala threw himself on the ground I had just cleared and remarked how comfortable it was compared with the jeep.

None of us thought of the panther — because up to this moment none of us knew about it!

The moon would not rise till late. We ate Merwan's contribution of chicken biriyani and pork vindaloo, two very delicious but over-rich dishes, and while Thangavelu was preparing the tea, drank water from the river. That is, all of us except Tiny, who was certain the river water contained cholera germs, typhoid germs, and bacteria of every variety. He said he would wait for the tea. Then Thangavelu stroked the camp fire that was to burn all night and we lay back and smoked and told stories, gazing at the starry sky beyond the canopy of leaves above our heads. We counted ourselves fortunate to be able to enjoy such bliss, which so many of our fellow creatures, crowded in stuffy cities all over the world, have never experienced for even a day in all their monotonous lives. And so we fell asleep.

I do not know why it was that I awoke with a start. My watch showed a few minutes past three. The camp fire had died down to a few glowing embers, for Thangavelu, who had undertaken to keep it alive, had long since fallen asleep. Donald, to my left, was snoring loudly. Merwan and Tiny, in that order to my right, had covered their heads with their bedsheets to ward off mosquitoes and the dew, and were sleeping soundlessly.

I wondered what had wakened me so suddenly. Perhaps some jungle noise. Perhaps an elephant breaking branches in order to feed on the higher, more tender leaves. I listened more intently and for a time heard nothing except Don's noisy, rattling snores.

Then I knew what had wakened me, for close at hand I heard a guttural rasping sound: 'Haa-ah! Haa-ah! Haa-ah!' The call of a hungry panther!

Now panthers in the forest are, as a rule, quite harmless

animals. Except when they turn man-eaters which is very rarely, or when they are wounded, they are shy, cowardly beasts that avoid the presence of man. No doubt the animal that was now calling, although apparently quite close, had not yet caught sight of the embers of our fire. As soon as it did so, in all probability it would hurry away as fast as it could. Or so I thought as I continued to listen sleepily to the sound.

The call came again, and louder. The hungry panther was certainly quite close. Surely, it must have seen our fire by now? I felt very sleepy indeed and comfortable. Drat the beast, I thought. Why doesn't it let me sleep?

That was when I heard the panther snarl! At last it has seen us, I thought; now it will vanish. But the panther snarled again, long and menacingly.

Strange, I thought, my eyes half-closed with sleep. It is either a very inquisitive or a very angry and daring panther. I mused; but why worry? I was safe in the centre of the party. Tiny was at one end, Don at the other, and Thangavelu by himself not far from the fire.

The panther growled again, low and long, and I sat up abruptly, groping for the torch I had kept near my pillow. Blinking to free myself from sleep, I directed the torch-beam towards the snarling that was growing louder.

It revealed a panther, crouching on the ground a few feet from Thangavelu and evidently preparing to spring upon him. There was no mistaking its posture: I could see its tail lashing to and fro, a sure indication of its malevolent intentions. I felt for my rifle, which I had kept loaded beside me on the ground.

And then Thangavelu ruined everything.

I suppose his jungle instinct was really responsible. It alerted him, but rather late, to the great danger that threatened. He sat up abruptly, and in doing so kicked over the *degchie* containing the water he had boiled for Tiny to drink. Perhaps the clatter it made, or Thangavelu's movement, or more likely my torch-beam, convinced the panther that its presence had been discovered, and before I could do anything with the rifle, handicapped as I was with the torch in my right hand, the brute leaped aside and disappeared behind the nearest bush.

All this time Thangavelu had been blissfully unaware of any danger. Still half asleep, he had not heard or seen the panther. I awoke the others and told them what had happened.

They were surprise at first. Then Don said, 'Dad, you've had a nightmare. Merwan's chicken biriyani and pork vindaloo are the cause of it. I haven't heard a sound all night and I doubt if there's a panther within miles.'

The others laughed and I was a bit huffed. How could Don say he had not heard a sound when he had been snoring all night? I clambered to my feet, still holding the torch and rifle?

'Come and see this,' I invited, shining my torch on the ground and walking towards the spot where the panther had been lying. But the earth there was hard and nothing could be seen.

'See what' asked Don, sarcastically, while Merwan wailed, 'Why did you wake me up for nothing?'

They all went back to their places and fell asleep again, including Thangavelu. Nobody had believed me. But I knew that the danger that had threatened us, and particularly the servant, had been very real and not part of a dream or my imagination.

I rekindled the fire with the wood that Thangavelu had gathered the evening before. Then with my rifle and torch at hand, I remained awake for the rest of the night with my back propped against my bedroll. I was convinced the panther I had seen had been a man-eater and that Thangavelu had been saved in the nick of time. The calls that had awakened me showed that it was hungry. The chances were it might return.

An hour later a sambar started calling on the hill-side half a mile away. It called for some time before the spotted deer scented or saw the source of the danger. Then they started calling too. Clearly the panther was retreating across the hillside.

By this time a crescent moon had arisen, outlining the immediate neighbourhood. The water in the river gurgled monotonously as it flowed over the rocks and I felt very sleepy. At last the dawn came, when Tiny was the first to awake. He saw me.

'Don't say you've been sitting up all night?' he asked.

'Wake Thangavelu and tell him to make some tea', was all the reply I gave. Then I went to sleep before the water could boil.

Tiny fished all day. He caught a ten-pound mahseer, a couple of seven-pounders and some smaller fish. Don tried his hand, but like me he is impatient and caught nothing. Merwan said he wanted to have a bath, and so as not to disturb the fishing, started to wander downstream with his towel across his shoulders. I thought of the man-eater which no one believed I had seen; and called after him, 'Wait a minute, I'll join you.' Picking up my rifle and swinging a towel, I followed him.

That afternoon we all felt sleepy, particularly myself, and the camp was once again hushed in slumber. But not for long. We heard a series of hollow sounds drawing nearer gradually, 'Boomp! Boomp! Boomp!'

Poachers! They were bombing the river and operating in broad daylight, too, evidently without fear of being caught. Soon, around the bend in the river appeared the usual two coracles, the first loaded with men and the other with fish. Catching sight of our party, they paddled frantically against the current to try to reach the other side.

This move incited us to act though. Don fired a shot into the air. Then he called out, 'Come here, or the next shot will be at you.'

The paddling stopped and the two coracles started drifting downstream. It was evident the men inside were debating whether to surrender or make a dash for it. Then Merwan shouted in English, which of course they did not understand. 'Come here, you bastards, or as sure as eggs we'll sink you.'

Slowly the men started paddling the coracles towards us, but stopped when they were a few yards offshore. From our slightly elevated position on the bank, we could look down on the hundreds of fish lying in the second coracle.

Then began a harangue which was as needless as it was foolish. Don threatened and admonished them alternately, for their wrongful activity. The men replied that they saw nothing wrong in it. The fish belonged to nobody in particular. Then why should the Government frame rules or demand fishing licences? And who were we to interfere? And so on, and so on.

Thangavelu, being about the wisest in our party at the time, said, 'Give us a couple of your best and largest fish. Then, go and blow yourselves up for all we care!'

In the midst of all this I asked, 'Look, is there a man-eating panther in these parts?'

There was a hushed silence. Then one of the men replied in a low tone, as if he did not wish to be overheard, 'Indeed, *dorai,* there is. It has killed many, many people. Only a few days ago it killed one of our own comrades, whose name was Balu. That's why we are now catching fish by daylight.

Normally, we would only do this on moonlit nights, but not a soul will stir out after sunset now.'

So I was right after all!

Don was excited. 'Come here. Come ashore,' he invited. 'Damn the fish. We'll not harm you. I want to know more about this panther. We're shikaris. We're interested and will try to shoot it.'

A chord having been established, the fishermen brought their coracles to the bank and tied them with ropes to the roots of trees. Then they stepped ashore and sat around us in a group. Don and I plied them with questions, and from their answers pieced together the story which I have already related. The men admitted the panther was not a man-eater in the strict sense. So far, it had not actually eaten any of its victims, but had contented itself with mauling and mutilating them hideously. Obviously the animal was female, possessed of unusual sagacity and with a quite abnormal memory, for most wild animals generally forget the past very quickly. This pantheress evidently remembered the slaying of her cubs and her feeling of hate for the human race seemed as fresh now as on that day. After hearing the story, our sympathies were with the aggrieved animal.

Eventually the boatmen asked to take leave of us. The sun would grow hot and the fish could not be bombed so easily, for they would swim into deeper waters. Disgustedly, we told them to get the hell out of it, but not before Thangavelu had remembered to pick out two of the largest and best fish for us.

'So you see, chaps, I was not dreaming after all,' was my first comment as the two coracles began to draw away. Tiny was the only one to think any more about fishing that day. The rest of us, Thangavelu included, went into close conference as to how to shoot this panther. Don and Merwan were particularly keen. For myself, I was of the opinion that the panther had a case.

From the start, the others felt we had a difficult problem in not having a regular man-eater to deal with. Here I disagreed. In my opinion, given the time, this pantheress would be far easier to come to grips with, because, filled with hatred for humans, she would go out of her way to try and attack us. As I saw the situation, we should operate individually in trying to find her. That would give us four chances to one. Correspondingly, the pantheress would most certainly come for any one of us whom she might see alone, although, according to the fishermen, she had not hesitated to attack a whole group of persons. This plan appeared to me to offer a much greater chance of success than the one proposed by Thangavelu, which was to go to Talainovu in the jeep and purchase two young bulls or buffaloes as bait. For these would then have to be driven on foot to the camp site and suitable spots selected before they were tied out. All this I knew would take considerable time and, as matters stood, there was far less chance of the panther attacking either of the baits than one of us.

Fortunately, Don had brought his .423 Mauser rifle along with his .12 bore shot-gun, while I had my .405 and my .12 bore too. This made two rifles and two shot guns, enough to arm all four of us.

We decided to have an early lunch, after which Tiny, with my shot-gun loaded with lethal shell, would walk downstream along the river bank for two hours or so, and then turn and come back. Merwan would do the same upstream, using Donald's gun. Don and I, armed with our rifles, would search the jungle separately and in different directions. Thangavelu would climb up a tree somewhere close by and await our return, while keeping an eye on the jeep and our camp kit which was lying scattered around. It was agreed that everyone should get back to camp by 5 p.m., at the latest.

We did this and, with parting admonitions to each other to keep a sharp look-out against surprise attack, scattered according to plan each hoping to be the lucky individual to come across the panther. I do not think any one of us quite realized till he was all alone that what he had set out to do, and was doing in fact, was to offer himself for the next four hours or more as a bait to a most dangerous wild animal that had all the advantages of ground and cover in its favour.

I had decided to go in the direction in which I had heard the sambar calling the previous night. Perhaps this led towards some cave and would afford a better chance of success than just roaming aimlessly in the jungle. A few minutes from the river I picked up a game-trail that led up the north-eastern slope of the same hill down which the jeep had travelled from Talainovu. It was a well-defined track, used by sambar and other animals in coming to water at the river during the summer months, and recent marks of deer and bear revealed the presence of a fair amount of game, despite the comparative silence of the previous night.

The path wound diagonally uphill, skirting boulders and heavy cover at a safe distance, as game-trails made by the members of the deer family usually do, for fear of some carnivore lying in hiding behind a rock or bush. This was in my favour, although I knew that a panther was able to conceal itself behind cover of any sort. My thoughts were uneasy and after a while I became anxious about Don and our other two friends. I hoped they were being as careful as I was.

It was too late — and too hot — for the birds to be calling, and so I proceeded in uncomfortable silence, keeping a sharp look-out to right and left while studying every bit of cover in front of me before I drew abreast of it. The real danger lay from behind, as I knew, since panthers and nearly all tigers for that matter, even when they have made a practice of attacking human beings, never completely lose their fear of man and in most cases spring upon their victims from behind.

And so I halted frequently to look behind me, trying to catch the least movement of leaf or blade of grass that might betray the pantheress as she prepared to pounce. As was to be expected, there were a number of false alarms. My searching eyes detected a twig shaking suspiciously, or a blade of grass springing suddenly upright from where it had been held down by the weight of some hidden presence. Sometimes I heard a rustle, or the distinct crack of a dried twig, often behind me and many times in other directions: Then I froze, half raised the .405, and stared intently towards the sound, expecting at any moment to see the spotted form come hurtling down upon me. Nothing happened. The rustling or the snapping of the twig was not repeated, and the forest remained uncannily silent. Or the twig that shook did so again, or the blade of grass continued to wave in the breeze. Then tension died within me, the hair at the back of my neck relaxed, and I realized there was nothing to fear. Thus I proceeded for some distance till some other movement frightened me once more.

This sort of thing went on for some time, till I realized my nerves were playing havoc with me and that I was behaving like a greenhorn. As likely as not, the pantheress was miles away. As I walked along, thinking my own thoughts, fits of alertness alternated with periods of carelessness and indifference. Time passed uneventfully, and I began to feel things were not as bad as they had been painted by the poachers. No doubt, like all villagers, they had exaggerated the matter grossly.

I reached the shoulder of the hill and began to descend

the other side into a lush valley of heavy bamboos. A faint rustle and swish of leaves, then the sharp crack of a frond betokened only one thing. An elephant!

I stopped and gazed at the spot whence the sound had come. Much depended upon whether it was a solitary animal or one of a herd. If solitary, I might expect trouble should I go too close. If I had stumbled upon a herd, it was almost certain that, upon discovering my presence, they would take themselves off. The game-trail I was following led directly towards the origin of the sound. If I now abandoned the trail to avoid the elephant, I knew I would not be able to go far, for very soon I would be foundering in thickets of bamboo and thorn, no place in which to meet an angry panther or an equally angry elephant. So I made up my mind to stick to the trail.

The breeze blew strongly from behind and there were no further sounds from among the bamboos in front. I waited awhile, but the silence continued. This indicated that the elephant had become aware of my presence, having scented me. Either he had moved away, or he was waiting for me to come closer.

No, had he moved away I would in all probability have heard him, for although these giant creatures can walk almost soundlessly, in that heavy undergrowth there would have been at least some faint sounds of his passage. I therefore concluded that he was waiting for me to approach. I delayed for another ten minutes, hoping the elephant would change his mind and avoid an encounter. He did not move. Perhaps he was thinking the same thing.

I should have waited longer, but I became impatient and decided to oust the beast. It was a wrong move, and one that nearly ended disastrously.

Thinking that a nonchalant approach on my part would

frighten him off, I began to whistle loudly and advanced boldly along the game-trail. The result was immediate. The elephant charged. He screamed in the way of all elephants when attacking, partly to inflate their own courage and partly to strike terror into their victims, and came crashing through the bamboos straight towards me. The green undergrowth parted violently to reveal a monstrous head with gleaming tusks, a trunk coiled inwards between them, and ears laid tightly back against the skull.

I thought quickly. No rogue elephant had been proclaimed in this area. Therefore, to shoot this monster would mean endless trouble for me with the people of the Forest Department. To run away would invite being chased and caught within a short distance. To try to stop him by wounding him, in the knee if possible, would be cruel and cause him endless suffering.

There was but one possibility. A very slight one, but I took it. Shouting loudly, I aimed the rifle over his head and fired a round into the air. If this did not stop him, I knew the next round would have to be at the elephant, if I intended to remain alive.

It worked! The giant animal braked hard by planting all four feet into the ground. There was a cloud of dust and fallen leaves as he slithered to a halt. Knowing his courage had failed him, I seized the advantage by running three or four steps forward and firing a second round into the air.

The huge beast turned about. The note of anger had died out of his scream when he trumpeted shrilly again, this time with a note of fear as he swayed in indecision and then bolted; the short tail which had been stuck out behind in the manner of all charging elephants was now between his hind legs like that of a whipped cur. The noise of his departure died away and I sat down disconsolately upon a nearby stone.

I was glad I had not been compelled to fire at the elephant, but I was disgusted at myself for not having exercised more patience by sitting it out rather than by advancing and so precipitating a charge. For my rifle shots, among those hills, had made a terrific racket. The hope I had entertained of the pantheress showing herself, or attacking me, was now gone. Only half-an-hour had passed since leaving camp. Would it be worth my while to carry on along the track I had been following for the remaining ninety minutes before turning back to the river as arranged?

A few moment's thought made me realize the futility of crying over spilt milk. So I stood up and continued along the trail. There was little danger from the pantheress for the next ten minutes or so. The noise of the rifle shots would have frightened her. The elephant, and any others like him, would now be far away. I made rapid progress through the bamboos, which eventually thinned out as the ground rose gradually higher from the basin of the Cauvery River. The vegetation changed slightly and I came upon a parkland of babul, boram and dwarf tamarind trees interspersed with areas of long grass, and here the friendly game-trail I had been following all the way from the big river gave out. Rather, it became lost among innumerable other paths that criss-crossed this parkland, which was obviously a favourite grazing ground for deer.

Little pellets of dung lay everywhere, that larger ones made by sambar and the smaller by spotted deer. To my right was quite a mound of tiny pellets underneath a fig tree, now laden with a rich red harvest fruit. Thousands of these figs had fallen to the ground, knocked down by monkeys and all manner of birds by day, and the huge fruit-bats, called 'flying fox' in India, by night. The maker of that large heap of tiny dung-pellets was a jungle-sheep, which we call 'kakar' or 'muntjac.'

These pretty animals, which reach the height of a small sheep and are coloured a uniform reddishbrown, are very gracefully shaped, the males having short, bifurcated horns. They love figs and other wild fruit. The stags, particularly, have the habit of coming all the way back to a chosen spot to pass their dung on alternate days. All hunters, human and animal, know this habit, and so all they have to do when they come across such a spot is to conceal themselves adequately and wait long enough for the return.

Carnivores are well versed in the habits and movements of the deer family and all the lesser animals that form their prey. They have to be, if they would eat. So this lovely parkland, filled as it was with deer, would be a very likely place in which to come across the pantheress and I redoubled my efforts to look for her.

I had gone some distance when, from a direction a little to the right and before me, I heard a series of bird-like calls. The cries grew louder as they approached rapidly. Wild dogs! A pack of them was hunting down a quarry and the chase was coming in my direction. I stepped quickly behind the sheltering trunk of a nearby tamarind tree.

The wild dog of the Indian forest is the cleverest of all hunters and the implacable foe of every living creature. Once a pack of these creatures scents or sees a deer and gives chase, its fate is sealed. They hunt it down mercilessly and intelligently. The main body of dogs run behind their quarry, giving voice to a hunting cry that resembles the high-pitched call of a bird more than anything else, while a few dogs gallop ahead at terrific speed and on both flanks of the quarry. These flankers then ambush the victim and worry it, if they are unable to bring it down themselves, till the main body catches up and completes the job. I have seen a sambar doe, worried by these flankers, cross a dry river bed with her entrails trailing in the sand for yards behind her, both eyes bitten out, and dogs hanging by their teeth to her throat and flanks.

I heard the clashing sound of horns against wood and a splendid sambar stag appeared. Foam flecked his mouth and sprayed backwards to his neck and shoulders, and his eyes were wide with terror as he galloped in headlong flight. The next instant there was a terrific roar and a mighty striped form launched itself through the air and directly on to the sambar' back.

My earlier thoughts had proved correct. A tiger had been patrolling the parkland in search of a meal. He had heard the wild dogs approach and knew they were pursuing a quarry that was coming his way. Ordinarily, tigers avoid wild dogs and fear them for their reckless bravery, their intelligence and their numbers. Probably this tiger would have avoided them too but for the chance that the hunted animal and his pursuers happened to be coming in his direction. So before he quite realized what he should do about it, he took the decisive step.

For this same reason, the tiger had not discovered my own approach from behind him. His keener hearing had appraised him of the wild dog's hunting cries before I had heard them and he had been listening intently in that direction and had not caught the faint sounds I may have made.

The sambar's back bent to the sudden weight of the tiger and he let out a hoarse bellow of terror. Their tightly entangled bodies sank from view into the long grass. I heard the sharp crack of bone as the vertebral column was broken skilfully by the tiger, and the drumming of the stag's hooves upon the earth as the twitching muscles and nerves of his four legs continued to respond to the last message to flee. Upon this scene, the next instant, burst the pack of baying snarling wild dogs!

Recovering from their momentary surprise at seeing

themselves forestalled, they quickly rallied. In a flash they surrounded the tiger and the body of the quarry they regarded as their own. I counted nine of them.

The bird-like hunting call that had been coming from the pack only a moment earlier changed abruptly to a series of long and plaintive notes. I had heard these cries on an earlier occasion, many years before, in the far-distant jungles of the Chamala Valley. There a pack of wild dogs had been chasing a tiger and this queer new cry was the same those dogs had made on that occasion. They were summoning reinforcements. Every wild dog within miles would hasten to their aid. It appeared to be an unwritten law of the species that no member dared disobey.

The tiger rose to his feet threateningly and I could see him clearly. His body turned slowly to enable him to see how many enemies beset him. His face, was contorted hideously as he snarled and roared with all the strength of his lungs, and his tail twitched from side to side spasmodically, a visible indication of nervous tension, rage, doubt and an unaccountable fear of these unruffled, implacable and cruelly clever foes.

The circle of dogs stood fast, legs firmly yet slightly outspread, each member of the pack now making that loud, shrill summons for help. The roars of the tiger and the yelping call of the nine wild dogs were pandemonium. The jungle echoed and re-echoed with the din.

The tiger realized that every second lost now counted in favour of his foes. In two bounds he charged the dog directly in his path. The dog skipped nimbly aside, while those behind leaped forward to attack from the rear. The tiger sensed this and whirled around, flaying wildly to right and left with his two forepaws. The dogs within reach of those mighty paws fell back helter-skelter, but one was too slow. The raking talons struck the dog's hindquarters, his body was thrown into the air with one leg almost torn off, and the dogs behind the tiger leaped forward to bite off chunks of flesh from his sides. Once more the tiger whirled around, once again his enemies scattered before him, while those at the back and on both sides raced forward to bite him where they could.

The tiger feinted and made a double-turn and the dogs from behind him that had rushed forward could not turn back. They met the full force of his powerful forelegs with their widely-extended talons. Two quick blows and two more dogs were torn asunder. One of them tried to drag itself away, but its nearness to the tiger tempted him to make a false move that immediately offset the advantage he had just gained by his clever double-turn. He pounced upon the disembowelled wild dog and buried his fangs in its body.

The dogs from behind and both sides now fell upon him and covered his body, tearing out scraps of the living flesh. The tiger roared and roared again, but now there was a note of fear in each roar.

The huddle of tearing rending beasts disintegrated and the tiger had freed himself for the moment. There were now but six dogs around him and some of them were injured. But the tiger was bleeding profusely from the many wounds he had received. He gasped for breath. The dogs would not relax. From all sides they renewed the attack, yelping and snapping. The tiger roared again, but not nearly so loudly. The will to continue the fight was ebbing. He was definitely afraid.

Just then quite another sound could be heard above the pandemonium: the distant cries of answering wild dogs, not from one direction, but from several, all at once. Reinforcements.

The harassed tiger heard them too, and the fight went out of him. He turned tail and raced away with the six dogs, despite their wounds and exhaustion, after him.

Within a minute the reinforcements began to arrive. First three dogs, then another, and yet another. They halted a moment at the scene of battle and sniffed the blood-tainted grass and the three mangled dogs. This roused them to a fury and they growled and snarled. Then they raced in the wake of the fleeing tiger and his six pursuers.

Soon a larger pack of about a dozen dogs arrived on the scene. In a few seconds they had taken stock of the situation and followed the five that had preceded them. The fate of that tiger was sealed, for by now there were two dozen wild dogs on his trail. They would not relax their pursuit till they had caught him and torn him to shreds.

The sounds of the chase died away in the distance as I stepped from behind the tamarind tree to look at the three dead dogs and the scene of battle. The sambar stag that the tiger had slain lay untouched a few feet away. After disposing off the tiger, no doubt the surviving dogs would return and eat their fill.

Tiny had returned by the time I arrived and Merwan showed up soon after. Neither of them had seen or heard anything. It was quite late when Donald returned. He had met the tracks of a panther and not long after had passed a cave. Associating the two, Donald had thrown stones into the cave, expecting and hoping the panther would emerge. Instead, a slothbear had dashed forth with two cubs riding on her back. She was greatly annoyed at being disturbed and Donald would have been compelled to shoot her in self-defence, had she seen him. Fortunately, his did not happen. The bear rushed blindly forward into the jungle, and that was the end of that. No panther could have shared a cave with a family of bears, and so Donald passed on.

Strangely enough, none of the party had heard the shots I had fired to frighten off the elephant and everyone was greatly interested in my account of the fight between the tiger and the wild dogs.

This time we all helped in gathering wood for the camp fire and arranged to take watch-turns of two hours, each. Then came an early dinner, followed by a smoke and a chat. Eventually the conversation began to die as, one by one, we became sleepy. It was only nine o'clock but time to turn in. We had chosen Thangavelu to be on watch for the first two hours. We did this deliberately, for later on he was bound to fall asleep anyhow. Merwan came next, followed by myself, Donald and Tiny. Merwan had tried hard to exchange turns with Tiny, but the big man was too clever for him.

As I fell asleep, a tiger began to roar somewhere over the hill, where I had been that day. I thought to myself that it must be the mate of the animal that the wild dogs had pursued and surely slain.

When Thangavelu called Merwan at eleven o'clock, he would not wake and the ensuing argument disturbed me. I told Thangavelu to throw cold water over him, but the former felt that such conduct by a servant might be misunderstood. So I had to get up and throw the water myself. Merwan sat up with a jerk and was very annoyed, but he took his revenge at 1 a.m., when the time came to wake me, for did so with cold water. Merwan is like that!

He told me that he had heard a panther sawing a few minutes after midnight, apparently on the hill behind us and pretty far away. Then he told me something that was very important indeed. Only a few minutes before he woke me, a bird, which he thought must have been a jungle-fowl, had clucked a noisy alarm and flapped away heavily. This had been quite close. Merwan remarked that he had almost forgotten to mention the incident; he thought it was a matter of no consequence anyhow!

I said nothing in reply as he covered himself up before falling asleep, but I knew the matter was of great consequence indeed. Why should a jungle-fowl be so alarmed that it had cried out and left the secure place where it had sat to roost the evening before, to risk changing its perch and a flight in darkness? They don't do that unless some potential danger has passed very close. Perhaps it was a python searching for food. Perhaps a wildcat or a tree-civet. Perhaps even a panther.

The more I thought about it, the more I felt that here was the animal we were seeking, that it had returned to our camp with the deliberate intention of stalking and killing one or more of us. I arranged another log on the fire to make more light to see by. Then I changed my position so that I sat with my back to the nearest muthee tree, that grew a few feet from the water. This enabled me to face the jungle, with my companions a little before me and to the right, while I was safe from an attack from the rear. Then I settled down to listen and watch intently.

Nothing happened till after two o'clock. The gurgling sound of the river as it cascaded over the rocks prevented me from hearing the more subtle noises of the forest. A fish plopped loudly in the water, followed by a yet greater splash, perhaps a bigger fish, or even a crocodile in pursuit of the first fish. On the opposite bank of the river a night heron raised a wailing, plaintive cry, and a dark shadow caught my eye against the lighter hue of the star-studded sky: a giant horned-owl, a species confined to the forests and feeding on the smaller mammals, including rabbits.

Just then I heard a faint hissing, rasping sound. I could scarcely distinguish it because of the murmur of the rushing water. It stopped and then was repeated, quite close at hand, from near a clump of bushes a little beyond my sleeping companions, where the jungle grew thickest and was pitch black. I had heard that sound before and recognized it at once.

I knew then that the pantheress was hiding in the thicket that was closest to the spot where Don and the others were sleeping, and that she was working up her courage for an attack. In a few seconds she would reach the point of springing upon them.

I could not see her. Only the blackness of the thicket. If I shone my torch on that blackness now, it might reveal the pantheress or it might not — according to whether or not she was sheltering behind some bush or shrub. Should the latter be the case, I knew full well she would disappear as soon as she saw the light. So I decided to wait a little longer.

But the pantheress decided to wait no more. She acted.

Voicing the short, sharp roars made by her kind when they charge, she sprang clear of the thicket to land a few feet from the sleeping men. With the next bound she would be amongst them.

I was waiting for this and it was fortunate that I had the rifle to my shoulder with my thumb on the light switch.

The torch-beam cut through the darkness like a knife and reflected the blazing eyes of the pantheress. She hesitated a second, taken completely by surprise and dazzled by the light. I was about to press the trigger when there was a shattering explosion, followed quickly by a second shot.

'Beat you to it, dad!' yelled Don, as he sprang to his feet, having wakened and fired his two shots while still lying on the ground.

Then the other sleepers awoke, and their surprise was indeed comical. Thangavelu just yelled. Tiny sat bolt upright and remarked, half asleep, 'Mother dear!' But Merwan surpassed them; he rolled about as if he'd been shot himself.

Then they saw the dead pantheress, or almost dead, I

should say. For she was gasping and twitching still, while life faded slowly from eyes that were held in my torch-beam. They died to a cold, watery blue and became still. Then I knew that the pantheress was dead.

We gathered around and examined her. A fine specimen of a female. Truly my heart had not been in that night's work and I regretted every part I played in hunting her from the time we heard her story. I consoled myself with the thought that what had to be done had been done, and I left it at that, but my congratulations to Don on his prowess were more heart-felt than he ever suspected.

Seven

*Sher Khan and the Bettamugalam Man-Eater**

MANY YEARS AGO A RETIRED BRITISH ADMINISTRATOR, POPULARLY known as the Collector in those days, had acquired for himself 300 acres of jungle land on the northern slopes of the Gutherayan range of hills in the District of Salem, where he built an incredible bungalow. He built it all of stone and to the pattern of a castle.

This man loved the jungle and he preserved it at a tremendous expense of himself by engaging an army of coolies to hack away the thorny undergrowth and the lantana plants which, in those years, were just beginning to envelop the forests of southern India.

Since then the lantana has grown apace and now covers

---

* For map, see Chaper 1.

thousands of acres of Reserved Forest land. Various government departments, including the Forest Department, have tried and are trying in vain to eradicate this scourge. Spraying with a poisonous solution can obviously be done only on a very limited scale. A white bug has been found which multiplies in millions; it covers the lantana bushes, blackens the stem, branches all leaves, and kills all the lantana in perhaps an acre or two of land. Then something happens to the bugs themselves: they die within a few days, from some poison absorbed from the lantana itself, which thus gains the ultimate victory.

Jungle fires rage periodically, particularly during the hot weather. The lantana is burnt to the ground, only to spring up again and flourish with the coming of the rains, fertilized by its own ashes.

Incidently, the juice from a few freshly-crushed leaves of this plant, rubbed upon a scratch or an abrasion on the skin, will assist the wound to heal completely. It is as effective as tincture of iodine, with the added advantage that it does not irritate.

But to return to the British Collector and his 300 acres: he called his place Bettamugalam Estate, after the name given to the local sub-taluk area, and his stone house he called 'Jungly Castle.' Cleaned of the strangling lantana, the natural forest grew apace. The grass that flourished in the glades between the trees attracted bison and deer, which in their turn brought their natural foes, tigers, panthers, and the still more voracious wild dogs.

Conditions then began to change. The British Collector died and Bettamugalam Estate, with Jungly Castle, was brought by an Anglo-Indian who did not have the means to keep the place up to the standard of the former owner. Once more the lantana started to encroach upon the grassy glades, and as a consequence the bison and deer decreased in numbers. But the carnivores remained and they grew hungry.

Then the Anglo-Indian died in his turn, and no legal owner came forward. Jungly Castle fell into disrepair. Villagers came on moonlit nights in bullock carts and stole the cut granite blocks, pulling down the walls to get them. For these stones, especially when they could be obtained free, offered first-class material with which to construct the walls of their own huts.

The bison had by this time vanished, and the herds or deer had almost disappeared. The tigers, panthers and wild dogs that congregated to eat the deer followed them. Only the jungle-fowl, spur-fowl and pea-fowl remained to increase in numbers, for the heavy undergrowth of lantana gave ideal cover. Otherwise, the whole area assumed a forlorn appearance. Now and again an odd tiger or panther would pass that way, hoping but generally in vain, for a stray spotted deer or jungle-sheep to break his fast. He was generally very hungry but there was nothing to be got.

Now, in the village of Aiyur, a little over for miles away, lived a man of about twenty-five years, whose name was Gurappa. Gurappa had married very late in life for one of his caste and status, the usual age being around seventeen to eighteen years for a boy and thirteen to fourteen years for a girl. But Gurappa's father could not get his son married earlier, for they were a poor family, and the parents of every prospective bride turned down the marriage of their daughter to a mere yokel, the son moreover of such a poor father. But a girl was found at last. I was told that she was very deaf and had walked with a limp from birth. Very likely these impediments had caused her parents to agree to the marriage with Gurappa, who was so poor.

Now another problem presented itself. The bride-groom

had no house. His father had sold the hut the family had lived in. Not even in India can a bride-groom bring his bride home on their wedding day to no house!

So Gurappa decided to build one in a hurry. True, he had no money, but fortunately a good number of stones still remained of Jungly Castle, although the best and largest of them had already been pilfered.

Scorning to wait for a moonlight night, the would-be bridegroom begged the village headman to lend him his cart. With a long-term policy in view of extracting free labour from Gurappa in return when the harvest came around, the village patel consented.

It is safer if there are no witnesses when one sets out to commit a felony. Gurappa knew this, so he set out alone after his midday meal, intending to collect the stones and be back by sundown. Working single-handed is invariably a back-breaking job, as he soon found out. To lever the stones out of the crumbling walls with the short crowbar he had brought for the purpose, and to carry each stone and load it on to the bullock cart, took much energy and time, calling for a fair number of resting periods. The sun had dipped behind the hills to the west and the nightjars were already calling from the sandy track along which the cart had come, when Gurappa decided to call it a day and bring away the first load. Tomorrow he would borrow somebody else's cart and fetch a second load.

So he beat the bony bulls with a piece of broken bamboo. They started to walk dejectedly homewards, for this strange man, who was not their owner, had not bothered to feed or water them all day. Gurappa followed behind leisurely, his mind at peace for the moment. Up to now there had been nothing to disturb the bridegroom. No sound had he heard to cause him any uneasiness.

The waiting tiger that had seen him must have been very hungry indeed, if not on the verge of starvation, to act as he did. Perhaps he was sick or wounded and had been disabled from hunting his natural prey. Certainly he was not a regular man-eater, for nobody had been killed in this area by a tiger for quite a time.

The bulls hauled the cart past a babul tree, the lower half of which was smothered in lantana. The tiger must have been hiding within that lantana, for that was where he sprang from. When I came to the spot with a Forest Range Officer, several guards, the sub-inspector of police and a constable, just twenty-four hours later, some of the stems still bent down by the weight of the animal as he had lain in wait for Gurappa.

Probably Gurappa had never known what happened till he found himself being carried away by a tiger. Then he must have struggled and screamed loudly, for the bulls took fright and bolted, hauling the heavily laden cart behind them. They did not get very far, for there was a curve in the track ahead, where it skirted some lower ground. In turning, the cart went off the track and down the khud, taking the bullocks with it.

Miracles often happen, even with bullock carts. While the vehicle was considerably damaged, there was no injury to either bull. Freed from the restraining yoke, they found their way back to Aiyur, terrified but unhurt, long after the sun had set.

Adjacent to the village of Aiyur is a Forestry Department school where officials already working in the department, along with students who have passed the required examination, undergo practical instruction in field forestry. A Range Officer is stationed at the school, along with two or three senior foresters and a number of guards and watchers, who look after the nurseries and departmental buildings.

The headman, alarmed by the fact that his bulls had returned without the cart, assumed that an elephant had attacked and smashed it, and had accounted for Gurappa in the process. With half the village trailing behind him, he sought the co-operation of the Range Officer for permission to send out a search party into the jungle. Permission was readily given, but there was a marked lack of enthusiasm among the villagers to volunteer. Finally four of five persons were persuaded to offer their services, but by this time darkness had already fallen. Even in broad daylight a wild elephant that has killed a man is something no villager will face. In pitch darkness an encounter of this nature is not to be thought of. So the search was postponed till the next morning. The headman must have spent a sleepless night thinking of his cart, while cursing Gurappa for being the cause of his misfortune.

Early next day the search party set out. It did not take them long to find the cart at the bottom of the khud, but of Gurappa there was no sign. The tracks of the cart wheels and the bullocks, made in the soft sand, showed that the animals had taken the corner at a gallop; hence the accident. What had caused them to do that?

Still suspecting that an elephant was to blame, the villagers back-tracked and soon found the real cause. The whole-story was written in the dry, soft sand of the track. There was blood, the pug-marks of a tiger, and a distinct drag-mark, left by some part of the victim that had trailed along the ground. Fear fell upon them then. It was dangerous enough to encounter a possible rogue elephant. But they were many in number and an elephant might be expected to hesitate before attacking such a large party. Not a man-eating tiger. He might reappear at any moment, from anywhere, with disastrous results.

Without further delay the group returned to Aiyur. Gurappa

was dead beyond doubt. What could be gained by searching for him?

By chance; I happened to be camping at Sivanapalli that day. This little village lies about five miles to the west of Aiyur. It is a favourite spot of mine, and being just over fifty miles from Bangalore, I often go there at week-ends. Incidentally, it marks the scene of the shooting of the only black panther that has ever been known in this region, the details of which adventure have been related in another story.*

The forest Guard of Sivanapalli, who had gone to Aiyur to meet his superior, the Range Officer, returned at about noon to tell me what had happened to the unfortunate bridegroom, Gurappa. Carrying a torch and my sweater, with a pocketful of dry biscuits and a flask of tea for dinner in case I was delayed, I set out for Aiyur within fifteen minutes of hearing the news.

A report had already been made to the Forest Department headquarters at Denkanikota, a small town eight miles to the north, by the Range Officer, so that shortly after my arrival the sub-inspector of police turned up on his motor-cycle, with a constable on the pillion seat. Thus it came about that the two police officials, the Range Officer, a retinue of guards and myself came to the lantana thicket at the foot of the babul tree from which the tiger hadsprung, almost twenty-four hours earlier, upon the unfortunate Gurappa as he had walked behind the bullock cart that was laden with stolen stones. The prologue of this story, as I have told it, had already been pieced together by me from scraps of conversation with the two officers and their assistants. The sub-inspector of police, who was a Brahman and a fatalist, remarked more than once

---

* See *The Black Panther of Sivanapalli.*

on the connection in the web spun by fate between the old British Collector, long dead and gone, who had owned Bettamugalam Estate and Jungly Castle, and the modern bridegroom, Gurappa, who had no house at all and had been striving to build one. Not quite seeing the point, I quipped that there might also be something in the thought that fate may have taken a dim view of the general situation and decided to punish someone who was in the act of robbing the dead. I meant this as a joke, but was surprised at the manner in which my suggestion caught on. The superstitious Brahman and the somewhat nervous Range Officer accepted my point completely.

Nobody was keen on looking for what was left of Gurappa.

As I have said, I found the spot in the lantana where the tiger had been hiding before it sprang upon its victim. The drag-mark was still faintly visible, although much of it had been obliterated during the night by the action of the wind upon the sand, grass and leaves, and the movements of ants and other insects.

However, we were able to follow for a hundred yards or so when, quite unexpectedly, our search ended. An 'aeroplane' tree was growing here — known thus by the local Tamil inhabitants because it sheds its seeds by a wonderfully cleaver and novel device. Each seed is situated at the junction of two three-inch-long leaf-like blades exactly resembling in miniature the twin propellers of an aeroplane. These blades fall from the parent tree and are spun and carried by the breeze, along with the seed, to incredible distances before they tumble to the ground. In the shade of this tree the grass was still green, and protruding from this grass, as if beckoning to us, was a human arm and hand, the five fingers spread and pointing upwards.

We had found Gurappa at last — what was left of him!

Peculiarly enough, the upper parts of his body, from breast to head, had been untouched. While one arm stretched upwards, the fingers of the other hand were stuffed into the mouth as if to stifle a scream. The eye sockets were empty, because the black ants had already eaten away the eyeballs. Then red ants had come, and these now swarmed over the face and skin. In many places the black outer skin had been devoured, exposing patches of white and red flesh, now rotting underneath. The reason why hyaenas and jackals had up to now not touched these toothsome portions was simple to guess. Red ants are notorious for their aggressive nature and painful stings.

But there was hardly anything left of Gurappa's body below his chest. The tiger had eaten his fill, while the scavengers of the night had removed the rest.

The foliage of the 'aeroplane' tree had hidden from the vultures what the tiger and the others had left, for had these birds arrived before us, nothing at all would have remained.

The stench of death and putrefaction hung heavily in the still evening air. Flies squatted in myriads on the stems of the surrounding grass, prevented from settling on the rotting flesh by the army of red ants that had already driven away their cousins. A terrific battle appeared to have been waged between the two species, as large numbers of dead, of both varieties, strewed the ground for a yard around Gurappa's head and arms. Now and again a sorely-wounded member of one of the opposing armies tired to drag itself away.

The tiger would certainly not return to eat the little that remained. Why he had left it in the first place was unaccountable; but he would anyway give the red ants a wide berth.

The sub-inspector ordered his underling to arrange for the removal of the remains. Then he wrote an unnecessarily verbose statement which I was asked to sign as a witness. It was getting dark when we returned to the Forest Rest House at Aiyur. The Range Officer offered me accommodation at his bungalow for the night, but the thought of the dry biscuits in my pocket made me decide to return to my camp at Sivanapalli and the corned meat that awaited me there. I had my torch, and after all the tiger might not be a confirmed man-eater.

So I started out to the dismay of the two officers, who shouted a warning behind me that I might never reach Sivanapalli. The path wound downhill mostly, between lantana, scrub and scattered babul saplings till, as a lower level was reached, the trees became loftier and clumps of heavy bamboo grew in among them. The darkness became intense, through which the beam from my torch cut only a narrow pencil of light.

Suddenly a feeling of great uneasiness came over me — rather, a feeling of mortal fear. Why, I could not imagine. I had heard no sound, nor had I caught any audible cries of alarm from the deer and other creatures in the jungle to warn me of danger. Complete silence reigned on every side. There was only the soft crunch of my own rubber-soled boots on the ground, and the occasional crack of a twig or crackle of a leaf as I trod upon it.

I halted abruptly and spun around, fully expecting to see the tiger stalking me from behind. But there was nothing to be seen, not even the glimmer of a firefly. There was nothing to be heard; not even the chirping of a friendly cricket.

Then I knew why I was so afraid: it was the idea of absolute loneliness. There was no living creature nearby to witness what happened to me. Nothing, and nobody to help. And, although I could not see him in the gloom, or hear him, even in that absolute silence, I was as certain of the presence of the tiger there as I was of my own.

I have found that at times of great peril in the jungle, the human reflexes act in one of two ways. The trumpeting scream of a charging rogue elephant, or the guttural roar of an attacking tiger or panther, sometimes galvanizes the victim into precipitate flight, or else he is so paralyzed by fear that he is rooted to the spot and quite incapable of movement. It is rare, indeed, that the victim can think at all, much less think clearly, of what he should — or rather could — do in the circumstances. There is no time for thinking.

But in this case there was no screaming elephant before me, nor a roaring tiger for that matter. Only silence, and the certain knowledge that the man-eater was there. And the reflex that came to me was to run, and to run fast, as fast as I could, away from that dreadful spot. I had the greatest difficulty in restraining myself, for I knew that if I started to run it would be just what the tiger would like me to do. For then he would attack. All tigers, including man-eaters, know that every other creature is afraid of them. They are accustomed to striking terror into the hearts and minds of their prey, and with that knowledge comes the greater confidence that enables them to hunt so successfully.

I knew at that moment that the only thing that could save me from the tiger would be to act otherwise. He was lurking somewhere, watching and waiting for me. Perhaps he was behind, perhaps ahead, or may be to one side or the other, waiting and watching for an opportunity to spring upon me. He would have done so long before had it not been for my torch and the bright beam of light that was cutting through the darkness. This had worried him. If I wanted him to attack, all I had to do was extinguish the torch and start running. Then he would come.

I thought quickly. And I kept on walking at a measured pace, flashing the torch behind me, to both sides and then in front. The path was narrow, not more than six feet wide at the most.

The track turned a corner and ahead of me the light revealed a rock, standing to the left and about a hundred yards away. It was a sloping rock and appeared to be about six to eight feet high. I felt that I could run up and on to it without difficulty, provided I had a sufficiently long start. For I had had an idea. Here was a suitable place at which to try to tempt the man-eater to show himself.

As I turned the idea over in my mind, I continued to walk forward. Those hundred yards were far too long to risk a show-down. The speed of a charging tiger is something fantastic and has to be seen to be believed. But when the rock was fifty yards away, I decided to take the chance.

Making certain my rifle was cocked, and fixing the location of the rock clearly in my mind, I suddenly extinguished the torch and ran as fast and as hard as I could.

The darkness, when the torch went out, was intense. I could not see a thing. That was why I had taken care to face the rock and fix its location before putting out the torch and starting to run.

It took quite a few seconds for the tiger to gather his wits and realize that his victim had actually done what he had been waiting for. As I ran, I was just beginning to think that perhaps there was no tiger at all and that my nerves had made a fool of me, when there was a shattering roar from behind and the man-eater launched his attack. I heard that roar, but I could run no faster anyway.

I was only a few feet ahead of the tiger when I reached the rock and ran up the slope. Then I whirled around, raised the rifle to my shoulder and pressed the torch-switch with my left thumb all simultaneously. The man-eater had reached the base of the rock and was crouched for the spring that would carry him to the top when the rifle went off, almost at point-blank range. With the crash of the explosion he somersaulted backwards while I worked the underlever of the .405 to place the second round in the breach. Then I pressed the trigger.

Nothing happened.

A moment later, with a loud snarl the tiger leaped to its left and disappeared into the long grass that grew there. Working the underlever again, I ejected the cartridge that had misfired and fired the next round at the spot where the tiger had just vanished.

I had been too frightened when I fired the first shot, but I distinctly remember hearing the echo of the second one reverberating against the slopes of Gulhatti hill, which I could not see in the darkness but which is within a mile of the rock I stood upon.

The growling had ceased. Had my second bullet found its mark? Had the tiger collapsed from the effect of my first shot? Perhaps both had taken effect. Or had I missed entirely? Worse still, perhaps I had only wounded the brute.

With the torch still shining upon the bushes where the tiger had vanished, I sat down on the rock to collect my scattered wits and control my breathing. Mostly, to try to think. Only then did I realize how narrow an escape I had had. Had the tiger been closer behind me, or to either side or ahead, he might have cut me off before I could reach the rock. Moreover, had the cartridge that had misfired been one ahead in the magazine of my rifle, it would have failed at the crucial moment and the man-eater would certainly have completed his spring.

When I grew a little calmer I began to wonder what had

happened to the man-eater. It seemed inconceivable that I could have missed him at point blank range. Then I remembered I had been running fast and had rushed up the rock at the last moment. Fear, excitement and exertion had made me breathe hard and this had evidently caused me to press the trigger unconsciously, causing me to miss entirely or perhaps just wound the beast.

It was impossible for me to follow up in that darkness. If I had missed him, he would have been scared away entirely. If he was wounded, it was very unlikely that the man-eater would resumed the pursuit if I continued on my way to Sivanapalli. So after a few moments I decided to do that and return the next morning to take up the trail.

I reached Sivanapalli without event and lay down in my little tent, still thinking of what should be done the next day. Then the dried biscuits in my pocket reminded me that I was hungry and I got up to make tea and open the tin of meat that had been the cause of the whole incident.

There are no Poojarees or aboriginal trackers at Sivanapalli, but there was Sher Khan, a character who had led a colourful existence and must at the time have been about forty years old. He was a Muslim, a poacher of game, a timber thief, and the suspected author of several dacoities on a minor scale, when bullock carts carrying sacks of grain to the villages of Denkanikota and Anchetty had been held up and robbed at night. The method of dacoity had been as simple as it had been effective.

The carts used to travel by night in order to save time. Generally, half-a-dozen of them would move, one behind the other for company and for protection from wild animals, particularly elephants, and of course the evil spirits that are said to be everywhere. Highway robbery, up to that time, was unheard of.

The first case reported to the police was by five cartmen who had been behind one another from Anchetty to Denkanikota. They were on the ghat road when it had happened, nine miles from their destination. The time was 1 a.m., and the bulls strained at their loads on the steep gradient. Each driver sat in his cart, more than half asleep. Suddenly a voice hailed them from the darkness of the roadside. It was harsh and loud. They saw no man, but the voice said that a gang of dacoits were hiding by the wayside. They had loaded muskets and would be well. Then followed the orders. They were very simple.

'Get down from your carts, all five of you, and walk back for a full mile. When you reach the tenth mile-stone, you may sit dawn. Light a fire and wait there till morning. When daylight comes, you may return to your carts. Remember, some of us will follow and keep a watch over you till down. If any one of you dares to disobey, he will be shot without further warning. Remember also that we promise we shall not harm your carts or animals. You are poor men and we do not want to hurt you. It is the rich men's belongings, carried in your carts, that we want.'

The cartmen obeyed. They were thankful they had been spared. Early next morning they found their carts, standing where they had been left. Some of the food-stuff had been stolen, but not all if it. Only the more valuable items. The gang could not have been a very large one after all, or they would have taken everything.

This happened two or three times more, on other roads and tracks leading to Denkanikota and Anchetty, before the carts stopped moving at night and police patrols took their place. Several suspects were rounded up, including Sher Khan. They were beaten and locked up. But all of them always affirmed complete innocence and all of them had alibis.

That was how I first met Sher Khan. He was returning to Sivanapalli after one such beating and complained aloud of the injustice that was rampant in this world. But there was a mischievous twinkle of insincerity in his eye as he spoke.

As I said, he was a Muslim, and the literal translation of his name is 'Chief among Tigers'. He was a ruffian, but a very likeable one, and that is how he became my friend. I would never fail, when at Sivanapalli, to visit his little house and drink tea with him, and he would never fail to return my call.

So I went to Sher Khan early on the morning after my adventure, and asked him to assist me. For I was confident that I had not missed the tiger when I had fired at point-blank range. I knew I must have hit it. That meant following up a wounded tiger in the jungle, and to do that there must be two persons. Following a blood trail through bushes, over leaves and on hard and stony ground requires concentration of eyesight and mind. One must look here, there and everywhere, for a speck of blood or a mere smear of the underside of a leaf, or against a stem or rock. While you are engaged in so looking, the wounded tiger might be just ahead, waiting for you, or he may be lying to the right or the left, concealed behind a tuft of grass, a clump of bamboo, a tree-trunk or a termite-hill, waiting till you come within springing distance. There is a third possibility, and that is he may be stalking you from behind even while you are looking for him. But you are blissfully unaware of his presence, because your attention is concentrated on the ground, following his trail. On the other hand, if you try to keep an effective lookout for the wounded beast, you will soon find you have lost the trail. You just cannot do both jobs effectively, and so a second person is essential. One of you concentrates on following the tiger's bloodspoor and tracks, while the other keeps a sharp look-out ahead, to the right, left and also behind. In the hands of this second person lies not only his own life, but the life of his companion.

Sher Khan volunteered to help without hesitation, but insisted that I drink the customary cup of tea with him before we set out. A clap of his hands and one of his four wives responded. He told her to make: 'Attcha-cha-first class!' for the sahib.

Being a Muslim, he was allowed to have four legal wives — and he had them. Most of us find it a problem to manage one, but he managed all four with ease! And this is how he did it.

Sher Khan showed no preference towards any one of his your epouses — either to the youngest or the most recent or the prettiest. They were all kept strictly *gosha* — that is to say, they were compelled to cover their faces with a *bourkha* when they went out in public. No man was allowed to look upon them. I, as a very particular friend, had the priviledge of seeing their faces, and even of speaking to them — but very sparingly, mind you — when I visited his house.

Sher Khan made it a practice to divide the household duties among his four wives on a weekly-roster basis. For a week one of them would be responsible for the cooking of all the food, with a second to assist her; the third would be responsible for washing all the utensils; the fourth for the household work such as sweeping, mending, washing of clothes, etc. The following week, the roster would change, and so on week by week thereby dividing all the work very equitably among all four. Sher Khan himself would not lift a finger to do any household work. He did the marketing — if his rather nefarious activities could be so described — and brought home the earning, or the money, whichever you my prefer to call it. The wife who did the hardest work for that particular week, namely the cook, he would sleep with two days in the week, the remaining three women one day each. Fridays and Sundays were 'off days' from that sort of thing. Days off rest' as he called them.

They were a poor family, but disciplined, happy and contented. The women never quarrelled with him and hardly ever among themselves. For if they did, a beating would be administered; fairly, equitably and impartially, each recalcitrant wife receiving an equal number of blows or cuffs according to the nature of the offence. And in spite of the often undeniably pressing demands made upon him, he had no children.

As soon as we had drunk our tea we were off. Sher Khan announced that he had no gun and brought a rusty sword with him instead. He remarked that it had belonged to his father, and to his father's father's father' father, who was a soldier serving under the great Tipu Sultan, the tiger of Mysore. The mathematics involved in the problem of checking whether this man's great-great-grandfather could have lived in Tipu's lifetime are rather too involved for me. In the meanwhile, we had walked out of earshot of all his wives and I raised an impersonal question, addressed perhaps to the air: 'A voice comes out of the darkness and threatens to shoot many cartmen. Yet there is no gun. How can that be, Sher Khan?'

The silence for a moment is complete. Then he replied. 'You may call me a liar if you wish, sahib. But that is exactly what happened. There was no gun at that time, nor any other. I never possessed one and still don't have a gun. And the gang consisted of myself and three of the wives, sahib. The fourth is too old. But she had the brains, and it was all her idea.

And, I believed him.

We were nearly at our destination. There stood the sloping rock from which I had fired at the man-eater the previous night. This time it was to my right. We approached in silence and looked at the ground. No blood was to be seen and the earth was too dry and hard for tracks. Without speaking, I pointed to the bushes bordering the path where the tiger disappeared from view.

I took the lead for the moment, with my Muslim friend directly behind. In spite of the prevailing dryness all around, it was evident that a heavy body had recently passed through. A couple of broken stems hung loosely, still joined to their parent-branch by the outer skins. A yard or two further and we saw it almost simultaneously: blood!

There was a splash of bright red on the carpet of dry, brown leaves that covered the ground. I touched it with my forefinger and rubbed it against my thumb. It was thick and coagulated, and by that I knew that my bullet of the night before had inflicted more than a mere surface wound. It had penetrated deeply.

We changed places now, and I put Sher Khan ahead of me. He would concentrate all his attention on following the blood-trail, while I would cover him — and myself — in all four directions.

The Muslim was no born tracker, but what he lacked in ability as an aborigine he made up for in intelligence. He fussed and fumbled around, taking far more time than would a member of any of the jungle tribes in following such a trail, but he found one blood spot after another. The tiger had bled far more freely now. The exertions caused by his bounds had no doubt opened the wound. Splashes and pools of blood lay all along the trail, making it easy to follow.

I caught sight of a slight movement ahead and lightly touched Sher Khan with my hand. He halted at the prearranged signal and froze. With rifle to shoulder, I watched the spot from whence the movement came. I also watched on both sides and even glanced behind us. For wounded tigers are notoriously clever in lying in ambush or in creeping upon their enemies from behind.

The movement came again. A small branch swayed ominously a few feet ahead of us. I prepared for the attack. Stretching out my hand, I gripped Sher Khan by the shoulder and pulled him unceremoniously behind me.

The branch swayed again. I stared at it for a minute. And then I relaxed. A false alarm. I noticed the leaves on the swaying branch were all upside down. That is because it had been broken by an elephant and was hanging suspended to the place from which it was broken by the stems of some creepers that were strong enough to bear its weight.

There must be no talking whatever in a situation like the present, so I reached backwards, gripped Sher Khan, and once again placed him in the lead. Then I nodded my head as a signal for him to press on. We proceeded slowly and passed the suspended branch.

Under a bush we noticed that the dried grass had been dyed deeply with blood. It seemed to be all over the place, on the leaves and stems of the bush as well. The tiger must have lain down here. Perhaps he rolled on the ground. Perhaps he covered his injured face with its paws and got them all covered with gore too. That would account for the blood, spread so widely under the bush before us.

I touched Sher Khan again to halt him, and we listened for a full five minutes. But we heard not a sound. As carefully and silently as we were moving the two of us would necessarily have made some noise in the undergrowth over that dry terrain. If the tiger was nearby, he must surely have heard us. Then he would either growl in warning, attack, or slink away silently. But nothing of the kind happened.

The blood-trail now unexpectedly veered to the left and we knew that the tiger was making for a small stream that skirted the foothills. The wound must have been taking effect, and thirst had driven him there for water. At that time of the year the stream was dry except for a few isolated pools here and there. The tiger was making for one of these pools and the chances were that when he reached it he would lie up in the vicinity till he recovered from his wound or died of it, a lingering, starving, horrible death.

I hate wounding an animal and spare no pains, when I have done so, to follow it up and put it out of its misery. From the amount and nature of the blood lost by the tiger it looked as if my bullet had inflicted a severe wound from which there was little chance of recovery. Once more I thought of the dreadful lingering death that was in store for this animal unless I succeeded in finding it.

I stopped Sher Khan and we conferred in whispers for a few minutes. I knew of a pool on the river bed which I judged to be at least two miles away, but Sher Khan said there was a closer one, smaller but which held water throughout the year, higher up the stream and less than a mile from where we now stood. So we continued to follow the blood-trail, and as the Muslim predicted, after a short distance it veered to the left and made for the smaller pool, now directly ahead.

The ground sloped as we approached the stream bed and I was made aware of its nearness by the repeated cries of jungle-fowl that sheltered in the thick belt of trees and undergrowth that lined both banks, sustained in summer-time by the water that was hidden from sight but still flowed beneath the dry sand. In a few minutes the short dry grass, withered by the sun, was replaced by long green stems, the heat and sight of the sun was shut out by a canopy of trees, and I knew we had reached the rivulet.

The blood-trail went straight ahead; we were in sight of the dry sands of the stream-bed, stretching to right and left.

I can imagine the agony of the wounded beast that came here last night or in the early hours of this morning in search of water to allay its burning thirst, only to be confronted by this waterless stretch.

But Sher Khan whispered that the pool was just around the corner to our left, now a stone's throw away, and unerringly the trail led in that direction. Once again I changed places with my friend and took the lead. Tracking was unnecessary now, as clearly the wounded tiger was making for the pool and I felt we would find it there. We turned a corner but I could see no pool. I stopped in silent perplexity, when Sher Khan came up from behind to point to an outcrop of flat rock which could just be seen above the sand of the stream and within a few feet of the further bank.

A plover rose the air from the rock, crying 'Did-you-do-it! Did-you-do-it! Did-you-do-it!', and I knew that water lay hidden from my view in a hollow of that rock. The stream had narrowed there and both banks had come very close to each other. The undergrowth was dense, and the forest loomed menacingly around and above us from the ground that dipped down to the bed of the rivulet.

We halted again. There was silence and no indication of the tiger's presence. I looked down and could see no blood-trail. Evidently in did not approach across the sandy bed, but kept to the cover of the undergrowth bordering the banks.

Forward we went once more. We were there at last, and what a sad story revealed itself in the water of the tiny pool and the sloping rock that led down to it. For the water was red with blood, and the rock was sticky with it, where the tiger had evidently lain in agony with his head in the water to assuage his thirst and to lessen the pain of his wound. His pugmarks were visible on the rock in several places, steeped in his own blood. Finally he had gone to the shelter of the bank and I knew that there was where I would find him; laying in the cool of the undergrowth like all striken animals, he would await his end with patience.

Then I remembered that this animal had been responsible for killing a human being, as far as could be made out for no apparent reason. If not brought to book, he would no doubt in time have became a confirmed man-eater. Motioning to Sher Khan to stay where he was, I advanced to meet him and finish him off.

I heard a slight sound behind me and looked around. Sher Khan was following. Perhaps he wanted to be present to witness the last scene in this drama. Perhaps he was just nervous at being left alone. We advanced into the dense undergrowth beneath the canopy of trees and were lost to sight.

The silence that had reigned all this while was then broken by a shattering roar that seemed to come from the very ground at my feet, and things began to happen very fast. Momentarily the undergrowth was agitated violently and then a mighty form launched itself past, and almost over me, on to Sher Khan who was not two feet behind.

The Muslim yelled and swiped wildly his rusty sword. The blunt edge met the bulk of the springing tiger and the impetus of both objects caused the blade to bite into the flank of the animal. Sher Khan went down, still screaming, and the tiger fell on top him.

Fortunately, Sher Khan had the presence of mind to cover his head and face with his two arms as the tiger sought to bite him. Leaning forward, I placed the rifle behind its neck, ensuring the bullet would not endanger my friend, and pressed the trigger.

I fired once again while Sher Khan scrambled to his feet

and leaped out of range of the dying creature's claws. Then the drama was over.

Strangely enough, my friend was practically unhurt except for a few scratches, and the reason was that my bullet of the night before had gone into his upper palate and come out above his nose. The whole frontal or nasal bone hung loosely by the flesh — a truly ghastly wound from which the poor beast could never have recovered.

It was fortunate that the blow my friend aimed at the tiger with his ancestor's rusty sword had met its marks for I was directly in line with it. Had he missed, Tipu, the Tiger of Mysore and his henchman of long ago, Sher Khan's ancestor, would have claimed one more victim! I would have been decapitated by the force of that blow.

Sher Khan laughed afterwards when I told him this. He said I had my own revenge when my bullet, fired into the tiger's neck, had passed but a few inches above his head. He asked me if he might have the skin of the animal as a memento of our encounter and I gladly gave it to him. For, despite his many faults and his rascality, Sher Khan is a brave man and a most likeable fellow. Above all, I admire the way in which he manages his four wives. Long may they be spared to him, and he to them.

We sat by the camp-fire before I left him and swapped yarns. He told me some of his adventures while I smoked my pipe and listened. Beyond the leaves all was lost in the darkness of the jungle night. Now and again a burst of sparks soared skywards as one of us threw a fresh log on to the fire to keep it brightly burning.

From behind his hut came suddenly the jungle chorus of the jackal pack: 'Oooo-ooo-oooh; Ooo-where? Ooo-where? Here! Here! Heere! Hee-yeah! Heeee-yeah!' Yah! Yah! Yah!'

After that there was an abrupt hush. A heavy, all-pervading

silence. You can hear it, you feel it, you know it. It is the silence that heralds the unexpected. As complete as if a switch had been turned.

Then, far away across the hill the second came rolling down to us, permeating the jungle and riding across the tops of the trees in the valley below.

'Oo-o-o-n-o-o-n! A-oongh - gah! A-oongh - gah! Oo — ugh! Oo - Ugh!'

A tiger roaring.

Jungles Long Ago

Introduction

AMONG THE PLEASURES OF WRITING BOOKS ARE THE LETTERS THAT often come to an author from readers all over the world. Some of them are highly flattering and add to the writer's vanity as they record the hours of enjoyment derived from his stories. A few ask questions and demand an early answer, while others seek to put the author on the spot in one way or the other.

Recently I received a letter from England in which I was asked why I preach animal preservation in nearly all my books, while most of my stories are about shooting them. But I feel that most of my readers will believe and understand me when I say that I have never killed for pleasure, at least not since I was very young. I do plead guilty for the sins of my youth; but the urge to slay wantonly died in me comparatively early; since then I have been able to kill only in cases of necessity.

Due to something I once told Malcolm Barnes, my publisher, which he included in his foreword to my last book, Tales of the Indian Jungle, I have received many letters urging me to continue writing, if for no other reason than to increase public interest in the jungles and the wild life that remains in India. So I have decided to try to do just that, but in this new book there are no stories of shooting man-eaters, or of shooting anything for that matter. Instead, you will find reminiscences of adventures in the jungle a long time ago. Some of the things we did then were pointless; some were just crazy and I would not have the guts to undertake them again today, now that I am, I hope, a wiser man. And there is a chapter on occult lore and another on jungle medicine.

All these reminiscences are jewels in a long chain of memories — precious jewels that sparkle for me brightly as I gaze at each and remember it once again, reliving those wonderful days — and nights — when we passed each exciting moment so happily, so fully, with never a thought of the what — might — have — happened or what — might — happen. The present was all that mattered and we lived each moment to the full.

Those were the times when there were no problems, no frustrations, no anxieties for the future. We were of and in the jungle, and that was all that mattered — with the trees and the animals and the sunshine about us in the daytime, and the moon and the stars and the fireflies, the croaking of frogs and the chirping of the crickets by night, we were in a paradise of contentment, the calls of frightened deer and the chorus of a pack of jackals were the music to which we fell asleep besides the embers of our fires, stoked now and again by the one whose turn it was to be on 'sentry-go', so to speak, as he added a bunch of faggots or a small log, when the sparks would leap skywards, pursued by a billow of smoke.

Camp life was relaxing in every sense of the word; but we were strict, very strict, very strict about the duties of the 'sentry' for two hours, which was the length of time each of the party was obliged to spend in protecting the camp, and for which we cast lots the evening before.

The 'sentry' was required to stoke the fire and keep his senses alert for the approach of elephants, particularly of a single bull. Also to listen to the sounds and cries of the night, from which his comrades would be able to learn what had happened in the forest while they slept. The offender who was caught dozing at his post not only became the butt of caustic comment, but was compelled to do a double duty the following night.

So imagine now that you are seated before this fire. You are in a glade of a great forest; towering trees surround you, clothed in a cloak of blackness broken by a thousand sparklets, the myriad tropical fireflies. Close your eyes and listen to my tales of tigers, of adventure and mystery, as the jungle breezes waft the night scent of the wild flowers on a cool current that fans your brow, and remember that you are in a land where time is of no consequence and the word 'hurry' is never spoken.

One

A Night in Spider Valley

ERIC NEWCOMBE, WHO FIGURES SO LARGELY IN THIS STORY, WAS AT school with me. We were great friends, and one of the reasons for this was that Eric had a very pretty sister.

Unfortunately, he was one of those people occasionally encountered who have an inevitable attraction for trouble. To make my meaning clear, if you were with Eric you could surely expect something unfortunate to happen. It was almost a certainty.

Sometime, as boys, we raided orchards, or we raided the girls' school at night, dressed as ghosts or Red Indians, or the dormitories of the convent, running the gauntlet of the nuns a dozen times; yet we always escaped, except when Eric was with us. For we tried it all again with him in the party. Dressed as 'yoemen' of old — Eric was 'Guy Fawkes', I remember — we had once terrified the girls in their beds at the convent and were making good our escape, pursued by various nuns with umbrellas, but vaulting over the wall to freedom, at whose feet do you think we fell? None other than our own headmaster, returning from a late night about which he was careful not to speak.

Eric was such a bumpkin that, not content with falling in love with a girl whose parents strongly disapproved, he had to fall off the wall he had climbed over in order to see her and to break his arm in the process. And when we were in pursuit of the 'The Killer of Jalahalli', a panther that had been wounded, whose story I have already told.[1] Eric, who was with me, had to go and get himself mauled. Not long afterwards we visited a circus and Eric conceived the idea of stroking a panther in its cage. As might have been expected, the panther resented this familiarity and badly clawed his hand. I might mention that for both of these catastrophies I got all the blame from his wife, for he had married that girl some years after falling off the wall.

Then one night we went to shoot wild-pig at Gulhatti. It poured with rain. We were sitting in a field for the pig, but I decided to give up and return to the forest bungalow. But not Eric. What was a little rain after all, we asked? He would bag a pig regardless. He got pneumonia instead, and his wife blamed me even for that!

I have told you about these incidents so that you might appreciate that I was not over-enthusiastic when this Jonah suggested we do a night jaunt into the jungle in search of adventure. To ensure we met with excitement in some shape or form, he stressed we should go unarmed but should carry torches and a supply of food. That was something at least. He was such a crazy character that I would not have been surprised in the least had he made in mandatory that we went torchless and foodless as well.

---

1. See: *Nine Man-Eaters and One Rogue.*

Eric was very likeable, extremely persuasive, very fond of nature and the wild, quite unassuming and altogether irresponsible. He was quite unaware of the possible trouble that some of his actions could bring to him and his unfortunate companions. I am always game for an adventure, but when I realised it was to be in the company of this amiable character, I do confess I felt a considerable degree of doubt.

Those of you who have read of my adventures with the tiger I have called 'The Novice of Manchi'[2] and my earlier story about 'The Marauder of Kempekerai',[3] will remember the valley I have described in those stories and which I called 'Spider Valley'. It is a deep and densely forested valley in the District of Salem, extending southward for about twenty miles from a little hamlet named Aiyur and enclosed between two lofty mountain ranges.

This valley is the bed of a stream, and a narrow footpath accompanies the stream, crossing it every now and then as the stream turns to right and left in an attempt to shorten the overall distance. The mountain ranges to west and east tower above the valley bottom, sometimes oppressively close, giving the traveller the impression that he is in a leafy tunnel. A delightful forest lodge, known as the Kodekarai bungalow, on the slopes of the Gutherayan peak at a height of over 4,000 feet, and to the east of the valley, overlooks the scene as the stream and the valley struggle onward to their ultimate junction ten miles away with the Chinar river, itself a tributary of the great Cauvery river, which is the biggest in South India.

We chose 'Spider Valley' for *ghoom* (a Hindustani word signifying to 'wander' or 'stroll') for a variety of reasons. It was a very densely forested area and abounded in those days

2. See: *The Tiger Roars*.
3. See: *Man-Eaters and Jungle Killers*.

with elephant, bison, tiger, panther and bear. Sambar and jungle-sheep, rather than spotted-deer, were plentiful because of the hilly terrain and adjacent mountain ranges. Rock snakes, commonly termed pythons, were said to be present in numbers, and smaller animal life was abundant. The tall, waving bamboos and the damp undergrowth were the home of millions of fireflies as well as of a luminiscent beetle and three varieties of 'glow-worm'. Finally, I knew it to be the only area in Salem District where, by virtue of the dampness the evergreen jungle, a hamadryad (king cobra) might be encountered.

In those early days I owned a fleet of Model T Fords, thirteen of them at one time in fact and all in running order. Purchased at various military auctions as scrap at prices ranging from Rs. 50/- to Rs.250 (£2.50 to £12.50), I tinkered with them and put them back upon the road for use on my trips to the jungle. The cheapest buy was an engine on its chassis and wheels for Rs.12 (about 60p.). Upon this chassis I fixed a body consisting of a dual-purpose box *machan* that could be rigged up on a tree or placed over a hole dug in the earth. Handles helped to fix this *machan* to a tree, while loopholes in the sides provided apertures for firing when it was employed to cover a pit dug in the ground. The whole contraption, as I have indicated, was clamped to the chassis of the model to form an inverted compartment in which to carry my tools, food, water and bedding. A comfortable cane chair, secured over the petrol-tank, made a fine driving-seat. As for mudguards, there were none. Nor a windshield. A pair of dark glasses served to keep the grit out of my eyes.

It is true I was covered with dust by journey's end, or bespattered with mud on a rainy day, but this added to the fun. a companion, if there was one, would be seated on a similar cane chair to my left, and I would delight in driving the left front wheel of this vehicle very skilfully through pools of rain-water or heaps of cow-dung, and laugh when he was showered with mud or worse.

Eric had a great liking for this vehicle which he called 'Sudden Death' and was adamant that we should make our journey in it, or rather on it, which would be a truer term, in preference to any of the other Model Ts.

I must tell you that it was, and still is, against the law to travel about on a chassis as a regular means of transport. The law requires that there must be a regular body of some sort on any vehicle. The question of registering 'Sudden Death' and obtaining a number for it had therefore to be solved. You will remember it was sold as scrap and had no number at the time. So I removed the number-plate from one of my other Model Ts and drove that vehicle down to the registration office for the needful action. On the application form that had to be filled in was entered both the engine number and chassis number of 'Sudden Death'. The engine and chassis numbers of the vehicle used as a substitute were doctored with a coating of shellac which made them indecipherable; it could be removed later by scraping and a few drops of petrol. 'Sudden Death' was duly registered and given a new number. That, too, under its very own engine and chassis serial numbers. The law was powerless after that to prosecute me for driving about on a chassis that did not have a regular body, for the portable *machan* could not officially be regarded as such. The car that had been presented in its place resumed its own identity when its own number was put back after the shellac coating had been removed.

There were two other features about 'Sudden Death' which I have still to record. The first was that I have fitted it with a special carburettor — also picked up as scrap — which enabled me to start the engine on petrol, and switch to kerosene when it had heated up. A Model To covered about twenty-four miles to the gallon. Petrol in those days cost fourteen *annas* per gallon (about £0.05), and kerosene 8 *annas* a gallon, or about half the price. So motoring on kerosene was economical indeed. Engine oil was 31/2 Rs. or £0.20 a gallon, while brand new tyres were around Rs. 15 or £0.70 each.

The other feature of 'Sudden Death' was a Ruxtel back axle. This provided a very low and a very high gear, in addition to the two transmission gears operated by pedal on every Model T. 'Sudden Death' could, therefore, because of her 22 hp engine and light weight almost climb a wall, and on the flat she could nip along under kerosene at a speed that made many a new car look like a tortoise. As for a failing sparkplug, I never bothered to carry a spare. Pending cleaning it when I had the time to do so, all that was required was removal from the cylinder head, for 'Sudden Death' would then snort along on three cylinders as if she had never had a fourth!

As we would be on the move all night, we planned to wear the lightest clothing, the proverbial khaki, while I donned the pair of knee-length, alpaca-lined, rubber-soled boots that I generally wore on such prowls. They are light, noiseless and soft, but thick enough to absorb the fangs of any Russell's viper or a cobra that might be lurking in the undergrowth and inadvertently stamped upon. Eric wore rubber-soled boots with the ends of his pants tucked into them. Snakes offer the greatest hazard at night, far greater than that of running into an elephant or a bear. Tigers and panthers, unless man-eaters, wounded or in the act of mating, offer practically no danger at all.

'Sudden Death' took us to the Aiyur Forest Lodge without incident. Here we had dinner. Then, carrying our food and a change of clothing in haversacks upon our backs, and a bag of spare torch-cells each, we set forth for Spider Valley, the best part of three miles away. I had a five-cell torch hanging in a cloth case at my side while I used a three-cell torch, handier for spotting. Eric carried a pair of three-cell torches.

There is a fire line leading through the forest in a southeasterly direction from the lodge. After nearly a mile this traverses the edge of a water-hole, then changes direction westwards and after some time meets a track leading up a hill to another forest lodge at a place named Gulhatti.

At this water-hole we have our first adventure. Our torches revealed a row of twin-pointed green lights on the opposite bank of the pool which kept bobbing up and down restlessly in an attempt to escape the unwinking stare of our torch-beams. A herd of spotted-deer have been caught in the act of drinking!

I sank to my haunches to watch them, but Eric left the path we were following and moved down towards the water. This was a mistake, for his clothing got caught in the wait-a-bit thorns that clustered around the pool. Apart from scratching himself, he made quite a lot of noise and made yet another mistake. He moved into the beam from my torch, thereby revealing to the deer that the bright objects they had been staring at all this while, but could not quite identify, were connected with their deadliest enemy — man. With a drumming of hooves the herd disappeared like magic. But a far more ominous sound took its place.

'Woof! Woof! Woof!' A bear had come down to drink. And he, too, had done the unexpected thing.

He must have been moving along the very pathway we had been following and had decided to drink. So he went down to the pool just ahead of Eric. Being hard of hearing and poor of sight, the bear did not hear us at first, nor notice our torch-beams. Maybe he had his head down and was drinking. But when Eric began to crash about and show himself in my light, and the spotted-deer thundered away in alarm, the bear realised that something was cooking and that something was directly behind him.

Like all his kind when they get alarmed, he did not wait to think. It did not even occur to him to run away. Instead, he rushed headlong at the intruder. Time enough for him to find out the nature of the intruder later. So he charged straight at Eric at top speed, and Eric at the moment was caught in the wait-a-bit thorns!

What did he do at this critical moment! He hurled his three-cell torch straight at the oncoming bear, then only a few feet away. Only he could have done such a thing.

Here was a bear coming hell for leather at the light when — behold!— the light came hell for leather at him! By luck the torch struck Bruin somewhere in the face, with the result that, as quickly as he had made up his mind to charge, he now made up his mind to run away. Veering to his left he disappeared in a crashing of bushes and loud'Woofs1' Eric left the thorns with some of his clothing adhering there, rushed to where I stood rooted to the spot, and exclaimed 'A bear!'

I remained silent.

We turned due west for some time and then south along a much narrower track, which was the pathway we were to follow for twenty miles till it met the Chinar river. It led downhill and we entered Spider Valley. The vegetation grew densely on all sides; the lantana bushes, with their clusters of red, pink and orange coloured flowers, visible in our torch-beams, were rapidly giving away to increasingly dense clumps of bamboo.

Then we heard the sounds of elephants: a crash as one of these monsters tore down a culm of bamboo, followed by a curious 'wheenk' as the tender upper leaves and outer skins of which elephants are very fond were peeled off. Finally the thicker base stem was cast away. Truly wasteful creatures they are; for the sake of a basketful of tender leaves and skin, a whole massive culm has been destroyed.

Was this animal alone, or was there a whole herd grazing at the head of the valley for which we were making? We squatted on the ground to await further evidence, and for a while there was absolute silence. Then we heard the swishing as the elephant beat upon the ground a bunch of leaves that he had gathered at the end of his trunk preparatory to stuffing the whole lot into his mouth.

Then silence again, but not for long: 'Phutt! Phutt! Phutt! Phutt!', followed by a prolonged 'whooshing' sound.

He was closer to us than we had thought for these sounds revealed that he was answering the call of nature. It was also becoming apparent that he was probably alone.

He was directly ahead of us and the breeze was blowing from us in his direction, so that it could only be a matter of minutes, if not seconds, before he caught our scent. Then one of three things might happen.

Normally he should just have melted away into the jungle as elephants have a habit of doing, regardless of their great bulk, when they get scent of man. On the other hand he might stand absolutely still, as motionless as a rock, hoping that we might either pass him by without noticing his presence, or if he was on mischief bent, to allow us to come close enough to enable him to charge down upon us devastatingly. The third, but most improbable alternative, was to charge us without further ado. Elephants, even when in 'musth' or in an other-irritable mood, are unlikely to do this. The majority think things over for a minute or two before acting.

I was about to grab Eric and move off to the left to start a long detour in order to avoid the creature when a fresh sound came to our ears: 'Quink! Quink! Quink!' The sound of a baby elephant nuzzling up to its mother.

We now knew we were in far less danger: unless one gets too close to such a baby, a herd will generally avoid human being. It is the solitary elephant one has to be careful of.

At least, that was way things ought to have gone.

But there were other factors. For one thing, it was night; for another, the beams from our torches would frighten the elephants, even annoy them. We had deliberately chosen a dark night, for although the jungle looks pleasantly ethereal in the moonlight, to move about in such light gives one's position away far sooner than in real darkness. Further, our torch-beams would not carry very far in moonlight and the reflection of the eyes of an animal would be far weaker than in pitch darkness.

We had already agreed to talk as little as possible, so I extinguished my torch and with my free hand reached out to grasp and turn off Eric's too. For a moment the darkness was intense, then as our eyes became accustomed to the gloom, the darkness softened and the glitter of the stars added considerable illumination to our surroundings.

The silence continued to be intense. It became oppressive. It got on our nerves. Eventually it became ominous as we began to feel we were being watched.

A low and continued rumbling like distant thunder came from our right. But the sky was clear and star-spangled, so the noise could not possibly herald rain. Where did it come from?

Eric was staring hard to the right as we heard the rumbling again. I could see he was a little alarmed. Finally he put his lips to my ear and asked in a whisper, 'Do you hear that? Can it be a tiger?'

I raised my finger to my mouth to enjoin silence, rubbed my stomach with my other hand, and stabbed my forefinger in the direction where we had first heard the elephants. The starlight was bright enough for us to see each other and Eric recognised my action. I was trying to tell him that the rumbling sound came from the digestive processes of an elephant's stomach.

There are five fundamental lessons a night-prowler should learn if he hopes to prowl with success, whether 'ghooming' like ourselves or reconnoitring the front lines of an 'enemy'. The first is not to talk, or even whisper, on any account. The second is to 'freeze' at sight or sound of an animal or an enemy as the case may be. The third is to keep to the shadows and avoid crossing open spaces. The fourth is to be careful where you place your foot, for even if it is too dark to see, taking a false step into thorns or causing the dried leaves to rustle, will give away your position. You must cultivate the habit on these occasions of moving each foot forward in the manner of soldiers on a ceremonial slow-step parade rather than raising the knee and bringing the foot downwards, as in normal walking. Of course, this requires a little practice, but more than that it needs conscious forethought, remembering to use the 'glide-step' in a night-time '*ghoom*' rather than lapsing forgetfully into your ordinary walk.

The fifth and least thing to remember at all times, especially when you 'freeze', is to 'freeze' literally and not keep fidgeting about, slapping at mosquitoes, scratching, raising your hands to your face, and such-like actions.

You should never forget that the faintest whisper becomes audible in the still night air, while the slightest motion attracts the attention of an alert animal, or an enemy, as the case may be, and will give you away. Bear these five tips in mind always if you have occasion to go out on a night '*ghoom*', or under different circumstances if you don't want to invite an enemy bullet in your direction. Eric had broken the very first of them by whispering to me and the nearest elephant had heard him.

An instant later there came an earth-shaking 'Tri-aa-ank! Tri-aa-ank'—the alarm cry of a frightened female.

These huge creatures are almost unpredictable. You can never say how they may react even under exactly similar circumstances, though with a wide experience of them in the wild, I can say that usually, under certain conditions, you may expect one of them to behave in this way or that.

After that alarm call, pandemonium reigned for a short time. Then followed a chorus of cries from all around us: 'Kakk! Kakk! Kakk!' as mothers summoned their young peremptorily, accompanied by 'Quink! Quink! Quink!' as a dozen baby-elephants hurried to shelter beneath their mothers' bellies. What was more frightening was a prolonged roar from the stream-bed now only a few yards in front of us.

'Ahha-a-a-a-a-ah!Ahha-a-a-a-a-ah!' A bull-elephant, probably the master of the herd, had herd the alarm signal of his mates; he cried his reassurance as he hurried to their aid, while another male, this time to our left but further off also answered with a roar. Then the first bull, coming headlong toward us, splashed through the water. We heard the squelching as he hurried across the stream, roaring as he came.

We were unarmed, remember, and on foot. I grabbed Eric by the elbow. We turned and scurried back along the path. No time, now, for cautious walking. Rather, we broke into a jog-trot.

Meanwhile the bull behind us, still roaring, rejoined the females who had raised the first alarm. He had stopped roaring now. Only the squeals and squeaks of the young and the coughing 'Kakk! Kakk!' calls of summoning mothers could be heard. The second bull, who had also been roaring, had probably joined them as well, for his roars stopped too.

If either or both the bulls decided to chase us now, as

likely as not they would start off in silence and only give vent to the shrieking trumpet-sound of attack when they actually saw or scented us. This would be quite different in timbre from the shrill cry of fear and alarm first voiced by the frightened cow. The attacking note is pitched higher and is more prolonged. There is no mistaking the quality of hatred, anger and menace that is put into such a sound, while the alarm-cry is lower-pitched and of shorter, quicker duration, rarely voiced more than twice in succession.

Instead, we heard crashing sounds which seemed to be receding behind us. The 'quicks' of the young had stopped. Evidently the leader had decided that discretion was the better part of valour and was taking his charges away. Now numerous splashings announced that the animals were crossing the stream. We stopped running and sat down to listen.

A few moments later complete silence reigned except for a distant 'Ponk! Ponk! Ponk! as a sambar doe, high up on a hillside to our right, who had heard all the commotion below, decided some danger might be afoot and voiced her own alarm.

Eric brought his lips to my ear again and whispered 'what now?'

I shrugged, held up the palm of a hand to signify we should wait a little and then, by pointing my forefinger down into the valley, indicated that we would continue our journey. Eric saw my point. Having stared, we were not going back just for the sake of a few elephants.

We waited perhaps fifteen minutes to allow the herd to move out of the way. Then we got up and continued our cautious progress down the valley. Very soon we reached the stream. It was perhaps twenty yards wide at this spot. The water reached almost from bank to bank, which accounted for the great amount of splashing we heard when the elephants crossed over, but it was barely knee-deep, as we found out of ourselves when we followed the path which cut across the stream for the first time.

The undergrowth on the farther bank was very dense. There was less lantana here and a great deal of 'vellari' shrubbery in its place, while mighty trees with trunks of great girth met overhead, their branches crowding and completely obscuring the starlight. Bamboos in profusion grew in massive clumps on both banks of the stream.

The darkness was stygian and a high breeze, which had just risen, blowing down the valley from behind us, caused the bamboos to creak and groan and their culms to bend and thrash wildly against one another. This breeze was unfortunate; we did not like it at all. Coming from behind, it would spread our scent far and wide and warn the animals ahead of our approach. Carnivora have a very poor sense of smell, so it hardly mattered as far as they were concerned, but deer and elephant would know we were coming long in advance of our arrival. We would not see many of the former, while the latter, unless on mischief bent, would give us a wide berth. At the same time, the noise made by the breeze filled the air and prevented us from hearing anything else.

I walked ahead, flashing my three-cell, while Eric followed closely. I had cautioned him not to use his torch, as its beams would fall upon myself and advertise my presence. Further, the light of a second torch from behind is very distracting to the person in front, for various reasons.

The elephant herd had taken itself off in some other direction, and for the time being, at least, there was neither sight nor sound of them, although we found ample evidence of their recent presence in the valley in the form of broken branches, chewed fragments of bamboo, and huge balls of dung all over the pathway.

A moment later something sticky and clammy clung to my

face. I could not see it although my torch was lit. Then I recognised what it was: I had walked into the web of one of those enormous spiders that live in large numbers in this valley, and for which reason I had called it 'Spider Valley'. These spiders are huge, often measuring as much as ten inches from leg-tip to leg-tip across the body. This one was not great in bulk, however, perhaps the size of a large marble. The abdomen and thorax were black with vivid stripes of yellow running around and across. The eyes were large and blood-red and reflected torchlight as if two large rubies were hanging side by side in mid-air. the legs were long, hairless, black and powerful, as if made of wire.

I had watched these creatures spinning their webs in daylight. They climb to a high branch and from there they let themselves drop, emitting a thread behind them. When they judge they have fallen far enough, they control any further fall by the simple expedient of not emitting further thread. In this position, head downwards, they hang till a gust of breeze blows the thread close enough to some leaf or branch, to which they immediately cling and attach the thread. If no breeze comes within an appreciable time, the spider climbs up the line of web thread by which it has descended, and tries all over again from a more advantageous position.

Having secured the first line of its thread as a sort of bridgehead, it climbs to the top of this second tree and repeats the action by dropping itself from there while adjusting the length of thread emitted from its abdomen till it meets the first line of web, to which it attaches this new strand. Waiting for the breeze again, it drops lower to reach some point a few feet off the ground and a little distance from the first tree from which it began its operation.

The spider has now spun a huge X, extending some fifteen to twenty feet across. It now returns to the point it had started from and begins to connect all four corners of the letter X to each other by running up and down the arms of the letter X until it has made a huge rectangle with the X in the centre.

The rest is simple; the spider moves around and around, weaving strands of web in parallel lines all around, and perhaps half-an-inch from each other. All this is mighty hard work, but the spider I watched one morning, just starting work on its web as I walked down this valley, had finished by the time I returned that way late the same evening: a wonderful exhibition of precision engineering for an insect of its size.

These creatures will devour anything that gets caught in their webs, butterflies, moths, beetles, and even the smaller species of birds whose blood it consumes. The strands of its webs, although no thicker than the finest thread are very elastic and incredibly strong. Even a single strand will not break easily under strain. Moreover, the substance that forms this strand is very sticky.

Once the work is done, the spider takes up its position in the centre of the web with its legs outstretched. In this position, due to its colouring, it looks like some leaf-stem or other insignificant object suspended in midair. It hangs motionless, but entirely alert. As soon as some creature flies inadvertently against the web, the sticky substance of which the strands are made adhere to it. The creature flutters and struggles, thus fouling other sticky strands.

Immediately, the spider in the middle of the web comes to life. It scurries towards its prey and scampers swiftly around and around it, emitting an endless flow of threads until the prey is entirely encased and enmeshed.

Then comes the final sad scene. The spider approaches its helpless victim, bites it and starts sucking out all its blood and body-juices, growing fatter and fatter itself in the process till frequently it more than doubles its own size. The prey, on the other hand, collapses as an empty bag of outer skin or as an empty shell, should the victim happen to be a beetle. When all is over, the spider repairs the damage done to its web in the struggle; it does this at once, without postponing the work till some future opportunity. Then it returns to its position in the centre, pending the arrival of its next victim. Spiders are voracious and seem to possess an insatiable appetite.

This spider is very pugnacious and will fight to the death against any one of its own kind who attempts to tresspass into its web. I witnessed this for myself years ago, when I deliberately placed one of these spiders upon the web of a companion of the same species. A battle royal ensued, in the process of which legs were quickly torn off each combatant. The tresspaser lost in the end, after five of its legs had been bitten off by the spider who owned the web and who had lost two of its own legs in the battle. Those that remained, however, were enough to enmesh the trespasser securely in a ball of webbing. then came the coup-de-grace, the blood-sucking process, at which stage I ended my observations.

I brushed the web from my face and continued on our way. The path became narrower and the forest on both sides became dense. My torch-beam danced from one grey tree-trunk to the next; the moss and lichens that covered them looked like the beards of thousands of old men hanging to the ground.

Suddenly a stillness fell upon the jungle, a hush that could be felt as well as heard. Eric observed it, too, and quickened his steps. His toes kicked against my heels and he involuntarily touched my elbow. I halted in my tracks and he bumped into me. I extinguished the torch and sank down upon my haunches. In a jungle, the closer one can get to the ground, the better one can hear. For a moment Eric wondered where I was and groped with his hands in the darkness about me. Then he whispered 'Scotchie?'

It is a nick-name by which I was known at school,-though I rarely hear it today. My old school-pals have practically disappeared. Many have gone abroad, while a large number have made the last journey we all must make. The thought makes me feel lonely at times.

I wondered what could be the cause of that hush, that almost palpable silence that hung so heavily about us. Reason told me there might be many explanations. The sudden cutting-off of the breeze that was blowing all this while from behind us by some hilly spur that we had circumvented in the darkness; an opposing breeze, blowing northwards up the great rift yawned before us in the night; a hush before a storm, a moment when all Nature appears to hold her breath in preparation for the fast approaching tempest.

The darkness was intense and there was no break in the gloom, even when I gazed upwards. the tree-tops were lost in obscurity and the stars that until a few moment ago were visible here and there through the canopy of leaves were now completely obliterated. That was when I came to know the reason for the strange silence that had fallen all around us. Indeed, a storm was approaching!

To witness such a phenomenon in the tropics is unforgettable, whether on land or at sea; but to have to undergo it upon the ground in a dense forest is hardly an enviable prospect. People sometimes run under a tree to shelter from the rain, but that is not the kind of rain we have in India, particularly in the jungles, and it certainly was no safe place when the tree itself might be split in two by lightning or torn up by the roots in the wind.

A moment later came a vivid flash overhead. It seemed to rend the canopy of the tree-tops and scatter the darkness with a single blaze of ethereal light. The heart of the storm was so close that it seemed but a fraction of a second before the thunder-clap followed in an outrageous, monstrous roar, as of thousand cannon firing in unison. The earth upon which we stood shuddered and the overhanging foliage quivered with the resonance of the thunder; the very universe seemed to tremble.

There was nothing to do but crouch close to the ground. To remain standing is to invite injury from falling branches. Together we scrambled towards the trunk of a nearby tree. I made certain it was one of medium height and not one of the greater specimens whose top would reach to the upper trellises of the jungle, for the loftier the tree the more it would present itself as a target for the lightning which, in violent electrical storms of this kind, can be expected to strike at any moment.

The hush and the darkness returned, but not for long. There was another, more intense flash, followed by an even louder clap of thunder. The third flash was not a flash at all. Like a great serpent of fire from the sky, the lightning struck a giant tree somewhere in the jungle and the thunder that followed seemed to burst our ear-drums and numb us with its intensity.

The next moment we heard a mighty, rushing uproar approaching towards us up the valley, like a hundred breakers in unison dashing upon a rocky beach. This was the wind and as it came closer one gained the impression that the trees of the forest were bracing themselves for the onslaught.

It was almost upon us now, and together with this fearsome, roaring sound we heard the staccato reports of hundreds of branches as they snapped like matchwood in the irresistible squall. Above the rushing of the wind we heard the louder thudding and crashing of falling branches and trees, and the creaking, tearing, and rending of timber. Here and there, trees of outstanding height or bulk, by reason of their top-weight and resistance to the wind, were uprooted from the earth and fell with resounding crashes, bringing down a host of minor trees and saplings that were unlucky enough to be sheltering below.

The gale continued for a few minutes only then passed as suddenly as it had begun. The trees lifted themselves again, many of them bereft of half their foliage. All was quiet for a short while except for the diminishing roar of the wind as it receded up the valley.

A new sound soon became audible, growing rapidly in intensity as it drew nearer: a continuous, hissing noise like escaping steam. The rain.

Now it was upon us. What was dry ground and foliage a moment earlier was in the twinkling of an eye converted into a sodden morass of mud and greenery. The best of umbrellas and raincoats would be of no avail in a downpour of this intensity, and we were carrying no umbrellas or raincoats anyway. Not only were we soaked to the skin, but the little equipment and food on our backs was equally saturated. Water poured down our bodies and flowed down our pants, filling our shoes, including my prized alpaca-lined boots, to the brim. This footwear was sold under a guarantee of being waterproof. It now proves the merit of that advertisement, but in an inverse manner. The water that had filled it remained where it was and refused to leak out.

The rain went on and on.

The little stream which was wont to purl and ripple over smooth, mossy stones as it meandered hither and thither, gliding down its course, did none of these nice things any longer. It dashed, lashed and smashed against the rocks in its course, accompanied by a thudding and grinding of torn branches and tree-trunks that were swept down by the flood. The water rose higher and covered the rocks and boulders that obstructed its path. it became a raging, unbroken flow, crested by the flotsam and jetsam that was whirled and tossed helplessly in the mad grip of the swirling flood.

The ground upon which we were standing was a foot deep in mud and there was not the slightest indication of the rain abating. But it lasted only a little more than an hour, and then it passed as swiftly at its precursor, the wind.

There were a million noises around us now, the dripping from the leaves, the gurgling rush of the stream, the frequent 'plop' from its banks as large section of earth, soaked by the rain and undermined by the raging torrent, collapsed into the flood.

We felt very miserable indeed. Unspoken thoughts turned to home, the comfort of bed and warm blankets, a steaming cup of tea, a relaxing pipe and a good book. What insane idea ever impelled us to start on a trip like this and place ourselves in such a predicament? Then recriminations passed. We forced ourselves to smile and begin to think what we should do next. We could only go back or press on. And who would think seriously of going back?

One thing was certain: we could not continue in our sodden clothing. As evaporation set in, our garments would grow colder and colder upon our bodies. Without clothes we could feel cold, admittedly, but at least we would not grow colder. However, logical or illogical this argument might seem, we divested ourselves entirely, poured the water from our boots and put them on again. Our wet clothes we secured to pieces of bamboo, which we shouldered in addition to our kit.

Now we were ready to continue but far from comfortable, I can assure you. The bamboo dug in itself into the flesh and the straps of our kitbags dug in too; thorns scraped our skins and our bare feet flopped about loosely in our boots; moreover, it was midnight and very cold.

Soon another hazard presented itself. We found ourselves slipping and slithering in the mud and ooze. The noise we were making by floundering along the soaked pathway and against the undergrowth on both sides of it would advertise our movements in the jungle for a furlong around. In any event, few animals would be on the move after the heavy downpour. Even the elephants would be inclined to call it a day — or rather, a night — and huddle together in some sheltered sport. Every creature would lie quiet; that is, every creature but the snakes! They would be up and about, hunting and gorging themselves upon the frogs that were making this night an occasion for rejoicing.

All around us we could hear these creatures croaking, particularly along the banks of the swollen stream. 'Korr! Korr! Korr! Quacker! Quacker! Quacker!' came the sound from a thousand bull-frog throats. The air droned with the noise. It vibrated and pulsated to the chorus of joy voiced by the what was obviously the whole frog-population of Spider Valley.

For this was mating-time, and the forest floor was littered with squashy, love-making couples upon which we could not avoid treading in the darkness.

For a moment I caught a glimpse of something white in the middle of the path. Then it was gone. Again it appeared briefly and then disappeared once more. I could see the ground where it vanished and got the impression of movement, although I could not recognise what it was.

I came to a stop and directed the torch-beam steadily upon the movement. Eric halted behind me. For a few second I could not make out what lay on the pathway, then I knew what it was: a snake!

I increased my pace, motioning to Eric to remain where

he was. Snake have no ears, but they make up for lack of hearing by an acute sense of feeling. Through the scale upon their bellies that rest against the ground they are able to sense danger from anything that moves by detecting the vibration caused by that movement.

The boots I was wearing had soft rubber soles and I was able to approach relatively undetected. The beam of my torch was directed upon the reptile but it did not appear to be disturbed. Coming from behind, the source of the torchlight was beyond the range of the snake's vision. Snakes' eyes are lidless and fixed, and cannot turn sideways or backwards. Nor did my approach register itself upon the reptile's brain which, at the moment, was completely engrossed upon the work in hand, the swallowing of a very large bull-frog in one piece.

I was close enough now to make out the details. The snake's jaws, not being hinged together, were distended grotesquely and the gullet swollen out of all proportion. The head and one fore-leg of the unfortunate frog had already disappeared down this passage, while the other three legs and the body hung limply outside. Normally, the creature should be kicking and struggling desperately to escape, but this frog was quite dead, and the reason was apparent. The snake was a cobra. The venom had killed the frog in a few seconds.

The cobra had not raised its hood in either alarm or anger, for it was still unaware of my approach, but the bulk of the bull-frog already in its gullet had sufficiently expanded the skin in the region to show up the characteristic V-mark. I was an ardent collector of snakes at that time, and the specimen before me was of outsize dimensions. I decided to catch it.

Unfortunately, the thick cloth bag I had brought for just such a purpose was with the kitbag on my back. I had to lay down the bamboo and my wet clothes before I could remove the kitbag from my back, and in all this movement the cobra became aware of our presence. It ejected the frog it had half-swallowed, turned around to face me and raised its hood, trembling with fury.

It was a magnificent specimen, but it would slither away in another second if I failed to put it into a fighting mood, so to do this I stamped my foot heavily upon the ground a couple of feet away. The cobra responded by raising itself still higher and then struck the ground at the spot where my foot had been but a moment before.

Meanwhile I was working feverishly to get kit-bag off my shoulders, unfasten the zip and grope with my hand amongst the many miscellaneous items in search of that snake-bag. The operation took a long time. The outside of the bag was soaking wet for one thing and I was working with one hand, unable to look for bag as I had to keep my eyes fixed upon the cobra.

At last I found it, pulled it out quickly and advanced towards the snake, which turned itself fully around to face me.

Catching a cobra is really very easy once you rivet its attention. It is only when the reptile is in rapid motion that the operation becomes difficult and entails considerable risk. In this instance, I stretched out my right hand, holding the cloth bag by its handle close to the snake's head. It quivered with fury, hissed loudly, and lunged at the bag. That is when I withdrew the bag so that the cobra, with hood fully distended, struck its head upon the ground for the second time.

One has to be quick at this moment, but there is really nothing to it. The quickness of action comes with practice. The length of bamboo on which I had slung my wet clothes was in my left hand. It came in handy now. I quickly pressed down upon the snake's neck, behind its head and above the hood, with the end of this bamboo about six inches from its tip. The ground was wet, so I has to be careful not to allow the head to slip free. Eric was to be of no assistance to me. I saw that he had retired a good ten yards away. I called to him urgently to come and hold my torch. He advanced reluctantly and took it from me.

'Hold the light steady,' I admonished. Then I stooped down, dropped the cloth bag and grasped the snake behind its neck with the thumb and forefinger of my right hand. Then I removed the bamboo. The snake coiled itself around my hand and forearm, but I uncoiled it with my left hand while urging Eric to pick up the bag.

He hesitated and I repeated, 'Hurry up; pick it up and open it.'

It seemed to me as if Eric was taking terribly long time to do just this, but eventually the bag was held in position and I forced the coils of the snake into it. Lastly I thrust the head inside, keeping the fingers of my left hand around the neck of the bag, released the snake's head and jerked my right hand out of the bag very quickly. Almost in the motion, I closed the neck of the bag with the fingers and thumb of my left hand.

That is all there is to catching a cobra. Some people have told me that it calls for nerve. Don't you believe that. In my opinion, it is just the opposite. There should be 'no nerve', or as few as possible. For it these are nerves, the snake-catcher may not be able to catch his snake. Worse still, he may hesitate in the middle of the operation, and that would be just too bad for him! The snake would catch him then with a bite upon his finger or hand.

I took care to tie up the neck of the bag very firmly and then thrust it back into my kitbag. A few minutes later we were on our way again.

For the next thirty minutes or so our discomfort increased because of the wet and cold. It would have been nice to stop and light a fire to dry our clothing and ourselves, but the whole jungle was sodden and such an operation was out of the question. However we were young and ardently keen upon adventure. Mind conquers such obstacles and we pressed on forgetful of our physical discomfort. Except for encountering the elephants at the head of the valley, we had had no fun and we were longing for something to happen.

The stream began to flow rapidly now among steep rocks; the ground became hard and the trees and bamboos were shorter and more sparse. Larger expanses of sky were visible, and we noticed that the clouds had cleared. Myriads of stars hung over us and shone brightly.

The parallel ranges of mountains to the right and left of us, as we walked southwards, corresponded respectively to the western and eastern banks of the stream. Now we observed that they seemed to be converging upon each other while the valley narrowed to the proportions of a ravine. We could see the dark, unbroken outline of ridges and mountain-tops on both sides as they towered upwards into the star-bedecked sky.

'Ayngh! Aa-u-ung! Oo-ooo ngh! Oo-ooo-ngh! Ooo-ooo-ooongh!'

We stopped in our tracks as we recognised that awesome sound. The canyon in which we were standing reverberated.

It was the call of tiger! The animal was to our left and close ahead. It had come down the eastern range and was about to cross the stream. We extinguished our torches and hurried forwards to try to intercept it.

'Ugh! Ugh! Ugha!Ugha! Oooo-h! Ooo-h! Ooo-ooo-nigh! Aungh-ha! Ugh!Ugh'!

The call was almost continuous now. The tiger was being very noisy. Was this a sign of impatience? I seemed to detect an imperious note. Then remembered that this was the month of February. Rather late in February, admittedly, but nevertheless February still — the mating season — or the tail end of it!

Here was the explanation of the prolonged semi-roars we were hearing. The beast was no tiger but a tigress. She was calling for a mate, and a tigress in this mood is not a very desirable creature to meet when unarmed.

As I have mentioned on many occasion, tigers are generally quite safe to meet, even when one is unarmed, with three exceptions — a man-eater, a wounded tiger, or a tiger in the mood for mating or in the act of mating. None of these conditions were literally fulfilled at that moment, but the third condition was very near.

The tigress continued her calling. She was but a short distance ahead now and still on our side of the stream. We were hurrying along that same bank. The stream was to our right. The flood water caused by the recent storm had abated considerably, but the stream must have been three or four feet deep at least. It the tigress intended to cross, she would have to swim.

As a rule tigers like water. Particularly in the hotter forests of Andhra Pradesh, I have come across them lying in shady pools to cool themselves when the temperature had reached over 110 degrees in the shade. But it was rather doubtful if this tigress would trust herself to cross the stream which was still foaming and frothing with the extra water fed to it from a myriad trickles reaching it from the forest on both sides.

At that moment my conjectures were interrupted by a fresh sound: 'Wrr-ung!Ar-ung! Arr-ungh! Oo-ooon!'

It was louder by far than the noise made by the tigress and the roar of water besides.

A tiger! He had heard and answered to the call of a mate. The tigress heard it too. She answered with a loud 'Ugh! Ahha-ha-ha-ha!' of delight.

We were still in darkness. To flash our torches now would make our presence known. Most probably both tigers would disappear, unless they actively resented our company. Things would not be so pleasant then. But if we remained in darkness our presence would probably not be detected, as tigers have no sense of smell, while the noise of the stream would muffle any noise we might inadvertently make.

Our eyes had accustomed themselves to the starlight as we came to a halt and stood behind a tree that bordered the track. A few feet to our right was the bank of the stream. Beyond that and to our left, the jungle was a wall of darkness lit by a thousand flickering, moving lights, the fireflies that dart to and for in ceaseless motion. The tumbling waters reflected countless stars, and here and there we could make out the darker forms of bushes or clumps of coarse grass on the bank. Of movement of any kind, we could see nothing.

Both tigers had now stopped calling. For them to meet, one or the other would have to ford the stream that lay between. The question was, which would be the one to cross? If the tigress crossed, we would be safe. If the tiger came over, both animals would be very close to us and would certainly resent our presence if they detected us.

The tigress clinched the matter by calling once more. This time she was almost mewing, like a very gruff and hoarse cat. Like all females in her circumstances, she was revelling in her position of advantage and was enticing the male to come to her; she would not condescend to go to him. Would the tiger be able to resist such a temptation.

He roared and roared again. It was a roar of defiance and challenge at the same time. Clearly he was warning all other tigers to keep away from his newly-founded mate. The tigress, still on our bank, continued her enticing mewing.

As I expected, the tiger could resist no longer. A long, dark silhouette emerged from the black wall of forest on the other bank, hesitated for a few seconds and then slid into the water of the stream.

I have already said that this watercourse is neither broad nor deep and it took him a very short time to cross. The silhouette became a solid grey form as he waded and then walked ashore, perhaps some fifty yards away.

All this while the tigress had not revealed herself. She now broke cover with a bound, herself another grey shape, leaped forward to meet the tiger with a loud growl and reared up on her hind — legs to slap him across his neck. The nock-fighting in which mating tigers indulge was about to begin. Neither animal intends to hurt the other, but frequently during this fighting, through excitement or a stray bite or scratch, tempers run high and the tigress invariably gets really rough. The tiger tolerates a lot until she at last goes too far. Then he loses his temper and sets about her in real earnest.

Both animals can be badly scratched and bitten and bleed freely by the time the repeated mating is over, but both animals appear to revel in the routine, soon forget their differences and cling together as a couple till the cubs are about to be born, at which time the tigress will separate herself from her lord for a while through fear that he might devour the cubs. Thereafter they will rejoin for maybe a year, along with their cubs, when they will part to seek fresh mates with the next season, approximately two years after the last, although the cubs sometimes remain with their mother for a few months more.

We had lost our chance of beating a retreat while the going was good before the tiger crossed the stream. Now that he was only a few yards away, and moreover because the tigress was with him, the slightest movement on our part would betray our presence to one or both the animals. If that should happen, our extinction was more than probable as both the felines, and particularly the male would not tolerate our eavesdropping on their lovemaking. it is equally likely that the tigress, in the excitement of mating, would resent our presence. It was too late now, anyway, to do anything about it. The only course open to us was to sink down to earth behind the tree-trunk that hid us and hope that the mating animals would not move in our direction.

For the next hour we were compelled to listen to a pandemonium of grunts, snarls, roars, prolonged mewing and a medley of other noises as the two animals pursued their lovemaking, the sounds differing in a accordance with their mood and temper at each moment. As the mating progressed to reach climax, the loveplay became rougher and rougher, until it reached a point when they were almost fighting each other tooth and nail. In mating the tiger bites the female in the neck and literally holds her down. They then separate a while and rest before starting all over again.

Several times, in the course of their gambols and struggles, they dashed hither and thither, on more than one occasion coming within ten yards of us. Occasionally, we thought we were discovered and prepared to make a dash for it, although we knew such a step would only hasten our destruction. The tree that hid us was too thick to climb, and the next was twenty feet away, but we could not climb it together. The first to reach it might possibly escape, provided the tigers did not follow him up, but the second man would be doomed. So we stayed where we were.

Finally the two felines tired of their efforts. The tigress curled up to rest like a cat, while the tiger sat on his haunches beside her to recuperate. And we wondered if they would never go away.

The placid scene was broken by a roar from the further

bank. Another tiger — a male — had heard the sounds of revel and had come to see if there was chance to join in. The first tiger at once sprang to his feet to give an answering roar in challenge to the newcomer. The tigress uncurled herself, stood on her four legs twitched her tail from side to side, and then settled down on her haunches. Clearly she was enjoying the situation, no doubt extremely pleased with herself at the prospect of two males about to engage in a titanic contest on her account.

The tiger on the further bank answered the challenge with roars of his own. Then he broke cover and stood revealed. Now the two males faced each other, the stream between them. The tigress, upon her haunches still, snarled mildly, mewed and almost purred in glee. It was obvious she was enjoying herself. This provoked the first tiger beyond endurance. Coughing a loud 'Whoff! Whoff! Whoff!,' he entered the stream and rushed at his rival. The level of the water appeared to have dropped appreciably, for this time he was able to wade the whole distance.

The challenge awaited his coming, coughing and roaring. the first tiger reached the other bank, crouched low for a moment, and then hurled himself at his rival.

But something quite unexpected happened at the last moment. All this while the newcomer had given every indication that he was prepared to stand and do battle for the handsome female across the stream, but as her first lover crouched for his final spring, his courage turned to water. He whirled around and bolted for dear life. Seeing this and gathering momentum the first tiger charged after him with a series of victorious roars.

The female on our bank, disappointed that there was not going to be a fight for her favours, but anxious now to endear herself to her lord, coughed once and galloped across the stream to follow the two males that had vanished into the blackness of the jungle.

At that Eric and I lost no time. We raced away to get out of the vicinity of the three tigers and leave them to settle their lovemaking problems. We stumbled along through the gloom for the best part of half a mile before we risked switching on our torches again, for we did not dare to attract the attention of the three animals who had gone up the rising ground across the stream and might return at any moment.

From the contours of the surrounding mountains as silhouetted against the sky, I knew we were approaching the hamlet of Kempekerai. It was here that I shot the tiger I called the 'Novice of Manchi'.4 At this point the pathway we were following crossed the stream and we waded through the water which now reached just above our knees. The track leads up a slope to the hamlet, and we followed it till we reached the mud-wattle huts of Kempekerai.

A cur barked but none of the inmates bothered to stir, and it was only after repeated calling that a very tousled and sleepy head was thrust from a slightly-opened doorway. The half-closed eyes blinked in the glare of my torch. The head and eyes were those of my old friend Byra the Poojaree, of whom I have told you in other stories. For the greater part of the year this man lived with his wife and children almost stark naked in burrow called 'gavvies' excavated in the steep banks of the Chinar river. When the rains came and the Chinar rose and the earth of the 'gavvies' turned too soft and was liable to collapse and close the burrow in which they lived, the whole family took service as cattle-grazers under some rich agriculturist, who sent his herd of cattle into the reserved forests to graze upon the long grass that spring up after the rains.

The agriculturist had to pay in licence to the Government

for grazing his cattle. In those days this fee was four *annas* (a fraction below four pence) per head for the whole period of five months grazing. The usual procedure was to buy a licence for about fifty head of cattle, paying the Government twelve-and-a-half rupees as grazing fee (at the rate of sixteen *annas* to the rupee), but to drive anything up to 200 head — or even more — into the forest. A small gratuity of five rupees to the forest guard would cover the grazing fee for the remaining 150 unlicensed animals.

To look after these 200 beasts, Byra and his family would have to build what was called a '*patti*', which was nothing more than a small clearing in the jungle. A smaller circular fence of thorns was constructed within this clearing for actually sheltering the cattle from wild animals at night. it was in the style of the African 'boma', with the difference that, as there are no lions in South India, the thorn fence would not be more than a yard in height and not very thick either. Tigers and panthers are not given to vaulting over thorn fences and carrying off their prey, as are the more daring lions of Africa that hunt in groups.

The hamlet of Kempekerai was nothing more than a multiple cattle '*patti*', accommodating not only Byra and his family but a number of other families as well, all of them engaged in looking after different herds of cattle belonging to different owners. As a result, the animals actually in residence at any of these multiple 'pattis' exceeded, by at least five times, the stipulated number of cattle permitted to graze in that area under licence from the Forest Department; the Government got less than one-fifth of the revenue in cattle-licences that it should have collected; the forest guard received an amount in bribes at least equal to, if not more than, his official salary; the owners of the herds had made a good arrangement; the grass, shrubs and the saplings of certain varieties of succulent trees were eaten down and destroyed over a large area of forest; the deer suffered by losing that amount of grazing; 'foot-and-mouth' disease, rife among village cattle, spread and decimated the deer, bison and wild-boar in the jungle; and everybody was happy, including the tigers and panthers in the area, who with easier hunting got a good deal more to eat, preying upon the domestic herds. Happiest of all were the jackals, hyaenas and vultures that ate the cattle that died, whether by disease or by being killed by other wild animals.

This is indeed a true picture of the state of affairs in those good old days till a certain deadly poison was introduced as an insecticide by the Government and made available to farmers, almost free of charge, to protect the crops from insect pests.

Some peasant then discovered that the insecticide, intended to kill caterpillars, beetles and other such pests, would also kill tigers and panthers that preyed upon the domestic herds and, far more important, unwanted mothers-in-law, brother-in-law, in fact all 'in-laws' of both sexes and all ages with happy impartiality, not to mention secret lovers, rivals, elder brothers who were so inconsiderate as to inherit the property when father died, and a whole host of other unwanted characters into bargain. To put it in a nutshell, opportunity was rife for those who were disgruntled in one way or another.

The carcasses of cattle killed by tigers and panthers were systematically doctored with the result that the felines died in hundreds and have been almost wiped out in Southern India. Along with them jackals, hyaenas and vultures, who shared these kills, perished in still larger numbers. There was also a sharp rise in the number of in-laws and other inconvenient people who began to succumb, suddenly, mysteriously and in increasing numbers, to violent stomachache and other alarming symptoms. Life is cheap and nobody worried unduly, while the statisticians were compensated slightly in the other graph they were maintaining with regard to the vexatious problem of 'Population Explosion and Family Planning' which happened to coincide with the advent of the poison.

To this day, unlicensed still exceed the licensed cattle by many times. The owners save that much money in license fees, the forest guards draw more than their salary now, the Government loses much more, and everyone is still happy. The only difference from the old days is that there are now no tigers, panthers, hyaenas, jackals or even vultures to join in the general rejoicing. Nearly all are dead — poisoned.

Incidentally, the villagers were not taking very kindly to the family-planning programmes. In fact, the greater number of them were distinctly annoyed about the whole thing. On the one hand, they were being urged to mechanise their farming methods and give up the old-fashioned, cattle-drawn wooden ploughs of their forefathers. At the same time, the cost of living and the prices of all commodities were rising day by day. The monsoon had a knack of not arriving when it should and of coming when it should not. Either way their crops failed. Landlords were more grasping and so were the money-lenders. The Government had tried to help all it could by distributing land, oxen and ploughs free of cost to any family in order to assist farmers who preferred to stick to the old style; but money, that root of all evil, was a temptation, and the oxen and ploughs were sold or mortgaged shortly after they were distributed. The land would have followed suit as well, but that was rather too great a risk to take, being immovable property.

Finally, the price of kerosene was increasing by leaps and bounds. One could not afford to burn the midnight oil. An early dinner and early to bed became the golden rule.

In the midst of all these troubles, the poor ryot had but one consolation left to him — his cherished and beloved wife. At least she belonged to him, to do with as he wanted. what with rising costs, no kerosenre, an early dinner and early to bed, he had at least some opportunity here. She was the one solid item that was entirely his own. but at his stage along came these Family Planning people with their ridiculous advice, offering strange devices their forefathers had never heard of and begrudging the poor farmer the one and only pleasure and recreation available to him in these hard days.

So the statisticians were worried at the still-steadily rising curve of population, although a trifle relieved that here and there would appear a slight kink in it, caused by the untimely demise of some in-laws and other who had succumbed to a sudden unaccountable and unbearable stomach pain that had come on immediately after dinner.

All of which brings us back to Byra the Poojaree, my old friend of the jungle. Byra was very happy when he discovered that the visitor arriving at such unearthly hour was none other than myself. He crawled out of the narrow doorway of his hut and offered the accustomed greeting of the Poojarees by touching his forehead to the ground before me. Then we sat down for a chat and I told him the reason for our presence.

The jungle man was surprised and not a little concerned at the fact that we were unarmed. He thought that we were taking too great a risk, especially with elephants, and gave us the disconcerting news that there was a particularly 'bad' elephant roaming that part of the valley we had yet to negotiate. Whereas this elephant had not yet been proclaimed a 'rogue', inasmuch as it had not actually killed anybody, it was an animal that charged on sight and only the fleetness of foot and jungle-cunning of the poojarees of Kempekerai have saved them, at least so far. Byra doubted that we had that fleetness or cunning and advised us not to continue our journey that night.

'Wait for daylight,' he advised. 'At least, then you will be able to see where you are running when he chases you, although I doubt that will do you much good.'

The other reason why Byra was annoyed by the fact that we were not carrying firearms was his hope that he might have persuaded one or other of us to shoot a sambar or spotted deer for his family and himself to eat. This was Byra's only weakness, his craving for meat. Every time we met it was the same thing. He would pester me to shoot a deer or sambar, and just as steadfastly I refused. Money I was ready to give him, but I had explained a hundred times that I do not like killing deer and sambar. Although he has never succeeded in his efforts to break me down on this point, Byra never fails to try and try again. Possibly he thinks that he will wear me down eventually, and so must have our preliminary struggle every time we meet.

Eric and I decided to eat and bring out our sandwiches. Unfortunately they contained beef, an ingredient that is forbidden to nearly all South Indians, including the humblest forest folk. The cow is sacred, and to eat its flesh is outrageously and unthinkably sinful. So although we did not make the mistake of offering him any, there was a distinct look of disapproval on Byra's simple face. Eating beef was one of two things that he held against me; of the other I have just spoken. On all other matters he felt we were buddies or, to use a slang expression, 'as thick as thieves'.

Considering he had never been to school, this man, aborigine as he was, was an authority on jungle medicines obtained from flowers, fruits, leaves, roots and barks of various trees and herbs. He was the 'doctor' of the surrounding poojaree community and had been summoned in emergencies to cure all sorts of illnesses. He had a secret remedy for snake-bite, and had not lost a single case, or so he said. I know for a fact he cured two cases of cholera when that dreaded epidemic spread to his community, and, as I have mentioned in one of my books, he delivered his own wife when she was having her baby.

I have witnessed this and his method was very simple. He prepared a shallow hollow in the sands of the nearest stream, and into this hollow he put a thick layer of green leaves. In this hollow his wife lay down on her back. Next he got a torn piece of saree cloth and tied one end to the soles of her feet. This cloth was only long enough to reach to her knees. Byra gave this end to hold with both hands, and to do so the woman had to part her thighs and knees, which she raised off the ground. Byra then instructed her to pull hard upon the end, where upon, with hardly a whisper, the baby was born and Byra welcomed it into this world by raising it by the heels and slapping it on the back. He had no scissors, so the sharp end of a stone or mussel-shell (which could be found along the banks of most steams), operating a flat stone, served to sever the cord.

Within half an hour of the appearance of the placenta, the wife rose, suckled her infant and walked away. Byra then shoveled the sand into the hollow until it was entirely filled.

Knowing my weakness for tea Byra had already made a fire, and on this I placed my canteen filled with water from the stream. It was very muddy and the resultant brew was rather sub-standard. I told the poojaree of our encounter with the three tigers not far upstream, and he said that these three were the only ones in residence there at that moment. There had been another female, but she had wandered away some months earlier and had not returned. He went on to say that frequently one or other of the three tigers would attack the herds while the cattle were grazing in the forest and kill one of the cows.

The tigress had been calling quite a lot recently, he confirmed. The poojarees in the hamlet had heard her only two nights earlier. All three animals were cattle lifters, but none of them had shown any inclination to attack the graziers, who had frequently driven them away from their kills to salvage the hides for drying and sale. he added that there was also a pair of panthers living on the other side of the stream that occasionally kill a stray cow if opportunity allowed. A month earlier, one of these panthers had pulled down a calf and was killing it when one of the tigers rushed out of the undergrowth, put the panther to flight and carried the calf away, slung across its back.

We stood up to leave, when Byra once again remonstrated about the great risk we were running with the 'bad' elephant. However, to remain in shelter at the *patti* for the rest of the night was not jungle 'ghooming', and ghooming was the purpose of the trip. We explained this to the poojaree and shouldered our loads, but not before I checked to make certain that the cobra was still safely secured.

Very well then; I will go with you', the little man announced. 'When the sun rises I will return. Till then, I shall remain with you and offer what protection lies in my power. I don't think you realise the danger you will be in if you happen to meet the elephant in this darkness', he stressed, 'for the beast will be upon you before you know where you are and crush you to a pulp.'

With these ominous words in our ears we left Kempekerai and headed downhill to the stream. I led, shining the torch; Byra followed me, while Eric brought up the rear. We reached and crossed the water and followed the narrow path before us into the labyrinths of the jungle. It was distinctly chilly and a jungle-cock, crowing among the bamboos, reminded us it was two in the morning. Like their cousins, the domestic roosters, wild-cocks follow the same habits in the jungles that are not unduly disturbed by men or too many wild cats. they crow at two and at four in the morning, and just after the false dawn, usually before six o'clock.

We might have covered a half-mile when Byra stepped up from behind and halted me with his hand upon my arm. He reached forward to extinguish the torch. Eric half-asleep now collided with us before he realised we had stopped. I strained my ears, but heard no sound. The jungle-cock had passed out of hearing range.

The stars cast a sheen over the forest that was quite different from moonlight. It was a soft and ethereal light that just succeeded in making itself felt in the darkness without breaking its dominion. The forest that surrounded us was as black as a bottomless pit, the starlight being enough only to see each other and the few yards around us.

I looked at Byra inquiringly. He touched his nose with the forefinger and thumb of his left hand, at the same time swinging his right arm, from elbow downwards, to right and left before him.

The elephant! Byra could smell it! It must be very close indeed, or the Poojaree would have whispered his message in my ear.

I wrinkled my nose in an effort to catch the scent. At the same time I turned my head sideways, one cheek in the direction we were moving and the other in the direction whence we had come. I fancied I could detect a peculiar odour which within a few seconds I began to associate with the presence of an elephant. These animals smell strongly when they are close. But perhaps it was a figment of my imagination.

My cheeks told me there was hardly a breeze blowing

from any direction, a fact that was neither good nor bad. Had the breeze been blowing from behind us, the elephant — provided there was one ahead — would have scented us by now. had the breeze been blowing from him to us, we might have been able, exercising the greatest caution, to creep past him undetected. As matters stood, with practically no breeze in any direction, our situation was one of stalemate. The elephant -- supposing there was one ahead — had not so far detected our presence. But he was bound to do so if we moved any closer. Even if he did not scent us, he would certainly hear us in that deathly silence.

Byra had come to the same conclusion much earlier. He raised his right palm at waist level. The signal was plain as if he had spoken: 'Wait!' Tensely we stood quite motionless.

The moments dragged by. We heard no sound. I could smell the strange odour still, but I could not associate it with an elephant. Perhaps Byra was wrong after all and there was no elephant before us.

Then the silence was broken. We heard a rustling sound, growing louder and heavier and moving along the pathway on which we were standing. Byra had been right. There was an elephant ahead, and he was moving through the undergrowth in our direction. It was only a matter of seconds before he would emerge upon the pathway.

Byra signalled to us to retreat and gave the lead by turning around and walking on tip-toe down the track along which we had just come. Eric followed, and I brought up the rear.

At that moment the breeze decided to take a hand. A gust blew strongly down the valley, passing over us and directly towards the elephant. The cat was now out of the bag!

The elephant scented us and in the next instant was crashing through the rest of the undergrowth. He came out upon the track behind me. Still retreating, all three of us turned around. We could see his colossal black bulk now, like a great big black rock astride the track. Two long streaks of white stood out against that blackness. His tusks!

A moment later and we knew, indeed, that this was the 'bad' elephant about which Byra had warned us. For no sooner did the beat set eyes upon us than he recognised us for his avowed enemies — men. he trumpeted his shriek of hate and came charging towards us, looking blacker and bigger at every instant.

To run away would be hopeless. At so short a distance no man can escape a charging elephant. Either Eric or myself, encumbered as we both were with our loads, would fall a prey to this monster. he would smash to a jelly whichever one of us he caught first. To try to dodge into the bushes either to right or left was equally hopeless because of the darkness. It looked as if only Byra would live to tell the tale.

I did the only thing possible in the circumstances. I took a very flimsy chance. It stopped, turned around. At the same time I yelled with all my might.

The bright beam fell fully upon the monster, scarcely ten feet away. In a peculiarly detached and interested fashion, I noticed that the animal had curled in his trunk, that his head was raised, showing a half-opened mouth, and that the points of his tusks were in line with his small, gleaming, wicked eyes. He lowered his head to bring those tusks into line with me and thus let the torch-light fully into his eyes. The next instant a cloud of dust hid the ground and the elephant's legs.

I was still screaming when I realised that the brute had come to a halt. Breaking suddenly, by planting his four great feet in the ground, was the cause of the dust.

I did not know it then, but seeing the peril I was in made Byra stop, turn around and come to my assistance. He was screaming too, I suddenly realised; words of ludicrous, vile abuse to the elephant, all of its kind and its ancestors. Eric had dashed past him and was still in full flight. He did not mean to desert me but had not realised that the elephant was so close as to compel me to turn around and face him.

The next few moments were electric. What was going to happen next was a matter of life or death. Would the pachyderm press his attack home, or would Byra and I succeed in turning him?

With sinking heart I remembered Byra's words of warning, uttered but a short while earlier. Once it charged, nothing would stop this elephant.

The monster shook his head from right to left and back again several times, with the purpose of avoiding the piercing beam of my torch that shone fully into his eyes. But I followed his movements with my torch, still shouting lustily.

The brute stood his ground. Then I took the last chance left. Yelling like a maniac, I stepped forward sharply, directing the beam fully into those small, wicked eyes. Then his courage broke. he turned half around so that his huge bulk, facing broadside on, straddled the narrow track.

Without speaking to each other, Byra and I knew that it was now or never. With concerted shouts, we rushed towards the monster, my torch still shining directly upon its head. The elephant was unnerved. Like all big bullies, he was accustomed to attack and see his enemies scatter like chaff before the wind. Never before had any puny creature dared to attack him.

That was exactly what was happening now. He could not get that glaring light out of his eyes and our discordant screams were unnerving him. So he lumbered up the pathway away from us, Byra and I behind him, still shouting at the top of our voices. To shake us off, he swerved sharply to the left and crashed through the undergrowth.

Byra and I came to a stop. We had accomplished his rout.

Now we had to get away as quickly as possible. Turning once again we walked back the way we had come. It would not do for us to run, for that might bring the elephant back. We could find no traces of Eric!

It was but half-a-mile to the spot where we had to cross the stream to return to Kempekerai, but Eric did not know the place. Probably he had passed it and continued along the track beyond.

Byra broke into a trot to try overtake him, while I walked rapidly on. I was not feeling so good. In fact, I was feeling awfully sick and I noticed that I was shaking as if in fever and did not seem to be able to stop. Also I was soaking wet — perspiration no doubt, although I did not remember perspiring so much. I toyed with the idea of sitting down for a few moments but the thought came to me that the black devil might change its mind and return to the attack. So I walked all the faster. Very soon I reached the ford leading to Kempekerai, and there was no sign of Eric or Byra.

I splashed through the stream and climbed the winding path to the hamlet. Reaching the huts I threw myself on the ground to get rid of the nausea that had not yet passed away.

It was some time before Byra arrived with Eric. The poojaree told me that my friend was a good runner. he had to follow for almost two miles before he succeeded in overtaking Eric. Eric's version was that when he glanced back, but could see neither Byra nor myself, he concluded that the elephant had got both of us. This had made him run all the faster.

Byra seemed quite unperturbed by our recent adventure. To him it was part of everyday forest existence. He suggested that we brewed some tea. If there was one thing Byra had a weakness for, it was tea. So have I, but for once I did not feel up to drinking any. Throwing down my haversack, I told him and Eric to help themselves. Then I lay down on the bare earth and fell asleep.

The sun was shining brightly when I awoke. Eric was sleeping soundly close by, lying neatly on his groundsheet, covered with a light blanket. Byra was coiled almost into a ball by the side of a small fire that had long gone out. His head was touching his knees.

My teeth were chattering with the cold. Lying on the ground with no covering had made matters worse. In the chill of the morning, when enthusiasm is usually at an ebb, I wondered if the risks we had taken the previous night were justified. I remembered reading in a article somewhere or the other, that it is at such a time — when one first awakens — that the influence of the subconscious mind is at its strongest, and the impressions one receives at the moment conveyed the wisest and best advice. It went on to say that, should the recipient follow this advice, he would prosper and avoid the pitfalls of living. But these few moments of good sense pass all too swiftly, the article continued, to give place to the individual's own individuality and way of thinking, and he then relapsed into his own fixed ideas.

I fear this is what happened to me, for those minutes of common sense were put aside. I aroused Eric and Byra, and while the latter relit the fire to brew our tea, Eric and I went down to the stream for a cold bath and brush-up. It is wonderful what a bath in a mountain stream will do for the cobwebs in one's brain, and for muscles that ache and eyes that are still heavy from insufficient sleep.

By the time we returned, Byra had not only boiled the water and made the tea, but had drunk more than half of it himself. He offered a ready excuse for this by saying that he felt the fever coming on, and as the *dorai* knows very well, plenty of tea is the only prescription for averting fever. I replied that the *dorai* had never known this but would bear it in mind by dishing out less of the ingredients that go to make the beverage the next time. Then Eric and I finished what was left.

A cold breakfast, followed by a smoke and some desultory chat, led Byra to ask what we intended doing next. I replied that we would sleep for most of that day and start again with nightfall to finish our journey at the point where the stream joins the Chinar river. This we expected to reach about midnight. After another short rest, we would start to return, accomplishing the trip this time by daylight. We hoped to get to Aiyur by dusk the following evening, when 'Sudden Death' ought to get us back to Bangalore in time for dinner.

The poojaree was not happy to learn our plans. He implied, by indirect comparison with a donkey which, in spite of being repeatedly beaten yet refuses to go forward, that we had failed to learn our lesson at the hands of the elephant, by wanting to pass through his domain once again after darkness. He suggested we start about two in the afternoon instead, when all pachyderms take, or should take, their siestas by standing asleep in the shelter of some thick clump of tress, so that by nightfall we should be well away from the places where pisachee (devil) usually hung out. Of course, if our luck was bad, he might have gone further afield, in which case we might still run into him, but at least that risk was not as great as would be the case by starting after dark. Byra also insisted upon accompanying us as far as the Chinar River and back again, saying he would not leave us till we were at least five miles on the return journey between Kempekrai and Aiyur, where we have left the car.

We discussed the matter and wiser, if less adventurous, counsel prevailed. We decided to follow Byra's plan and, as there was nothing better to do, we fell asleep. Soon after midday we ate a cold lunch, followed by more tea, and at exactly two o'clock were on our way again, retracing our steps on the narrow pathway along which we had so precipitously bolted the night before. But this time we could look about us and take all possible precautions by testing the wind and keeping a sharp look-out for signs of the elephant.

We were unlucky from the start. A strong wind was blowing from north to south, that is, down the stream from behind us and in the direction we were going. It would inform the rogue of our approach should he be anywhere ahead.

Plainly, on the damp earth of the narrow pathway, we could see our own footmarks: the blurred impressions of Eric's rubber shoes, the larger marks made by my own alpaca-lined boots, Byra's bare footsteps, and imposed upon them all the ponderous, almost dish-sized tracks left by the elephant that had chased us the night before.

Byra was in front. Every now and then he stopped to test the wind by plucking a few blades of grass from the ground and dropping them from shoulder-height. Imperceptibly, they fell to earth at a slight angle ahead of us. The wind was still blowing from behind.

Byra stopped to listen. We halted and listened too. The forest was athrob with life. Birds twittered all round. We could hear their more distant calls from the hill-sides to right and left. Cicadas and crickets of all varieties chirped in different cadences. The single, shrill resonance of the plains-cicada is here mixed with the rising and falling sonority of the hill variety, smaller in size than its cousin of lower-lying areas but capable of emitting a far louder sound. Then a myriad crickets of all sizes, ensconced beneath leaves or hidden under rotting logs of wood, joined in the general vibration of insect vociferation, filling the air with the sound of throbbing, omnipresent life.

Far ahead of us a barking-deer learned of our approach. The wind blowing down the valley told him. 'Kharr!' he cried, and again and again 'Kharr! Kharr!'

The langur monkeys, high up on both hill-sides, heard him. 'Whoomp! Whoomp! Whoomp!' they shouted in sheer glee, leaping from branch to branch and rock to rock. But the little barking-deer continued his alarm-cry.

This worried the langurs. Their whoomps of joy died down. Now they were silent. I could picture the langur-watchman, seated on tree top, peering hard into the valley below, trying to discover the nature of the danger that had alarmed the little deer. The shaggy brows in his round black face must be beetled with worry and uncertainty; his large, round, black eyes must be searching the stream-bed far below and such gamepaths as were visible to him from that height, in an effort to see the foe. He was responsible for the safety and lives of the numerous she-monkeys and babies of the tribe gamboling in innocence around him. Should he fail in his duty, by failing to give the alarm, one of them would die. No doubt he thought that at any moment he would see the stripes of a tiger or the spotted coat of a panther slinking from bush to bush.

He saw nothing, for we were yet too far away.

Nevertheless the little deer, whose keen sense of smell had told him of something the langur could not see, announced our approach by continuing to bark and bark, 'Kharr! Kharr! Kharr!'

The langur-watchman became increasingly uneasy. What kind of foe was this, approaching but invisible?

At last he could stand the tension of uncertainty no longer. he had to warn the tribe. 'Harr! Ha!' he shouted gutturally, and again in quick succession, 'Harr! Ha! Harr! Ha!'

The alarm had its effect at once. Although we could not

see or hear them, there followed a hundred thuds as langur-mothers clutched their babies to their breasts and leapt prodigious distances to safety in the loftiest treetops. Others scampered up rocks or ran up the hillside. A hundred black faces turned in anxiety to their watchman. What enemy had he seen? His next action would tell them.

If a tiger or panther were approaching, the watchman would, surely leap from his tree-top to another. He would stand on his two feet, with long tail erect to keep his balance, look downwards and abuse the enemy in langur-language.

The watchman did none of these things. He still had not seen us. So he continued his alarm, 'Harr! Ha!' and again 'Harr! Ha!' A sambar stag, resting on a bed of high grasses somewhere up the mountain-side to our left, heard the commotion. He sprang to his feet and cried 'Dhank! Dhank! Honk!' These signals of alarm from the different denizens of the forest had not sounded in vain. They were heard by listening and understanding ears. Ponderous ears, indeed. For at that precise moment the elephant struck again.

Decades old, and wise in the ways of the jungle, he had been hearkening and hiding in motionless silence. He had heard the alarm-cry of the barking-deer, the calls of the langur-watchman and the belling of the disturbed sambar stag. Undoubtedly he had smelt us, too, for he was standing much nearer and knew that it was the hated human foe who had come again.

He made up his mind quickly. This time he was not going to fail in his purpose. His purpose was to destroy one of the hated, two-legged foes. he would wait in silence till we walked right up to him. Then and then only would he charge. By this means he was sure to catch one of us.

We knew nothing of his presence or what was passing in his evil mind. Despite his size, he remained hidden by a rock to our left behind which he had taken up his position. For once Byra, man of the forests as he was and versed in jungle-lore from childhood, and with unnumbered generations of jungle-ancestors before him, was deceived. Walking warily in the lead, with Eric and myself following light-footed behind, he moved forward step by step.

Byra saw the big rock to his left and halted to study it carefully. We saw it, too, and stopped to look. It was a large, high, loaf-shaped rock, almost black in colour except for two large patches of grey lichen growing upon its surface. A fig tree clung to one side of it. We noticed that some of the roots of this tree had run over the rock. One root strayed down the side, resembling a long, thick, light-coloured snake going into the ground.

All this we saw. But we did not see the elephant hiding behind that rock, because he made neither sound nor movement.

Byra was satisfied that there was no danger and that it was safe to proceed. he walked forwards slowly. We followed.

Now we stood abreast to the rock. Now we began to pass it. The elephant knew then that in another second we would see him. He also knew that now we were so close that he must be able to catch at least one of us. He made up his mind.

An ear-splitting scream rent the silence: 'Tri-aa-aa-ank!'

The he was upon us. He meant business this time for he did not utter another sound. From behind the rock his black form emerged. the great trunk was coiled inwards like a giant snake, behind high-thrown head and flattened ear. His mouth was half-open.

Eric, in front of me, turned and ran. So did I. Instinctively, Byra knew that if he followed he would be caught, as he would be a third man running behind two others, who would baulk him. He decided to swerve and try to escape by running downhill and across the stream which flowed parallel to the pathway we were following.

He had no chance. The elephant was upon him. It uttered a short and muffled half-scream, above which I heard Byra's shriek of despair. There was 'whoosh' followed by a thud.

The elephant then gave vent to his rage by trumpeting repeatedly: 'Tri-aaa-ank! Tri-aaa-ank! Tri-aa-ank!'

I was running as fast my clumsy boots would let me. Eric younger in years, lighter in build, and wearing soft shoes, overtook me and disappeared ahead. I am ashamed to say that I continued to run. I know I should have stopped and gone to Byra's aid. Of small consolation was the thought that unarmed as I was, there was nothing I could do, and as the elephant was thoroughly enraged my shouts would not deter him. The night before, my torch beam in the darkness had confused him. Now he would finish me off as well.

The elephant had stopped. I could hear him screaming still. He was probably trampling poor Byra to pulp.

I reached the crossing. Eric was on the other side of the stream. A short distance higher lay Kempekerai and safety. As hurriedly as possible we recruited all the Poojarees in the hamlet. Torches of wood and grasses were made. Embers to light them were carried in broken pots. Two dozen in number, we recrossed the stream, set the torches alight, and with the whole party shouting at the top of their voices, we set forth to gather what remained of my poor friend.

The elephant was silent, although we expected him to show at any moment. Would he charge our party?

I did not think so. We were two dozen strong and we are making a terrific noise.

The next moment we saw him. He was standing squarely upon the pathway. Irritably, he was shaking his head from side to side, his great trunk wagging along with the motion. His ears were flapping forwards. We could see his bloodshot little eyes staring at us. Clearly he was undecided as to whether to charge or beat a retreat.

Each member of our party excelled himself that day. Every one was shouting louder still, if that were possible. The elephant continued to hesitate. Then his nerve failed. He turned about; then he faced around again. Unexpectedly, he made off up the hill to our left. We advanced cautiously, continuing to yell.

At each moment we expected to come across the remains of the luckless Byra, squashed to a pulp. I could picture the little man before me, his grin spreading from ear, and two jet-black little eyes gleaming with laughter. The vision choked me. I could join in the shouting no longer. The little man had sacrificed his life to save us. Had he escaped, the elephant would have followed and got one of us. Eric, walking beside me, looked grim, although he continued to yell with the rest.

But we could not find the remains of what had once been Byra, although we searched everywhere. Could he have escaped?

We spread out to search in an ever-widening circle, but still there was no sign. Hope began to dawn in each of us. Just then, I heard what sounded like a faint groan. A couple of the poojarees near me had heard it too. We stopped to listen, but there was no other sound.

My companions, always superstitious, began to grow afraid. Three of us had clearly heard that groan. Some spirit must have made the sound. Maybe Byra's spirit. The two who heard cast fearful glances at me. A few moments more and perhaps they would take off.

Then I clearly heard the word 'Dorai'. It came very faintly, but there was not doubt about it. But from where? There was nothing in sight but grass and trees—and the big black rock.

The solution came in a flash. Byra was alive, and he was on top of that rock. How did he get there? Why, the elephant threw him there, of course!

I told my two companions the good news. In a trice they had clambered up the steep sides of the rock, and then we heard their joyful shouts: 'He's alive! Byra is alive!'

All of us grouped around the rock while the two men on top called out that Byra had said the elephant had thrown him up in the air. Luckily, he had fallen on top of the rock, where the beast could not get at him again. Had he fallen back to the ground, he would certainly have been crushed.

Then came bad news: 'His leg is broken, *Dorai*. Broken at the thigh.'

Removing my clumsy boots, I managed to get up the rock aided by my two companions pulling from above and others pushing from below. I found Byra with his thigh broken, but he was still smiling!

Possibly the elephant had seized him by the leg and broken the bone when it threw him. Perhaps falling on the hard rock was the cause. However, the all-important fact was that Byra was still alive. We made a stretcher out of branches, jungle-vines and soft, green leaves. As tenderly as we could, we moved him on to this. Meanwhile I sent for ropes from Kempekerai. Fastening these to the ends of the rough stretcher, we lowered him off the rock as gently as possible. Then we carried him back to the hamlet.

I had a difficult task to persuade Byra to let me take him to hospital in Bangalore. he wanted to remain at Kempekerai until the ends of his broken thigh-bone joined.

Many jungle medicines and leaves posses marvellous healing properties. No doubt the end of the broken bone would unite. But would they join straight? Would Byra be able to walk normally again? I stressed these things and urged him to let me take him to hospital, but it was nightfall before I got his consent. The peoples of the forest are very afraid of our hospitals.

We set forth for Aiyur at break of day, willing hands bearing the stretcher, but it was very difficult to fasten the stretcher across the open box-*machan* that formed the body of 'Sudden Death,' my Model T Ford. At last it was done and by slow driving, avoiding the many potholes, it still took us a long time to reach the hospital at Bangalore.

There we created a sensation. Every doctor, nurse and ward-boy present, and every patient who could hobble and was not at death's door turned out to see the strange sight. It is not often that one comes across a car without a body, with no mud-guards or driving seat, but with only an open box tied to it behind, and balancing precariously upon that open box a fragile stretcher of jungle wood, vines and leaves holding a small man, practically naked, with a broken thigh.

In four months Byra could walk as well as ever. The broken thigh-bone joined perfectly. The doctor said he had been a good patient. I know that the only thoughts that had sustained him throughout this period of pain and adversity were visions of his beloved jungles, and their mountains and streams.

It was a glad day when I took him back by car to Aiyur and walked with him to Kempekerai. We had to do it in slow stages. This time you may be sure I did not take Eric. For one I did not want to tempt the jinx that seemed to accompany this friend of my school-days.

I almost forgot to relate that I was compelled to release the cobra I had caught two nights earlier when we were carrying Byra to the car. It would have been an added burden and a nuisance on the journey.

Two

The Medical Lore of India

THE POORER PEOPLE OF SOUTHERN INDIA CANNOT AFFORD TO GO TO a doctor to find cures for their ailments, for the very good reason that a single visit would take a large bite out of a week's earnings.

To give you an example: suppose a man has a sore or is suffering from a recent injury to a finger or leg, what would be the doctor's charges? Well, an injection of some sort would be indicated, probably antitetanus or penicillin in some form. Then there might be a dressing to be applied, together with tablets of some sulpha drug. The injection would cost at least, 1.50 rupees. The dressing and tablets another rupee. The doctor's professional fees would be around 3.50 rupees, so that the bill would be in the region of six rupees, a figure that represents three day's earnings at two rupees a day, if the patient is an unskilled labourer or a farmhand, and a full day's earning if he happens to be

604

'skilled'. So the ordinary man will think many times before going to a doctor.

So what does he do? He simply walks out on to the roadside where, within a few yards and in a minute or two he will undoubtedly come across a nice, warm flat mass of dung recently deposited by one of the many cattle that wander at will all over the streets and country-side. Our patient dips one or two of his fingers into the mess and comes up with a wet, sticky lump of dung which he applies to wound, tapping the same in smartly till it covers the whole surface of the injury in the shape of a small saucer.

That is all there is to it. Does it work? Incredibly it does in the great majority of cases. If, perchance, the treatment should fail and the wound not get better, or even gets worse, the reason (to the patient) is as plain as the nose on his face, and simple too. There was something wrong with the cow that passed the dung, and so sets out to repeat the treatment with another sample of excreta.

'But tetanus germs live in a cow dung' you exclaim. 'The medical books say so.' Undoubtedly they do, but you would have a real hard time getting that idea across to the patient. He would not believe a word of what you said, for one thing. For another, he would not believe there were such things as germs. When you tell him they are so small that he cannot see them with his eyes, he concludes the tale is a figment of your imagination or ignorance, deliberately told in order to frighten him into seeing a doctor. Very likely you are a doctor yourself.

Cobwebs of the species of spider that lives in holes in the ground, and those of the variety that spins its webs between the branches of small bushes, where they scintillate with multicoloured light like clusters of jewels when the rising sun falls upon the dew that has gathered upon them, are sterling remedies when gathered freshly and plugged into freely bleeding wounds.

Juice from freshly broken pods of garlic is said to allay the irritation caused by mosquito bites, while for any form of eye-trouble the patient should stand facing the rising sun and squeeze orange-peel into his eyes. Equal quantities by weight of finely-powdered indigo seeds and finely powdered tobacco-leaf, put into the eyes at night, is reputed to cure cataract, although the patient is cautioned to expect some sensation of burning.

The bottle-bird or Indian tree-sparrow performs a wonderful feat of architecture and tailoring when she builds her long, bottle-like nest of closely-woven fibres and suspends it by a single strand from a tall date palm. After laying her eggs, the mother bottle-bird searches the landscape later in the evening, at an hour when she would otherwise be safely in her nest, for an early fire-fly or more than one fire-fly if she is lucky. Injuring the fire-fly sufficiently to prevent if from escaping but not seriously enough to kill out-right, the wise little bird now introduces the insect into the nest through the cleverly-constructed entrance that, strangely enough, is at its lower end.

What does our villager do when hurrying home unduly late of an evening and happens to notice the glow of the fire-fly through the interstices of a nest? He does not stop and climb the tree right away to break down the nest and procure the elfin within. That would take too long. He is already late and soon it will be quite dark. Moreover, he is alone. This is the hour when devils begin to emerge from their lairs beneath tombstones, from the trunks of neem and banyan trees, and from holes in the ground. In fact, the variety known as 'minnispurams' are known to live in tall trees. Or, if he is near jungle, there is the possibility of encountering a wild beast. So he makes a note of the position of the tree in which the nest swing with its tiny lantern inside, and he hastens on his way.

The following morning he is back. Date-palms are notoriously difficult to climb because of their thorny trunks and spiked leaf-tips. Our yokel therefore brings with him from the village a long bamboo pole, or if any grow nearby he proceeds to lop one of suitable length.

With this he brings down the nest by beating the single strand that secures it to a frond, and then he hoses on time in extracting the fire-fly. That tiny glimmer is invisible now in the dazzling sunshine, but the village knows it will shine again once the sun goes down and darkness covers the land.

He may keep if for good luck! Or he may eat it, for he reasons that the light will shine inside him, just as it shone in the nest, and will illuminate all the nooks and corners of his intestines so that the good spirit that looks after his welfare may be able to see and cure anything that is not quite right.

If young birds or eggs happen to be in the nest, he will throw them away with the rest of the nest, or if he is of a lower caste he might even eat the fledgelings.

Some of the wild creatures of this land are in great demand as medicine and are killed as soon as they are seen, if they are not lucky enough to get away. The black-faced grey langur monkey perhaps heads this list. Once common throughout the country, in southern India he has been slain mercilessly till the few of his kind that remain have moved into the innermost recesses of the forest. Even there they are shot by marauding bands of poachers, although their slaying is prohibited by Government. all this is being done in the belief that the flesh of a langur monkey is one of the most effective aphrodisiacs any failing male can hope to find.

Another unfortunate creature that is sacrificed to make medicine for the same purpose is the elegant Indian slender lorris, mistakenly called a 'sloth'. It is a pretty little monkey, delicately made, with no tail and two large, limpid brown eyes that reflect the rays of a torch as if they were made of pools of crimson fire. As it moves rather slowly, this poor creature is easily captured. Then its two eyes are torn out of their sockets while it is still alive to make a marvellous aphrodisiac for some man who has spent a lifetime in womanising and has reached a stage when he can womanise no more. The lorris, still alive but bereft of its two eyes and totally blind, is thrown aside to fend for itself. Unhappily, these little beasts possess a good deal of vitality and linger for days, till they eventually die of starvation.

Once I happened to find one in this state. I took it home, attended to its torn eye-sockets as best as I could, and fed it with milk. Despite its ghastly wounds the little monkey recovered.

For a long time it would not trust me, nor allow me to touch it, and bit viciously. But could anybody blame the tiny creature for being distrustful of human beings after the terrible ordeal it had suffered at their hands? Eventually, however, this little animal understood that I meant it no harm and was trying to befriend it. From that moment it changed its attitude towards me. No more affectionate and gentle little creature have I kept as a pet at any time.

A third mammal that suffers greatly in southern India because of a belief that may or may not have any foundation is the large Indian fruit-bat commonly referred to as the 'flying-fox'. The flesh of this mammal is reputed to be a very effective remedy for asthma, and as this complaint is widespread in the land despite its tropical climate, the flying-fox is diligently shot, or netted, whenever the opportunity offers. However, in this instance the mammal is killed outright and the flesh cooked, as in the case of the langur monkey, and so it escapes the awful fate that befalls the slender lorris.

Snakes that are non-poisonous also suffer a hard fate. The poisonous ones are killed and then burned (to prevent them from coming back to life), but the large and harmless snakes, as the dhaman or 'rat-snake' are skinned alive and then thrown aside. It is terrible to see the poor reptile, white without its outer skin, writhing and twisting in its agony. The outer skin is roughly cured with salt and copper sulphate and then sold for a couple of rupees to make a belt or purse, being unsuitable for making shoes unless it is fully tanned.

Doctors of another school speacialise in what they proudly call 'gem therapy'. This is the art of curing sicknesses by the use of semi-precious stones. It is performed in three ways:

1. Certain stones are burned to ashes and these ashes taken on the tongue or in water. The Ayurvedic System employs this method, but it is a practice of only the very rich.
2. A single stone — or perhaps a number of them — is soaked in water for a week, and this water is distributed, in half-ounce doses, as the medicine. Eleven jewels in particular are employed, namely the diamond, ruby, emerald, sapphire (both blue and white), moon-stone, coral, cat's eyes, gomed, pearl, amethyst and topaz. A twelfth, the opal, is made use of only in the case of eye ailments. A combination consisting of a number or these gems is allowed to 'cook' in water for a week. This water is then administered in small doses in cases of a more obstinate nature.
3. What is considered the highest form of gem treatment employs the principle of radiation and vibration. When a complaint is diagnosed and the gems that form the remedy are decided upon, the patient is seated directly in front of an electric fan, to the blades of which the required gem, or number of gems in little bags of netting

are attached. The current is then switched on and the blades made to rotate at high speed for fifteen or twenty minutes. The idea is that radiations of cosmic colour-force are thrown off from the gem or gems attached to the fan-blades directly upon the patient. This form of therapy is claimed to cure a sufferer from most long-standing complaints within a few weeks.

This therapy can also be used upon a patient residing miles away or in another country, even at the opposite end of the world. In such a case an object, intimate with person, is employed. it may be a photograph, a smear of blood upon blotting-paper, a lock of hair, a finger-nail or even handkerchief. This object, called 'the sample', is attached to a wooden frame which in turn is positioned six inches in front of the electric fan, to the blades of which the gems have been previously attached in small bags of netting. The current is switched on and the blades allowed to rotate at high speed for several hours, instead of just fifteen to twenty minutes, as when the patient is present in person. Astonishing cures have been reported.

But we have all heard of the Tibetan prayer-wheel which is used to rotate continuously with a prayer or a wish that has been enclosed within, while the petitioner concentrates upon it. He believes his wish will thus be granted, and very often if comes to pass. There could be connection between the crude revolving prayer — wheel and the revolving blades of the electric fan, of course, and the gems in their net-bags might simply be factors to aid the concentration of thought.

While the blades of the electric fan employ the principle of radiation, 'vibration' is used in employing an electric 'vibrator' or even a radio loud-speaker. The patient is seated directly in front of such a vibrator, upon which the selected gem or gems are placed and the current switched on, when the cosmic rays are said to be vibrated from the gems to the patient. Distant treatments are also undertaken in the same manner as with the electric fan. The patient's 'sample' is attached to a frame placed six inches in front of the vibrator. In some cases a variation is achieved by vibrating the 'sample' along with the gems in their net-bags, placing them all together upon the vibrator or at the centre of the loudspeaker's cones and switching on the current. For distant treatments, as in the case of the electric fan, the vibrator is made to work for some hours. The trembling vibration is said to impart the cosmic colour-force of the gems from the vibrator to the patient or his 'sample'.

These 'samples' as are said to represent the patient and to identify with him in all respects, no matter how far away he may be, and the radiations or vibrations falling upon them amount to those radiations or vibrations falling upon the patient directly.

Sometimes prayers or urgent wishes are written down upon a piece of paper and made to rotate on the blades of a fast-working fan for some hours or are placed upon a vibrator. Invariably these prayers or wishes become reality. In all instances the 'sample' or the piece of paper with the prayer or wish written upon it, absorb the cosmic rays thrown upon it or vibrated to it, and as these articles represent the actual person or the actual wish, patient gets cured even if he lives at the far end of the world, or the prayer becomes as actuality and is granted.

Space does not permit me into details, but I would like to give you a very brief résumé of this system:

Diamond. For energy. Prescribed in case of sterility, venereal disease, leucorrhoea, drunkenness, old age and all rundown conditions.

Ruby. Prescribed for cases of heart disease, headache, indigestion, sprue, eye diseases, loss of appetite and mental troubles.

Emerald. Prescribed in case of stammering, childishness, stomach disorders, the habit of telling lies, want of intelligence, mania, thieving, dumbness and deafness.

Pearl. Prescribed in cases of diabetes, tuberculosis, dropsy, diarrhoea, bladder diseases, jaundice, restlessness, vices of all sorts and a weak mind.

Coral. Prescribed for liver and blood diseases, measles, high blood pressure, piles, toothache, orchitis, diseases of the joints and urine troubles.

Topaz. Prescribed mainly for mental and personal lapses such as spendthriftness, hypocrisy, talkativeness, fondness for law suits, insanity, paralysis, rheumatism, diseases of the throat or palate and liver, obesity and tumours.

Sapphire. For cases of neuralgia, deformity, enlarged spleen, dropsy, hysteria, epilepsy and all forms of nervousness.

Gomed. For mental fears, suicidal tendencies, uterine troubles, constipation, diseases of the brain and glands, tomours and liver abcess.

Cat's Eye. For boils, skin diseases, cancer fissure, itching, smallpox.

Opal. Mainly for all troubles involving the eyes.

The reader will undoubtedly be amused by the idea that gems might be able to effect any cure whatever, especially by the theory that 'radiation' or 'vibration' could be used on behalf of any patient thousands of miles away. But the proof of the pudding is in the eating, and there appears to be some justification.

From the beginning the Government of India has not imposed a ban upon any of the many systems of medicine practiced in this country, nor has any preference been shown officially for any particular practice. This policy was followed because of the numerous casts and creeds, some of whom have a marked liking for a particular system. The western systems are allopathy and homeopathy, from which we have the offshoots of elctro-homeopathy and Dr Schusscler's biochemical system of the 'twelve tissue remedies'.

The standard Hindu system is Ayurveda, in which the medicines are prepared from the leaves, bark, roots, seeds or flowers of herbs, plants and trees, with its sister system of Siddha, which is practically identical but practiced chiefly in southern India. I can vouch for the efficacy of both these systems, which have claimed numerous successes where all other systems have failed.

Unani medicine is preferred by the Muslim community and depends for its ingredients not only upon plants, but upon minerals and precious stones as well. Chromopathy is followed by many, particularly in Hyderabad State (now Andhra Pradesh). A simple system, it employs the main colour of red, dark blue, sky blue, green yellow and their intermediary blendings, to effect its cures. These colours are used in two ways. Glass bottles of the different colour are filled to three-quarters of their capacity with plain water and allowed to 'cook' in brilliant sunlight for two days. An ounce of this water forms each dose of medicine. Along with this internal dose, the affected part of the human anatomy is exposed to coloured sunlight for twenty to thirty minutes at a time, the rays of the sun being allowed to shine upon the part through a sheet of glass of the required colour.

It is difficult, nowadays to procure glass bottle, and even sheets or fragments of glass of the required colours or of their blends, so this snag is generally surmounted by purchasing transparent material like cellophane of the different hues, such as employed for making decorations. This coloured paper is wrapped once, twice or thrice around a white glass bottle, according to the depth of colour required. Blends of colours are obtained by wrapping paper of first one colour and the another around the bottle; for example red paper, and then blue, to make purple. In place of coloured glass sheets, paper of the required hue is placed directly over the affected part, which is then exposed to strong sunlight.

You will probably think that chromopathy is a lot of nonsense, but I can assure you it is not.

We have all heard of diabetic carbuncles and of how difficult they are to cure, invariably requiring to be lanced. But let the sun shine on your carbuncle through blue glass or paper for thirty minutes twice a day, and at the same time drink four ounces of 'blue' water (water exposed to sunlight in a blue glass bottle or a bottle wrapped in transparent blue paper). The sun must be done at noon and 3 p.m., when the days are at their hottest.

If you are anaemic, procure three large white glass bottles, wrap bright red, transparent cellophane twice around each, and tie the paper in position with red thread. Fill each bottle to three-fourths capacity with pure water and place the bottle in brilliant sunshine for two days. Mark the letter A, B and C on the corks of the respective bottles.

On the third day, finish the contents of bottle A in four or five doses. Refill the bottle immediately and place it back in the sunlight next day, while you drink the contents of second bottle, marked B. Refill that and finish the third bottle, marked C, on the third day, refill it and put it back in the sun. On the fourth day, use the first bottle, marked A, once again, and so on. Your anaemia will begin to disappear in a week to ten days and cost of treatment will have been the price of three sheets of transparent material.

To cure a wart or group of warts, procure a magnifying

glass, wrap transparent yellow cellophane around it, and allow the sunlight to pass through the glass upon the wart, focussing the same to a point insufficiently concentrated to burn the skin. Expose the part from ten to fifteen minutes twice daily and the wart will shrivel up.

What is known as the 'urine system' is practiced largely in the state of Gujarat. The basis of treatment is that the patient is kept on a low diet, amounting almost to complete fasting in some cases, and is given only his own urine to drink. No water, milk or other liquid is permitted. The system is prescribed for all complaints and is highly recommended in certain cases where allopathy and other methods have failed. Mr. Morarji Desai, a former Indian statesman, is a strong advocate of this system.

The 'de Chane system', originating in Hyderabad, is the skilful combination, by a very clever doctor, of the maxims of allopathy, homeopathy and Ayurveda. It has some astounding cure to its credit.

Diagnosis of complaints by the use of electro-or permanent magnets and a pendulum, or by plain intuition, is widely practiced. Samples from the distant patient in the form of a bloodstain, a strand of hair, a silver or finger-nail, a photograph or a bit of personal clothing act as substitute for the patient in his absence, and the operator not only correctly diagnoses the complaint from these substitutes without setting eyes upon the patient, but indicates, according to whichever system of medicine the patient himself may prefer.

Healing by Yogic exercises, pranic breathing, relaxation and meditation are prevalent, while we have our quota of magnetic healers employing passes and the laying on of hands, or using auto-suggestion and the direct spoken command to the genes and body-cells of the patient.

I have witnessed a practitioner of the last-mentioned

system in action when treating a patient with severe dysentery. Laying one hand upon the patient's abdomen and the other on the small of his back, this practitioner almost shouted at the cells of the recalcitrant bowels to do their work properly, while at the same time addressing the genes in a cajoling, persuasive manner, telling them to instruct the wayward cell to do their duties properly. The dysentery stopped within twenty-four hours.

The reciting of *mantrams*, the performance of magical rites, the taking of oaths to give money or other gifts to some saint when a cure has been effected, are all forms of auto-suggestion that amount to self-hypnotism, a very important, and efficacious branch of the science of hypnotism, which again is a method of contact with the subconscious mind. The subconscious mind is the real centre of each one of us. It can accomplish any reasonable wish.

Black art is employed in India mostly for destructive ends but is also occasionally used for healing. It has always proved effective upon those who believe in it.

Cases of 'miracle' healing, under which heading I include religious healing, are often heard of, and the four great Indian religions — Hinduism Islam, Christianity and Buddhism — claim successes in about equal numbers.

In giving this brief review of the general system of healing in use in India I have by no means covered all. Others remain that claim many cures. For instance we have the humble village soothsayer who corresponds to the medicine man of an African hamlet. This individual is the confidant of everyone, from headman and *patel* to the lowest *mochee* or cobbler, 'sweeper' and scavenger. He is called upon to heal any one of them when they are sick, to cure their cattle when bitten by snakes or rabid dogs, or their poultry when they get the Ranikhet disease. he foretells periods of drought and when the monsoon rains will break, and even when floods are likely. He gives advice when crops fail. he helps in arranging marriages, settling disputes and quarrels over land, locates runaway wives and settles domestic problems. This nosey parker knows the business of everyone in the village. To what can we ascribe his general success? Are there hidden sciences and arts in which he is really a master? Or is he just exceptionally astute, a skilled psychologist, mind and character reader, a hypnotist to degree and a smooth talker to a much greater degree? Or is he simply one who has a great deal of common sense and knows how to use it? But every villager will acclaim him his 'guru' (teacher).

Are there such things as 'secret potions' that can bestow good health, freedom from general sickness, perhaps from particular complaints? May be something that can bestow long life? Most people today will find this hard to believe, and about 'long life' I am not prepared to argue, having my own ideas on the subject. But I can tell you this much, and the information is culled from very ancient documents. There are three herbs that grow in India, and one in China, that are said to do just this. what's more, I have all three Indian varieties growing in my garden, while the Chinese plant, or rather an extract made from it, is available in Calcutta. But I can tell you for certain that there are herbs that keep away sickness, sustain the human heart, lower (or raise) the blood-pressure, ensure against arteriosclerosis, cure asthma, diabetes, leprosy, leucoderma, rheumatism and many other complaints, and protect you totally against colds and 'flu.

I have a circular tin-box filled with small blue glass bottles. Each contains one of these 'secret' herbs in powder form: I take a pinch from each of these bottles early in the morning and last thing at night and as far as possible carry this tin-box with me wherever I go. People who have caught me in the act of swallowing these 'medicines' have been astounded at the number of them. And they have scoffed, but I am not perturbed. Touch wood (or my tin box), I just cannot catch a cold. The 'flu' lays out all the members of my household except myself at least twice each year. They get fever and various aches and pains, particularly when they are caught in the monsoon rains. I get soaked, too, and like it. I am sixty-three years old (1972) and can still walk a score of miles a day, especially in the jungle with the animals around me, and be fit for a few more.

For all of which, including the tin box and its contents, I thank God.

Three

Occult Lore and Other Matters

MATTERS OCCULT AND PERTAINING TO THE UNSEEN ARE TAKEN AS much for granted by the folk of southern India as are any of the material objects that they can see. Illness of any kind, a calamity, material losses or a spot of ill-luck, whether of great consequence or small, are all ascribed to one of two causes. The first is the 'bad-time' of the day (*rahukalam* as it is called), or maybe the 'bad-time' of the recipient himself; the second is the deliberate machination of some evilly disposed enemy employing a black magician to cast a spell. In these circumstances, black magicians, spell removers (and those who cast spells), soothsayers and fortune-tellers of all descriptions are in great demand, and there never seems to be enough to go around.

In the larger towns, of an evening you will find these people seated cheek by-jowl in long lines on the pavements. All kinds of fortune-tellers. Some employ a parrot or a lovebird

619

which upon command from the owner, picks out certain playing-cards from a pack or simply cards with fortunes inscribed in close lettering upon them.

Then there are fortune-tellers who ply their trade by consulting the cards directly or by throwing dice. The brotherhood of palmists is strongly represented. A few specialists tell fortunes by reading in the sand, or by charcoal-marks on the pavement, or by studying the shadow thrown by the client at midday. Whatever their methods, none of them appear to want for clients, and as the fees range from one rupee to three for a consultation, the soothsayers seem to earn a very lucrative living.

It would be futile if you were to try to dissuade any of these clients from wasting their money. They would consider you a fool or an ignoramus. The Indian mind inclines strongly to the disposition of Fate, and the parrot or the love-bird, the playing cards, shadows and the rest are all agents that can be made to foretell one's future when handled by a skilled guru.

Most illnesses are ascribed to demon visitation, and for every patient who consults a qualified doctor, there is at least another — probably many more — who seek out 'medicine-man'. I have been a direct witness to many of these cases and the *modus operandi* is almost always the same. I will quote the case of young Niklas (Nicholas actually, but nobody appeared to be able to pronounce that word properly).

He was perhaps nineteen years old, rather short, very black with a handsome cheerful face, long wavy black hair and two rows of perfect teeth that showed prominently when he grinned, which was quite often. A pleasant, hard-working lad, he was popular with everybody up to the day his father was killed suddenly.

'Titch', the father, was what is known in India as a 'lineman'.

He was employed by the Electricity Department, and his duty was to be on hand at certain hours to answer emergency calls regarding electrical installations that went out of order suddenly. It was Titch's job to answer such calls and set the trouble right.

A call came through rather later one Thursday night, and Titch responded. Unfortunately, that Thursday happened to be the first of the month and Titch had drawn his salary earlier in the day. More unfortunately, Titch had been drinking. Not too much, but a little more than he should have, for Titch always celebrated payday with four or five shots of arrack. It did not cost much — about a shilling for two drams.

There had been a strong wind-storm about an hour earlier and the branch of a tree had fallen across the overhead cables, causing a short-circuit and some damage. It was pitch dark when Titch climbed the pole, and the miserably dim ray from the two-cell torch with its almost exhausted batteries supplied by the Department hardly showed up the tangled wires. Just then it began to rain heavily and a sudden gust of wind set free the tangled wires from there they had been hanging, while the rainwater aided conduction. Once wire fell across Titch's neck and the other almost missed his bare feet. Almost — but not quite! Seven thousand volts of electricity flashed through his body and Titch fell from the pole, bringing the wires with him. He was a ghastly sight two hours later after the storm had abated and they picked him up. The wire across his neck had burned its way into his flesh and he was very dead man.

This event upset Niklas, but not nearly as much as his mother's conduct with the same month. She went to live with a neighbour, a young bachelor, for a week, and then the neighbour brazenly moved into house that had belonged to Niklas's father, Titch to live openly with the widow,

Anthonyamma. All this shocked young Niklas, who spoke to his mother about it at the first opportunity. Was this how she respected the name and memory of her late husband, his father? Anthonyamma complained to her paramour, who threw Niklas out of the house that should have by rights been his and threatened to kill him should he dare to return.

Poor Niklas ran to his uncle, Arokiaswamy, for shelter, and the very next night had his encounter with a person who could have been none other than the Devil himself; or so the neighbours said. When I asked him about it, Niklas assured me he saw and spoke to this person as clearly as he was seeing and speaking to me at that moment.

There being no latrine in his home, Niklas had gone behind the nearest bush, as was the custom with all the members of the family, both male and female, in answer to the calls of nature. This had been at about nine o'clock at night, when it was quite dark. Ordinarily he would have been asleep by this time, but that night, for some reason, he did not feel sleep. Niklas said he had been particularly careful, as it had rained an hour earlier and everyone knew that cobras came out of their holes in the ground to hunt for frogs after the rain.

He was down on his haunches when a tall man, dressed entirely in white, appeared before him. The man called him by name and bade him follow. Despite the position he was in at that moment, young Niklas had been impelled to obey and had followed behind the white figure, which maintained a distance of a dozen paces ahead despite Niklas' attempt to catch up. Another thing he had noticed was that the figure appeared to grow taller and taller but not to touch the ground.

They reached the great banyan tree that was growing half-a-furlong away, the figure in white still leading, before it finally halted. This enabled Niklas to catch up at last. He was not clear what happened next. At one moment the figure appeared to rise up vertically into the hanging roots of the old banyan. Then he could see it no longer. What he did recollect a tremendous slap across the back of his neck, after which he remembered no more.

When Niklas failed to return, his cousin brought the fact to the notice of her mother and his uncle. Thinking nothing unusual, they had paid no attention till some time had passed. Then all three set out to look for the missing boy. The white shirt and pants Niklas had been wearing were what caught his aunt's eye, and they found him lying under the old banyan tree and carried him home. That tree was hundreds of years old and reputed to be haunted; therefore they reasoned that the lad's condition was clearly the outcome of some evil spiritual agency or agencies.

From that time on Niklas suffered from mysterious fits, at least once each day, and sometimes as many as three or four. These fits were not epileptic, as Niklas was never unconscious in their throes. In fact he spoke clearly, but in a language nobody could comprehend, though it appeared to concern his mother and her lover. he seemed, moreover, to be in towering rage during these attack, for his eyes flashed and his teeth gnashed. He would become so violent that the combined efforts of all three persons in the household quite failed to control him. At times he would strike them or try to bite. At other times he would roll upon the ground, froth at the mouth and rave at everyone around him. Each attack lasted from ten to fifteen minutes. Then Niklas would return to normal slowly. It took about half-an-hour before he regained his composure. In a few days these attacks increased in intensity, becoming more frequent and of longer duration, while Niklas grew more and more violent.

It was quite late one night when my servants announced

that he had just been summoned to come to Niklas, who had become unusually violent. The lad was some very distant relative of his, but in India nearly everybody is a relative, even if the relationship be removed seventy times seven. Besides, nobody ever misses the opportunity to delve into somebody else's affairs, particularly when such a good excuse as being a relative offers itself.

'Master would like to come?' invited my retainer. 'Tonight Debbil Man come all the way from City Market to drive away this Pey (evil-spirit). My mother's sisters' husband's brother's daughter's son pay him fifty rupees to drive debbil out of poor Niklas, who is son by second marriage to eldest brother of father-in-law of my cousin-brother, and therefore a close relative of mine.'

My senses reeled at the prospect of attempting to unravel Niklas' real relationship to my servant, but I supposed it could be done if sufficient tenacity was applied to the problem. But I am always interested in the occult and here was a chance of witnessing something special. Not that I thought this to be genuine case of spirit obsession. There could be many other explanations, all of them mundane in character. Niklas could be putting on an act. I knew he hated his mother's new boy-friend. Perhaps he was afraid of this man when he had lived under the same roof with him. he might influence his mother to poison the man, or he might poison the man himself or poison the uncle who had befriended him. As likely as no, this was just a case of hysteria. Yet there might be something more to it.

'I'll come along,' I announced and soon we were both standing at the door of the tiny house occupied by Arokiaswamy, the uncle, and his family.

The place was thronged with people and reeked with tobacco-smoke from numerous beedies (small native cigarettes wrapped in the leaves of the peepul-tree). Men and women were seated in tight circle around Niklas, gaping to see what was going to happen next. Just then the boy appeared to be completely in his senses. He saw me enter the room, called a respectful greeting and invited me to come and sit next to him. With difficulty I climbed on the ground beside Niklas, opening the conversation by inquiring how he was.

Niklas answered that he was quite all right. Further conversation was interrupted by the entrance of the 'Devil Man' who was to exorcise the evil spirit.

He was a tall, cadaverous, very black individual, with unusually large eyes set in sunken sockets and great mop of black hair that surrounded his head like a woolly cap. He was dressed in a flowing black robe that reached to ground. From looking at Niklas, his eyes fell upon me and he halted in his tracks. There was hostility in his looks and in the words that fell from his lips.

'What does the *Dorai* want here?' he asked arrogantly. "If he is a preacher and wishes to pray, let him do so. If he is a doctor and has brought medicine, let him give it. I shall go.' With these words he turned back to the door, when many voices were raised to dissuade him from departing.

I got to my feet and called out: "Let the driver-away-of-evil-spirits do his work in peace. I came but to see the lad, and having seen I shall return.'

The black magician (for such he was and as such I shall allude to him in the rest of this story) appeared mollified: 'Let the *Dorai* remain and watch me drive out the spirit, if he so wishes. I know all white men are consumed with curiosity regarding such things. Only he must not interrupt me by word or deed.'

'I shall not,' I promised, and sat down in my former place by the side of Niklas.

The black magician advanced, seated himself directly before Niklas and summoned his uncle Arokiaswamy, a lanky middle-aged individual, to bring the black cock and the bottle of arrack that had already been procured for the ceremony.

When the liquor and the trussed fowl were handed to him, the magician drew a dirty-looking pocket-knife from the recesses of his clothing, unfolded the blade and began to saw with its blunt edge upon the throat of the unfortunate bird. The cock began to flap its wings but the magician continued till he had completely severed the head from the body. The thick red blood that gushed from the stump contrasted strongly with the cock's black feathers. The magician allowed as small quantity of this blood to run into a diminutive aluminium drinking mug, while the rest of it dripped on to the dry earthern floor of the hut and was absorbed.

From his pocket he brought out some dry resinous powder wrapped in paper and allowed it to spill on to the floor. The magician borrowed a match from me and set fire to the powder after several attempts. It burned with a greenish flame. Then he picked up the aluminium mug and held it over this flame for a few seconds while he closed his eyes and started muttering incantations in a sing-song voice. I noticed that the green flame burnt itself out pretty soon but the magician continued with his mantras.

At last he finished, opened his eyes and, lifting the mug, ordered Niklas to drink. The lad appeared to be in some kind of a trance. His eyes were opened but turned upwards, so that I could see the whites. His lower jaw was slack and partly open, and he was rocking himself backwards and forwards to the rhythm of the magician's droning voice. He stretched out his hand obediently and the magician placed that mug in his grasp, closing the boy's fingers firmly around the vessel so that he would not drop it.

Once again he commanded 'drink', and at one gulp Niklas swallowed the hot red blood.

The magician now seized the boys's right wrist in his left hand, and left wrist in his right hand, and raising his voice, commenced shouting the vilest obscenities at the evil spirit said to be within the lad, calling it strings of unmentionably bad names and commanding it to be gone forthwith.

Niklas started to twist and to turn and then to struggle violently with the man who was holding him down, but the magician clung to his wrists and shouted further abuse upon the demon within, commanding it to come forth at once.

Niklas became more violent; then he started to scream aloud. But his shouts were coherent: 'Go away from here. Why do you torment us? We have not place to live and you are ordering us out of the only shelter we have been able to find for so long.'

The words almost turned into a plea. The magician released Niklas' wrists to enable himself to fill the aluminium mug to the brim with raw liquor from the bottle, and tossed the contents down his own throat. He quickly repeated this action, then laid the mug down, grasped the boy's wrists once more and recommenced ordering the demon to leave Niklas.

The lad started to struggle violently, so much so that the magician was compelled to call upon some members of the assembly to help. While this was being done, he did not lose the opportunity to fortify himself still further with yet more arrack. Things came to head a moment later when Niklas gave vent to a piercing screech, jumped to his feet in spite of the many pairs of hands that were holding him, and then fell to the ground as if poleaxed. He kicked spasmodically a few times, stretched his body tautly while grinding his teeth (which sound we all could hear), then threw his arms above his head and ceased to move.

A low wail came from the audience. Clearly most of them thought the boy was dead, but as I watched his chest I could detect rise and fall of his breathing.

The magician was now pointing dramatically to the corner of the room where the light from an oil-lamp hanging from a nail on the wall could barely reach. 'Do you see them?' he quavered. 'Not one spirit, but two. A man and a woman.'

Everyone looked in the direction he was pointing. Of course, nothing could be seen, but the people seated nearest to that corner scrambled hastily to their feet and backed away.

Sensing he was master of the situation, the magician then started to engage in a garbled argument with the spirits that only he could see and hear.

'No, you shall not come back,' he yelled. 'No, not even if you pay me a thousand rupees. These are poor folk. The miserable advance they have paid me for my services is but a pittance. I know they will pay me much more before I leave, so I won't take any part of the one thousand rupees you are offering me.'

'Stand aside,' he ordered. 'Stand away from the door-way. The two spirits are leaving now. Can't you see them? A man and a woman; both completely naked. The woman is very beautiful. She is bedecked with jewels. She has a very pretty face and a lovely figure, but she is evil—very, very evil. For the woman is a devil, you must know.'

'Stand aside,' he continued while the crowd, and particularly the menfolk, began to gape in hope of a glimpse of this lovely, naked girl. 'Stand, I say. For if she gets within reach of you she may change her mind about leaving and enter into you instead, then you will know all about it.'

There was a general stampede to the opposite side of the room, which being filled with people already, caused considerable pushing and shoving. At that moment my eye caught the magician's. I could swear there was a twinkle of laughter in his. He seemed to be saying to me: 'If people want to be fooled so easily, let me fool them. Don't spoil things.' So I remained a silent spectator.

'Ah, now they are leaving' went on the magician. Then, after a moment, 'They have left. Now nobody should go outside for at least half-an-hour to allow the spirits to get clear away.' As a result, I was obliged to remain another thirty minutes in that congested room. It would not have been fair to leave earlier and let the magician down.

This may well have been a farce from start to finish; I agree. Niklas was either an accomplice and played his part well, or this was a simple case of hysteria, since his mother's conduct had upset him greatly. And as Niklas had gained nothing by acting, so we must conclude that Niklas' subconscious mind, in a tremendous state of frustration at being turned out of his own home, wanted to draw attention to his own unenviable position in the new household that his mother had set up with her boy-friend. The fact remains, however, that from that time Niklas was completely cured. He never again suffered from fits and all the credit went to the black magician, the driver-out-of-evil-spirits, for his wonderful performance. We may regard the whole performance as a smart bit of work, but no other person living in these regions will agree: it was to them clearly and simply a case of possession by evil spirit.

Now let me relate the story of Maria, which is far more difficult to explain. Of course, I cannot give you the lady's real name, but Maria will serve the purpose. She was an Anglo-Indian of slightly less than middle-age, respectably married, with four children. A good housewife and a hard worker, she did not care for servants whom she maintained were more a hindrance than a help. And she abhorred mendicants.

Now if there is anything for which India is notorious, it is its beggars ; they swarm everywhere. They throng the roads and accost you in the market-place, and as if that is not enough, they call at your front door and will not go away till you give them alms.

Many such mendicants were in the habit of vising the house where Maria lived, and among them was one in particular who annoyed her immensely. He was a tall, very black man with long hair and a great black beard that streamed down over his chest. He had the most piercing black eyes she had ever seen. This fellow generally wore the accepted costume of a yogi; a long saffron robe reaching to the ground. It was far from clean, as was also the saffron cloth he wore loosely around his head as an untidy turban. Caste marks of white and red on his forehead, a necklace of large amber beads and a stout staff completed his dress. He was always barefooted.

Maria detested the fellow for two reasons. The first, his arrogant manner of demanding alms. Here was no beggar, he made one feel, but someone whose demand had better be met or ... The second reason was more subtle. The man's piercing black eyes seemed to Maria to undress her each time he looked at her. It made her feel as if the clothes she wore — she was invariably a chic dresser — might just as well be dispensed with for all good they did in hiding her nakedness.

One day Maria was particularly busy and the beggar particularly demanding, with the result that she ordered him to get out. Resenting this, the mendicant argued back, when, true to the habits of almost all Anglo-Indians in this hot country, Maria started to abuse him in no uncertain manner.

The response to this was quite unexpected. The visitor said not a word but just glared at her, and those terrible eyes of his seemed to grow larger and to come closer and closer. Now they appeared but a few inches away, and as Maria stood rooted to the spot, they came yet nearer and the next instant were inside her. Or so it seemed.

A still small voice now spoke to her. It was not that of the magician's which was deep and sonorous. This was a high pitched, treble voice, the sort of voice one would associate with a boy of eight years or so. And it always laughed before it said anything. Maria was to come to know of this to her cost very soon. Always that high-pitched, cackling, treble laughter before the words came.

'At last,' chortled the child-like voice, 'I have managed to get back into a human body. It has been so many years, so many long years. But at last I have succeeded. You are mine, Maria, and I will never let you go.' The words rose to a crescendo. 'Never will I leave you, nor will I let you leave me, Maria. From this day forth we two shall be one. Husband and wife, my dear. it has been such a long, long time.'

Maria told me this story afterwards and said that from that moment all sense of privacy was lost to her. Never, at any moment, did she feel alone. 'The Voice,' as she called it, was always with her day and night and it was particularly the nights that she dreaded.

As time passed, this demon within her began to make itself more and more felt. It would always be talking to her in its high-pitched, treble voice, making the most obscene suggestions. Worse still it was always laughing. When she undressed or took her bath, it would scream with glee and shout, 'I can see you! I can see you!' When she lay down to sleep at night it would say the filthiest things to her and make the most vulgar suggestions, ending with 'I, want you. I must have you.'

Matters grew worse as the Voice began to make its demands more and more pressing. Maria would awaken with a start, a sense of a heavy weight upon her as if somebody was lying on top of her. At other times she would feel herself clasped tightly in a pair of strong invisible arms.

Gradually Maria began to change in her own conduct and nature. She had always been an upright person of good character, but I expect the continuous flow of lewd suggestions and the actions that these suggestions awakened wore Maria down till she herself started to welcome, and finally follow, those continuous promptings. By this time the people who had known her and noticed the change began to talk about it, and in our town rumours spread rapidly.

Thus it was that I came to hear of Maria, and being always interested in such matters, lost no time in contacting her through the friend who had told me.

Maria did have short respite now and again from the prompting of the Voice, although this was not very often or for long. Luckily, it was on one of those occasions that I first met her and I had time to gain her confidence and hear her story before the Voice suddenly came back and took hold of her. There was no mistaking this, for Maria abruptly stopped speaking to me in mid-sentence and her voice changed to an almost childlike treble lisp: 'How nice of you to visit me. Do come and sit closer, it will be so cosy for both of us.'

Maria was handsome in appearance and of pleasing build and it was easy to understand how her change in habits and her newly acquired intimate and sexy behaviour was going to get her into a lot of trouble. The friends who had told me about her and probably nearly all those who had heard the story were convinced her's was clear case of possession. The mendicant whom Maria had ordered away so abruptly had laid a curse upon her, one of the worst curses that can be put upon anybody in the East: the curse of obsession by an evil entity or spirit. Millions of people believe in this sort of thing. The events clearly pointed to it. There could be no other possible explanation, they would say.

I have travelled a lot in India in my time, during which period I have never lost an opportunity to investigate, as far as possible, every case of occult happening that has come my way. I have read a lot about these things, met and spoken to a number of black magicians and delved into the matter as deeply as I could. Indeed, I have gone as far as to become initiated into the cult of black magician by preforming certain rites that, under the oath of secrecy, I cannot reveal.

Anyone who has delved into these matters deeply enough and gained sufficient experience develops sort of uncanny sense for knowing whether a case he may encounter is actually the result of a black magician's spell or not. As I have said already, nearly everything of an abnormal kind that happens in India is attributed to the occult and to black magic, but to those who, like myself, have studied the subject, this is far from being so. A fair percentage of people who suddenly begin to act queerly do so for quite natural reason. Hysteria plays a very large part in the lives of people in the East, both men and women, but more particularly among women at the time of menstruation and menopause.

Then again, people in the East are far more emotional then those in the West. Little injuries done to them assume gargantuan proportions, and they brood and brood over their wrong till, quite frequently, their minds give way. At best, there is but a narrow margin in the minds of us all between sanity and insanity, and it does not take very much or very long for that small barrier to break down and the same to become insane, at least to some degree or in certain ways. So before attributing anything to occult influence, we should not fail to consider whether suggestion and auto-suggestion may have played a part in influencing the person concerned to act in a given manner. Repeated and powerful suggestion upon the subconscious mind of practically any ordinary individual will soon cause that person to act in the way intended while hypnotism, which is after all but a well-harnessed form of suggestion, undoubtedly acts as a most powerful factor.

Hypnotism, powerful and almost instantaneous, is an art well known and widely practiced in India by some pseudo-yogis and other interested person, and I felt certain Maria's case fell entirely into this category. She had repeatedly stressed that the mendicant's piercing black eyes' seemed to bore right through her, to undress her, as she said, to the point that she felt it was useless for her to wear any clothing. His gaze and his concentrated silence had brought her under his hypnotic influence undoubtedly, and she was but carrying out in practice the suggestions he had forced upon her.

The only solution was to break that hypnotic spell, but to do so successfully would require an indirect approach. I knew it would be useless for me to tell her that she had been hypnotised and that I would try to remove the hypnotic influence that had been brought to bear upon her. Without doubt, one of the first commands her visitor had given her under his spell was to resist any suggestion that he was influencing her. I would have to hypnotise her myself without her knowing what was happening, and then put the counter-suggestions required to nullify the orders of the mendicant.

Luckily I was wearing my heavy silver ring, set with a blue stone, a gift to me from a close friend from Ghana, so I decided to play upon Maria's clear belief that she had been bewitched by using this belief to hypnotise her.

'Maria,' I began, 'I am wearing a ring that has come all the way from Ghana in Africa. It belongs to a very powerful witch-doctor who gave it to me. Now, if you will stare at the blue stone on this ring without closing your eyes, I will invoke the magic that is in the ring to free you of your trouble for all time.'

Maria was a simple sort of woman, obviously not well read, and the mendicant's suggestion in the form of the Voice continued its cackling, followed with a lewd suggestion each time, for many minutes, while I persisted with my magic ring. But at last she quietened down and agreed to look at the ring. Removing it from my finger, I laid the ring upon a small table that I placed close before her.

I asked her to stare at it without blinking her eyes. Maria then started to do as I had asked.

At first her gaze would wander, but I brought it back each time till I finally succeeded in rivetting her attention upon the blue stone. Slowly I made the sleep suggestion and in a surprisingly short while Maria was sound asleep under my hypnotic influence.

The rest was easy. I made the counter suggestions required to nullify the mendicant's earlier commands and continued for some time, till I felt my orders had supplanted the mendicant's earlier evil commands. I told her that never again would she be troubled by the Voice. That had been only her own imagination. She had never heard any such voice. There never had been a voice. I had been a nasty dream. Entirely her own imagination. No such thing as a Voice! It then woke her up.

The lady, as I have told you, was basically a good woman and I am glad to be able to record that she was quite cured from that moment. No longer did she hear the high-pitched treble voice (which, incidentally, was her own voice pitched to a treble key under hypnotic instruction), urging her to do and speak obscene things. No longer did it speak to her night and day. Maria had been freed and neither the devil nor any evil spirits had played any part in entering into her.

Nevertheless, I have come across some well-authenticated cases of spirit-possession and I will now tell you about one of these. I have already mentioned the case of Ossie Brown in some detail in my earlier book, *The Call of the Man-Eater.* The story begins in much the same way as Maria's. A fakir in a yellow robe was wont to present himself on the first day of every month at the pay-counter of the premises where Ossie was working and demand alms from him and the other staff-members as they received their salaries.

In time, Ossie resented this peremptory attitude and threatened to hand the man over to the police. Hot words followed, ending with the fakir cursing Ossie and a statement that he would put 'someone' into my friend who would take up his abode there and remain till death.

That very night Ossie awoke with the curious sensation that he was not alone. He opened his eyes to see a dark figure outside his mosquito-net. The figure came closer and closer and appeared to merge with him by actually getting inside him. Thereafter, Ossie started exhibiting strange mannerisms at work. His voice and behaviour would change. Apparently he did not know where he was, or who he was. He would ask gruffly how he came to be there. Then he would walk out of the room. Sometimes he would return after a lapse of thirty minutes or an hour quite oblivious of his behaviour or of how he left his work spot. Occasionally he would collapse, as if in a fit. When he recovered, he was quite normal and was very surprised at being told of his behaviour.

Just about this time, rather foolishly, I invited Ossie on a trip of the jungle. We camped that night on the banks of a great river, far from human habitation. A herd of wild elephants were grazing close by. We could hear them trumpeting and breaking the branches off trees, and we lit large camp-fire to keep away any stray elephants that might come our way. Suddenly, a strange gruff voice addressed me, demanding to know who I was. It came from Ossie, but as I looked at him I saw quite another person looking back at me. The eyes, the face, everything was different. This entity repeated his demand. Who was I? Where were we?

I tried to pacify Ossie by saying we had come out shooting, whereupon he demanded that I should give him my gun. Fortunately, he did not notice that my rifle was against a tree directly behind him. I know that if he got hold of it he might shoot me. So distracting his attention to the elephant, I pounced upon the weapon and threatened to shoot him if he came any closer.

Regardless of my threat, he advanced upon me. I knew only too well that in a physical struggle I would be no match for this person, evil spirit or not. I would be compelled to shoot and at least wound my friend and that would not be an easy thing to do with a heavy calibre .405 rifle.

When he was only five feet away the solution came to me. I fired the rifle so that the bullet just whizzed over his head. Ossie halted abruptly, shuddered and passed a hand over his forehead wearily. The next second the possessing entity had gone and my friend spoke to me in his normal voice.

The sequel to this story is that Ossie went to Calcutta where, one day, he threw himself from the second-floor of a building and was killed. To me this case was a clear example of spirit-possession. You will notice it differed from Maria's in one very important fact. Maria fancied she heard a voice in her own head telling her to do things. She did not change or act differently herself. By that I mean her personality remained the same. In Ossie's case the change was in himself, physically as well as outwardly. His manner, appearance and voice all changed in the twinkling of an eye. Secondly, Maria could always remember what the inner voice, prompting her, had said. In Ossie's case he was quite ignorant of all that had happened to him and could remember nothing.

The reason for the difference appears obvious. Maria's conscious and subconscious minds were overshadowed by the orders of the mendicant, delivered while she was under hypnosis and in his control. Nevertheless it was Maria's own conscious and subconscious minds that were functioning under the orders of an outsider disguised under an assumed identity of a childlike, treble voice. With Ossie, both his conscious and subconscious minds were not only dominated, but temporarily taken possession of by quite another identity, this time a discarnate entity under the orders of the fakir, who must have been a powerful medium as well as master of black magic. As a result, Ossie's conscious and subconscious minds were not functioning at all at the time and so he remembered nothing of what had taken place.

There are quite a number of persons living in India today who perform each day, and sometimes several times in the course of each day, the miracle of what are known in spiritualistic parlance as 'the phenomenon of apports'.

In the darkness, or the dim red illumination the seance room, spiritualists claim that small objects such a flowers or other trivial articles are brought to them by the spirits and laid upon their laps even though all doors and windows have been closed. The mystics of India go much farther than this. To begin with, they operate in broad daylight, in an open space, sometimes with hundreds of people looking on.

Sai Baba the reincarnated, generally referred to as Sathya Sai, who is a personal friend whom I have known as a lad and who claims to be the reincarnation of the original Sai Baba the great, who died many years ago, once stretched out his hand in front of me and closed it over a little metal image which appeared to materialise and his fingers were closing upon it! Baba, as he is affectionately referred to by his personal acquaintances, gave it to me as a keepsake and I put the little figure in my purse.

Years later a pickpocket relieved me of this purse, with my money and the figurine inside, as I was boarding the last night-bus from Bangalore to Whitefield, twelve miles away, where I was living at the time. I knew nothing of the theft at the time, but about halfway to my destination the conductor came round collecting tickets. I put my hand into my pocket for my purse.

It was gone! Worse still, I did not have another coin on my person.

Yet there was something small and hard in the corner of that pocket. I felt again and drew out the small figurine that Baba had given me. It had been inside one of the compartments of the missing purse. The purse itself had been taken. How had the little image come back into pocket?

The conductor was looking hard at me. Suspicion came into his face when I withdrew my hand, empty except for the tiny figure between my fingers. The conductor pulled the cord to stop the bus. We were about seven mile from Whitefield and it was five minutes to midnight. Moreover, it was raining. I had the prospect of a long walk before me.

I explained that my pocked had been picked. The conductor grinned sardonically, 'Tell that to the Marines,' he said in the local dialect. Only, having never heard of the Marines, he used another name in its place, a very rude word with a very, very dirty meaning that I cannot possibly repeat. Then his eyes fell upon the figurine. His manner changed. He pulled the cord twice, which was the signal for the driver to proceed.

'We'll risk it,' he said. 'No inspector is likely to check at this time of night.'

I thanked that conductor when I alighted from the bus. He confided that he was a devotee of Baba's. I have often wondered whether Baba, when he produced the figurine out of the air that day and gave it to me, knew what good purpose it was to serve in saving me from a long, wet, midnight walk.

The second time I went to Baba was when I was in a spot of real trouble. Before I could ask him, he told me my trouble. He also told me what were to be the consequences. He gave me that answer nearly thirteen years ago and everything he said came to pass exactly. Before parting, he stretched out his hand for me to shake. As he did so, I noticed that he closed his fingers over something. Then he handed me as small piece of ash.

'Keep it in a small box, carefully,' he advised. 'Should you have any trouble at any time, or a problem, open the box and look upon the ashes. Picture my face in the ashes. I think your trouble, or problem, whatever it is, will disappear very soon after that.'

I did exactly what Baba told me. I cannot say I have been trouble-free. But whatever my trouble, they have since turned out to be but little ones. And I still have that box with the ashes in it.

However, this is a digression. The question is, how do people like Baba get these apports? There seem to be only two solutions. The first is obvious. Trickery, in the form of sleight-of-hand. Something that our fathers, grandfathers and great-grandfathers have seen on the stage for years. The second solution defies explanation.

Let us consider trickery first. Did Baba successfully 'palm' the figurine and the ashes upon me, right under my nose, without my noticing how he did it? I deny it, but what is the use arguing? So let me tell you some of the other occurrences which he bought to pass. You will then be in a better position to judge whether 'palming' could have been possible.

A sick girl was brought to him. She had been suffering from a permanent headache for months. By apport, Baba produced a small bottle of very strongly scented balm. The first application of this balm upon her forehead cured that headache for good.

Baba was once invited to an alfresco tea-party. The tables were spread beneath a grove of large and beautiful mango trees. The month was November. No fruit grows on mango trees in November. April to June are the months for mangoes in India.

Somebody remarked, 'What a pity there are no mangoes now.' To which Baba replied, 'But there are.' In his hand was a stalk, to which three ripe mangoes and a couple of leaves were attached.

One more incident. Baba was travelling by car from Bangalore to his permanent abode in Putlipatli. Short of his destination by about fifty miles, the car stopped. The driver had not put sufficient petrol into the tank. They would either have to beg some passing lorry for petrol, or Baba must go by bus for the rest of the journey.

Baba stepped out of the car, walked to the rear and stretched the palm of his hand over the petrol-tank. Then he reseated himself. 'Drive on,' he instructed. 'We now have enough petrol to complete the journey.' And they had.

So, if these things are not done by sleight-of-hand, how are they done? At least, how do people in India say they are done?

There are two current explanations. Basically, they amount to the same thing, although in modus operandi they are quite dissimilar. The general opinion is that the apports are brought to the master desiring them through the agency of what are known as 'Kutti shaitans', diminutive little sprites generally invisible, but which at times take on the appearance of tiny, naked, very black people, no more than six inches in height and of both sexes. On to the degree of occult power possessed by the master depend the number of 'Kutti-shaitans' in the band that serves him or her, and it may vary from a single one to two dozen.

Elaborate methods are prescribed as to how a person may gain control over one or more of these little elfs, but they are said to be quite dangerous people once you have anything to do with them. The trouble is that when you set yourself to acquire one or more of them, they in turn acquire you and the contract is for life; you cannot revoke it at any period, and if you try to do so the direst of repercussions await you in the form of great misfortune, sickness and eventual death. Moreover, the sprites do not serve you for nothing: they with will obey you and get you what you want, provided you in turn agree to their terms and give them what they want. And their terms and wants are always of a horrid nature.

Once a week, mostly on Fridays, but with some magicians on Thursdays, time must be set apart at midnight on which these payments are to be made to the little sprites in a room specially appointed for the purpose. Blood is frequently demanded: Pig's blood, the blood of a black cock, human blood from a vein in your own or somebody else's arm, or menstrual blood. Sprites of a lower order demand that you commit the greatest sacrilege against the dictates of your own religion, whatever it may be, by saying things, doing things and submitting religious objects to deeds that are the most blasphemous possible.

Nor is that all. No master may marry. If he wants to cohabit with a woman he must first get permission from his Kutti-shaitans to do so. This is only bestowed after incurring a heavy penalty. Financially, the master can never be in abundant circumstances. He will receive only enough money to live in moderate comfort. Never may he become rich.

To acquire one of these sprites, he must first become a black magician of which there are many orders. Actually to capture the sprite he is required to visit a buffalo-kraal at midnight on the night of the Amavasa, which is the darkest

night of the month, exactly halfway between full moon and
the succeeding new moon. He should hide himself in a corner
of the kraal along with the buffaloes, arriving at least an hour
before midnight. When the time comes and the hour strikes,
if he looks earnestly enough he will generally notice something
rather like a big moth or a small bat flitting about on the back
of one of the buffaloes. The seeker should approach it quietly
and make snatching motions with his arms and hands, as if
trying to seize this flitting creature.

Of course he would never really be able to seize a sprite.
His motions are only symbolical and signify his earnest desire
and intention to succeed.

The sprite, or Kutti-shaitan, will then speak to him,
normally by means of mental rather than spoken conversation.

'What are you trying to do?' it will ask.

'I mean to capture you,' the seeker will reply.

'Why? What do you want of me?' the sprite will ask.

'I mean to catch and conquer you. I want you for my
servant; to do my bidding and get me whatever I may desire.'
The seeker is required to be very firm and positive in this
assertion.

The sprite may remonstrate at first, or begin to bargain
straight away. Often it may lay down extremely difficult, if
not quite impossible, conditions in return for its services. The
seeker is strongly advised to refuse straight away and then to
try to drive as hard a bargain as possible, for he must remember
that, once it is made, the pact is sealed for the rest of his
lifetime. It may never be broken, renounced or cancelled.
Many instances are on record of black magicians who, for one
reason or another, but principally for the sake of contracting
a marriage, have tried to nullify their agreements with their
Kutti-shaitans, either by straight-forward renunciation of
trickery. The direst penalties have befallen them in the way

of misfortune, sickness, loss of sight or limbs, or even death. So you should really think twice before you enter into an agreement of this sort, even if your self is able to bring you so many nice things.

The other common belief, and this is more prevalent in northern India than in the south, is that the familiar who brings the apports, and is known by the name of the hamzad, is merely your own astral self, resembling you in every way, including appearance, mannerisms and even clothing. The hamzad is believed to be capable of travelling to the ends of the earth in the twinkling of an eye, of carrying enormous weights and of being able to do anything for you and get you whatever you want. It is understood of course that everything the hamzad brings is made invisible in course of transit and is made to resume is substantial appearance when the hamzad presents it to his master.

You are required to work hard before you can capture the services of your hamzad. This is done by following certain very secret formulae. As in the case of the Kutti-shaitan, a two-way bargain must be entered into between the seeker and his hamzad for service to be rendered and this bargain is mandatory for life. Penalties of the most frightful character, including the violent termination of the seeker's life, follow the breaking of this pact by the human partner.

It may be interesting to note certain fundamental differences as well as some basic similarities, between western black magic and the Indian brand of black magic.

The main difference seems to lie in the fact that, whereas European black magicians, generally known as wizards and witches, more or less make undisguised convenants with Lucifer, the spirit of the morning, and other terms synonymous with Satan, or more commonly, the devil; ('shaitan' being the name in Hindi and 'pey' or 'pisachee' in Tamil) plays any part in the bargain. Kutti-shaitans, of the hamzad or, on some occasions a particular spirit variously known as a 'minispuram' in the south and in western India as a 'rakash', are the entities invoked for this purpose and they are by no means considered to be devils, nor do they bear any resemblance to one. The Indian seer firmly believes that he is dealing with one or more very powerful spirits who are definitely not of an evil disposition, although they may at times be tempted or driven to outbursts of the most severed anger or revengefulness, or plain malevolence. He will very strongly deny that he is having any truck with the devil and will become most indignant if you insist that this is so.

At the same time, considering that the aims of the two schools are about the same, while the result attained are more or less equal, one cannot but wonder whether the devil or any other spirit, has really anything to do with it. Of course, the westerner will claim that the devil and the minispuram or spirit are one and the same. The Indian will stoutly deny it: his minispuram is far from being a devil.

Maybe, however, the much maligned devil and the greatly feared minispuram have nothing whatever to do with it, and that it is black magician's, or which's own subconscious mind that is at the bottom of the whole affair, assuming and playing the part of the devil or the minispuram, just to satisfy its owner?

It will be noticed that in all cases a bargain is mandatory. Without this pledge on the part of the black magician on the one hand and the entity on the other, no deal can transpire, no pact may be made. Why is this so? The religious-minded person will claim that by striking a pact of this kind, the devil will win over the witch's soul to himself, with eventual damnation and hell. The black magician of India will say that his minispuram must naturally require, and receive, some sort of reward and satisfaction for his labours on his master's behalf.

May it not also be a fact that the existence of a pact serves to remind the magician always of his contacts with the other sides, the devil or spirit who is under an obligation to him and to whom he is equally beholden every moment of the day and night. The pact serves to rivet the attention of his conscious and his subconscious minds at all times.

Therein lie the essential ingredients that make black magic work. The strong awareness on the part of both the conscious and subconscious minds of the magician, western or eastern, that he has struck a bargain with some supernatural power possessing the attributes of ability and willingness to work for him with assured success, and get him what he wants, in return for possession of his very self. The magician and this power thus becomes welded into one force, as it were, and this though is with at all times, giving him a boost of selfconscious assertiveness and confidence in himself that he would not normally possess.

Conversely, all self-assertiveness and self-confidence completely disappear in a victim in India, even if he should by nature have these attributes, when he finds himself pitted against a black magician. Generations of upbringing together with the frightening tales drilled into him from childhood, make him quite certain that he is absolutely helpless before the man of magic and entirely in his power.

Thus we have a person all filled with confidence, in a supernatural power that is helping him day and night opposed to another who has known from childhood that he is helpless against a foe who has supernatural assistance. The result is a foregone conclusion and the man of magic always wins.

Latent hypnotism plays a major part in both the casting and removal of 'spells' in India. Everyone has heard of 'mantras' and 'mantrams', words used in relation to magical formulae of one kind or another. The words are identical in meaning and apply to everything from coherent sentences, uttered either in ancient Sanskrit or in the local vernacular (it should be remembered that there are about three hundred vernaculars in use throughout India and Pakistan) in either prose or poetry, to incoherent and meaningless phrases. Mantras are employed to bring good luck, employment, a suitable partner in marriage, a male child, protection against sickness or danger, a cure for any sickness and for a host of other purposes. In fact, their employment is practically synonymous with the use of talismans, but with a rather wider range.

It is the repetition of such a mantram, over and over again, that serves to focus the attention upon a particular purpose or objective. It serves to keep the mind from straying away from that purpose or objective. Thus one attains a determination, together with a large degree of auto-suggestion, which in itself is nothing but auto- or self-hypnotism.

A third factor is also present ; a great impelling desire, coupled with great personal emotion. The person is all worked up, in all his being, to achieve and to acquire what he wants. So we save here the ingredients necessary for attaining success in any field. Firstly determination, the great driving factor; secondly, a great desire to attain it, a sort of burning need for it; thirdly, belief or faith that what is being striven for will be achieved; and fourthly, great emotion to keep the mind and nerves stretched.

The mantrams of the East are therefore, a very clever way to apply in practice all the four great rules of 'How to Get What You Want in Life', and would appear in any normal person as nothing more.

But, does this explanation apply to every case? Let me relate a true story to which thousands now living in India will testify.

Shri Narsiah was a humble stationmaster of the very

unimportant railway station at Polreddipalayam on the Southern Railway in the state of Andhra Pradesh. But this humble and self-effacing man was the means of saving the lives of hundreds of persons bitten by poisonous snakes, including cobras, vipers and the deadly kraits. Should anyone be bitten by a poisonous snake anywhere in India, it was only necessary to send a telegram to Shri Narsiah at his station mentioning the name and address of the afflicted person. People in those parts are extremely poor and most can hardly afford to pay the cost of an express telegram. With this in mind, there is an unspoken understanding in the minds of the telegraphists throughout the region. When such a message is handed in, everyone handling the message, as well as the telegraphists receiving it, gives the message priority over every other telegram, even 'express' messages, however important they maybe. So we could expect Shri Narsiah to receive the telegram in reasonably short time. Nevertheless, so terribly fast does the bite of a cobra work that the patient would be near to death anyway.

Growing to one side of the single platform at Polreddipalayam railway station is quite a short tree. It is a very peculiar tree indeed, different from all others. For it is a sacred tree and is the means by which the cobra's victim, perhaps a thousand miles away, can be saved from death. This little tree is festooned with small pieces of white rag, tied to every conceivable part of it within reach. Those little pieces of white cloth are torn from corners of Shri Narsiah's *dhoties*, or anklelenght loin-clothes, for the stationmaster does not wear trousers of the ordinary western style. He is a high-caste Brahmin and bears caste-marks upon his forehead. The climate is hot and he is bare-bodied invariably but his loincloth, wound tightly around his waist and extending to his ankles is his stock-in-trade for curing snake-bites wherever they may occur.

Each time Shri Narsiah receives a snake-bite telegram, he hastens to the little sacred tree, tears a strip of about six to eight inches from the bottom corner of his dhoti, ties it to a branch of the tree and mutters a secret mantra half aloud. The snake, provided it has not already been killed, is said to die at this instant. Narsiah then goes back to his work as stationmaster in the little cabin which is his office as if nothing untoward has happened. Maybe a thousand miles away the patient, lying on the ground in a coma with saliva dripping from the corners of his mouth, and with only a few moments more to live, suddenly opens his eyes, sits up and then stands erect. He has been completely cured!

Bear in mind that the victim was unconscious, at death's door. He certainly could not practice hypnotism nor could he be hypnotised. Nor could he indulge in auto-suggestion, nor even in prayer. He could not do anything, for that matter, to help himself.

In distant Polreddpalayam, Shri Narsiah, interrupted in his duties, certainly did not waste time on any such practices. He had simply hurried to the tree, torn a strip from the lower end of his dhoti and uttered a mantra while he tied that strip to the tree. Then he returned to his duties. And the patient recovered!

If you were to ask Shri Narsiah how it was done, I do not think he will tell you.

At one time of my life I worked in the Telegraph Department for nearly thirteen years, and I transmitted many such messages to Shri Narsiah. To satisfy my curiosity, I have subsequently telegraphed the snake's victim at the address given on the distress message. In every single case the man had been cured! What is more to the point, I was bitten by a cobra myself and a telegram was sent to Shri Narsiah on my behalf.

I had just returned from duty. The time was about 3 p.m.
A hue and cry was suddenly raised by one of our tenants.
'Snake!' She screamed. Then, as she saw the spectacled hood,
'Cobra! Cobra!'

I had been catching snakes since I was eight years old and
so thought nothing of it. Without difficulty I secured the
cobra by grabbing its tail, while I put a stick across the back
of its head. Quickly releasing the tail, I transferred my grip
to the back of the cobra's neck. Then I lifted it up. The snake
was completely helpless. I carried it to the box I generally
keep ready for such eventualities and was in the act of throwing
it in when the snake wound the free end of its tail around
my other arm. It was quite a long specimen for a cobra. A
female, if I remember correctly.

As the snake restricted my movements I was unable to open
the lid of the box, so I called my servant-boy (known as a
'chokra') to remove the tail that was coiled around my arm.

The chokra started to do so timidly when the cobra
transferred its tail-coils to the boy's wrist. He panicked. he
gave a violent jerk to free his wrist and in doing so wrenched
the head of the cobra from between my fingers. That reptile
was fast, and before I could act, it had buried its fangs in the
ball of my thumb.

I threw the wretched cobra into the box, closed the lid,
and as I did not have too much faith in mantrams and
stationmasters, hastened in my car to the local hospital for
an antivenine injection.

But my people at home had firm faith in Shri Narsiah,
and as the telegraph office was but two furlongs distant, the
telegram to him was on its way before I reached the hospital.

There was considerably confusion when I told the nurse
at the emergency section what had happened. She said I must
see the duty doctor and went in search of him. The doctor

came back with her and asked what had happened. I told him. He asked whether I was certain it was a snake Finally, he went in search of the serum.

He came back looking rather bothered. Apparently the hospital had run out of stock. He told me to hurry to another hospital which was over two miles away. I was feeling giddy by now with a pain in my thumb and hand. I got into the car and made for the other hospital, where I was given 10 cc of antivenine serum intravenously.

But my people had sent a reply-pad telegram to Shri Narsiah and to this he had replied, 'Don't worry. Patient cured. Snake dead.' The hospital detained me for about four hours to see how I fared. Except for severe urticaria set up through serum reaction, I felt more or less none the worse for my experience. The giddiness had passed and there was no pain in the region of the bite.

Finally I returned home and was handed Narsiah's reply. I read it and went directly for the box where I had put the cobra. I opened the box. The snake inside was quite dead. Not only dead, coiled up inside as rigid and stiff as if it had been made of metal.

How and why did that cobra die? It had not been injured by me or by anyone else. Also, it takes at least twenty-four hours for a dead snake to become so rigid. In this case only four hours had passed, yet the cobra had become so rigid that I could not uncoil it again, although I tried.

Not a very good case, it may be said, because I had been given the injection after the telegram had been sent. I should have waited for the stationmaster to act. But who would have done so in the circumstances? In any case, why did the cobra die? Why did it stiffen so soon.

Almost everyone who has lived in India for any length of time will be able to tell you instances of black magic. They abound in every corner of the land.

Sammy Soanes was a friend of mine. He had originally come from Goa then a Portuguese possession, and had bought a small property and settled down in Bangalore. A gentleman from Malabar bought the neighbouring house and moved in with quite a large household. Quarrels started between Sammy's people and the neighbours. My friend was of a quiet, non-interfering disposition, but these quarrels reached a pitch when he was compelled to make a police report as well as take legal proceedings.

Now his neighbour, the man from Malabar, although a recent-comer, had already become notorious as a black magician. He called Sammy to the stone wall that separated their respective properties and told him flatly that if he did not withdraw both cases against him forthwith, he (the neighbour) would make Sammy bedridden for life.

Sammy laughed at him. The man from Malabar turned on his heels and walked away.

As I have said, Sammy was a good-tempered soul. He forgot about the incident in a couple of hours and that night went to bed at his usual early hour. But he could not rise early the following morning. He could not get out of bed at all, for he was unable to raise himself. He was paralysed from the waist downwards.

Panic seized him as he remembered the happenings of the previous day. Mrs Saones, who had overheard the neighbour's threats, pleaded with her husband to allow her to carry his abject apologies to the man from Malabar. Perhaps he would be merciful and forgive. Then Sammy would be able to get out of bed once more.

There is a strange quality that docile persons possess. You can drive them just so far, but suddenly they will reach a point when they can be driven no further. The neighbour's threats had reached that point. Sammy refused to apologise. Instead, he urgently summoned a Nambodripad, also from the West Coast of India, who was a personal friend and had himself settled down in Bangalore a couple of years earlier.

Krishnan, Sammy's friend, duly answered the summons and declared at once that the neighbour was responsible for Sammy's paralysis. He said, after some further consideration, that the magic used to bring about Sammy's incapacity was the work of a powerful 'yaksha'. So powerful, indeed, that his own familiar was not strong enough to undo it and put Sammy upon his feet again. What he could do, however, was to bring a similar spell to bear upon the neighbour, so that he would become paralysed himself and confined to his bed in turn.

Sammy gave the green signal to this and by the same evening the man next door suddenly lost his power to stand upright and within the hour found that he, in turn, could not move from the waist downwards. This led to a sort of contest in casting spells between this nasty neighbour and Sammy's Nambodripad friend, working on behalf of Sammy, in which the latter very definitely came off much the worse. Sammy was stricken with high fever, was unable to eat or drink, and the paralytic stroke that had afflicted him showed no signs of abating. He had to be fed in ravenously. The neighbour, on the other hand, had managed to overcome the Nambodripad's spell and was back on his feet again.

It was at this stage that Mrs Soanes, unknown to her husband, visited the black magician next door to beg his pardon. When he opened the door to let her in, he remarked 'I knew you would come. It was just a matter of time.'

This man was a haughty fellow and spurned her apologies for a long time. Finally he agreed to remove the spell and restore Sammy to health in return for a sum of five hundred rupees, the full amount be paid in cash and in advance.

Mrs Soanes never doubted for moment that he would keep to his terms. But where was she to lay hands on five hundred rupees without her husband's knowledge? Then she remembered the heavy gold chain lying at the bottom of her steel trunk. That and two gold bracelets she had bought after years and years of hard labour and saving.

She took the article to Borilal, the local money-lender. They were worth over two thousand rupees, but after much pleading and begging, that skinflint agreed to give her six hundred rupees in loan, although he did not actually present her with this amount in cash. Rather, he deducted the full interest for one month which he claimed came to just one hundred rupees, in advance, and gave the balance of five hundred rupees to his client.

Mrs Soanes hastened to her neighbour's house and timidly knocked at his door. After a while the black magician answered her summons. He nodded perfunctorily and allowed her to enter. Gruffly he commanded, 'Give me the money.'

Meekly, Mrs Soanes handed over five hundred rupees in notes. The man counted the money. Then he rudely dismissed her, saying, 'You may go. Your husband will be able to stand by this evening.'

Mrs Soanes did not dare to ask any questions, but almost fled from that awful presence. As the sun set that evening, Sammy suddenly told his wife that he felt well again, and to substantiate his words he scrambled to his feet. Mrs Soanes never told him about her chain and bracelets. She was too poor to redeem the articles, so she had to fake a burglary and say they had been stolen. Sammy believed her.

This story is true. I knew Sammy Soanes personally for years and visited him when he was paralysed. At that time he told me about the spell cast by his neighbour, and his own friend's (the Nambodripad's) unsuccessful efforts to free him. Mrs Soanes told me the rest in confidence, later on.

I do not wish to repeat myself, but there is a case of my own which I have related in an earlier book. A person who knew this art took a dislike for me. As a result I was awakened around 3 a.m. for several days with a feeling of being choked by a heavy weight upon my chest. I also heard measured footsteps outside my window, but there was never anybody there. Upon a whim, I consulted a local magician, who is very famous in my home town. Before I could speak, he told me the exact purpose of my visit. He also told me to go home, measure a certain distance from my window and dig down into the earth a certain depth. I was to destroy what I found there, whereupon I would be left in peace.

I measured out the stated distance, dug down the required depth, and found a small effigy with hair fastened to it. That hair looked remarkably like my own. I destroyed the effigy and was never troubled again.

I could relate many more tales of this sort, but they would become boring. It is sufficient to impress the fact that the people of India and especially those in the south of this peninsula, are brought up with black magic as an acknowledged fact from their earliest days. Nobody would ever think to question or doubt the reality; black magic is so involved in everyday life in this land that hardly any adult male of any community, other than westerners — who are considered not to believe in anything anyway — will go out alone after nine or ten o' clock at night until about five o'clock in the morning, by which hour evil spirits are considered to have gone to rest.

To carry pork, raw or cooked, after sunset is to invite being struck down by an evil entity. This is more so if you happen to be walking barefoot. It is safe, however, to carry pork provided you also carry a piece of charcoal. The devil will then leave you alone.

The members of certain tribes and communities are

accredited with being steeped in magic from their childhood and the average Indian will avoid having anything to do with such a person, as if he had the plague. Three of these communities (actually they are part of particular tribes of aborigines who have been in the land from the beginning of time so to speak) come to my mind. They all speak the Telegu dialect and belong to what is now the State of Andhra Pradesh, located in the centre of southern India. These tribes are the Theyli Marajas, who speak Urdu as well, the Koya Mamas, and the *Dawa*-Lokey (Dawa means medicine and 'Lokey' means people. Hence 'people who give medicine', literally 'medicine men').

All three of these tribes have woven a strong superstition around themselves in the course of generations. When they walk down a village street, children run inside and adults close and fasten their doors. All of them live as mendicants, but they are mendicant with a difference. These people do not beg humbly for food, clothing and money. They demand these things and present their demands under open threat of reprisals if they are not met, so that few dare to deny them.

The Theyli Marajas dress in loose *jabbars* (kneelength shirts), covering *dhoties* wrapped around each leg individually, and wear turbans ending in a decorative fan above their heads, with the other end hanging down their backs. Falling over the shirt, both back and front, is a sort of apron reaching from shoulder to ankles. They carry small, two-stringed violins, consisting of a tin or box body with a bamboo extension, the tin or box employed being gaily decorated with cowrie-shells. There is no bow to this instrument and no attempt is made to play it. Apparently it is not intended to produce music, but rather to announce the arrival of its owner, who plucks the strings with his fingernails. The resultant 'ting-ting' announces that a Theyli Maraja has come, and people hastily get something ready to give him in the way of grain or money to induce him to depart as quickly as possible.

These people are professional palmists, and in return for the gifts they receive will tell fortunes with surprising accuracy. So clever are they, in fact, that most people would rather not have their fortunes told for fear of hearing of coming sickness or early death. Rather they present their gifts hastily and invite the wandering Maraja to be on his way.

The Koya Mamas are a tall, very dark tribe of mostly lean men with coal-black, piercing eyes. They wear long hair, rolled up in a coil upon their heads and decorated with peacocks' feathers or a long-toothed comb. Invariably bare-bodied, with strings of gaily-coloured glass beads, they wear a long, tightly-fitting dhoti in the manner of a skirt. Another division of this tribe hails from the wilder parts of the country. Its representatives wear little or no clothing, except for a short loin-cloth. These people decorate their arms with amulets and bracelets made from the roots of trees or carved from bone, wear necklaces made from the coloured seeds of wild-plants and trees. As beggars they are very demanding and have knack of rubbing the base of the palms of both hands together when soliciting alms, while rapidly announcing: 'Look, it's coming soon ... See, it's on its way ... Soon, now. Very very soon it will be here ... Ah, I can see it now; there just there. Oh there, come, come this way.

The people from whom they are begging, when they hear these words, attach great significance to what, or whom, the 'It' mentioned by the Koya Mama might be, and hastily force a gift upon him, inviting him to go and visit the neighbour next door.

The Koya Mamas have a further knack of introducing a strand of horse hair between the heels of their palms when they rub them together. A tiny charm is attached to this hair;

after vigorous rubbing the strand seeks to unravel itself, thus causing the little charm literally to dance on the Koya Mama's palm. If you give him a rupee, he will present you with this charm (minus the horse-hair of course) as a very lucky keepsake.

The Dawa Lokey generally send their women-folk out to beg, even this task being considered beneath their menfolk, apart from being too strenuous. These women wear no jackets, but move from house to house barebreasted and dressed in single-coloured cotton sarees. Their 'doctor's bag' consists of a quilted cloth with the four corners meeting together over a short stick, which they carry across their shoulders in the manner of a gun. Inside the cloth is an assortment of roots, herbs and powders in small boxes. This forms their pharmacopoeia. There is no illness for which they have no cure, and they will try to impress one by answering in a different language from the one by which they are addressed. Should one happen to be conversant with this second language and answer in that dialect, the medicine-woman will then try third.

These itinerant doctresses announce their arrival at your front-door in peculiar sing-song voices with the words 'Dawa Lokey' repeated over and over again. Strictly speaking they are not beggars, as they earn their living by dispensing their herbal medicines. Depending upon the sagacity of the individual concerned, some of the roots and leave and powders they sell are singularly efficacious.

Every married couple in India desires to have children. This for two reason. The first and most important because to be childless carries a great stigma on the wife as barren and incapable of bearing offspring. Very few people stop to consider that it might be the man who is to blame, and not the woman, for it is at once taken for granted that the woman is barren, and barrenness in India is a terrible affliction. It is thought that the gods are unfavourably disposed to such a woman; maybe she is immoral and has lost the capacity to bear offspring, or maybe she is diseased. But whatever the reason the poor woman gets all the blame and she not her husband is looked down upon with a mixture of pity and contempt, and suffers too, from the attitude of superiority among her fertile neighbours.

The other reason for this fear of childlessness is, of course, the desire for the continuation of the family, and for this reason it is son who is desired and not a daughter.

There is in India a vast difference between having a son and having a daughter, and if a man is lucky enough to be the father of a number of sons he is considered to be on top of the world. For each of the sons, at the time of marriage, brings in a dowry. This dowry generally takes the form of a couple of thousand rupees or more, jewellery, land, a house or lower down the scale a car, a radio-set or transistor, or maybe a pair of gold rings or an automatic gold watch.

If, on the other hand, the man is unfortunate enough to have a daughter for whom he has to find a husband, that man is at the other end of the stick. For it is he who will have to do all dowry-giving to the bridegroom, who gives nothing in return, and if that man is unfortunate enough to be the father of several daughters he is indeed undone, as he will have to park with as many dowries as he has daughters. Nor will he be able to dodge the issue by keeping his daughters unmarried. To have even one daughter unmarried carries with it a fearful disgrace, for everyone will say that she is a bad girl and not a virgin; hence nobody will marry her. to have a number of unmarried daughters is to reach the bottom in public esteem. No girl is allowed to marry until her elder sister is married before her. Hence, if the father is poor and cannot afford to pay the required dowries, none of his daughters can marry and they are all dubbed as prostitutes, for to the person in the street there is only one reason for any girl to remain unmarried. Otherwise, surely someone or the other would have come forward to marry her. The reason why nobody has done so must surely be that the girl, and very likely her whole family, are immoral. The question that the father might be too poor to pay the dowries is conveniently overlooked.

As a consequence of this custom, the parents of every boy try to get a wife for him who brings the highest dowry. Conversely, the parents of a girl must look for a boy whose parents, in their turn, are prepared to accept a dowry of as little as the girl's parents can afford. And it is all left to the parent of both sides to bargain and barter. The boy and girl have no say in the matter, or in the choosing of their mates.

Money, having become paramount in India, as indeed it has throughout the world, the outcome is that it is comparatively easy to get your boy married and correspondingly difficult to get your girl married. As in most other countries, the birthrate, or survival rate of female children in India exceeds that of males, so the situation grows more difficult as the years pass for those unfortunate people who consider themselves to be cursed with a family of daughters.

In the overall picture, as people do not want to be childless for the reason I have already mentioned, the work of the government and of family planning organisations is extremely difficult. The significance of the threatened 'population explosion' is entirely lost on the average Indian ryot and poor person.

Poverty today is so great, and the cost of living so high, that a married couple can never think of having any form of hobby or recreation, however simple. Nor can they furnish their houses or buy any of the good things of life, not to mention food. This hand-to-mouth existence creates a deadly routine. Both husband and wife can afford to partake only of a very frugal *nasta* (breakfast), consisting of a small rice cake and a sip of coffee. Then both go out to work. The midday meal is equally frugal, and when they return in the evening the wife has to cook dinner, which again is frugal enough and consist of only a little curry and rice. After that, the couple retire for the night. They do not read, as they are illiterate. Even if they could read, they are too poor to afford the electricity or the kerosene required to illuminate their tiny rooms, many of which are hardly better than hovels.

What is there, anyway, for them to lie and discuss? The scarcity of food? The rising cost of living? Life's problems, and more problems and yet more? The only recreation that remains to these poor people is sex. it costs nothing. Further it does bring with it a measure of forgetfulness, of satisfaction, and a certain joy. Thirdly, when both are bullied at work by grasping employers, who drive them all day for what they can get out of them in the form of labour all day in return for a miserable pay, the realm of sex is something in which the man, and more rarely the woman, can at least dare to boost their frustrated egos. They can really let themselves go without fear.

Now, into the midst of this picture, admittedly dismal, comes a group of people who preach that even this one remaining pleasure should be eschewed. They are the members of the Family Planning Centre, introduced by the Government at the behest of the UNO (who are all foreigners anyway), and they say that a married couple should have no, or at most two children, and not more. These people say that the world is too full of children, and soon will be too full of men and women, and there will not be enough food to go around. As if there was enough food even now! The way to avoid all this, say the Family Planning people, is for each man and woman to undergo an operation. Alternatively, the woman may wear a loop, or swallow a pill now and then, or use some other sort of device.

So the villagers ask themselves: what in the world is life coming to? Our fathers, our grandfathers, our great grandfathers, all enjoyed sex! We enjoy sex! Now these people tell us these things. They are trying to take away from us the only pleasure that remains to us. We have nothing else to enjoy but the act of sex. Must we give that up, too? Because one day some years hence, the world will be too full of men and women and there will be no food to eat! Where will we be then? We are starving now anyway, and we may not live another five years. Maybe not even another one. Certainly not for twenty or thirty years? So leave us in peace to enjoy the one and only pleasure left. Mind your own business and leave us to mind ours. Why, only the other day when we went to the coffee shop for a sip, we heard all the people there laughing heartily. 'What is so funny?' Some of us asked, 'Let's share the joke.'

It was sometime before anyone could stop even to speak. At last one said, 'Remember the Family Planning doctor who used to lecture to us daily? And remember the nurse who fitted our women with loops, and distributed pills among them. Well, he has made her pregnant and now she is on maternity leave.

'Ho! Ho! Ho! Ha! Ha! Ha! Her own loop must have fallen off!'

On the other hand, my friend 'Samiar' (a term of religious respect), who lives on a little hillock not far from my land near Pennagram, in Salem District, plies a more popular and a far more lucrative trade.

Just over five feet tall, little Samiar (who is getting on in years now) enhances his stature by wearing several coils of very dirty black false hair upon his head. He has brilliant, piercing black eyes and wears huge earrings. On ceremonial occasions he decorates his forehead with white and red caste marks. For the forty years or more that I have known him, Samiar's reputation as a medicine man who can make barren women children has not ceased to soar. Hundreds of women have been brought to him, and as many have come of their own accord.

Samiar charges a very low professional fee for this service; just ten rupees for a poor woman and a fifty for a very rich one. The other condition is that the woman must be left alone with him in his hut during the hours of daylight. (To make such a condition extend into the hours of darkness would be scandalous, would it not? But surely nothing could possibly happen while the sun was shining, and after all, he is a 'Samiar', is he not?) Not so strangely, about half of the women become pregnant, but what is more strange is that most of those who do become pregnant have husbands who are sickly or otherwise wanting.

As I have hinted, I know Samiar extremely well. What very few others know is that he is a powerful hypnotist; also a rascal of the first degree, although an extremely jolly and likeable rascal. What is strangest of all is that many of these children, as they grew older, become rascals too, but jolly and likeable ones, and all of them have brilliant piercing, black eyes.

I have wandered in this country all my life, in its jungles, in its villages. I have mixed with hundreds of its poorest folk and talked to them. What I have written is only what they have told me in their own words. Of course, I understand the threat of 'population explosion'. I know, and can and do appreciate what the Family Planning Units are trying to do. But I greatly fear it will not work. The poor Indian, like everybody else, is human even if he is poor. He wants something concrete for himself, here and now, and is scarcely interested in what happens in the future, even only twenty or thirty years hence. He does not expect to live that long himself. And he could not care less what happens to those alive at that time.

Since there is no alternative recreation for him, since the conditions of living will continue to be as hard and difficult, and will grow harder and more difficult from day to day, he (and she) are not going to give up or even curtail in any way the one and only recreation they have left to them — the pastime of 'sex'.

India is being flooded by young people of all nationalities who come to the country in the thousands every month. Except for Russians, we meet folk from the Americas and from Western Europe, even from Japan, wandering about the streets of our cities and towns. Some are 'hippies' but the majority are not, although it will be difficult for you to find any in normal western dress. On the contrary, some adopt the saffron gown and heavy head necklaces of the Yogi, the short loin-cloth and bare body of the Indian labourer, the loose pants with outside shirt of the northern Indian, with hair-styles varying from long hair and heavy beard through all the intermediary stages to no hair at all on either head or face. Mostly they are to be seen with hair flowing wildly in the breeze and in other cases wound around the head in elaborate hair styles. The women of these groups appear equally odd: a few wear sarees draped around themselves rather clumsily and not in the graceful manner of an Indian woman, while others wear the 'kameez' and 'calva' (the shirt and tight trousers) of the northern Indian ladies. Some come in ultra-mini skirts, while a number are at the opposite extreme, wearing dresses of ankle-length that defy definition.

Curiosity has urged me to talk to a number of these

visitors in an effort to understand them, and this much I have gleaned, that almost every one has confessed that he or she has found no place in the world like India. Some of them have travelled widely, and all of them hope to spend the rest of their lives in India. I have then inquired what it is they have found so attractive, but to this question I found a great variety of answers. Some say this country is very peaceful, the people very nice, the climate excellently warm, the sunshine superb, food and living very cheap. Others say they have a great urge for matters spiritual which they cannot satisfy in their own country, where the rush and bustle is too great. All are agreed on one thing. Time counts for nothing in India; there is no hurry about anything and there is always a tomorrow.

A large number of these people have attached themselves to ashrams or to individual Yogis in different parts of this peninsula. One of the main centers is at Pondicherry where men and women of races have joined the Sri Aurobindo Ashram with hopes of settling down in the inter-racial township of Auroville, already planned and now under construction. This township promises to be utopian in character, where people of all nations, colours and religions may live together in peace and harmony — the only township of its kind in Asia. Many others have joined the following of the reincarnated Sai Baba at Whitefield. They are happy in their search for peace of soul, peace of mind and peace of living.

But all of these visitors are apt to forget a very important factor; actually, the most important factor of the lot. They have money sent out to them from their home countries, and if it were not for these remittances they would not be able to live in India at all, whether in an ashram or elsewhere, for as visitors and foreigners they are not allowed to take up work and be paid for it. It would be well for them to bear this fact in mind always, and not to speak so bitterly against their own lands as some of them do. For I repeat, it is their own country that gives them the money on which they find they can live so happily in India. Should these remittances for any reason cease, these visitors would have to go back to their countries and the 'rat-race' from which they have fled. And they will have to go back in a terribly great hurry, for each day they delay would make them that much more hungry.

But we have another type of foreign visitor, one who appears to want to break all the laws of the host-country and escape the consequences by virtue of the fact that he is a citizen of another land. I am certain these people would never think of behaving in their own lands as some of them do in India. No doubt the comparatively easy living, the lack of the time factor, the probability that they will get away with it nine times out of ten, if not ninety-nine times out of a hundred, tempts them to act in this way, not realising (or caring) that their action boomerangs back upon themselves, and upon their own countrymen wanting to visit India, and lastly on unfortunate people like myself who have chosen to remain in India and make it our home. Because of such wayward behaviour, we are classed with them as undesirable, as pestilential white folk who have no business to remain in India, who should go back without further delay to wherever we, or our ancestors, come from. In the stress of situations created by thoughtless visitors, it is only natural for Indians to forget that some of us settlers, whose families have been in this land for generations, by virtue of our living and experience are as much, if not more Indian, than they are themselves. We have helped to build India into what it is.

But let me return to matters more strictly Indian, from which I appear to have strayed. Rarely will an Indian of the working classes, man or woman, know his or her own age or date of birth. Little attention is paid to this event, although the anniversary of a death is always remembered. This is because a whole set of ceremonies has to be performed for the dead person, year after year on the anniversary of a death. No importance, however, rests on a birthday. This is not true, however, of the upper classes. Not only is the day of birth recorded but the exact time to the very minute. The reason is that each individual man and woman of the middle-classes or above is required to have his or her horoscope cast. It is incumbent upon the parents to do this for their children, and astrologers, who earn a very comfortable living in India casting horoscopes, require to know exact details of time and place of birth to be able to cast the horoscope correctly.

The one thing that may be regarded as the curse of our country, and which the Government from the time of Independence has tried, and is still trying hard to stamp out, albeit with little success, is the caste system. This system concerns only Hindus and not the other communities inhabiting this vast land. In simple words it means that every living Hindu, man, woman or child, must belong to one or other of the numerous castes that go to form the Hindu community. They belong to a caste, whichever it may be, by virtue of being born into it through parents of that same cast.

No person can change his or her caste under any circumstances. He can never promote himself to a higher caste whatever his merits or achievements. He is of that caste because his parents belonged to it and his great-grand parents before them, and his great-grandparents before that, and so on. His caste is as unalterable as the laws of the universe. Some of these caste classifications are governed by the trade the individual follows. It goes without saying that his father, grandfather and so on, followed the same trade before him.

For example, scavengers or sweepers, as they are called, are at the lowest rung of the caste ladder. Cobblers, or 'clucklers' as these are termed, are a slight step higher, and so on till we come to the warrior caste and the highest of all, the priests or Brahmins.

To give you an idea of how the caste system operates, let me show you true-to-life example. About fourteen miles south of my home-town of Bangalore is a wild and hilly area known as Bannerghatta, where I own farmstead consisting of a furnished house, a stone-lined well, and five acres of land, which I purchased for less than Rs. 10,000 (about £556). Half a mile from this farmstead are two hamlets. The name of one is Sampigehalli, and the name of the other is Byrapanahalli. Each consists of less than 200 homes. About two-thirds of these building are brick-and-mud structures, and the remaining one-third are wattle-and-thatch huts. The population of each settlement is well within 1,000 souls. Nevertheless in each of these hamlets there are no less than seven castes. Among these, the Brahmins and Lingayats are the highest in status; then come the Vakalgiries, working down to Kurubus, Maloles, Waddars and Madigols.

The Government has built wells in both places for the use of all the inhabitants. But do you think that anyone or everyone is allowed to draw water? Not a bit of it. The lower castes are strictly debarred. Incidentally, I myself am debarred from drawing water although I am not a Hindu and do not belong to any caste. The reason in that I eat beef. As a beefeater, I am considered as belonging to the lowest category of human being, lower even than a Madigol, if that were possible. Is not the cow a sacred animal? And I dare to eat it.

Then men, of course, never draw water. In a home such a task is considered to be beneath the status of a husband as master of the household. Only the women go to the village well. Yet, should a woman of one of the lower castes require water, she may go to the well with her pitcher, but that is all she can do. She must wait till a woman of a higher caste comes along; then she may ask this woman to be kind enough to draw a pot of water for her use. If the woman obliges, well and good. Should the woman be in too great a hurry and unable to spare the time, the low-caste woman must wait till some high-caste housewife, who can spare the time and is kind enough to oblige, draws the water for her.

One of the servants at my farmstead is named Ramiah. He is an old man and a Madigol. He lives with his son and daughter-in-law and two grandchildren in a wattle-and-thatch hut in Byrapanahalli hamlet. One night we had a great storm, with high winds and torrential rain. Ramiah's hut fell down about midnight. Do you think the family could shelter in one of their neighbour's huts or house? No! They were Madigols, that is of the lowest caste! So Ramiah, his son, daughter-in-law and grandchildren sat in the pouring rain all night amidst the remains of their fallen hut and continued to sit there till noon the following day, by which time the sun had partly dried both them and the hatch scattered upon the ground. Then they got together to rebuild what they could of their hut before nightfall. There was no alternative if they were to avoid sitting in the open for another night.

The hamlets of Sampigehalli and Byrapanahalli are still there and these customs continue to this day. The Government has tried hard to eradicate them. But the customs are centuries old and, as everyone know, old habits die hard. particularly does the caste habit, because everyone of a higher caste has such a glorious opportunity to exploit all the castes below him.

The Government has tried also to help the tillers of the soil. It has given many of them a couple of acres of land per head, a plough and two head of cattle, along with a loan to build a hut for themselves. As often as not the recipients of these gifts sell the plough and the oxen within a month of receiving them, and try to sell or mortgage the land as well. That is going rather far, however, and nobody has sufficient nerve to conclude this last transaction by buying the land.

Ryots have been invited to take generous loans from banks on security of the title-deeds of their lands. The money is intended to develop the land for agricultural purposes by digging wells, fertilising fields and so on. The loans carry very low interest, are for ten years, and may be repaid in easy instalments. But the ten years come and go, and no instalments, easy or otherwise, are paid, nor interest. The lands are not fertilised or developed, nor are wells dug. The ryot has spent the money on his daughter's dowry and wedding or on himself, in having a good time. The lockers of the banks are filled with peoples' title-deeds and the banks are wondering what they are going to do with them.

Major organised crime is rare in India. Murders are frequent, but they are generally motivated by infidelity, jealousy or disputes over land. Suicides are common and people kill themselves for every conceivable reason. The folk are emotional and temperamental, and suicide follows in the wake of a normally simple everyday problem which might have been easily solved.

Far down in the crime-scale are pocket-picking, petty cheating and pilfering. To the last two groups there is no limit; it is taken for granted that your neighbour will cheat you should he get half a chance to do so and if you have not been clever enough to cheat him first.

By and large, the rich classes are very rich and the poor very poor. Between these two extremes is a vast middle-class of people forming perhaps a third of the population. The very poor make up the remaining two-thirds, the rich people being but a tiny fraction of the whole population. These rich people — landlords, business tycoons, cinema stars and so forth —

have little to do with the very poor and as a rule are not in the least considerate to them. The poor, comprising the bulk of the population, have been poor all their lives and for generations before, having descended from a long line of ancestors who have always been poor. Prior to independence in 1947, for hundreds of years they had been ruled and oppressed by foreigners as well as their own kith and kin in the form of maharajahs, chieftain, princes, zamindars, landlords and money-lenders. They think in terms of having had no past, a present that is extremely bad, and a future that is without hope.

With all this background of poverty, misery and general hopelessness, we should not be too hard on those petty faults and weaknesses which are but the natural outcome of generations of exploitation and overpowering sense of inferiority. It is to be hoped that the time will come when the races of India realise at last that they are an independent people and not just talk about it.

India is a beautiful land, inhabited by a nice, friendly people, more appreciated by foreigners than by themselves. The majority of Indians think in narrow terms of caste, religion and community rather than nationality. The rulers are doing what they can to correct them and create a sense of national unity, but they have an uphill task, with many ancient customs and prejudices to overcome — the chief of which is the caste system — and a host of self-interested people to beat. Old habits die hard, and in this instance it is particularly difficult to kill the old caste bogey for the very cogent reason that millions of persons classed as of high caste, live and benefit by it, as their ancestors did before them for untold generations. It is only natural that they are disinclined to relinquish a way of living that has been and still is of daily gain to themselves in every sphere — in their employment,

671

their official, social and financial and domestic status —
merely in order to satisfy an ideal of improving the country,
when they know quite well they will not be nearly so well
off should the caste system disappear.

Four

Some Indian Game Sanctuaries

I HAVE HAD THE PRIVILEGE OF VISITING FIVE OF THE GAME SANCTUARIES of northern India. These five, and a number of others, have been created by the Government in a last minute attempt to save some of the noblest animals of the subcontinent from extinction. Among these creatures are the Asian lion that is found only in the Gir forest of Gujarat State, the one-horned rhinoceros that lives in the north-eastern extremity of the country in the State of Assam and in Nepal, the Indian wild buffalo, found roughly in the same localities as the one-horned rhino, and the swamp deer, sometimes called the barasingha (meaning 'twelve-horned deer'), because of the twelve tines that adorn this magnificent animal, six upon either antler.

I began a tour of five sanctuaries in the company of two American friends and a Canadian, and as I maintained a day to day record of all that happened, I had better present the facts as they occurred. As far as I was concerned, the journey started when I left the airport of Bangalore for Bombay on the morning of March 3, 1970. It was a smooth fast flight, with nothing much of interest to see. We flew over Belgaum and soon saw smoke rising from several forest fires that were raging on the ghats between Poona and Bombay.

In exactly one and a half hours we touched down at the Santa Cruz airport at Bombay, whence I went by taxi to the Nataraj Hotel, which was the arranged rendezvous with the other members of the party, whose plane, however, arrived only after a fifteen-hour delay.

Eventually we started one morning for the small airport of Keshod in Gujarat State, from which point air-passengers are conveyed to the heart of the Gir forest, where we had booked rooms in the spacious forest lodge, where travellers are generally accommodated. The plane — a Dakota magnificently dolled up and in excellent flying condition — carried us across the small strip of the Arabian Sea which separates the city of Bombay from the peninsula of Saurashtra, which forms the western portion of Gujarat State. We flew over several steamers and noticed shoals of dolphins leaping from the waves.

The airport of Keshod is a few miles inland. There we were met by the van that was to convey us to the settlement of Sasan Gir, fifty-five miles distant, in the heart of the forest of the lions. En route we passed the port of Veraval with its ancient Somnath temple. There is a legend here that when the Mohammedan invader, Mohammed of Ghazni, planned to destroy this edifice in 1026, two thousand Brahmins poured holy water, brought all the way from the Ganges River, upon the idols, and strewed flowers over them night and day, to win the grace of the Gods and avert disaster. Mohammed of Ghazni never destroyed the temple.

The road was dry and dusty and the forest, when we reached it, was equally dry, rather open, sprinkled with babul trees and interspersed with dwarf teak and not too many thorns. Except for the teak, the scenery was reminiscent of Africa.

The 'Guest House', which is the grandiloquent name given to the forest lodge, was comfortably furnished and the khansamma (cook-butler-tableboy) laid out a welcoming meal. We found the officials of the Forestry Department most obliging and co-operative.

What is popularly called the 'lion show' had been arranged for five o'clock that evening. A live buffalo-bait had been tied up about eight miles away and the pride of lions that had been located in the vicinity actually 'called' to the spot by the junior forest officials, corresponding in rank to the forest guards of southern India, but known in Gir as shikarees or chowkidars. Many of them are quite old, and have been in the employment of the Forestry Department when the Gir forest belonged to Junagadh State, when ruled by a Muslim prince. This prince flew to Pakistan when India annexed his territories, and that was how the Gir forest became part of the province of Saurashtra in the Indian State of Gujarat. The shikarees and chowkidars were transferred to service in the government of Gujarat, but many of them still proudly display the letters J. F. (for Junagadh Forests) in polished brass on their tunics.

Incidentally, no visitor is allowed to watch the actual killing of the buffalo-bait by lions. The authorities consider that this might encourage the taking of life. But there is no objection to watching the lions feeding once that bait has been killed by them. The bait costs the visitor Rs. 150, and there is also a fee for using still or cine cameras.

It is interesting to watch the shikarees and chowkidars actually calling the wild lions. There are generally two of these men present, and they make a 'Khik! Khik! Khik!' sound with their mouths, followed by a 'Kroo! Kroo! Kroo!' noise with their lips. The wild lions appear to respond to these calls, if they do not recognize the persons who are making them and actually approach quite close to the caller.

To be on the safe side, the guards are armed with single-barrelled guns of .12 bore, loaded with buck-shot. I examined the weapons carried by the men who had called the lions and found them to be as ancient as the men themselves assuredly hailing from the days of the old Junagadh forests. I then questioned the men as to why they carried these weapons, and the older of the two replied that sometimes, although very rarely, a young lion in his prime would resent the presence of onlookers in numbers, armed with camera big and small, who keep moving around while he and the other members of the pride are eating. This animal then becomes aggressive, begins to growl and excites the rest of the pride. Then anything might happen.

'I have been dealing with lions since I was a boy, sahib,' he confided in Hindustani, 'and my father before me, and his father, and his father before that. Always watch the tail, sahib, then the eyes. And listen to any noise the animal might make. When the tail begins to twitch and rise above his back, when those large green eyes lose their roundness and start to half-close, when the whining sound he is making — or perhaps he is making no sound at all, or maybe he is just grunting — changes to a rumbling growl, he is about to charge you. Run for your life then, if you think you can. Actually it will be useless, for you won't run very far. Should none of these things happen, you are safe, although it might only be fore the moment. Never can you tell when these *shaitan log* (devil people) suddenly become angry. You should always watch, watch, watch. The tail sahib, and those big green eyes!'

Apparently the purpose of the ancient gun and its load of buskshot was to fire in the air if necessity arose, rather than at the offending animal should it begin to evince signs of rising excitement. My informer said that the noise of the shot invariably had the effect of calming it down. Personally, I think the main purpose of the old guns was to boost the courage of those who carried them.

There was a pride of six lions on the kill when we arrived shortly after five o'clock. It consisted of two full-grown lionesses and four half-grown cubs, two cubs belonging apparently to each lioness. Unlike tigers and most other animals, all the lions seemed to be on friendly terms with each other and there were no signs of quarrelling.

As we grew bolder, we went closer and closer, till we were within thirty feet of the feasting animals. My friends, who were equipped with cameras, were taking photographs as fast as they were able. At one stage one of the lionesses, possibly disgusted at our close presence, seized the kill by a hind leg and pulled so hard at it as to break the tethering rope. She started to drag the dead buffalo away.

Then an amazing thing happened. The two chowkidars ran forward, caught hold of the dead animal by a foreleg, and started to pull in the opposite direction. It was an incredible spectacle. A tug-of-war between two human beings and a wild lioness, with five other lions looking on and a crowd of human spectators. I would never have believed it had anyone told me. The foresters were no match for the lioness, who started dragging them along with the kill. Then, amazingly, they let go of the leg they were pulling and ran forward towards the lioness, shouting in unison at the pitch of their lungs. The lioness released her hold, leaped backwards, and stood erect to look at the two men wistfully.

The other five lions were watching the scene with interest.

We continued to regard it with amazement. Hastily, and not without considerable effort, the two men dragged the bait back to the tree to which it had been secured, and re-tethered it. I then lost my regard for the ferocity of the lions of Gir. As if nothing whatsoever had happened, all the lions returned to their meal, and in less than an hour there was not much left of the buffalo but bones.

The cubs, now replete with meat, began to take an interest in us. Their mothers, also full, rolled on to their sides and went to sleep. The sun was low in the western horizon.

Seeing themselves free of parental interference for once, two of the youngsters bounded playfully towards us, making guttural, mewing noises. Clearly they were purring as lion cubs usually do.

'Get back, sahib! Get back!' cautioned the elder chowkidar in a low voice, at the same time motioning urgently with his hand for us to retreat. Rather surprised at his unexpected concern at the approach of the cubs we nevertheless obeyed.

'If the mother wakes up and sees them near you,' he said by way of explanation, 'she will think you are going to harm them. Then all hell will break loose. You will come to know what the 'shaitan log' are really like.

Very soon the two lionesses awoke and returned to the remains of the kill which, as I have said, now consisted mainly of bones. One of the spectators, a professional photographer from Austria, got the chowkidars to drive the lionesses back for a moment while he hung a microphone from a branch of the tree beneath which the bones lay. Then he photographed the lionesses teasing the bones while he tape-recorded the sounds.

Just about this time one of the lionesses had a small fracas with a cub that was worrying her. The Austrian recorded this too. Then he played the tape back. It was amusing to observe the expressions on the lion's faces when they heard their own growl and snarls.

Suddenly the pride stopped feeding. With one accord all heads, including those of the cubs, were turned away towards a nullah a few yards distant. We could see nothing. We heard nothing. The next moment, silently, from between the stems of teak and babul, a magnificent lion in his prime stepped forth, his mane was only slightly less heavy than that of his African cousin. Even at this distance and in the fading light, we could see the tufts of hair protruding from the elbows of this forelegs.

Our clowkidars became perturbed. They backed away from the pride and motioned to us to follow. We did so, retreating the fifty yards to where the van awaited us. We got inside.

'It is the bad lion, sahib,' said the older forester. 'When he turns up, the lion show must come to an end at once. For he brooks no spectators and is no respector of cars or persons. See even the other lions fear him.'

We turned to see the pride of six scatter in all directions. There came a thundering growl as the newcomer walked up to the bones, sniffed at them, and raised his head to regard us balefully.

The light was bad, but the photographers in the party wanted to stay to photograph the lion. The two chowkidars, however, were obdurate. To remain would be to court trouble, if not tragedy. They urged the driver to start the vehicle and drive away. When we complained the older man replied, 'Sahib, we are responsible for the safety of all of you. that the animal is a shaitan personified. If he had made up his mind to charge, these ancient weapons we carry would not stop him. Allah himself knows whether the cartridges would go off, for they are very. old. We give him a wide berth when he appears. So also do the other lions, as you can see for yourself.'

It was dusk when we left the bad lion in undisputed control of the situation and began the return journey. We passed a few spotted deer, some late pea-fowl and a four-horned antelope a mile or so further and then, just as it was getting too dark to see, we heard a lion roaring a few paces from the track.

The elder chowkidar motioned to the driver of the van to stop, then banged the metal door with his hand while making the 'Khik-Khik!' sound with his mouth and the 'Kroo-Kroo!' noise with his lips. Within a few minutes a half-grown lion stepped out of the gloom, halted and gazed at the van expectantly. Clearly, he was hoping for something to eat in the way of live bait. We watched him for some minutes, then stepped out of the vehicle, whereupon the lion melted away into the shadows.

More excitement awaited us upon our return to the Guest House. Not content with the lion show, the enterprising Range Officer in charge had laid on a panther show as well. After dinner we were invited to attend this exhibition by following a pathway which led from the bungalow through scrub-jungle to a spot scarcely 300 yards away. A goat had been tied up to a post earlier in the evening and killed by a panther which was, apparently, a regular visitor to the spot, as he got an easy meal almost every second day in order to allow visitors to watch him eat. As with the buffalo-bait and the lions, spectators were not permitted to see the actual killing but there was apparently no harm in watching the panther eat once it had killed the goat. Incidentally, that goat cost us about Rs. 60.

All was ready. The panther had killed the goat — a black one — earlier, and then been driven off, being held at bay by a chowkidar with a big stick, squatting beside the dead goat. As darkness had fallen already, the scene was faintly illumined by concealed floodlights. The path we followed led into a big, circular iron-barred cage similar to what one sees at a circus but with this difference. At the circus the animals are in the cage and the spectators outside. Here, we were in the cage and the panther outside.

Once we had assembled, the chowkidar with the big stick who had been keeping the panther off the kill, left his post, bringing his stick with him, and entered the iron cage with us. Then he secured the door behind him.

The panther had been watching and waiting for this moment. Obviously he was well-practiced in the procedure and may often have wondered to himself what it was all about. Perhaps he was wiser and wondered how stupid human being were to go to all this trouble just to watch him eat.

Up he trotted within a few moments and fell with gusto upon the goat. The floodlights were gradually increased in intensity until, in about ten minutes, the scene was brightly lit. The panther became aware of this and must have felt uncomfortable, for he made one or two attempts to drag the goat away. But the tethering rope held fast, and the panther eventually resigned himself to tucking-in to meal under brilliant flood-light.

What might have been a rather unexciting exhibition was fortunately ended by the unexpected arrival of a hyaena. Perhaps this animal thought that he should also be given an opportunity to show himself. He sneaked up from behind, but the panther discovered him. With a snarl the panther left the kill to chase the hyaena away. The hyaena bolted, with the panther behind him, and the lights were dimmed.

Soon the panther returned, and a little later the hyaena too. Another loud snarl and another chase. Back came the panther followed by the hyaena who, growing bolder, showed himself. This time there was much snarling and growling on the part of the panther, and shrieking by the hyaena, but they never came to actual grip. Clearly the panther was not going to have everything his own way.

In the meantime the chowkidar, a young man this time, who had been through it all many times before and was manifestly bored, remembered that he had a young wife at home and felt that she would be in need of him. he coughed vigorously and clapped his hands. At the same time the floodlights were put out.

The panther show had come to its end. In the darkness we could scarcely find the exit from the iron cage, but eventually we got back to the luxurious forest lodge and the foam-rubber mattresses and pillows on its beds.

At midnight I went out on the verandah. My companions were sound asleep. In the distance a lion roared. From the low hills on the opposite side came a chorus of roars in answer: 'Aaauuungh! Aaauuungh! Aauungh! Aauungh! Aungh! Aungh! Aungh! Aung! Aung!' The bewitching sounds died away into silence. I wondered if the 'bad' lion was calling to the frightened pride.

Before six o'clock the following morning we were on our way in the van to a jungle lake half-a-dozen miles away and reached it in time to glimpse a lovely sunrise over the jungle-clad hills to the east. The morning was pleasantly chilly in spite of the fact that we were in midsummer and in one of the arid areas of India.

A spotted stag brayed his challenge by the lakeside and in a few moments we saw him break cover and approach the water to drink, a dark silhouette against the golden path laid by the rays of the risen sun across the limpid water. A bevy of peafowl, quite twenty birds in all, followed one another to within a hundred yards of where the spotted stag was still drinking, and at that moment a magical sound rent the air.

A lion roared in a low valley beyond the roadside and another answered from a short distance further off.

A sambar-stag, hearing those roars, belled his alarm from a distant hill-top. I was excited, perhaps even more than my three friends from overseas. For I am familiar with the habits of tigers which are quite different from those of lions, and the calls of the lions enthralled me. I tore down the hill in the direction of the sounds and my friends followed closely behind.

Soon we arrived at a sandy stream. Impressed freshly upon the soft earth of the further bank were huge pugmarks. And they had not been made by a tiger — for there are no tigers in the Gir forest. They were the pugmarks of a lion.

We hastened onwards and were in time to catch a glimpse of the animal leap into the undergrowth and vanish. Clearly it had known that we were strangers and not the chowkidars to whom it was undoubtedly accustomed. We could not see much of his mane in the few moments the lion gave us. It was probably a young animal; certainly not 'bad' lion, which was just as well.

The sun had risen by the time we got back to the car. The road circumvented a hill-side and we were able to look down upon a vast sheet of water. Floating upon it in several places were what appeared to be logs of wood, but which I recognised as crocodiles. Then we began the return journey, passing more spotted-deer and peafowl on the way. Also a small sounder of wild pigs.

The jungle-track past several hamlets occupied by Maldharis, the name given to a pastoral sect of people who live in this area and bring their cattle into the Gir forest for grazing. They are a colourful race. The men wear loosely-gathered jackets and voluminous trousers, a turban or head-band of coloured cloth, a metal necklace with large ornaments, sometimes bangles of bone, and inevitably carry wooden staves. The women dress rather like the Indian gypsies, with ample brightly-hued sarees, tight-fitting jackets that reveal wonderful figures, no Western women could hope to approach. necklaces, bangles, ear-rings of silver, beads and imitations ivory. They are most handsome. The children look like miniatures of their elders but are even more brightly clothed.

In days past there was an abundance of water and grass in the Gir jungle. Animals were plentiful too. The lions had their natural prey and were not much interested in eating the livestock owned by the Maldharis, a species of buffalo, large and with curved, looping horns, which the peasants were mostly able to protect successfully.

The Maldharis were poor but happy in the forest with their buffaloes, whose milk and milk products they sold to the local *sahukars* or money-lenders to whom they were in debt. But with the passing of the old Junagadh State came unexpected problems. More and more cattle from all over Saurashtra and Kutch were driven into the forest, their numbers estimated at about 48,000, a year, in addition to the 21,000 stock owned by the resident Maldharis, who inhabit 129 'nesses', or hamlets, corresponding to the cattle pattis in the jungles of southern India. The Gir forest then became a vast cattle camp, which created an acute shortage of water and grazing, for which the Maldhari now has to travel a long distance. With the continuous increase in cattle came cattle diseases that spread to the wild fauna. The shortage of grazing also cut the wild fauna down in numbers, and so did the increase in promiscuous poaching.

All these changes affected the lions; they began to kill the cattle and buffaloes of the Maldharis in greater numbers The Maldharis became poorer with the rising cost of living; they could not afford to purchase cottonseed and groundnut cake to feed their herds. Municipal taxes made the sale of their milk products difficult and they were denied the benefits extended by welfare schemes in the towns for the sale of butter and ghee for the reason that they were not urban folk.

In desperation the Maldharis, who were generally not able to procure firearms, began to poison the lions that killed their stock by poisoning the flesh of the cattle that had been killed. When the lions returned for a second meal, they ate the poison and died in agony.

This is the same sort of thing that has led to the almost complete extinction of tiger, panthers and even hyaenas in southern India. But the position is even worse in the Gir; for whereas tigers and panthers almost always hunt alone and are therefore poisoned one at a time, the Gir lions, like their African cousins, hunt and feed in prides and are thus poisoned in numbers. We were told that nine lions had been poisoned in this manner very recently. This was shocking news, considering the fact that the lions of Gir arc the only representatives of their species in the whole of Asia.

The Gir itself has also been intruded upon by cultivation around its perimeter, so that the area now comprising this forest is but 13,00 square kilometers of 576 square miles in extent. A census of the lions remaining in this jungle, conducted in 1955 by measuring and counting footprints, indicated about 247 animals. the next census in 1968 showed only 177 lions, a decrease of about forty per cent. The fate of the Gir lion is, indeed, hanging by a thread.

A century ago, the forests of Gir covered three times the present area. Recent statistics reveal that sixty-three per cent of the land surrounding the Sanctuary is under cultivation. With the felling of the forest and advent of more and more cattle, together with the presence of poachers and the poisoning of kills, the noble lion of Gir seems doomed to extinction.

The Sanctuary is now estimated to support a wild-life population of less than twenty-five per cent of its original strength, compelling the lions to rely almost solely on the buffaloes of the Maldharis for food. Their ability to get enough to eat is severely taxed. Although this animal is by nature a nocturnal hunter, existing conditions compel it to hunt by day because the Maldharis corral their stock at sundown.

The Maldhari settlements past which we drove in the van that morning proved to be small mud huts, thatched with sticks and leaves. Allowing a vacant space for the cattle, the whole area of each ness is enclosed by a strong, tall thorn fence, very reminiscent of the thorn bomas of African herdsmen, or in some instance by rock-and-mud walls. Indeed, the whole scenery in the forest is much like that of the thorny scrub-jungles of Africa except for the occasional stunted teak tees growing in between.

Should a lion succeed in jumping one of these fences or walls and killing a buffalo, his effort is vain, since he cannot get his kill over the obstruction to freedom. Should a lion succeed in killing one of the herd in the jungle, he generally loses most of the meat when the Maldhari herdsmen combine to drive him away to salvage the hide.

Incidentally, this also happens in southern India when the herdsmen drive a tiger or panther off the cow it has just killed. Occasionally the feline resents this intrusion and attacks a herdsman, mauling him even occasionally killing him. That, in turn, has often led to the tiger or panther becoming a man-eater. I was told that the same thing has happened in Gir, although infrequently. Now and then a lion has taken to killing men and eating them; it has then had to be shot.

It is estimated that of the domestic stock killed within the Sanctuary fifty per cent are taken by lions and outside the

Sanctuary up to eighty per cent. Panthers account for the remaining kills. As I have said before, there are no tigers in the area.

Because he is mostly deprived of his victim, either as soon as he kills or when he returns to the carcass to find the hide removed by the owners, the lion is of necessity compelled to kill more often than would be the case if he were allowed to gorge his fill. Statistics show that twenty-three per cent of the kills are not eaten at all, while the lions are barely able to consume ten kilograms of meat from a further twenty per cent of kills.

This cycle of unfortunate circumstances has brought the lions of Gir forest into conflict with the Maldharis who occupy the 129 nesses they have established all over the Sanctuary, as well as the owners of thousands of visiting cattle. Enraged herdsmen do not hesitate to shoot or poison such lions as they are able to if they will not be detected.

The Government pays compensation to the owner whose animal has been killed by a lion outside the Sanctuary, but not when it has been killed within. This is not good enough. The Sanctuary, which was primarily created for the protection of these Asiatic lions, is not being allowed to function as it should and fulfil the purpose for which it was instituted.

Of the natural wild fauna three-quarters have disappeared. Most of the fertile valleys in the Sanctuary have been cultivated and a continuous strip of cultivation has already cut the Sanctuary almost in two. The felling of trees — mainly teak — continues, while the hordes of domestic livestock prevent saplings from replacing them. Nearly two million kilograms of grass fodder are removed from the Sanctuary every year. The Sanctuary has been reduced to an impoverished, artificial and heavily-exploited zone. The presence of the few remaining Asiatic lions alone has aroused world-wide interest, but only the Government of India can save the situation at this last-minute stage.

I am glad to be able to record that the Central Government has risen to the occasion and has entrusted the State Government of Gujarat with a scheme called The Gir Lion Sanctuary Project, which started in January 1972. The Governor of Gujarat, Shri Shriman-Narayan, envisaged a two fold target, the first object of which was to protect the lions of Gir in particular, as well as other wild life, from poaching, poisoning and dangerous diseases. The second object is the socio-economic improvement of the Maldharis' condition.

Many meetings were held and resolutions passed, resulting in formal orders being issued by the Government of Gujarat to: (1) Close the Sanctuary permanently to grazing by migrant cattle. (2) Enclose the whole area with an effective physical barrier. (3) Allot land outside the Sanctuary to the Maldharis at present inhabiting 129 nesses inside it, and to shift them, with their families and livestock, out of the Sanctuary in a phased programme. It remains to be seen how far these aims are carried out. One fact is certain. Should the programme fail to be executed, the Gir lion is doomed to extinction within the next decade. Any number of meetings and resolutions, stacks of orders that exist on paper, speeches by the highest officials, drawings, plans and schemes supported by statistical data will not save the lion. What is required is action, and that quickly.

It is discouraging to learn that, after the passage of a whole year, the Maldharis were still where they have always been, in their nesses within the Sanctuary.

After breakfast, at about ten o'clock, we left the forest lodge in the van to motor the dusty roads to the capital of the old Muslim ruler, a town named Junagadh, which is filled with ancient Muslim tombs and mosques. A quick lunch at the Circuit House and we were away again, this time bound for the Royal Palace of Wankaner, where we were to spend a night and day as guests of His Highness the Maharajah and the Prince Yuvaraj of Wankaner. The distance from Sassan Gir to the palace is 105 miles by road.

Petrol trouble delayed us, but we were more or less on schedule when we reached the palace at 5.30 p.m. where the Maharajah and the Prince greeted us with old-world courtesy, garlanding us to the particular delight of my friends.

Next morning the Prince took us out in a tourist cart to his father's private jungle of some 3,800 acres, situated about six miles away. The country consisted of low, rolling hills; the soil was very dry and clothed with dwarf babul. The Yuvarajah complained that the townspeople from Wankaner made inroads into his father's forest, cutting the sparse timber for firewood and poaching, if they got the chance.

We came to a palisaded house where the private salaried Range Officer and two Forest Guards in the employment of the Maharajah resided. These turned out and gave the Yuvarajah — and ourselves — a big salute.

Picking up one of the guards, we motored along the rough tracks winding around the hills and sometimes across them, if the ground permitted, meeting sixteen blue bulls, the colloquial name for Nilgai, in small batches, the largest consisting of five members, all male. We also disturbed two chinkara, a species of antelope smaller in size than black buck, a lone fox, and numerous sand grouse. The Yuvarajah told us that black partridge and sand grouse visited the area in large numbers during the monsoons, but went away with the approach of summer. The estate was covered with Porcupine diggings and burrows.

The Yuvarajah invited us to stop over another day and motor with him to see the famous 'wild asses of Kutch.' These animals, of the donkey family but standing almost as high as mules, live in an area of this dry land somewhat over a hundred miles to the north of Wankaner. Unfortunately we were bound to a tight programme and just could not spare the time. Returning to the palace, we were struck by the large numbers of wild peafowl that strutted about and called to each other. Even the extensive grounds of the palace were full of them. Nobody shoots these beautiful birds in Gujarat. 'Pea-or! Pea-or!', their cries echoed from all around.

The Yuvarajah, who had appointed himself as our guide, took us next to his private farm, situated on the outskirts of the township of Wankaner, where we were shown around a lovely guest house that he was remodelling, with excellent furniture and, of all things, an up-to-date swimming pool, something unheard of in this arid land.

Close by was an ancient well, with steps of pure marble leading down to two terraces built into the sides of the well. From the centre of the well spouted a fountain of water that reached up to the higher terrace and then splashed down to cover everything, including part of the lower terrace, with a fine mist. We felt delightfully cool, as if we were standing on an air-conditioned verandah.

After lunch we left to motor to the capital city of Ahmedabad, 140 miles distant. I felt as if I were in another world, the countryside being totally different from that southern India. It was a parched area, semi-desert, and this fact was emphasised by the strings of camels we passed on the road, their numbers sometimes assuming the proportions of a caravan. Seated on these animals were wild-looking men and women in curious array. Other camels carried their household effects, string-costs, all size of pots and pans, immense heaps of clothing tied into bundles, and miscellaneous other articles that could scarcely be identified. The afternoon was exceedingly hot. As we approached Ahmedabad, the country became slightly greener. It was evening when we reached our destination.

Part of our programme the following morning was to visit the Nal Sarovar lake, a bird sanctuary and a bird-watchers' paradise, but this had to be dropped. Due to two very severe summers in succession when the monsoons had failed, the lake had dried up completely. So we visited the local zoo instead, where we saw a large variety of animals and a collection of birds from all over the world that is really excellent. I was particularly interested in the snake-pit with its jet black cobras. No doubt owing to the colour of the local soil, which is very dark and known in these regions as 'black-cotton-soil', nature has arranged that the creatures that live upon it should also be dark in colour to prevent them from being conspicuous, which would otherwise be the case.

Amidst a collection of tigers and panthers, and a pair of lions from Africa, were a Gir lion and two lionesses. This lion we discovered to be far fiercer than any of the wild lions we had met at Gir, even putting the 'bad lion' to shame. He repeatedly charged at his keeper and us, stopping only at the bars of his cage. Even the African lion was unfriendly. Assuredly, the big felines are far more docile in their wild condition.

That afternoon we took off by plane for the city of Udaipur, where we landed after a very bumpy flight of fifty-five minutes, due perhaps to flying over heated, almost desert land, barren, rocky and unfriendly to look down upon. From the airport we motored to the edge of a large and magnificent lake, boarded a motor-launch and chugged across to one of a series of islands that dotted the water. But this island was different from the rest, for upon it has been built a beautiful hotel, known as the Lake Palace Hotel, with sixty-five rooms that, for the most part, directly overlook the water. The building encloses an open-air garden, abounding with trees and flowering shrubs. It is the private property of the Maharana of Udaipur, till recently one of the important ruling princes of India. He has converted it into a tourist hotel and is running it himself.

In the evening we went by launch to visit one of the neighbouring islands, where the Maharana has a palace which is also being converted into a twenty-room guest house with a magnificent swimming pool. Some of the carving we saw in this palace were wonderful, being old Moghul and Rajput work of ancient origin. The Maharana has a huge palace on the mainland, too, and yet another on the top of a neighbouring hill. From where we stood, the hill-top palace seemed almost inaccessible, perched like an eagle's nest upon rocks at summit, it gleamed a pale pink in the rays of the setting sun.

The Prince also owns a number of shooting boxes scattered about the low scrub jungle of rolling hills that surrounds the lake. Around the city of Udaipur itself are the remains of a continuous wall, once built to protect it against the invading Muslim hordes of the great Moghul conquerors.

When the sun began to set behind the western hills and cast a rippling red-gold pathway across the waters of the lake, we heard raucous voices and saw a strange sight. Thousands upon thousands of green parakeets flocked across the lake from every direction to roost upon the huge trees that grew on the island. It is estimated that over 10,000 birds fly here to roost each evening, coming from areas to feed, but return punctually once more the following evening. This has been going on for centuries, as on the orders of successive Maharanas no one may molest the parakeets; this protection makes it possible for them to increase in numbers every year.

Packs of jackals could be heard that night, howling on the mainland: familiar and welcome sound, it brought back a hundred memories of nights spent in jungles, now far away in the south. The packs called and answered each other from shore to shore: 'Here! Here! Here! Heee-hah! Hee-yah! Hee-yah! Hee-yah! Yah! Yah!'

Then the following morning we took the launch for the shore, where a car conveyed us to the Maharana's main palace, a wonderful structure of white and black marble, with coloured glass windows, amazing carvings, and a rare collection of old armour and swords. Nearby was an ancient temple. And in the afternoon we set out for Jaisamal lake and game sanctuary, thirty-five miles away, passing through dry jungle in hilly country enroute.

In a little over an hour we arrived at the lake, an immense expanse of water. The Maharana has yet another two palaces here, on opposite shores. The lake appeared to be well-stocked with fish, and we could see them leaping out of the water and falling back again. The evening was bright and sunny.

We motored five miles into the heart of the adjacent, Jaisamal game Sanctuary to view a 'Panther show' of a different sort. The jungle was fairly heavy, but very dry. We passed two herds of spotted deer by the wayside, some of the stags carrying exceptionally fine heads. Our destination was an abandoned watch-tower, constructed by a bygone Maharana and converted by his descendant into a shooting box. It was built of stone and was three floors high, and the walls were filled with loop-holes presumably for firing through. It looked like miniature fort, and overlooked a narrow, shelving valley, through the middle of which passed a dry streambed. On the further side of this valley was a gentle, sloping hillside. There were small glades clearly visible to us between the trees and low bushes.

About fifty yards beyond the shooting box a wooden platform, roughly five feet high, had been erected. It stood upon four legs and was a more or less permanent structure. the unfortunate goat, this time a brown one, was tethered on top of it and beneath was a trough, filled with water.

We were invited to enter the stone tower, where four cars were already parked, through a low doorway at its foot and to climb a narrow stairway to the third floor. There we found a full house of people assembled; they were seated in chairs before all the available loop-holes that overlooked the platform and its goat. In this gathering were a film star and her friends. All of them were chattering, smoking, moving about and hailing each other in very audible voices.

It soon became clear that, so great was the audience, if we wanted to see anything we would have to go down to the floor below. This we did and chose four loop-holes before any more people came along.

I could not resist the temptation of asking the agreeable Forest Range Officer in charge of the operations whether the authorities felt any harm was being done by allowing us to watch the panther kill the goat, telling him that in the Gir had not been allowed to see either the lions kill the buffalo or the panther kill the goat prior to the 'show', as that was considered as encouraging the taking of life. The F. R. O. smiled disdainfully. 'We are Rajputs', he vouchsafed by way of explanation. 'Those fellows are Gujaratis.'

He then went up the stairway to where the film star and her friends were gathered, and soon the chattering ceased. He must have impressed on the party that this was no rehearsal.

Staring through the loophole, I glimpsed a single spotted doe across the dry stream in the mid-distant, soon followed by bevy of after bevy of peafowl. Then dark forms filtered through the undergrowth: a sounder of wild pigs. Then a slight movement behind a bush in the foreground caught my eye. I stared hard. A panther crouched close to the ground.

I had not seen him arrive. No one had. It was 6.15 p.m. The panther remained where he lay without moving. Obviously he was aware of people watching and preferred the greater darkness before he showed himself.

At 6.30 p.m. he moved slightly, but still did not risk an attack. It was seven o'clock and getting quite dark when the panther could contain its hunger no longer. From where it was crouching, the spotted cat leaped neatly on to the platform, walked calmly up to goat that had turned around to face its attacker and was straining backwards at its leash, and almost unconcernedly seized it by the throat. The goat bleated once and kicked feebly. Then the feline pressed the head of its prey to the platform and held it there for a long time, till life was extinct.

It was getting more and more difficult for us to see anything in the increasing darkness when the Ranger pressed the switch that was to bring the spot-light into play, but there was no response. The current had failed.

We could barely see the panther tearing at the goat's throat to suck the blood from the jugular vein. A few minutes later it leaped down from the platform and drank deeply at the trough of water. Clearly this panther had been through the performance very often before and knew exactly what to do. Then it became too dark to see more.

The film star gave us a winning smile as she brushed ahead on the narrow stairway in the ground, and soon we were heading for Udaipur.

The next day was idle till the afternoon, when we left for the airport. We were bound for the distant city of Nagpur, from where we were scheduled to motor to the Kanha National Park. But there were many delays on the way, due partly to bad weather and partly to an argument at Delhi between the pilot and a passenger who turned up after the engines had been started, so it was not until early next morning that we landed at Nagpur. Rain was still falling.

But we had to be up again at seven o'clock to set off on a journey by car of 210 miles. Our entourage was of two vehicles: a car for travelling and a Land Rover for our use in the sanctuary, where some of the tracks, up and around steep hills, cannot be negotiated by an ordinary car. Meanwhile the Land Rover was hauling trailer tightly packed with camping kit, a cook, a butler, a table-boy, and all manner of food for our use while we were 'in camp'. Also any number of bottles of Coca-Cola for my American friends. These stood upon ice in large ice-box, in rows like soldiers on parade. Nagpur is situated in Maharashtra State, while Kanha is in Madhya Pradesh. thus we had to cross an inter-state frontier and in doing so were required to sign a form. Our kit and food-stuffs were also examined with awe. It is not clear what the searchers were looking for, but what they saw must have puzzled them beyond belief. They passed us on without further argument.

Forty miles short of our destination the car became stuck in the mud. It had been raining heavily an hour or so earlier and the road was morass. We got out to help and discovered we also had a flat tyre. To jack the car in that mud was a problem. There seemed nothing to do but wait for the Land Rover to catch us up.

Luckily it appeared fairly soon. We climbed aboard, changing places with the cook and the other two servants whom we transferred to the car. We left them to help the driver in his struggle in the mud.

The road was in a terrible condition due to the recent heavy rain and it was difficult journey, even for the Land Rover, encumbered as it was with the heavy trailer behind. We passed through three forest chowkies, or checkposts, in succession, at each of which were displayed numerous notice boards with warnings against poaching and other offences. At every one of these a fee or tax of some sort was collected from us. At last we arrived at the guest houses, for there were quite a number of them.

When, as we unloaded the trailer, I saw all the food that had been provided for us, I was lost in amazement. How different was this fare from what I took on my own trips in the south! There, after the second day, my diet invariably consisted of dried chappatti, often without butter. Roast beef was the luxury, but only on the first day. Thereafter there were chappatties only, and of course lots of tea. Here we had turkey, duck, chicken, mutton fish, fruits of every sort. Not one chappatti could I see anywhere, nor any sign of beef!

So we set off for the jungle in the Land Rover, a forest guard seated beside the driver to direct him. Within a furlong we met herd after herd of spotted deer, some of the stags carrying amazing horns. Grazing along with these animals, and sometimes by themselves, were herds of black-buck. Now and again we could pick out the almost black form of mature stag with its white belly, but for the most part the males were young. Does, along with their fawns, were quite numerous. Peafowl were plentiful, and we saw two red jungle cocks. One flew across the track ahead of us while the other ran along the roadside for a while before dodging into cover.

The red jungle fowl of central and northern India is quite different from the silver-hackled bird of the south. Neither species changes its habitat: the central and northern bird is slightly smaller, dark in colour with rusty-red wing feathers, and crows somewhat like a domestic cock. The southern bird is larger, with a silver-grey hackle, and wing feathers that look as if they have been painted with heavy oil-colours in a very dark brown border with dark spots. Feathers of the same kind adorn the hackle in addition to those of silver-grey. It has a

very distinctive call: Wheew! Kuck! Ky'a! Ky'a! Khuckhm!'
It is by far the more beautiful of the two varieties.

We returned to the guest house at sunset to find that the
cook had performed a miracle and our supper was ready. The
dining-room lay just off the verandah, so that while we ate
we were able to listen to all the sounds of the jungle. Soon
we heard a series of strange sounds, the like of which I had
never heard before. Loud, trumpet-like cries, somewhat like
the braying of a spotted stag, but with much more of the
brassy resonance of a male sambar's note of alarm: 'Aa-hh-
harmm! Aa-hh-harmm! Aa-hh-harmm! Aa-hh-harmm!'.

This was the call of a male barasingha! It is rather difficult
to imitate that memorable sound on paper, but when you hear
it, it is distinctive. And it is sad to think that in a few more
years it will be heard no more. The barasingha, or twelve-
horned deer, derives its name from its magnificent head of
twelve tines, six upon either side, the word 'bara' signifying
twelve in Hindi, Urdu and Hindustani. It is only very slightly
smaller in size than a sambar, but is dark-brown as distinct
from the brownish-grey of the sambar. Like the sambar, the
stags have coarse, long hair on their flanks and around the
neck and throat, where it almost resembles a mane. They are
far larger than spotted deer.

Unfortunately, these creatures seem to be rather silly, lacking
the alertness of both sambar and spotted deer. They move
slowly, heavily and sedately, and are slow to take alarm, slow
to react, slow to run away. Nor can they run as fast as sambar,
although the latter is bigger. The stags have the same habit
as the nilgai or blue bull: they congregate in small herds of
half-a-dozen without a single doe.

These characteristics have led to their downfall, inasmuch
as they fall easy prey to the poacher, their principal enemy,
in addition to marauding tigers and panthers, as well as wild

dogs and even hyaenas. Barasingha, once plentiful in India, are now almost extinct. The Kanha Sanctuary, designed for their protection especially, holds but fifty-five of these beautiful animals. Kaziranga, and a few other sanctuaries, have rather more ; but everywhere they are alarmingly scarce. Their future in India, together with the lion of Gir and the one-horned rhinoceros of Kaziranga in the north-east, is very bleak indeed.

I had not yet fallen asleep that night when I heard a tiger roaring. He must have been half a mile from the guest house. How good it was to hear that memorable sound again: 'Oo-oongh! Aa-oo-oongh! Aungh! Oo-oo-ongh!'.

We were away by six-thirty the next morning and very soon found the group of barasingha that had been calling the night before: five stags, all in a bunch together. Hardly a mile further on we encountered four doe barasingha, these also in a group by themselves. Not far from them we passed three groups of black-buck and many herds of spotted deer, one of them over a hundred animals. Bevy after bevy of peahens, and some isolated cock birds, scattered to right and left of us. It was a peaceful scene until we observed two jackals slinking through the grass close by, silent reminders of the sudden death that can overtake the creatures of the jungle at any moment.

Leaving the park-like country that is the abode of the deer, the Land Rover took us into the low hills that surrounded it. Soon we saw a pair of bison staring at us from under the tall sal trees. The jungle of Kanha are very different from those of southern India. Stately sal trees clothe the former, tall and straight and beautifully green. The absence of lantana undergrowth is noticeable, also of the 'wait-a-bit' or Segai thorn, both of which make wandering in the south very difficult at times. This, and the absence of wild tuskers, which are dangerous and a positive hazard for the unwary hunter or greenhorn naturalist on foot, make Kanha a paradise for 'ghooming', the Hindi name for wandering about. On the whole, I would say the Kanha jungles are about the best for this purpose that I have ever visited.

The next morning we drove through heavy forests, covering over thirty miles or so of rising, hilly country to a high ridge where the natural teak opened on to an extensive maidan or expanse of low grassland, entirely surrounded by the jungle.

We were agreeably surprised to be told that the Government of India Tourist Department plans to convert this area into a landing-ground sufficiently large to operate a Dakota plane service from Nagpur for the convenience of foreign tourists and local sightseers, thus obviating the long car-journey of 210 miles from Nagpur.

This plateau overlooks a famous former shooting block, the Bandla Block, which still goes by the same name. Many old hunters who have spent their early years in Madhya Pradesh, which was previously known as the Central Provinces, will remember this area with nostalgic affection as one that produced some of the most magnificent tigers, for which these forests were world-renowned. On the return journey we encountered as many as seven sambar together, quite an exceptional number for creatures that generally graze in solitude ; also many families of langur monkeys and any number of red jungle-fowl, and the small barking-deer or muntjac. Returning to the low, and the country, we passed the usual families of spotted deer and blackbuck.

In the morning we were back again in the Land Rover, meeting once again large herds of spotted deer and blackbuck, any number of peafowl and a few barasingha. In desperation the authorities are now planning to enclose the barasingha within a high wire fencing of fairly close mesh, covering an area of a few square miles, to protect them against their natural enemies, tiger, panther and wild dog, and of course poachers. It is to be hoped this succeeds, although by its adoption these animals could hardly hereafter be classed as living in a truly wild state. Still, I suppose that fifty barasingha within a fence are better than no fence and no barasingha!

By this time we were tired of driving about in the Land Rover. Three elephants, belonging to the Forest Department, were obtainable on hire, so we changed over to the backs of a couple of pachyderms and went searching the borders of some *nullahs* in the hopes of seeing a tiger or panther. But we saw only the usual barasingha and blackbuck.

At about four o'clock we took the Land Rover again to look for tiger, but we saw only spotted deer, peafowl, red jungle fowl and langur monkeys. A couple from New Zealand, who had booked elephants for that evening, were more lucky. They had one separately on their respective mounts, and while Jack Doon, the husband, was returning he came across a spotted stag struggling on its back. A few yards distant crouched the panther that had attacked it, caught in the act of slinking away. The stag was evidently badly mauled and its spine had been broken. The elephant Jack was riding upon had only recently come to Kanha. A nervous female, it bolted twice upon seeing the stag and its assailant. When the mahout finally succeeded in controlling and bringing it back, Jack discovered the panther again and took pictures of it for nearly thirty minutes, during which time it climbed up a tree, jumped down again and then went up a low rock. Margaret Doon, while returning on the other elephant, came across a dead spotted fawn. For some reason its killer had abandoned the meal and now the fawn was being devoured by a pack of jackals.

That night an official who had arrived at the guest house insisted that we go out with him at nine o'clock and use his spot-light to try to see bison or a tiger. As a matter of fact, such journeys in vehicles with spot-lights are strictly disallowed in Kanha, but being the boss himself, and for our sakes, he made an exception. We found a very large bull-bison, followed by a cow a few paces behind, but no tiger ; and when returning met the usual herds of spotted deer and blackbuck and, close to the bungalow, a couple of sambar.

At dawn the following morning the official took us out again, this time using our own Land Rover and driving it himself. We went to a natural salt-lick, where a tower had been constructed, with a ladder reaching to a covered platform. This tower overlooked a large jungle pool in which the water was partly covered with beautiful pink-petalled lotus flowers. Within a few yards of this pool was the salt-lick in a hollow in the ground. A sambar stag that had been at the salt-lick thundered away at out approach, while from the pool came the flapping of a myriad wings and swarms of spot-bill and brahmini ducks arose, spiralling into the air with a whir of wings. As they flew around and around they uttered sharp cries of alarm.

We also disturbed other creatures: a herd of about fifteen adult bison with half-a-dozen calves, all of them led by a huge master-bull. They had been drinking at a smaller pond opposite the watch-tower and we had not seen them at first. This pond was to the west of the track we were motoring down, and in the park-like section of the country, while the watch-tower and the lake and salt-lick, surrounded by forest, were to the east. Thus the track formed a sort of natural boundary between the two types of country. The master-bull, with his following, saw us and attempted to cross the track to get back into the forest. We prevented them from doing this by racing the Land Rover ahead, or in reverse when the need justified it, so that the bison always found our vehicle between them and the jungle.

Maybe a dozen times we drove forwards or backwards at express speed, by which time we could see that the herd was becoming restive and the master-bull distinctly annoyed. The bison were within thirty yards and less of us they made attempt after attempt to cross the track. Then the bull uttered a shrill, whistling sound and pawed the ground, shaking his monstrous horns at our driver with increasing anger. Then we let him pass. The herd presented an imposing sight when it finally thundered across.

The morning mists had not yet lifted when, little further on, we came upon a sambar stag grazing in the open, and still further two barasingha stags wanted to do just the opposite-cross over the open country.

In both our cases our official followed the same tactics, driving the Land Rover backwards and forwards to prevent them. This allowed my companions to take some good photographs. Finally we drove on and allowed the stags to go where they wished.

The usual herds of spotted deer and blackbuck were everywhere, accompanied by families of peafowl, and we were all in high spirits that morning by the time we got back for breakfast. At lunch our friend had a pleasant surprise for us. He announced that a tiger had killed a buffalo-bait he had ordered to be tied up the previous day. So our official inquired if we would like to accompany him on elephant-back to try to see the tiger, and of course we all agreed. Thereupon he ordered all three elephants to be got ready, one for ourselves, one for another party of visitor who had arrived that morning, and the third for a young German and his wife who had also just turned up.

We sent the elephants ahead and followed in half an hour in our Land Rover, with two jeeps from the Forestry Department carrying the other people. We found the elephants awaiting us in a shady section of jungle and transhipped. Our official rode with us on the largest. Following each other in single file, the three elephants approached the buffalo kill.

As is the case very often, the carcass was not where it should have been, and where it had been lying a couple of hours earlier when the scout for the Forestry Department had spotted it and come to report its death. In all probability, the tiger had spotted the scout in turn, and no sooner had the man departed when the tiger had succeeded in breaking the buffalo's tethering rope and dragging the dead animal away. The ground was thickly covered with dried leaves, but from my perch upon the elephant I could detect no signs of a drag-mark. It looked as if the tiger had not dragged his victim away after all, but had shifted it bodily by carrying the kill across its back.

Some tigers adopt this strategy when they want to be particularly secretive, so leaving no drag-marks behind. Others prefer it as being more convenient than a kill that is dragged along the ground and gets caught by bushes and thorns. In the former case instinct appears to tell them that its is more difficult to trace a kill that has been carried away rather than one that has been dragged, while in the latter case it is entirely a matter of convenience.

As there were no thorns and scarcely any bushes at this spot, it was apparent the tiger had carried it kill away to prevent it from being traced by the scout whom he had seen snooping around. There was also another possible reason: the disquieting fact that there were hide-hunters in the Kanha Sanctuary (just as there were at Gir), who remove the hides of animals killed by carnivora in order to sell them. Perhaps this tiger had already lost some of his kills in this way and was taking no chances.

The practice of removing natural kills can have disastrous

consequences. When the killer is frightened away, he does not return to his kill. Thus he is getting less food than normal and he is forced to kill some other jungle animal unnecessarily, or a domestic animal (as so frequently happens in Gir), which enrages the owner and leads to retaliation against the carnivore. Moreover, after the skin has been removed, it is a strong temptation to the skinner to poison the raw carcass lying exposed in the jungle. Deadly poison — in the form of Folidol — is very easy to obtain on the explanation that it is required as preventive against crop pests, for which purpose it is supplied plentifully by the Government. Also, it is so very cheap. The owner of the cow reasons that his beast has cost time and a great deal of money, and that after consuming the poison the killer will not be able to wander far and will soon die. Then the grazer will take the tiger skin, too, and the money obtained for it will help to defray the loss sustained by the death of the milch cow.

Anyway, to carry its kill particularly a buffalo, this particular tiger must have been a large and powerful specimen. No cub, and very few tigresses, could accomplish such a task.

I dismounted from the elephant to examine the ground. A freshly broken leaf above waist-level and, a little further, a snapped green twig at about the same height, confirmed that the tiger had indeed carried the buffalo away bodily. There being a thick carpet of dried leaves on the grounds, no pugmarks were discernable; had the tiger dragged away its kill the dried leaves would have revealed it.

The tiger had headed directly downhill. The official whispered that a small stream, holding water in places, wound around the base of the hillock where we now stood. It was about a furlong away. With little doubt, the tiger had made for the stream.

I remounted the elephant, and spreading out to distance

of a hundred yards from one another, the three elephants with their parties now moved slowly downhill in line. The elephant on which I and my friend were riding was in the centre ; the German and his wife were to our right, and the other party to our left. A belt of thickly-growing green trees revealed the presence of the stream, and as we reached the high bank overlooking it we heard a low growl to our right and were just in time to see the hind-quarters of a tiger in full flight with its tail. The German couple heard the growl too, and from their position to our right had a clear view of the tiger as it came bounding along the stream-bed. The next instant it saw them, changed direction abruptly, and scrambled up the further bank of the nallah, to vanish from sight.

Down below us lay the half-eaten remains of the dead buffalo within a foot of a pool of water trapped in the drying bed of the stream. Of the tiger we heard or saw no more. Much disappointed, we returned to where we had left the Land Rover and the two jeeps, changed into them, and were soon back at the guest house. In the afternoon we were on our way back to Nagpur.

On our journey we came to a large tank that was on the verge of drying up. Although there had been rain at Nagpur and Kanha, the area midway appeared to be suffering from drought. The entire village population had turned out and men, women and children of all ages were a foot deep in water, scooping the helpless fish into their baskets. Some of these were quite big, weighing four to five pounds each.

It was two in the morning when in drizzling rain we caught the plane from Nagpur to Calcutta. We were not scheduled to spend any time in Calcutta on this stage of our journey; we were to catch the next flight to Jorhat, a town in north-eastern Assam, in an area known as the North-East Frontier Agency, from where we would have to drive by car to India's greatest game sanctuary, Kaziranga, to see the famous one-horned rhinoceros in its wild state, in addition to wild-buffalo, barasingha, tiger and elephant.

I approached the booking-clerk to verify our seats on this plane and book our luggage, when he blandly told me that the official concerned would attend to this work only at 6.15 a.m. The flight to Jorhat was scheduled for 7.05 a.m.

The one thing passable about the Calcutta airport is its dining-room. We had tea there and waited till the clerk arrived. He scanned a list and said our names were not among those of the passengers on the Jorhat flight. He admitted we had been 'booked', but that was not enough ; our names had not been 'confirmed'. Mere booking was not enough, he said. Any clerk could 'book' your name. But the airline authorities had to 'confirm' that there was a place for you on the plane. For us this had been done. And the plane was already full.

He advised us to wait another fifteen minutes or so. The airline coach would be coming from the city, which was nine miles away, ringing the passengers for this flight. Our luck might be good. Maybe four persons had cancelled their flights, in which case there would be room for us.

The coach turned up at 6.30 a.m. What was more wonderful, four seats were available! Then an official asked to see our 'permits'.

'What permits?' we asked in unison.

'What permits?' he repeated. 'Don't you know that you are all foreigners? Foreigners are not allowed to enter the N.E.F.A. area without permit signed by an official of the Government of India as represented by the Assamese Office in Calcutta, because Jorhat is close to the Nagaland border, where foreigners are not allowed.'

We did not know, and said so with some heat. We wanted to go to Kaziranga to look at rhinos, and were not bothered

THE KENNETH ANDERSON OMNIBUS

about N.E.F.A. or Nagaland. He shrugged and said we could not board the plane. Then he turned away.

Joe, one of our American friends, was professional photographer. He had made the journey to India to take pictures and publish them in a series of articles about animals. Every moment was of consequence to him in terms of money. He really blew his top at the news. The airline official merely smiled. 'You will not be able to go to the Assamese Office in the city today,' he added. 'You see, there is a general strike in progress and you will not be able to get a taxi. All motor-traffic is off the road.'

'You might walk the nine miles,' he went on, 'but the office is certain to be closed, due to the strike.'

Yet, in spite of the gloomy picture he had painted we had a little luck. We succeeded in finding a conveyance to the city. It took us to one of the largest and best hotels in Calcutta, where we were fortunate to find accommodation. The strike that had been threatened did not materialize, but a 'hartal' (which amounts to the same thing) was in progress. We managed to get a taxi and went posthaste to the office of the representative of the Assamese Government for our permits. Here our passport numbers were noted and questions asked. We were told it would take a day or two for counter-checks to be made before the required permits could be given. Joe again blew his top. We just managed to get him out of the office in time. A few seconds more, and we would never have got those permits.

'We decided to fill in the time while waiting by seeing as much as we could of Calcutta. Then it would not be necessary for us to stop over when returning from Jorhat.

We visited the zoo first. There we saw the three famous white tigers and their three half-grown white cubs. Light-grey almost white in colour, they are certainly unique. One of the tigers is a beast of outsize proportions. Each of the six animals is housed in separated quarters. Then there is a gayal, a large animal with the body of a bison but with straight horns. It comes from Eastern Assam and the Burmese border. Also, of course, the Indian rhino and a number of Gir and African lions. A feature of the zoo is a large lake within its boundaries to which great numbers of wild-duck of all varieties, migrants from beyond the Himalayas, find their way and spend four months of the year.

For the time being Joe was happy and seemed to have got over his irritation at the delay in reaching Kaziranga. But his pleasure was short-lived, for when we got back to the hotel at 5.30 p.m. we received the bad news that Indian Airlines had suspended all their flights to and from Calcutta owing to another hartal, called with immediate effect, due to the resignation of the West Bengal Government.

The news made Joe furious. He wanted to charter a special plane to Kaziranga or go by car. Since neither of these things could be done, he became grumpy and sulky. The situation grew rather unpleasant.

All this happened on Monday, March 16, 1970. The last we heard before dinner was that, if the local government could sort itself out, we might be able to fly to Jorhat on the 7.05 a.m. flight on Wednesday, the 18th — if the permits came by then.

Tuesday (the 17th) was an uneventful day. We did some sightseeing by taxi in the morning and called at a few shops. By afternoon, however, the political situation had deteriorated ; taxi were off the road and were replaced by truckloads of armed policeman patrolling the streets. We were warned not to attempt to step out of the hotel. Calcutta is crammed with over a million-and-a-half homeless people who dwell on the pavements. They cook and eat there, sleep there, and of course hardly ever get the opportunity to wash. It is unsafe for anybody to go out on the streets on foot during periods of political trouble of any sort, for these pavement-dwellers are not slow to take advantage of the first opportunity that comes their way, and when law and order go away, to knife a passer-by in the back. They have no interest in the contesting political factions.

The only ray of hope that reached us that afternoon was in the form of our four permits. Frankly, I had not expected these to arrive for a long time. We ate our dinner early and retired, to wake up before 5 a.m. and get ready for the air journey we hoped to make at seven.

I had to carry my own suitcase and airbag down the stairway from the third floor, as the lift was not working. Nor were the servants willing to be helpful in this hotel, because of rule that they must not be tipped. The airline office was bedlam. Nobody would pay us the least attention and it was impossible to find out whether we could proceed on the 7.05 a.m. plane, or even if that plane was taking off. The airport was another bedlam. Nobody knew if our names were on the list of passengers.

Seven o'clock, then eight and finally three in the afternoon. We were still firmly upon mother earth. None of us had lunch and we were all exhausted — what with Joe wanting to do this thing and that, claim a refund in Court, send a telegram to the President of India with copies to the Prime Minister and the American Consulate, and the incessant chattering of the Bengalis around us, which reminded me of the noise made by the thousands of mynah-birds when they return in the evenings to roost on the tall trees surrounding my home at Bangalore. It was a nerve-wracking experience.

Nobody could say at what time our flight to Jorhat would take place ; indeed, nobody knew whether the plane would fly or not. To make matters worse, the official suddenly received instructions from their union to go on a 'work to rule strike', while the porters were told to go on 'total strike'.

At last, at 3.15 p.m., the loudspeaker crackled, somebody coughed, and prepared to speak. Flight No. 211 was cancelled! We were lucky to find a taxi to take us back and drop us at the hotel from which we had started early that morning.

Being of a stubborn sort, I made a jaunt on my own to the airlines office the same evening, to find that our luck had changed at last. All four of us were booked on Flight No. 249 at 6.10 the following morning, Thursday the 19th. Returning to the hotel in triumph, I found I had lost my old room; someone else had already taken it.

We left at 4.45 a.m. the following morning to find Dum Dum Airport in the same state of strike and confusion. The fate of Flight. No. 249 was greatly in the balance. However, with the use of much animal cunning, elbow grease and some surreptitious baksheesh, we managed to work a transfer to a combined flight of Nos. 205 and 249 in a Viscount aircraft which, seemingly to the surprise of the airport officials themselves, and most assuredly to our own, took off at last at 9.30 a.m. None of us glanced earthwards at Calcutta as we left the city behind.

The Annabiddahalla Tigress

'ANNABIDDAHALLA' LITERALLY MEANS IN THE VERNACULAR 'THE hollow into which the elephant fell.'

A stream winds downwards in southerly direction, having its source quite close to the forest hamlet of Kempekerai in the mountainous jungle stretch to the north of the town of Pennagaram in the District of Salem in Tamilnadu — formerly the Madras Presidency. This stream drops sharply at one point. It is a fall of about two hundred feet and it occurs in region of granite rocks, so that the water has worn a deep hollow through striking the stream bed over a period of perhaps thousands of years.

In the rainy season the water fills this hollow and rushes madly onwards in its course, but in summer, when the stream ceases to flow, a deep pool of still, dark and forbidding water fills the hole. Nobody knows its exact depth. Probably it is well over thirty feet. As summer advances and the heat increases, the level of the pool descends, leaving a sheer, circular wall of smooth rock all around, covered with slime and moss, up which nothing that has fallen into the pool can ever hope to climb back to safety.

That is what gave the place its name. For an elephant came along one hot season in search of water. The animal came to the pool and must have extended its trunk to suck up some of water. Probably the water was just out of reach. The elephant extended too far, slipped on the slimy sides skidding down into the pool.

Elephants are excellent swimmers, but nothing and no one except a fish can continue swimming for ever. Some cartmen who were travelling along the nearby road to Muttur heard the elephant's screams and gurgles of fear and suffocation. They left their carts, seated themselves on the rocks, around the pool and gloated over the drowning beast's efforts to escape.

It is said that the elephant made prodigious but vain efforts to get a foothold on these slimy rocks. It slipped back each time.

The cartmen were so interested that they lit fires on the rocks and camped there the whole night. The elephant finally disappeared beneath the surface with a last shriek and gurgle in the early hours of the morning. It took over a fortnight before sufficient gas could collect in the stomach to float the carcass to the top. By this time the stench was awful, and it grew worse and worse as the thick hide and flesh fell apart in decomposition to expose huge chunks of rotting meat.

After that no creature came near that pool for a very long time. That is, not for at least thirty years, when a tiger that had been roaming the area and had started to prey upon men repeated the whole act by slipping into the pool itself. But that's another story.

Tigers rarely remained in this area for long, yet it was in fact the bend in a regular 'tiger beat' that resembled a rather wide letter U if laid upon its left side, that is with the opening facing left. The lower side represents the bed of the Chinar river, from the point where it empties itself into the larger Cauvery and for a little over seven miles up its course. At what point the stream from the north, along whose course lies the deep pool of Annabiddahalla, empties itself into the Chinar.

Tigers were occasionally in the habit of swimming across the Cauvery and wending a leisurely way up the course of the Chinar, killing what spotted deer, sambar or pig they could find, and an occasional heifer or buffalo at the cattle *pattis* at Panapatti and Muttur along the way, to turn northwards up the course of the Annabiddahalla stream, skirting the big pool and climbing the hill above it. They then continue another seven miles as the crow flies till they reached the bed of another stream, euphemistically known as the 'Talavadi river' although it is really little more than a deep and rocky nullah, flowing westwards for perhaps fifteen miles to empty itself into the Cauvery river at a point maybe seven miles above where the Chinar river itself joins the Cauvery. The Talavadi stream, of course, is represented by the upper side of the letter U lying on its left side.

As I have related, these wandering tigers from across the Cauvery would stroll eastwards up the Chinar river, then turn northwards up the Annabiddahalla stream and finally return westwards down the Talavadi nullah to reach the Cauvery and swim across it once more to the Kollegal bank on the opposite side.

It was interesting to note that the tigers always followed this course and never came in the opposite direction — that is, from the Talavadi to the Annabiddahalla stream down to the Chinar and back to the Cauvery. I wandered across this area for many years and found it always so. I even questioned the poojarees who have spent all their lives in these forests, and they said the same thing. It is one of those jungle mysteries that appears to defy explanation.

These feline hunters had always been harmless, confining themselves to hit and run raids on the cattle *pattis* that lay along the beat if they were not lucky enough to find wild game.

What came in time to be called the 'Annabiddahalla Tiger' was no exception. In fact it was no tiger, but a tigress. She would follow this beat approximately every four months. At times the interval would be longer. From what people living in the mud-and-wattle huts along the Cauvery told me, she would take a month to six weeks to complete the journey. Then they would find her pug-marks coming down the rocky Talavadi water-course, taking advantage of the cooler sandy stretches that skirted the edges of the stream where the rushes grew, and the tall clumps of the 'orchid' or 'muthur' grass, till once again she had reached the banks of the Cauvery. Here, as her pugs indicated, she had spent no time hesitating. they led to the water's edge where, whether the season was dry and the water low, or the monsoons had broken and the Cauvery in flood, they would disappear from sight. The tigress must have been a strong swimmer.

Clearly, she had her home on the Kollegal bank of the river, probably in some cave at some lonely spot on one of the lofty mountains that rose abruptly in tiers from the river bank. Very definitely her mate was there too, for suddenly she failed to return to her old beat and a whole year passed. Even more than a year, in fact.

Then the tigress returned. Once more her familiar tracks were seen on the sands of the Chinar river as it wound past the cattle *patti* of Panapatti and this time she was not alone.

715

Two sets of pugs accompanied her, one upon each side. They were small pugs, about the size of the tracks that would have been made by large Alsatian dogs. The tigress had brought her two cubs along.

It was most unfortunate that she had done this, for it brought trouble to the cattle, the herdsmen that attended them and finally to the tigress herself and her cubs.

The cattle that had been killed hitherto by passing carnivore, both tigers and panthers, had been few, and the herdsmen who attended them had not taken the matter very seriously. They could always get away with an occasional lie by telling the owner that the animal had died of a sudden sickness, or slipped and fallen down a *khud* or steep *nullah* and broken its neck.

But this tigress, finding the cattle many in number and comparatively sleek in condition, decided to settle down in the area with her two cubs. It was so much easier to kill and to feed her cubs upon fat heifer or buffalo calf than have to wander for miles in search of food and then perhaps find none: she would have to go to sleep on an empty stomach and, worse still, so would her cubs. She knew from experience that when they were in that condition, as large as they had grown, they would still persist in trying to drink milk from her and that was a very painful experience. For the cubs had long and sharp claws that would tear into the fur and skin of her belly, and they had grown sharp and strong teeth that bit into her udders.

Kills began to take place in quick succession now, on almost every third day, for the cubs had keen appetites. No longer could the excuse of sickness or an accident be put forward to account for missing animals. They became far too many. So the poojarees and other low-caste villagers, who comprised the herdsmen that attended on the large assortment of cattle and buffalo kraaled at Panapatti, sent out a call for help to my shikari and camp-follower, Ranga by name who live at the small town of Pennagaram, about eight miles away.

I have told you something about Ranga in other stories. He and a poojaree named Byra and I had wandered in these forests, mile upon mile, for many years, and there was hardly a corner of any of them that was unknown to one or all of us. Byra had been a poacher, and he remained one till he died. Ranga was a far more versatile fellow. Starting as a poacher, he had climbed the ladder of status to that of cartmen, shikari, cultivator, and finally to that of a miniature landlord. He had attempted to kill his first wife and gone to jail for it, because he made the mistake of getting caught. Profiting from this experience, he had murdered his second wife after making sure he would not get caught by leaving a complicated lead to her uncle. Thereafter, realising it would be far too much of a risk to attempt a hat-trick by murdering his third, he had solved the problem by marrying a fourth, leaving the two women as a check upon one another while he got tied up with a fifth.

Leaving this place of many marriages for the moment and returning to the subject of the tigress, Ranga received the call for help and took it very seriously. He had an old muzzle-loader in those days. But it was a good weapon, inasmuch as it had laid low many a sambar hind that Ranga had ambushed over a water-hole in summer, many a spotted deer, doe or fawn that had come to drink at the same water-hole, and many a wild pig that had been so daring as to wander into the sugar-cane fields near Pennagaram on a moonlit night. Ranga was certain that he could account for the tigress with his trustly firearm without any trouble at all.

He sent word by the men who had come to summon him that the herdsmen should carefully conceal the remains of the next cow or buffalo killed by the tigress with branches of trees so that vultures would not find and finish it, and then to call him immediately. He would come at once, keep watch over the carcass and finish off the tigress as soon as she had returned for a second meal.

The plan worked well up to a point. The tigress killed a buffalo and with her two cubs ate nearly half of it. The herdsmen concealed the remains under branches cut from nearby trees and sent for Ranga. Ranga came without delay, bringing his trusty matchlock.

The only fly in the ointment was that there was no convenient branch close enough to the carcass for him to build a *machan* upon which to sit up for the tigress. There had been one and only one, and it had been just in the right place. But the foolish herdsmen of Panapatti had lopped it down just to get at its leaves and smaller branches to cover the cadaver! Could they not have brought the leaves from somewhere else? The whole jungle lay before them for this purpose. They had been far too lazy. Why walk so far when a convenient bough was to be found so close at hand?

So Ranga had to look for another site for his *machan*. He found it. There was another branch on another tree. But it was from eighty to hundred yards away. The range was rather too far for a muzzle-loader, particularly at night when everything appears so distorted. Some of these old blunderbusses are wonderfully effective at impossible ranges for a shot gun to be of any good. But on a dark night, when it would be difficult to bring off a good shot even with the aid of torch-light the odds were stacked against Ranga.

The tigress came along with her cubs. Ranga had heard them coming. Soon he knew the tigress had started her meal; he could hear the growls made by the mother and her offspring as they quarrelled over the meat.

That was when he pressed the button of the electric torch he had tied with string to the barrels of his muzzle-loader. The cells were probably half-exhausted, for Ranga said he could hardly pick up the eyes that shone back a whitish-red in his direction. Trusting to luck he pressed the trigger.

There was the usual roar of the explosion, the explosion, the bright flash of the ignited black gun-powder, and the heavy pall of smoke that covered the whole branch upon which he was seated. Ranga knew he had not missed. He could hear the tigress roaring loudly and angrily.

To reload the muzzle-loader in the darkness, balanced precariously on a hastily constructed and unstable platform, was not easy, but he managed it at last. The roaring had ceased when he timidly depressed the switch of the flash-light a second time, but now he saw nothing beyond the dim, dark blur of the carcass lying upon the ground. Of tigress or cubs there was no sign.

When daylight came, my henchman and the herdsmen, who had heard the shot at night and came from their huts, saw that the tigress must have been hit. There were drops of blood upon the ground, and later, by dint of careful stalking, they found the trail with smears and spots of blood on the grass and upon the leaves. It led downhill and across the Chinar, which at this time of the year carried running water hardly a foot in depth.

On reaching the further bank, a heavy out-crop of orchid-grass showed where the tigress and her two cubs had passed. More smears of blood upon the green stems indicated that the tigress had been hit somewhere in the right flank. There was no evidence that her right shoulder or thigh had been damaged, as the pug-marks she had left in the soft sand showed no signs of a limp, nor did the wound appear to be a serious one, as the blood trail was comparatively light. After the clump of orchid-grass, the tigress and her family had crossed a low thorny hill, on the further side of which the trail had petered out. Either the wound had gradually ceased to bleed, or layer of fat or hide had worked itself across the cavity to stop the bleeding.

In the usual optimistic fashion of the Indians, Ranga and his companions congratulated each other that between them they had got rid of this troublesome animal. No doubt it would die of its wounds somewhere in the jungle or be drowned when it tried to swim back across the Cauvery in its weakened state. Of the fate of its two cubs they never thought or cared.

It was a dark night, just over two months later, when a string of bullock carts bumped and jangled down the three sharp hairpin bends in the track that led from the higher-levels of the hill above the Annabiddahalla pool to the lush valley through which the little stream purled on its way to the Chinar. The vegetation was dense in this valley, and elephants and sloth bear, sambar and jungle-sheep abounded. The felines and spotted deer kept for the most part to the more open forest slightly higher up; the deer because they disliked getting into heavy vegetation where they could be easily ambushed by carnivore and the even more dangerous wild dogs, and the felines because the valley was full of insect pests and they hated the big ticks, the mosquitoes and, strangely enough, the tiny fleas that were a feature of this forest.

The leading bullock-cart carried a dimly burning lantern hanging from the yoke securing the two buffaloes that drew it ; it hung just behind their hind-quarters. There was a reason for this. The domestic buffalo is an abnormally stupid animal. If the lantern had been suspended anywhere near its neck or face, it would refuse to draw the cart. Nobody knew just why. Maybe the beasts that drew the cart thought that they were

home, so why go further? With the light behind them and
darkness ahead, they thought they had still to go on. Rather
illogical reasoning, I admit, but maybe buffaloes are illogical
creatures. The cartmen had to use them in preference to the
usual bulls, for the loads of cut bamboos were unusually heavy
and the track stoney and steep. Buffaloes have more strength
than bulls.

Admittedly, to hang the light behind rather than in front
had the obvious disadvantage. Nobody, not even the buffaloes,
could see what lay ahead. And when there was only one
lantern to the whole convoy of a dozen carts, it did not help.
But perhaps it was better not to see too much, on the principle
that to see no evil was to know no evil. What I mean is, an
elephant might be standing just around the corner or just off
the track. Ordinarily, he would not be visible at night. Also,
ordinarily, unless he was a 'bad' elephant, he would take no
notice of string of bullock-carts passing by. So why see him
unnecessarily and become unnerved?

However, this did not always work. If perchance the
elephant was not so good, or even slightly bad, he might not
relish this disturbance of his privacy. Yet there was nothing
the cartmen could do about it anyway. They certainly could
not turn back. Try turning a bullock cart around hurriedly on
a narrow track on a pitch-black night, with eleven more carts
and eleven friends driving them behind you. Of course they
could all come to a halt instead; at least the leader could.
Number two would bump into him and stop. Number three
would bump into the number two and so on. Would it help?
Better to keep going. If the beastly elephant comes too close,
beat the empty kerosene tin in the cart behind you, kept there
for just that purpose. That should stop him. And if it does
not? Jump out of the cart and leg it down the line of carts
behind you. But do not lose your head and run into the jungle;

there may be a other elephant there. By the time the elephant smashes up your cart, throws one or both your buffaloes into the air in his exhilaration and then turns his attention to cart number two, you have enough time to be well out of the way. Besides, there are eleven other fellows behind you. By the time they wake up and realise all is not well, the elephant will have had a roaring time. The main thing is to save your own skin.

But what about snake? Poisonous snakes crossing the road? One of the buffaloes might step upon one; in which case, within two hours there would be only one buffalo less.

The cartman should always ride in his cart, not walk behind it for fear of elephants. One such cartman never kept to this rule. He had met a herd of elephants on this very track, but about seven miles further on. It had been evening and he had been alone in his cart; so he had returned to the camp of the bamboo — cutters, to set forth before dawn the next morning. This time he walked behind the cart, so that if he bumped into the elephant he could fade away without being spotted.

However, the buffaloes escaped treading on a cobra in the track, but one of the cart-wheels broke its back. The next thing the cobra saw was the man's foot. So he bit it. The cartman walked another mile or so, reaching the Muttur Forest Bungalow, where I was encamped, at break of day. I cut the wound to bleed it, and walked him about vigorously.

All to no avail. the poor fellow died in about two hours, and the police gave me no end of trouble for two days. Apparently, the fact that I had cut his foot with a knife to cause bleeding was highly suspicious. Perhaps if I had done it with some blunt instrument and concealed the blood things would have been okay. I just could not get them to understand the reason. I think I have told this story somewhere else, but it suffers repetition as it has direct bearing on bullock-carts that travel through jungles by night.

However, no elephant ambushed this particular convoy. But a very hungry tigress did, accompanied by two equally hungry cubs. They let the convoy pass, that is all but one. They attacked the last cart.

The driver was sound asleep when it happened, hunched up over the scraps of rope he used as reins, and rolled up in a coarse black blanket. He awoke with a start, to the sensation of falling through space, as the cart toppled down into a nullah bordering the road. He could hear deafening sounds; growls, snarls and the bellowing of his own two buffaloes. He did not know it just then but riding on the back of one of them, with her fangs embedded in its throat, was a tigress. A cub, slightly less than half-grown, but ineffectually into its side, while another clung to the hindquarter of the other buffalo.

The cart and all the creatures involved in this melee landed with a crash at the bottom of the nullah, which was luckily not deep. The cartman was thrown free, while the yoke holding the buffaloes snapped. The buffalo that had been attacked by one of the cubs broke away and bolted down the nullah, leaving the bewildered cub to join its mother and the other cub that were attacking the remaining buffalo. In another two minutes it was dead.

The cartman, hastily extricating himself from the entangling blanket, saw struggling black forms and heard frightful noises. By the light of the stars he scrambled up the side of the nullah to regain the track the convoy had been following. Away in the distance he heard the jangling and thumping of the other carts as they raced away from the scene. Those of the drivers who had been awake and heard the pandemonium that had broken out behind them had guessed that something terrible was happening to their companion behind. Exactly to which companion they did not care nor stop to find out ; the buffaloes yoked to the carts needed no goading to speed their pace. They knew the roars of a tiger when they heard them! Galloping behind each other in a jagged line, the convoy bounced and thudded down the precarious track, while running for his life, the luckless driver whose cart had been attacked ran behind to catch them up.

News of this event spread far and wide and the bullock-carts ceased to travel by night. This did not help the tigress, who became more hungry, and she had to feed her cubs besides herself. Nobody knew it then, but her right shoulder had been badly hurt ; in fact, the bone was split by the lead ball from an old, old musket. It was Ranga's musket that had done the damage.

Driven by hunger, the tigress started to attack cattle by day light. In this she was joined by her cubs, who were rapidly learning the art of killing, though the methods were crude and amateurish as befitted their inexperience. Their mother could not do much better, handicapped as she was by a smashed shoulder. Thus it transpired that each kill made by this trio of animals presented a nasty spectacle of mangled living flesh and torn hide and bone, a victim that had been partly eaten alive. It was all so different from the kill made by a normal tiger ; a neat job in which the neck of the prey is neatly broken with a minimum of bloodshed.

These attacks continued for the best part of six months, during which time the cubs grew apace. They now required no help, but could kill expertly by themselves. Curiously, they remained with their maimed mother instead of breaking away and fending for themselves as cubs begin to do when about a year old. The killings of cattle and buffaloes increased as the cubs grew older and larger and their appetites increased.

Probably nothing more exciting would have happened had not Mariappa, the cowherd, instead of running away as fast as he could, as did all wise cowherds, rushed to defend his milch-cow when the three tigers attacked it at the edge of his field. He might have succeeded had the attacker been a single beast, but numbers bring courage, both to human being and to tigers.

If you should be 'ghooming' in a jungle — that is wandering about with the hope of seeing what animals you come across — or should you meet a pair of tigers or a tigress with cubs (both of which are today most unlikely to happen, I might tell you), halt and above all do not move. Do not start to run away, for that will attract the attention of the tigers which, just like your dog, love to chase things that run away from them. Take cover, by all means, if you know how, without floundering about and advertising your presence. Above all, remain absolutely motionless. And never, I strongly advise you, start to follow them to see where they are going. There is a fair chance that you can do this in perfect safety with a single tiger, or even with a pair of panthers. But when a pair of tigers are involved, or a mother with cubs, the chances are small. Tigers do not like their family privacy disturbed for one thing, while numbers definitely bolster their courage. With elephants it is quite the opposite. Leave 'Jumbo' alone if he is by himself, and avoid a female with a calf, though a herd of thirty, even if you are all by yourself, you can drive like cattle almost with impunity.

Mariappa committed the grave error of rushing towards three tigers lying over the lovely cow which they had just killed. I suppose he thought he would be able to save it. Very brave of him, but equally foolish. The next instant he was dead. Which of the three feliness killed him nobody knows.

Six

In a Jungle Long Ago

IT ALL HAPPENED AT PANAPATTI MANY YEARS AGO. *PATTI*, AS I HAVE explained in earlier stories, signifies 'a cattle-camp', and Panapatti was one such camp. It is situated on the southern bank of the Chinar river, about three miles and a half from its confluence with the Cauvery, which is the largest river in southern India. The Chinar holds water only in the monsoons, and possibly a couple of months after that. For the remaining six months of the year it is a dry nullah, although both banks for a dozen mile or more from where it empties itself into the great river are clothed with heavy jungle, acres of bamboo, with muthee, tamarind and jumlum trees and other varieties in between.

When the monsoons end vegetation dries quickly in India. As a consequence the grass and the stalks of chollam, ragi and rice, harvested from the fields and given to the cattle after the ears of grain have been removed, becomes exhausted too and there is nothing for the domestic herds to eat. That is when the owners of the herds turn covetous eyes upon the forests, where the grass still grows and certain varieties of leaves and shrubs provide grazing.

Grazing licences are purchased from the Forest Department, and thousands of domestic cattle are driven into the jungle, where they are kept till the advent of the next monsoons, when they are driven back to the village again once local grazing becomes possible as the grass and crops spring up. As this an annual performance regular campsites have grown up in all the forests where the cattle are kraaled during the summer months. These sites in the south are the 'pattis'.

Panapatti is in the District of Salem of what is now Tamil Nadu State and was formerly the Presidency of Madras; hardly anybody outside a radius of twenty miles knew or heard of its existence. To my knowledge on only two occasions occasion did excitement in any form come to Panapatti. The first of these was with the advent of an elephant that killed a few people, including a hunter that had come after it. This animal came to be known as 'The Rogue Elephant of Panapatti'. I have told the story in an earlier book.[1]

There was a lull of several years after that. Then notoriety visited the little camp for the second time with the advent of 'The Avenging Spirit', which I am going to tell you about. Let me hasten to add that this spirit was not a human phantom but a tiger that appeared suddenly from nowhere, earned a ghostly fame, and then disappeared as mysteriously as it had come.

The owners of most of herds kraaled at Panapatti were rich landlords inhabiting the large town of Dharmapuri, about twenty-eight miles away as the crow flies. Three or four, of

---

1. See: *Nine Man-eaters and One Rogue.*

lesser importance, hailed from the smaller town of Pennagaram situated just ten miles distant. The herdsmen to whom the cattle were entrusted during their stay at patti, were the lowest caste of villagers from Pennagaram, augmented by a few 'poojarees', who were jungle-men belonging to an aboriginal tribe, living in the forest all the year round, sheltered in little thatched huts or in *gavvies* or hollows dug into the banks of the Chinar river at spots where that stream ran through hilly country and the banks were steep and high. This protected the inmates from elephants that crossed the Cauvery and walked up the bed of the Chinar river in the dark hours of the night.

Such a poojare was Kaiyara. He had been one of the graziers regularly employed for quite a number of years in looking after the herds that came to Panapatti during the summer months. On an average the cattle remained in this camp for about six months in the year, and Kaiyara's wage was ten rupees (about 50p) for the entire period, plus a weekly allowance of rice or chollam or ragi. Not all together, mind you, for that would be gross over-payment. Say about ten pounds in weight per week, whichever grain was the cheapest available in the market at that time.

When Kaiyara had first taken service several years ago, he had had his wife with him and an only child, a daughter named Mardee. Then the krait came. It had been a very hot night and the slim, jet black snake with the infrequent white notches across its neck and back, had slithered into the grass-thatched hut occupied by the little family and coiled itself around the base of the dark earthen pot in which the drinking water was kept. No doubt the reptile was feeling the heat, too, and relished the cool of the pot.

Kaiyara's wife had very long hair. When she lay on the floor of the hut at night, it had a habit of getting knotted or falling across her face and disturbing her. So on that occasion she had decided to tie it up with the strip of black rag that she kept for the purpose.

But where was that rag? By the water-pot. Talking to her husband as she did so, the women stooped and her fingers close around what she thought was the rag. Unfortunately it was the krait she had grasped.

The snake struck at what it thought was an enemy, burying its small fangs just above her wrist. Then it disengaged itself, slithered behind the water-pot and passed through the wattle hut wall into the jungle outside.

The woman hardly saw what had bitten her. Something cold and black, she knew, and then it was gone. She called to her husband and held out her arm for his inspection. Kaiyara looked and saw two tiny drops of red blood on her back skin. They were hardly half-an-inch apart. The poojaree recognized the marks for what they were, punctures inflicted by the fangs of a venomous snake.

He got busy. There was no doctor, no anti-venom injection, no hospital within twenty-eight miles. Only his dirty cloth bag, containing some powdered herbs and roots, could help.

Kaiyara knew nothing about lancing the wound and bleeding it. So he stepped outside, picked up some soft cow-dung, made a mixture of it with some of the powder from his bag, and smeared the paste thickly over the wound. Then he started muttering a mantra, over and over again.

Within thirty minutes his wife complained of great pain in her wrist. Also shooting pains in her abdomen. She said she was beginning to feel giddy. After another thirty minutes she could not speak. The last she had said was that she had great pains in her stomach. Saliva was pouring from the corners of her mouth. Her breathing was heavy. Yet another thirty minutes later there was hardly any sign of breathing. The woman was cold and limp. Her eyes had rolled back in their sockets. A few minutes more and she was dead. Kaiyara was left alone with his little girl, Mardee, to look after.

The years passed. Mardee was now a comely lass. She had grown into full womanhood, mature and well developed in body. Handsome, too for a poojaree aboriginal. She was her father's mainstay and looked after him well, cooking all the meals and doing the chores in their tiny household. She also went out with the cattle at dawn and grazed them till sunset, returning with the herds of beasts as they ambled home in the evenings when the sun sank behind the jagged hillocks to the west on the bank of the Chinar.

Many of the poor herdsmen and a number of the poojarees coveted her and came to Kaiyara with proposals of marriage. To strengthen their suits, some were prepared to forego the usual dowry which every father had to pay the bridegroom and his family before a daughter could be married. Mardee spurned all her suitors. Young as she was, the girl was of a determined nature; she would have nothing to do with common herdsmen or poojarees.

Then one day, Sathynarayan came to Panapatti. He was the eldest son of his father, Gopalswamy of Dharmapuri, a rich landlord and merchant who owned over two hundred head of cattle grazing at Panapatti. Sathynarayan was also married and had a wife and young son. But they stayed behind at Dharmapuri when he came to Panapatti to inspect his father's herd. Sathynarayan arrived at a comfortable time of the morning when the herds had already been taken out for graze: about nine o' clock. The cattle had been driven out as the sun's rays were just rising above the Muttur Ridge, four miles to the east, to melt away the heavy mists that clothed the valley of the Chinar and the sloping land on both its banks, and to send the wild elephants into the dense bamboos for shelter, and the sambar into the hills.

He left his car on the main road with his chauffeur and walked the two miles of jungle track that brought him to the patti. It was a filthy track, Sathynarayan thought; the earth was several inches deep in layers of cow-dung, deposited year after year by successive herds of cattle and buffaloes. He stepped delicately, avoiding the more recent patches of dung for fear of soiling his shoes.

Soon he stood at the doorway of Kaiyara's hut and coughed loudly; then he spat. It was utterly beneath his dignity to call the inmate by name. The poojaree had watched his employer's son approaching. He crawled through the low doorway and prostrated himself on hands and knees, touching his forehead to the ground, the customary salutation of a poojaree in the old days.

'What news?' inquired the young man curtly.

'All is well, Swamy,' replied the poojaree regaining his feet. 'By the grace of the gods, none of your revered father's cattle have been taken away by the ferocious wild beasts that fill this forest nor stricken by the cursed foot-and-mouth sickness. I give thanks daily to the gods for their mercy. The animals have been driven out to graze under the care of my unworthy daughter.'

'So that is how you earn your keep?' asked Sathynarayan pointedly. 'By sending the cattle out in charge of girl while you sleep in your hut. What can she do if a wild animal should attack?'

The father was silent, then he thought of a brilliant excuse: 'I was sick of the fever, with pains in my stomach and diarrhoea all last night, your honour, else I would have gone with the herd myself.'

'You lie!' accused the landlord's son. 'However, as I have come to see the animals for myself, you must now guide me to where your daughter has driven them.'

731

Thus it came about that Sathynarayan saw Mardee for the first time and lusted after her greatly. He could not speak to her straight away. That would have been beneath his status, particularly with her father looking on. He would have to look for some better opportunity.

The young man took a great interest in his father's herd after that day. His parent was rather surprised suddenly to discover that his son-and-heir, who had hitherto shown little liking for his business and none whatever for cattle, had developed an unexpected thirst for knowledge. So he smiled indulgently and decided to encourage his son. Probably it was just a passing fad and would soon wear off, when the boy would become as useless as before. Of, course Sathynarayan's wife could not comment. Women in India are not permitted to question the comings and going of their men.

Sathynarayan timed his visits to a later hour, when he knew the animals would be grazing in the forest. Moreover, he avoided the *patti* and went directly to the grazing ground. Thus he met Mardee for the second time, and third and fourth time, and many times thereafter.

Although she was still a child, her woman's instinct told the poojaree girl that the young man had fallen in love with her, a sentiment which he was not slow to encourage with small gifts of money. Mardee had always aimed high, far above the local cattleboys and poojarees, and here was the answer to her dreams. A very rich young man; her employer's only son to boot!

Sathynarayan lost no time in seducing her. The jungle offered plenty of scope for that and Mardee became pregnant. Of course, the lovers thought that nobody knew of their clandestine affair. Actually everybody in the *patti* knew about it. The herd-boys had seen from a distance. The poojarees had gone one better: they had stalked the lovers and peeped on their most intimate moments at close range. Then they had run back and told Kaiyara.

The old man was astounded. Such a thing was unheard of; it had never happened before. His employer's son was a brahmin of highest caste. Moreover, he had his own wife and son. Mardee, his own daughter, as a poojaree was of the lowest caste! How could this thing be? If he should dare to question the young man, the matter would be reported, and his employer, the father, would undoubtedly throw Kaiyara out of his job. So he kept the matter to himself for five months until it was evident his daughter was going to have a baby. He questioned the girl. To his dismay, she appeared to be not in the least ashamed. She admitted that Sathynarayan was the father and declared he was in love with her and had promised to marry her.

At the very next opportunity Kaiyara screwed up enough courage to question the young man.

Sathynarayan flew into a towering rage. 'What are you talking about?' he thundered. 'Would I defile myself with your daughter, a slut of the lowest caste, like yourself? Who told you this absurd tale?'

'She told me herself' answered the old man flatly.

Sathynarayan scowled, but said nothing in reply. He turned his back and walked away.

The next morning Mardee took the herd out again for grazing. It was clear she had not slept the night before. There were rings under her eyes and they were red. She had been crying. This could be understood, for her father had said that the young man had denied having touched her and had called her a low-class slut.

It was long past the sunset hour when the herd struggled back that evening. They came in twos and three, and a few of them did not come at all. And of Mardee there was no trace.

Darkness fell before Kaiyara fully realized what had happened. He begged the other men to come with him in search of his daughter. Some agreed. Others pleaded that they were indisposed.

There were no lanterns in the *patti*. Nor did anyone possess and electric torch. Each little hut had just one small oil-light of its own, a tiny taper of wick, floating in a little earthenware bowl of oil. There was no moonlight either, for it was time of *amavasa*, the darkest period of the month. Moreover, this is also the most inauspicious and dangerous period to be out at night, the time when devils of all kinds roam at will: evil spirits that sometimes appear as men and women, sometimes as elephants, tigers and other wild animals, and often as tall white pillars reaching to heaven. They would cackle and scream with unholy laughter when they came across defenceless mortals to kill.

In this atmosphere of terror the little party set forth, treading their way along the trails left by the cattle as they grazed in the forest. The only lights came from the stars that blinked down through the foliage. Inky darkness covered the ground. A demon might be anywhere, behind tree-trunk or bush, and might strike at any moment. A tiger or panther might lurk round any corner. Even an elephant could be three paces away and would be entirely hidden in that gloom. The men walked together, in a bunch, those at the sides making considerable noise as they brushed through the thorns bordering the pathways and getting their skins well lacerated in the process because nobody wanted to be the last man in line.

It was common knowledge that it was the last man who always fell prey to the attack of a tiger, a panther or an elephant. At least, if that happened, he would cry out and warn the others, who would have a chance to run away. But if a demon attacked him he would just disappear in silence.

Nobody would know about it. Then the next last man would vanish, and the next, and so on. No one would know a thing till all had disappeared.

In this fashion the little party crept forward, faltered and then came to a stop. Each member had worked himself into a state of abject fear and the feeling was infectious. By mutual consent they came to a halt.

'Mardee', screamed her father in desperation. 'Mardee, Mardee, where are you my child?'

There was no answer but the sough of the jungle breeze as it began to blow down the valley. Far away a tiger roared. Just ahead an elephant heard the roar and trumpeted in challenge. A sambar stag on the further bank of the Chinar caught the scent of human beings and belled in alarm. Once, twice and many times. A langur monkey, higher up the hillside, woke to the disturbing noises and grated his repeated warning to the other members of his tribe.

The search party wavered no longer. They turned and hastened back to the *patti*. Indeed, they walked so fast it was impossible to do so in a bunch. Somebody had to be last. But this time the gods were good: no wild beasts attacked him, nor did a demon strike him down. They all got back to the *patti*, but without Mardee.

As the girl had vanished in broad daylight, everybody thought she had been taken by a tiger. Had an elephant killed her, or a panther for that matter, some trace of her would have been found. But although Kaiyara, and every other resident of the *patti*, combed the surrounding jungle for a week, not a trace of the missing girl did they come across.

Then there came a clue. A long cartman, struggling to get his vehicle up the steep incline of the Muttur track leading through the jungle to Pennagaram, remembered that he had been forced off the road-way into the ditch by a big car that had come up from behind and was trying to get ahead of him. Because of the gradient, all carts were hauled by buffaloes, as they were more sturdy than the customary bullocks, and more sure-footed. Unfortunately, they were also more stupid. When the car had come up from behind, the cartman had noticed that, strangely, the driver had not even once sounded his horn. Instead, he had attempted to overtake the cart in swift silence, with the result that the buffaloes had shied and run down into the steep ditch beside the road, capsizing the vehicle with its load of bamboos. Luckily, the cartman had been thrown clear, and as he hit the ground he had looked up to see who was responsible for this callous behaviour.

The car was Sathynarayan's. The cartman knew it well by sight. Somebody else was driving but he recognized Sathynarayan in the back seat. He had been holding on to a woman. He had caught a glimpse of a red sari as the car lurched past at high speed. He said he did not know who the woman was. But Mardee had been wearing a red sari on the day she disappeared. Slowly the pieces of the puzzle came to fit together.

Normally, one could expect the Muttur track to be deserted on the early hours of the morning. The presence of the carman was something unexpected. If a car were parked at a bend in the track where it wound around a stony hillock called Karadimedu (Bear's Mill), the owner could follow a short cut through the forest that would take him in about twenty minutes to the grazing ground where Mardee had driven the cattle.

The whole thing seemed to lead to a choice of two conclusion. Either the lovers had made an appointment which the rich young man had used as an opportunity to abduct her, perhaps with the intention of murdering her later; or unknown to her, he came upon her by stealth and had taken her away against her wish.

Kaiyara reasoned all this out in his mind aided by one or two of his companions whom he felt he could trust. He dared not speak of it openly. There were informers everywhere and none knew who could be trusted. Word would be carried to the young man, or his father, Gopalswamy. Kaiyara would then be sacked. That would be the least that could happen. He remembered he was up against moneyed people. They could pay *goondas* (ruffians) to beat him up, perhaps murder him. For that matter, they could bring a false charge against him of theft or something else. He would be locked up in the police station and be beaten up mercilessly. His cronies advised him to leave well alone. Treat the whole matter as the will of God, and forget about it.

But Kaiyara was a father. Further, he held a reputation at least among the herdsmen and his brother poojarees at Panapatti, of being a black magician who could cast powerful spells, and if he did nothing he would lose the reputation for good and all. He would be scorned as an imposter, a coward. His companions would say to each other: he called himself a black magician, but where is his magic now? If he were genuinely what he claimed to be, he would cast a spell upon the man who had committed this crime and that man would fall very sick and die. For everybody at the *patti* had reasoned out for himself what had happened, although none dared to speak of the matter openly.

A few days later, the night of *amavasa* came again, the darkest night of the month, when evil spirits are afoot and magicians cast their most potent spells. When the camp-fire burned fitfully at Panapatti after the evening meal and the herdsmen sat around to chat for a few minutes before retiring to their huts for the night, Kaiyara stepped into their midst and addressed them. He had adorned himself for the occasion. Red and white marks changed his face into a fearsome sight.

A silver armlet above his right elbow identified his status as a black magician. A necklace of the large serrated seeds of the oudarrachamani plant encircled his neck, and another of large, black, glass beads.

He cleared his throat and began to speak: ' Brothers, as you all knew some evil man has beguiled my daughter. Not only has he done wrong, but he has taken her away and perhaps murdered her. The days are bad and we are poor people. There is none we can approach for help. None will stretch forth a finger to aid us, for we have no money, while the evil man who has done this thing is very, very rich. But I do have this power which neither he nor all his money, influence and friends can take away from me. It is the power to curse him and his family, from the realms of the living to those of the dead. I will go in search of my beloved daughter. Maybe I will find her, maybe not. Maybe, I myself will not return. Should any harm befall me at the hands of this evil man, I want you to bear witness that I now curse him and his family. His life, and the lives of his dear ones, will be swallowed up for the life of my beloved daughter and my own. I curse him! I curse him! I curse him! By this thrice repeated curse, it shall be as I say.'

Next morning Kaiyara went forth from the *patti*. Only his close companions knew he had gone to Dharamapuri boldly to announce to his employer, the rich business man and cattle-owner, what Sathynarayan had done to his daughter.

Kaiyara never came back. He was never seen again! The herdsmen soon forgot about him and the words he had uttered. Possibly his special friends thought about it and felt sorry. The poojaree had been foolish enough to put his head into the tiger's mouth, so to say.

Six months passed. It was the festival of Pongal and everybody was enjoying themselves. In the village the bullocks' horns were gaudily painted, red, blue, green, bright yellow. Upon their foreheads were long red and white marks of ochre too. Games were arranged and sometimes mock fights between men and bulls.

Sathynarayan and his wife and son, accompanied by his father, motored from Dharamapuri through Pennagaram to the point on the road where they had to leave the car in the care of the driver and walk the distance to Panapatti.

In fact this trip had been entirely the father's idea. Sathyanarayan certainly did not want to go to Panapatti ever again. The place held too many awkward memories for him. That damned poojaree girl had taken him seriously. She had actually believed the silly stories he had spun that he was going to marry her and make a lady out of her. To make matters worse, the wretched girl had the misfortune to fall pregnant, and to crown matters she had told her father all about it. The affair had cost him a thousand rupees, which he had to pay to the chauffeur, Das, to gain his silence about the day they had abducted the bitch. Luckily not even Das knew what he had done with her body. He had made the driver get out of the car so that there would be no witness.

As if that were not bad enough, the damned girl's father had had the temerity to come all the way to their family home at Dharamapuri to inquire about his daughter's whereabouts. By a stroke of good fortune, his father had gone to Madras the day before. That incident had cost him another thousand rupees. This time Das knew, for it had been Das who had taken the dead body late at night in the spare car. He and driver had weighted in with stones and the latter had dragged it out of the car and thrown it into a large tank forty miles away, along the road to Salem.

But all this meant that Das knew too much. Last week the driver had approached him with a demand for five hundred rupees. Sathynarayan had started to refuse, but had stopped short when he saw the smirk upon the driver's face which told its own tale.

Then Sathynarayan made a plan. Immediately after Pongal he would go for a big shoot, and he would take Das with him. There would be a shooting accident and the driver would be killed! Of course, a lot of awkward questions would be asked by the police, but he knew that his father would come forth with bags of money and the questioners would fall silent.

Now why, of all place, did his father want to visit Panapatti for the Pongal festival? Sathynarayan had tried to put the old man off. But as everybody knows, old people are very stubborn. His parent had got quite hot about it. He had even chided the young man with the disappointment he had felt when the latter's sudden interest in the cattle herd at Panapatti had as suddenly ended. And so the four of them were trudging through the jungle to Panapatti, having left Das to look after the car. The chauffeur had worn another of his nasty smirks as he caught his eye before parting. Sathynarayan resolved that he would have to stage that hunting trip and the accident that was to go with it, without further delay. Das was becoming far too dangerous.

The four visitors reached the patti where the herdsmen and the few poojaree had made ready to welcome them. As the august patrons were of the highest caste no refreshments of any sort could be prepared by them or pass through their defiled hands before being presented. Thus the gifts took the form of green coconuts, which had to be broken before the water could be drunk, and huge sweet-limes called 'sathgoodies', from which the outer skin had to be removed to get at the pulp. Gifts of this sort would be readily accepted, as there was no chance of the ingredients being contaminated.

The painted and gaudily decorated cattle were displayed

and a couple of mock-fights between men and bulls were staged. As the animals were roped and held in restraint by half-a-dozen men on each side, these encounters were farcical and excited nobody except perhaps those who took part in them. The evening closed with the usual felicitations and, after consuming more coconut water, the visitors prepared to depart. They had taken care to ascertain from the herdsmen that there were no elephants in the vicinity and so they dawdled till a later hour than they would otherwise have done. Once again the sun was sinking behind the jagged hills across the western bank of the Chinar, but with normal walking they would reach the main road where the car awaited them before dusk.

It happened somewhere midway between the *patti* and the main road. Sathynarayan and his father were walking ahead together, probably discussing a business deal of some sort. The young man's wife, as behaves all respectable and dutiful Indian married women, was obliged to walk a few paces to the rear. This she was doing, leading, her small boy by the hand. The child was tired and bored to death by the whole proceeding. He was crying.

It is not good for the young of any creature to cry in the forest. The jungle recognizes no law of pity for the young and helpless, only the rule of survival of the fittest, which certainly does not include the young. There was a sudden snarl ; at the same time a great tawny body with black stripes materialized from nowhere to seize the crying child in its jaws. The mother saw this and instinctively hurled herself at the beast's head to save her child. The two men in front heard the snarl and swung around. They saw the tiger with the child in its mouth rear up and strike the mother with its front paws. They waited to see no more.

Sathynarayan, who was younger, ran faster and reached

the car first. His father fell from exhaustion several times before he also made it. Then Das drove the car at break-neck speed to Pennagaram to get help. No help was forthcoming at that hour, for the shades of night had already fallen. The next morning a vast concourse of people armed to the teeth, retracted the steps of the fleeing man and came upon the tragedy.

Mother and the son lead a yard apart. The tiger's great teeth had bitten through and through the little boy. His mother had been killed by the two great blows that had been dealt to her. Not a morsel of flesh had been eaten from either victim. Upon the hard ground were no traces of pug-marks.

As may be imagined, pandemonium reigned at Pennagaram and in the nearby villages and forest pattis. No man-eating tiger or panther had been heard of for a hundred miles around. As a matter of fact, at this particular time the herdsmen of Panapatti and the fishermen at Uttaimalai and Hogenaikal and the other hamlets on the other banks of the great Cauvery river confirmed that there was a distinct lack of carnivores of any sort in the area. Being the dry season, and this year a particularly hot one, the sambar had taken themselves to the mountains and the spotted deer had gone to less dry area. Such carnivore as had existed, and these were few, had gone with them.

Where the killer had come from, nobody, could tell. Why he had killed and then not eaten was a still greater mystery.

I had been on a visit to my land at Anchetty, a hamlet in the same forest but about twenty miles to the north when all this happened, but no news had reached Anchetty yet. I had later left Anchetty, walked to another *patti* named Gundalam, and then sixteen miles down the course of a stream I have called the 'Secret River' to its confluence with Cauvery river. From there I had come another ten miles to

742

uttaimalai, where the fishermen were very excited at having heard of the happenings near Panapatti.

There is a short-cut across the foot-hills which brought me to the bed of the Chinar river two furlongs below Panapatti. I found the herdsmen and poojarees gathered under a tree discussing the recent event. They had not driven the herds of cattle into the forest for grazing for the last two mornings for fear the killer might attack either the animals or themselves — that is, the one or two herdsmen who minority.

All the poojarees, without exceptions, and the rest of the herdsmen were of the opinion that they and the herds were quite safe. The tiger that had killed was not a man-eater, for it had not touched the bodies of the woman and child it had slain! Nor was it a game-killer, for they had come across no bones or carcases of sambar or spotted-deer. The vultures had not soared in the sky nor quarrelled over the remains of a kill for a long time.

In fact, this was not a tiger or a panther at all — at least, not one of flesh and blood! It was the spirit of Kaiyara, the poojaree, who had avenged the murder of his only daughter and of himself. The poojaree had assumed the form of a tiger to fulfil the curses himself had placed upon the braggart Sathynarayan.

'Nor is this the end, *dorai*, the eldest of the poojarees at the *patti*, and one who had been a particular crony of Kaiyara's, confided to me in an undertone. 'Not by a long chalk. It is but one half of the curse. The lesser half, if fact. The two really guilty ones have yet to die, the murderous Sathynarayan and the rascally car-driver who helped him.

It is a rare thing for an India to confide his innermost thoughts to a man of western origin persons of another and unspoken proscription exists against persons of another race and colour, to whom it is considered most unwise to impart secret information of any importance. There is a general belief that westerners are extremely foolish, very callous, most disbelieving and, in fact, grossly ignorant of all matters not directly involving the five material senses. This prejudice is everywhere in the land and perhaps strongest in the minds of simple folk from the villages and jungles. It took me more than two hours of subtle and adroit questioning before I could wheedle from the old man the facts which I have already set forth in this story. Considering moreover, that I have mixed with jungle folk and villagers from the time I — and they — could walk and talk, I consider myself extremely lucky to have been able to get all the facts. I eventually collected.

To me, of course, all this was but jungle-talk, the sort of thing one could expect to hear from superstitious folk. In my opinion, the tiger was just a tiger and nothing more. Perhaps it was a wounded animal and in pain when it saw the woman and child and attacked them in sheer rage. Maybe the crying of the child attracted and enticed it, perhaps even annoyed it. Maybe a hundred other reasons, but it was only a flesh-and-blood tiger. From this followed the next thought that, although for some unaccountable reason it had not eaten either of its victims, it might attack again at any time. Accordingly I made arrangements to try to shoot it. At that time I was not working, so the time factor did not count and I was in not hurry to return to city life.

As I have related in other books, most man-eaters follow a regular 'beat' in the territory where they operate. By this I mean that they follow a definite itinerary in moving from one jungle area to another, past particular villages, up the beds of or across certain streams, or along certain game-trails and fire-lines, in moving from one locality to another. Having moved this way once and killed and eaten a human or two here and there, they come back along the same trails and routes after a certain period of time, and do this over and over again. So, with patience and care, it is possible to map out the 'beat' followed by such a man-eater and to forecast with considerable accuracy when and where to wait for him in ambush, or try to entice him with a bait or by some other means.

All this did not apply in the present case. This animal had not killed any other human being anywhere for miles around. As I have said, it had not even attacked a single cow in any of the herds, 'nor had it killed a deer or pig as far as was known.

I enlisted the aid of the poojaress and herdsmen in the *patti* and scoured the bed of the Chinar river, both up and down, for several miles in each direction in order to find its pug-marks and ascertain it was a male or female. Search as we did, we found no pug-marks anywhere.

This tiger must have come from the east, therefore, where lay comparatively open country, scrub jungle which petered out into cultivation for miles around. No tiger could live, or conceal itself, in such conditions. It had to come from the forest. Tigers do not live in fields!

I prevailed upon the herdsmen to lend me four cattle from the herd that belonged to Sathynarayan's father, promising to pay for any one that was killed. I knew that the owner would not object under the circumstances, but nonetheless sent one of the herdsmen to Dharamapuri to inform the owner of what I was doing.

I found the poojarees in the *patti* disinclined to be cooperative in the proceedings from this point onwards. The ancient one among them told me, flatly that I could not expect him and his clan-members to help me to lay a trap for their dead companion when the turned up in the form of a tiger — not that he would be so foolish as to kill any of the baits I had tied up, or allow himself to be shot at. It was well known that no bullet made of lead could penetrate a spirit. Nevertheless, it was the motive of their actions in helping me by which they would be judged. They could not, and would not assist me in trying to shoot this tiger.

Money talks and so I was able to entice the herdsmen who were not poojarees to aid me. After much inquiring and tramping up and down, I chose four places as being the most likely for a tiger to turn up. All that I could do now was to wait complacently till one of the baits was taken.

Rather than be idle meanwhile, I scoured the forest from dawn to dusk searching for the pugs of the tiger up and down the banks of the Chinar river. As the herdsmen and poojarees at Panapatti were not keen on helping me. I sent for my old friend Byra, himself a poojaree, who lived at Annabiddahalha, another patti about fifteen miles distant, and for Ranga who had accompanied me on many adventures. Both these men were expert trackers and knew the area for miles around. But the three of us searched in vain: not a single tiger-pug did we find. The killer had disappointed as silently and as suddenly as he had come.

Time ran out on me and the day came to go back to Bangalore. I returned the four baits I had borrowed together with a small gratuity. Normally, it is not possible to come to an arrangement of this sort and the hunter is compelled to purchase his baits outright. But this case was an exception because they knew for certain hat none of the baits would be harmed. how could they, when there was not tiger to harm them?

About two months elapsed and Das, the driver, was returning alone to Dharamapuri in the big family car from the city of Salem, sixty-five miles away, where he had taken Sathynarayan's father for admission to hospital for removal of a cataract. Das had left the old man there and was hurrying back for dinner. He had forty miles to go to reach his home in Dharamapuri. The road narrowed down to traverse the winding bund of a large deep tank. There appeared to be no traffic in sight and Das accelerated.

Then something must have happened to the steering, or may be a front tyre blew out. Nobody knows for certain. The only witnesses were two villagers hurrying homewards who saw the whole incident. The car left the roadway suddenly at a point where the road turned left, crashed through the thin brick wall bordering the bund directly ahead and plunged headlong into the tank.

Das had closed the windows. He was trapped in the car and his body was recovered a week later when the vehicle was hauled out by the police.

Was it coincidence that he was drowned in the very tank into which he had thrown the body of Kaiyara after his master and he had murdered the poojaree and weighted the body with a stone? Sathynarayan heard the news and madness fell upon him. First, his only son, them his wife. Now the chauffeur, Das.

Sathynarayan remembered the murder of the old poojaree and his daughter before him. Tales had been carried to him about the curse the old man had uttered against him and he became convinced it was his turn next. At that moment, Sathynarayan realized he must die. Thus his mind gave way. His father returned from hospital to find his son a lunatic. The old man did not spare expense. He took Sathynarayan to Salem and consulted the best of doctors. They boy repeating names of Kaiyara and Mardee in his raving but the doctors could do nothing to cure him.

Sathynarayan was then taken to Madras, and admitted to a mental home. The psychiatrist discovered that the mania arose from some connection in the madman's mind with the two persons those names he kept muttering. However, no treatment was effective and the father became reconciled to the fact that his son and heir was permanently insane. The young man was brought home, where he was given two male attendants to look after him night and day. His father hoped that he would improve with time.

In this he was doomed to disappointment His son became worse and grew violent, whereas before he had been but a gibbering maniac. The old man reluctantly decided that he would have to put him into the asylum at Madras as a permanent inmate. But this was not to be, for the curse of Kaiyara had yet to exact its full toll — or so people said!

Sathynarayan was missing from his room when his attendant brought his breakfast early one morning. He had been there the evening before. A search was made all over the town but nobody remembered to have seen him anywhere. They young man was well known and somebody would have noticed his movements. It was four days later when vultures spiralled the sky above the track that leads from the main road to the cattle kraal at Panapatti. They flew in wide circles, which narrowed as the birds of prey rapidly increased in numbers. Then, one after another, they plummetted to earth, their wing-feathers emitting a loud rattling noise as they tore through the air.

Byra saw the vultures and heard the sound. He had taken employment that year among the graziers at Panapatti and was driving a herd of cattle to the forest for grazing. He knew the vultures had spotted a 'kill', and being a hunter from childhood he went to investigate. Perhaps there might be some meat for him to eat.

The kill was easy to find. The discordant screeching noise made by the vultures led him to it unerringly. The birds were gathered round in a circle and had not yet begun to feed. For they were afraid!